TRAVELLER'S LITERARY COMPANION

SOUTH & CENTRAL AMERICA

TRAVELLER'S
LITERARY COMPANIONS

Read your way around the world

In Print

1993

Titles in the Traveller's Literary Companion series:
South and Central America (1993)
Africa (1993)
Eastern Europe (1994)
The Indian Subcontinent (1993)
Japan (1993)
South-east Asia (1993)

British Library Cataloguing in Publication Data: A catalogue record for this book is
available from the British Library.

Paperback ISBN 1 873 047 45 2
Hardback ISBN 1 873 047 40 1

Cover design by Russell Townsend
Front cover and spine photograph of an Indian burial ground near La Paz in the Bolivian
    Andes by Andrew Wood
Back cover photograph of Pablo Neruda's house 'La Chascona' by Tomasina Wilson
Maps drawn by Tomasina Wilson
Additional artwork by Zana Juppenlatz
Typeset by MC Typeset Ltd
Printed by Utopia Press

First published in 1993 by
In Print Publishing Ltd, 9 Beaufort Terrace, Brighton BN2 2SU, UK. Tel: (0273)
682836. Fax: (0273) 620958.

SERIES FOREWORD

This series of *Traveller's Literary Companions* is the series I have been looking for all my travelling life. Discovering new writers and new countries are amongst the greatest pleasures we know, and these books will greatly increase the enjoyment of all who consult them. Each volume is packed with scholarly and entertaining historical, geographical, political and above all literary information. A country lives through its literature, and we have here an illustrated survey not only of a country's own writers, but also of the views of foreigners, explorers, tourists and exiles. The only problem I foresee is that each volume will bring about a compulsive desire to book a ticket on the next flight out.

The writers take us back in the past to each country's cultural origins, and bring us right up to the present with extracts from novels, poems and travel writings published in the 1980s and 1990s. The biographical information about the writers is invaluable, and will give any traveller an easy and immediate access to the past and present state of each nation. Conversation with hosts, colleagues or strangers on trains will be greatly assisted. An enormous amount of work has gone into the compiling and annotating of each volume, and the balance of fact and comment seems to me to be expertly judged.

I particularly welcome Jason Wilson's volume on South and Central America, the first in the series. This is a very considerable undertaking, covering in fascinating detail each country of that continent, and transporting us from vast Brazil to Surinam, from Mexico to Guatemala, from Magic Realism to Symbolist poetry. Familiar companions like Graham Greene and V.S. Naipaul mingle with Voltaire, Robert Lowell, and Aphra Behn, and the range of Latin American writers, some like Borges and Isabel Allende already famous in the English-speaking world, and some relatively unknown, is most impressive. Wilson's love of his subject is evident. It is a book that makes one long to read and see and see and read.

Margaret Drabble

About the author

Jason Wilson lectures on Latin American literature at University College, London. He has published books on Octavio Paz (Cambridge University Press, 1979; Twayne, 1986), on Latin American Literature in English translation (Institute of Latin American Studies, 1989), and numerous essays and reviews on contemporary Spanish American writers. He has an edition of Alexandre von Humboldt's *Travels* in Penguin Classics (forthcoming as this book goes to press), and a study of W.H. Hudson and Charles Darwin awaiting publication. He is currently working on Anglo–American writers who have travelled in Latin America. Jason Wilson is married, with three daughters, and has himself travelled widely in Latin America.

CONTENTS

LIST OF MAPS

Introduction

This literary guide is aimed at non-Spanish speakers, and offers them background information on 21 South and Central American mainland republics, with extracts in English from foreign visitors, usually writers, as well as passages from native writers if translated into English. The idea is to give a sense of how foreigners see these cultures, and how they see themselves through their writers. In general, travel writers have been included only if they are also imaginative writers. Biographical details help direct readers to explore the relationship between individual writers and specific places.

Certain assumptions lie behind *Traveller's Literary Companion to South & Central America*. A primary one concerns the overpowering presence of geography and climate in the lives of the people, even in the urban areas. Huge distances, inaccessible zones from Mexican *mesetas* to Brazilian rainforests, the empty *pampa*, the frozen fiords of Chile and extreme climates and contrasts lead to ways of life marginalized from the overcrowded, expanding cities. Material poverty and day-dreams about Western technology explain the drift of the landless to the varying shanty-towns. A lot of 'American' writing comes from uprooted urban authors exploring their own hinterlands, with their archaic beliefs and customs, often still deeply pre-Colombian, and Indian. Change has often been radical so that past ways of life have been wiped out, not only in the disappearing tribes, but also in the rapidly modernizing cities, demolishing and rebuilding within a writer's own lifetime. The stability of tradition in the Americas is not strong, and is easily ignored as elusive notions of being modern drive these young cultures haphazardly forward. Much 'American' fiction was written to educate, inform, describe, record, or just name rural regions and urban lifestyles on the wane, just as foreigners write to confront alien ways of life and sights for the stay-at-homes.

Most of the novels excerpted are realistic, sharing a basic belief that language, contrary to recent academic dogma, reflects and recreates something really there, empirically real, even if in the past. Even Jorge Luis Borges grounds his fictions in some sense of shared place. However, a sense of place is not the only basis for realism. A sense of lived history is also crucial. Further definitions of the 'American' experience invoke the fragility of democracy, colonial dependency, and the omnipresence of the military-backed dictatorships of the left and the right. There is a protest vein in American writing that is angry and moving, especially in those areas most afflicted. Witness literature is painfully realistic. Shrinking all 'American' literature to 'realism' is justifiable for this *Companion*, but not for literary history, for much good subjective writing would remain excluded, especially poetry, and experimental, allegorical, and metaphysical explorations, including '*literatura fantástica*'.

One way of reading 'American' literary history into this guide is to view much American writing, as well as the many foreigners writing about America, as a kind of report or travelogue. The overlap between fiction – a report on a strange and distant land – and travel books is enormous, for both fiction and travel books can be read as chronicles, a term that García Márquez from Colombia and Roy Heath from Guyana have used to define their purpose and work.

I employ the adjective 'American' because I have wanted to cross the arbitrary national boundaries, and not evaluate extracts along purely nationalistic lines. By using the term 'American' I include not only Brazilian authors, but also Guyanese, and Europeans and North Americans who have written their reports on the lands south of the Rio Grande.

In compiling my extracts and biographies, and linking writing to geography, history and politics, I have turned to many useful books, including Jean Franco's *The Modern Culture of Latin America: Society and the Artist*, 1967 (still relevant today); Gerald Martin's *Journeys Through the Labyrinth*, 1989 (though opinionated, does stimulate); Selden Rodman's travels in quest of writers, *South America of the Poets*, 1970; and countless histories, encyclopaedias and dictionaries. Of the many travel guides consulted, my favourites remain the *South American Handbook*, and the *Mexico and Central American Handbook*, both edited by Ben Box, always quirky and packed with information. For further reading material I have suggested biographies where possible, rather than literary studies, for biographies relate a writer's life and work to place.

Given the brevity of shelf-life in today's bookselling world, many of the books from which I have taken extracts are out of print. When it comes to Latin American literature in translation, much has been translated (see my *An A–Z of Modern Latin American Literature in English Translation*, 1989) but can be obtained only from good public libraries.

I would like to thank Andrea for help in researching out-of-favour writers, my daughters Camila, Lucinda and especially Tomasina, for her photos and maps, my attentive and encouraging publisher John

Edmondson, Anthony Edkins, Frank Tuohy, Alastair Dingwall, Martín Cullén, and the cultural attachés Raúl Ortiz, Alicia Torres, Gonçalo de Mello Mourão, and Elvira Velásquez. However, any errors are mine alone.

May this *Companion* be read for pleasure whether actually trekking out there, or just as a bedside guide, and be informative to all students of the area.

Jason Wilson
London SW6

Short Glossary

The following short list explains words which are used several times in the book. Other Spanish words and phrases are translated in the text as they occur.

adobe sun-dried mud brick
aguardiente brandy, rum, any strong liquor (in Spanish it means 'burning water')
audiencia a hearing, interview, high court
cacique a Carib word, meaning chief, boss, local tyrant
cantina bar
caudillo leader, head of state, tyrant
cholo in Bolivia and Ecuador, someone with mixed Spanish and Indian blood; in Guatemala and Peru, a Westernized Indian or half-caste; in Peru it can be synonymous with 'Peruvian'
criollo creole, someone native to Spanish America; a Spaniard born in the Spanish American colonies; used as an adjective it means 'typically national'
encomienda land and people granted to Spanish *conquistador*
estancia farm in Argentina (it means a 'room' in Spain)
gringo in Mexico a North American; in Argentina any foreigner, but today usually a North American; all over Latin America, an obvious fair-haired Westerner (from the Spanish *griego* or Greek, perhaps from the song 'green grow' – *gringo* – 'the rushes-o')
hacienda farm in most of Latin America (it means 'cattle' in Argentina)
ladino Spanish-speaking Indian (from *latino*, Latin-speaking); in Guatemala, a half-caste or Westernized Indian
machete broad-bladed knife for cutting sugar cane, and paths through the jungle
mestizo half-caste or half-breed, usually between Westerner and Indian
peón originally a foot-soldier, a pawn in chess, and usually a farmhand or manual worker
pulque fermented alcohol made from the maguey cactus
rancho shack

Using the Companion

Each country has its own chapter and each chapter is divided into four distinct sections: (1) an introduction to the geography and cultural and political background; (2) a Booklist giving full publishing details of all the books mentioned in the introduction and extracted; (3) a selection of extracts; (4) biographical details and summaries of major works.

Extracts are ordered alphabetically by place and each is assigned a number to make it easy to locate from elsewhere in the chapter. A quick list of all the works extracted in a chapter can be obtained from the **Booklist** where extract numbers are highlighted in bold type. Full source references for the extracts are included under 'Acknowledgments and Citations' at the end of the book.

Publication **dates** are given throughout. A date after an English title for a book originally written in Spanish refers to the date of publication of the translation. In the Booklist, the date in square brackets is the first publication date of the book in its original language.

The **symbol** ◊ after an author's name indicates that there is a biographical entry in the chapter. If there is a biographical entry in another chapter, the author's name is followed by the symbol and the title of the relevant chapter in parentheses – eg 'Malcolm Lowry (◊ Mexico)'.

Bold type is used to highlight references to places, whether cities and towns or museums and writers' houses.

There is an **index of authors** at the end of the book.

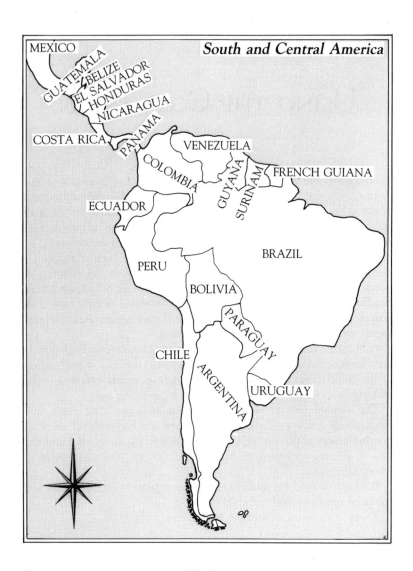

South and Central America

MEXICO

> 'A brief mountain pass took us suddenly to a height from which we saw all of Mexico City stretched out in its volcanic crater below and spewing city smokes and early dusklights.'
>
> Jack Kerouac, On the Road

Mexico, or the Estados Unidos Mexicanos, is probably derived from Mexitli, one of the names of the Aztec god of war, or from *metzli* (moon) and *xictli* (navel) – that is, the town in the middle of the lake of the moon (Lake Texcoco). It is pronounced *Mehico* and spelt with a 'j' by Spaniards (*Méjico*). It is the most populous Spanish-speaking country in the world, with 88.6 million in 1990. The country has 1 959 038 sq km, a 2494 km border with the USA, and southern borders with Guatemala and Belize. The core of the country is the arid Mexican high plateau, roughly bordered by north–south mountain ranges called the **Sierra Madre Occidental** and the **Sierra Madre Oriental**, with specific regions like the fertile **Sonora** plains with sugar cane; the **Baja California** peninsula; the **Yucatán** limestone platform peninsula; the **Gulf of Mexico** coastal plains with swamps, oil and cattle ranches; the tropical south with the **Chiapas** highlands; and the volcanic **Southern Plateau** with its dormant and active volcanos, continuous earth tremors, and earthquakes (the 1985 quake in Mexico City claimed over 20 000 dead). The subtropical and tropical climates depend on elevation and range from *tierra caliente* to *tierra templada* and *fría*. What is clear is that landscape, climate and geography determine many elements of Mexican cultural life, as reflected in the titles of the stories of writer Juan Rulfo ◊ in his two collections *El llano en llamas*, 1953 (*The Burning Plain and Other Stories*, 1967) and *Pedro Páramo*, 1955 (*Pedro Paramo*, 1959 – Extract 7) where the surname of the *cacique* means 'high plateau'.

Fifty per cent of Mexico's population lives in the Southern Plateau, with polluted **Mexico City**, at 2255 m, reaching an estimated 19 million in 1990, an alarming rise in urban population from 1928 when

Mexico City reached 1 million. The smog today has obscured the view of the two volcanoes **Popocatépetl** (5349 m) and **Ixtacihuatl** (5286 m), the 'smoking mountain' and 'white lady', both snow-covered and landmarks in Malcolm Lowry's ◊ novel *Under the Volcano*, 1947 (Extract 5) and Carlos Fuentes's ◊ ironic *La región más transparente*, 1958 (*Where the Air is Clear*, 1960), his fictional attempt to come to grips with the vastly expanding and alienating city of the late 1950s (Extract 18). An equally engrossing, and at the time scandalous, attempt was Oscar Lewis's reordered tape recording of a poor slum family's history, *The Children of Sánchez: Autobiography of a Mexican Family*, 1962.

From Hernán Cortés's capture of the Aztec empire in 1521, when he used his mistress La Malinche as interpreter, the Spaniards interbred and created a predominantly *mestizo* population (60%) with some 12% pure Indian who resisted Christianization and assimilation. Cortés also imposed the Spanish language, so that some 89% of the population speak Spanish, and only some 3.8% the main Indian languages that survived – Nahuatl, Zapotecan, Totonacan and Maya-Quiché. The Indians, whether Spanish-speaking or not, have fascinated writers like D.H. Lawrence ◊; B. Traven ◊; the surrealist Antonin Artaud (who visited a Tarahumaran shaman in Mexico in 1936 to take *peyotl*); Carlos Castaneda (and his elegy to Yaqui sorcerers); and Gregorio López y Fuentes (1897–1966), whose novel *El indio*, 1935 (*They That Reap*, 1937) shows that despite the Revolution little has changed for the Indians. The Revolution tried to 'Mexicanize' the 8 to 10 million Indians divided into over 50 ethnic/linguistic groups, a programme symbolized in José Vasconcelos's (◊ Argentina) essay *La raza cósmica*, 1925, where the idea of an ethnic melting pot promised a super-race. The National Indian Institute was set up in 1948 to work at Indian integration (writer Juan Rulfo was on the staff), but this was abandoned in 1981 when the idea of assimilation was questioned (see Alan Riding, *Mexico: Inside the Volcano*, 1987).

THE AZTECS

The Mexican flag, with an eagle, a snake in its beak and a cactus, symbolizes modern Mexico, and its roots in the Aztec past. The nomadic Aztecs arrived in the high plateau in 1325, picked the spot for their principal city **Tenochtitlán** (razed and rebuilt as Mexico City in the sixteenth century) when they saw a snake and eagle on a cactus, and built a Venice-like city of causeways in the saline Lake Texcoco. Their theocracy was dependent on ritualistic wars, priests, and vassals. Apart perhaps from the fair and bearded Quetzalcóatl, the Plumed Serpent who fascinated D.H. Lawrence, the Aztecs had developed quite divorced from European influences. When Hernán Cortés arrived on the Mexican **Caribbean coast**, he founded the first Spanish settlement at **Veracruz** (the 'true cross'). After burning his boats he set off to conquer the Aztecs, with massive help from defecting Tlaxcalans, and his Indian mistress La Malinche. When Cortés stood on the crater looking down on to Tenochtitlán, one of his foot soldiers, Bernal Díaz ◊ could only compare the sight to a fabulous city in a chivalry novel (Extract 16).

This period has caused wonder in successive generations of Europeans at the artistry and wealth of the Aztecs under Moctezuma, wealth that underpinned Spain's sixteenth century expanding empire. When Cortés was away, his underling, a henchman called Alvarado, massacred 200 Aztec nobles, and had to retreat as they revolted. The *noche triste* of 1521 led to the decimation of the city and its later rebuilding without canals in 1525, using the stones of the *teocalli* (sacrificial temples) in the cathedral. From that date, with only a few defenders (like Bartolomé de las Casas), the Aztec world, with its poets and beautiful codices, disappeared until rediscovered in the 1940s by Mexican scholars when Nahuatl poetry was translated into Spanish, and then English (see Michael Schmidt and Edward Kissam, *Flower and Song: Aztec Poetry*, 1977).

How the Aztec world disappeared has puzzled non-Mexicans. John Dryden wrote *The Indian Emperor* in 1665 about Moctezuma; W.H. Prescott's *The History of the Conquest of Mexico*, 1843, romanticized the achievement of Cortés; Rider Haggard wrote a typical romance, *Montezuma's daughter*, in 1893. Later, in the 1920s, the iconography of Mexico's revolutionary muralists like Diego Rivera and David Alfaro Siqueiros turned the Aztecs into noble savages, or healthy Stalinist peasants; Cuauhtemoc's revolt, and suicide (1520), made him the first of Latin America's resistance fighters for Chilean poet Pablo Neruda (◊ Chile). The Aztecs' sudden collapse has entered the Western imagination. No wonder there are virtually no statues to Hernán Cortés in Mexico. The Nahuatl language also passed words into most European languages, like tomato (*tomatl*), chocolate (*chocolatl*) and avocado (*ahuacatl*). For a glimpse of their closed world, see Jacques Soustelle, *The Daily Life of the Aztecs*, 1955. For a wonderful understanding of their culture, see Irene Nicholson, *Firefly in the Night: A Study of Ancient Mexican Poetry and Symbolism*, 1959.

COLONIALISM TO INDEPENDENCE

New Spain was quickly conquered and Christianized. From 1535, New Spain had its first of 62 viceroys; from 1533 its university; and over the years some 10 000 churches were built to preserve the faith. In 1531 an

Indian virgin appeared to Juan Diego on a hill to become Mexico's patron saint, la Virgen de Guadalupe, housed in the **Basílica de Guadalupe**. Octavio Paz's ◊ prose poem 'Obsidian Butterfly' (Extract 23) described how an ancient Aztec goddess of fertility called Tonantzin was worshipped on the same spot. The fate of the Indians was silence over the 300 colonial years. They worked as virtual slaves on *encomiendas* and in the mines. A penetrating description of life in the later viceroyalty emerges from Octavio Paz's biography of the intellectually brilliant poet-nun Sor Juana Inés da la Cruz (1645–94), who was forbidden to write by her male superiors (see *Sor Juana: or, the Traps of Faith*, 1988). Sor Juana's work has been translated as *Sor Juana's Dream*, 1986 and *A Sor Juana Anthology*, 1988. She was the most important writer in New Spain – an early feminist. The convent where she lived is now the **Museo del Claustro de Sor Juana**, Plaza de San Jerónimo 47, Downtown, Mexico City. At the end of the eighteenth century Alexandre von Humboldt (◊ Venezuela) wrote the first systematic study of the colony, *Political Essay on the Kingdom of New Spain*, 1811. The house in **Taxco** where Humboldt wrote this study is a museum.

As with the rest of Spain's colonies the French invasion of Spain in 1808 gave a voice to the *criollos* seeking more control over their land. In 1810 a priest, Father Miguel Hidalgo from a village called **Dolores** set about transforming New Spain with his famous *grito* (echoed every 16 September, Mexico's national day). He sought racial equality and a redistribution of land, for the church owned more than half of all land in Mexico. But he was put to death by the *gachupines* (Spaniards). Another priest, padre José María Morelia, tried again in 1813–14, but he was caught, defrocked and executed. By 1820, Iturbide had made himself Emperor and declared Mexico an independent monarchy. In Mexico the conservatives had triumphed. But Iturbide was shot in 1822. From then on, Mexico was a republic, and anarchy prevailed, with the colourful and vicious General Santa Anna six times president, and the power behind the scenes. When Texas declared its independence in 1836 he sacked the Alamo. The Americans were furious, and in 1846 declared war on Mexico, occupying Veracruz, then Mexico City in 1847. In the Treaty of Guadalupe in 1848, Mexico lost all its territory north of the Rio Grande: California, Montana, Arizona, Florida, etc.

The disasters associated with Santa Anna ended with the Reform movement, where the pure-blooded Zapotec Indian, Benito Juárez, a liberal, came in with his secular and progressive ideas. He instated civil marriage, and anti-clerical laws. Just when he was on top, the French invaded because impoverished Mexico had not paid interest on a debt. Napoleon III put Maximilian, younger brother of Austria's Emperor Joseph, on the Mexican throne in 1864. Maximilian and Carlota lasted

Octavio Paz

long enough to catch the West's imagination. Maximilian was a naturalist, and politically a moderate, but when the French withdrew in 1867 Benito Juárez's forces caught and executed him in **Querétaro.** Carlota went mad, and died years later in 1927 in Belgium. Their palace in **Cuernavaca** plays a crucial role in Malcolm Lowry's failed love story *Under the Volcano*; the Mexican playwright Usigli has a play *Crown of Shadows*, 1946, on their tragic love affair; and Fernando del Paso a recent untranslated novel, *Noticias del Imperio*, 1987. Victor Hugo wrote a manifesto from exile on Guernsey urging Juárez to fight Maximilian, and Manet painted famous pictures of the 1867 execution.

Juárez was a radical president and remained in power until 1872, installing railroads and schools. Porfirio Díaz took over from him, re-electing himself until 1911. He allowed foreign capital in, developed mining, oil and textiles, and let Mexico be run by technocrats called *científicos*. A perceptive view of nineteenth century Mexico comes from Fanny Calderón de la Barca's letters, *Life in Mexico*, 1842, while Octavio Paz's essay *El laberinto de la soledad*, 1950 (*The Labyrinth of Solitude*, 1961) remains today a fine, passionate review of Mexico's cultural heritage.

REVOLUTION

But the lot of the Indians and common workers did not improve. Ninety five per cent of the rural population had their *ejidos* (common land) appropriated as private ownership was deemed more efficient. The resentment was explosive. A classic account of this Indian resentment is John Kenneth Turner's *Barbarous Mexico*, 1911, while Traven's novels, like *The Rebellion of the Hanged*, 1936 (Extract 1), *The Carreta*, 1931, and *The General from the Jungle*, 1940 (opening with the Revolutionary cry *Tierra y libertad!*) capture the mood of the Indian peasants in **Chiapas.**

In 1910, an idealist (and vegetarian) called Francisco Madero opposed Porfirio Díaz's re-election platform, and was elected president. He was overthrown by General Huerta, a move that led to civil war with factions in the south under the peasant Emiliano Zapata, in the north under cattle rustler Pancho Villa, and others under Obregón and Carranza. Huerta fled in 1914 and there was a convention in **Aguascalientes** to decide on options. This period from 1910 to 1914 is brilliantly captured in Mariano Azuela's ◊ cinematic novel *Los de abajo*, 1916 (*The Underdogs*, 1929 – Extract 8) about the effects of the Revolution on peasants and intellectuals, naming actual places, and battles. This was the first of a group of novels exploring the Revolution: others available in English include Martín Luis Guzmán, *El águila y la serpiente*, 1928 (*The Eagle and the Serpent*, 1930) and *Memorias de*

Malcolm Lowry

Pancho Villa, 1940 (*Memoirs of Pancho Villa*, 1965). The effect of the violent Revolution on traditional provincial and very Catholic towns like **Zacatecas** and **San Luis Potosí** has been vividly recorded in Ramón López Velarde's poetry ('Better not to return to the village, / subverted Eden now silent / mutilated by the din of machine guns . . .'). The house he died in is a museum in **Avenida Alvaro Obregón, Mexico City**. There are many later books like Carlos Fuentes's *La muerte de Artemio Cruz*, 1962 (*The Death of Artemio Cruz*, 1964) or *Gringo viejo*,

Graham Greene

1986 (*Old Gringo*, 1986) that turn back to these violent revolutionary years. Octavio Paz's *The Labyrinth of Solitude* focuses on the Revolution as the ambiguous foundation of modern Mexico. A readable historical account is Ronald Atkin's *Revolution! Mexico 1910–1920*, 1969.

THE CONSTITUTION AND MEXICAN IDENTITY

By 1917 Carranza was in charge, and the Mexican constitution was drafted, a revolutionary programme of land reform and curtailment of church power. The *ejido* was brought back. But the violence continued. Zapata was murdered in 1918, and Obregón overthrown in 1920. It was in the Mexico of the 1920s coming to terms with its own Revolution that Kate fell for the Mexican reincarnation of Quetzalcóatl in Lawrence's *The Plumed Serpent*, 1926 (Extracts 9 and 21). For many years, in a unique relationship with power, the president was a virtual elected dictator, with a monolithic party that from 1946 was called PRI, the Institutional Revolutionary Party.

The cultural politics of the period were dramatic. José Vasconcelos (◊ Argentina) was Minister for Education, and gave over public wall space to the muralists who created a propagandistic art for the people, with the Revolution as main transforming theme. Vasconcelos also invited educationalists like the Chilean Nobel winning poet Gabriela Mistral to help. The revolutionary fervour at the same time created cultural opposition from many poets, centred round the magazine *Contemporáneos* (1929–31) that was cosmopolitan, a source of Octavio Paz's revision of what it meant to be a writer in Mexico. The work of some of these poets can be read in the anthology *New Poetry of Mexico*, 1970. The debate was about whether being a Mexican meant closing yourself to outside sources, or incorporating them. The late 1930s saw a recrudescence of anti-clerical persecution when priests were not able to give mass. Graham Greene ◊ has captured this paranoic period in **Tabasco** state in *The Power and the Glory*, 1940 (Extract 32), his novel about the whisky priest on the run, and in his travel book *The Lawless Roads*, 1938 (Extract 3). Earlier the priests had actually taken to guns and the hills during the Cristero revolution, narrated by Rulfo in *El llano en llamas*, 1953 (*The Burning Plains*, 1967), and earlier in Traven's novel *The Treasure of the Sierra Madre*, 1927 (Extract 6).

The radical presidency of Lázaro Cárdenas from 1934–40 nationalized the railways in 1937 and oil in 1938 (when the alcoholic consul in *Under the Volcano* lost his job as Britain broke relations with Mexico), and distributed over 50% of cultivated land to peasants, putting the 1917 constitution into practice. He also opened Mexico to Spain's Republican civil war exiles. Mexico never recognized Franco. After Cárdenas not much was done over the war years. However, Trotsky, exiled in **Mexico City**, and living in Diego Rivera's house, was assassinated (see Tomlinson's poem, Extract 24), not long after the surrealist leader André Breton had visited him in Mexico in 1938. **Trotsky's house** can be visited, near the **Frida Kahlo Museum** (she was Rivera's surrealist painter wife) in **Coyoacán**.

Through the 1950s little changed. Juan Rulfo's novel *Pedro Páramo* shows how the Revolution just passed the peasants by. One of his short stories, 'And They Gave Us the Land' is ironic about the desert given to peasants in the name of land reform.

All Mexican writers and intellectuals have participated either directly or as critics in the formation of Mexican identity and nationhood, with all the questionings, right from the early Ateneo group with Vasconcelos and Alfonso Reyes (1889–1953 – see his essay *Mexico in a Nutshell and Other Essays*, 1964), whose house at **Industria 122** in **Mexico City** can be visited, though his wonderful library has been moved to the Instituto Tecnológico in Monterrey, through Samuel Ramos's psycho-historical approach in 1934, *El perfil del hombre y de la cultura en México* (*Profile of Man and Culture in Mexico*, 1962) where he studied the *pelado* (who appears in Lowry's *Under the Volcano*), to Paz's Freudian approach to Mexico revealing its dark secrets through sex, swear words, US–Mexican relations, death, and the Pachuco, forerunner of the Chicano, in his *The Labyrinth of Solitude*. Most Mexican writers pit their fictions against the socio-historical backcloth, and set their characters in a recognizable Mexico.

Mexico is also the nearest foreign country for North Americans who arrive to discover how different the Mexicans are, and write about it; see for example the biographies and extracts of such writers as Bowles (Extract 28), Burroughs (Extract 13), Kerouac (Extract 20) and Porter (Extract 11). North American influence, given the shared boundary, is also crucial in Mexico with the wet-backs and *pochos* (North-Americanized Mexicans), Hollywood films and TV, summarized as 'Pepsicóatl culture' by Carlos Fuentes.

The Impact of the Sixties and New Writing

In 1968 Mexico hosted the Olympic games, and also massacred over 300 protesting students in **Tlatelolco Square**. Paz resigned as Mexican ambassador in India, and wrote about this massacre in *Posdata*, 1970 (*The Other Mexico: Critique of the Pyramid*, 1972), as did Elena

---

Notes to map (facing page): [a]*Kate in D. H. Lawrence's The Plumed Serpent, 1926, watches a bullfight;* [b]*Kate moves to Sayula (Chapala) on Lake Sayula (Chapala);* [c]*D. H. Lawrence lived in Oaxaca from November 1924 to February 1925, and wrote Mornings in Mexico, 1925. Malcolm Lowry's consul in Under the Volcano, 1947, recalls his stay in Oaxaca. Lowry stayed there in 1936, spending Christmas in jail, and again in 1946. Richard Ford's novel The Ultimate Good Luck, 1981, is set there;* [d]*Malcolm Lowry lived in Cuernavaca (15 Calle Humboldt) where he set his novel Under the Volcano, alluding to the volcano Popocatépetl;* [e]*Graham Greene's whisky priest in The Power and the Glory, 1940, moves between Villahermosa and Tuxla Gutiérrez, as did Greene himself in his travel account The Lawless Roads, 1938, which includes a map of his journey. Hollow circle = capital city.*

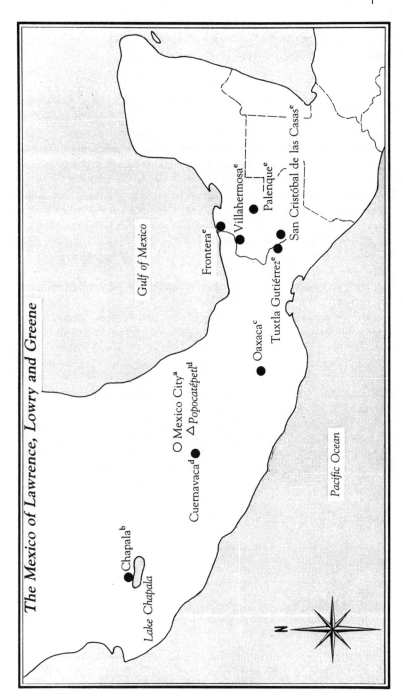

The Mexico of Lawrence, Lowry and Greene

Gulf of Mexico

Pacific Ocean

Lake Chapala

Chapala[b]

O Mexico City[a]
△ Popocatépetl[d]
Cuernavaca[d] ●

Oaxaca[c] ●

Frontera[e]

Villahermosa[e]
Palenque[e]
Tuxtla Gutiérrez[e]
San Cristóbal de las Casas[e]

N

Poniatowska in *La noche de Tlatelolco*, 1971 (*Massacre in Mexico*, 1975) which launched her as one of Mexico's most exciting writers. The 1960s saw an enormous change, as Mexicans came to terms with the youth culture from the north, which even affected older writers like Fuentes, whose *Cambio de piel*, 1967 (*A Change of Skin*, 1968 – Extract 2) is both a happening, and a critique of Mexico's official past. The Aztec/Indian past continues to figure, and to visit the **Museum of Anthropology** is a national duty for Mexicans. Paz entitled a long ambitious poem *Piedra de sol*, 1957 (*Sun Stone* – there are 5 different translations), based on the Aztec calendar stone in the museum.

After a depressed, indebted 1970s and 1980s, Mexico has a young president, with signs of an economic boom deriving from free-trade agreements with the USA and Canada. Mexico is the world's fourth largest producer of petroleum, and receives some 4.6 million tourists every year, 85% from the USA. The 1985 earthquake traumatized the country, but the emergency showed Mexicans that they had a pride and unity rare in other Latin American countries. The literary scene, from prizes to cultural supplements, publishing houses and magazines, is alive, with much foreign fiction being translated. Many of Mexico's more exciting writers have been translated into English, among them Juan José Arreola (1918–), *Confabulario and Other Inventions*, 1964 and *The Fair*, 1977; Emilio Carballido (1925–), *The Norther*, 1968; Rosario Castellanos ◊; Fernando del Paso (1935–), *Palinuro of Mexico*, 1989; Sergio Galindo (1926–), *The Precipice*, 1969, *Rice Powder*, 1978, and *Mexican Masquerade*, 1984; Elena Garro (1920–), *Recollections of Things to Come*, 1969; Margo Glantz ◊; Jorge Ibargüengoitia (1928–83), *The Dead Girls*, 1983, *Two Crimes*, 1984, and *Lightning of August*, 1986; José Revueltas (1914–76), *Human Mourning*, 1989; Gustavo Sáinz (1940–), *Gazapo*, 1968, and *The Princess of the Iron Palace*, 1987, while many others figure in several anthologies. The variety and sophistication range from post-Borgesian ironists to social realists, available in Joanna Labon (ed), *Storm 7–8: New Writing from Mexico*, 1992.

BOOKLIST

The following selection includes all titles which are extracted in this chapter as well as those mentioned in the introduction which are available in English. In *general, paperback editions are given when possible. The editions cited are not necessarily the only ones available. For most of the extracted works, the original* publisher in English can be found in 'Acknowledgments and Citations' at the end of the volume, as can the exact location of the extracts and the editions from which they are taken. The date in square brackets is the original publication date of the work in its original language. Extract numbers are highlighted in bold for ease of reference.

Arreola, Juan José, *Confabulario and Other Inventions* [1962], George D. Schade, trans, University of Texas Press, Austin, TX, 1964.

Arreola, Juan José, *The Fair* [1963], John Upton, trans, University of Texas Press, Austin, TX, 1977.

Atkin, Ronald, *Revolution! Mexico 1910–1920*, Macmillan, London, 1969.

Azuela, Mariano, *The Underdogs* [1915], E. Mungía, Jr, trans, Jonathan Cape, London, 1930/ Signet, New York, 1962. **Extract 8.**

Bellow, Saul, *The Adventures of Augie March* [1953], Penguin, London, 1966/Random House, New York, 1953. **Extract 30.**

Bowles, Paul, 'Señor Ong and Señor Ha', in *Collected Stories*, Black Sparrow Press, Santa Barbara, CA, 1980. **Extract 28.**

Burroughs, William, *Queer* [1984], Picador, London, 1986/Viking Penguin, New York, 1984. **Extract 13.**

Cain, James M., *Serenade* [1938], Picador, London, 1985/AMS Press, New York. **Extract 10.**

Calderón de la Barca, Fanny, *Life in Mexico* [1842], Century Hutchinson, London, 1987.

Carballido, Emilio, *The Norther* [1958], Margaret Sayers Peden, trans, University of Texas Press, Austin, TX, 1968.

Carver, Raymond, *In a Marine Light: Selected Poems*, Picador, London, 1988. **Extract 14.**

Castellanos, Rosario, 'Balún Canán', in *Another Way to Be: Selected Works of Rosario Castellanos*, Myralyn Allgood, trans, The University of Georgia Press, Athens, GA, and London, 1990. **Extract 4.**

Cruz, Sor Juana Inés de la, *Sor Juana's Dream*, Luis Harss, trans, Lumen Books, New York, 1986; and *A Sor Juana Anthology*, Alan S. Trueblood, trans, Harvard University Press, Cambridge, MA, 1988.

Deighton, Len, *Mexico Set* [1984], Panther, London, 1985/Ballantine, New York, 1989. **Extract 15.**

del Paso, Fernando, *Palinuro of Mexico* [1977], Elizabeth Plaister, trans, Quartet, London, 1989.

Díaz, Bernal, *The Conquest of New Spain* [1576], J.M. Cohen, trans, Penguin, London, 1963. **Extract 16.**

Dryden, John, *The Indian Emperor, or the Conquest of Mexico by the Spaniards* [1665], H. Herringham, London.

Ford, Richard, *The Ultimate Good Luck* [1981], Flamingo, London, 1990/Random House, New York, 1987. **Extract 25.**

Fuentes, Carlos, *A Change of Skin* [1967], Sam Hileman, trans, André Deutsch, London, 1987/ Farrar, Straus and Giroux, New York, 1968. **Extract 2.**

Fuentes, Carlos, *Constancia and Other Stories for Virgins* [1989], Thomas Christensen, trans, André Deutsch, London, 1990/ Farrar, Straus and Giroux, New York, 1990. **Extract 17.**

Fuentes, Carlos, *The Death of Artemio Cruz* [1962], Sam Hileman, trans, Secker and Warburg, London, 1977/Farrar, Straus and Giroux, New York, 1964.

Fuentes, Carlos, *Old Gringo* [1986], Margaret Sayers Peden, trans, Picador, London, 1987/Farrar, Straus and Giroux, New York, 1986.

Fuentes, Carlos, *Where the Air is Clear* [1958], Sam Hileman, trans, Farrar, Straus and Giroux, New York, 1977. **Extract 18**.

Galindo, Sergio, *Mexican Masquerade* [1964], John and Carolyn Brushwood, trans, Latin American Literary Review Press, Pittsburgh, PA, 1984.

Galindo, Sergio, *The Precipice* [1960], John and Carolyn Brushwood, trans, University of Texas Press, Austin, TX, 1969.

Galindo, Sergio, *Rice Powder* [1958], Bert and Lara Patrick, trans, Perivale Press, Van Nuys, CA, 1978.

Garro, Elena, *Recollections of Things to Come* [1963], Ruth L.C. Simms, trans, Sidgwick and Jackson, London, 1978/University of Texas Press, Austin, TX, 1969.

Glantz, Margo, *The Family Tree* [1981], Susan Bassnett, trans, Serpent's Tail, London, 1991. **Extract 19**.

Greene, Graham, *The Lawless Roads* [1939], Penguin, London, 1971. Published in the USA as *Another Mexico*, Viking Penguin, New York, 1982. **Extract 3**.

Greene, Graham, *The Power and the Glory* [1940], Penguin, London, 1962/Viking Penguin, New York, 1991. **Extract 32**.

Guzmán, Martín Luis, *The Eagle and the Serpent* [1928], Harriet de Onís, trans, Dolphin Books, New York, 1965.

Guzmán, Martín Luis, *Memoirs of Pancho Villa* [1940], V. Taylor, trans, University of Texas Press, Austin, TX, 1965.

Haggard, Rider, *Montezuma's Daughter*, Longmans, Green and Co, 1893.

Humboldt, Alexandre von, *Political Essay on the Kingdom of New Spain* [1810], Knopf and Oklahoma University Press, Norman, OK, 1972. **Extract 12**.

Huxley, Aldous, *Eyeless in Gaza* [1936], Grafton, London, 1977/Carroll and Graf, New York, 1989. **Extract 29**.

Ibargüengoitia, Jorge, *The Dead Girls* [1974], Asa Zatz, trans, Chatto and Windus, London, 1983/Avon Books, New York, 1983.

Ibargüengoitia, Jorge, *Lightning of August* [1964], Irene del Corral, trans, Chatto and Windus, London, 1986/Avon Books, New York, 1986.

Ibargüengoitia, Jorge, *Two Crimes* [1979], Chatto and Windus, London, 1984/Avon Books, New York, 1984.

Kerouac, Jack, *On the Road* [1957], Penguin, London, 1972/Viking Penguin, New York, 1991. **Extract 20**.

Lawrence, D.H., *The Plumed Serpent* [1926], Penguin, London, 1950/Knopf, New York, 1951. **Extracts 9 and 21**.

Lópes y Fuentes, Gregorio, *El Indio* [1935], Anita Bremner, trans, Ungar, New York, 1961 (published in 1937 by Bobbs-Merrill in the USA and under the title *They That Reap* by Harrap, London, 1937).

Lowry, Malcolm, *Dark as the Grave Wherein my Friend is Laid*, Penguin, London, 1972. **Extract 26**.

Lowry, Malcolm, *Under the Volcano* [1947], Picador, London, 1990/New American Library, New York, 1984. **Extract 5**.

New Poetry of Mexico, Mark Strand, ed, Secker and Warburg, London, 1972/Dutton, New York, 1970.

Nicholson, Irene, *Firefly in the Night: A Study of Ancient Mexican Poetry and Symbolism*, Faber and Faber, London, 1959.

Olson, Charles, *Mayan Letters* [1953], Jonathan Cape, London, 1968. **Extract 34**.

Pacheco, José Emilio, 'Battles in the Desert', in *Battles in the Desert and Other Stories* [1981], Katherine Silver, trans, New Directions, New York, 1987. **Extract 22.**

Paz, Octavio, *The Collected Poems, 1957–1987*, Eliot Weinberger, ed, Carcanet, Manchester, 1988/ New Directions, New York, 1987.

Paz, Octavio, *The Labyrinth of Solitude: Life and Thought in Mexico* [1950], Lysander Kemp, trans, Penguin, London, 1985/Grove Press, New York, 1961.

Paz, Octavio, *The Other Mexico: Critique of the Pyramid* [1970], Lysander Kemp, trans, Grove Press, New York, 1972.

Paz, Octavio, *Selected Poems*, Charles Tomlinson, ed, Penguin, London, 1979. **Extract 31.**

Paz, Octavio, *Selected Poems*, Eliot Weinberger, ed, New Directions, New York, 1984. **Extract 23.**

Paz, Octavio, *Sor Juana: or, The Traps of Faith* [1986], Margaret Sayers Peden, trans, Harvard University Press, Cambridge, MA, 1988 (published as *Sor Juana: Her Life and Her World*, Faber and Faber, London, 1988).

Paz, Octavio, *Sun Stone* [1957], Muriel Rukeyser, trans, New Directions, New York, 1962.

Poniatowska, Elena, *Massacre in Mexico* [1971], Helen Lane, trans, Viking Press, New York, 1975.

Prescott, W.H., *The History of the Conquest of Mexico*, R. Bentley, London, 1843.

Porter, Katherine Anne, *Flowering Judas*, The Modern Library, New York, 1935. **Extract 11.**

Ramos, Samuel, *Profile of Man and Culture in Mexico*, University of Texas Press, Austin, TX, 1962.

Revueltas, José, *Human Mourning* [1943], Roberto Crespi, trans, University of Minnesota Press, Minneapolis, MN, 1989.

Reyes, Alfonso, *Mexico in a Nutshell and Other Essays*, University of California Press, Berkeley, CA, 1964.

Riding, Alan, *Mexico: Inside the Volcano*, I.B. Tauris, London, 1987.

Romero, José Rubén, *Notes of a Villager: A Mexican Poet's Youth and Revolution* [1932], John Mitchell and Ruth Mitchell de Aguilar, trans, Plover Press, Kaneohe, HI, 1988. **Extract 27.**

Rulfo, Juan, *The Burning Plain and Other Stories* [1953], George D. Schade, trans, University of Texas Press, Austin, TX, 1967.

Rulfo, Juan, *Pedro Paramo: A Novel of Mexico* [1955], Grove Press and John Calder, New York and London, 1959. **Extract 7.**

Sáinz, Gustavo, *Gazapo* [1965], Hardie St Martin, trans, Farrar, Straus and Giroux, New York, 1968.

Sáinz, Gustavo, *The Princess of the Iron Palace* [1974], Andrew Hurley, trans, Grove Press, New York, 1987.

Schmidt, Michael, and Kissam, Edward, *Flower and Song: Aztec Poetry*, Anvil Press Poetry, London, 1977.

Soustelle, Jacques, *The Daily Life of the Aztecs* [1955], Penguin, London, 1964.

Storm 7–8: New Writing from Mexico, Joanna Labon, ed, 1992 (distributed by Cape, London).

Tomlinson, Charles, *Notes from New York and Other Poems*, Oxford University Press, Oxford, 1984. **Extract 24.**

Traven, B., *The Carreta* [1931], Allison and Busby, London, 1984/ Schocken, New York, 1987.

Traven, B., *The General from the Jungle* [1940], Allison and Busby, London, 1985/Schocken, New York, 1987.

Traven, B., *The Rebellion of the Hanged* [1936], Charles Duff, trans, Penguin, London, 1970/ Schocken, New York, 1987. **Extract 1.**

Traven, B., *The Treasure of the Sierra Madre* [1927], Basil Creighton, trans, Picador, London, 1983/ Hill and Wang, New York, 1984. **Extract 6.**

Turner, John Kenneth, *Barbarous Mexico* [1911], University of Texas Press, Austin, TX, 1969.

Usigli, Rodolfo, *Crown of Shadows* [1943], William Stirling, trans, Wingate, London, 1946.

Yáñez, Agustín, *The Edge of the Storm* [1947], Ethel Brinton, trans, University of Texas Press, Austin, Texas, 1963. **Extract 33.**

Extracts

(1) CHIAPAS

B. Traven, *The Rebellion of the Hanged*

Traven opens his relentless novel about Indian exploitation during Porfirio Díaz's dictatorship in the logging woods in Chiapas with a description of one of his main Indian characters.

Candido Castro, the Mexican Indian of Tsotsil race, lived with his wife Marcelina de las Casas and the two children Angelino and Pedrito in a hut which was in the 'independent' or self-constituted agricultural colony of Cuishin, not far from Chalchihuistan. His modest piece of property amounted to about five acres of stony, parched and calcinated soil, so that to feed his family he had to work extremely hard.

The big landowners – the *finqueros*, as they were called – of the surrounding districts of Jovel and Chilum more than once tried to persuade and entice Candido, their aim being to get him to abandon his miserable little dwelling and come to work for them as a *peón* or hired man, bringing all his family with him. Those landowners were unceasing in their quest for new Indian families – indispensable labour for their estates – and they had no scruples about the means they employed to uproot Indians from their settlements . . .

The colony, the group of huts, was made up of five families belonging, like Candido, to the race of Tsotsil Indians. Their patches of land were as desolate as his. Their miserable hovels were made of palm-leaves crudely mixed with mud, and in that place they led an existence such as only those humble rural Mexican Indians are capable of enduring. Nevertheless, all efforts on the part of landowners to turn them into hired workers had produced the same results as in the case of Candido. The Indians knew that, in many ways, life on the big estates was sweeter than on their arid, dry and sun-baked soil – the colony well merited its name *Cuishin*, which means 'burning' – but they preferred their precarious existence, with the perpetual anguish of seeing their harvests ruined, to the yoke of a landlord boss, though this servitude might have given them a Garden of Eden in exchange for the lost freedom. They preferred to be racked with hunger in their own independence and liberty rather than grow fat under the orders of a master.

(2) CHOLULA

Carlos Fuentes, *A Change of Skin*

A group of trendies drive to Cholula (a town in Puebla state of about 20 000 inhabitants), a symbol of Christianized Mexico with some 70 churches atop a huge ruined Aztec pyramid. Fuentes opens his novel by making them unaware of the history of Cortés's destruction of the earlier city.

When the four of you entered today all you saw was the narrow filthy streets and the packed houses that are all alike, all of one storey, all a blind wall with a too wide door of cracking wood, all daubed yellow and blue. Sure, I know, now and again you passed a dwelling that crowed money, an elegant home with windows that watch the street and boast those touches Mexicans find so irresistible, fancy wrought-iron grilles, projecting awnings of cross-ribbed canvas. But where, Isabel, were the good citizens who live behind those windows? Did they come out to welcome you to town, or did they leave that office to the dust and the filth, the misery crowded around you, the barefoot women with dark faces wrapped in shawls, the heavy pregnant bellies, the naked children, the packs of street dogs. Packs of mongrels that drift everywhere, go nowhere. Some yellow, some black, all lost, listless, strengthless, hungry, scratching at their infestations of sores and fleas, poking along gutters for garbage scraps, crippled, emaciated, with the slanted red and yellow eyes, dripping infection, that betray their coyote ancestry; white-nosed, hair worn off, bare hides splotched with scabs, torpid and purposeless as they whine the slow rhythm of this torpid purposeless town that once upon a time was the pantheon of an ancient Mexican world. Cholula, town of misery today, festering today, this Sabbath the eleventh of April, 1965, with diseased dogs and women with swollen wombs who pad the dust barefoot and laugh silently as they exchange their joking secrets and their secret jokes in voices that cannot be heard, words thinly inflected, fused chains of inaudible syllables.

(3) CIUDAD DE LAS CASAS

Graham Greene, *The Lawless Roads*

In the spring of 1938 Greene was sent to Mexico to report on the persecution of priests in Tabasco and Chiapas, where he rode for three days on mule back to Las Casas (today known as Ciudad de las Casas, Chiapas).

It was a lovely town to wake to in the early morning light, as the donkeys went plodding round laden with bright chemical gaseosas for the saloons – low single-storey houses with brown tiled roofs and little flowery patios, the mountains crouched all round like large and friendly dogs; twenty-two churches, of which five were open, but no priest allowed inside.

The finest church is the old colonial church of Santo Domingo sharing a little green square with La Caridad and the prison – once the presbytery. A long flight of steps down into the square, barley-sugar pillars up the facade – the colour of pale terra-cotta – statues headless where the troops have reached them; inside flowers and white drapery had been set for Easter, the church was scrupulously clean, a heavy curtain hung before the altar, and Christ lay dead among flowers. The walls were crammed with dark old eighteenth-century portraits of bishops and saints set in heavy and tortuous gilt. It gave an effect of fullness – and of emptiness, like a meeting when the leader had gone. Nothing meant anything any more; it was just sentiment to spread flowers and drapery; the Host wasn't here. There was no more reason to remove the hat than in a ruin, than in the church on the hill above the city, smashed and shady with love-initialled walls and snaky chambers. Santo Domingo, La Caridad, La Merced with a ruined cavalry barracks next door in what was once the presbytery, a broken square outside with a rotting bandstand in the middle of a rubbish dump – well, it was Easter, we were celebrating the death of God. This emptiness and desolation was right, in a way.

(4) COMITAN

Rosario Castellanos, *Balún Canán*

The young girl narrator in Rosario Castellanos's novel is brought up on her father's estate in Comitán, Chiapas (near the Mexican/Guatemalan border, with a population of some 55 000), observing the Indian life around her. Extracted from Another Way to Be: Selected Works of Rosario Castellanos – see Booklist.

In Comitán we have several fairs every year, but none is as joyous and lively as that of Saint Caralampio. He has the reputation of being a miracle worker, and people make pilgrimages from far away to pray before his image. It was carved in Guatemala and shows him in a kneeling position, with a long white beard and a saintly glow, while the executioner has the fatal axe poised over his head. (All we know about the executioner is that he was a Jew.) But now the people of the village have to stop outside the doors of the church, since it is closed like all the rest, on orders from the government. That isn't sufficient reason to call off the fair, so in the plaza booths and promenades are being set up.

Peddlers come down from San Cristóbal with their loads of goods: dried fruit, pickles, badly made rag dolls with their cheeks scandalously painted red to leave no doubt that they are from the cool highlands, pottery shepherds with thick ankles, little sheep made of cotton, boxes of varnished wood, and rustic weavings.

The merchants – all wrapped up in woollen blankets – spread their wares on rush mats on the ground. They proclaim them to the multitudes with voices hoarse from smoking strong tobacco. They haggle patiently and stubbornly over prices. The rancher in his bright satin jacket gapes in astonishment at the abundance spread before him. After thinking long and hard he pulls a homespun handkerchief from his pocket, unties the knots that guard his money, and buys a pound of hazelnuts, a bundle of cigars, and a small violin. Down the way the lottery is being held.

(5) CUERNAVACA

Malcolm Lowry, *Under the Volcano*

Lowry's novel about the breakdown and final pathetic death of the lovesick, alcoholic, failed-writer Firmin opens with a description of Quauhnahuac (Cuernavaca) on the Day of the Dead in 1938, where two friends recall the same day the year before in 1937.

Two mountain chains traverse the republic roughly from north to south, forming between them a number of valleys and plateaus. Overlooking one of these valleys, which is dominated by two volcanoes, lies, six thousand feet above sea-level, the town of Quauhnahuac. It is situated well south of the Tropic of Cancer, to be exact, on the nineteenth parallel, in about the same latitude as the Revillagigedo Islands to the west in the Pacific, or very much farther west, the southernmost tip of Hawaii – and as the port of Tzucox to the east on the Atlantic seabord of Yucatan near the border of British Honduras, or very much farther east, the town of Juggernaut, in India, on the Bay of Bengal.

The walls of the town, which is built on a hill, are high, the streets and lanes tortuous and broken, the road winding. A fine American-style highway leads in from the north but is lost in its narrow streets and comes out a goat track. Quauhnahuac possesses eighteen churches and fifty-seven *cantinas*. It also boasts a golf course and no fewer than four hundred swimming-pools, public and private, filled with the water that ceaselessly pours down from the mountains, and many splendid hotels.

The Hotel Casino de la Selva stands on a slightly higher hill just outside town, near the railway station. It is built far back from the main highway and surrounded by gardens and terraces which command a spacious view in every direction. Palatial, a certain air of desolate splendour pervades it. For it is no longer a Casino. You may not even dice for drinks in the bar. The ghosts of ruined gamblers haunt it . . .

What had happened just a year ago today seemed already to belong to a different age. One would have thought the horrors of the present would have swallowed it up like a drop of water. It was not so. Though tragedy was in the process of becoming unreal and meaningless it seemed one was still permitted to remember the days when an individual life held some value and was not a mere misprint in a communiqué. He lit a cigarette. Far to his left, in the north-east, beyond the valley and terraced foothills of the Sierra Madre Occidental, the two volcanoes, Popocatepetl and Ixtaccihuatl, rose clear and magnificent into the sunset. Nearer, perhaps ten miles distant, and on a lower level than the main valley, he made out the village of Tomalín, nestling behind the jungle, from which rose a thin blue scarf of illegal smoke, someone burning wood for carbon. Before him, on the other side of the American highway, spread fields and groves, through which meandered a river and the Alcapancingo road. The watchtower of a prison rose over a wood between the river and the road which lost itself farther on where the purple hills of a Doré Paradise sloped away into the distance. Over in the town the lights of Quauhnahuac's one cinema, built on an incline and standing out sharply, suddenly came on, flickered off, came on again. 'No se puede vivir sin amar,' M. Laruelle said . . . 'As that estúpido inscribed on my house'.

(6) DURANGO

B. Traven, *The Treasure of the Sierra Madre*

Dobbs thinks he has got away from his companions with the gold dust they discovered in the hills. He spies Durango (with a population of 600 000 and a cathedral built in 1695) in the distance, meets three Mexican mestizos, and offers them a peso to help him with his donkeys. But they attack him, slice off his head with a machete, and unwittingly spill the gold dust into the sand.

Towards noon of the next day when the path went over a hill, he could see Durango in the distance. Durango, the lovely jewel of the Sierra Madre, which, bathed in golden light and softly fanned by gentle breezes caressing it with the tenderness of a feminine hand, nestles between protecting hills. 'The Town of Sunshine' it is called by those who, once having seen it, are homesick for its endearing loveliness. Mother Earth, who is not stingy when once she has a mind to make a present, has placed on one side of it one of her miracles of nature, the 'Cerro del Mercado', a mountain of pure iron, six hundred million tons of pure iron ore.

That evening he camped for the last time. Next evening he would be in Durango and on the following morning in the train for Canitas. The sale of the donkeys and the rest of his gear would take little time, as he would ask no more than he stood in need of for his journey.

He was jubilant. He was in sight of port. When the wind was in the right direction he could hear the whistle of the goods trains in the silence of the night. And this shrieking whistle of the engines, which often sounds so mysterious and ghostly, made him feel that he was already in an hotel close to the station. It was the cry of civilization and this cry was his assurance of safety. He had a longing for law and order, for the solid masonry of the town, for everything which would serve to guard his treasure.

(7) JALISCO

Juan Rulfo, *Pedro Paramo*

Guided by his mother's memories, Juan Preciado arrives in Comala to find out who his father is. Comala is an invented Mexican town that could be any of the ghost towns in Jalisco.

I didn't intend to keep my promise. But then I began to think about what she told me, until I couldn't stop thinking and even dreaming about it, and building a whole world around that Pedro Páramo. That's why I came to Comala.

It was in the dog-days, when the hot August wind is poisoned by the rotten smell of the saponaria, and the road went up and down, up and down . . .

'What's the name of that village down there?'

'Comala, sir.'

'You're sure it's Comala?'

'Yes, sir.'

'Why does it look so dead?'

'They've had bad times, sir.'

I expected it to look the way it did in my mother's memories. She was always sighing for Comala, she was homesick and wanted to come back, but she never did. Now I was coming back in her place, and I remembered what she told me: 'There's a beautiful view when you get to Los Colimotes. You'll see a green plain . . . it's yellow when the corn is ripe. You can see Comala from there. The houses are all white, and at night it's all lighted up.' Her voice was soft and secret, almost a whisper, as if she were talking to herself . . .

The heat shimmered on the plain like a transparent lake. There was a line of mountains beyond the plain, and beyond that, nothing but the distance.

'What does your father look like?'

'I don't know,' I said. 'I just know that he's called Pedro Páramo.'

. . .

After we crossed the ridge we started downhill again. We left the warm air up there and walked down into pure heat without a breath of air in it. Everything looked as if it were waiting for something.

'It's hot here,' I said.

'This is nothing. Just wait, you'll be a lot hotter when you get to Comala. That town's the hottest place in the world. They say that when somebody dies in Comala, after he arrives in Hell he goes back to get his blanket'.

(8) JUCHIPILA, NEAR AGUASCALIENTES

Mariano Azuela, *The Underdogs*

Azuela's jaded revolutionaries pass through Juchipila, on a river of the same name, near Aguascalientes in 1914. Their motives for fighting have turned into bloodlust and alienated the peasants.

They entered the streets of Juchipila as the church bells rang, loud and joyfully, with that peculiar tone that thrills every mountaineer.

'It makes me think we are back in the days when the revolution was just beginning, when the bells rang like mad in every town we entered and everybody came out with music, flags, cheers, and fireworks to welcome us,' said Anastasio Montáñez.

'They don't like us any more,' Demetrio returned.

'Of course. We're crawling back like a dog with its tail between its legs,' Quail remarked.

'It ain't that, I guess. They don't give a whoop for the other side either.'

'But why should they like us?'

They spoke no more.

Presently they reached the city square and stopped in front of an octagonal, rough, massive church, reminiscent of the colonial period. At one time the square must have been a garden, judging from the bare stunted orange trees planted between iron and wooden benches. The sonorous, joyful bells rang again. From within the church, the honeyed voices of a female chorus rose melancholy and grave. To the strains of a guitar, the young girls of the town sang the 'Mysteries'.

'What's the fiesta, lady?' Venancio asked of an old woman who was running toward the church.

'The Sacred Heart of Jesus!' answered the pious woman, panting.

They remembered that one year ago they had captured Zacatecas. They grew sadder still.

Juchipila, like the other towns they had passed through on their way from Tepic, by way of Jalisco, Aguascalientes and Zacatecas, was in ruins. The black trail of the incendiaries showed in the roofless houses, in the burnt arcades. Almost all the houses were closed, yet, here and there, those still open offered, in ironic contrast, portals gaunt and bare as the white skeletons of horses scattered over the roads. The terrible pangs of hunger seemed to speak from every face; hunger on every dusty cheek, in their dusty countenances; in the hectic flame of their eyes, which, when they met a soldier, blazed with hatred. In vain soldiers scoured the streets in search of food, biting their lips in anger. A single lunchroom was open; at once they filled it. No beans, no tortillas, only chili and tomato sauce.

(9) Lake Chapala

D.H. Lawrence, *The Plumed Serpent*

*In his novel, Lawrence changed actual Lake Chapala in Jalisco
to Sayula. The house where he wrote it still exists, as does the
church on the lakefront at the end of the novel. Sybille Bedford
stayed on the same lake in the 1950s in A Visit to Don Otavio:
A Traveller's Tale from Mexico.*

Sayula was a little lake resort; not for the idle rich, for Mexico has few
left; but for tradespeople from Guadalajara, and week-enders. Even of
these, there were few.

Nevertheless, there were two hotels, left over, really, from the safe
quiet days of Don Porfirio, as were most of the villas. The outlying
villas were shut up, some of them abandoned. Those in the village lived
in a perpetual quake of fear. There were many terrors, but the two
regnant were bandits and bolshevists.

Bandits were merely men who, in the outlying villages, having very
often no money, no work, and no prospects, take to robbery and
murder for a time – occasionally for a lifetime – as a profession. They
live in their wild villages until troops are sent after them, when they
retire into the savage mountains, or the marshes.

Bolshevists, somehow, seem to be born on the railway. Wherever
the iron rails run, and passengers are hauled back and forth in railway
coaches, there the spirit of rootlessness, of transitoriness, of first and
second class in separate compartments, of envy and malice, and of iron
and demonish panting engines, seems to bring forth the logical
children of materialism, the bolshevists.

Sayula had her little branch of railway, her one train a day. The
railway did not pay, and fought with extinction. But it was enough.

Sayula also had that real insanity of America, the automobile. As
men used to want a horse and a sword, now they want a car. As women
used to pine for a home and a box at the theatre, now it is a 'machine'.
And the poor follow the middle class. There was a perpetual rush of
'machines', motor-cars and motor-buses – called *camiónes* – along the
one forlorn road coming to Sayula from Guadalajara. One hope, one
faith, one destiny; to ride in a *camión*, to own a car.

There was a little bandit scare when Kate arrived in the village, but
she did not pay much heed. At evening she went into the *plaza*, to be
with the people. The *plaza* was a square with big trees and a disused
bandstand in the centre, a little promenade all round, and then the
cobbled streets where the donkeys and the *camiónes* passed. There was a
further little section of real market-place on the north side.

The band played no more in Sayula, and the *elegancia* strolled no
more on the inner pavement around the *plaza*, under the trees. But the

pavement was still good, and the benches were still more-or-less sound. Oh Don Porfirio's day! And now it was the peons and Indians, in their blankets and white clothes, who filled the benches and monopolized the square.

(10) MEXICO: AN INDIAN HUT

James M. Cain, *Serenade*

> James Cain's failed opera singer is driving with a whore to help her run a brothel in Acapulco. They stop on the way from Mexico City to visit her Indian parents. Later they are stranded in a church, become lovers, and he recuperates his voice.

Maybe you never saw an Indian hut, so I better tell you what it looks like. You can start with the coloured shanties down near the railroad track in New Orleans, and then, when you've got them clearly in mind, you can imagine they're the Waldorf-Astoria Hotel and that the Mexican hut is a shanty standing beside it. There's no walls, or roof, or anything like you're used to seeing. There's four sides made of sticks, stuck down in the ground and wattled together with twigs, about as high as a man's head. In the middle of the front side is a break, and that's the door. The chinks between the twigs are filled up a little bit with mud. Just plain mud, smeared on there and most of it falling off. And on top is a thatch of grass, or palmetto, or whatever grows up on the hill, and that's all. There's no windows, no floor, no furniture, no pictures of the Grand Canyon hanging on the walls, no hay-grain-and-feed calendars back of the clock, with a portrait of a cowgirl on top of a horse. They've got no need for calendars, because in the first place they couldn't figure out what the writing was for, and in the second place they don't care what day it is. And they've got no need for a clock because they don't care what time it is. All I'm trying to say is, there's nothing in there but a dirt floor, and the mats they sleep on, and down near the door, the fire where they do their cooking.

(11) MEXICO: MAGUEY FIELDS

Katherine Anne Porter, *Hacienda*

*In her satirical story about the chaotic filming during the 1930s
of Eisenstein's unfinished epic Viva Mexico, Katherine Anne
Porter here mocks Kennerly (Upton Sinclair), Eisenstein's
backer, as they go by train to the hacienda where they are to
film. 'Hacienda' is a story in the collection Flowering Judas – see
Booklist.*

The sun was shining when we left Mexico City, but mile by mile
through the solemn valley of the pyramids we climbed through the
maguey fields towards the thunderous blue cloud banked solidly in the
east, until it dissolved and received us gently in a pallid, silent rain. We
hung our heads out of the window every time the train paused, raising
false hopes in the hearts of the Indian women who ran along beside us,
faces thrown back and arms stretching upward even after the train was
moving away.

'Fresh pulque!' they urged mournfully, holding up their clay jars filled
with thick gray-white liquor. 'Fresh maguey worms!' they cried in
despair above the clamor of the turning wheels, waving like nosegays
the leaf bags, slimy and lumpy with the worms they had gathered one at
a time from the cactus whose heart bleeds the honey water for the
pulque. They ran along still hoping, their brown fingers holding the
bags lightly by the very tips, ready to toss them if the travelers should
change their minds and buy, even then, until the engine outran them,
their voices floated away and they were left clustered together, a little
knot of faded blue skirts and shawls, in the indifferent rain.

Kennerly opened three bottles of luke-warm bitter beer. 'The water is
filthy!' he said earnestly, taking a ponderous, gargling swig from his
bottle. 'Isn't it horrible, the things they eat and drink?' he asked, as if,
no matter what we might in our madness (for he did not trust either of
us) say, he already knew the one possible answer. He shuddered and for
a moment could not swallow his lump of sweet American chocolate: 'I
have just come back,' he told me, trying to account for his extreme
sensitiveness in these matters, 'from God's country', meaning California. He ripped open an orange trademarked in purple ink. 'I'll simply
have to get used to all this all over again. What a relief to eat fruit that
isn't full of germs. I brought them all the way back with me.' (I could
fairly see him legging across the Sonora desert with a knapsack full of
oranges.) 'Have one. Anyhow it's clean.' . . .

'It's these Mexicans,' he said as if it were an outrage to find them in
Mexico. 'They would drive any man crazy in no time . . .'.

(12) MEXICO: MESCAL AND MAGUEY

Alexandre von Humboldt,
Political Essay on the Kingdom of New Spain

The German explorer and scientist Alexandre von Humboldt was curious about everything. He recorded his omnivorous, encyclopaedic fascination with all that he saw during his five years in South and Central America in thirty volumes on his return from his travels in 1804.

A very intoxicating brandy is formed from the pulque which is called *mescal*. I have been assured that the plant cultivated for distillation differs essentially from the common maguey. It appeared to me smaller, and the leaves not so glaucous, but not having seen it in flower I cannot judge of the difference between the two species. The Spanish government has long been very severe against the mescal which is strictly prohibited because the use of it is prejudicial to the Spanish brandy trade. However, an enormous quantity of this maguey brandy is manufactured in the intendancies of Valladolid, Mexico and Durango . . .

But the maguey is not only the vine of the Aztecs; it can also supply the place of the hemp of Asia and the papyrus of the Egyptians. The paper on which the ancient Mexicans painted their hieroglyphical figures was made of the fibres of agave leaves, macerated in water, and disposed in layers like the fibers of the Egyptian papyrus. I brought with me several fragments of Aztec manuscripts written on maguey paper of a thickness so different that some of them resemble pasteboard while others resemble Chinese paper. These fragments are particularly interesting as the only hieroglyphics which exist at Vienna and Rome are on Mexican stag skins. The thread which is obtained from the maguey is known in Europe by the name of pite (pita) thread, and is preferred by naturalists to every other because it is less subject to twist. The juice which the agave yields when it is still far from the period of efflorescence is very acrid, and is successfully employed as a caustic in the cleaning of wounds. The prickles which terminate the leaves served formerly, like those of the cactus, for pins and nails to the Indians. The Mexican priests pierced their arms and breasts with them in their acts of expiation.

(13) MEXICO CITY

William Burroughs, *Queer*

Burroughs had escaped to Mexico City, which he hated, threatened with arrest on a drugs charge. In this autobiographical novel, his rich junkie protagonist Lee begins in Mexico City in the late 1940s, and ends up fruitlessly looking for yage, the hallucinatory drug, in Ecuador. In this passage he asserts his superiority over a Mexico City cab driver.

'Three pesos to Insurgentes and Monterrey,' Lee said to the driver in his atrocious Spanish. The driver said four. Lee waved him on. The driver muttered something, and opened the door.

Inside, Lee turned to Allerton. 'The man plainly harbors subversive thoughts. You know, when I was at Princeton, Communism was the thing. To come out flat for private [property] and a class society, you marked yourself a stupid lout or suspect to be a High Episcopalian pederast. But I held out against the infection – of Communism I mean, of course.'

'*Aquí.*' Lee handed three pesos to the driver, who muttered some more and started the car with a vicious clash of gears.

'Sometimes I think they don't like us,' said Allerton.

'I don't mind people disliking me,' Lee said. 'The question is, what are they in a position to do about it? Apparently nothing, at present. They don't have the green light. This driver, for example, hates gringos. But if he kills someone – and very possibly he will – it will not be an American. It will be another Mexican. Maybe his good friend. Friends are less frightening than strangers.'

(14) MEXICO CITY

Raymond Carver, *The Young Fire Eaters of Mexico City*

Carver shows in this poem (from In a Marine Light: Selected Poems – see Booklist) how some of Mexico City's slum kids survive as street performers.

They fill their mouths with alcohol
and blow it over a lighted candle
at traffic signs. Anyplace, really,
where cars line up and drivers
are angry and frustrated and looking
for distraction – there you'll find
the young fire eaters. Doing what they do

for a few pesos. If they're lucky.
But in a year their lips
are scorched and their throats raw.
They have no voice within a year.
They can't talk or cry out –
these silent children who hunt
through the streets with a candle
and a beer can filled with alcohol.
They are called *milusos*. Which translates
into a 'thousand uses'.

(15) MEXICO CITY

Len Deighton, *Mexico Set*

In Deighton's spy thriller Bernard is sent out to 'enrol' a KGB colonel in Mexico City, with trips down to the Mexican Pacific coast and all over Mexico City. The plot involves Bernard's defected spy wife, and scenes in London and Berlin.

You look out for the *tacheria* which always has smoke from the open fire and a line of people waiting for the fresh tacos. Across the road there are the buses that bring pilgrims to the Shrine of Guadalupe. Buses of all shapes and sizes and colours. Huge air-conditioned monsters that bring people from the big international hotels downtown and bone-rattling old wrecks which convey pilgrims from across the mountains. But the customers buying tacos are not all from the shrine; locals come here too.

Next door to the smoky *tacheria* is the place where I was to meet Stinnes. It is a large, shed-like building with a ramshackle frontage. Across the bright-red overhang, 'Angel – body shop' is crudely lettered in bloody script. Inside there are trucks and motor cars in various stages of repair and renovation. And always there is the intense flashing light, and the intermittent hiss of the welding torch. There is always work for the skilled car-repair men in Mexico City.

I got there early, drove through the workshop, and parked in the backyard. Angel Morales, a small, sad-eyed man with dark skin and a carefully trimmed moustache, came out to see who it was. 'I'm meeting someone, Angel,' I said. 'It's business.' I passed him an envelope containing money.

Angel nodded mournfully. Angel was a friend of a friend of mine but we'd put things on a proper business footing from the time we first met. It was better than using any of the safe houses that the SIS people at the embassy would provide for me. He took the envelope and tucked it into a pocket of his oily overalls without looking inside it. 'I want no trouble,' said Angel. That must have been the only English that Angel knew, for he'd said the same words to me on the two previous meetings.

'There'll be no trouble, Angel,' I said, giving him the sort of wide smile that I'd seen on carefree men with easy minds.

He nodded and went back to shout abuse at an Indian youth who was bolting a new section of metal on to the back of a badly broken truck.

(16) Mexico City (Tenochtitlan)

Bernal Díaz, *The Conquest of New Spain*

This is Bernal Díaz's classic account of first peering on to Tenochtitlan in 1519. Tenochtitlan was the island capital of the Aztec empire, never even dreamed of by Europeans. It was razed and rebuilt as Mexico City in 1525.

Next morning, we came to a broad causeway and continued our march towards Iztapalapa. And when we saw all those cities and villages built in the water, and other great towns on dry land, that straight and level causeway leading to Mexico, we were astounded. These great towns and *cues* and buildings rising from the water, all made of stone, seemed like an enchanted vision from the tale of Amadis. Indeed, some of our soldiers asked whether it was not all a dream. It is not surprising therefore that I should write in this vein. It was all so wonderful that I do not know how to describe this first glimpse of things never heard of, seen, or dreamed of before.

When we arrived near Iztapalapa we beheld the splendour of the other *Caciques* who came out to meet us, the lord of that city whose name was Cuitlahuac, and the lord of Culuacan, both of them close relations of Montezuma. And when we entered the city of Iztapalapa, the sight of the palaces in which they lodged us! They were very spacious and well built, of magnificent stone, cedar wood, and the wood of other sweet-smelling trees, with great rooms and courts, which were a wonderful sight, and all covered with awnings of woven cotton.

When we had taken a good look at all this, we went to the orchard and garden, which was a marvellous place both to see and walk in. I was never tired of noticing the diversity of trees and the various scents given off by each, and the paths choked with roses and other flowers, and the many local fruit-trees and rose-bushes, and the pond of fresh water. Another remarkable thing was that large canoes could come into the garden from the lake, through a channel they had cut, and their crews did not have to disembark. Everything was shining with lime and decorated with different kinds of stonework and paintings which were a marvel to gaze on. Then there were birds of many breeds and varieties which came to the pond. I say again that I stood looking at it, and thought that no land like it would ever be discovered in the whole world, because at that time Peru was neither known nor thought of. But today all that I then saw is overthrown and destroyed; nothing is left standing.

(17) Mexico City

Carlos Fuentes,
Constancia and Other Stories for Virgins

Through his narrator, Fuentes shows how the dramatic changes in Mexico City have created a special nostalgia.

My house in Las Lomas de Chapultepec has one outstanding virtue: it shows the advantages of immortality. I don't know how people felt about it when it was constructed, when the forties were dawning. The Second World War brought Mexico a lot of money. We exported raw materials at high prices and the farmworkers entered the churches on their knees, praying for the war to go on. Cotton, hemp, vegetables, strategic minerals; it all went out in every direction. I don't know how many cows had to die in Sonora for this great house to be erected in Las Lomas, or how many black-market deals lay behind its stone and mortar. You have seen such houses along the Paseo de la Reforma and the Boulevard de los Virreyes and in the Polanco neighborhood: they are architectural follies of pseudo-colonial inspiration, resembling the interior of the Alameda movie house, which in turn mimics the Plateresque of Taxco with its cupolas, towers, and portals, not to mention that movie house's artificial ceiling, dappled with hundred-watt stars and adorned with scudding little clouds. My house in Boulevard de los Virreyes stopped short of that.

Surely the Churrigueresque delirium of the house I have lived in for more than twenty years was an object of derision. I imagine two or three caricatures by Abel Quezada making fun of the cathedral-like portal, the wrought-iron balconies, the nightmare ornamentation of decorations, reliefs, curves, angles, madonnas, cornucopias, fluted plaster columns, and stained-glass windows. *Inside* reproduces *outside*: once again, in a hall that rises two stories, we encounter the blue-tile stairs, the iron railing and balconies overlooking the hall from the bedrooms, the iron candelabra with its artificial candles dripping fake wax of petrified plastic, the floor of Talavera tile, the uncomfortable wood-and-leather furniture, straight and stiff as if receiving a sentence from the Holy Inquisition. What a production . . . !

But the extraordinary thing, as I was saying, is that this white elephant, this symbol of vulgar pretension and the new money of the entrepreneurs who made a profit off the war, has been converted, with time, into a relic of a better era. Today, when things are fast going downhill, we fondly recall a time when things were looking up. Better vulgar and satisfied than miserable but refined. You don't need me to tell you that. Bathed in the glow of nostalgia, unique and remote in a new world of skyscrapers, glass and concrete, my grotesque quasimodel home (my Quasimodo abode, my friends, ha ha! it might be hunch-backed, but it's mine, all mine!) has now become a museum piece . . .

(18) MEXICO CITY

Carlos Fuentes, *Where the Air is Clear*

In this, his first novel, Fuentes attempts to convey the mess of Mexico City through a representative bunch of interlocked characters, many of them named in this extract.

One more, One more, signaled the fingers of peso-cab drivers. Cars raced, zigzagging, squeezed into packs, *tan-tar-ran-ta-tan-tan.* Their horns woke Rodrigo Pola; the city's impenitent racket filtered through cracks into his inside room on Rosales Street. On the roof of her home surrounded by the hills of Las Lomas, Norma Larragoiti de Robles spread cushions and made herself comfortable on them, took off her silk wrapper, and with care, aware of the smallest of her pores, anointed her body with an opal oil. Sun tan. Hortensia Chacón, forever in darkness, waited for sounds from Tonalá Street, waited for the moment when the school would let out in the afternoon, and for the sound of a key in its lock. And on Avenida Mixcoac men were opening a new way through wine stores and third-rate movies and little sales-stalls and the roar of steamrollers and air-hammers and asphalt heaters, slowly and dustily, but none of that reached the sealed room where Rosenda Pola slept, as always in delirium, captive of a lucidity that could not be put alive into the world, that clotted and stuck inside her trembling emaciated throat. Charlotte, Pierrot, Silvia Régules, Gus, Prince Vampa, Pichi, Junior, all were sleeping. Only Pimpinela de Ovando was ready for the new day, straight and perfumed, wearing dark glasses and walking along Madero toward Roberto Régules's office. From Robles's high window, Mexico City spread itself like a fanned deck of playing cards . . . the Ace of Spades at Santo Domingo street, the three of hearts in Polanco . . . from the dark tunnel of Mina, Canal del Norte, and Agentina, mouth open, searching for air and light while coughing up lottery tickets and gonorrhea carriers, to the straight but not strait propriety of

Reforma, indifferent to the crowded minor vices of Roma and Cuauhté-
moc's brittle-faced rising walls. From his office Robles looked down
upon ungainly cluttered rooftops . . .

(19) MEXICO CITY

Margo Glantz, *The Family Tree*

*Margo Glantz's novel about her immigrant parents' adaptation
to Mexico compares the past to the present in a city that has
dramatically transformed itself over the past 40 years.*

Every day I go down the street now renamed after Miguel Angel de
Quevedo, an early ecologist known as the Apostle of the tree. Miguel
Angel de Quevedo would turn in his grave if he could see that the
tallest of the Mexican cypress trees that used to grow along the narrow,
beautiful avenue have been torn up and destroyed. Now the remaining
trees will be isolated and their roots (that you can see through the soil)
will be crushed by the yellowish pavement and by all the heavy trucks
that pass over them, with the result that the trees will lose their colours
and the rest of us our clean air. I can't feel any satisfaction when I go
down Zamora Street in Coyoacán which has been virtually dis-
embowelled for some months now because they are laying huge pipes
inside its delicate belly. Even the drunks in the El Combate bar are
upset about that!

Still, I suppose we should console ourselves. Lima is pretty horrible
too, and streets are being destroyed in Buenos Aires, and art nouveau
buildings are being torn down in Montevideo, though those countries
are all further down the road to underdevelopment. Even Caracas has
traffic jams and buildings are replacing trees and the mountains are
disappearing from the horizon, though that seems impossible, since
Venezuela has only just become an oil rich nation and we have all kinds
of natural resources here in Mexico.

Nevertheless, I can't do anything but sink back into nostalgic
recollection whenever I go into a museum and see on a wall a painting,
sometimes a huge one, by Velasco, and I am faced with the former
crystalline magnificence of this region. There is an almost epic quality
to the light.

(20) MEXICO CITY

Jack Kerouac, *On the Road*

*Sal Paradise and Dean Moriarty reach Mexico City in 1950
after smoking 'tea' and whoring in Gregoria on the way down by
car 'on the road' through Mexico.*

A brief mountain pass took us suddenly to a height from which we saw
all of Mexico City stretched out in its volcanic crater below and
spewing city smokes and early dusklights. Down to it we zoomed, down
Insurgentes Boulevard, straight toward the heart of town at Reforma.
Kids played soccer on enormous sad fields and threw up dust. Taxi-
drivers overtook us and wanted to know if we wanted girls. No, we
didn't want girls now. Long, ragged adobe slums stretched out on the
plain; we saw lonely figures in the dimming alleys. Soon night would
come. Then the city roared in and suddenly we were passing crowded
cafés and theaters and many lights. Newsboys yelled at us. Mechanics
slouched by, barefoot, with wrenches and rags. Mad barefoot Indian
drivers cut across us and surrounded us and tooted and made frantic
traffic. The noise was incredible. No mufflers are used on Mexican cars.
Horns are batted with glee continual. 'Whee!' yelled Dean. 'Look out!'
He staggered the car through the traffic and played with everybody. He
drove like an Indian. He got on a circular glorietta drive on Reforma
Boulevard and rolled around it . . . 'This is traffic I've always dreamed
of! Everybody *goes!*'

(21) MEXICO CITY

D.H. Lawrence, *The Plumed Serpent*

*Kate, the novel's heroine, looks over the Valley of Mexico and
the volcanoes Popocatépetl and Ixtacihuatl in 1921, before
leaving hated Mexico City for Lake Chapala in Jalisco and her
affair with Quetzalcóatl reincarnated.*

Ixtaccihuatl, the white woman, glittered and seemed near, but the other
mountain, Popocatepetl, stood further back, and in shadow, a pure
cone of atmospheric shadow, with glinting flashes of snow. There they
were, the two monsters, watching gigantically and terribly over their
lofty, bloody cradle of men, the Valley of Mexico. Alien, ponderous,
the white-hung mountains seemed to emit a deep purring sound, too
deep for the ear to hear, and yet audible on the blood, a sound of dread.
There was no soaring or uplift or exaltation, as there is in the snowy

mountains of Europe. Rather a ponderous, white-shouldered weight, pressing terribly on the earth, and murmuring like two watchful lions.

Superficially, Mexico might be all right; with its suburbs of villas, its central fine streets, its thousands of motor-cars, its tennis, and its bridge parties. The sun shone brilliantly every day, and big bright flowers stood out from the trees. It was a holiday.

Until you were alone with it. And then the undertone was like the low, angry, snarling purring of some jaguar spotted with night. There was a ponderous, down-pressing weight upon the spirit: the great folds of the dragon of the Aztecs, the dragon of the Toltecs, winding around one and weighing down the soul. And on the bright sunshine was a dark steam of an angry impotent blood, and the flowers seemed to have their roots in spilt blood. The spirit of place was cruel, down-dragging, destructive.

Kate could so well understand the Mexican who had said to her: *El grito mexicano es siempre el grito del odio* – The Mexican shout is always a shout of hate. The famous revolutions, as Don Ramón said, began with *Viva!* but ended always with *Muera!* Death to this, death to the other; it was all death! death! death! as insistent as the Aztec sacrifices. Something for ever gruesome and macabre.

Why had she come to this high plateau of death? As a woman, she suffered even more than men suffer; and in the end, practically all men go under. Once, Mexico had had an elaborate ritual of death. Now it has death, ragged, squalid, vulgar, without even the passion of its own mystery.

(22) Mexico City
José Emilio Pacheco, *Battles in the Desert*

A child narrator evokes his mother's catholic values after the family moved from provincial Guadalajara to the enormous and expanding capital in the 1950s. He refers to the scandal of his love for Mariana, sexy mother of a schoolfriend and mistress to a politician. Extracted from the collection Battles in the Desert and Other Stories – see Booklist.

My mother always insisted that our family – that is to say, her family – was one of the best in Guadalajara. Never any scandals like the one I had created. Honorable, hard-working men. Devout women, self-sacrificing wives, exemplary mothers. Obedient and respectful children. Then came the Indian hordes seeking their revenge against decency and good blood. The revolution – the old chieftains, that is – confiscated our ranches and our house on San Francisco Street on the pretext that there were too many Cristeros in the family. On top of that, my father – who, despite his degree in engineering, was held in contempt for being the son of a tailor – squandered the inheritance from his father-in-law on one absurd business venture after another, like trying to set up an air route between cities in the interior of the country or exporting tequila to the United States. Then, using money borrowed from my maternal uncles, he bought the soap factory that did well during the war and then went under when the North American companies invaded the domestic market.

And that's why my mother never tired of repeating: We've ended up in this accursed Mexico City. Infamous place, Sodom and Gomorrah awaiting the fire again, a hell where horrors, the like of which were never seen in Guadalajara, like the crime I had just committed, were daily occurrences. Sinister Capital City where we had to live among the worst elements. Contagion, bad examples. Birds of a feather flock together. How could it be, she insisted again and again, that a supposedly *decent* school would accept a bastard (what's a bastard?), the illegitimate son of a kept woman? Because there really is no way of knowing who the father is when you consider how many clients that prostitute must have, that corrupter of youth. (What does that mean, an illegitimate son? What's a kept woman? Why do you call her a prostitute?)

(23) MEXICO CITY

Octavio Paz, *Obsidian Butterfly*

> This extract is the opening of the prose poem 'Obsidian Butterfly', 1949, spoken by an Aztec fertility goddess in the shape of an Obsidian Butterfly, an artefact from the Anthropological Museum in Chapultepec Park, Mexico City. Extracted from Selected Poems (edited by Eliot Weinberger) – see Booklist.

They killed my brothers, my children, my uncles. On the banks of Lake Texcoco I began to weep. Whirlwinds of saltpeter rose from Peñon hill, gently picked me up, and left me in the courtyard of the Cathedral. I made myself so small and gray that many mistook me for a pile of dust. Yes I, mother of flint and star, I, bearer of the ray, am now but a blue feather that a bird loses in the brambles. Once, I would dance, my breasts high and turning, turning, turning until I became still, and then I would sprout leaves, flowers, fruit. The eagle throbbed in my belly. I was the mountain that creates you as it dreams, the house of fire, the primordial pot where man is cooked and becomes man. In the night of the decapitated words my sister and I, hand in hand, leapt and sang around the I, the only standing tower in the razed alphabet. I still remember my songs:

Light, headless light
Golden-throated light
Sings in the thicket green

They told us: the straight path never leads to winter. And now my hands tremble, the words are caught in my throat. Give me a chair and a little sun.

In other times, every hour was born from the vapor of my breath, danced a while on the point of my dagger, and disappeared through the shining door of my hand mirror. I was the tattooed noon and naked midnight, the little jade insect that sings in the grass at dawn, and the clay nightingale that summons the dead. I bathed in the sun's waterfall, I bathed in myself, soaked in my own splendor. I was the flint that rips the storm clouds of night and opens the doors of the showers. I planted gardens of fire, gardens of blood, in the Southern sky. Its coral branches still graze the foreheads of lovers . . .

(24) Mexico City

Charles Tomlinson, *At Trotsky's House*

In his poem 'At Trotsky's House', Tomlinson describes the house in Coyocacán in Mexico City where Trotsky was assassinated in 1941 while staying with Diego Rivera and his wife Frida Kahlo. The house can now be visited. Extracted from Notes from New York and Other Poems *– see Booklist.*

A barrel-organ
assails the suburb
with *Tales from the Vienna Woods*:
in Calle Viena
the garden is guarded
by wall and turret
and an aleatory score
of bullet holes
pocks the interior.
Lev Davidovich slept here
and this is the table
at which he wrote,
the goatee shedding its stray hairs
over the books, the pamphlets.
Words, words . . . there are cylinders

for the silent dictaphone
and a bottle of Waterman's Ink long dry.
And this is the way he
left things
the day of the assassination?
Más o menos, sí.
He is courteous in three languages
the great man's grandson –
Does he never return to Europe?
De temps en temps.
Under the palm outside
whose rind is peeling,
Europe, or one's part of it,
seems a distant planet:
and the Moscow
to which the urn of ashes
is awaiting its return
lies kremlined forever in historic snow.

(25) OAXACA

Richard Ford, *The Ultimate Good Luck*

*Ford's love story is set in a druggy, corrupt and violent Oaxaca,
with guerrillas, bomb attacks, and a disgusting prison.*

At two o'clock he got out of bed, turned off the light and did pushups
till his arms ached, then walked out into the walled patio where he
could see the city against the black Sierra and breathe the bougainvil-
lea. In the war, this was scrounge time, when things got dicey. The
incomings wasted you out of sleep, slammed your face in the dirt,
clawing the deck for a flak vest and helmet. He didn't want to be asleep
at two o'clock anymore. He preferred to be alert to whatever there was
to hear. The bungalow sat on a long, eucalyptus-shaded hill that
humped back toward the big mountains north of town. It was the
suburbs. Americans rented there because the bungalows were cheap
and neat and had grassy lawns and no deposits were taken. But he
didn't know the American girls next door, and now Rae was coming
with the money, and the hard part was done and Sonny was coming
out, he wouldn't have the chance. He had begun, in a month of
waiting and passing through offices and anterooms, and seven months
living alone, to feel like he was losing a freedom of some kind, getting
cautious without any gain back in precision. Bernhardt said it was the
American experience abroad, the long decline in expectation until you

could see the immediate world like a native, but without the native's freedom. It should be a great unburdening, Bernhardt said, but to Americans it was always a hardship. Bernhardt thought Americans thrived on protecting privileges nobody else would ever want. Bernhardt liked explanations. It was a lawyer's vice.

Oaxaca sparkled like a matrix of platinum sequins laid over velvet. The dark played out into the valley south toward Chiapas, so that where the land stopped and the sky began was a boundary lost to sight. He counted landmarks every night. The pink rotator on the airport tower, the blue Corona Cerveza on Bustamante, the hollow lights that shone all night on the cathedral opposite the zócalo, and the red Pepsi script shimmering far out in the Mixtec barrios beyond the river. There was never a sense of intimacy. The town seemed to function practically in the visible distance, though the empty air in between became enticing and silent and still. The American Highway curled down the mountains, split, circled the city two ways, then reunited, and the only detectable movement there was the lights of an overland truck gearing down before flatting out into the valley. Americans were off the road hours ago. The trucks and the Dinas would blink their lights, then run you off the cliffsides.

(26) OAXACA

Malcolm Lowry,
Dark as the Grave Wherein My Friend is Laid

In this passage from Lowry's posthumously published novel, Sigbjørn Wilderness (Lowry's alter ego) and his wife take a bus from Mexico City down south to Oaxaca (531 km away), a magical place that figures in Under the Volcano, and which Lowry first visited in 1936 and again in 1946.

They left for Oaxaca the next morning at eleven thirty. At first it was all desert, too high even for trees, just a few scrub oaks and cactus and mesquite and sage. They had seats in the back, as usual, this time in a first-class bus, which was still climbing, going up and up and up and round and round and round; beyond Huehuepan the driver, tired – he had driven from Puebla that morning – Godlike, took his hand off the wheel altogether and the bus conductor just steered from the right: Sigbjørn had the feeling the bus was steering itself: up, up, up, into the cruel strength of the country, but suddenly they saw a green valley, a sparkling river and then a waterfall. Afterward the country seemed still crueller; it was as if the bus were driving into a gigantic slab of stale cake, or a country the color of a rusty gasworks, cliffs, parched earth, sheer hillsides of rock, and dead trees; the bus always in second or first gear, very very slowly, winding, purring, then down and on, on, on, and up. This is the Tierra Colorada.

Nonetheless, it was Oaxaca, and Oaxaca, he kept saying over and over to himself. Oaxaca! Grand canyons opened off right, where vast cataclysms had cracked the earth. A cool breeze blew in through the window. They passed small villages of adobe, with tiled roofs and neat farms, and the cattle seemed well fed. True he had not been this way before but it seemed to him there was a vast improvement in the human lot, and all this he put down to Ejidal. Fernando had his hand in this, he thought; everywhere he seemed to read the work of his friend. What a contrast too from the terrible railroad journey through Puebla he had taken with Hölscher, the eternal fields of cactus, the fetid, slow, crowded train stopping at every desolate boiling station, the delirium, rubbing the baby with tequila, the heat, and the misery. It seemed to him that there was a lesson in this, that he had won through to this, he was taking the same journey, and yet by a more elevated route, it was almost as though he were flying. It was much, indeed, the same feeling that he had had on arriving in Mexico.

(27) Patzcuaro

José Rubén Romero, *Notes of a Villager*

In his fictionalized autobiography, Rubén Romero recounts how, as a poor young man, he arrived at Pátzcuaro (population about 65 000, at an altitude of 2110 metres), near the famous lake of the same name, south south west of Morelia.

Arriving at Pátzcuaro, we didn't know what direction to take. Toward Mexico City? No. Still very much alive in our memories was our recent misery there. To Cotija? Also no. How could we arrive there flat broke and expect to support ourselves when everything in that place had ended so badly for us? And it was in Pátzcuaro that we decided to stay without any plan whatsoever, buoyed by that faith in the unseen that characterizes the poor in their struggle to survive.

Punctually, like a hotel employee, I went down daily to the depot to meet the train, perhaps hoping Providence would arrive. The rest of my hours I passed either in the College Garden, reading whatever novels of realism fell into my hands or I climbed as far as Calvary Hill to contemplate, enraptured, the stupendous panorama that opened up there.

A Japanese drawing with colored inks over black lacquer of a jewel box: armies of pines in an interminable grand march, swift canoes cutting the wavy surface of the lake, and scattered in the depths of the landscape, the five ancient islands – *Janitzio*, *Jarácuaro*, *Pacanda*, *Yunuén*, and *Tecuén* – guarding the doors of the past.

Fridays, at market time, I installed myself on a stone bench to see the parade of fancy young gentlemen of the village, who went from green grocer to green grocer, dickering over the cost of vegetables.

Near me, the Tarascan women gave forth their sharp cry: 'Buy my tortillas or I'll throw them away.' They are short, stocky, with cocoa-colored skin and go everywhere barefooted, taking the short, swift steps of the followers of Siddartha.

They wear skirts of navy blue, pleated at the waist and held only by a sash of showy colors. A white, embroidered blouse gives evidence of their ample bosoms, and the two ebony braids are lost in a profusion of ribbons and multicolored bows.

On the mule skinner's sleeping mat were displayed, all mixed together, the varnished avocados of Tácambaro, the velvety *chirimoyas* of Ario, the meaty *mameyes* of Pedernales, and the fragrant guavas of Jacona, all appearing like resplendent uncut gems from a treasure in an oriental tale . . .

Those same Friday evenings there was a serenade of stringed instruments that could hardly be heard because the square was the size of a large cattle yard. The people took refuge against the cold under the arcades, that stubborn cold of Pátzcuaro that lasts almost the entire year and brings forth from the coat racks the most unlikely outer garments.

(28) TAPACHULA

Paul Bowles, *Señor Ong and Señor Ha*

Bowles opens his short story 'Señor Ong and Señor Ha', written in 1947 about a boy (Nicho), his mother's Chinese lover (Ong), a drug dealer (Ha) and this boy's need for revenge in a village close to Tapachula near the Mexican/Guatemalan border. Extracted from Collected Stories – see Booklist.

At the end of the town's long street a raw green mountain cut across the sky at a forty-five degree angle, its straight slope moving violently from the cloudy heights down into the valley where the river ran. In the valley, although the land was fertile, there were no farms or orchards, because the people of the town were lazy, and did not want to bother clearing away the rocks that strewed the ground. And then, it was always too hot for that sort of work, and everybody had malaria there, so that long ago the town had fallen into its little pattern of living off the Indians who came down from the mountains with food and went back with cheap cloth, machetes and things like mirrors or empty bottles. Life always had been easy; although no one in the town was rich, still, no one ever went hungry. Almost every house had some papayas and a mango tree beside it, and there were plenty of avocados and pineapples to be had in the market for next to nothing.

Some of this changed when the government had begun the building of the great dam up above. No one seemed to know exactly where the dam was; they were building it somewhere up in the mountains; already the water had covered several villages, and now after six years the construction was still going on. This last was the important part, because it meant that when the Indians came down from above they now brought with them not only food but money. Thus it had come about that certain people in the town had suddenly found themselves rich. They could scarcely believe it themselves, but there was money, and still the Indians went on coming down and leaving more and more of it on the counter of the shops. They did not know what to do with these unexpected pesos. Most of them bought huge radios which they kept going from early morning until night, all tuned in full strength to Tapachula, so that when they walked the length of the main street they were never out of earshot of the program and could follow without a break. But they still had money. Pepe Jimenez had brought a bright new automobile in the capital, but by the time he had arrived back in town with it, after driving it over the sixty miles trail from Mapastenango, it was no longer an object to excite admiration, and he felt that he had made an unwise purchase. Even the main street was too bumpy and muddy for him to drive it up and down, and so it stood rusting in front of Mi Esperanza, the bar by the bridge. When they came out of school Nicho and his companions would play in it, pretending it was a fort.

(29) TAPATLAN

Aldous Huxley, *Eyeless in Gaza*

Anthony Beavis leaves London for arid, mountainous Southern Mexico with a Bolshevik schoolfriend Staithes who runs a coffee finca, to help him support a Mexican revolutionary, but everything goes wrong. Huxley was there in 1933.

In the hotel at Tapatlan, where they spent the night, Anthony was bitten for the first time in his life by bed bugs, and the next morning it was an attack of dysentery . . . . On the fourth day he was well enough to go out and see the sights. The last earthquake had almost wrecked the church. A dense black fruitage of bats hung, like ripe plums, from the rafters; an Indian boy, ragged and bare-footed, was sweeping up the droppings; from the altars the baroque saints flapped and gesticulated in a frozen paroxysm of devotion. They walked out again into the market-place, where, secret and as though ambushed within their dark shawls, the brown Indian women squatted in the dust before their little piles of fruit and withering vegetables. The meat on the butcher's stall was covered with a crust of flies. Rhythmically shaking their long ears the donkeys passed, on small quick hoofs, noiseless in the dust. The women came and went in silence, carrying kerosene tins of water on their heads. From under hat-brims, dark eyes regarded the strangers with an inscrutably reptilian glitter that seemed devoid of all curiosity, all interest, any awareness even of their presence.

'I'm tired,' Anthony announced. They had not walked very far; but at Tapatlan, it was an immense fatigue even to be living and conscious. 'When I die,' he went on after a silence, 'this is the part of hell I shall be sent to. I recognize it instantly.'

(30) TAXCO

Saul Bellow, *The Adventures of Augie March*

Augie March and his lover travel to Acatla (probably Taxco) to hunt iguana with a tamed eagle. The town of Acatla is filled with American eccentrics and artists living in Mexico on the cheap.

From the porch where we ate we had the town and the cliffs before us. Nearly immediately below was the zócalo, the dippy bandstand and its vines, the monstrous trees around. The cathedral had two towers and a blue-varied belly of dome, finely crusted and as if baked in a kiln, overheated, and in places with the mutilated spectrum that sometimes you split out of brick. It was settled uneven on the stones of the square, and occasionally in the midst of admiration gave you a heavy, squalid, gut-sick feeling, so much it incorporated all that was in the surroundings. The bells clung like two weak old animals, green and dull, and the doors opened on a big gloom in which stood dead white altars and images slashed and scratched with axes, thorns, raked with black wounds – some of these flashy with female underpants on their hips, nail-cloven and hacked as they were, and bleeding as far as their clothespin white fingers. Then on a hill to one side was the cemetery, white and spiky, and on another side and higher in a star of connecting gullies was a silver mine, and there you could see where the force of great investment had dented. The mountainside was eaten for some distance by machine. I was intrigued and climbed up there one day. It certainly was odd what mechanisms you saw all over Mexico, what old styles there gnawed and crawled, pit or tunnel makers, and machine scarabaeuses, British and Belgian doo-jiggers, Manchester trolleys or poodle locomotives at the head of sick cars covered with blanketed men and soldiers.

Within the town still, along the road to the mine, the garbage was thrown into a little valley, hummocky with soft old decays; the vultures hung over it all day. At one of the highest points you could see, in a cliff, there was a waterfall. Sometimes it was covered in a cloud, but there usually flew the slight smoke of water, paler than the air, above the treeline. A good deal below were the pines, at the widow's peaks of wrinkled rock; and then more tropical trees and flowers, and the hot stone belt of snakes and wild pigs, the deer, and the giant iguanas we had come to catch. Where they hung out the light was very hot.

(31) Teotihuacan

Octavio Paz, *Hymn Among the Ruins*

Paz wrote this poem in Naples in 1948 where the ruins are the great cities and the mood is post-war depression; the 'hymn' is what poetry can do. This second stanza shows how Mexicans do not understand their roots. The poem is translated by the American poet William Carlos Williams and can be found in Selected Poems *(edited by Charles Tomlinson) – see Booklist.*

Night falls on Teotihuacán.
On top of the pyramid the boys are smoking marijuana,
harsh guitars sound.
What weed, what living waters will give life to us,
where shall we unearth the word,
the relations that govern hymn and speech,
the dance, the city and the measuring scales?
The song of Mexico explodes in a curse,
a coloured star that is extinguished,
a stone that blocks our doors of contact.
Earth tastes of rotten earth.

(32) VILLAHERMOSA

Graham Greene, *The Power and the Glory*

Greene evokes the atmosphere of Villahermosa in tropical Tabasco in the opening sequence of the novel that 'gave me more satisfaction than any other I had written'. It was renamed The Labyrinthine Ways in the USA, and in 1947 John Ford made it into a film – The Fugitive.

Mr Tench went out to look for his ether cylinder, into the blazing Mexican sun and the bleaching dust. A few vultures looked down from the roof with shabby indifference: he wasn't carrion yet. A faint feeling of rebellion stirred in Mr Tench's heart, and he wrenched up a piece of the road with splintering finger nails and tossed it feebly towards them. One rose and flapped across the town: over the tiny plaza, over the bust of an ex-president, ex-general, ex-human being, over the two stalls which sold mineral water, towards the river and the sea. It wouldn't find anything there: the sharks looked after the carrion on that side. Mr Tench went on across the plaza.

He said '*Buenos días*' to a man with a gun who sat in a small patch of shade against a wall. But it wasn't like England: the man said nothing at all, just stared malevolently up at Mr Tench, as if he had never had any dealings with the foreigner, as if Mr Tench were not responsible for his two gold bicuspid teeth. Mr Tench went sweating by, past the treasury which had once been a church, towards the quay. Half-way across he suddenly forgot what he had come out for – a glass of mineral water? That was all there was to drink in this prohibition state – except beer, but that was a government monopoly and too expensive except on special occasions. An awful feeling of nausea gripped Mr Tench in the stomach – it couldn't have been mineral water he wanted. Of course his ether cylinder . . . the boat was in. He had heard its exultant piping while he lay on his bed after lunch. He passed the barbers' and two dentists and came out between a warehouse and the customs' on to the river bank.

The river went heavily by towards the sea between the banana plantations: the *General Obregon* was tied up to the bank, and beer was being unloaded – a hundred cases were already stacked upon the quay. Mr Tench stood in the shade of the customs house and thought: what am I here for? Memory drained out of him in the heat. He gathered his bile together and spat forlornly into the sun. Then he sat down on a case and waited. Nothing to do. Nobody would come to see him before five.

(33) YAHUALICA, JALISCO

Agustín Yáñez, *The Edge of the Storm*

Yáñez opens his novel by evoking the repressive atmosphere of a provincial village near Guadalajara, just before the Mexican Revolution of 1910 will change it forever.

There are no fiestas in the village; only the daily dance of myriads of sunbeams; the only music is the sound of the bells that toll the passing of the dead, or the tuneless, plaintive melodies of religious chants that express the latent sense of oppression. Never any parties. Dancing is held in horror . . . Not even to be thought of . . . never, never. Families visit each other only at times of bereavement or illness, or possibly to welcome home a long-absent member.

It is a barren village; there are no trees or orchards; no trees even at the entrance or in the Cemetery. In the Square, only watered plants. For most of the year the river is dry; river of large, smooth stones, shining in the sunlight. A landscape of barren ridges stretching tier behind tier to the horizon . . . barren ridge on barren ridge.

There is no 'alameda' in the village. The streets lie parched under the blazing sun. Worn pillars of stone and mortar stand in the squares and at the corners of the houses. Village of black-robed women, hermetic and solemn.

Only the general cleanliness of everything reveals the hidden life. The streets are well swept, the houses whitewashed. Not a single one, not even among those by the river, is unkempt. The men are clean shaven; old men with lean faces, young men with ruddy cheeks, pale adolescents, all wearing clean shirts, clean trousers. Cleanliness pervades the village; clean young men, clean horsemen, clean white trousers worn by the workers in the fields. Clean are the pale-faced, black-robed women, the pale women clad in black, who are the life of the church precincts, the sunswept streets, the furtively open doors. Well-swept streets bring a note of freshness at noonday, at eventide, and in the long hours of the night. Black-robed women, rising early, sprinkle cleanliness from secret wells.

Each house has its well, hidden from the curious gaze of the outsider, like the pots of flowering plants in the hidden patios and inner passageways, smelling of freshness and peace.

(34) YUCATAN

Charles Olson, *Mayan Letters*

The poet Charles Olson was puzzled by the mysterious Mayan civilization. He spent time excavating and speculating, writing letters home to American poet friends like Robert Creeley.

lerma campeche monday april 23 51

. . . Bushed, hoy. And precisely the verb. For, the bush, of Jaina, leaves me so. Jesus, what a job these lands are, in the sun! Impossible, the way, the sun drags you down – in one half hr it is eating you, its clawing having pulled off yr pins. Wicked. I tried, for awhile, to scratch away at the walls of the graves (one leaps in to holes which are exactly like the stage holes into which Hamlet leaps). But there, with what breeze there is coming from the sea (and there was good breeze yesterday) cut off, one can't take more than 5 minutes! I'm telling you, lad, one thing is hugely proved: one can't touch this Yucatan (or I'd gather, any place of these Maya) without full expeditionary equipment. Which, of course, means, institutions. Ergo, mal.

Any one place requires, instantly, two to three days: that is, all one can do the first day, is to get there. For by that time the sun is too far up to do anything but sleep in some place out of the sun. So that evening, and the next morning, early, are the only work times. Which means, almost, the 3rd day, for return. All of which is too expensive for the likes of one sole adventurer as me!

Biographies and important works

AZUELA, Mariano (1873–1952). Born in **Lagos de Moreno** in **Jalisco**, on 1 January 1873, Azuela graduated in medicine from **Guadalajara** in 1899, and practised as a doctor in Lagos in 1909. He began writing in 1896. In *Mala yerba*, 1909 (*Marcela, a Mexican Love Story*, 1932), and in *Andrés Perez, maderista*, 1911, he dealt with Madero's defiance of dictator Porfirio Díaz's plan to re-elect himself. When the revolution broke out, Azuela supported Francisco Madero, and in 1911 was appointed Director of Education for Jalisco state. In 1914, after Madero's assassination, he joined the revolutionary group of General Julián Medina in northern Mexico as a doctor. On the run after Pancho Villa's defeat, he wrote his classic about the violence of the Mexican Revolution, *Los de abajo* (*The Underdogs*, 1929 – Extract 8) in El Paso, Texas, in 1915 in 23 serials for a newspaper. It was not recognized until 1925. The novel follows the rise and fall of a revolutionary peasant group lead by Demetrio Macías as they fight General Huerta's *federales* in 1914, with a motley horde of sinister characters from a turncoat intellectual called Cervantes to La Pintada, a sadistic guerrillera. The novel catches the speed of events, and the Revolution's effect on local peasants. The battle of Zacatecas, and the 1914 Aguascalientes convention date the action at 1914, in the middle of the civil war/Revolution. In 1917, Azuela settled in **Mexico City** (where he died in 1952) as a doctor, famous as an author. He wrote further novels dealing with the trauma of the revolution: *Los caciques*, 1917 and *Las moscas*, 1918 (*Two Novels of Mexico: The Flies and The Bosses*, 1956); *Las tribulaciones de una familia decente*, 1919 and *La luciérnaga*, 1932 (*Three Novels: The Trials of a Respectable Family, The Underdogs and The Firefly*, 1963). See S.L. Robe, *Azuela and the Mexican Underdogs*, University of California Press, Berkeley, CA, 1979.

BELLOW, Saul (1915–). Bellow was born in Lachine, Quebec from an immigrant Jewish background in 1915, and moved to Chicago in 1924, attending the University of Chicago, Northwestern University and the University of Wisconsin, and becoming a university lecturer from 1938. He published his first novel in 1944 and all his subsequent fiction is packed with the anguish of surviving in urban hells, and the drama of the mind-life in a godless century. In 1976 Bellow won the Nobel Prize. In *The Adventures of Augie March* (Extract 30), we read Augie's picaresque, street-wise life told by himself from his childhood in hoodlum Chicago. The Mexican part of the novel takes Augie with his latest rich mistress and an eagle to hunt iguanas down south in Mexico, the first time that Augie gets abroad. In Mexico he undergoes a crisis and emerges back in the States with his future wife, a beautiful actress, and a theory about 'axial' lines and his own fate. The Mexico that Augie discovers is an expatriate one where Americans who hate the States can live 'cheaper'. It is also where Augie glimpses Trotsky (Bellow saw him in his coffin in August 1940), and where he comes into confrontation with 'all the old things'. Bellow knows about the eagle, Mictlan, sacred dogs, fiestas, and is good on iguanas, the Hotel Regis (where D.H. Lawrence had stayed and which was at **25 Calle de Uruguay**), which he calls 'Regina', the *zócalo* (main square) and cathedral of Acatla (Taxco), the dust and peasants. He was in Mexico for three months in 1940. He also wrote 'The Mexican General' (a story), 1942, and *Mosby's Memoirs*, 1968, set in Mexico.

BOWLES, Paul (see under Guatemala). Bowles went to Mexico in March 1937, to distribute 15 000 stickers saying *Muera Trotsky* ('Let Trotsky die'), met the Mexican composer Silvestre Revueltas, and travelled to **Tehuantepec**, and **Tapachula**. In June 1940 Bowles was back in **Mexico City**, and **Cuernavaca**. With his wife Jane Bowles (◊ Panama) he rented a *hacienda* 80 km from **Jajalpa**, with a view of the **Toluca volcano**. He spent some 4½ years in Mexico. In *Without Stopping: An Autobiography*, 1972, his account of his Mexican days reveals a more politicized person than ever appears in the fiction.

BURROUGHS, William (1914–). Born in St Louis, Missouri on 5

William Burroughs

February 1914, Burroughs graduated from Harvard. He was arrested for possession of drugs and firearms and escaped to **Mexico City** in October 1949, where he lived until the case was dropped in 1952. Kerouac ◊ stayed with Burroughs and his wife Joan in **212 Orizaba, Mexico City** where in March 1952, playing the William Tell overture, Burroughs accidentally shot his wife dead, and spent two weeks in a Mexican prison. His experiences as a Morphine addict living the 'easy' life in Mexico appeared in the novel *Junkie*, 1953. He travelled through Panama to Colombia and Ecuador in 1951 and again in 1953. He later lived as an expatriate in Paris and Tangier, and achieved underground notoriety with his novel *Naked Lunch*, 1959. In 1963 he published *Yage Letters* to and from the Beat poet Allen Ginsberg, dealing with the search for *yage*, an Amazonian hallucinatory drug. In 1984 he published *Queer* (Extract 13), a short autobiographical novel (sequel to *Junkie*) about lust, boredom and

travel. A junkie who shoots morphine ends up fruitlessly trying to find *yage* somewhere in tropical Ecuador, or Peru. He is a rebel, likes boys, and is rich; he hates middle-class America, and has weird theories about telepathy. He despises Mexico City – 'little jerkwater country' – Panama, Quito and Guayaquil. *Queer* is also extracted in the chapters on Panama and Ecuador (see pages 148 and 209). See Ted Morgan, *Literary Outlaw: The Life and Times of William S. Burroughs*, The Bodley Head, London, 1991.

CAIN, James (1892–1977). Cain was born in Annapolis, Maryland. He graduated from Washington College and set out to become a professional singer, but instead became a journalist. He published his first novel *The Postman Always Rings Twice* in 1934, which put him on the best-seller lists, and which has twice been made into a film. In this story of lust and murder, the bum who works for a Greek petrol pump owner and seduces his sexy wife runs off for a while with another woman after they fail to kill the Greek, and goes down to **Ensenada** in Mexico for a dirty weekend, before returning and accidentally killing his pregnant mistress, and hanging for murder. *Serenade*, 1938 (Extract 10) is about a singer who loses his voice and roughs it in low-life **Mexico City**. He fancies a whore (who dates a famous bull-fighter), but she drops him when he tries to sing to her. Later she offers him a job running a brothel for *gringos* in **Acapulco**. There is a wonderful description of the drive from Mexico City to Acapulco via an Indian village, a storm when they hide in a church with an extraordinary scene of cooking and making love in the church, where this once impotent man finds his manhood and his singing voice. The couple escape the whore's powerful lover, and go to California where he makes it big in films. But his girl is despised for being a Mexican, and finally in New York she realizes that he was once homosexual, and she kills his gay ex-lover. They both run off and live incognito in Guatemala, until she leaves him and is murdered in the street in Mexico. The novel is realistic, laconic and a compulsive read. Cain himself had worked for 17 years in Hollywood. *Serenade* was made into a film in 1956.

CARVER, Raymond (1939–1988). Carver was born in Clatskanie, Oregon. As a short story writer (see *Stories of Raymond Carver*, 1982), he led America's 'dirty realist' authors, dealing with middle America, divorce, drink, work problems, etc, and conveying a bleak view of wasted human lives. His poetry reads like someone casually talking (see *Selected Poems*, 1988). Carver taught at several universities. He lived with writer Tess Gallagher until he died.

CASTELLANOS, Rosario (1925–1974). Although she was born in **Mexico City** (on 25 May 1925) Castellanos was brought up on her father's *hacienda* in **Comitán de las Flores**, near the Guatemalan border. She died by accidental electrocution when she was Mexican ambassador in Tel Aviv in 1974. Her experiences in **Chiapas** with the Mayan-speaking Indians dominated her later writing. She gave back her father's land to the Indians, and worked in the National Indian Institute in **San Cristóbal de las Casas**. Her fiction deals with the racial conflict between the Indians and *ladinos* (Europeanized Mexicans). Castellanos writes from inside her

characters, not ideologically. Her first novel, *Balún-Canán* (Extract 4) was published in 1957 (*The Nine Guardians*, 1959). It is lyrically narrated by a child who learns about Indian myths, customs and legends through her *nana* (nanny). Further fiction includes the untranslated *Ciudad real*, 1960 (short stories) and *Oficio de tinieblas*, 1962. She collected her poetry in 1972 as *Poesía no eres tú*, translated in A *Rosario Castellanos Reader*, 1988; *The Selected Poems of Rosario Castellanos*, 1988; and *Meditation on the Threshold: a Bilingual Anthology of Poetry*, 1988.

DEIGHTON, Len (1929–). Born in London, Deighton went to St Martin's School of Art after his national service, then on to the Royal College. Later he became a cookery expert, and then spy thriller writer. *Mexico Set*, 1984 (Extract 15), the second volume in a trilogy, is placed in a believable Mexico, topographically exact as one would expect, as it weaves its tale of spies and a secret world around Mexico and London.

DIAZ, Bernal (1492–1581). Díaz was born in Spain and died on his estate in Guatemala. He wrote *The Conquest of New Spain* (Extract 16) when he was 76 years old to set the record straight concerning Cortés's conquest of Mexico as recorded by the official chronicler Francisco López de Gomara. Díaz was a foot soldier, without much learning, but the notion of a counter-history, of telling the plain truth, initiated a tradition in Latin American culture visible today in writers like Carlos Fuentes and Gabriel García Márquez, who write fiction in order to tell the truth about what happened in history. Robert Cunninghame Graham (◊ Paraguay)

Rosario Castellanos

wrote *The Life of Bernal Díaz*, 1915. Earlier the American historian W.H. Prescott based much of his *History of the Conquest of Mexico*, 1843, on Bernal Díaz's honest account.

FORD, Richard (1944–   ). Ford was born in Jackson, Mississippi, and now lives in Montana with his wife. He trained as a marine, and as a boxer, and studied law which he never practised. He has written novels (*A Piece of my Heart*, *The Sportswriter*) and short stories (*Rock Springs*) that deal with rough middle America. His Mexican novel *The Ultimate Good Luck*, 1981 (Extract 25), follows

Carlos Fuentes

Quinn, a tough Vietnam vet trying to buy his brother-in-law Sonny out of **Oaxaca jail**. His ex-girl friend Rae flies down with the money to pay the *mordida* (bribe) as the assassinations start. The novel is partly a love story, a revenge story, a mafia and drugs story, and a study of the differences between Americans and Mexicans. Mexico, like Vietnam, appears as evil, violent and unpredictable.

FUENTES, Carlos (1928–). Born on 11 November 1928 in Panama City where his father was Mexican ambassador, Fuentes moved to Rio, then to Washington for seven years where his first language became English (which he speaks and writes perfectly), and then to Santiago and Buenos Aires. Fuentes graduated as a lawyer from **Mexico City** in 1946, studied at Geneva University in 1950–51, qualified in 1955, but never practised. He joined Mexico's Foreign Service until he could live from his royalties. He has taught at universities (Cambridge, Harvard) and was Mexican ambassador to Paris in 1975–78. Fuentes is a genuine cosmopolitan, and travels and lectures round the world, promoting his radical view of Mexican and Latin American politics and history. He visited Cuba in 1961, and in 1968 Czechoslovakia, with Kundera and García Márquez, his close friends. He has won numerous prizes for his fiction, including Premio Biblioteca Breve in 1967 and the Premio Cervantes in 1987. He has written film scripts, plays, excellent journalism, and literary criticism like *Myself with Others*, 1988, which includes an autobiographical essay.

He published his first novel in 1958, *La región más transparente* (*Where the Air is Clear*, 1960 – Extract 18), an attempt to capture modern **Mexico City** (where the air is no longer clear) through a spectrum of characters centering around a powerful banker who goes bankrupt called Robles. The novel is precise in its urban locations. In 1962 he published *La muerte de Artemio Cruz* (*The Death of Artemio Cruz*, 1964), telling the last 12 hours of a dying macho *cacique* whose life mirrors the historical unfolding of twentieth century Mexico from its problematic Revolution in 1910 to the late 1950s, narrated experimentally with some sections exposing Cruz's bad conscience, and others his struggle to power. Since then Fuentes has been prolific, with 12 novels translated into English including *Cambio de piel*, 1967 (*A Change of Skin*, 1968 – Extract 2), a pop novel about a trip to **Cholula** with four characters in 1965 (with Beatles songs, drugs, etc), and flashbacks to their loves and alienated pasts; *Terra nostra*, 1975 (*Terra nostra*, 1976), an ambitious Buñuelesque rewrite, with surreal historical licence, of Philip II's Spain and the building of the Escorial; *Gringo viejo*, 1986 (*Old Gringo*, 1986, filmed in 1989), dealing with Ambrose Bierce's imagined suicide in Revolutionary Mexico (Bierce disappeared in 1913 in Mexico); a surrealist mystery about doubles and witches, *Aura*, 1962 (*Aura*, 1966); *Una familia lejana*, 1980 (*Distant Relations*, 1982), with overlapping families; and his more recent Joycean and Sternian *Cristóbal nonato*, 1987 (*Christopher Unborn*, 1989) – Christopher is about to be born on a beach in Acapulco in 1999 in the hope of winning a prize and recounts his history from the womb, with a dismal view of Mexico ('Makesicko City') and Latin America. Fuentes sees his role as Balzacian, chronicling his country's social and personal history from the Discovery to the present, via a unique Revolution, with special focus on **Mexico City**. His purpose is to understand Mexico, its cities, peasants, plutocrats, landscape and history, and to strip it and his characters of false masks and search for true identity. Fuentes is excellent at realistic detail, a good satirist, and engagingly incorporates intellectual debates into his fiction. See Luis Harss, *Into the Mainstream: Conversations with Latin American Writers*, Harper and Row, New York, 1968.

GLANTZ, Margo (1930–). Glantz was born in Mexico, daughter of Jewish immigrants from the Ukraine. She is a novelist, has worked as a journalist, lectured at university (UNAM in **Mexico City**), was married to a diplomat, and has a daughter. She recently lived for two years in London as Mexico's cultural attaché. She has published some 16 books, including

Margo Glantz

Genealogías, 1981 (*The Family Tree*, 1991 – Extract 19) which recounts the history of the arrival of her parents (especially her bohemian father) in post-Revolution Mexico and their adaptation to it, with photos, in a witty post-Borgesian way. See Andrew Graham-Yooll, *After the Despots; Latin American Views and Interviews*, Bloomsbury, London, 1991.

GREENE, Graham (1904–1991). Born in Hertfordshire on 2 October 1904, Greene went to Berkhamsted School where his father was headmaster, then on to Balliol College, Oxford. He went into journalism, and became film critic for the *Spectator* in 1935. His first trip abroad was to Liberia (*Journey without Maps*, 1936); his second to Mexico, from February to May 1938. His Mexican novel *The Power and the Glory*, 1940 (Extract 32), opens in **Villahermosa** in the state of **Tabasco** (but kept nameless) with the dentist Mr Tench walking out into the 'blazing' Mexican sun. Vultures, heat, sharks and indifference. A state with prohibition, and priest-hunting 'reds'. Following this laconic opening chapter, we meet the priest-chasing lieutenant, with the Chief of Police with toothache, and hear about a priest on the run who passes himself off as a *gringo*. These opening chapters catch the Mexico that Greene 'loathed'. The 'whisky' priest has reached rock bottom in his beliefs and habits, yet stubbornly refuses to surrender. In a mirror he sees himself as 'fat and ugly and old and humiliated'; he had fathered a daughter, and craved brandy. Yet he remained a priest, hidden by his 'wife' ('women are appallingly practical') and is even imprisoned by the lieutenant as a smuggler. In the jail he feels 'extraordinary affection' for the criminals. But finally he is betrayed, knowingly, by a *mestizo* for the reward.

In his travel book on Mexico, *The Lawless Roads*, 1938 (Extract 3), known in the USA as *Another Country*, Greene refers to Garrido Cannabal's 'isolated swampy puritanical state' where 'every priest was hunted down or shot, except one who existed for ten years in the forests and swamps, venturing out only at night'. His travel book records his disgust at this priest-hunting – 'the fiercest persecution of religion anywhere since the reign of Elizabeth'. Tabasco is far from tourist Mexico where Americans swoon over ruins, and read *Life* and *Time* and drink coffee in Sanborne, 'impervious to Mexico'. Mexico City was simply not connected with Tabasco. On mule-back, Greene cursed the mosquitoes, the smells, vultures, ticks and rats. He had crossed from **Villahermosa** to **Palenque**, **Yajalón**, **Cancuc**, **Las Casas**, **Tuxtla** and back to **Mexico City**. Greene had borrowed details for the priest in *The Power and the Glory* from Jesuit priest Padre Miguel Pro, who was hunted and finally executed shouting '*Viva Cristo el Rey*'. Padre Pro was canonized by the Pope in 1988. Another possible source for the whisky priest was Father Macario Aguado (see Norman Sherry, details below). Greene died in Antibes, France, on 3 April 1991. See also under Argentina, Paraguay and Panama, and see Norman Sherry, *The Life of Graham Greene. Vol 1: 1904–1939*, Jonathan Cape, London, 1989.

HUMBOLDT, Alexandre von (see under Venezuela).

HUXLEY, Aldous (1894–1963). Huxley was born in Godalming, Surrey and died in California. He visited

Aldous Huxley

to look after a coffee *finca* in Mexico, and help a revolutionary Jorge Fuentes to power. We follow their arrival at **Colón**, then **San José, Puerto San Felipe** and **Tapatlán** where there is a scene of danger and violence. The barren landscape, the *ranchos* at **Miajutla**, pulque country, are well observed by Huxley. The Mexican episode ends in fiasco. See Sybille Bedford, *Aldous Huxley: A Biography. The Apparent Stability*, William Collins and Chatto and Windus, London, 1973.

Central America with his wife Maria from January to June 1933, travelling mainly in Guatemala and Mexico, visiting the Copán Maya ruins in Honduras by small plane. Most of this journey is recounted in *Beyond the Mexique Bay*, 1934, although he did not write about one unpleasant incident in the village of **Ejutla** (Mexico) where a drunk tried to shoot at him because he thought he had been snubbed. Huxley's novel *Eyeless in Gaza*, 1936 (Extract 29) charts a group of prep school friends and their family life and development up to the eve of the second world war. They are numbed intellectuals incapable of love, and protecting themselves in books and theories and purely sexual affairs, looking at the stupidity of the world from the outside, in despair at their own sterility. In this sense it is a critical novel of a whole English generation. Huxley uses a jigsaw-puzzle effect of shifting dates that range from 1904 to 1935 where Mexico presents an opportunity for Anthony Beavis to try and free himself through action. Beavis follows the Bolshevik Staithes

KEROUAC, Jack (1922–1969). Kerouac was born in Lowell, Massachusetts, and graduated from Columbia University in New York in 1941. He was a merchant seaman and one of the original 'Beats' travelling from the west to the east coast of America, befriending Burroughs ◊ and Ginsberg, and especially Neal Cassady, the real-life model for Dean Moriarty of his novel *On the Road*, 1957 (Extract 20). This novel is narrated by a budding writer searching for experience who latches on to bohemian petty crook Moriarty, and follows his whimsical philandering and drug-taking over the years 1947 to 1950. Sal Paradise and Dean Moriarty end up crossing the 'magic border' into **Nuevo Laredo**, Mexico, which in their naive, excited eyes is a 'Holy Lhasa' where everything is different, the people direct, sincere, and cool ('There's no *suspicion* here . . .'). They drive through **Sabinas Hidalgo, Monterrey, Montemorelos** and in **Georgia** smoke 'tea' ('ma-ree-wa-na'), and have an orgy in a brothel. They reach **Mexico City** where Sal gets dysentery and Dean beats it like a 'rat'. Kerouac spent the summer of 1950 with William Burroughs in **Mexico City** (**212 Orizaba**, near the **Cine Mexicano**), returned in

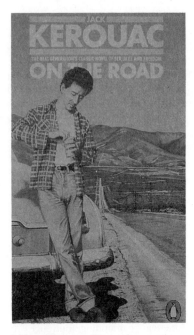

1952 and wrote *Doctor Sax*, and was back in 1955 and 1956. He wrote jazz poems about Mexico City over one month there in his no-corrections style (*Mexico City Blues*, 1959); and in *Tristessa*, 1960, he recalls a Mexican girl, in reality called Esperanza, who supplied Morphine and was a junkie and a whore, from the Mexico City slums. See Ann Charters, *Kerouac: A Biography*, Picador, London, 1978/Straight Arrow, San Francisco, CA, 1973.

LAWRENCE, David Herbert (1885–1930). Born at Eastwood in Nottinghamshire, Lawrence began writing poems from 1909 and in 1911 published his first novel, *The White Peacock*, followed by *The Trespasser*, 1912, and *Sons and Lovers* in 1913. In 1912 Lawrence met Frieda, wife of a Nottingham University professor, and after her divorce in 1914 went to live with her in Germany. Lawrence spent the first world war years in Cornwall, and then lived a nomadic life, moving from Ceylon to Australia, New Mexico and Mexico. He was in **Mexico City** (the Hotel Regis, moving to the Monte Carlo Hotel) from March to May 1923, when he settled in **Chapala** on the lake shore until July 1923, renting **Los Cuentales** on **Calle Zaragoza**. In September he was back in Mexico until he left to join Frieda in England in late November 1923. From 8 November 1924 to February 1925 he lived in **Oaxaca**, writing his Mexican novel. It was in 1925 in **Taos**, New Mexico, when he first discovered the symptoms of the TB that killed him.

Lawrence's Mexican novel, *The Plumed Serpent*, 1926 (Extracts 9 and 21), is a complex exploration of Mexico in the light of its recent socialist revolution (1921 is a date from the novel), with a lot of religious details, and long songs extolling Quetzalcóatl. Lawrence was fascinated by the 'otherness' of the Indians, and repulsed by **Mexico City**. He is acute on its weather, and local details from the cooking to the landscape. The novel opens with middle-aged Kate going to the last bull-fight of the Mexico City season with two American friends. The tone is satirical, and well-observed. It is mainly through Kate that we learn about the 'Mexican city-bred inferiority complex' that explodes in aggressions. Mexico City is a place without glamour, or charm. It is packed with 'the mongrel men of a mongrel city'. No ambivalences: 'She loathed Mexico' and 'The spirit of place was cruel, down-dragging, destructive'. Later she casually reads a cutting from a newspaper about the revival of the old Aztec gods Tlaloc and Quetzalcóatl. She discovers that Mexico 'was still a strange beam of wonder and mystery, almost like hope'. The theme of the novel is the

D.H. Lawrence

possibility of rebirth: 'Even the gods must be born again. We must be born again'. It is through Kate's friendship with Ramon and his Quetzalcóatl cult, and Cipriano, embodiment of Huitzilopochtli, and what happens around this (from the desecration of the church, to the attempted murder of Ramon on his *hacienda*, to her final, fulfilling marriage and submission to Cipriano after witnessing human sacrifice) that Lawrence embroiders his views on complex Mexico. Kate reflects on Cipriano, later to be her lover: 'His education lay like a film of white oil on the black lake of his barbarian consciousness'. About the look of an Indian she recognizes 'the peculiar gleaming far-awayness, suspended between two realities . . .' This sense of an alternative reality attracts Kate: 'She felt she could cry aloud for the unknown gods to put the magic back into her life, and to save her from the dry-rot of the world's sterility'. Mexico is antidote to industrialized Europe. Lawrence is

excellent on the twin volcanoes **Popocatépetl** and **Ixtacihuatl**, and on the countryside around Lake Sayula (in reality **Lake Chapala**) and its 'sperm' coloured, shallow water: 'It was a place with a strange atmosphere: stony, hard, broken with round cruel hills and the many and fluted bunches of the organ-cactus behind the old house, and an ancient road trailing past, deep in ancient dust.' Much of the novel is travelogue. Kate is all the time explaining to English readers typical Mexico, from the bull-fights Lawrence watched in Mexico City in March 1923, to its church ceremonies, its trains and buses. Evelyn Waugh wrote: 'Every traveller to Mexico must read *The Plumed Serpent*' (*Robbery Under Law: the Mexican Object-Lesson*, 1934).

Lawrence's story 'The Woman who Rode Away', 1925, placed in the wilds of the **Sierra Madre** in the state of **Chihuahua**, concerns a blonde, blue-eyed, nameless woman, married to a silver mine owner, with children, trapped in his house. She manages to escape, and sets off to reach the mysterious mountain Indians. Here she is captured, and finally sacrificed to their cruel gods, for she had longed for this ritual, already 'dead' in life. The story 'The Princess', 1925, invokes a woman, a ride up into the savage mountains, a Mexican, a desired rape . . . but this one ends ironically, with her marriage to a tame older man after the passionate, reckless Mexican is shot dead by forest rangers. In *Mornings in Mexico*, 1927, written during a stay in **Oaxaca** from November 1924 to February 1925 in a rented house in **Pino Suárez** street south of the main park, Lawrence is fascinated by how Mexican Indians calculate time ('a vague foggy reality') and prefer to live in the 'naked moment', and see distance as always relative to feelings about the place referred to; and by how nature in the New World is alien – 'Nowhere more than in Mexico does human life become isolated, external to its surroundings . . .' He died in France in March 1930. See Jeffrey Meyers, *D.H. Lawrence: A Biography*, Macmillan, London, 1990.

LOWRY, Malcolm (1909–1957). Lowry was born in Wallasey, Cheshire, son of a Liverpool stockbroker. He ran away from school and sailed to China, though he eventually returned to finish a degree at Cambridge. In 1933 he published his first novel. In 1936 he went to live in **Cuernavaca** at **15 Calle Humboldt** with his first wife, whom he had married in 1933. He spent 20 months there, including Christmas 1937 in **Oaxaca jail**. He divorced in 1940. In 1947 Lowry published *Under the Volcano* (Extract 5), the story of a hopeless, intelligent alcoholic, Geoffrey Firmin, and his dramatic failure in love. The novel is dated on the Day of the Dead, 1938, with England at 'war' with Mexico over President Cárdenas's expropriation of British oil companies. Firmin, British consul, is *persona non grata*, seen as a spy. Lowry sets his inquiry into loss of will power and the failure of love in a realistic **Cuernavaca** and its landscape. This novel is stylistically Joycean, stream-of-consciousness, bundling the reader into twenty-four hours through various eyes, packed with puns, jokes, bilingual associations, hints, in long sentences, and lots of subclauses. The literary experimentation is held in check by Lowry's attempt to write a modern tragedy.

The novel changes the name of the town from Cuernavaca to the original Aztec Quauhnahuac, meaning in Nahuatl 'among the trees'. The 18 churches, 57 cantinas, 1 cinema and 400 swimming pools, the hill, the tortuous streets and Maximilian's ruined love-palace, exist as if in a Baedeker, always 'dominated by two volcanoes', **Popocatépetl** and **Ixtacihuatl**, threatening the expatriates. Apart from this symbolic geography, Lowry copies down signs, notices, buses and cantinas, littering his novel with foreign inscriptions. A crucial place in Firmin's love memories is **Oaxaca**. In Oaxaca Lowry stayed in the same hotel – **Hotel Francia** – in 1936 and 1946 as D.H. Lawrence had in 1924.

Geoffrey Firmin, in his spiralling descent into a private hell, is shot like a dog as a *pelado* by the corrupt and drunk Mexican police at the novel's end, as if it were a mercy killing. Firmin, by the end, has fallen to the bottom of the Mexican social order, has become Mexican, is without 'socks', with the pariah dog that follows him around as his mirror image. Firmin's alcoholic fall into hell is not a nostalgic patriot's; he prefers to 'die in Mexico'. Outside his own degradation the Consul views Mexicans positively. *Under the Volcano* was rewritten four times, turned down by twelve publishers, and in two years sold only two copies in Canada where Lowry was living (near Vancouver in a shack with his second wife). Lowry had been to jail, had brushed with bureaucracy, was expelled from Mexico, talked of spies and dogs and drunks, and like his Consul, dabbled in esoterica. Lowry's subsidiary aim was to put Mexico on the literary map: the 'slow melancholy tragic rhythm of Mexico itself', hoping to capture a 'sympathy and understanding of Mexico and her problems and people'. *Under the Volcano* was made into a film in 1984, directed by John Huston. Of Lowry's posthumously published works, an overwritten novel *Dark as the Grave Wherein my Friend is Laid*, 1969 (Extract 26), set in Mexico, sees Sigbjørn Wilderness in quest of his friend Juan Fernando Martínez who worked for the Banco Ejidal. Martínez was a fellow drunk who was murdered in **Villahermosa** in 1939. In December 1945 Lowry had flown to **Mexico City**, bussed down to **Cuernavaca** and **Oaxaca** to find that his friend was dead, and then left via **Acapulco**. The novel *La mordida* (Mexican for 'bribe') remained unfinished. Lowry died in East Sussex in 1957. See Douglas Day, *Malcolm Lowry: A Biography*, Oxford University Press, 1974.

OLSON, Charles (1910–1970). Born in Worcester, Massachusetts, Olson taught at several US universities, and was rector at the famous Black Mountain College from 1951 to 1956. Fascinated with Mayan hieroglyphics, he travelled to **Yucatán** in 1950 and wrote letters to his poet friend Robert Creeley. These became the book *Mayan Letters*, 1953 (Extract 34), an intriguing glimpse into a cranky obsession. The same year he began writing his 'projective verse', based on open form, and lines determined by breath, collected as *The Maximus Poems*, 1960. He also wrote an idiosyncratic study of Herman Melville: *Call Me Ishmael*, 1947.

PACHECO, José Emilio (1939–). Pacheco was born on 30 June 1939 in **Mexico City**. He took to writing early, and published his first book of short stories in 1958 as well as editing the literary review *Estaciones*. He has published nine books of poems, including *No me preguntes cómo pasa el tiempo*, 1969 (*Don't Ask Me How the Time Goes By: Poems 1964–1968*, 1978), as well as a *Selected Poems*, 1987. He has written an untranslated experimental novel about Nazism and

problems of narrating fiction (*Morirás lejos*, 1967) and further short stories, some of which are available in English in *Battles in the Desert and Other Stories*, 1987. The title novella of that collection (Extract 22) is about a boy growing up in the **Mexico City** of the 1950s, falling for a friend's sexy mother, declaring his love for her, and rebelling against his family. Pacheco has been a journalist, has taught at various universities in the USA and Canada, and for one year at Essex University in the UK. He won the Guggenheim, and the National Poetry Prize in 1969, prepared anthologies, translated literature into Spanish (Beckett, Pinter), and is a fine critic. Pacheco writes an ironic poetry, putting the self-centred poet on trial, using quotations and allusions in a collage way. His poems tend to be brief and assert that 'poetry' is no longer popular, and the poet no longer a bard or visionary.

PAZ, Octavio (1914–). Paz was born in **Mexico City** on 31 March 1914 and was brought up in the suburb **Mixcoac** (his home at that time is now a convent on the **Plazuela de San Juan**). His father was a lawyer who represented the peasant revolutionary Emiliano Zapata in New York. Paz published his first poem in 1931, and founded the first of his many literary reviews. In 1933 he published his first book of poems. In 1936 he dropped out of university and went to work in **Yucatán**, where he wrote a long protest poem about the misery of the sizal workers. In 1937 he married the writer Elena Garro, and the Chilean poet Pablo Neruda invited him to visit Republican Spain and attend the Writers' Congresses in Madrid and Valencia (1936–37). On his return a year later, Paz founded the magazine *Taller* (1938–41) with exiled Republican Spaniards as collaborators. In 1943 Paz, disenchanted with left-wing politics, went to live two years in the USA on a Guggenheim award. He joined the Mexican Foreign Service as cultural attaché in Paris from 1945 to 1951, and took part in the post-war French surrealist group, befriending André Breton.

In 1949 he collected his poems in *Libertad bajo palabra*, using the same title in 1960 and 1968. In Paris, Paz wrote his seminal essay on Mexicanness, *El laberinto de la soledad*, 1950 (*The Labyrinth of Solitude*, 1961) which psychoanalyses the Mexican character through sections on machismo, US/Mexican stereotypes, love and death, and a critical examination of the Mexican Revolution. It is a passionately written attack on official revolutionary ideology from a surrealist poet's perspective. In 1951 Paz published his prose poems *¿Aguila o sol?* (*Eagle or Sun*, 1970) and, after visiting Japan and India, returned to Mexico where he published further important collections of poetry – *Semillas para un himno*, 1954; *Piedra de sol*, 1957 (there are five published English translations), a long, ambitious poem based on the Aztec calendar stone dealing with history, love, and recovery of a harmonious life; and *La estación violenta*, 1958. In Mexico he also wrote one of the best books in Spanish on the role of the Romantic poet–critic, *El arco y la lira*, 1956 (*The Bow and the Lyre*, 1973). Paz was sent back to Paris in 1959–62, and published *Salamandra*, 1962. From 1962 to 1968, he was Mexico's ambassador to India, where he married his second wife Marie-José Tramini. His long Indian years led to many poems and speculations on the contrasts between East and West, Mexico and India, from *Blanco*, 1967, borrowing a Tantra form dealing with erotic love and

thought, to his essays *Conjunciones y disyunciones*, 1969 (*Conjunctions and Disjunctions*, 1974).

In 1968 Paz resigned his post in protest at the massacre of students just before the Mexican Olympic Games. He lectured at Harvard as Charles Eliot Norton Professor (1971–72), and published *Children of the Mire* in 1974. From 1971 to 1976 he edited the literary magazine *Plural*. In 1975 he published an autobiographical poem *Pasado en claro* (*A Draft of Shadows and Other Poems*, 1979). In 1976 he founded the magazine *Vuelta*, which is still running, and published a collection of poems also called *Vuelta*, evoking his return to Mexico after years of nomadic living. In 1979 he collected all his poems as *Poemas (1935–1975)*, and in 1987 he published his latest book of poems *Arbol adentro* (*A Tree Within*, 1988).

Nearly all Paz's poetry exists in English: *Early Poems, 1935–1955*, 1973, and *The Collected Poems of Octavio Paz, 1957–1987*, 1987, contain translations by Elizabeth Bishop (◊ Brazil), Charles Tomlinson ◊, and many others. Extract 31, from 'Hymn Among the Ruins', is translated by William Carlos Williams. Paz's critical essays have been collected in a series of books (*Marcel Duchamp: or the Castle of Purity*, 1970; *Claude Lévi-Strauss: an Introduction*, 1970; *Alternating Current*, 1973; *The Siren and the Seashell and Other Essays*, 1976; *One Earth, Four or Five Worlds: Reflections on Contemporary History*, 1985; *On Poets and Others*, 1987; *Convergences: Essays on Art and Literature*, 1987). In 1982, Paz published his intellectual biography of the Mexican seventeenth century nun forbidden to write by her male superiors, *Sor Juana Inés de la Cruz o las trampas de la fe* (*Sor Juana: Her Life and Work*, 1988), combining erudition and insight, and crossing many genres. Paz has won innumerable literary prizes, culminating in the Nobel prize in 1990. He lives in **Mexico City**, and has always courted polemics, as a lyric poet fighting for values against the pressures of contemporary politics and history. See Jason Wilson, *Octavio Paz*, Twayne, Boston, MA, 1986.

PORTER, Katherine Ann (1890–1980). Porter was born in Indian Creek, Texas. After leaving school she went into journalism, and then lived as an expatriate in Mexico. Her short stories *Flowering Judas*, 1935, confront Mexico. In the story 'Flowering Judas' Braggioni, a revolutionary, woos Laura, an introspective *gringa* teacher working at **Xochimilco** and living in **Mexico City**. The period is post-Revolutionary Mexico. In 'The Martyr', a fat muralist painter in Mexico loses his spiteful, daring, skinny mistress to a rival muralist. He dies of grief, eating *tamales* in a café. 'That Tree' evokes an American poet who goes to Mexico for the 'idle, free, romantic life of a poet' where the cheap life allows him to live like a bohemian with an Indian mistress. However, he insists on marrying a chaste Mid-western schoolteacher who cannot accept living in a 'beautiful dangerous place among interesting people'. In the end, after years of separation, she returns to her ex-husband, preferring his chaos, and artistic failures (he has become a well paid hack journalist) to her home town in the USA. 'Maria Concepción' deals with illiterate Indians living in their *jacal*. One day Maria catches her husband with another girl, and swears revenge. Her husband and the girl run off to the Revolution. On their return he is arrested as a deserter and Maria then murders her rival, is protected by her husband, and the whole village supports her.

She even adopts her rival's baby. 'Hacienda' (Extract 11) conveys Porter's ironic views of how foreigners adapt to Mexico. A woman writer observes the behaviour of several people on a film set at a *pulque hacienda* (at **Tetlapayac**) waiting for one of their local actors to be released from jail. She notes down details about the American producer (Upton Sinclair), and the Russian director (Sergei Eisenstein) whose camera catches an 'unchanged Mexico' where Indians' faces were 'closed dark faces . . . full of instinctive suffering, without individual memory', a Mexico unaffected by the Revolution of some 10 years before.

Porter visited Eisenstein and reported on his unfinished film *Viva México!* She translated Mexico's first novel (José Fernández de Lizardi, *The Itching parrot* [1816], Doubleday, New York, 1942). She arrived in Mexico in 1920, and lived there on and off until 1931. She met Diego Rivera, Siqueiros, Covarrubias, and shared her house in **Mixcoac** with the drunk, homosexual poet Hart Crane. Her long novel *Ship of Fools*, 1962, begins on board ship at **Veracruz** before setting off for Europe. For Porter, Mexico was 'my much-loved second country'. See Joan Givner, *The Life of Katherine Anne Porter*, Jonathan Cape, London, 1983.

ROMERO, José Rubén (1890–1952). Born in **Cotija de la Paz** in **Michoacán**, Romero's family moved to **Mexico City** when he was six, but business went badly and they returned to Michoacán where Romero grew up. When the 1910 Revolution erupted, Romero fought against Porfirio Díaz, the dictator, and joined the Revolutionary government, ending up as Mexican ambassador to Cuba in 1939. His first novel, *Apuntes de un* *lugareño*, 1932 (*Notes of a Villager*, 1988 – Extract 27) follows the growing up of his *alter ego*, poet and young Revolutionary. Equally autobiographical, *La vida inútil de Pito Pérez*, 1938 (*The Futile Life of Pito Pérez*, 1963) continues the theme of life in the provinces in Mexico.

RULFO, Juan (1918–1986). Rulfo was born on 16 May 1918 in the village of San Gabriel (today **Venustiano Carranza**), **Jalisco**, and was brought up in **Sayula**. His father and uncle were murdered in the violent 'Cristero' revolution (1926–29) of priests against the Revolutionary government. Rulfo placed all his fiction in this poor, desert area with its *mestizo* peasants clinging to reactionary beliefs, and communicating through violence. He was sent to an orphanage in **Guadalajara**, and in 1933 left for **Mexico City** to live with an uncle. Rulfo worked for immigration, travelling all over Mexico, on an irrigation project, and for a rubber company from 1947 to 1954. In 1962 he joined the Instituto Indigenista, protecting Mexico's Indians. He published the first of his stories in 1942, collecting them in *El llano en llamas*, 1953 (*The Burning Plain and Other Stories*, 1967), all set in **Jalisco** where the arid geography conditions the characters, betrayed by the promises of the Revolution. These stories involve a relentless undermining of ideals – family, love, hope, communication – but they are not documentaries. Rulfo writes a quirky, poetic prose, enlivened by black humour, with laconic monologues and dialogues. His only novel *Pedro Páramo*, 1955 (*Pedro Paramo, a Novel of Mexico*, 1959 – Extract 7) is situated in an arid geography (*Páramo* means 'plain', and *Pedro* is linked to *piedra*, 'stone') where in complicated

flashbacks we are given the fragmented portrait of a *cacique*, in a town he owns called Comala, his loves and violence, and bastard sons seeking him out. Half way through, the reader realizes the characters are all dead, that Comala is a ghost town, one of the many in Mexico. The Revolution had passed this town by. Rulfo worked in films, wrote scripts, and tinkered with an unpublished novel all his life.

TOMLINSON, Charles (1927–). Tomlinson was born in Stoke-on-Trent. He is Professor of English at Bristol University. His first poems came out in 1955, and were collected in 1985. A painter, he writes a sharply visual, tautly controlled poetry. He has travelled in Mexico, and befriended Octavio Paz ◊, whose work he has translated (see Octavio Paz, *Selected Poems*, Penguin, 1979), collaborating with Paz in *Renga*, 1971, and *Airborn/Hijos del aire*, 1981. See his *Translations*, Oxford University Press, Oxford, 1983.

TRAVEN, B. (?–1969). Traven was probably born in the Polish village of Swiebodzin in 1882, 1890, 1891 or 1901 – nobody has ever found out. He lived in Germany as an actor and revolutionary journalist under the pseudonym Ret Marut. As leader of the brief revolutionary government in Bavaria he was sentenced to death, but escaped, found work on a Norwegian ship, and stayed on in Mexico when he first landed there in the summer of 1924. He lived in tropical **Tampico** near the oil-fields in a bungalow for six to seven years, writing in German. In Tampico he befriended and supported the Nicaraguan revolutionary Augusto Sandino. His first novel, *The Death Ship*, came out in

1926. His second, *The Cotton Pickers*, about the wobblies, was also published in 1926 (the 'wobblies' were the Industrial Workers of the World, a revolutionary trade union movement founded in Chicago in 1905). Traven travelled as a photographer to **Chiapas** on an official Mexican government expedition, and returned there many times. He wrote an untranslated travel book, with his own photos, called *The Land of Spring*, 1928. From 1930 to 1955 he lived in an *adobe* shack at a small hotel in **Acapulco** called **El Parque Cachú**. It was here that a Mexican journalist and novelist, Luis Spota, blew his anonymous cover in an article in 1948. In 1957 Traven married and lived in **Mexico City (61 calle Mississipi)** where he died on 4 March 1969. In 1951 he had become a Mexican citizen. Traven was notoriously elusive, hated journalists, and pretended he was Hal Croves. He wrote 12 immensely popular books in German in the Jack London tradition. The most famous, *The Treasure of the Sierra Madre*, 1927 (translated in 1934 – Extract 6), was filmed by John Huston in 1948 (starring Humphrey Bogart). It is about three American bums from the **Tampico** oil-fields who find gold in the hills. They kill off Mexican bandits, then one is hacked to death, and they lose all their gold powder. The two survivors choose to live with the Indians, rather than go back to 'white' society's gold-fever. The action takes place during prohibition in the 1920s, and is rabidly anti-American. Equally powerful is Traven's *Rebellion of the Hanged*, 1936 (Extract 1), where *peones* at a mahogany lumber camp, with fierce guards and sadistic overseers, finally rebel. It is set during Porfirio Díaz's dictatorship; the 'hanged' refers to a punishment. Traven is acute on Tsot-

sil Indian psychology, and suffering. The action is relentless about losses, and takes place in tropical Mexico near **Jalotepec**. The cry '*Tierra y libertad*' (Zapata's cry) ends the novel, as the Mexican Revolution begins. *La Carreta*, 1931, is about an Indian oxen-cart driver, sold to different owners, and is a vivid picture of the *indio*'s sordid life before the Revolution. Traven also deals with Mexico in *The White Rose*, 1929, *The Bridge in the Jungle*, 1929, and *General from the Jungle*, 1940. See Karl Guthke, *B. Traven: the Life Behind the Legends*, Lawrence Hill Books, New York, 1991.

YANEZ, Agustín (1904–1980). Born in **Guadalajara** on 4 May 1904, Yáñez trained as a lawyer, was a university lecturer, Governor of the State of Jalisco from 1953 to 1959, and then Sub-Secretary to the President 1962–64, and Minister of Public Education 1964–70. He was a member of the Colegio Nacional and Director of the Academia Mexicana de la Lengua. He published his first novel in 1942, and the book that brought him fame, *Al filo del agua* in 1947 (*The Edge of the Storm*, 1963 – Extract 33), in which the storm that is about to break is the Mexican Revolution of 1910; for this novel studies a provincial village (**Yahualica** in **Jalisco**) in 1909–10 under Porfirio Díaz, especially the oppressive role of the church, laying bare the hypocrisy and sexual repression in the society of those times in a modernistic style with inner monologues and flashbacks. *Las tierras flacas*, 1964 (*The Lean Years*, 1968) is set in the 1920s and portrays a conflict over modernization between a *cacique* who dominates an estate called Tierra Santa and his illegitimate son who wants to introduce technology.

GUATEMALA

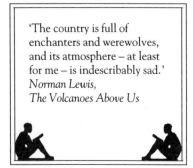

'The country is full of
enchanters and werewolves,
and its atmosphere – at least
for me – is indescribably sad.'
Norman Lewis,
The Volcanoes Above Us

Guatemala, the República de Guatemala, is named from the Indian word *Guhatezmalha* meaning 'mountain of vomiting waters'. Its land mass is 108 889 sq km, with 88 km of Caribbean coast, and 260 km of Atlantic coast. It lost Chiapas to Mexico in 1842, only fixing its Mexican boundaries in 1899, and its Honduran one in 1933. It still claims Belize, formerly British Honduras.

Its population rose to 9.2 million in 1990, 67% of which was pure Indian, the highest percentage in Latin America. Five per cent are negro on the Atlantic Coast, and the rest are *ladinos* and *mestizos*. **Guatemala City** at its centre, 1485 m high, has some 2 000 000 inhabitants.

The Indians speak 18 different languages, with Maya-Quiché as the trading language, and are descended from the Mayas whose civilization mysteriously ended in 600 AD. They have been recreated in the works of Guatemala's Nobel prize winning novelist Miguel Angel Asturias ◊. From his first published work *Leyendas de Guatemala*, 1930, his translations of Mayan classics like the *Popul Vuh* (translated into English as *The Book of Counsel: The Popol Vuh of the Quiche Maya of Guatemala*, 1971) to his masterpiece *Hombres de maíz*, 1949 (*Men of Maize*, 1975 – Extract 11) and *Mulata de tal*, 1963 (*The Mulata and Mister Fly*, 1967), he has explored imaginatively their way of life, and psychology so that his work becomes the best entry into their closed world. Equally sympathetic, but from abroad, Norman Lewis ◊, in *The Volcanoes Above Us*, 1957 (Extracts 2, 4 and 5) and in his essays, has also focused on the silent, resisting Indians, in their *huipils* (blouses), who work on *milpas* (maize patches), play *marimbas* (kind of xylophone), and are strangely religious, adapting Roman Catholicism to their earlier beliefs. Maya peasant leader Rigoberta Menchu, winner of the 1992 Nobel Peace Prize, exposed the Indians' plight in her autobiography *I Rigoberta Menchu*, 1984. An exotic view of the Mayans and their treasure emerges in Rose Macaulay's ◊ *Staying with Relations* (Extract 8).

Guatemala's **Mayan ruins**, with those in Yucatán and Honduras, came into Romantic prominence in the nineteenth century thanks to John Lloyd Stephens's two travel books *Incidents of Travel in Central America, Chiapas and Yucatán*, 1841 and *Incidents of Travel in Yucatán*, 1843, beautifully illustrated by Frederick Catherwood's detailed prints of the forgotten jungle-strangled ruins. The best excavated sites are at **Tikal** in Guatemala, and Palenque and Chichen Itzá in Mexico. The astronomical, calendar and mathematical sophistication of the mysterious Mayans, with a zero, and computer-like accuracy of astronomical predictions, as well as their sudden disappearance, and only recently decoded hieroglypic script, have been well described by Charles Gallenkamp in *Maya: The Riddle and Rediscovery of a Lost Civilization*, 1959.

Guatemala was conquered by bloodthirsty Pedro de Alvarado, coming south from Mexico, and remained part of the Spanish colonial system until 1821. Antigua was the ancient capital destroyed by a volcano in 1527 and again in 1773 (there are 28 volcanoes in the densely populated highlands, the highest being **Tajumulco** at 4220 m. The capital was moved to Guatemala City, in a zone known as the *tierra templada* (as opposed to *tierra caliente*). After two years as part of Iturbide's empire, Guatemala joined the Central American Federation, until it declared its independence in 1847. Most of the nineteenth century was dominated by the rivalry between liberals and conservatives, with the liberals in power until 1944. Rubén Darío, the Nicaraguan poet (◊ Nicaragua), depended on some of these forgettable dictators for patronage. During these years the dictator Estrada Cabrera ruled from 1898 to 1920, the model for the black-suited president in Asturias's surreal and grotesque novel *El señor presidente*, 1946 (*The President*, 1963). He was followed by another dictator, Jorge Ubico, from 1931 to 1944. Ubico, known as 'Tata' to the Indians, was paternalist, and sold the first concessions to the Frutera, or United Fruit Company of Boston, in 1906. Bananas became one of Guatemala's main exports. Asturias's novels, especially *El papa verde*, 1954, denounced US imperialism through its control of banana production. Following Juan José Arévalo's election as president from 1945 to 1951 came Arbenz, the man who initiated Guatemala's recent turbulent history.

Arbenz Guzmán, a revolutionary who was supported by the Communists, expropriated unused land from the United Fruit Company as part of his agrarian reform and threatened the USA. US pressure forced him to veer to the left of what began as a nationalist revolution, and he was toppled by a coup armed from Honduras by the USA and led by Castillo Armas in 1954. At the source of this conflict lay Guatemala's feudal land-owning structure, and isolated Indians. Two per cent of the people controlled 66% of the land; in 1984 the wealthiest 20% received 57% of the country's income. This period has been well caught in Norman Lewis's *The Volcanoes Above us*, and the threatening atmosphere of Guatemala is vividly evoked in Paul Bowles's *Up Above the World* (Extract 9).

The thirty-year war between the guerrillas and the military began in the 1960s leaving some 100 000 dead. Guatemala has the dubious distinction of having invented death squads, right-wing paramilitary groups 'disappearing' people. The guerrilla poet Otto René Castillo (1936–67) was one of the victims (see his poems *Let's Go*, 1971 and *Tomorrow Triumphant: Selected Poems*, 1984). Ramírez ◊, ex-Sandinista Vice-President, sets his novel *To Bury Our Fathers* (Extract 7) during these violent times. Ronan Bennett's recent political novel *Overthrown by Strangers* begins in Belfast and ends in Guatemala. In 1986, the centrist Christian Democrat Vinicio Cerezo won 70%, the first civilian president in 16 years. In 1991, Jorge Serrano was elected. That some sense of everyday life existed during Guatemala's virtual civil war is the theme of Rodrigo Rey Rosa's ◊ fiction (Extract 1).

Miguel Angel Asturias's work transforms the sad reality of the Indians, and the oppressive US interventions, in a series of mythical novels, and a later series of denunciatory novels more in the realist vein, so that he can be considered the chronicler of his country's twentieth century history. That Guatemala is also a beautiful country of lakes and high volcanic peaks, that two thirds of the land is forested, with a tropical climate, home to the quetzal bird, can be seen in Jonathan Evan Maslow, *Bird of Life, Bird of Death: A Naturalist's Journey Through a Land of Political Turmoil*, 1986. See also Paul Theroux, *The Old Patagonian Express: By Train Through the Americas*, 1979; Patrick Marnham, *So Far From God . . . A Journey to Central America*, 1985; and Anthony Daniels, *Sweet Waist of America: Journeys Around Guatemala*, 1990. For an earlier more learned (and waffly) view see Huxley ◊, *Beyond the Mexique Bay*, 1934 (Extract 6). An excellent, but untranslated, essay on Guatemala has been written by Luis Cardoza y Aragón (*Guatemala, las líneas de tu mano*, 1955). Younger Guatemalan writers feature in recent anthologies like *And We Sold the Rain: Contemporary Fiction from Central America* (ed Rosario Santos), 1989 (Extract 3) and *Clamor of Innocence: Central American Short Stories*, 1989, with political poets included in *Volcán*, 1983. Most Guatemalan literature is political in intention, countering the long repressive history of dictatorships and US interventions.

BOOKLIST

The following selection includes all titles which are extracted in this chapter as well as those mentioned in the introduction which are available in English. In general, paperback editions are given when possible. The editions cited are not necessarily the only ones available. For most of the extracted works, the original publisher in English can be found in 'Acknowledgments and Citations' at the end of the volume, as can the exact location of the extracts and the editions from which they are taken. The date in square brackets is the original publication date of the work in its original language. Extract numbers are highlighted in bold for ease of reference.

And We Sold the Rain: Contemporary Fiction from Central America, Rosario Santos, ed, Ryan, Peterborough, 1989/Four Walls: Eight Windows, San Francisco, CA, 1989.

Asturias, Miguel Angel, The Green Pope [1954], Gregory Rabassa, trans, Jonathan Cape, London, 1971/Delacorte Press, New York, 1971.

Asturias, Miguel Angel, Men of Maize [1949], Gerry Martin, trans, Verso, London, 1989/Delacorte Press, St Lawrence, NY, 1975. **Extract 11.**

Asturias, Miguel Angel, The Mulata and Mister Fly [1963], Gregory Rabassa, trans, Penguin, London, 1970/Delacorte Press, New York, 1967.

Asturias, Miguel Angel, The President [1946], Frances Partridge, trans, Gollancz, London, 1963 (published as El Señor Presidente by Atheneum, New York, 1969).

Bennett, Ronan, Overthrown by Strangers, Hamish Hamilton, London, 1992.

The Book of Counsel: The Popol Vuh of the Quiche Maya of Guatemala, Munro Edmondson, trans, Tulane University Press, 1971.

Bowles, Paul, Up Above the World [1967], Arena, London, 1984/Ecco Press, New York, 1982. **Extract 9.**

Castillo, Otto René, Let's Go! [1965], Margaret Randall, trans, Cape Goliard, London, 1971/Curbstone, Willimantic, CT, 1984.

Castillo, Otto René, Tomorrow Triumphant: Selected Poems, Magaly Fernandez and David Volpendesta, eds, Night Horn Books, San Francisco, CA, 1984.

Clamor of Innocence: Central American Short Stories, Barbara Paschke and David Volpendesta, City Lights, San Francisco, CA, 1989.

Darío, Rubén, Autobiografía [1909], **Extract 10** (Jason Wilson, trans).

Daniels, Anthony, Sweet Waist of America: Journeys Around Guatemala, Century Hutchinson, London, 1990.

Gallankamp, Charles, Maya: The Riddle and Rediscovery of a Lost Civilization, [1959], Penguin, London, 1981.

Huxley, Aldous, Beyond the Mexique bay [1934], Penguin, London, 1955/Greenwood Press, Westpoint, CT, 1975. **Extract 6.**

Lewis, Norman, The Volcanoes Above Us [1957], Arena, London, 1989. **Extracts 2, 4 and 5.**

Lloyd Stephens, John, Incidents of Travel in Central America, Chiapas and Yucatán [1841], Dover, New York, 1969.

Lloyd Stephens, John, Incidents of Travel in Yucatán [1843], Dover, New York, 1963.

Macaulay, Rose, *Staying with Relations*, Collins, London, 1930. **Extract 8.**

Marnham, Patrick, *So Far from God . . . A Journey to Central America*, Penguin, London, 1986/ Viking, New York, 1985.

Maslow, Jonathan Evan, *Bird of Life, Bird of Death: A Naturalist's Journey Through a Land of Political Turmoil*, Penguin, London, 1987/Viking, New York, 1986.

Menchu, Rigoberta, *I Rigoberta Menchu: An Indian Woman in Guatemala*, Ann Wright, trans, Verso, London, 1984.

Payeras, Mario, 'Story of a Maestro', in *And We Sold the Rain: Contemporary Fiction from Central America*, Rosario Santos, ed, Ryan, Peterborough, 1989/Four Walls:

Eight Windows, San Francisco, CA, 1989. **Extract 3.**

Ramírez, Sergio, *To Bury Our Fathers: A Novel of Nicaragua* [1977], Nick Caistor, trans, Readers International, London, 1984. **Extract 7.**

Rey Rosa, Rodrigo, *Dust on Her Tongue*, Paul Bowles, trans, Peter Owen Publishers, London, 1989. **Extract 1.**

Theroux, Paul, *The Old Patagonian Express: By Train Through the Americas* [1979], Penguin, London, 1980/Houghton Miflin, Boston, MA, 1989.

Volcán: Poems from El Salvador, Guatemala, Honduras and Nicaragua, Alejandro Murgía and Barbara Paschke, eds, City Lights, San Francisco, CA, 1983.

Extracts

(1) EL PETEN

Rodrigo Rey Rosa, *Dust On Her Tongue*

This short story of the revenge taken by the widow Lucy Ward on her servant describes the El Petén region in northern Guatemala, famous for its Tikal ruins, chicle (chewing gum) and timber. It lies on Lago Petén Itzá, with a population of some 5000.

Richard Ward, an American, had come to the Petén nine months earlier, and had purchased a piece of land facing the lagoon of Itzá, where he built a small cottage. He intended to retire there with his wife Lucy, who was waiting in Wisconsin for news of him. Two weeks before the body was found, Richard Ward had been seen in a shop in Flores, and then he had disappeared. His servant Rafael Colina was taken to the police station, where he was questioned. No result came of this, nor of the search made of his hut, on Ward's land. They kept him for a few hours, and after administering the customary beating, let him go.

Lucy Ward arrived in Flores one wet Sunday in September. She was stout, with graceful arms and legs. At the police station they gave her the little box containing the ashes: 37, she read on the cover, Sr. R. Ward. A police car took her to the property, where Rafael was expecting her.

She wandered around the terrain, examining the landscape with the questioning expression of someone looking at an abstract painting he fails to understand; and then she realized with some surprise that it pleased her. She went into the cottage, looked around, and decided to spend the night there. Later, on her way to sleep, she thought of her husband, and was grateful to him for having found this place. She decided to try living there for a while.

From the outset it was as though the absence of human companionship, an absence she had dreaded, was compensated for by the feverish life of the plants, the activity of insects, and the tenuous presence of Rafael. Little by little she became aware of the forest's tiny miracles, and she learned how to resign herself to the inconveniences: the ever-present ants, the constant sweating, the mosquitoes at twilight and at dawn.

(2) GUADALOUPE

Norman Lewis, *The Volcanoes Above Us*

Lewis's narrator takes a train up to Guadaloupe (near the beautiful Lake Atitlán) to find out what has happened to his expropriated coffee finca.

The thing to remember about Guadaloupe was that it was a ladino town. There are one or two places in Guatemala, like the City itself, which are accepted as being 'white', and there are many pure Indian villages in the mountains; but most of the small towns like Guadaloupe are peopled by ladinos, who are a strong and recent mixture of two races. They are a people who dress in Western fashions as well as they can afford, who like to ride rather than walk, to work without soiling their hands, to promenade at set hours and in the proper places, to marry their daughters well, to dabble in politics and accumulate money. An infinite distance separates them from the Indian side of their ancestry.

The ladinos of Guadaloupe live unheedingly among grandiose vestiges of the past. It is a town of majestic ruin, cracked splendour and tarnished gilt. The old stone houses are blind-walled, with rare windows defended by massive grilles and enormous doorways through which a man could ride without dismounting from his horse. The main square known as the plaza is enclosed by superb colonial buildings, including a church like a cathedral. There are other streets and squares, but the streets are narrow and ill-paved, and the squares are hidden among decaying buildings decorated with the stone escutcheons of extinct nobility.

There are also shops, and drinking dives called cantinas, all of them single-storeyed and painted in fierce colours. The fronts of the shops are painted with pictures which dramatize the goods sold inside: a bull charges at you head down and nostrils distended from the façade of the butchers . . .

(3) GUATEMALA: IN THE JUNGLE

Mario Payeras, *Story of a Maestro*

> *Mario Payeras's 'Story of a Maestro Who Spent His Whole Life Composing a Piece for the Marimba', opens with Patrocinio setting off into the woods to make his own marimba – the Guatemalan version of the xylophone. This extract is taken from* And We Sold the Rain: Contemporary Fiction from Central America *– see Booklist.*

Patrocinio Raxtún went into the jungle when he began to get old. Originally, he was from the region of *guarda-barrancas* birds and the *palos voladores*.[1] He left that world because all his material possessions consisted of three orange groves spoiled by time. He knew how to play the marimba from childhood, but the daily preoccupations of worldly goods exposed to the vicissitudes of light and to the voracity of the migrations left him no time for music. Searching for happiness, he spent long weeks descending the humid slopes of the Cuchumatanes mountains, entering deep into the boisterous universe of parrots in the rainy season.

By the time the torrential rains had stopped, he had arrived at an old village, on the banks of the Chixoy River, where no one seemed to be living. Life passed by in the shade of the big *sapodilla* trees. There he fixed up an abandoned house, scraped clean its sprouting beams, and organized an economy inaccessible to the laws of trade and to the predatory species of the air. The band of monkeys, who from their solitude spy on the affairs of men, saw when the mouse-eating boa, which until then had occupied the house, slipped imperceptibly away. As soon as he had taken care of his material needs, the maestro began building his marimba . . . So, with the arrival of the season when the parrots create an uproar from daybreak on, Patrocinio Raxtún went into the forest in search of the *hormigo* tree. It is a sonorous species which, despite its passion for rain and its canary's calling, makes the axe reverberate. It took him two days, besieged by swarms of bees that turn the salt of ordinary physical labour into sweet forms of energy, to chop one tree down and separate a piece large enough to obtain twenty-six keys.

[1] Poles used in an ancient Mayan dance.

(4) GUATEMALA: VOLCANOES AND INDIANS

Norman Lewis, *The Volcanoes Above Us*

Lewis's narrator Charles Williams summarizes his experience of living in Guatemala.

For anyone who has lived in Guatemala, other countries, by contrast, are lacking in savour. The problem confronting the people who want to promote a prosperous tourist industry is how to take out this over-strong flavour so that only the safely picturesque remains. This is difficult in a country which lies under the shadow of thirty-two volcanoes, its towns rattled constantly by earthquakes, like dice in a box, its villages peopled by a race who never smile, but sometimes giggle in a foolish way in the presence of tragedy. Tourists who visit the Indian fiestas are chilled by the fact that they are conducted in silence, and that the natives are unresponsive to kind words or gestures on the visitors' part. Worse still, if the visitors persist in staying until the evening, by which time most of the Indians are drunk, they may see machete fights when still the only sound is that of the clash of steel and the chop of a blade into a muscle and bone. The volcanoes are a scenic attraction, regular in shape and most beautiful, their ashen cones pale against the sky. It is unsafe to climb to the tops of some of them because the Indians sacrifice to their gods on altars set up on the edge of the craters, and violently resent any intrusion. The country is full of enchanters and werewolves, and its atmosphere – at least for me – is indescribably sad.

(5) Guatemala City

Norman Lewis, *The Volcanoes Above Us*

Charles Williams has entered Guatemala City with the victorious army toppling the 'communist' president (Arbenz fell in June 1954, although he is not named in the novel.)

I was taking it easy and enjoying myself. The outer suburbs of Guatemala City always appealed to me. They are like the last-century frontier towns you see on the screen, but they are painted in all colours; houses and shops and taverns painted blood-red and blue and yellow and strung out in all directions. After a while I began to notice that there was something unusual about this particular afternoon. The doors and the window shutters were closed and there were no half-breeds full of aguardiente sitting in the dirt outside the cantinas. Later I passed three abandoned ice-cream barrows in a row, and while I was wondering about this some Regular Army soldiers came out into the sunshine ahead, and one of them fired a tommy-gun at me. I was surprised, but not very surprised, because there is something in the atmosphere of Guatemala that keeps you in a state of preparation for this kind of thing. People shoot at each other with very little provocation, and frequently – as in this case – they are well out of range.

The outskirts of Guatemala City are seamed with narrow ravines called barrancas, and as this street ran along the edge of one I crossed it and looked over the edge. There was a great deal of garbage in the ravine, both clinging to its sides and in the bottom, with a few black turkey-vultures limping about picking it over.

(6) Guatemala City

Aldous Huxley, *Beyond the Mexique Bay*

Huxley visited a market outside Guatemala City in 1933.

Outside in an overflow market we saw an old Indian woman selling iguanas. They were cheap; you could buy a miniature dragon with three feet of whip-lash tail, all alive, for twenty or thirty cents. Flayed and gutted, the dried carcasses of several more lay in a neat row on the pavement, a pale meat crusty with flies. Near them stood an enormous bowl, full of iguana eggs. Curiosity wrestled with prejudice and was at last defeated; we moved away, leaving the eggs untasted. That evening we happened to pass along the same street. Business in lizards had evidently been slack; the old woman's pitch was still crawling with monsters. While we were looking, she began to pack up her wares for the night. One by one, she took up the animals and dumped them into a circular basket. The tails projected, writhing. Angrily she shoved them back into place; but while one was being folded away, another would spring out, and then another. It was like a battle with the hydra. The abhorred tails were finally confined under a net. Then, hoisting the lizards on to her head, and with the bowl of their eggs under her arm, the old woman marched away, muttering . . .

(7) GUATEMALA CITY

Sergio Ramírez, *To Bury Our Fathers*

Sandinista guerrillas kidnap a military attaché and drive out of Guatemala City towards Antigua on their way to Nicaragua.

The dilapidated blue and white taxi pulled off down Sixth Avenue. The two of us, separated by the colonel's bulk, did not even dare to look at each other, frightened we would give everything away with an indiscreet smile, as we left the Panamerican Hotel behind us, and the neon sign of the *Jardín de Italia* which had just come on with the others in the dusk, their vertical lettering twinkling or gloomily static: *El Cielito papi K Listo de la Luz y Fuerza La Casas de los Abrigos N*. Polanski, the poster announcing *The Holy Shroud* at the *Lux* projecting out into the street, the lid of the glovebox tied up with a piece of wire rattling constantly, and every block we travelled meant he was that much more in our hands. We were suffocating on the gasoline fumes, but at least we had passed the police headquarters, the Parque Concordia, and the neon lights were getting fewer and fewer; we reached 20th Street, still worried because even now he might suddenly say – stop, I want to get out; but we arrived at the avenue by the cemetery with no problems, its interminable white wall still bright, though above it the cypresses were gradually losing their outlines as night fell; the shadowy forms of headstones, crosses, and the statues of angels littering José Esposito's stonemason yard, tiny eaveless houses with yellow skirting, blue doors and narrow gardens glimpsed through cement block walls; corn mills, butchers shops, dimly lit bars, the rain-streaked figure of the goddess of luck on an adobe wall

10 centavos and you'll be poor no more
Chica lottery offers you the chance of your
LIFE

Then out onto the Antigua Highway, past the windows of the Roosevelt Hospital, the lights of the city further and further behind us, the air streaming in through the badly fitting windows cooler now as we rattled along, until with a loud backfiring explosion the driver slowed down for the 13 kilometre police post.

(8) LAKE SALVADOR

Rose Macaulay, *Staying With Relations*

Catherine, the novelist protagonist, arrives at Puerto Barrios to spend a holiday with English friends on a finca in the jungle, and takes the train from Livingstone to San Pedro. This weakly plotted novel reads like a guidebook, even though Rose Macaulay never visited Guatemala.

The light railway ran, leapingly, fifty miles back from Livingstone port, among forests, mangrove swamps, coffee plantations, maize patches, sugar canes, valleys and mountains, and ended at the little lake, which was called Salvador. It had taken the little train four hours to reach the little lake, and it was now noon. The travellers leaped thankfully from the little train and went their several ways, some taking to mules along forest paths, some to various kinds of craft on the lake, others to their homes in the minute pueblo of Ceniza, which stood like a brown toadstool patch festooned with scarlet creepers at the lake's head.

For Catherine there waited at a little jetty a white and scarlet motor launch. To this vehicle she was conducted by her cousin Isie, by Benet Cradock, and by an Indian mozo, for these had come to meet her train and convey her up the little lake and the river Merces to San Pedro, where the mule journey would begin. Catherine's luggage was disposed by the mozo in the launch's hold, and the party embarked. A half-breed priest meanwhile talked to them from the jetty in bad Spanish about how he, too, would, if it should be no inconvenience to them, make the journey up to San Pedro in their launch. Benet, in Spanish nearly as fluent as his and more correct, apologised for not being able to take another passenger, owing to the great weight of Catherine's luggage. They continued the conversation until the launch was some way down the lake and the noise of its locomotion drowned that of the clergyman's voice.

'We could have taken him quite well really,' Catherine said. 'However, I suppose you don't like him.'

Isie and Benet agreed that this was the case, Isie adding that the clergyman was a pain where it hurt the most.

'He is the parish priest in our village,' Benet said. 'If we let him come on the launch we should have him with us all the way through the forest. Talking. He always talks when he's drunk. When he's sober he's silent, and rather morose. To-day he's drunk, naturally, after a week in Livingstone.'

(9) PUERTO BARRIOS

Paul Bowles, *Up Above the World*

In this 1967 novel, the Slades, typical American intellectual tourists, have arrived at a Guatemalan Caribbean town (Puerto Barrios, fictionalized as Puerto Farol), and have to confront local attitudes.

Dr Slade looked out of the doorway across the veranda with its broken wicker furniture, past the waterfall of rain that splattered down from the door, to the empty garden beyond. A large buzzard suddenly appeared and settled clumsily on the bare plank that was the veranda's railing. For a moment he thought it was going to topple over. Like a mass of charred newspaper it wavered there for an instant, then steadied itself, folded its wings and let its raw red head fall to one side of its breast.

The man picked his nose with his forefinger now as he spoke. 'There is a place called Paraíso only thirty-two kilometers from here. There are the ruins of San Ignacio. Very interesting. Big stones in the jungle, with faces in them. They'll give you nightmares!'. His laugh broke into a cough, and he spat straight down from where he stood, watching the mass of sputum fall to the floor. Then he seemed to be doing a little dance by himself behind the desk as he scuffed it with the sole of his shoe. '*Sabe lo que son, las pesadillas?*'

'Yes, yes, of course,' said Dr Slade. 'We'll be taking the train tomorrow morning, and we'll need at least three men to help with our luggage. I just wanted to let you know.'

'It's fantastic!' Mrs Slade exclaimed, looking up at her husband. 'A town as big as this without a single taxi!'

'A town as big as this with only this hotel,' he retorted. 'The walk's nothing. Fifteen minutes. But God, we've got to sleep here. And we've got to eat here. The taxi's the least of my worries.'

The man behind the desk was tearing the skin from another mango; the tart varnish-like odour filled the hall. Mrs Slade spoke very little Spanish. '*Mango bueno?*' she said to the man.

'*Regular*,' he answered without looking up.

They wandered out onto the veranda; the buzzard did not move. The air smelled of flowers, and there was a constant tapestry of insect sound audible behind the roar of the rain.

(10) San Jose

Rubén Darío, *Autobiografía*

Darío, the Nicaraguan poet, recalls an incident in the Guatemala of the 1880s in his autobiography (extract translated by Jason Wilson).

General Cayetano Sánchez, backer of President Barillas, was a reckless soldier given to drinking who could do whatever he wanted. One moonlit night I had been invited to a dinner in the San José castle with my old teacher the Pole José Leonard, and the poet Palma. We had been served local dishes, especially one called chojín, tastily prepared for us by General Toledo, who aspired to the presidency of the Republic. It was bitter, and hot, and consisted mainly of radishes. As usual there was plenty of wine and coffee followed by innumerable brandies. We were all more than merry, but General Sánchez was almost hotheaded in his drunkenness. As we strolled along the fortifications he pointed out the twin towers of the cathedral in the moonlight, and then had a crazy idea: 'Let's see who is in charge of this cannon!'. An officer came forward. Cayetano, as we called him, said to us: 'See that lovely target? We're going to knock down one of the cathedral towers' and ordered the cannon to be loaded. The soldiers obeyed like zombies. As General Sánchez was capable of anything, we realized this was a dicey moment. The poet Palma came up with an excellent idea. 'Alright Cayetano, but first let's improvise poems about this matter. Tell someone to fetch more brandy!' We all understood, and heroically swallowed more and more alcohol. Palma served enormous glasses to the General. He and I recited poems, and then when we had emptied the bottle, the General fell asleep. And so Guatemala was saved from being woken up at midnight by a cannonade fired as a practical joke. Not much later Cayetano Sánchez came to a tragic end.

(11) San Miguel Acatan

Miguel Angel Asturias, *Men of Maize*

Asturias's novel about Indian mythic psychology ends with a postman whose wife has run off, and who has lost his Indian roots living as a ladino and delivering mail in San Miguel Acatán.

The wife of Señor Nicho the postman ran away, while he, on foot, made his way across mountains, villages and plains, trotting to arrive more quickly than the rivers, more quickly than the birds, more quickly than the clouds, at the distant township, with the mail from the capital.

Poor Señor Nicho Aquino, what will he do when he gets there and finds her gone?

He will tear his hair, he will call her, not Chagüita, as he called her before they were married, nor Isabra, as he called her after, but what every woman who runs off is called, 'tecuna'.

He will call her tecuna, tecuna, his heart chafing him like saddle sores, and he will bite, yes bite his own tail, but bite it alone, all alone in his unlit rancho, his dark solitary shack, whilst the Germans who trade in the town will read two or three times over the letters from their friends and family and the business letters from overseas brought by Señor Nicho, devoted as a dog, from the capital to San Miguel Acatán, a small town built on a shelf of golden stone above abysses where the atmosphere was blue, the color of the sea among pinewoods of dark green shade and fountains of rock, sewing boxes from which streamed threads of water born to line the fields with marigolds, ferns, fire lilies and begonias with heart-shaped leaves.

Poor Señor Nicho Aquino, what will he say when he gets there and finds her gone?

He will be left speechless, trembling, rags, sweat, dust, and on finding his tongue, his speech, a voice to unburden himself, he will call her tecuna, tecuna, tecuna!, while many a mother will sniff back big, swelling, salt tears, needless tears, but tears nonetheless, as they read the letters from their sons away studying in the capital, and the justice of peace and the local commandant will read letters from their wives, and the garrison officials the letters from some lady friend telling them she's well, even if she's sick, and that she's alone and faithful, even if there's someone with her . . .

How many lies that night in San Miguel Acatán after the arrival of the unshod beast, the postman!

How many pious lies emerged from all those envelopes to surround the naked truth that awaited Señor Nicho Aquino!

How many letters in that minuscule town of houses built on mountainsides, one on top of the other like hencoops, whilst Señor Nicho, after shouting his wife's name, will shrivel up like a worm disemboweled by fate as he calls her tecuna, tecuna, tecuna! until he tires of calling her that, and of wearing out his feet on the solitude of the rancho!

The mail, when it was Señor Nicho, arrived with the evening stars. Open doors and windows watched him go by, with the neighbors behind them, spying, to be sure he really had arrived, and to be able to tell themselves and others: The postman's here . . . Señor Nicho's arrived, did you see! . . . Two bags of mail, yes, two bags he had with him! Those who expected a letter and those who didn't, which of us is not always expecting a letter, all of them waiting, sitting in doorways or leaning out of windows, watching out for the postman, ready to break open the envelope and take out the folded sheets of paper, and read them straight through the first time, and with pauses and comments the second and third times, those who could read or half read, or get someone to read it out to them in the case of the tough-skinned peasants, eyes mossy with sleep, who could only gaze at the letters scrawled across the pages.

Señor Nicho's footsteps rang down the main street. Someone said he was showing off a new outfit, had new sandals on. Must be wanting to make a good impression on his wife, all done up like that, little knowing what was in store for him. The postman's steps rang out across the cobbled square perfumed with jasmine.

Biographies and important works

ASTURIAS, Miguel Angel (1899– 1974). Asturias was born on 16 October 1899 in **Guatemala City**. His mother was a schoolteacher and his father a magistrate who became president of the Supreme Court, but was banished to the country (where Asturias grew up) for refusing to have students shot. In 1920 Asturias was involved in student riots against the dictator Estrada Cabrera. In 1923 he graduated in law from the **Universidad de San Carlos** with a thesis on the social problem of the Indians, wrote his first short story, and went to London, then Paris where he lived from 1923 to 1933 on the fringes of the surrealist group, and studying Guatemalan anthropology at the Parisian Musée de l'Homme. In Paris, he translated a French book on the Maya into Spanish, and in 1927 helped translate the Mayan *Popol Vuh* into French. In 1930 he published *Leyendas de Guatemala* (translated into French in 1931 with a prologue by Paul Valéry), retelling stories heard as a child. Back in Guatemala in 1933 he founded the newspaper *Diario del aire*, which lasted eleven years and published four books of poems.

In 1946 he published his surreal novel on dictatorship begun in the 1920s, *El Señor Presidente* (*The President*, 1963), modelled on Estrada Cabrera's 1898–1920 dictatorship but combining elements from all Latin American dictators. Asturias uses dreams and surrealist techniques and grim realism to create his depressing world of corrupt power (we never see the dictator) and puppets. A beggar is killed, and others are forced to tell lies, a general is arrested, his daughter raped by the President's favourite, Cara de Angel, who then falls in love and marries her, annoying the dictator who imprisons him. A plot outline cannot convey the poetic and unpleasant details. Asturias wrote more direct political protest novels dealing with US banana imperialism, like

Miguel Angel Asturias

Viento fuerte, 1950 (*The Cyclone*, 1969, or *Strong Wind*, 1969) where the Indians' magic world is contrasted with US business and a cyclone is called up by a shaman. *El Papa verde*, 1954 (*The Green Pope*, 1971) follows the rise to riches of a US banana king. In 1947 Asturias was posted as Guatemalan ambassador to Buenos Aires until 1953. His masterpiece *Hombres de maíz*, 1949 (*Men of Maize*, 1988 – Extract 11) is a novel about the degeneration of the Indian since the Mayan days in terms of two views of maize, originally sacred, but today sold for money. The six-part novel begins with a dense recreation of the Mayan world view through a guerrilla, Gaspar Ilom, and ends with a postman who has betrayed his Indian roots, and seeks his lost wife. Asturias blends surrealist dream and myth exploration with social protest. *Mulata de tal*, 1963 (*The Mulata and Mister Fly*, 1970) contrasts Indian magic and catholicism in an extravagant novel dealing with the secret life of Guatemala.

After the fall of the radical Arbenz government in 1954, Asturias lived in exile in Argentina until 1962 and then in Paris. In 1967 he was awarded the Nobel Prize for literature. He died in Madrid in 1974.

BOWLES, Paul (1910–). See also under Mexico. Bowles was born in New York City. He went to Paris as a composer, and edited an avant-garde magazine, before marrying Jane Bowles (◊ Panama), and writing fiction, first based on his experiences travelling in Mexico, Central America and Colombia, and then on his long sojourn in Tangiers from 1952. He is also a translator (see under Rodrigo Rey Rosa). He once spent three weeks in Guatemala. Settled in Mexico, Bowles visited Panama in 1938, and Costa Rica, Limón, **Guatemala City** and Chichecastenango. Earlier in 1934 he had visited Colombia, getting ill in Santa Marta. In *Without Stopping: An Autobiography*, 1972, we see that he had read Bioy Casares and Borges in the original, and edited a special number on Latin American literature for *View* in 1945, translating Borges. He learnt Spanish by reading Huidobro's long poem *Altazor*, only to discover that Huidobro invented his vocabulary. In his novel *Up Above the World*, 1967 (Extract 9) we meet the Slades, in a deserted tropical town, waiting to

Paul Bowles

board a ship. Thus begins their descent into hell, and final destruction. It is as if Bowles takes his sadistic revenge on a stereotypical, liberal, impatient couple of American tourists. Dr Slade is a 67-year-old, married for a second time to the much younger Day. They silently torment each other. They disembark at Puerto Farol in a nameless Central America, probably Guatemala, with Indians and high mountains. The novel explores the Americans' fear, their anxieties about being abroad in a place where bats give rabies. Many of Bowles's short stories are realistically located in tropical Central America, with local place names, but never naming the country itself. Bowles thus roots his civilized Americans and Spaniards in off-the-beaten-track places in order to submit them to humiliations. Gore Vidal, in the introduction to Bowles's *Collected Stories, 1939–1976*, 1980, summarizes the stories as evoking 'the plain incomprehension of Americans in contact with the natives of Mexico'. The best stories are 'The Echo', 'Call at Corazón', 'Under the Sky', 'At Paso Rojo' and 'Tapiama'. They also deal with off-beat sexualities. In general, Bowles places his fiction carefully in landscapes he has travelled through. See Christopher Sawyer-Laucanno, *An Invisible Spectator: A Biography of Paul Bowles*, Bloomsbury, London, 1989; and *Paul Bowles, By His Friends*, Gary Pulsifer, ed, Peter Owen, London, 1992.

DARIO, Rubén (see under Nicaragua).

HUXLEY, Aldous (see under Mexico).

LEWIS, Norman (1919–). Born in Enfield, North London, Lewis has travelled widely, written twelve novels, and travel books about Spain and Latin America. As a journalist, he first drew the world's attention to the plight of Brazilian Indians in 1968. His vivid autobiography, *Jackdaw Cake*, 1987, describes his marriage, and then his move out to Cuba under Batista as rootlessness drives the couple round the world in search of a place to live. His essay *The Missionaries*, 1988, returns to his years in Guatemala in the 1950s. His Guatemalan novel *The Volcanoes Above Us*, 1957 (Extracts 2, 4 and 5) tells the story of 38-year-old Charles Williams, a Welsh coffee *finca* owner, waiting to get his farm back after the overthrow of Werner (Arbenz), the left-wing Guatemalan dictator. But the novel is really about the plight of the Indians, for Williams is a pensive anthropologist. Lewis shows us the real Guatemala, focusing on the opacity of the Indian mind behind a conventional plot about his narrator reaching a new level of awareness about himself and love. He tells his readers: 'The Indian is vanishing. He is withdrawing himself silently, dying out or being changed into a ladino.' The novel shows an English reader what Guatemala is really like: 'It had this wonderful sparkling climate all the year round, and the countryside was beautiful, but in an unearthly way, and very sad and silent.' He vividly describes an earthquake where the lights 'snap' out and glass shatters like 'cracking ice'. The **Tamanzun volcano** seems 'remote and unreal', the clue to Guatemala for Lewis. This land of 'cactus and orchid and the sad, senseless cries of brilliant birds' is opposed to England where 'nothing changes', and monotonous life continues in its bourgeois predictability. Lewis has set further realistic novels in Colombia (*Flight from the Dark*

Norman Lewis

Equator, 1972) and in 1959 Cuba (*Cuban Passage*, 1982).

MACAULAY, Rose (1881–1958). Macaulay was born in Cambridge, one of four daughters of a classics lecturer. She grew up in Italy and later graduated from Somerville College, Oxford. The first of her 14 novels appeared in 1906. In 1930 she

published *Staying With Relations* (Extract 8), a vaguely plotted novel about over-cultured Brits in jungly, Mayan Guatemala, an American crook neighbour, a kidnap and a long car-journey in Mexico up Baja California. The novel is a pretext to observe and satirize Bloomsbury types in the jungle. The protagonist is a female novelist visiting friends, recording the oddities of people. The

Rodrigo Rey Rosa

novel describes her arrival at **Living-stone**, her trip by train to **San Pedro**, the lake, Mayan ruins, the *hacienda*, the jungle. She reports on 'alligator pears' (avocados), the Lacondon Indians, the rain, the *chicleros* (*chicle* or chewing gum collectors), earthquakes, copal balls. The novel is topographically exact. However, Macaulay never visited Guatemala, her 'dream country'. In 1929 she took a two-month trip from Florida to the US Pacific coast, but because her sister was a nun they were not allowed to enter Mexico (during the Cristero uprising). Rose Macaulay also wrote *They Went to Portugal*, 1946. See Jane Emery, *Rose Macaulay: A Writer's Life*, John Murray, London, 1991.

PAYERAS, Manuel (1950–). Born in Guatemala, Payeras has been active in the guerrilla movement, writing about it in *Days of the Jungle*, 1983. His study of Guatemalan ecology came out in 1990.

RAMIREZ, Sergio (see under Nicaragua).

REY ROSA, Rodrigo (1958–　). Rey Rosa was born in Guatemala. *The Beggar's Knife*, 1985, and *Dust On Her Tongue*, 1989 (Extract 1), both translated by Paul Bowles ◊ consist of laconic, suggestive stories, usually narrated in the first person. Some deal with children's sudden, devious awarenesses, others with outsiders and subtle revenges. One ends with a Chinaman implicitly accused of wanting to kill the young narrator. Another has the widow of a dead American, possibly murdered, chucking out her servant's pet toad. Another has a boy who for a whim kills a driver from a bridge, accuses a peasant boy his own age, and tells the truth to his family over a meal so that they think he is a liar. Bowles wrote: 'The action of the tales takes place in Guatemala – not the Guatemala of the news broadcasts but that of the people whose life continues more or less the same as always, in spite of the violent events that threaten the continuation of that life.' Rey Rosa's novel *The Pelcari Project*, 1991, translated by Bowles, allegorically narrates an experiment with parrots as a means of political indoctrination in Central America.

EL SALVADOR

'As I waited to cross back over the Boulevard de los Heroes to the Camino Real I noticed soldiers herding a young civilian into a van, their guns at the boy's back, and I walked straight ahead, not wanting to see anything at all.'

Joan Didion, *Salvador*

El Salvador, or the República de El Salvador, means 'Saviour' in Spanish, and is the most densely populated country in the Americas. Its land area is 21 041 sq km, with no Caribbean coastline, and its population reached some 5.3 million in 1990. **San Salvador**, the capital, had a population of 453 000 in 1983. The country is 80% *mestizo*, with few Indians left except for the Izalco Indians. The language is Spanish, and the religion mainly Roman Catholic.

El Salvador is intensely cultivated (the world's third largest producer of coffee). It has a chain of some 20 cone-shaped volcanoes, some active, along the Southern coast with **Santa Ana** at 2355 m the highest and **Izalco**, at 1885 m, famous for the massacre of peasants in 1932, and Claribel Alegría's ◊ and Roque Dalton's ◊ eye-witness novels about it (see Extracts 2 and 9). Between the high mountain ranges there are broad agricultural plateaux. The climate is tropical, divided into a rainy and a dry season.

In Pre-Columbian times the Pipil Indians of El Salvador were city builders, with a hieroglyphic writing, close to that of the Mexican Aztecs – the Nicaraguan poet Ernesto Cardenal (◊ Nicaragua) has written about them. Their capital was **Cuzcatlán**, still used as an alternative name for El Salvador (as in Manlio Argueta's ◊ novel – see Extract 5). In 1524 Pedro de Alvarado entered the country on his way from Guatemala and founded the capital **San Salvador** in 1525. From then El Salvador remained part of the Spanish colonial empire until 22 September 1821, when El Salvador declared its absolute independence from Spain, resisted inclusion into Mexico, and joined the Central American Federation (1823–29). On 30 January 1841, it became its own country. For the next 45 years the conservatives and liberals fought for power as coffee growing grew in importance. There is no history of democratic institutions as the oligarchy allied itself with several military juntas. The oligarchy is famously known as the '14 families', who run everything in the country: until the fierce guerrilla wars of the 1970s and 1980s they were also very nationalistic, investing their wealth back into the country. An acerbic account of El Salvador appears in *The Old Patagonian Express* (Extract 10) by Paul Theroux (◊ Honduras).

In 1932 there was a *peón* uprising in **Izalco** which resulted in at least 15 000 peasants killed by '*El Brujo*' Maximiliano Martínez, in power from 1931 to 1944. He was ruthless, but he also invested in roads and public works so that the country has a good road system. In 1969 El Salvador fought what was known as the 'Football' or '100-hour war' with neighbouring Honduras. The cause was the Honduran agrarian reform of 1969 which forbade any but Honduran-born from owning land, when many Salvadorans escaped their overpopulated land to work in Honduras. After two matches between the countries competing for a place in the 1970 World Cup due to be held in Mexico, El Salvador invaded, planning to open a passage to the Caribbean. But the Organization of American States intervened and forced a peace that left 2000, mainly Honduran, dead. Since the late 1970s El Salvador has been torn apart in what is virtually a civil war between the guerrillas (the FMLN) and the military which has ruined the thriving economy. In 1979 the British Embassy was evacuated and disappearances, death squads and torture became the daily staple of life (as Joan Didion ◊ describes in *Salvador* – Extract 8). Some 75 000 have been killed over these years. The archbishop Oscar Romero, who was outspoken about the poor, was murdered during Mass in the **Cathedral** on 24 March 1980 (incorporated into Oliver Stone's bitter film *Salvador*, 1985, criticizing US policy). Recently (November 1989) the Jesuit rector of the **Catholic University** and several other priests were murdered in their residence. In February 1992 there was an effective cease-fire.

Salvadoran writers have been deeply politicized by the events since 1932 and their work belongs to that branch of witness/denunciation/propaganda literature inevitable in such a situation, and epitomized by Dalton, Claribel Alegría, Manlio Argueta, and anthologies like *Mirrors of War: Literature and Revolution in El Salvador*, 1985; *Volcán*, 1983; *Lovers and Comrades: Women's Resistance Poetry from Central America*, 1989; Rosario Santos, ed, *And We Sold the Rain: Contemporary Fiction from Central America*, 1989 (Extract 4); and Barbara Paschke and David Volpendesta, eds, *Clamor of Innocence: Central American Short Stories*, 1989 (Extract 1).

BOOKLIST

The following selection includes all titles which are extracted in this chapter as well as those mentioned in the introduction which are available in English. In general, paperback editions are given when possible. The editions cited are not necessarily the only ones available. For most of the extracted works, the original publisher in English can be found in 'Acknowledgments and Citations' at the end of the volume, as can the exact location of the extracts and the editions from which they are taken. The date in square brackets is the original publication date of the work in its original language. Extract numbers are highlighted in bold for ease of reference.

Alegría, Claribel, *Ashes of Izalco* [1966], with Darwin J. Flakoll, Curbstone, Willimantic, CT, 1989. **Extract 9.**

And We Sold the Rain: Contemporary Fiction from Central America, Rosario Santos, ed, Ryan, Peterborough, 1989/Four Walls: Eight Windows, San Francisco, CA, 1989.

Argueta, Manlio, *Cuzcatlán* [1986], Clark Hansen, trans, Chatto and Windus, London, 1987/ Aventura, New York, 1987. **Extract 5.**

Argueta, Manlio, *One Day of Life* [1980], Bill Brow, trans, Chatto and Windus, London, 1984/ Aventura, New York, 1985. **Extract 6.**

Clamor of Innocence: Central American Short Stories, Barbara Paschke and David Volpendesta, eds, City Lights Books, San Francisco, CA, 1989.

Dalton, Roque, *Miguel Mármol* [1982], Kathleen Ross and Richard Schaaf, trans, Curbstone, Willimantic, CT, 1987. **Extract 2.**

Dalton, Roque, *Poems*, Richard Schaaf, trans, Curbstone, Willimantic, CT, 1984.

Didion, Joan, *A Book of Common Prayer*, Penguin, London, 1977/ Penguin Books, New York, 1986. **Extract 3.**

Didion, Joan, *Salvador*, Chatto and Windus, London, 1983/Penguin Books, New York, 1988. **Extracts 8 and 7** (Roque Dalton's poem 'San Salvador' translated by Edward Baker).

Escudos, Jacinta, 'Look at Lislique, See How Pretty It Is', George Yúdice, trans, in *And We Sold the Rain: Contemporary Fiction from Central America*, Rosario Santos, ed, Ryan, Peterborough, 1989/ Four Walls:Eight Windows, San Francisco, CA, 1989. **Extract 4.**

Gavidia, Francisco, 'The She-Wolf', Steve Hellman, trans, in *Clamor of Innocence: Central American Short Stories*, Barbara Paschke and David Volpendesta, eds, City Lights Books, San Francisco, CA, 1989. **Extract 1.**

Lovers and Comrades: Women's Resistance Poetry from Central America, Amanda Hopkinson, ed, The Women's Press, London, 1989.

Marnham, Patrick, *So Far from God . . . A Journey to Central America*, Penguin, London, 1986/ Viking Penguin, New York, 1985.

Mirrors of War: Literature and Revolution in El Salvador, Gabriela Yanes, Manuel Sorto, Horacio Castellanos Moya, and Lyn Soto, eds, Zed Books, London, 1985.

Theroux, Paul, *The Old Patagonian Express: By Train Through the Americas* [1979], Penguin, London, 1980/Houghton Miflin, Boston, MA, 1989. **Extract 10.**

Volcán: Poems from El Salvador, Guatemala, Honduras and Nicaragua, Alejandro Murgía and Barbara Paschke, eds, City Lights Books, San Francisco, CA, USA, 1983.

Extracts

(1) CACAHAUTIQUE

Francisco Gavidia, The She-Wolf

Gavidia's early short story describes Cacahautique in an autobiographical mode linking personal and national history. The story is available in the anthology Clamor of Innocence *– see Booklist.*

Cacotique, now pronounced and written with total vulgarity as Cacahautique, is a village high in the mountain of El Salvador, facing Honduras. The brave general Don Gerardo Barrios was born there; later, as president of the Republic, he built a recreation ranch in Cacahautique, with four acres of rosebushes and four more of citrus, coffee slopes that yielded nine hundred sacks, and a house fit for the first lady, a woman of extreme beauty and elegance. A vast cement and stone patio, a pulp mill, and a trough to wash the coffee; a small stream that burbled day and night by the side of the house, all constructed on the hanging slope of a hill so high up that it dominated the plains, the valleys, and the rolling hills of coffee covered in blossoms; the nearby mountain where woodcutters with axes on their shoulders descended almost perpendicular roads; to one side, forests; to another, a sugar mill, at times processing cane, driven by oxen that moved in circles turning the mill, at times, sheathed in a shroud of waste pulp, solitary and silent under a broad tree; further yet, magnificent peaks, one notched in the middle; bordering the farm, a ravine in whose abyss a torrent raged, hurling out drowned cries; cold air, splendid sky, and five or six pretty young women in town – these are the memories of my childhood.

My father bought the ranch from the president's widow and, leaving San Miguel, we lived on it for three years. I would have been about eight. I'd like to write about that village, but there isn't time; however, I won't forget to mention one of the most magnificent spectacles that could be seen. From the small Plaza del Calvario a valley is visible that unfolds to the width of forty or fifty kilometers. In other times, forming forests of spikes, quivers on their shoulders, the innumerable armies of Lempira passed. In the bottom of the valley the river Lempa crawls like a silver lizard. One side of the river, as far as San Salvador, is called Tocorrostique; the other side to San Miguel is called Chaparrastique. Farther on from the valley extends the leaden green of the coastal forests; and farther, like the edge of a disk, the steel-blue curve of the Pacific. A tempestuous sky frequently wraps up the gigantic panorama in the passing clouds of a storm. Just as the valley extends to the sea, so from the sea hurricanes come howling for two hundred kilometers to lash at the trees in the mountains of Honduras. That's why you will hear that occasionally a traveler has passed the heights of Tongolón, where the two oceans are visible, only to be caught by ferocious winds and thrown from the horrible precipice.

Cacahautique is a village that palpably represents the transition from an indigenous camp to a Christian community. The thatched roofs are interspersed with Arabian tile roofs that were adopted into colonial architecture without reservation. Hunters use shotguns and arrows. The vocabulary is a picturesque mix of Castilian and *lenca*[1], and the creation myth mixes Catholicism with the terrifying pantheism of the local tribes. I still remember the dread I felt as a child when I passed by the hut where a woman lived, who, I was assured, turned herself by night *into a pig*.

[1] An indigenous dialect, more obscure than *pipil*, the common Indian tongue of El Salvador. [Translator's note.]

(2) El Matazano, Soyapango

Roque Dalton, *Miguel Mármol*

> *Dalton's documentary novel about the 1932 peasant rebellion is narrated by Miguel Mármol, survivor of the firing squad, whom Dalton interviewed before writing up his notes as a 'novel'.*

They smashed in Serafín G. Martínez' mouth and teeth with the barrel of a rifle. Finally, we stopped in a really dark place that is part of the canton of El Matazano, jurisdiction of Soyapango. Back then there was a local, very dusty, dirt road. Nowadays it's the road to the airfield or Army Boulevard, the part in front of the Royal Motel, a little beyond the ADOC shoe factory. The moon was bright, but the trees kept the place shaded in darkness. They got everybody out of the truck at the point of a barrel. I pulled myself up as much as I could but was planted on the floor. A policeman came over to help me out and then with a slap knocked off my hat. But I shoved him hard and he backed off and stopped fucking around with me. When I joined the group, they pulled Bonilla and Bondanza out and put them against the wall. Serafín Martínez, with his mouth full of blood and broken teeth, told Captain Alvarenga not to kill Navas because he had five children. Serafín had a big heart. But I, who had always been crude and bad-tempered, yelled at him: 'Don't ask anything from these son-of-a-bitches who've brought us here to murder us.' The truck's headlights lit up the scene. Fifteen policemen made up the firing squad, while the other two and the driver and the commanding officer were pointing at us. The commanding officer gave the order: 'Ready, Aim, Fire' almost in one breath. I'd say he was nervous. But the troops were really nervous too and the first round only slightly wounded our two comrades. The second round wounded them pretty badly but the comrades didn't go down, standing proud and firm, though you could see death in their faces. Sometimes I still dream about the way they looked. Bondanza shouted out: 'Long live the Communist Party!' The third round was on target and they went down. Captain Alvarenga asked: 'Let's see which one of you wants to die next?' 'Me,' I shouted, and I took a step forward. The firing squad was on one side of the road and the wall on the other. The police were sweating, despite the summer chill. My whole body itched and I couldn't scratch myself because my arms were tied. I started to cross the road when I heard a calm voice: 'I will die alongside comrade Mármol.' It was the Russian. As best we could, we joined hands behind our backs, uniting us, and we stood against the wall together feeling proud. The commanding officer gave the order and the first round went over our heads. They didn't touch us, and I thought they were just fucking around, to prolong the torture. 'You haven't even learned to shoot straight, assholes,' I calmly said to them. The police unloaded two more rounds that only grazed us, and Captain Alvarenga started to curse them up and down.

(3) EL SALVADOR: 'BOCA GRANDE'

Joan Didion, *A Book Of Common Prayer*

Joan Didion's novel is set in fictional Boca Grande, near Costa Rica and Managua, whose capital has the same name as the country (El Salvador/San Salvador). Boca Grande also resembles the Caribbean coast of Colombia, which Didion visited.

In at least two of the several impenetrably euphemistic 'Letters from Central America' which Charlotte wrote during her stay here and tried unsuccessfully to sell to *The New Yorker*, she characterized Boca Grande as a 'land of contrasts'. Boca Grande is not a land of contrasts. On the contrary Boca Grande is relentlessly 'the same': the cathedral is not Spanish Colonial but corrugated aluminum. There is a local currency but the American dollar is legal tender. The politics of the country at first appear to offer contrast, involving as they do the 'colorful' Latin juxtaposition of *guerrilleros* and colonels, but when the tanks are put away and the airport reopens nothing has actually changed in Boca Grande. There are no waterfalls of note, no ruins of interest, no chic boutiques (Charlotte went so far as to rent a storefront for one such boutique, but my son Gerardo turned the storefront to his own purposes and it has been since the October Violence a Pentecostal reading room) to provide dramatic cultural foil to voodoo in the hills.

In fact there is no voodoo in the hills.

In fact there are no hills, only the flat bush and the lifeless sea.

And the light. The opaque equatorial light. The bush and the sea do not reflect the light but absorb it, suck it in, then glow morbidly.

Boca Grande is the name of the country and Boca Grande is also the name of the city, as if the place defeated the imagination of even its first settler. At least once each year, usually on the afternoon of the Anniversary of Independence, the Boca Grande Intellectual Union sponsors a debate, followed by a nohost cocktail party, as to who that first settler might have been, but the arguments are desultory, arbitrary. Information is missing here. Evidence goes unrecorded. Every time the sun falls on a day in Boca Grande that day appears to vanish from local memory, to be reinvented if necessary but never recalled. I once asked the librarian at the Intellectual Union to recommend for Charlotte a history of Boca Grande. 'Boca Grande has no history,' the librarian said, and he seemed gratified that I had asked, as if we together hit upon a catechistic point of national pride.

(4) LISLIQUE

Jacinta Escudos,
Look at Lislique, See How Pretty It Is

This short story shows how politics and guerilla life cut people off from their home towns, like Lislique, in the provinces. The story is available in the anthology And We Sold the Rain – see Booklist.

Ah, to return to Lislique, return to its trees, its fresh and quiet afternoons. Lislique. But the Lislique I knew as a kid – with its cobblestone streets, its white houses full of ancient secrets, and the *niña* María on the corner telling her apes to come back home, not to go too far, and those pains in the ass sneaking into neighbors' farms and stealing oranges and guayabas. Then would come the complaints, the fights with the woman next door, and you're in deep shit with the mayor . . .

Lislique, where Jaime once dreamed of joining the Eagles, 'eight time national champs and one time almost of the Central American Cup.' He said he was as good as Cariota Barraza, and he was, or even better, although he wasn't a lefty, but he was the best halfback in the Cornelio Reyna Soccer Club. He wanted to go to the capital, to play on the Flor Blanca Club, but he'd never been any farther than La Unión, which he liked a lot, swearing that maybe that's what San Salvador was like. If he had gone there, for sure he would've gotten scared by so many buildings, streets, people, cars.

Lislique and the mango tree nearby on the road where Jaime and I used to tease the girls that went by, or where we'd sit and shoot the bull, or take cover when the *guardia* came looking for anyone they might grab and draft by force.

(5) SAN SALVADOR

Manlio Argueta, *Cuzcatlán*

Argueta's novel about peasant poverty, and guerillas, describes a first visit from the countryside to the capital and General Castaneda Castro's 1945 coup.

One day – it was one of only two times I ever went to San Salvador – a couple of friends and I decided to go to Soyopango and then on to the capital; they did have trains back then, but they weren't meant for poor people and we didn't dare take one. Our plan was to go the plaza where they were celebrating the August Fair. This must have been around 1946. We got as far as the corner of La Garita when we heard gunshots.

We had two choices: either go north in the direction of Aculhuaca, and wait for the shooting to stop, or keep on going into San Salvador and pay no attention to the gunfire.

So we got as far as La Tiendona, where there was lodging for the poor; besides, it was a fun place right in the heart of the August Fair. Suddenly we saw a demonstration, a handful of people coming down the main street. We asked what was going on and some people told us it was a demonstration organized by General Castaneda Castro, who had recently been installed as President of the Republic. The men and women in his group were wearing blue and white, the colors of his party as well as those of the national flag. Coming from the opposite direction we could see another group of demonstrators, all dressed in red and white. These were the supporters of Dr Arturo Romero, who, according to them, was the presidential candidate of the poor. Both groups were coming from opposite directions, and met at the corner. When they met there was a lot of shouting, since they were armed with only sticks and stones; Castaneda Castro's people were carrying pistols – after all, his was the party of the military.

We had barely enough time to duck into a doorway which, fortunately for us, was open, since most people locked their doors once the shouting began. We heard more shots. We were crouching there in the doorway when the owner of the place shows up and asks what we think we're doing, because he's about to lock up and we'd better get lost before he calls the police. We told him we didn't know San Salvador well and gunfights were new to us. Well, you'd better get used to them, he said, then gave us a shove. 'Eat shit, shepherds, Easter's over,' he added.

(6) SAN SALVADOR

Manlio Argueta, *One Day of Life*

Argueta's novel is an unofficial history of El Salvador's peasants
– an oral, counter-version, narrated by a 'we', of a rebellion.

Today we went to occupy the Cathedral in San Salvador. It all began with the death of my uncle Justino Guardado, a few days after the demonstration at the Bank. On the road to Ilobasco where he had his house. One night, four members of the civil authority, those who were armed, went to his house, they dragged him out under a shower of blows and decapitated him, they dragged his wife and children out, and set fire to the house. My uncle Jacinto.

Who knows where they took him. The next day his body was found beaten and beheaded. His head stuck on a *jiote* post, those that are used to mark off property. The rest of his body was thrown in a ditch nearby.

The whole town was outraged, without knowing what to do because we all loved Justino and he did not deserve to die that way – he was a hard worker and a good son, one of the mainstays of his family and of my grandmother Lupe. He always helped her with her little chores.

But the four who took him away were well known in the region. Then the men of the region got together.

'Justino's hands were never stained with blood. He was a good man.'

'All Justino did was help organize the demonstration at the Bank to demand a discount on seeds and fertilizer. That's all.'

'So what are we going to do in memory of our companion?'

And a group was formed to find the murderers. Armed with clubs and machetes, the men went from house to house.

And we dragged them out, one by one. There stood the four of them, trembling like nesting hens.

'But we are not murderers,' said the men.

And they forced the four to dig a grave for Justino. Right there where they'd murdered him.

And to kneel and ask the dead man for forgiveness.

And to recite the Credo for him. Under the sun. Praying in the hot sun, while we surrounded them with our machetes at the ready.

'We are the civil authorities,' they said.

'You are the assassin authorities,' our men said.

And each of the four had to throw at least one shovelful of dirt to give satisfaction to the dead man. After the burial they were set free.

'From fear of God more than anything else and because we're not murderers.' We pardoned them.

Justino was avenged and the account of his death was settled. Justino was my uncle, son of Mama Lupe.

We never imagined the grief we would suffer as a result of the incident with the civil authorities.

When the officers realized what had happened, truck-loads of guardsmen and even a helicopter and an airplane were sent. The slaughter was brutal: there were many deaths, houses were burned, women raped, children beaten. Even the animals had to pay a price. They took care of the chickens and the pigs with gunshots.

The oxen and the horses were done away with knives. Some men were able to escape to the mountains with their women and children. Through mountains and along roads we wandered.

Five days later, we started reappearing in the region; we couldn't stand the hunger. And our little brothers and sisters, their bodies couldn't stand the bites of mosquitoes and other nocturnal insects. The houses in seven villages were searched. From Ilobasco to Chalate the government's repression extended.

Almost all the houses in the area where Justino's death had been avenged were destroyed.

None of this appeared in the newspapers. They never say anything in favor of the poor. No one could work in this situation.

That's how the taking of the Cathedral came about.

(7) SAN SALVADOR

Roque Dalton, *San Salvador*

Dalton mocks literacy in his poem titled after his country's capital. This translation, by Edward Baker, appears in Joan Didion's Salvador.

In San Salvador
in the year 1965
the best sellers
of the three most important
book stores
were:
The Protocols of the Elders of Zion;
a few books by
diarrhetic Somerset Maugham;
a book of disagreeably
obvious poems
by a lady with a European name
who nonetheless writes in Spanish about our country
and a collection of Reader's Digest condensed novels.

(8) SAN SALVADOR

Joan Didion, *Salvador*

Novelist Joan Didion also wrote acutely as a journalist, refusing the easy ironies over an incident in San Salvador.

The place brings everything into question. One afternoon when I had run out of the Halazone tablets I dropped every night in a pitcher of tap water (a demented *gringa* gesture, I knew even then, in a country where everybody not born there was at least mildly ill, including the nurse at the American embassy), I walked across the street from the Camino Real to the Metrocenter, which is referred to locally as 'Central America's Largest Shopping Mall'. I found no Halazone at the Metrocenter but became absorbed in making notes about the mall itself, about the Muzak playing 'I left my Heart in San Francisco' and 'American Pie' ('. . . *singing this will be the day that I die* . . .') although the record store featured a cassette called *Classics of Paraguay*, about the *pâté de foie gras* for sale in the supermarket, about the guard who did the weapons check on everyone who entered the supermarket, about the young matrons in tight Sergio Valente jeans, trailing maids and babies behind them and buying towels, big beach towels printed with maps of Manhattan that featured Bloomingdale's; about the number of things for sale that seemed to suggest a fashion for 'smart drinking', to evoke modish cocktail hours. There were bottles of Stolichnaya vodka packaged with glasses and mixer, there were ice buckets, there were bar carts of every conceivable design, displayed with sample bottles.

This was a shopping center that embodied the future for which El Salvador was presumably being saved, and I wrote it down dutifully, this being the kind of 'color' I knew how to interpret, the kind of inductive irony, the detail that was supposed to illuminate the story. As I wrote it down I realized that I was no longer much interested in this kind of irony, that this was a story that would not be illuminated by such details, that this was perhaps even less a 'story' than a true *noche oscura*. As I waited to cross back over the Boulevard de los Heroes to the Camino Real I noticed soldiers herding a young civilian into a van, their guns at the boy's back, and I walked straight ahead, not wanting to see anything at all.

(9) SANTA ANA

Claribel Alegría, *Ashes of Izalco*

The novel's narrator is a woman who was tortured but refused to betray her husband who was involved in the 1932 uprising. Here, she recalls her home town of Santa Ana (compare with Paul Theroux's extract below).

Santa Ana is small. It stretches from the church of Santa Lucia, where the stolid virgin offers her eyes – two fried eggs on a platter – to idlers lounging in the park across the street, and continues as far as the knotted, elephant-leg ceiba, whose branches are themselves horizontal trees shading the bright-skirted women selling *pupusas*. Its branches shelter the fortress gate where a sentry fights his immobile battle against sleep; they shade the colonel, hands behind his back, frowning down at his tenacious enemy: the dust which dulls his polished boots.

In the other direction, Santa Ana extends from the railway crossing (Stop! Look! Listen!) where the road from Chalchuapa carries oxcarts and barefoot peasants to market, through the business district to Don

Jaime's modern coffee mill (Largest In The World!) and the five wedding-cake houses of Don Jaime and his sons . . .

The market this morning (María padding along behind me with her basket!) brought back the small, familiar world of childhood: mounds of nances and candies; odors of sweat, urine, tamarinds; live iguanas with malevolent red eyes, thick tongues, short, ugly legs strapped behind their backs. Nothing has changed: the same starving dogs with marimba ribs and bony tails tucked between their legs slink among the stands; potbellied, naked children dart like fish through the dust and garbage; beggars with open sores await alms and death along walls tattooed with filth, spittle, and peeling posters.

(10) SANTA ANA

Paul Theroux, *The Old Patagonian Express*

Theroux arrived at Santa Ana, El Salvador's second city, near the frontier with Guatemala, in the 1970s. Patrick Marnham's So Far From God . . . A Journey To Central America, *published in 1985, altered his view.*

The town only looked Godforsaken; in fact, it was comfortable. It was a nice combination of attributes. In every respect, Santa Ana, the most Central American of Central American towns, was a perfect place – perfect in its pious attitudes and pretty girls, perfect in its slumber, its coffee-scented heat, its jungly plaza, and in the dusty elegance of its old buildings whose whitewash at nightfall gave them a vivid phosphorescence. Even its volcano was in working order. My hotel, the Florida, was a labyrinthine one-storey affair, with potted palms and wicker chairs and good food – fresh fish, from nearby Lake Guija, was followed by the crushed velvet of Santa Ana coffee, and Santa Ana dessert, a delicate cake of mashed beans and banana served in cream. This pleasing hotel cost four dollars a night. It was a block from the plaza. All Santa Ana's buildings of distinction – there were three – were in the plaza: the Cathedral was neo-gothic, the town hall had the colonnaded opulence of a ducal palace, and the Santa Ana theatre had once been an opera house.

In another climate, I don't think the theatre would have seemed so special, but in this sleepy tropical town in the western highlands of El Salvador – and there was nothing here for the luxury-minded or ruin-hunting tourist – the theatre was magnificent and strange. Its style was banana republic Graeco–Roman; it was newly whitewashed, and classical in an agreeably vulgar way, with cherubs on its façade, and trumpeting angels, and masks of comedy and tragedy . . . There were columns, too, and a Romanesque portico, and on a shield a fuming volcano as nicely proportioned as Izalco, the one just outside town, which was probably the model for this emblem.

Biographies and important works

ALEGRIA, Claribel (1924–). Alegría was born in Estelí, Nicaragua, on 12 May 1924, but she grew up in El Salvador, where her father was exiled. She could return to Nicaragua only in 1979, with the Sandinista revolution. In 1943 she graduated from George Washington University (where she studied with the poet Juan Ramón Jiménez), and in 1947 married Darwin J. Flakoll, with whom she has produced important anthologies like *New Voices of Hispanic America: An Anthology*, 1962, and a joint novel *Cenizas de Izalco*, 1966 (*Ashes of Izalco*, 1989 – Extract 9) based on the massacre of peasants at Izalco in 1932. Flakoll is also one of her translators. She has published 14 books of poems, including *Flowers from the Volcano*, 1982. She has won the Cuban Casa de las Américas prize. All her writing is politically concerned with the fate of peasants and women in El Salvador and Nicaragua, exemplified in her novel *No me agarren viva: la mujer salvadoreña en lucha*, 1983 (*They won't Take me Alive, Salvadoran Women in Struggle for National Liberation*, 1986) – a biography of Eugenia, a Salvadoran guerrilla leader who in 1981 was tortured by the military. She memorized her torturers' names, and they are repeated in this text. Alegría has also written about her childhood in *El detén*, 1977, and *Album familiar*, 1982 (*Family Album: Stories of Catholic Girlhood*, 1990). Her books were banned in El Salvador. She lives in Nicaragua

and Mallorca, and is active in Central American liberation movements.

ARGUETA, Manlio (1936?–). Born in **San Miguel**, El Salvador on 24 November 1936 or 1935 (sources differ), Argueta has been persecuted and exiled for his opposition to the military. He is a poet, with two of his four novels published in English: *Un día en la vida*, 1980 (*One Day of Life*, 1984 – Extract 6), based on the life of a peasant woman from the village of **San Antonio de los Ranchos**, whose husband had his eyes put out and who she refused to recognize as that would mean her death; and *Cuzcatlán, donde bate la mar del sur*, 1986 (*Cuzcatlán*, 1987 – Extract 5), dealing with the impoverished, illiterate peasants of El Salvador. A character in *Cuzcatlán* says of the US advisers helping to eradicate subversives: 'They don't speak Spanish. How are they going to understand us like that?' Argueta's novel provides the answers. With day dreams, inner monologues and laconic conversations, a silent Indian family voice their tale of humiliation in the context of a growing need to support the guerrillas in the El Salvador of the 1980s. The novel turns back to the 1932 revolt and massacre, and ends with a popular guerrilla tribunal pardoning an ex-peasant turned *guardia*. Through this minimal plot about a forcibly conscripted Indian who returns to his village as a despot, Argueta strives to raise his reader's consciousness showing us the *peóns'* mythic inner life, and their will to survive and recover their old, pre-Spanish kingdom, Cuzcatlán.

Since 1972, Argueta has lived in Costa Rica, the founder–director of the Salvador–Costa Rican Institute. Argueta said to Greg Price (*Latin America: The Writer's Journey*, 1990), 'I have thought of the novel as a way of making our reality more widely known. In a way, it is also a work of sociology or history.'

DALTON, Roque (1935–1975). Dalton was born in **San Salvador**. He studied law at university, and joined the Communist Party in 1955. He was several times imprisoned and sentenced to death, and lived in exile for 13 years. In 1969 he won the Casa de las Américas poetry prize for *Taberna y otros lugares*, translated in *Poems*, 1984, written in a down-to-earth, sarcastic style. In 1973, he returned to El Salvador and joined the guerrilla group ERP (*Ejército revolucionario del Pueblo*), and continued to write militant poetry. On 10 May 1975 he was assassinated by a faction of his own party. His eye-witness novel *Miguel Mármol*, 1982 (*Miguel Mármol*, 1986 – Extract 2) is based on a real person who was present at the 1932 massacre in **Izalco**, a founder-member of the Salvadoran Communist Party who recounted his life and political experiences to Dalton.

DIDION, Joan (1934–). Didion was born in Sacramento, California on 5 December 1934. She graduated in English at Berkeley, worked on *Vogue*, and freelanced as a journalist. In 1963 she published her first novel. In 1964 she married John Gregory Dunne. She now lives in New York. Her novel *A Book of Common Prayer*, 1977 (Extract 3), is set in the imaginary Central or South American state of Boca Grande, near Costa Rica and Managua and on the equator. The narrator is an American anthropologist married into a family that runs the tropical backwater as it wants, even 'playing' with the *guerrilleros*. This dying woman dispassionately watches Charlotte Douglas, a *gringa* tourist who accidentally ends up in Boca Grande, and whose daughter is a Berkeley revolutionary on the run. Didion profiles a spoilt, sexy, Californian drifter, who is finally murdered during a *guerrillero* attack. The novel plots Charlotte's life and husbands and is about the blindness of the Americans to their neighbours down south, epitomized by the naive US ambassador colluding with those in power. Boca Grande is a tropical dump where 'nothing changes'. There is no past, no history, no future, just a present that sinks without trace. Charlotte's sin was her *gringa* view of Boca Grande, with its 'colourful' sites, its safe Jockey Club, its 'enchanting' children selling contraband Marlboro, its amusing street musicians. She believed firmly in the reality of the US embassy and the airport and never suffered the 'weightless isolation' of the place. Her American quirk was 'that the world was peopled with others exactly like herself', and taking everything literally leads to her tragedy.

Sources for Boca Grande come from Joan Didion's *Salvador*, 1983 (Extract 8), a superb documentary study of 'the exact mechanisms of terror' in El Salvador, and from the essay 'In Bogotá' from *The White Album*, 1979, which opens with a description of Cartagena in coastal Colombia as 'hot, fevered'. There is the same speculating about how Latin

Americans view history: 'When Colombians spoke about the past I often had the sense of being in a place where history tended to sink, even as it happened, into the traceless solitude of autosuggestion'. She found Colombia a place of dislocations, with unpleasant CIA Americans hovering around the US embassy. The hopelessness of Colombian politics, the attitudes of the USA, the climate, the view of history, are transformed into Boca Grande. She has also written on Cuban exiles in *Miami*, 1989.

ESCUDOS, Jacinta (1961–   ). Born in **San Salvador**, Escudos has published one novel, and several short stories. She lives in Nicaragua and works making documentary films.

GAVIDIA, Francisco (1875–1955). Gavidia was born in El Salvador. He wrote short stories, plays, and poems, and translated French poetry.

THEROUX, Paul (see under Honduras).

BELIZE

Belize (*Belice* in Spanish), comes from an ancient Mayan word for the Belize River on which Belize City is situated. It was formerly British Honduras, becoming independent in 1981, and long claimed by Guatemala (in 1975 British troops were sent out because of a threat of invasion). Its land area is 22 965 sq km and its population some 176 000. When **Belize City**, with about 40 000 inhabitants, was destroyed by a hurricane in 1961 the administrative capital was moved inland to **Belmopan**, with some 3000 inhabitants. The country is racially mixed, with one third negroes, both English and Spanish speaking, one sixth Indian, and around 6000 Carib-speaking negroes (the Garifuna) on the coast. One third of the population live in Belize City. Sixty per cent are Catholics, and 35% Protestant. Ninety per cent of the land is broadleaf forest, with sapote and mahogany logged and exported. Most of the interior is inaccessible. The highest peak, Victoria, is 3680 m. The area is subtropical, with a dry season. In 1931 and in 1961, severe hurricanes hit Belize.

In the seventeenth century Britain occupied this coast; by 1638 logwood (used for dyes) cutters had settled there. Spain tried to reclaim its colony on the coast with a fleet in 1798. By 1862 Belize was officially a British Colony. In 1812 **St John's Cathedral** was built, followed in 1814 by **Government House**. In 1964 full internal self-government was granted, and in 1981, full independence. Belize is a constitutional monarchy. Most writing about the country has come from passers-by, like Greene (◊ Mexico and Panama), Huxley (◊ Mexico), Stone (◊ Honduras), and Naipaul ◊. One exception is

100

Belizan born Nigel Lewis whose thriller *The Cold Chain*, 1988, is set realistically in 1981 Belize.

Tourism is being developed along Belize's 140 m reef, and cays. Mayan ruins are being unearthed (at **Caracol**, for example). Martha Gellhorn, over 80, visited in 1990: 'It is astonishing at my age to stumble on a new country.'

BOOKLIST

The following selection includes all titles which are extracted in this chapter as well as those mentioned in the introduction which are available in English. In general, paperback editions are given when possible. The editions cited are not necessarily the only ones available. For most of the extracted works, the original publisher in English can be found in 'Acknowledgments and Citations' at the end of the volume, as can the exact location of the extracts and the editions from which they are taken. The date in square brackets is the original publication date of the work in its original language. Extract numbers are highlighted in bold type for ease of reference.

Greene, Graham, *Getting to Know the General: The Story of an Involvement* [1984], Penguin, London, 1985/Viking Penguin, New York, 1985. **Extract 2**.

Huxley, Aldous, *Beyond the Mexique Bay* [1934], Penguin, London, 1955/Greenwood Press, Westport, CT, 1975. **Extract 1**.

Lewis, Nigel, *The Cold Chain*, Hamish Hamilton, London, 1988.

Naipaul, V.S., *The Overcrowded Barracoon* [1972], Penguin, London, 1976. **Extract 3**.

Stone, Robert, *A Flag for Sunrise* [1977], Picador, London, 1982/Random House, New York, 1992. **Extract 4**.

Extracts

(1) BELIZE AS BRITISH HONDURAS

Aldous Huxley, *Beyond the Mexique Bay*

Aldous Huxley visited British Honduras in 1933, and wondered at the eccentricity of this particular piece of imperialism.

If the world had any ends British Honduras would certainly be one of them. It is not on the way from anywhere to anywhere else. It has no strategic value. It is all but uninhabited, and when prohibition is abolished, the last of the profitable enterprises – the re-export of alcohol by rum-runners, who use Belize as their base of operations – will have gone the way of its commerce in logwood, mahogany, and chicle. Why then do we bother to keep this strange little fragment of the Empire? Certainly not from motives of self-interest. Hardly one Englishman in fifty thousand derives any profit from the Britishness of British Honduras. British Honduras goes on being British because it has been British.

(2) Belize City

Graham Greene, *Getting to Know the General*

Greene travelled to Belize with his guide Chuchu on a Panama-nian plane in 1978.

We were met and driven into the city which, poor as it is, had an odd beguiling charm, with wooden houses standing on piles seven feet high above the wet streets and mangrove swamps all around. Perhaps the charm comes from a sense of the temporary, of the precarious, of living on the edge of destruction. The threat is not only from Guatemala, the threat too is from the sea, which seems to be steadily, quietly seeping in, like some guerrilla force which one day will take over the city as it nearly did in 1961 when Hurricane Hattie struck with a tidal wave ten feet high.

(3) Belize City

V.S. Naipaul, *The Overcrowded Barracoon*

The novelist V. S. Naipaul was in Belize in 1969. In this extract he surveys the scene from Government House and extends his speculations to the history and settlement of the country.

White water-skis and fishing rods lean against the wall of the Governor's office, airy and light. A half-open umbrella hangs from the grey steel safe. There is a wall-map: this all but empty British territory – 9,000 square miles, 100,000 people – incongruous in Latin America: Mexico the industrial giant to the north, Guatemala of the high mountains, the political assassinations, the temperate flowers and fruit, the Spanish and Mayan antiquities, to the west and south. The wire-netted windows of the Governor's office show the sparse gardens of Government House, the two tall royal palms. Just beyond the garden wall is the Caribbean, not blue here, thick with catfish, restless scavengers of the waters of this city built on swampland.

The Empire here was never grand. It began as a seventeenth-century coastal intrusion on the Spanish American Empire. The territory doubled its size in the last century. But it was acknowledged as an intrusion and was never settled; it never became a land of plantations. The first interlopers came with their Negroes to cut logwood; their successors went further inland to cut mahogany. The mahogany forests have all been cut down. Bush remains, and scattered little bush communities: Maya Indians, who move among the mighty ruins of their civilization like any other degraded immigrant group; Black Caribs, transported from the West Indian island of St Vincent, considered by Negroes to be very black and ugly, with a bad smell; Spanish and mestizo refugees from Yucatan; and, in the last ten years, some thousands of Mennonites, a Bible-reading German–American sect, who have transformed many square miles of tropical bush, bought at fifteen shillings an acre, into the landscape of pioneer America. The descendants of the Negro log-cutters, now two-thirds of the population, and confirmed lovers of city life, live in the overcrowded coastal capital, Belize City.

(4) BELIZE CITY

Robert Stone, *A Flag for Sunrise*

Stone's embittered American protagonist Holliwell passes through Belize City.

Then he woke up and they were circling Belize City, preparing to land. From the air, the city looked much more pleasant than it actually was. The sea beside it was a gorgeous light green; the sparkling beaches down the coast were crescents of summery sunlight.

Holliwell frowned out at the tropical abundance, recalling his dream . . .

At the airport, the Union Jack flew over the terminal building; shirtless, red-necked gunners lounged beside emplacements covered with camouflage netting. When the cabin door was opened a warm wet wind sifted through the compartment – and looking out at the palm trees and the guns and the lines of parked deuce-and-a-halfs it was impossible for him not to think back. But of course it was not at all the same, only the comic rumor of a war that would never be fought between the Sherwood Foresters and a phantom army of Guatemalan conscripts.

Two men with fishing-rod cases got off at Belize.

Biographies and important works

GREENE, Graham (see under Mexico and Panama).

HUXLEY, Aldous (see under Mexico).

STONE, Robert (see under Honduras).

NAIPAUL, V.S. (1932–). Naipaul was born in Chaguanas in Trinidad but the family moved to Port of Spain in 1938. In 1949 he won a scholarship to Oxford and has lived in the UK ever since. He published his first novel in 1957, and since then has written some of the most exciting serious fiction in English. Naipaul has also written travel books, and collected lucid articles (*The Overcrowded Barracoon*, 1972, on Belize, etc – Extract 3). In *The Middle Passage*, 1962, he evokes his 1960 trip to Guyana. Although he has not set any fiction in Latin America, he knows it well, and has written a history of Trinidad under the Spanish, *The Loss of El Dorado: A History*, 1969 (concentrating on Raleigh and de Berrio's quests), and a brilliant essay on Argentina (and on Borges, whom he visited in 1972), *The Return of Eva Perón*, 1980.

HONDURAS

'The view from the ship had been a picture, but now we were inside that picture. It was all hunger and noise and cruelty.'
Paul Theroux,
The Mosquito Coast

Honduras, or the República de Honduras, one of Central America's poorest, means 'depths' in Spanish, and refers either to the deep sea nearby, or the deep valleys cutting into the mountains. It has a land mass of 112 088 sq km, with 644 km of swampy Atlantic Coast and 80 km of Pacific Coast. Its population in 1990 was 5.1 million. The capital **Tegucigalpa** lies 975 m above sea level, was founded in 1524, and in 1986 had 605 000 inhabitants. It is a *mestizo* country, with some 6% pure Indians. Spanish is the main language, with Indian and English spoken by ex-Jamaican negroes on the Atlantic coast. Roman Catholicism is predominant. The country is tropical, with a rainy season lasting from May to mid-November. It is mainly mountainous (80%), with no active volcanoes, and frequently devasted by hurricanes.

Honduras was part of the great Mayan empire before the Discovery. The ruins of **Santa Rosa de Copán** cover 20 sq km reclaimed by the jungle and rival Palenque·in Mexico. By the time Columbus touched land at Honduras on his fourth voyage (1502) the Mayans had disappeared. Over the first half of the sixteenth century, Cortés in Mexico and Pedrarias in Panama squabbled over Honduras. Then the Spaniards fought the hostile Indians led by Lempira (today his name is the currency). In 1539 Honduras was incorporated into the Captaincy General of Guatemala. But it remained without communications, especially on the Atlantic Coast which became a haven for pirates, and the British, who felled timber for ships, virtually controlled the whole of the **Mosquito Coast**, still sufficiently wild for Paul Theroux ◊ to set his novel about self-sufficiency there (Extract 4).

In 1821, following Mexico, Honduras seceded from Spain to form the Central American Federation, but this failed, and Honduras declared independence on 5 November 1838. Since then, there have been swings between democracy and dictatorships, with the *caudillo* Tiburcio Carías in power from 1932–49, a US invasion under President Taft in 1911, and continuous border problems leading to the 'Football War' with El Salvador in 1969. In 1990 Rafael Callejas was elected president.

Honduran political and cultural life has been dominated by the monoculture of bananas with two huge US companies, The United Fruit Company (La Frutera) and the Standard Fruit Company, accounting for as much as 50% of the country's total exports. For some 60 years these companies ran the economy, and became hated, leading to the dismissive term 'banana republics'. The United Fruit Company, for example, owned some 1 750 000 hectares of plantations, with a peak exportation of 29 million hands of bananas in 1929. Although the US companies did some good – higher wages, clearing swamp lands, etc – their policy of 'peace at any price' hindered the crucial building of roads, and exploring of the country's potential wealth. It is this experience that forms the basis of O'Henry's ◊ mocking linked stories (Extract 3). However, the reality in literary terms is a small, poor, illiterate country where a writer is inevitably politicized, like the poet Roberto Sosa ◊, as revealed by the interviews with him in Jim Lindsey's translation of *The Difficult Days* (Extract 2). For a contemporary account, see Patrick Marnham, *So Far From God . . . A Journey to Central America*, 1985, and for some recent fiction see *And We Sold the Rain: Contemporary Fiction from Central America*, 1989 (Extract 6), and *Clamor of Innocence: Stories from Central America*, 1988 (Extract 1).

BOOKLIST

The following selection includes all titles which are extracted in this chapter as well as those mentioned in the introduction which are available in English. In general, paperback editions are given when possible. The editions cited are not necessarily the only ones available. For most of the extracted works, the original publisher in English can be found in 'Acknowledgments and Citations' at the end of the volume, as can the exact location of the extracts and the editions

from which they are taken. The date in square brackets is the original publication date of the work in its original language. Extract numbers are highlighted in bold type for ease of reference.

Escoto, Julio, 'April in the Forenoon', Gregory Rabassa, trans, in *And We Sold the Rain: Contemporary Fiction from Central America*, Rosario Santos, ed, Ryan,

Peterborough, 1989/Four Walls: Eight Windows, San Francisco, CA, 1989. **Extract 6.**

Lewis, Norman, *The Volcanoes Above Us* [1957], Arena, London, 1989. **Extract 7.**

Marnham, Patrick, *So Far from God . . . A Journey to Central America*, Penguin, London, 1986/ Viking Penguin, New York, 1985.

O'Henry, *Strictly Business and Other Stories*, Hodder and Stoughton, London, 1973. **Extract 3.**

Salarrué, 'We Bad', Thomas Christensen, trans, in *Clamor of Innocence: Central American Short*

Stories, Barbara Paschke and David Volpendesta, eds, City Lights Books, San Francisco, CA, 1988. **Extract 1.**

Sosa, Roberto, *The Difficult Days*, Jim Lindsey, trans, Princeton University Press, Princeton, NJ, 1983. **Extract 2.**

Suasnavar, Constantino, in *Anthology of Contemporary Latin–American Poetry*, Dudley Fitts, ed, New Directions, Norfolk, CT, 1942. **Extract 5.**

Theroux, Paul, *The Mosquito Coast*, Penguin, London, 1981/Avon Books, New York, 1983. **Extract 4.**

Extracts

(1) THE CHAMELECON

Salarrué, *We Bad*

'We Bad' is a sad and hopeless story about a father and son on the run, hoping for a better life across the Honduran frontier. The Chamelecón is a river, and an impenetrable region, near the Honduras border with Guatemala. The river flows out to the Caribbean. 'We Bad' is available in the anthology Clamor of Innocence – see Booklist.

They laid up for a nap under the whistling and aromatic pines. Over an ocote-wood fire they warmed up coffee. Rabbits huddled in an uneasy quiet in the *sapote* grove, browsing. Goyo and the boy were approaching the wild Chamelecón. Twice they saw traces of the *carretía* snake, thin as the track of a belt. When they stopped to rest, they put on a fox trot and ate tortillas with Santa Rosa cheese. For three days they made their way through mud up to their knees. The boy broke down crying; the old man cursed and laughed at him.

The priest in Santa Rosa had cautioned Goyo not to sleep in the shelters, because gangs of thieves constantly patrolled for travelers. So at nightfall Goyo and the boy went deep into the underbrush; they cleared a little spot at the foot of a tree and there they spent the night, listening to the singing of cicadas and the buzzing of blue-tailed mosquitoes as big as spiders, not daring to breathe hard, trembling with cold and fear.

'Dad, you seen *tamagases* snakes?'

'No, boy, I checked the trunk when we turned in, and there weren't any hollows.'

'If you smoke, pull down your hat, Dad. If they see the embers they'll find us.'

'OK, take it easy man. Go to sleep.'

'It's just I can't sleep all bunched up.'

'Stretch out, then . . .'

'I can't, Dad, it's freezing.'

'The devil with you! . . . Curl up against me then!'

And Goyo Cuestas, who had never in his life hugged his son, took him against his foul skin, hard as a rail, and, circling his arms around him, warmed him until he was sleeping on top of him, while he, his face twisted in resignation, waited for daybreak to be signalled by some far-off rooster.

The first daylight found them there, half frozen, aching, worn out with fatigue, with ugly mouths open and drivelling, half folded up in their ragged blankets, dirty, and striped like zebras.

But Honduras is deep in the Chamelecón. Honduras is deep in the silence of its rough, cruel mountains; Honduras is deep in the mystery of its terrible snakes, wildcats, insects, men . . . Human law does not reach to the Chamelecón; justice does not extend that far. In the region, as in primitive times, it is up to men to be good- or bad-hearted, to be cruel or magnanimous, to kill or to spare according to their own free will. Clearly the right belongs to the strong.

(2) Honduras

Roberto Sosa, *Mi Padre*

Sosa's long indignant poem 'Mi Padre', 1967, opens with a reference to the fact that many Hondurans came from over-crowded El Salvador. This poem is published in The Difficult Days – see Booklist.

From beyond Cuscatlán, my father came.
The south was his anchor.
In his fingers were lakes that had leapt to their death.

He knew the sweetness of the summoning horizon.
He loved winters,
morning,
waves.

He worked without words
to give us bread and books.
It was his way of dealing hunger's stacked deck.

. . .

To my memory
irresistibly
come the forts we visited together,
the shouting of crowds
at fireworks bursting in the air,
the icons closely guarded
by cautious village friars.

. . .

(3) HONDURAS: 'ANCHURIA'

O'Henry, *Strictly Business*

Originally published as Cabbages and Kings in 1904, O'Henry's collection of linked short stories is set in the Central American Republic of Anchuria (that is Honduras, where O'Henry was on the run from the law), with its invented capital San Mateo, 80 miles up inland, and a tropical coastal town without a port called Coralio.

A jiggety-joggety journey it was; ice-cold and hot, wet and dry. The trail climbed appalling mountains, wound like a rotton string about the brows of breathless precipices, plunged through chilling snow-fed streams, and wriggled like a snake through sunless forests teeming with menacing insect and animal life. After descending to the foothills it turned to a trident, the central prong ending at Alazan. Another branched off to Coralio; the third penetrated to Solitas. Between the sea and the foothills stretched the five miles' breadth of alluvial coast. Here was the flora of the tropics in its rankest and most prodigal growth. Spaces here and there had been wrested from the jungle and planted with bananas and cane and orange groves. The rest was a riot of wild vegetation, the home of monkeys, tapirs, jaguars, alligators and prodigious reptiles and insects. Where no road was cut a serpent could scarcely make its way through the tangle of vines and creepers. Across the treacherous mangrove swamp few things without wings could safely pass . . .

Stone sidewalks, little more than a ledge in width, ran along the base of the mean and monotonous adobe houses. At the outskirts of the village these streets dwindle to nothing, and here were set the palm-thatched huts of the Caribs and the poorer natives, and the shabby cabins of negroes from Jamaica and the West Indian islands. A few structures raised their heads above the red-tiled roofs of the one-storey houses – the bell-tower of the Calaboza, the Hotel de los Estranjeros, the residence of Vesuvius Fruit Company's agent, the store and the residence of Bernard Brannigan, a ruined cathedral in which Columbus had once set foot, and, most imposing of all, the Casa Morena – the summer 'White House' of the President of Anchuria. On the principal street running along the beach – the Broadway of Coralio – were the larger stores, the government bodega and post-office, the cuartel, the rum-shops and the market-place.

(4) LA CEIBA

Paul Theroux, *The Mosquito Coast*

Theroux's novel, narrated by the eldest son of the crank inventor Fox, describes his family's arrival at La Ceiba (Honduras's main port) on their way to their self-sufficient oasis in the coastal jungle.

Seven pelicans with dark freckled feathers flew low over the green sea in formation like a squadron of hedge clippers. Father said, 'I hate those birds.' There were gulls and vultures too. 'There's something about a coast that attracts scavengers,' he said. There was a cow on the beach, and railway boxcars on the pier, and the low town of La Ceiba looked yellow and jammed. Hundreds of men met our ship, not to welcome us but to quarrel with each other. Everything was backwards here. Father said, 'You kids can go on ahead – you've got your knapsacks,' but we were so alarmed by the heat and noise we waited for him to finish with the passport official and load his tools and seed bags into a black man's cart. Then we followed with Mother, who seemed to be holding her breath.

The Spellgoods, still gospelling, were met by a troop of black girl choristers in pink dresses and tipped-back straw hats. The Bummicks were hugged by people who looked just like the Bummicks – a boy, a woman and two old men in khaki. There were wooden motor launches tied up at the pier, loading crates of dried soup and sacks of rice. They had canvas awnings instead of cabins, and names like *Little Haddy* and *Lucy* and *Island Queen.*

I never saw so many people doing nothing except sitting and standing and calling names. But where the pier met the main road they were selling baskets of fruit and greaseballs wrapped in green leaves. There was a fat black woman in a torn dress with a white cockatoo on her shoulder. She wore a dirty pair of blue bedroom slippers and was selling oranges. Father bought six oranges and said to us, 'How much were these at the A & P in Springfield?'

Clover said, 'Thirty-nine cents each.'

'And I just bought six for a quarter. I guess we came to the right place!'

(5) SAN PEDRO SULA

Constantino Suasnavar

Suasnavar's ironic poem mocks poverty. San Pedro Sula is Honduras's second city, founded in 1536, with some 320 000 inhabitants. The poem is published in Anthology of Contemporary Latin-American Poetry – see Booklist.

> I have lost my shoes
> in the great Valley of Sula.
> Crossing over rivers
> by slumbering bridges
> under the cloak of the moon.
> To the rustling of banana groves
> and the roars of the puma
> here I come, *caramba!*,
> Here I come, shoeless,
> to San Pedro Sula.

(6) TEGUCIGALPA

Julio Escoto, *April in the Forenoon*

Escoto's story about a coup includes the following dialogue between two officers. 'April in the Forenoon' is included in the anthology And We Sold the Rain – see Booklist.

That weekend Colonel Sanabria had returned hurriedly from abroad and appeared at the presidential office soon after he landed at the airport. General Fernández was standing in front of the large window in his office watching the light fall on a garden thick with gardenias and banana trees in bloom and contemplating in the distance the city orphaned by the sea. December was sewing needlework of cold onto the glass, and the north wind coming out of the mouth of the dormant volcano was beating against the window-panes. The general sensed a breath of circumspection in the room.

'What do the newspapers out there say?' he asked without turning round.

'Bad things, everything bad,' the colonel answered, observing the curved back, the sagging shoulders, the protuberance around the president's waist, as if he were being embraced by a rattlesnake, a circus performer, an automobile tire. 'They're calling it the barefoot revolution,' he went on to explain, 'and they're sure the days of your government are over.'

(7) TEGUCIGALPA

Norman Lewis, *The Volcanoes Above Us*

Lewis's protagonist waits in the Honduran capital Tegucigalpa (meaning 'silver hill', with some 800 000 inhabitants in 1990) in 1954 before crossing the border into Guatemala with a revolutionary force and witnessing foul machete battle scenes.

Tegucigalpa at this time was full of shark-fishers, pearlers, students of the occult, men who were going to sail round the world on balsa rafts, men who had seen flying saucers, claimants to Polish titles, explorers who had located the lost gold mines of the Cuna Indians of Panama, divers who had charted the position of bullion-laden wrecks in shallow water. The papers had been instructed always to refer to us as 'heroic crusaders in the Guatemalan people's struggle for liberty', and we had one thing in common, an infinite capacity for self-delusion. The Hondurans treated us with great kindness and courtesy. The men hugged and kissed us in the streets, although they kept their womenfolk out of sight when we visited them in their homes. At night they surrounded our camp with police armed with machine-guns. These precautions did not prevent one-third of our number falling victims to venereal disease before we were given twenty-five dollars apiece, American war-surplus uniforms all made to fit the same fat man with a dwarf's legs, a purple banner per company embroidered with hearts and daggers and so they sent us down to the frontier. Here in the tropics at the height of the rainy season, it rained for several hours daily, and a third of those that V.D. had spared were shortly sent back to the capital suffering from malaria.

Biographies and important works

ESCOTO, Julio (1944–). Escoto was born in **San Pedro Sula**, Honduras on 28 February 1944. He was a lecturer, and then became director of an institute in San Pedro Sula. He has written novels, stories, and children's books. Escoto founded the Centro Editorial in **Tegucigalpa**, a prestigious publishing house. He now lives in Costa Rica.

LEWIS, Norman (see under Guatemala).

O'HENRY (1862–1910). William Sydney Porter, alias O'Henry, was born in Greensboro, North Carolina, son of a doctor. At 15 Porter left school, and soon began working in a bank. He was accused of embezzling, fled the country, and became involved with other criminals. He lived in Mexico on his stolen money, then travelled down to Honduras until his dying wife made him give himself up. He spent three years in prison in Columbus, Ohio, borrowing the name O'Henry from a prison guard, and writing *Cabbages and Kings*, 1904. These linked short stories (Extract 3) are situated in the Central American Republic of Anchuria, close to Honduria as 'ancho' (wide) is close to 'hondo' (deep). In this tropical state, O'Henry places a capital, San Mateo, 80 miles up inland, and a coastal town without a port called Coralio, inhabited by different crooked Americans, and presidents and revolutionaries on the run. Coralio is so tropical that nobody works and nothing happens, and markets open at 11 in the morning. It is full of loungers, half-clothed Caribs, mangrove swamps, coconut palms and jungle, with a *cordillera* behind. People eat iguana, aguacate, and banana. Women walk about at night with fireflies in their hair. There is a *pulpería* (bar), a *calaboza* (prison) and a *cuartel* (barracks) and all is controlled by the Vesuvius Fruit Co. Into this O'Henry has dropped his misfits, and he writes in a light, corny and colourful style linking all the stories with 'business' and missing millions. A typical example is the story 'Ships', in which the American Consul plays a joke that backfires about selling shoes to the barefoot Indians. A man arrives with crates of shoes, and the American, in love with his daughter, has to import 'Cockleburs', then scatter them over the village to force the natives to buy shoes. In 1912 O'Henry's collected works were published in 12 volumes. The dialogue and characters of his stories, the street-wise quality and crackerbarrel wit, all come from his lawless life on the run, and the types he bumped into.

SALARRUE (1899–1975). Salvador Salazar Arrué, was born in San Salvador. He was editor of a newspaper *La Patria*, and was cultural attaché for his country in Washington. He published his first book *El Señor de la burbuja* in 1927, followed by *Cuentos de barro*, 1934, dealing with peasants, and many others. His selected poems were published by the University of El Salvador. He was also a painter.

SOSA, Roberto (1930–). Sosa was born in **Yoro**, Honduras. He is a professor of literature at the **University of Honduras**. In 1971 he won the Cuban Casa de las Américas prize for his poems *Un Mundo para todos dividido* (*The Difficult Days*, 1983 – Extract 2), banned in Honduras. His poetry is political and populist in the manner of Vallejo (◊ Peru). Sosa said: 'For Central American writers there is no road left but to be in favor of the oligarchies or against them'.

SUASNAVAR, Constantino (1912–1974). Born in **Puerto de San Lorenzo**, Honduras. Suasnavar edited magazines and the newspaper *El Norte*. He began writing his witty poems in 1936, collecting them in 1949. He died in **Tegucigalpa**.

THEROUX, Paul (1941–). Theroux was born in Massachusetts and

Paul Theroux

lived in London from 1971 to 1989. He wrote his first novel in 1967, and lectured in East Africa for five years and in Singapore for three years. Theroux has written travel books, and novels about Westerners in Africa and Malaysia, and Americans in London.

The Mosquito Coast, 1981 (Extract 4), a counter-blast to *Swiss Family Robinson* and all dreams of self-sufficiency and getting away from consumer civilization, is narrated by the eldest son of an inventor crank who hates America. The 'awfulness of America' on the East Coast in Northampton, near Boston, spurs this man to find a 'blank map'. The family take a cargo ship from Baltimore to Honduras, with missionaries on board. From La Ceiba, a town 'damaged by sunlight', they move upriver to a plot of land, Jeronimo, bought from a German, and begin to put into practice his dreams of self-sufficiency. They clear the land, build, plant, and make an ice-machine ('ice is civilization'). *Zambus* ('zambos' – half-breeds of Negro and Indian parentage) help, and the local lingo is Creole. The rain falls 'as big as marbles' and slowly the children realize their father is a tyrant, and mad. There is a confrontation with a missionary, a visit to the local Miskito Indians to sell ice, and three threatening mercenaries who turn up, and are killed when the crank explodes his ice-machine. The family moves to Brewer's Lagoon, a muddy coast and during floods they go up the **Patuca River** with an old outboard engine. Finally they reach the missionaries. The crank destroys their Cessna plane and is shot just as his sons plot to kill him and return to 'civilized' America. The background detail sets off Theroux's picture of Fox, his growing madness, his refusal to go native, eat wild fruit and enjoy life as he pretends not to sleep, and punishes idleness. The novel was made into a film in 1986, directed by Peter Weir.

In *The Old Patagonian Express: By Train Through the Americas*, 1979, from Boston to Patagonia by rail, Theroux reaches the **Mosquito Coast** by train from San José, Costa Rica: 'It is wild and looks the perfect setting for a story of castaways'. Limón in Costa Rica (a 'dreadful place, and the town stank') is similar to La Ceiba in *The Mosquito Coast* with its stink, noise, mess. Theroux takes a boat trip up along a river choked with hyacinths, notices the 'mangy vultures', and asks: 'Was there a dingier backwater in the world?'.

NICARAGUA

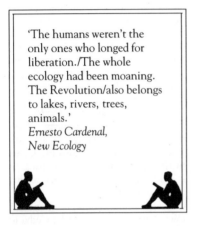

'The humans weren't the only ones who longed for liberation./The whole ecology had been moaning. The Revolution/also belongs to lakes, rivers, trees, animals.'
Ernesto Cardenal,
New Ecology

Nicaragua, or the República de Nicaragua, means either 'here near the lake' or is derived from Nicarao, the name of an Indian chief from the lake shore. It is the largest Central American republic, with a land area of some 130 000 sq km, 480 km of Caribbean coastline, and 320 km of Pacific coastline. In 1990 the population was 3.9 million. The capital city **Managua**, with a population of 682 000, was devastated by an earthquake in 1972 that killed over 10 000; it had previously been destroyed in 1931. Sixty-two per cent of the population live on the volcanic slopes and the low plains. The majority are *mestizo*, with some 10% negroes living on the Atlantic Coast, with Miskito, Sumo and Rama Indians. Ernesto Cardenal ◊ has written moving poems on these Indians in his *Homage to the American Indians*, 1973. The main language is Spanish, with English spoken on the Atlantic Coast (see Paul Theroux's travels there), and Miskito among the Indians. The religion is Roman Catholic. Nicaragua consists of a chain of 27 volcanoes (8 active ones); the highest is **Viejo** at 1745 m and the most famous is **Momotombo** (immortalized by Victor Hugo). Both the naturalist Thomas Belt ◊ in the nineteenth century and US novelist Robert Stone ◊ in the twentieth century relate the volcanic mountains to the psychology of the people.

Columbus on his fourth voyage landed near **Bluefields** on 16 September 1502. The first Spaniard to enter inland was Gil González de Avila but he could not establish a settlement. Pedraria Dávila, from Panama, was in **León** by 1526. Today León is famous as the site of the poet **Rubén Darío's** ◊ **tomb**. From 1570 to 1786 Nicaragua was ruled as part of the *audiencia* of Guatemala. During those years, especially

1740–86, the **Mosquito Coast** was virtually British, and **Bluefields** is named after a Dutch pirate. The independence movement was characterized by a rivalry between the two towns of **León** and **Granada**, and Nicaragua was not fully integrated as a state until 1826, finally seceding from the Central American Federation in 1838. Managua was created its capital to placate the León/Granada rivalry in 1857.

Nicaraguan history since independence concerns its close relationship with the USA. From the 1840s Nicaragua was used as a shorter route to Californian gold than crossing the USA itself, and plans were made to build a canal. In 1855 a five-foot filibuster from Tennessee called Walker (the subject of Alex Cox's 1987 film *Walker*) landed on the Atlantic, conquered the country, and declared himself President of Nicaragua, re-establishing slavery, making English the official language, and annexing the country to the American South. After trying to invade Costa Rica, he was defeated and executed in 1860 in Tegucigalpa in Honduras (see Cardenal's poems *With Walker in Nicaragua*, 1984). Later, US marines helped Adolfo Díaz to power and remained in the country from 1909 to 1933 (bequeathing a National Guard and a passion for baseball). This continual American interference led to Augusto César Sandino's liberation movement in the 1920s; he was finally murdered by 'Tacho' Somoza in 1934 at a banquet, and gave his name to the Sandinista party that finally overthrew Anastasio Somoza after an 18-month war in 1979. Sandino was one of the poet Pablo Neruda's (◊ Chile) great liberators ('Sandino, with his guerillas, / was a jungle specter, / a coiled tree / or a sleeping tortoise . . .'). His birthplace in **San Juan del Norte** is a museum.

Nicaraguan history has been marked by Somoza nepotism. The first Somoza came to power with American backing in 1936. He used anti-communism to enrich himself and his family, censor the press, and eliminate the opposition. He was assassinated in 1956. For a while Luis Somoza succeeded, then a stooge, until the head of the National Guard, Anastasio Somoza, took over. When he was ousted he had accumulated a $500 million empire, owning a quarter of all Nicaragua's farmland. He was assassinated in Stroessner's Paraguay.

The overthrow of Somoza in 1979 was known as the 'Sandinista Revolution'. Elections were held in 1984, and 67% voted for the Sandinistas. That same year the USA imposed trade sanctions, and Nicaragua sought Soviet aid. Over these years Nicaragua became the focus of leftist enthusiasm and **Managua** a cosmopolitan centre, visited and written about by Julio Cortázar ◊ and Salman Rushdie ◊ among many others. By 1980 Nicaragua approached Cuba and Argentina as the most literate countries in Latin America; particularly interesting were the poetry workshops. Equally notable was the role of writers in government, with Minister of the Interior Tomás Borge, a poet and writer (see his *Have You Seen a Red Curtain in My Weary Chamber*, 1989), novelist Sergio Ramírez ◊ as Vice-President, and priest–poet Ernesto Cardenal ◊ as Minister of Culture. The revolution did not proceed without opposition; the newspaper *La Prensa*, run by the husband of the current president Violeta Chamorro (he was assassinated), was censored; 10 000 Miskito Indians were forcibly moved; and a virtual civil war broke out with the American-backed Contras. By 1985 over 4000 people had been killed. The Sandinistas surprisingly lost the elections to a coalition that let in Violeta Chamorro in April 1990.

Poetry in Nicaragua has a startlingly rich tradition, beginning with Rubén Darío (Extract 1) the cosmopolitan modernist; to Cardenal (Extracts 2, 7 and 8); to Pablo Antonio Cuadra's mythical poems dealing with Indians and translated as *The Jaguar and the Moon*, 1972, *Songs of Cifar and the Sweet Sea: Selections 1967–1977*, 1979, and *The Birth of the Sun: Selected Poems 1935–1985*, 1988; to the young revolutionary Gioconda Belli (1948–   ) translated in *From Eve's Rib*, 1989, and *Nicaragua Under Fire*, 1989. Poets Carlos Mejía Godoy, Luis Enrique Godoy and Julio Valle-Castillo appear in *The Nicaraguan Epic: Canto Epico to the FSLAN*, and *Nicaraguan Vision and Other Poems*, 1989, with many further poets in *Poets of Nicaragua: A Bilingual Anthology 1918–1979*, 1982.

A readable travel book, with chapters ferreting out Walker, Darío and Sandino, is *Hurricane in Nicaragua: A Journey in Search of Revolution* by Richard West.

BOOKLIST

The following selection includes all titles which are extracted in this chapter as well as those mentioned in the introduction which are available in English. In general, paperback editions are given when possible. The editions cited are not necessarily the only ones available. For most of the extracted works, the original publisher in English can be found in 'Acknowledgments and Citations' at the end of the volume, as can the exact location of the extracts and the editions from which they are taken. The date in square brackets is the original publica- *tion date of the work in its original language. Extract numbers are highlighted in bold for ease of reference.*

Belli, Gioconda, *From Eve's Rib* [1978], Steven F. White, trans, Curbstone Press, Willimantic, CT, 1989.

Belli, Gioconda, *Nicaragua Under Fire*, John Lyon, trans, Warwick Greville, London, 1989.

Belt, Thomas, *The Naturalist in Nicaragua*, John Murray, London, 1874. **Extract 6.**

Borge, Tomás, *Have You Seen a Red Curtain in My Weary Chamber?*, Russell Bartley, Kent Johnson and Sylvia Yoneda, trans, Curbstone Press, Willimantic, CT, 1989.

Cardenal, Ernesto, *Homage to the American Indians* [1969], Monique and Carlos Altschul, trans, Johns Hopkins University Press, Baltimore, MD, 1973.

Cardenal, Ernesto, *Marilyn Monroe and Other Poems* [1965], Robert Pring-Mill, trans, Search Press, London, 1975. **Extracts 2 and 8.**

Cardenal, Ernesto, *From Nicaragua with Love: Poems (1979–1986)*, Jonathan Cohen, trans, City Lights Books, San Francisco, CA, 1986. **Extract 7.**

Cardenal, Ernesto, *With Walker in Nicaragua and Other Early Poems, 1949–1954)*, Jonathan Cohen, trans, Wesleyan University Press, Middletown, CT, 1984.

Cortázar, Julio, 'Return to Solentiname', in *Nicaraguan Sketches*, Kathleen Weaver, trans, W.W. Norton, New York and London, 1989. **Extract 3.**

Cuadra, Pablo Antonio, *The Birth of the Sun: Selected Poems 1935–1985*, Steven F. White, trans, Unicorn Press, Greensboro, NC, 1988.

Cuadra, Pablo Antonio, *The Jaguar and the Moon*, Thomas Merton, trans, Unicorn Press, Greensboro, NC, 1972.

Cuadra, Pablo Antonio, *Songs of Cifar and the Sweet Sea: Selections 1967–1977*, Grace Schulman and Ann McCarthy de Zavala, trans, Columbia University Press, New York, 1979.

Darío, Rubén, *Selected Poems*, Lysander Kemp, trans, University of Texas Press, Austin, TX, 1965. **Extract 1.**

The Nicaraguan Epic: Canto Epico to the FSLAN, and Nicaraguan Vision and Other Poems, Dinah Livingstone, trans, Kantabis, London, 1989.

Poets of Nicaragua: A Bilingual Anthology 1918–1979, Steven F. White, trans, Unicorn Press, Greensboro, NC, 1982.

Ramírez, Sergio, ' Bed of Bauxite in Weipa', in *Stories* [1976], Nick Caistor, trans, Readers International, London, 1986. **Extract 9.**

Ramírez, Sergio, *To Bury Our Fathers: A Novel of Nicaragua* [1977], Nick Caistor, trans, Readers International, London, 1984. **Extract 10.**

Rushdie, Salman, *The Jaguar Smile: A Nicaraguan Journey* [1987], Picador, London, 1987/Viking Penguin, New York, 1988. **Extract 4.**

Stone, Robert, *A Flag for Sunrise* [1977], Picador, London, 1983/ Random House, New York, 1992. **Extract 5.**

West, Richard, *Hurricane in Nicaragua: A Journey in Search of Revolution*, Michael Joseph, London, 1989.

Extracts

(1) CORINTO
Rubén Darío, *Noon*

Darío describes landmarks, here the Pacific port of Corinto (Nicaragua's main port), in this stanza from his poem 'Noon'. 'Noon' is published in Selected Poems of Rubén Darío *– see Booklist.*

This is the island of Cardón, in Nicaragua.
I think of Greece, of Zacynthos or the Peloponnese,
for a tropical Corinth arises before me
in the gleam of the sun and the fondness of the water.
Green plumes of the palm trees. Far off,
rough with antiquity, solemn with myth,
stands the stone tribe of old volcanoes
which, like all else, await their instant of infinity.

(2) LAKE NICARAGUA
Ernesto Cardenal, *On Lake Nicaragua*

Cardenal describes a ferry journey on Lake Nicaragua (148 km long), where his Solentiname commune was located. This extract is from Marilyn Monroe and Other Poems *– see Booklist.*

Slow cargo-launch, midnight, mid-lake,
bound from San Miguelito to Granada.
The lights ahead not yet in sight,
the dwindling ones behind completely gone.
Only the stars
(the mast a finger pointing to the Seven Sisters)
    and the moon, rising over Chontales.
Another launch (just one red light) goes by
and sinks into the night.
We, for them:
    another red light sinking in the night . . .
And I watching the stars, lying on the deck
between bunches of bananas and Chontales cheeses,
wonder: perhaps there's one that is an earth like ours

and someone watching me (watching the stars)
from another launch, on another night, on another lake.

(3) LAKE NICARAGUA

Julio Cortázar, *Return to Solentiname*

*Cortázar visited Cardenal's island commune in Solentiname on
Lake Nicaragua. This extract is taken from Nicaraguan Sketches
– see Booklist – which also includes a story that Cortázar wrote
on this visit.*

. . . let me talk about my trip to San Carlos and the launch which took
me down the San Juan River to Santa Fe, to that house of friends where
for endless hours I would watch the broad waters, teeming with fish and
festooned with islands of floating plants, waters idly seeking their outlet
in the Atlantic.

Looking out at the river I thought of Langston Hughes's poem (*I've
seen rivers . . .*) and of how time and space seemed strangely to fuse
along that flowing road (as the ancient Egyptians called the Nile). I
regret that I'm not better at describing landscapes. I would have liked
to send the reader off into that languid heat, scored by the fine white
herons on the shores of the San Juan. I'd like the reader to feel what
Europe so long ago lost: the vague fear of the unknown, of the mystery
that begins on river shores and which the double green curtain of jungle
and mangrove swamp hides from the eye. No point in consulting the
map, where uncertain references show tributaries, hills and volcanoes,
with rarely any hint of human life – a scattering of tiny towns in a
sonorous solitude, whose sounds are calls of alarm: the agorero bird, the
sudden roar of wild animals, the jeering screech of monkeys. Awesome
shades of Orellana, Gonzalo Pizarro, Lope de Aguirre, their almost
unthinkable courage as they penetrated for the first time this watery
world which still today teems with danger and death: no longer the
poisoned arrow whistling out of the brush, but the grenade of the
counterrevolutionary, the military ambush which has cost so many
lives in Nicaragua.

Later we went on horseback to Solentiname. I mean, we crossed the
vast lake in a launch that galloped on breakneck waves which forced us
instinctively to seek out footholds or restraints of some kind so as not to
be wildly thrown about. Then the archipelago, and the island which
sheltered Ernesto Cardenal's community. Signs of the Somocista
vandalism were still visible: the burnt out craft workshop, the ran-
sacked houses – yet everything is being rebuilt, white and sweet as in
those brightly detailed paintings the world now knows. The church was

left untouched, and the delectable childlike decorations on the walls still shine with all the colors of the local fish, hens, thatched huts, alligators and little airplanes. Cardenal will return in April to a house that they are finishing for him now. The guest house is already in use. Over a long lunch with friends we saw the lake rise under a wind that put our return in danger.

(4) MANAGUA

Salman Rushdie, *The Jaguar Smile*

Rushdie flew into Managua in July 1986, beginning his three-week visit to Nicaragua.

Later, however, as the plane wheeled over the green lagoon in the crater of the volcano of Apoyeque, and Managua came into view, I recalled another, darker text, from Neruda's poem Centro America . . .

Managua sprawled around its own corpse. Eighty per cent of the city's buildings had fallen down in the great earthquake of 1972, and most of what used to be the centre was now an emptiness. Under Somoza, it had been left as a pile of rubble, and it wasn't until after his fall that the mess was cleared up and grass was planted where downtown Managua used to be.

The hollow centre gave the city a provisional, film-set unreality. There was still a serious shortage of houses, and Managuans were obliged to improvise with what was left. The Foreign Ministry occupied an abandoned shopping mall. The National Assembly itself sat in a converted bank. The Intercontinental Hotel, a sawn-off concrete pyramid, had unfortunately failed to collapse. It stood amidst the wraiths of old Managua like an omen: an ugly American, but a survivor, nevertheless. (It became impossible, I discovered, not to see such a city in symbolic terms.)

(5) MANAGUA

Robert Stone, *A Flag for Sunrise*

In his fictional country 'Tecan', Stone changes Managua to 'San Ysidro', but the lake and buildings are the same.

Entering the capital, the Pan-American Highway made a brief promenade into town, running along the lakefront past several blocks of crumbling incongruously Victorian mansions and lit by cast-iron streetlamps of antique Parisian design. After less than half a mile of this, it broke up into unpaved narrow streets. San Ysidro, in its tuck of the lake valley, was losing the light. The cramped streets near the lake were suddenly dark, scantily lighted, but alive with the din of a half-seen crowd. Driving slowly, Zecca put his head out of the car window to see past the screen of dust and crushed insects that fouled his windshield.

On corners, vendors sold roasted maize from pushcarts, barefoot families made their way along the damp walls, ready to press back against them as cars passed. At the intersection where there was a little light, groups of young men in bright plastic shirts stood together drinking rum, listening or singing to someone's guitar. There was much music to be heard – but these streets were not festive or lyrical. The mood was restless – febrile, Holliwell thought – furtive. The songs were short on melody, driven and mocking, calling forth from those who listened a hard humorless laughter. Holliwell could not understand a word of the shouted, perversely inflected Tecanecan Spanish . . .

(6) MATAGALPA

Thomas Belt, *The Naturalist in Nicaragua*

Matagalpa, with a population of some 70 000, 24 km from Managua, was visited by British naturalist Thomas Belt in 1872.

Matagalpa does not rise above the dullness of other Nicaraguan towns; and there is a stagnation about it, and utter absence of aim or effort in the people, that are most distressing to a foreigner used to the bustle, business, and diversions of European cities. A few women washing in the river, or making tortillas or cigars in the houses, was all I saw going on in the way of work. The men, as usual, lolled about in hammocks, smoking incessantly. There are no libraries, theatres, nor concert rooms. No public meetings nor lectures. Newspapers do not circulate amongst the people, nor books of any kind. I never saw a native reading, in the central provinces, excepting the lawyers turning over their law books. Night sets in at six o'clock. A single dim dip candle is then lighted, in the better houses, set up high, so as to shed a weak, flickering light over the whole room, sufficient to read by. The natives sit about and gossip betwen eight and nine, then lie down to sleep.

(7) NICARAGUA: AFTER THE REVOLUTION

Ernesto Cardenal, *New Ecology*

In this poem, written after the 1979 Sandinista revolution, Cardenal links his liberated land to the 'New Ecology'. The poem is included in From Nicaragua with Love – see Booklist.

In September more coyotes were seen near San Ubaldo.
More alligators, soon after the victory,
   in the rivers, out by San Ubaldo.
     Along the highway more rabbits, raccoons . . .
The bird population has tripled, we're told,
   especially tree ducks.
The noisy tree ducks fly down to swim
   where they see the water shining.
Somoza's people destroyed the lakes, rivers and mountains, too.
   They altered the course of the rivers for their farms.
The Ochomogo had dried up last summer.
The Sinecapa dried up because the big landowners
   stripped the land.
The Rio Grande in Matagalpa, all dried up, during the war,
   out by the Sébaco Plains.
They put two dams in the Ochomogo,
   and the capitalist chemical wastes
spilled into the Ochomogo and the fish swam around as if drunk.
   The Boaco River loaded with sewage water.
The Moyuá Lagoon had dried up. A Somocist colonel
robbed the lands from peasants, and built a dam.
The Moyuá Lagoon that for centuries had been so beautiful.
   (But the little fish will soon return.)
They stripped the land and they dammed the rivers.
   Hardly any iguanas sunning themselves,
     hardly any armadillos.
Somoza used to sell the green turtle of the Caribbean.
They exported turtle eggs and iguanas by the truckload.
   The loggerhead turtle being wiped out.
José Somoza wiping out the sawfish of the Great Lake.
In danger of extinction the jungle's tiger cat,
   its soft, jungle-colored fur,
and the puma, the tapir in the mountains
   (like the peasants in the mountains).
And poor Rio Chiquito! Its misfortune
the whole country's. Somocism mirrored in its waters.
The Rio Chiquito in León, fed by streams

of sewage, wastes from soap factories and tanneries,
white water from soap factories, and red from tanneries,
plastics on the bottom, chamber pots, rusty iron. Somocism
left us that.
(We will see it clear and pretty again singing toward the sea.)
And into Lake Managua all of Managua's sewage water
and chemical wastes.
　And out by Solentiname, on the island La Zanata:
a great stinking white heap of sawfish skeletons.
But the sawfish and the freshwater shark could finally
　　breathe again.
Tisma is teeming once more with herons
　　reflected in its mirrors.
It has many grackles, tree ducks, kingfishers, teals.
　The plant life has benefited as well.
The armadillos go around very happy with this government.
　We will save the woodlands, rivers, lagoons,
We're going to decontaminate Lake Managua.
The humans weren't the only ones who longed for liberation.
The whole ecology had been moaning. The Revolution
also belongs to lakes, rivers, trees, animals.

(8) Nicaragua: Politics
Ernesto Cardenal, *Zero Hour*

In this poem, priest–poet Cardenal summarizes Central American political life. 'Zero Hour' is included in Marilyn Monroe and Other Poems – see Booklist.

　　Central America: tropical nights,
　　volcanoes and lagoons beneath the moon
　　and lights in presidential palaces;
　　barracks, and sad bugle-calls at dusk.
　　'I frequently decide the death of man
　　while smoking a cigarette'
　　says Ubico, smoking a cigarette . . .
　　In his palace, which is like a pink-iced cake,
　　Ubico has a cold. The crowd outside
　　has been dispersed with tear-gas bombs.
　　San Salvador, at night: distrust and spying,
　　muttering in the homes and small hotels,
　　and screams in police stations.
　　The crowd stoned the palace of Carías,

breaking just one window of his office,
but the police opened fire on the crowd.
And Managua: covered by deployed machine-guns
from its palace, which is like a chocolate cake:
steel helmets out patrolling in the streets.
Watchman, what of the night?
Watchman, what of the night?

(9) Puerto Cabezas

Sergio Ramírez, *A Bed of Bauxite in Weipa*

*A woman in this short story recalls her home town Puerto
Cabezas on the Caribbean coast. 'A Bed of Bauxite' is included
in Stories – see Booklist.*

There's no place as bad as Puerto Cabezas in the rainstorms, when the
streets turn to muddy fields. On Sunday mornings we had to leap the
puddles on our way to service at the Moravian Church, set in a deserted
square lined with bare oaks, clouds of mosquitos swarming around the
wooden spire. The sea is warm and oily, full of coconut tree branches
swept along by the currents together with kerosene cans, broken chairs,
the sea a garbage dump, one day the spongy corpse of a drowned man
floating beyond the bushes, a boat whose towrope the wind has snapped
drifting from its moorings to the dismay of the shouting, wide-eyed
fishermen, howling like banshees on the shoreline, hurricane at
midnight clawing at the corrugated iron roofs, water flooding the land,
up to the very top of the house stilts, dawn revealing the whole
landscape flooded and filthy.

(10) San Juan del Norte

Sergio Ramírez, *To Bury Our Fathers*

*San Juan del Norte, isolated on the border with Costa Rica, is
lyrically evoked in this novel about revolution in Nicaragua.*

San Juan del Norte, with the sea roaring in the distance beyond white
dunes like polished glass; the ruins of stores and banks, hotels, casinos,
and brothels, steamship agencies and consulates, mansions with the
bare bones of their algae-encrusted towers exposed to the wind, their
owners' names or effigies carved in crumbling pediments, the thick
knotty roots of eucalyptus and tamarind trees from once planned groves
now thrusting up through the cracks in marble slabs, heaving them up;

branches pushing their evergreen fronds in at french windows; a bar once upon a time *La Maison Dorée* now open to the sky like a walled garden, slender Viennese chairs still clustered around its iron tables which in the mists of dawn look as though they have just been vacated at the end of a party; a safe as tall as a man thrown in the middle of the street, a semicircle of golden letters on its door: *F. Alf. Pellas and Co.*; tombstones from the foreigners cemeteries with their Hebrew, German, Italian names, washed by the rains down to the beach, where the women use them to dry their clothes on; in the mouth of the river a dredger, towering immobile above the clumps of weeds swaying slowly with the tides, like a green plain, bending before the Atlantic wind, herons from the jungle that swoop down with raucous cries onto the oily beach, clouds of mosquitos and gnats swarming around the oil-lamps at night; the growling of pumas and the chorusing frogs, and in the darkness, the breeze wafting all round the harbour the whispers of the men who are squatting down at the quayside piled high with caged monkeys. Sometimes he wakes in the bandstand, terrified of their howling, their cages strewn now not only all over the jetty but along the coast at the rivermouth, on the dunes, and inside the ruined houses, more hunters emerging from the jungle every night with their captives in wicker cages, the monkeys' cries rising from every corner of San Juan del Norte.

Biographies and important works

BELT, Thomas (1832–1878). Born in Newcastle-upon-Tyne in the UK, Belt was a geologist. He travelled to Australia in 1852–62, then to Nova Scotia. In 1868 he was appointed to run the **Chontales** Gold Mining Co in Nicaragua where he lived until 1872. He wrote his *The Naturalist in Nicaragua: A Narrative of a Residence at the Gold Mine of Chontales; Journeys in the Savannahs and Forests* (Extract 6) on his way home in 1873 and it was published in 1874. It is dedicated to H.W. Bates (◊ Brazil), and is filled with precise and prejudiced descriptions of Nicaragua. Belt was a Fellow of the London Geological Society.

CARDENAL, Ernesto (1925–). Born on 20 January 1925 in Nicaragua's third city **Granada** on the shore of **Lake Nicaragua**, Cardenal was a student in Mexico City from 1943 to 1947 and then at Columbia University, New York from 1947 to 1949 where his poetry came under the crucial influence of Ezra Pound. It was from these years, and translations of Pound (published in 1961) that Cardenal's poetry found its voice. From Pound he developed a way of writing about history, the pre-Columbian past and political repression by using documents, quotations, and the classics. He learnt to move away from the subjectivity of traditional lyrical poetry. From 1954 to 1956, Cardenal worked on a cycle of poems dealing with US interference in Central America. In 1956 he underwent a spiritual conversion, and decided to become a priest, joining Thomas Merton's Trappist monastery at Gethsemani, Kentucky. From there he went to a Benedictine monastery in Cuernavaca, Mexico, and then La Ceja in Colombia. He was ordained in 1965, and in 1966 founded his commune on the island of **Mancarrón** in the **Solentiname archipelago** on **Lake Nicaragua**, finally closed by Somoza. Cardenal's 'second conversion' came about during his visit to Castro's Cuba in 1970, so that he supported the Sandinista Front until it toppled Somoza in 1979. Over the years of the Sandinista government, Cardenal was Minister for Culture. He reads his poetry very effectively, and is a charismatic figure with his white beard and beret, appealing to a radical blend of Christianity and revolutionary politics that has spoken for many in Latin America. He has been well translated into English collections, including *Marilyn Monroe and Other Poems*, 1975 (Extracts 2 and 8); *Apocalypse and Other Poems*, 1977; *Zero Hour and Other Documentary Poems*, 1980; *From Nicaragua with Love. Poems 1979–1986*, 1986 (Extract 7); and *Nicaraguan New Time*, 1988.

CORTAZAR, Julio (see under Argentina). He visited Nicaragua several times in his later years. See his *Nicaraguan Sketches*, 1989 (Extract 3).

DARIO, Rubén (1867–1916). Darío's real name was Félix Rubén García Sarmiento. He was born in Metapa, Nicaragua (today **Ciudad Darío**) on 18 January 1867. After the separation of his parents he was brought up by an aunt in **León**. He was a child prodigy, and became famous as a poet early in his life. After reading all he could in the **National Library** at **Managua** Darío sought to escape the provinciality of Central America and left for Santiago, Chile in 1886 where he read the latest French Parnassian and Symbolist poets, befriended the president's son, published *Rimas* in 1887, and, crucially, *Azul* in 1888. These prose pieces and lyric poems established Darío as the most outrageous innovator of his day, welding his French readings on to his tropical Spanish in a style alien to peninsular Spaniards, who were shocked at his daring, and risks. He returned to Nicaragua and married in 1890. For the rest of his life Darío was on the move, a nomadic bohemian, who sought out and encouraged other poets. From Central America in 1892 he went to Madrid and Paris, cultural Mecca of the times, and then down to Buenos Aires, the most cosmopolitan city he ever knew, where he lived from 1893 to 1898, working for the newspaper *La Nación*, and publishing his most extravagant, sensual and shocking book *Prosas profanas*, 1896 (*Prosas profanas*, 1922), as well as a book of essays *Los raros*, 1896, on heroes like Poe, Verlaine and Rimbaud. As correspondent for *La Nación*, Darío left for Europe in 1898. In 1905, in Madrid, he published *Cantos de vida y esperanza*, in which a series of poems deal with depression, but there are also circumstantial political poems. See Rubén Darío, *Selected Poems*, 1965 (Extract 1). His later, alcoholic days were spent in Mallorca where he lived with a peasant woman, Francisca Sánchez, but he returned to die in Nicaragua on 6 January 1916. The house in **León**

Ernesto Cardenal

where he grew up is the **Museo Archivo Rubén Darío** (originally on Calle Real, today called Darío). A plaque on the house commemorates his death, and he is buried in the **cathedral**. See Charles D. Watland, *Poet-Errant: A Biography of Rubén Darío*, Philosophical Library, New York, 1975.

RAMIREZ, Sergio (1942–). Ramírez was born in **Masatepe**, Nicaragua. He got his law degree in 1964, and lived in exile in San José, Costa Rica, where he worked in the Consejo Superior Universitario Centroamericano, becoming its Secretary General. He spent two years in Germany (explored in stories), edited a literary magazine, and founded a publishing house in 1969. He has edited anthologies of Nicaraguan writing. In 1979 he became Nicaragua's vice-president. His short stories *Cuentos*, 1963, and *Nuevos cuentos*, 1969 (*Stories*, 1986 – Extract 9) explore ironically Nicaragua's dependency on the West with stories about Jackie Onassis's yacht not stopping there, about a Venezuelan in Berlin who has to act Father Christmas, about baseball. *¿Te dio miedo la sangre?*, 1977 (*To Bury our Fathers*, 1984 – Extract 10), based on documents, is a complicated novel concerned with Nicaragua's struggle for freedom from 1930 to 1961, with three friends surviving and challenging Somoza.

RUSHDIE, Salman (1947–). Rushdie was born in Bombay, went to school in England, and university at Cambridge. Apart from his well known novels, Rushdie visited Nicaragua in July 1986 for three weeks and wrote *The Jaguar Smile: A Nicaraguan Journey*, 1987 (Extract 4), visiting the English-speaking Atlantic coast **Bluefields**, and President Daniel Ortega, his poet wife Rosario Murillo, Ernesto Cardenal ◊ and Vice-President Sergio Ramírez ◊, as well as Violeta Chamorro (three years later elected president).

STONE, Robert (1936–). Born in Brooklyn, Stone served in the US Navy as a journalist, then in the Merchant Marine in the Caribbean. His third novel *A Flag for Sunrise*, 1977 (Extract 5), set in Tecan, Central America, is an adventure story with a relentless plot and serious undertones. Through isolated charac-

ters who meet at the end in a destructive orgy, Stone comments on contemporary history, with a bleak post-Vietnam vision of sinister Americans and naifs abroad in 'this rotten fucked world', as if only gun-runners, drug addicts, faithless nuns, revolutionaries, depraved cops and mad missionaries survive down 'South'. The main character, who murders and betrays his nun lover to survive, is an anthropologist invited out to give a lecture, who then wanders down to the Caribbean coast in Tecan (*Tico* in Spanish means Costa Rican) on a vague CIA hunch. Holliwell is a semi-alcoholic lout drifting into middle age. In Stone's novel the various American characters all have to face up to deeper, more destructive revelations than any available back home. When Justin, the despairing nun, asks a practical question she is told, 'Its such a North American question'. At another moment Justin meditates: 'Can it be, she wondered, that I have come to understand this country? Impossible, she decided.' Here Americans sink into 'primordial dreams' for Central America is still in contact with bloodthirsty gods. Father Egan, the raving, dying missionary, and a child murderer on the run from a Mennonite community, at some Mayan ruins, with glyphs, hippies and stellae, talk about sacrifice, the devil and blood as if the *place* affects the mind. Stone makes his Tecan a place where you take 'a ride on the edge, among half-seen and unseen things . . .'. The 'Vietnam flashes' make Central American a tropical nightmare, a land that induces lust, 'mud and mangrove swamps and darkness'. Holliwell's moral is the last line of the novel: 'A man has nothing to fear . . . who understands history'.

COSTA RICA

Costa Rica, or the República de Costa Rica, means 'rich coast' in Spanish, probably because Columbus discovered gold jewelry on local Indians, though another explanation is that the name is derived from a corruption of Costa de *Oreja* ('ear'). Its land area is 51 100 sq km, and the population reached 3 million in 1990. The capital **San José de Costa Rica**, at an altitude of 1188 m, was founded in 1727, and became the capital in 1823.

Costa Rica has been called a 'white man's country', with only 1.8% negroes and mulattos. There are a few Indians remaining, with some 30 families of the Guaymí tribe, protected on the Nicoya peninsula. Seventy per cent of the population live on the **Meseta Central** between 900 and 1400 m high. Spanish is the main language, and Roman Catholicism the religion. There is a very high literacy rate. Costa Ricans are known as 'Ticos', from their habit of saying '*momentico*' for '*un momento*'.

Two-thirds of the land comprises high volcanic cordilleras, with **Chirripó** the tallest peak at 3820 m. The volcano **Irazú** exploded in 1963, and **Arenal** in 1968. The coasts are tropical: the Caribbean coast accounts for 25% of the land total (but only 6% of the population). In the rolling Meseta Central, where most people live, the average temperature is 26.7°C; above that it is *tierra fría*. Broadleaf evergreen forests cover 60% of the country. As Costa Rica is a 'safe' country, many North Americans retire here.

Costa Rica was discovered by Columbus on his fourth voyage in 1502, when he saw traces of gold. Early on the place was called Nueva Cartago, and by 1540 it was a province of the Captaincy General of

131

Guatemala. During the colonial period, Costa Rica remained a backwater, a place of poor farmers, with no large landowners, and no mineral wealth. It gained independence with all Central America on 15 September 1821. In 1824 it joined the Central American Federation, and began its policy of isolation in 1838 by going its own way. It settled its disputed boundary with Nicaragua in 1896, and only after nearly going to war with Panama in 1941. It has been one of the most democratic of all Latin American states.

In 1948 there was a brief civil war over elections being anulled. It lasted two months with the triumph of the socialist landowner José Figueres. With a quickly conscripted army he bombed government troops in **Puerto Limón**, and set the rightfully elected president back in power. By then Figueres had transformed the country. He disbanded the army and turned the barracks into a **Fine Arts Museum**. He signed the recipcrocal-assistance Rio treaty, which states that an attack on Costa Rica is an attack on the whole Western hemisphere; he nationalized the banks; set up free education, pensions and free medical aid. Since 1948, then, Costa Rica, has been without an army, an extraordinary feat in Latin America. In 1983 this neutral policy was confirmed. Don Pepe, as José Figueres was known, was twice elected president (1953 and 1970) before retiring to his coffee farm. Costa Rica has been a refuge for many persecuted Central Americans, like Salvadoran Manlio Argueta (◊ El Salvador), as well as for Rómulo Betancourt, from Venezuela. In 1986 the then president Oscar Arias Sánchez, for his work for peace in the area, was awarded the Nobel Peace prize. This island of democracy is celebrated in Cardenal's poem, 'Carters Sing' (Extract 1).

Laureano Albán (1942–   ) is the only Costa Rican poet in translation, with his historical and mythic poems in *Autumn's Legacy*, 1982, and *The Endless Voyage*, 1984. Carlos Gagini ◊ wrote a descriptive novel, dealing with the theme of US influence (Extract 2) and Carmen Naranjo ◊ is Costa Rica's best known living writer (Extract 4), with *There Never was a Once Upon a Time*, 1990, in English. For an impression of the land see Paul Theroux (Extract 3) and Patrick Marnham's *So Far from God . . . A Journey to Central America*, 1985.

BOOKLIST

The following selection includes all titles which are extracted in this chapter as well as those mentioned in the introduction which are available in English. In general, paperback editions are given when possible. The editions cited are not necessarily the only ones available. For most of the extracted works, the original publisher in English can be found in 'Acknowledgments and Citations' at the end of the volume, as can the exact location of the extracts and the editions from which they are taken. The date in square brackets is the original publication date of the work in its original language. Extract numbers are highlighted in bold for ease of reference.

Albán, Laureano, *Autumn's Legacy* [1980], Frederick H. Fornoff, trans, Ohio University Press, Athens, OH, 1982.

Albán, Laureano, *The Endless Voyage* [1981], Frederick H. Fornoff, trans, Ohio University Press, Athens, OH, 1984.

Cardenal, Ernesto, 'Carters Sing', in *Marilyn Monroe and Other Poems* [1965], Robert Pring-Mill, trans,

Search Press, London, 1975. **Extract 1**.

Gagini, Carlos, *Redemptions: A Costa Rican Novel* [1918], E. Bradford Burns, trans, San Diego State University Press, San Diego, CA, 1985. **Extract 2**.

Marnham, Patrick, *So Far from God . . . A Journey to Central America*, Penguin, London, 1986/ Viking Penguin, New York, 1985.

Naranjo, Carmen, 'And We Sold the Rain', in *And We Sold the Rain: Contemporary Fiction from Central America*, Rosario Santos, ed, Ryan, Peterborough, 1989/ Four Walls: Eight Windows, San Francisco, CA, 1989. **Extract 4**.

Naranjo, Carmen, *There Never Was a Once Upon a Time* [1984], Linda Britt, trans, Latin American Literary Review Press, Pittsburgh, PA, 1990.

Theroux, Paul, *The Old Patagonian Express: By Train Through the Americas* [1979], Penguin, London, 1980/Houghton Miflin, Boston, MA, 1989. **Extract 3**.

Extracts

(1) COSTA RICA: FREEDOM

Ernesto Cardenal, *Carters Sing*

Cardenal compares trouble-free, democratic Costa Rica with his own Nicaragua in his poem 'Carters Sing'. Thanks to this poem Cardenal was threatened with arrest by Somoza and fled Nicaragua. 'Carters Sing' is included in Marilyn Monroe and Other Poems – see Booklist.

In Costa Rica, carters sing.
Men on the roads with mandolins.
And ox-carts bright as parrots.
And oxen with coloured ribbons,
bells, and flowers on their horns.
At coffee-harvest time in Costa Rica.
When all carts are heaped high with coffee beans.

And bands play in village squares
and the windows and the balconies of San José
are full of girls and full of flowers.
And girls there go for walks in parks.
And the President can go on foot in San José.

(2) NEAR IRAZU

Carlos Gagini, *Redemptions*

Gagini's protagonist, a local poet in love, rides to an estate near the alive Irazú volcano (3432 m).

The little road, always climbing, passed in a straight line through the town of Guadalupe, emerged from the coffee zone, divided in two the village of San Isidro, and then zigzagged through farms and meadows. Finally, hidden beneath the trees, it disappeared into the forests crowning the mountains.

Behind the rider a dazzling panorama slowly opened. To the north, the Barba Mountains and to the south the Aserri Mountains stretched out like the jaws of a pair of pliers whose axis was the Irazú Volcano. In the center of the expansive valley lay San José, the capital, like an urban island in a verdant agrarian sea. Along the mountainside small villages of whitewashed houses resembled piles of seashells thrown against the rocks. To the west where the enormous jaws of the pliers had not quite closed, the blue hills of the coast hid the Gulf of Nicoya. The eye could easily distinguish on the slopes and in the glens the varied uses of land: the yellow blotches of sugar plantations, the green squares of coffee estates, the wide meadows with their grazing herds, the silver threads of rivers, and the ruddy brush ready to be burned . . .

The road became steeper and lonelier. Stones replaced the dust over which the horse had trotted. The noble animal showed no signs of fatigue, nor did it ever break step. Suddenly at the top of a hill, it turned to the left like one who knows the land well to follow a path shaded by two lines of orange trees whose branches hung heavily laden with the fruit.

Like someone who had suddenly awakened, the rider raised his eyes, the recognition of these surroundings filled him with joy. Sitting upright in the saddle, he wiped his face with his handkerchief and then brushed off his clothing. In a couple of minutes he stopped at an iron gate which he opened without dismounting.

About a hundred feet from there in the midst of a meadow stood an elegant and spacious adobe house of one story. A large garden surrounded it. A stately old fig tree dominated that beautiful landscape.

The western side of the house boasted an ample veranda with sliding stained glass windows, supported by iron columns painted white and crowned by golden capitals. A multitude of flower pots displayed a dazzling variety of plants which adorned the veranda furnished with rattan chairs and sofas and little lacquer tables. Above the veranda a terrace with a jasper balastrade offered an admirable view of the magnificent panorama already described as well as in the opposite direction a view of the bleak cone of Irazú, blackened by eruptions.

(3) Puerto Limon
Paul Theroux, *The Old Patagonian Express*

Theroux took a train to Puerto Limón on the Caribbean coast, the country's main banana-exporting port.

The next day I gave to roaming Limón, but on closer inspection Limón did not look any better than it had that first night, a steaming stinking town of mud puddles and buildings discoloured by dampness. The stucco fronts had turned the colour and consistency of stale cake, and crumbs of concrete littered the pavements. In the park there were three-toed sloths creeping in tree branches, and in the market and on the parapets of the crumbling buildings there were mangy vultures. Other vultures circled the plaza. Was there a dingier backwater in all the world? Columbus had come here with his son Ferdinand. Ferdinand, fourteen at the time, had written an account of that fourth voyage, and he had described Limón as 'lofty, full of rivers, and abounding in very tall trees, as also on the islet [Uva Island, the Indians called it Quirivi] where they grew thick as basil, and full of very lofty groves of trees . . . For this reason the Admiral [Columbus] called it La Huerta [The Garden].' It might have been so; but the accounts of this voyage are contradictory. Ferdinand sometimes saw things differently from his father. In Limón, Ferdinand wrote, to calm the fears of the sailors, the Indians sent out an old man with 'two girls, the one about 8, the other about 14 years of age . . . the girls showed great fortitude, for despite the Christians being complete strangers to them in appearance, manners and race, they gave no signs of grief or fear, but always looked cheerful and modest. So the Admiral showed them good usage.' In his *Lettera Rarissima* to the Sovereigns, Columbus gave a different version of this. 'On Cariai [Limón] and the neighbouring lands,' he wrote, 'there are sorcerers. They would have given the world for me not to stay there an hour. As soon as I got there they sent right out two girls, all dressed up; the elder was hardly 11, and the other 7, both behaving with such lack of modesty as to be no better than whores. They had magic powder concealed about them. As soon as they arrived, I gave orders that they be presented with some of our trading truck and sent them directly ashore . . .'

(4) SAN JOSE

Carmen Naranjo, *And We Sold the Rain*

Carmen Naranjo's allegorical/political satire describes a city that resembles San José. This story is included in the anthology of the same title – see Booklist.

The hunger and poverty could no longer be concealed: the homeless, pockets empty, were squatting in Parque Central, the Parque Nacional, and the Plaza de la Cultura. They were camping along Central and Second Avenues and in a shantytown springing up on the plains outside the city. Gangs were threatening to invade the national theater, the Banco Central, and all the nationalized banking headquarters. The Public Welfare Agency was rationing rice and beans as if they were medicine. In the marketplace, robberies increased to one per second, and homes were burgled at the rate of one per half hour. Business and government were sinking in sleaze; drug lords operated uncontrolled, and gambling was institutionalized in order to launder dollars and attract tourists. Strangely enough, the price of a few items went down: whiskey, caviar and other such articles of conspicuous consumption.

The sea of poverty that was engulfing cities and villages contrasted with the growing number of Mercedes Benzes, BMWs and a whole alphabet of trade names of gleaming new cars.

The minister announced to the press that the country was no longer on the verge of bankruptcy. The airlines were no longer issuing tickets because so much money was owed them, and travel became impossible; even official junkets were eliminated. There was untold suffering of civil servants suddenly unable to travel even once a month to the great cities of the world! A special budget might be the solution, but tax revenues were nowhere to be found, unless a compliant public were to go along with the president's brilliant idea of levying a tax on air – a minimal tax, to be sure, after all, the air was a part of the government's patrimony. Ten *colones* per breath would be a small price to pay.

July arrived, and one afternoon a minister without portfolio and without umbrella, noticing that it had started to rain, stood watching people run for cover. 'Yes,' he thought, 'here it rains like it rains in Comala, like it rains in Macondo. It rains day and night . . . If we could only export the rain . . .'

Biographies and important works

CARDENAL, Ernesto (see under Nicaragua).

GAGINI, Carlos (1865–1925). Gagini was born in Costa Rica. His work debates Costa Rican identity, in terms of nationalism, and concern about the dominance of the USA. *El árbol enfermo*, 1918, (*Redemptions*, 1985 – Extract 2), dramatizes the amorous conflict between a Costa Rican poet Fernando Rodríguez, forced into exile, seeking the hand of Margarita, a rich landowner's daughter, and Mr Ward, a powerful, practical American businessman, wooing the same girl. The title suggests how the Costa Rican 'redeems' Margarita. The background is realistic, and the issues still crucial. Gagini's novel is didactic, pointing out Costa Rica's political corruption.

NARANJO, Carmen (1930–). Born in Costa Rica Naranjo obtained her MA in 1953, and rose to the positions of ambassador to India (1972–74), Minister of Culture (1974–76), and representative of UNICEF in Guatemala and Mexico. In 1969, she was at the Iowa International Writing Program. She runs the Central American University Publishing House (EDUCA). Carmen Naranjo has published seven books of poems, and is also a short story writer and novelist.

THEROUX, Paul (see under Honduras).

PANAMA

'Now one glides through a narrow canal, gorgeous jungle like a wall on both sides, 2 minutes lost here would mean death, or a very peculiar new life – monkeys, birds, orchids, sinister orchestrations from the jungle. Hot here as a Turkish bath in hell.'
Malcolm Lowry,
Through the Panama

Panama, or the República de Panamá, the smallest republic in Latin America, was named after a local forest tree, and has a land area of 77 082 sq km, with a population reaching 2.4 million in 1990. It remains nominally Roman Catholic (despite incursions from Protestant missionaries) and Spanish speaking. The capital, **Panama City**, had 386 000 inhabitants in 1980. The people are *mestizo* with Indian, negro, oriental and European strains. The land consists of hills and rough mountains with an active volcano, **Chiriquí**. On the tropical coasts there are mangroves and palms. Sixty per cent of the land is covered by rainforest. **Barro Colorado** island in **Gatún Lake** is a tropical forest reserve.

Panama came into being in 1821 when the Spanish Empire was divested of most of its American colonies. For the rest of the nineteenth century, this tropical and mountainous isthmus remained a province of Gran Colombia, liberated by Simón Bolívar, and ruled from Bogotá. Its strategic importance had long been noted by the USA who passively supported a Panamanian revolt against Colombia in 1903 by sending a battleship to prevent the Colombians reclaiming Panama. The USA was the first country to recognize the new republic. Because of the Canal, the USA kept open its option to intervene in Panamanian affairs should the need arise, which it did in 1908, 1912, 1918, and under President Bush in December 1989. A succint account of this history is told by Graham Greene ◊ in *Getting to Know the General*, 1984 (Extracts 9 and 10).

Christopher Columbus in his fourth voyage touched land at Panama,

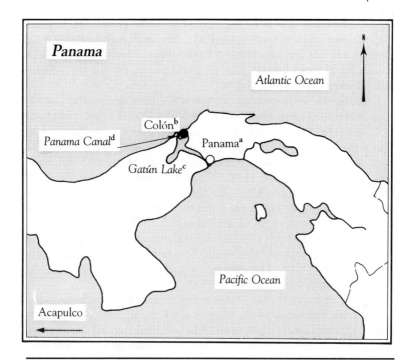

Notes to map: [a]*Panama City features in Malcolm Lowry's story 'Through the Panama', where Lowry himself passed in 1947; in William Burroughs's novel Queer, 1984; in Iain Banks's novel Canal Dreams, 1989; in Jane Bowles's novel Two Serious Ladies, 1943; in Graham Greene's novel The Captain and the Enemy, 1988; and in Greene's memoir Getting to Know the General, 1984;* [b]*Also known as Aspinwall. See extracts by Jane Bowles, Aldous Huxley (who was there in 1933) and Henryk Sienkiewicz (Extracts 2, 3 and 1);* [c]*Gatún Lake features in Banks's Canal Dreams;* [d]*Lowry's 'Through the Panama' narrates a detailed trip through the Canal. Hollow circle = capital city.*

part of Terra Firma, in 1502. Ill, he stayed for four months in **Belén** until forced out by hostile Indians. He called the land 'Veragua'. In 1513 Vasco Núñez de Balboa (confused by Keats ◊ with Cortés – Extract 4) crossed the isthmus and discovered the Pacific Ocean, called by him *El mar del Sur*. In 1519 **Panama City** (the oldest city on the Pacific coast of all the Americas) was founded, and in 1531 Francisco Pizarro sailed from Panama City for Peru. From then on the isthmus became the main road for all the loot from Peru, carried on mules along the *camino real* to **Portobelo** and Nombre de Dios (no longer on the map) – see Extract 10 for Greene on Portobelo. These were the monopoly ports used by the annual Spanish fleets from Cádiz, and so attracted many sallies from pirates. In 1572 Sir Francis Drake attacked

Nombre de Dios, and in 1595 he burnt it to the ground. In 1596 he died of fever and was buried in a lead coffin in **Portobelo** harbour (as Graham Greene and Iain Banks ◊ have noted), which has never been found. Sir Henry Morgan, another grand pirate, crossed the isthmus and attacked **Panama City** in 1671.

Crossing the fever-infested isthmus was crucial during the Californian gold rush of 1848, the 'Road to Hell'. By 1855 the first railway was built between the Atlantic and Pacific seaboards, travelled on by Anthony Trollope in the 1850s, who set his story 'The Journey to Panama' partly there, and later by Theroux (◊ Honduras). But ships still had to round Cape Horn. Many able men had speculated on digging canals for ships. Alexander von Humboldt (◊ Mexico) planned nine different routes. However, it was the Suez canal builder Ferdinand de Lesseps who first set about achieving this dream in 1881. After ten years of appalling death rates due to malaria and yellow fever (some 40 000 died) Lesseps had to give up. The painter Paul Gauguin was in Panama at that time. The Americans took over, and completed the sluice lock canal by 15 August 1914.

In order to assure the use of this essential canal for American trade a **Canal Zone** was ceded to the USA in 1903. It ran 8 km either side of the 82 km canal, with its artificial lakes (see Banks again). It is owned, operated and controlled by the USA. It consists of 938 sq km with some 60 000 civilians (or Zonians) living under American law (once again, Greene in both his fiction and travelogue is acute on Zonians). In 1977, after many negotiations, President Carter and General Torrijos agreed that the Canal Zone (the 'Big Ditch') would revert to Panama on 31 December 1999, with a clause allowing the US to intervene. A toll is demanded; it takes some eight hours to work through the locks that lift ships some 26 m above sea level and save them about 15 000 km round the Cape (details recorded by Malcolm Lowry ◊ in 1947 – Extract 5).

The squalor of the country is recreated by Huxley (Extract 3), and later Burroughs (Extract 7). Jane Bowles ◊ places the protagonist of *Two Serious Ladies* in the **Hotel Washington** in Colón (Extract 2), a refuge from sordid Panama.

In the past decade Panama has come into the news due first to General Omar Torrijos, a left-wing populist, and friend of Graham Greene, who came to power in 1968 after toppling the Arias family's domination of Panamanian politics, and then was mysteriously killed in a plane crash in August 1981. The man who took over, General Manuel Noriega, languishes in prison in the USA convicted of drug trafficking, and was the cause of the US invasion of 1989.

Panama City is a free port that attracts shoppers passing along the Canal (as in Iain Banks's novel *Canal Dreams* – Extract 6).

Iain Banks

The problems facing Panamanian writers are the small size of their country, its illiteracy, and its recent status as an independent nation, leading inevitably to questions about national identity, and protests against the USA. So far none of its writers (like Joaquín Beleño Cedeño, Demetrio Korsi, Rogelio Sinán or Ricardo Miró) have been translated, other than through occasional appearances in anthologies. A curiosity: the US novelist Sherwood Anderson died in Panama in 1941.

See Paul Theroux, *The Old Patagonian Express: By Train Through the Americas*, 1979, and Rosario Santos, ed, *And We Sold the Rain: Contemporary Fiction from Central America*, 1989.

BOOKLIST

The following selection includes all titles which are extracted in this chapter as well as those mentioned in the introduction which are available in English. In general, paperback editions are given when possible. The editions cited are not necessarily the only ones available. For most of the extracted works, the original publisher in English can be found in 'Acknowledgments and Citations' at the end of the volume, as can the exact location of the extracts and the editions from which they are taken. The date in square brackets is the original publication date of the work in its original language. Extract numbers are highlighted in bold for ease of reference.

And We Sold the Rain: Contemporary Fiction from Central America, Rosario Santos, ed, Ryan, Peterborough, 1989/Four Walls: Eight Windows, San Francisco, 1989.

Banks, Iain, *Canal Dreams*, Abacus, London, 1989. **Extract 6.**

Bowles, Jane, *Two Serious Ladies* [1943], Virago, London, 1979/ Dutton, New York, 1984. **Extract 2.**

Burroughs, William, *Queer* [1984], Picador, London, 1986/Viking Penguin, New York, 1987. **Extract 7.**

Greene, Graham, *The Captain and the Enemy* [1988], Penguin, London, 1989/Viking Penguin, New York, 1989. **Extract 8.**

Greene, Graham, *Getting to Know the General: The Story of an Involvement* [1984], Penguin, London, 1985/Viking Penguin, New York, 1985. **Extracts 9 and 10.**

Huxley, Aldous, *Eyeless in Gaza* [1936], Grafton, London, 1977/ Carroll and Graf, New York, 1989. **Extract 3.**

Keats, John, 'On First Looking into Chapman's Homer' [1816], in *The Poetical Works of John Keats*, Oxford University Press, London, 1967. **Extract 4.**

Lowry, Malcolm, *Hear Us O Lord from Heaven Thy Dwelling Place* [1961], Picador, London, 1991/ Carroll and Graf, New York, 1986. **Extract 5.**

Sienkiewicz, Henryk, 'Lighthouse-Keeper of Aspinwall', in *The Masterpiece Library of Short Stories, Vol XIII*, The Educational Book Co, London, undated. **Extract 1.**

Trollope, Anthony, 'The Journey to Panama', in *The Complete Short Stories, Vol 5*, William Pickering, London, 1991.

Extracts

(1) ASPINWALL

Henryk Sienkiewicz,
Lighthouse-Keeper of Aspinwall

Sienkiewicz's old man in the lighthouse in Aspinwall (the old name for Colón) will be ruined by receiving a book of poems in Polish that will flood him with nostalgia, so that he forgets to light his lights, and wrecks a boat. This short story was published in The Masterpiece Library of Short Stories – see Booklist.

The old man grew accustomed to his tower, to the lantern, to the rock, to the sand-bars, to solitude. He grew accustomed also to the sea-mews which hatched in the crevices of the rock, and in the evening held meetings on the roof of the lighthouse. Skavinski threw to them generally the remnants of his food; and soon they grew tame, and afterward, when he fed them, a real storm of white wings encircled him, and the old man went among the birds like a shepherd among sheep. When the tide ebbed he went to the low sand-banks, on which he collected savoury periwinkle and beautiful pearl shells of the nautilus, which receding waves had left on the sand. In the night by the moonlight and the tower he went to catch fish, which frequented the windings of the cliff in myriads. At last he was in love with the rocks and his treeless island, grown over only with small thick plants exuding sticky resin. The distant views repaid him for the poverty of the island, however. During afternoon hours, when the air became very clear he could see the whole isthmus covered with the richest vegetation. It seemed to Skavinski at such times that he saw one gigantic garden – bunches of cocoa, and enormous musa, combined as it were in luxurious tufted bouquets, right there behind the houses of Aspinwall. Farther on, between Aspinwall and Panama, was a great forest over which every morning and evening hung a reddish haze of exhalations – a real tropical forest with its feet in stagnant water, interlaced with lianas and filled with the sound of one sea of gigantic orchids, palms, milk-trees, iron-trees, gum-trees.

(2) COLON

Jane Bowles, *Two Serious Ladies*

The Copperfields arrive in Colón, and begin to separate, as Mr likes sleazy pensions and jungle, while Mrs becomes fascinated with a Panamanian whore, who initiates her into a sensual naturalness at odds with her inhibitions. The Hotel Washington still exists.

She looked out of the window of the taxicab and she noticed that there was a terrific amount of activity going on around her in the streets. The people, for the most part Negroes and uniformed men from the fleets of all nations, were running in and out and making so much noise that Mrs Copperfield wondered if it was not a holiday of some kind.

'It's like a city that is being constantly looted,' said her husband.

The houses were painted in bright colors and they had wide porches on the upper floors, supported beneath by long wooden posts. Thus they formed a kind of arcade to shade the people walking in the street.

'This architecture is ingenious,' remarked Mr Copperfield. 'The streets would be unbearable if one had to walk along them with nothing overhead.'

'You could not stand that, mister,' said the cab-driver, 'to walk along with nothing over your head.'

'Anyway,' said Mrs Copperfield, 'do let's choose one of these hotels quickly and get into it.'

They found one right in the heart of the red-light district and agreed to look at some rooms on the fifth floor. The manager had told them that these were sure to be the least noisy. Mrs Copperfield, who was afraid of lifts, decided to go up the stairs on foot and wait for her husband to arrive with the luggage. Having climbed to the fifth floor, she was surprised to find that the main hall contained at least a hundred straight-backed dining-room chairs and nothing more. As she looked around, her anger mounted and she could barely wait for Mr Copperfield to arrive on the lift in order to tell him what she thought of him. 'I must go to the Hotel Washington,' she said to herself.

(3) COLON

Aldous Huxley, *Eyeless in Gaza*

Huxley's protagonist, the numbed intellectual Anthony Beavis, goes off to fight in Mexico with his 'Bolshevik' prep school friend Staithes. They land at Colón on their way to ignominy at Tapatlán in Mexico.

At Colon they drove in a cab, at evening, along the esplanade. Whitish, like a vast fish's eye, the sea lay as though dead. Against a picture postcard of sunset the immoderately tall thin palms were the emblems of a resigned hopelessness, and in the nostrils the hot air was like a vapour of wool. They swam for a little in the warm fish-eye, then returned through the deepening night to the town.

For the rich there were, after dinner, cabaret shows with expensive drinks and genuinely white prostitutes at ten dollars. For the poor, in the back streets, the mulatto women sat at the doors that opened directly in to lighted bedrooms.

'If one were really conscientious,' said Anthony, as they walked back late that night to the hotel, 'I suppose one would have to go and infect oneself with syphilis.'

The smell of sweat, the smell of alcohol, the smells of sewage and decay and cheap perfumes; then, next morning, the Canal, the great locks, the ship climbing up from one ocean and down again to the other. A more than human achievement that made it possible, Mark explained, smiling anatomically, to transport whores and whisky by water instead of overland from Colon to Panama.

(4) DARIEN

John Keats,
On First Looking into Chapman's Homer

Keats described the thrill of reading Chapman's translation of Homer by comparing himself to one of the great conquistadores, but it was Balboa who stood on a peak in Darién, not Cortez (actually, Cortés), the conqueror of Mexico. Darién is today a town in the central hills of Panama.

Much have I travelled in the realms of gold,
And many goodly states and kingdoms seen;
Round many western islands have I been
Which bards in fealty to Apollo hold.
Oft of one wide expanse had I been told
That deep-browed Homer ruled as his demesne;

Yet did I never breathe its pure serene
Till I heard Chapman speak out loud and bold:
Then I felt like some watcher of the skies
When a new planet swims into his ken;
Or like stout Cortez when with eagle eyes
He stared at the Pacific – and all his men
Looked at each other with a wild surmise –
Silent, upon a peak in Darien.

(5) The Panama Canal

Malcolm Lowry, *Through the Panama*

Lowry dates his entry to his autobiographical story, narrated by Sigbjørn Wilderness, of a log of a sea trip down from Vancouver to Panama as 27 November 1947. Lowry placed notes in the margin taken from Helen Nicolay's book on the building of the Canal, The Bridge of Water, concerning William Patterson and the Darién expedition. 'Through the Panama' appears in Hear Us O Lord from Heaven Thy Dwelling Place – see Booklist.

Going down, at 7 am, between bouys, passing, at bouy 7, going the other way, the SS *Parthenia*, out of Glasgow; emerald palm trees, a road house on piles blinking its light, to the right; very green to right and left; to the left an island like a cupcake, completely flat, marshy land and a stretch of emerald jungle like chicory salad, and palms, with white houses showing through and what looks like a nice beach, bouys like little Eiffel Towers – ahead, the green light marks the first écloue (lock) – really beautiful beach to the left now beneath the chicory salad round the corner; Balboa to the right as we approach first buoy, palm trees and objects that look like country clubs, golf courses; left it gets more jungly – 20 or 30 frigate birds to the right, then a launch comes alongside and 20 Negroes carrying canvas bags climb up a pilot ladder
. . .
    The first lock: Miraflores: 1913. Gigantic iron-studded gates very high but looking too narrow for a ship to steer into – but we do.
    We ascend 54 feet through double lock.
    1000 birds of bad omen.
    Second lock: Pedro Miguel: 1913.
    We ascend 31 feet in second, single lock (symbolic) in 10 minutes.
    Culebra cut.
    Blackest history of canal's horror, failure, collapse, murder, suicide, fever, at Culebra cut. Now one glides through a narrow canal, gorgeous jungle like a wall on both sides, 2 minutes lost here would mean death,

or a very peculiar new life – monkeys, birds, orchids, sinister orchestrations from the jungle. Hot here as a Turkish bath in hell. Jungle has to be chopped every day.

Memorial tablet on a rock.

Apparatus as for foghorns, remote waterfalls. Besetting fear, as a writer taking notes, of being taken for a spy.

(6) PANAMA CITY

Iain Banks, *Canal Dreams*

Banks apparently has not visited Panama, but he sets his gripping novel there – a story of US trickery on ships stranded in the Panama Canal, on Lake Gatun. The reader is led into Panama City through the guidebooks that Hisako Onoda, the Japanese musician heroine, reads.

Mr Mandamus stirred his mint tea and looked out on to the Avenida Central, where the clogged traffic honked and hooted furiously, and outrageously decorated buses full of brightly dressed people contrasted with the matt camouflage of the Guards' jeeps and trucks.

They had started at the Santa Ana Plaza, where Mr Mandamus, guidebook in hand, led them down Calle 13 after having his shoes polished twice. Hisako, Mr Mandamus said, was the only Japanese person he'd ever encountered who didn't own – indeed had never owned – a camera. She agreed it was unusual. Officer Endo took photographs of everything, in a manner Mr Mandamus obviously considered a much more satisfyingly traditional Japanese fashion.

Hisako spent much time and money on Calle 13. The street was packed with shops and shoppers. She bought Kantule perfume from the San Blas archipelago, a *chaquira* necklace made by the Guaymí Indians, a ring with a small Columbian emerald set in it, a *chácara* bag, a circular *pollera* dress, a *montuna* shirt and several *molas*, a small pillow, a bedspread, and three blouses. Mandamus bought a hat. Broekman stocked up on Cuban cigars. Endo bought a *mola* for his wife and two extra diskettes for his camera. The men helped her carry all her shopping. Broekman thought some of the natives looked shifty, especially as Hisako had collected enough loot on her shopping expedition to make a *conquistadore* jealous.

They trooped down to the docks and through the fish market, then got lost in a maze of small, crowded, noisy streets. Mr Mandamus was delighted; the area was called 'Sal si puedes', which meant 'Get out if you can', and it was traditional to get lost in it.

(7) PANAMA CITY

William Burroughs, *Queer*

*Burroughs's tough gay junkie Lee passes through Panama City
('how I hate your cheatin' guts') in the late 1940s on his way to
find yage, the hallucinatory drug, in Ecuador.*

Every time I hit Panama, the place is exactly one month, two months,
six months more nowhere, like the course of a degenerative illness. A
shift from arithmetical to geometrical progression seems to have
occurred. Something ugly and ignoble and subhuman is cooking in this
mongrel town of pimps and whores and recessive genes, this degraded
leech on the Canal.

A smog of bum kicks hangs over Panama in the wet heat. Everyone
here is telepathic on the paranoid level. I walked around with my
camera and saw a wood and corrugated iron shack on a limestone cliff
in Old Panama, like a penthouse. I wanted a picture of this excresc-
ence, with the albatrosses and vultures wheeling over it against the hot
gray sky. My hands holding the camera were slippery with sweat, and
my shirt stuck to my body like a wet condom.

An old hag in the shack saw me taking the picture. They always
know when you are taking their picture, especially in Panama. She
went into an angry consultation with some other ratty-looking people I
could not see clearly. Then she walked to the edge of a perilous balcony
and made an ambiguous gesture of hostility. Many so-called primitives
are afraid of cameras. There is in fact something obscene and sinister
about photography, a desire to imprison, to incorporate, a sexual
intensity of pursuit.

(8) PANAMA CITY

Graham Greene, *The Captain and the Enemy*

*Greene's protagonist has arrived in Panama City during Gener-
al Torrijos's rule (1968–81), and is shown the city by his
left-wing guard.*

To escape boredom I asked Pablo not only to guard me – from what? –
but to show me his city. It was a city of steep hills and torrential
rainstorms which lasted for less than a quarter of an hour and yet made
miniature Niagaras down the streets, leaving cars stranded. It was also a
city of slums as Mr Quigly had mentioned to me, not only of banks. In
the quarter which was called ironically Hollywood it was a shocking
contrast to see the tumbledown shacks on which the vultures lodged

and in which whole families were crowded together in the intimacy of complete poverty only a few hundred yards from the banks, where the high windows glittered in the morning sun, and it was even more of a shock to gaze into the American Zone across the mere width of a street, and see the well-kept lawns and the expensive villas on which no vulture ever cared to settle. On our side of the road which was called the Street of the Martyrs, and had been named, Pablo told me, after some old conflict between American Marines and students, it seemed I was subject to Panamanian law, while on the other side I would be in the American zone and I could be hauled away there for any infringement of the American law and tried in New Orleans. More and more I wondered what had induced the Captain to settle in this city, for there were no signs of any gold outside the coffers of international banks and I doubted his capacity to break a bank.

One day Pablo took me for a drive the whole length of the immaculate green Zone. I felt all the more astonished that such riches could exist in sight of such poverty without any customs officer or frontier guard to keep the inhabitants of Hollywood from breaking in. I forget what words I used to express my amazement, but I remember Pablo's reply. 'This is not only Panama. This is Central America. Perhaps one day . . .' He patted the holster at his side. 'One needs better weapons than a revolver, you understand, to change things.'

(9) PANAMA CITY

Graham Greene, *Getting to Know the General*

In 1977, Greene visited the slums in Panama City.

In the absence of Chuchu it was the Sandinistas who arranged for me to visit Hollywood, the slum lying on the edge of the American Zone. A visit, they told me, was unsafe without the escort of an inhabitant, but one of their number knew of one who would ensure our safety.

Hollywood proved to be a horrifying huddle of wooden houses sunk in rain water like scuttled boats and of communal lavatories which stank to heaven and leaked into the water around. At a sheltered corner an old woman sat selling marijuana, and we were followed step by wet step by a smoker who was half-senseless with the drug and who asked us questions which we didn't answer and wanted to lead us where our guide and protector had no wish to go.

I thought with wonder of the neat lawns, and the golf courses, and the fifty-three churches half a mile beyond the unmarked frontier.

(10) PORTOBELO

Graham Greene, *Getting to Know the General*

Greene evokes the history of Portobelo, once the port for all the
Spanish crown's Peruvian booty.

Portobelo is fantastically beautiful. Little seems altered since Drake's
day when the town stood at the end of the gold route from Panama
City. Here is still the treasure house where the gold awaited shipment
to Spain, the three forts guarding the town, the ramparts which are
lined now with vultures: vultures too were sitting on and around the
cross of the cathedral. From the door of the cathedral one could see
nothing of the village, only the jungle descending like a curtain, dark
and impenetrable, to within fifty yards of the door. There seemed little
room among the stone ruins even for the small population of two
thousand. The statue of a black Christ presided over the altar. It had
been shipwrecked on the way to the Viceroy of Peru and salvaged by
the Indians.

Biographies and important works

BANKS, Iain (1954–). Banks was
born on 16 February 1954 in Fife,
Scotland, and now lives in Edinburgh. His *Canal Dreams*, 1989 (Extract 6), is a brilliantly crafted revenge story. The title refers to a
Japanese cellist who hates flying, and
who, on her way to give concerts in
Europe by boat, finds herself trapped
on the **Panama Canal** during a local
war, with awful nightmares that turn
out to be true. The novel was written
before Bush's 1989 US invasion.
Three ships are stranded on the lake,
with skeleton crews. One night they
are boarded by *venceristas* (cf Che
Guevara's battle cry 'Venceremos' –
'We will overcome') but when Hisako
is asked to play the cello to the leader
she discovers he is blond, a *gringo*.
Her lover, and the crews, are slaughtered, and she is raped, before she

escapes and slowly kills off all the fake
revolutionaries in this 'quite lawless'
place. Between scenes from the present in **Lake Gatun** in the Panama
Canal we learn about Hisako's
Japanese life: her poor mother, her
music training, her fear of flying and
her lovers, and how she once killed a
policeman during a student riot. The
CIA dress up as *venceristas* in order to
shoot down a plane-load of US sena-
tors, and then blame the real *venceristas*, in order to eliminate them. The
secret CIA leader tells Hisako that he
has perpetrated this fake revolutionary attack to keep trade free.

BOWLES, Jane (1917–73). Born in
New York, Jane Bowles started writing early. In 1938 she married the
composer, and later writer, Paul

Bowles (◊ Guatemala), and lived a nomadic life in Central America, Mexico, Sri Lanka, settling in Tangiers in 1947. In 1957 she suffered a cerebral haemorrhage, and had to stop writing. She died in Málaga, Spain, in 1973. Her only novel, *Two Serious Ladies*, 1943 (Extract 2), creates two separate stories about upperclassy, asexual ladies breaking away from their moneyed and educational privileges. The idiosyncratic Christina Goering and Mrs Copperfield meet up in a bar at the end. There are no explanations for the odd behaviour of the characters. Mrs Copperfield's fascination with a Panamanian whore, Pacífica, in **Colón**, allows Jane Bowles to explore the differences between Latin and American women. Pacífica was 'completely natural'; Mrs Copperfield begs, 'if only you could stop me thinking'. It is a novel about fantasies, suggested lesbianism. In 1944, Jane Bowles published a short story, 'A Guatemalan Idyll', about a timid US travelling salesman in a Guatemala City *pensión*, and the strange guests. Again, American-ness is put into question: 'Here we are in a crazy Spanish country'. 'Señorita Córdoba', another story, takes the same *pensión*, and deals with the fantasy of Paris in the mind of a woman intent on seducing a man for money. In 1938 Jane visited Panama with Paul Bowles. See Millicent Dillon, *A Little Original Sin: The Life and Work of Jane Bowles*, Virago, London, 1988.

BURROUGHS, William (see under Mexico).

GREENE, Graham, (1904–1991). See also under Mexico, Argentina, Paraguay. His Panamanian novel, *The Captain and the Enemy*, 1988 (Extract 8), takes as narrator a typic-

al, ignorant Brit and sends him to a dangerous Central American republic in the final section. This narrator is attracted to an eccentric, lawbreaking adventurer and ends up in 'lawless' Panama. Much of the novel is based on dialogue. Apart from fleshing out the realities of Panama for a British reader, the novel deals with the 'complexity of human love'. Part 3 is set in Torrijos's 'poor, beautiful, bizarre' Panama. The reader is led slowly into Panama, a 'little capitalist state with a socialist general, split in two by the Americans'. **Panama City** has hundreds of banks and the climate is violent and tropical. There are clear divisions between the **American Zone**, with its well kept lawns, and the slums. The Captain is on the side of Torrijos, the socialist general, and flies arms to the Sandinistas in the hills. The narrator's bodyguard Pablo also wants to 'change things' violently. We meet Colonel Martinez, head of intelligence (allegedly based on Noriega), but less informed than the CIA. Both the Captain and the narrator are killed by the CIA, echoing Torrijos's own mysterious plane crash and death.

In *Getting to Know the General: The Story of an Involvement*, 1984 (Extracts 9 and 10), Greene tells the love-story of his five trips to Panama. Latin American politics gripped him because it was a matter of 'life and death'. He outlines a history of Panama from Drake to Torrijos's death in 1968. Greene befriended his interpreter, the womanizing Chuchu, a professor of mathematics called José de Jesús Martínez, a sergeant in Torrijos's security guard. He confesses, 'I had little Spanish with which to communicate', even in Mexico in 1938 he managed only 'the present tense'. Despite this Greene travels round the country visiting the island of **Taboga**, **Portobelo**, the slum ironically called

Graham Greene in 1982

Hollywood, Nombre de Dios (no lon-ger on the map), the **Canal Zone** itself, as well as neighbouring Belize, Costa Rica and Nicaragua, with the *South American Handbook*, relieved about 'its habitual frankness'. He meets Ernesto Cardenal (◊ Nicar-agua), and befriends García Márquez (◊ Colombia), with whom he travels to Washington on a Panamanian passport to witness the Carter–Torrijos signing of the new Canal treaty.

HUXLEY, Aldous (see under Mex-ico).

KEATS, John (1795–1821). Keats, who was born in London, never travelled further than Rome, where he died of tuberculosis. However, a sonnet written in 1816 alludes to Panama, the newly discovered Pacific Ocean, and a peak in Darién, though 'stout Cortez' is wrong (Extract 4).

LOWRY, Malcolm (1909–1957). See also under Mexico. His autobiog-raphical story 'Through the Panama' (Extract 5) appeared posthumously in *Hear Us O Lord from Heaven Thy Dwelling Place*, 1961, and follows Sigbjørn Wilderness and his wife as jotted down in a boat trip journal from Vancouver to France, through the **Panama Canal** in 1947. As the boat passes the Mexican coast, Wilderness remembers Acapulco as a 'filthy mean little place' (no wonder, for in 1946 Lowry was kicked out of Mexico' a second time). When the Liberty ship reaches Panama the reader is shown a complete immigration form in Spanish and English. He gives us facts and figures on the Canal. He describes arriving at **Balboa**, and the locks.

SIENKIEWICZ, Henryk (1846–1916). Sienkiewicz was born in Wola Okrzejska, Poland, and died in Vevey, Switzerland. From poor gentry, he studied at Warsaw, became a journalist and published his first novel in 1872. His fame rests on his historical novel dealing with Nero, *Quo Vadis*, 1896, translated in 1941. In 1905 he won the Nobel Prize. A selection of his short stories, set all over the world, including Panama (Sienkiewicz was a perpetual traveller) came out in English in 1931 (Extract 1).

COLOMBIA

'One morning, after almost two years of crossing, they became the first mortals to see the western slope of the mountain range. From the cloudy summit they saw the immense aquatic expanse of the great swamp as it spread out toward the other side of the world.'
Gabriel García Márquez,
One Hundred Years of Solitude

Colombia, or the República de Colombia, is named after Christopher Columbus, although he never set foot in present-day Colombia. The country today is twice the size of France, and the fourth largest in South America with 1 138 908 sq km of territory. It is bounded by Venezuela, Brazil, and Ecuador, and has both Pacific and Caribbean coasts. The land is split by three mountain chains. The main one is the Cordillera Central of the Andes, with several peaks of more than 5000 m (the **Nevado de Huila**, the **Nevado de Ruiz**, etc) and a Western and Eastern chain. The Eastern chain is the most densely populated, with the capital **Bogotá de Santa Fe**, at 2640 m, the cool, misty and once most Catholic city in South America. In 1985 the population of Colombia was 29 482 000, with that of Bogotá reaching 4 185 000. Bogotá remains the cultural capital, but unlike many other Latin American countries does not have a high proportion of the country's population. The main reason for this is that the high mountain chains and deep *barrancas* have cut the regions off from one another. Both Joan Didion (◊ El Salvador) and Christopher Isherwood ◊ have described the capital (Extracts 2 and 3). Colombia's second city is **Medellín**, with a population of 2 069 000 in 1985, in the Western chain, today the centre of the incredibly lucrative cocaine business, but traditionally the business and industrial centre of Colombia. The *antioqueños* (from the **Antioquía** region) are said to have derived from Sephardic Jews (expelled from Spain in 1492). The third city is **Cali** in the Cauca River valley with a population of 1 398 276 in 1985. Around Cali are sugar cane fields.

THE THREE ZONES

All Colombia lies in the tropics with a wet and dry season, but the climate depends more on height than latitude. The country can be divided into three well defined zones, known in Spanish as *tierra caliente*, *tierra templada* and *tierra fría*. In the hot zones, particularly on the Pacific Coast with a high rainfall, you find a predominantly negro population (negro and *zambo* – negro and Indian interbreeding – account for some 18% of the country). The Caribbean coastal lowlands hold around 17% of the population, and the oldest towns. **Cartagena** was founded in 1533, and for centuries was the Crown monopoly port for all Peruvian silver and gold. Cartagena was sacked by Sir Francis Drake in 1586 who extorted a fabulous ransom which he sent home to the Queen. This deed surfaces in Gabriel García Márquez's ◊ fiction as folk memory. It is in this region that the great **Magdalena River** (1545 km long) runs into the sea among vast swamps (*ciénagas*). The river is a waterway that links these lowlands with the distant capital, and features in many García Márquez novels (*Love in the Time of Cholera* (Extract 5) and *The General in his Labyrinth* (Extract 9). Alexandre von Humboldt was one of the earliest to try to map this river when he went upstream in 1802. And the liberator Simón Bolívar died on his way downstream in 1830. Christopher Isherwood ◊ travelled upstream in 1947.

On the Caribbean coast you find **Barranquilla**, **Santa Marta**, and **Aracataca** (founded in 1885, with a population of 35 000 in 1987), supposedly the Macondo of *One Hundred Years of Solitude* (Extract 4), and *García Márquez's birthplace*, where there is today a small museum (**Carrera 5, 6–35, Aracataca**: you can take the Fundación bus from Santa Marta bus station and ask to get off at the Las Palmeras cafe – most of the locals know the museum, which is pictured in the 'Biographies' section of this chapter). This coast was devoted to banana production, mainly owned by the United Fruit Company. The 'banana fever' led to a boom in investment there, most of which left for the USA. In 1928, there was a strike, and workers were machine-gunned to death outside the railway station in **San Juan de la Ciénaga**: the incident is recreated in a chapter in *One Hundred Years of Solitude*. The whole of this isolated region forms the vivid background for García Márquez's fictional worlds. One of the appeals of García Márquez's fiction is that a forgotten, isolated region like the Caribbean coast entered the literary map of Colombia. For another novelistic recreation by a friend of 'Gabo' from the coast see Alvaro Cepeda Samudio (1926–), *La casa grande*, 1962 (*La Casa Grande*, 1991).

The second zone is the **Oriente**, the vast plains or *llanos* that end up in luxuriant jungle. Here there are cattle farms, and rubber tapping was important early in the century. On the whole, it remains wild and isolated and the picture that emerges from Rivera's ◊ novel *The Vortex* (Extract 8) has not changed much. The Colombian Amazon region contains 38.5 million hectares of jungle, with nearly 75% still forested and incredibly rich in species diversity (over 4000 species of butterflies). The Colombian government today is carrying out a pioneering scheme to preserve this jungle and give land back to the jungle Indians. This takes the form of *resguardos* or reservations.

The third zone is the **Andean** which includes Bogotá and has 78% of the country's population, including most of its Indians (some 300 000 today). Colombia is really a *mestizo* country, but some 26% could be said to be pure white.

Under Spanish Rule

Before discovery the Andean chain was home to the Sinú and Chibcha Indians whose stunning gold artefacts are today housed in **Bogotá's Gold Museum.** There are traces of earlier Indian civilizations, such as the recently discovered **San Agustín statues** in the **Magdalena River valley,** or the **Ciudad perdida** of the Taironas found by tomb robbers (*guaqueros*) in the jungle near **Santa Marta.** When the gold hungry Spaniards first arrived and travelled up the Magdalena seeking El dorado in 1525 they had no time to understand or preserve these Indian civilizations, and imposed Catholicism and Crown rule, making them work on *encomiendas*, or in mines. **Bogotá** was founded by Gonzalo Jiménez de Quesada in 1538. Pablo Neruda's (◊ Chile) poem about him pleads with nature to stop him – 'Now they've entered the forest: / now they're plundering, biting, killing. / O Colombia, defend the veil / of your secret red jungle' – but it was hopeless and Quesada murdered the Indians in his way.

Colombia under Spain was made an *audiencia* from 1550 to 1740, and then the Viceroyalty of New Granada from 1717–1723, and definitively from 1740 until Independence. This area included Venezuela and Ecuador. A good account of life during the later years can be read in Alexandre von Humboldt's (◊ Venezuela) *Travels.*

Colombia has always been known for its emphasis on education, especially under the Viceroy Caballero y Góngora, 1782–88, and early appointed a botanist, Celestino Mutis, to record its flora (his drawings have been recently rediscovered in Madrid).

As with all the Spanish American colonies the French invasion led to secession from Spain. The first uprising in Colombia on 20 July 1810 is today celebrated as Independence Day. It led to civil war, with the Spaniards reconquering their colony in 1814–16 to be finally defeated by Simón Bolívar at **Boyacá** in 1819. A new entity called Gran

Gabriel García Márquez

Colombia was set up under Bolívar, and his underling Santander but this collapsed while Bolívar was in Peru. For a while he returned as dictator in 1828–30, but, as we learn in García Márquez's novel *The General in his Labyrinth*, 1990 (Extract 9), about Bolívar's last journey down the Magdalena in 1830 to die in **Santa Marta**, he was completely cynical about his dreams for a federal Latin America. It is here that he wrote: 'America is ungovernable. He who serves a revolution ploughs the sea'.

The rest of nineteenth century political life was a battle between conservatives and liberals, with further civil wars in 1840–42, until in 1886 what is today Colombia was finally declared a Republic. A good portrait of the country at this time is Isaac Holton's *New Granada: Twenty Months in the Andes*, 1857. The background to Jorge Isaac's ◊ romantic novel *María* (Extract 7) also alludes to this period. The conservatives were in power from 1886 to 1930, with a further massacre called 'The War of a Thousand Days' in 1899–1902, seeing some 100 000 dead. Colonel Buendía in *One Hundred Years of Solitude*, and the anonymous Colonel from *Nobody Writes to the Colonel* fought on the liberal, losing side. This period also saw the loss of Panama in 1903 with the cynical complicity of the USA (see chapter on Panama), not finally recognized by Colombia until 1921.

The next period in Colombia's history, following a deal between conservatives and liberals to share power, emerged after the street assassination of the popular leader Jorge Gaitán in 1948, which led to three days of violence known as the *bogotazo*, a stage of seige lasting from 1949 to 1958, a period known as *La violencia*, or sectarian killings, that ended with over 260 000 corpses. Many Colombian novels try to recreate and understand this vicious period, including Daniel Caicedo's *Viento seco*, 1954; Eduardo Caballero Calderón's *Cristo de espaldas*, 1953, and *Siervo sin tierra*, 1954; and Manuel Mejía Vallejo's *El día señalado*, 1964. All are set in isolated communities, but, apart from García Márquez's earlier fiction, few of these novels have been translated. An exception is Manuel Zapata Olivella's *En Chimá nace un santo*, 1963 (*A Saint is Born in Chimá*, 1991), in which a cripple is saved from dying in a fire; it is called a miracle and this cripple becomes a cult for the poor, and a symbol of their resistance to the Church authorities. Colombia has had few military coups, but General Rojas Pinilla thought he had to put order into his land and came to power in 1953 and remained until 1958.

Since then, Colombia has returned to democratically elected presidents. However, the tenor of life changed in the 1960s when guerrilla groups took to the hills and jungles, and the drug barons started their own war. This has led to many further deaths, culminating in the guerrillas' seizure of the *Law Courts* and killing of 11 judges in 1985. One charismatic person to emerge from the violent 60s was father Camilo Torres, a priest who took to the armed struggle and was killed in 1966.

CONTEMPORARY CULTURE

As in all Latin American countries, there is a marked split between the cultured urban and Europeanized cities and the hinterlands. Most of Colombia's writers have lived in the urban centres, and their work reflects their problems, as in the case of José Asunción Silva, Colombia's first modernist writer, who committed suicide in 1896 and whose work recreates in *Bogotá* the inner conflicts of European city inhabitants, such as the rise of a new moneyed bourgeoisie and the spiritual values of art.

Another constant of Latin American culture is the problem of 'nationalistic' art. Silva has as much in common with fellow Latin Americans like Darío (◊ Nicaragua), and European poets, as with

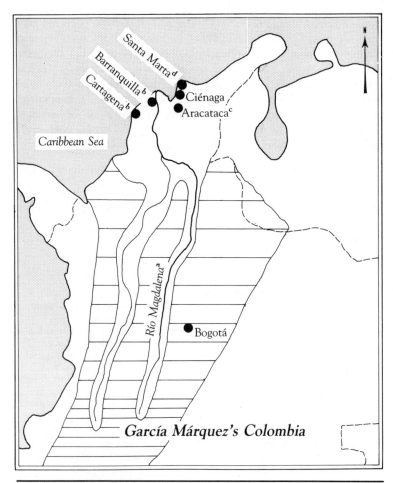

García Márquez's Colombia

Notes to map: [a]*It is up the Magdalena that García Márquez's aged lovers go in Love in the Time of Cholera, 1985, and down which a moribund Simón Bolívar descends in The General in his Labyrinth, 1989;* [b]*See Love in the Time of Cholera, and Chronicle of a Death Foretold, 1981;* [c]*García Márquez's birthplace (now a small museum), probably the 'pueblo' (village) in his No One Writes to the Colonel, 1961, and source for Macondo in One Hundred Years of Solitude, 1967;* [d]*also described by Joan Didion and Paul Bowles.*
Ruled area = mountainous region.

fellow 'Colombians'. Just as Silva reacted to the trends of his day from a cosmopolitan position, so did all the later avant-garde movements in Colombian literature, especially in their version of 'Beat' poetry, the *Nadaístas*. Another writer from the surrealist tradition awaits translation – Alvaro Mutis (1923–   ). One of the best younger poets of today, Juan Gustavo Cobo Borda (1949–   ), has taken an ironic view of having been born in Colombia. In his poem 'Bogotá D.E.', the grand past shrinks to a loud *bolero*, for the music of *cumbia*, Mexican television and soap operas mean more than literature. Colombia's grand old man of letters, Germán Arciniegas (1900–   ), has written outstanding essays explaining his country and continent for outsiders, including a biography of Quesada, *The Knight of El Dorado*, 1942, and a history of the Caribbean, *Caribbean: Sea of the World*, 1946.

BOOKLIST

The following selection includes all titles which are extracted in this chapter as well as those mentioned in the introduction which are available in English. In general, paperback editions are given when possible. The editions cited are not necessarily the only ones available. For most of the extracted works, the original publisher in English can be found in 'Acknowledgments and Citations' at the end of the volume, as can the exact location of the extracts and the editions from which they are taken. The date in square brackets is the original publication date of the work in its original language. Extract numbers are highlighted in bold for ease of reference.

Arciniegas, Germán, *Caribbean: Sea of the World* [1945], Harriet de Onís, trans, Knopf, New York, 1946.

Arciniegas, Germán, *The Knight of El Dorado* [1942], Mildred Adams, trans, Greenwood Press, Westport, CT, 1968.

Bowles, Paul, 'Call at Corazón', in *Call at Corazón* (short stories), Abacus, London, 1989/*Collected Stories*, Black Sparrow Press, Santa Barbara, CA, 1980. **Extract 10.**

Didion, Joan, *The White Album* [1979], Penguin, London, 1981/ Farrar, Straus and Giroux, New York, 1990. **Extract 2.**

García Márquez, Gabriel, *Chronicle of a Death Foretold* [1981], Gregory Rabassa, trans, Jonathan Cape, London, 1982/Knopf, New York, 1982.

García Márquez, Gabriel, *The General in His Labyrinth* [1989], Edith Grossman, trans, Jonathan Cape, London, 1991/Knopf, New York, 1990. **Extract 9.**

García Márquez, Gabriel, *Love in the Time of Cholera* [1985], Edith Grossman, trans, Jonathan Cape, London, 1988/Knopf, New York, 1988. **Extract 5.**

García Márquez, Gabriel, 'Tuesday's Siesta', in *No One Writes to the Colonel and Other Stories* [1961], J.S. Bernstein, trans, Picador, London, 1983/Harper and Row, New York, 1968. **Extract 1.**

García Márquez, Gabriel, *One Hundred Years of Solitude* [1967], Gregory Rabassa, trans, Jonathan Cape, London, 1970/Harper and Row, New York, 1970. **Extract 4.**

Holton, Isaac, *New Granada: Twenty*

Months in the Andes [1857], Southern Illinois University Press, Carbondale, IL, 1967.

Isaacs, Jorge, *María: A South American Romance* [1867], Rollo Ogden, trans, Harper and Brothers, New York, 1890. **Extract 7.**

Isherwood, Christopher, *The Condor and the Cows*, Methuen, London, 1949. **Extract 3.**

Olivella, Manuel Zapata, *A Saint is Born in Chimá* [1963], Thomas E. Kooreman, trans, University of Texas Press, Austin, TX, 1991.

Rivera, José Eustacio, *The Vortex* [1924], Earle K. James, trans, Putnam, New York, 1935. **Extract 8.**

Samudio, Alvaro Cepeda, *La Casa Grande* [1962], Seymour Menton, trans, University of Texas Press, Austin, TX, 1991.

Solano, Armando, in *The Green Continent*, Harriet de Onís, trans, Poetry London Editions, London, 1947. **Extract 6.**

von Humboldt, Alexandre, *Travels* [1834], Jason Wilson, trans, Penguin, London, 1993.

Extracts

(1) Aracataca

Gabriel García Márquez, *Tuesday's Siesta*

A mother and daughter, dignified but very poor, arrive in the 'Pueblo' (Aracataca) to lay flowers on the tomb of her son, who was shot dead as a thief by an old widow. They arrive in siesta time – hence the title of the story – and wake the dozing priest for the key to the cemetery. 'Tuesday's Siesta' is in No One Writes to the Colonel and Other Stories – see Booklist.

By twelve the heat had begun. The train stopped for ten minutes to take on water at a station where there was no town. Outside, in the mysterious silence of the plantations, the shadows seemed clean. But the still air inside the car smelled like untanned leather. The train did not pick up speed. It stopped at two identical towns with wooden houses painted bright colors. The woman's head nodded and she sank into sleep. The girl took off her shoes. Then she went to the washroom to put the bouquet of flowers in some water.

When she came back to her seat, her mother was waiting to eat. She gave her a piece of cheese, half a cornmeal pancake, and a cookie, and took an equal portion out of the plastic sack for herself. While they ate, the train crossed an iron bridge very slowly and passed a town just like the ones before, except that in this one there was a crowd in the plaza. A band was playing a lively tune under the oppressive sun. At the other side of town the plantations ended in a plain which was cracked from the drought.

The woman stopped eating.

'Put on your shoes,' she said.

The girl looked outside. She saw nothing but the deserted plain, where the train began to pick up speed again, but she put the last piece of cookie into the sack and quickly put on her shoes. The woman gave her a comb.

'Comb your hair,' she said.

The train whistle began to blow while the girl was combing her hair. The woman dried the sweat from her neck and wiped the oil from her face with her fingers. When the girl stopped combing, the train was passing the outlying houses of a town larger but sadder than the earlier ones.

'If you feel like doing anything, do it now,' said the women. 'Later, don't take a drink anywhere even if you're dying of thirst. Above all, no crying.'

The girl nodded her head. A dry, burning wind came in the window, together with the locomotive's whistle and the clatter of the old cars. The woman folded the plastic bag with the rest of the food and put it in the handbag. For a moment a complete picture of the town, on the bright August Tuesday, shone in the window. The girl wrapped the flowers in the soaking-wet newspapers, moved a little further away from the window, and stared at her mother. She received a pleasant expression in return. The train began to whistle and slowed down. A moment later it stopped.

There was no one at the station. On the other side of the street, on the sidewalk shaded by the almond trees, only the pool hall was open. The town was floating in the heat. The woman and the girl got off the train and crossed the abandoned station – the tiles split apart by the grass growing up between – and the street to the shady sidewalk.

It was almost two. At that hour, weighted down by drowsiness, the town was taking a siesta. The stores, the town offices, the public school were closed at eleven, and didn't open until a little before four, when the train went back. Only the hotel across from the station, with its bar and pool hall, and the telegraph office at one side of the plaza stayed open. The houses, most of them built on the banana company's model, had their doors locked from inside and their blinds drawn. In some of them it was so hot that the residents ate lunch in the patio. Others leaned a chair against the wall, in the shade of the almond trees, and took their siesta right out in the street.

(2) BOGOTA

Joan Didion, *The White Album*

Novelist and journalist Joan Didion visited Bogotá, and its
nearby underground salt cathedral Zipaquirá, in 1974.

First there was the mine. Tunneled into a mountain in Zipaquirá, fifty
kilometers north of Bogotá, is a salt mine. This single mine produces,
each year, enough salt for all of South America, and has done so since
before Europeans knew the continent existed: salt, not gold, was the
economic basis of the Chibcha Empire, and Zipaquirá one of its
capitals. The mine is vast, its air oppressive. I happened to be inside
the mine because inside the mine there is, carved into the mountain
450 feet below the surface, a cathedral in which 10 000 people can hear
mass at the same time. Fourteen massive stone pilasters support the
vault. Recessed fluorescent tubes illuminate the Stations of the Cross,
the dense air absorbing and dimming the light unsteadily. One could
think of Chibcha sacrifices here, of the *conquistador* priests struggling to
superimpose the European mass on the screams of the slaughtered
children.

But one would be wrong. The building of this enigmatic excavation
in the salt mountain was undertaken not by the Chibcha but by the
Banco de la República, in 1954.

(3) BOGOTA

Christopher Isherwood, *The Condor and the Cows*

The British novelist passed through Bogotá in October 1947 with
the painter William Caskey on his way down to Buenos Aires.

Obviously, the Hotel Astor was once a private house. It is a gloomy
rambling old place, built around an interior court-yard which the rain
has filled with dismal puddles. Downstairs there is a long dark
dining-room, decorated and furnished in a style which Caskey describes
as Hollywood Baronial; it has a massively carved mantelpiece and
several sideboards stacked with heavy silver plate. At tea-time this is
the rendezvous of Bogotá's upper class ladies. Mostly in elegant black,
with furs and jewels, they form big gaily chattering groups, eat
enormously and later retire to play bridge. The food is very good here,
but you get far too much of it. The waiters seem quite dismayed because
we can't manage five courses.

There is no public lounge, unless you count a large half-lit,
windowless hallway out of which several bedrooms open, on the upper

floor. It has little furniture; one sofa, two or three chairs and a telephone which would appear to have been installed here in order that the maximum number of people can overhear a conversation. We have already noticed that the acoustics in Bogotá are almost painfully good. Perhaps this is because of the altitude. Nothing escapes you – no sound in the next room, no voice in the courtyard, no footstep on the stairs. As for the traffic outside, it seems noisier than Third Avenue; the taxi-horns jab at your nerves like pins. We have to sleep with the windows closed. This doesn't matter much, however, because our room is enormous and anyway very cold.

The Carrera Septima, on which this hotel stands, is one of Bogotá's main business streets. It has no character, beyond a superficial North American showiness. There are neon lights, US advertisements with Spanish captions, movie theatres with Hollywood films, bars decorated in New York style, department stores full of US gadgets, fashions and drugs.

(4) The Caribbean Coast: 'Macondo'

Gabriel García Márquez,
One Hundred Years of Solitude

Macondo is the haunting name Márquez gave to his fictive Caribbean coastal town, near the Magdalena River. It is a backwater far removed from Bogotá. Although it does not exist on the map, Macondo is a microcosm of a Colombian small town, with its military, whores, intrigues, and incests. The novel encapsulates Macondo's history, from its founding in the nineteenth century up to the banana boom and massacre in the 1920s and its eventual transition to a ghost town.

One morning, after almost two years of crossing, they became the first mortals to see the western slopes of the mountain range. From the cloudy summit they saw the immense aquatic expanse of the great swamp as it spread out toward the other side of the world. But they never found the sea. One night, after several months of lost wandering through the swamps, far away now from the last Indians they had met on their way, they camped on the banks of a stony river whose waters were like a torrent of frozen glass. Years later, during the second civil war, Colonel Aureliano Buendía tried to follow that same route in order to take Riohacha by surprise and after six days of traveling he understood that it was madness. Nevertheless, the night on which they camped beside the river, his father's host had the look of shipwrecked people with no escape, but their number had grown during the crossing and they were all prepared (and they succeeded) to die of old age. José Arcadio Buendía dreamed that night that right there a noisy city with houses having mirror walls rose up. He asked what city it was and they answered him with a name that he had never heard, that had no meaning at all, but that had a supernatural echo in his dream: Macondo. On the following day he convinced his men that they would never find the sea. He ordered them to cut down trees to make a clearing beside the river, at the coolest spot on the bank, and there they founded the village.

José Arcadio Buendía did not succeed in deciphering the dream of houses with mirror walls until the day he discovered ice. Then he thought he understood its deep meaning. He thought that in the near future they would be able to manufacture blocks of ice on a large scale from such a common material as water and with them build the new houses of the village. Macondo would no longer be a burning place, where the hinges and the door knockers twisted with heat, but would be changed into a wintry city.

(5) CARTAGENA

Gabriel García Márquez,
Love in the Time of Cholera

Doctor Urbino, who married Fermina and left her secret lover in the cold, goes to the poor quarter of Cartagena to visit the mistress of his chess-playing companion who has killed himself.

In his effort to find a shorter route, the coachman braved the rough cobblestones of the colonial city and had to stop often to keep the horse from being frightened by the rowdiness of the religious societies and fraternities coming back from the Pentecost liturgy. The streets were full of paper garlands, music, flowers, and girls with colored parasols, and muslin ruffles who watched the celebration from their balconies. In the Plaza of the Cathedral, where the statue of The Liberator was almost hidden among the African palm trees and the globes of the new streetlights, traffic was congested because Mass had ended, and not a seat was empty in the venerable and noisy Parish Café. Dr Urbino's was the only horse-drawn carriage; it was distinguishable from the handful left in the city because the patent-leather roof was always kept polished, and it had fittings of bronze that would not be corroded by salt, and wheels and poles painted red with gilt trimming like gala nights at the Vienna Opera. Furthermore, while the most demanding families were satisfied if their drivers had a clean shirt, he still required his coachman to wear livery of faded velvet and a top hat like a circus ringmaster's, which, more than an anachronism, was thought to show a lack of compassion in the dog days of the Caribbean summer.

Despite his almost maniacal love for the city and a knowledge of it superior to anyone's, Dr Juvenal Urbino had not often had reason as he did that Saturday to venture boldly into the tumult of the old slave quarter. The coachman had to make many turns and stop to ask directions several times in order to find the house. As they passed by the marshes, Dr Urbino recognized their oppressive weight, their ominous silence, their suffocating gases, which on so many insomniac dawns had risen to his bedroom, blending with the fragrance of jasmine from the patio, and which he felt pass by him like a wind out of yesterday that had nothing to do with his life. But that pestilence so frequently idealized by nostalgia became an unbearable reality when the carriage began to lurch through the quagmire of the streets where buzzards fought over the slaughterhouse offal as it was swept along by the receding tide. Unlike the city of Viceroys where the houses were made of masonry, here they were built of weathered boards and zinc roofs, and most of them rested on pilings to protect them from the flooding of the open sewers that had been inherited from the Spaniards. Everything looked wretched and desolate, but out of the sordid taverns came the thunder of riotous music, the godless drunken celebration of Pentecost by the poor.

(6) Cartagena

Armando Solano

Here is a picturesque description of Cartagena ('One of the most interesting towns in South America' – South American Hand-book) by a Colombian historian. The passage is extracted from the anthology The Green Continent – see Booklist.

To the eager visitor who reaches its gates Cartagena is like a vision of the Orient. It is a white city, whose roofs and façades are wildly ablaze with violent colours of African intensity. Cupolas, balconies, windows, under the vivid light of the sun, make the sight one of aerial festivity. In its upper stories the city lives a fantastic life, a fitting counterpart to that of its narrow streets flanked by broad windows with grilles of wrought iron, high sidewalks, storied doorways which permit a glimpse of the dewy shadows of broad, flowering Andalusian patios with the dark and green mirrors of their thirsty cisterns. Neither Toledo nor any other city of old Spain can have preserved a purer or more genuinely Spanish air than this quiet city of Colombia where the colony left such a deep and indelible trace. There is not a single detail that breaks this exquisite harmony. Even the language of the populace, even the graphic exclamations and insults which the negroes hurl at one another from the driver's seat of their little carts when they get in one another's way, have the most typical and genuine flavour that can be imagined. These people use words of old Spanish, words that are no longer in circulation in the language of educated people and which are rollicking and dashing in their old age. And the agreeable impression this causes wherever one goes, in the market-place where the glittering fish are strewn upon the sand and the turtles paddle in little fenced-off mud puddles, at the doors of the churches, in the public square, is intensified and reinforced by the background against which it is set. There are dark, gloomy shops which offer for sale delicious traditional confectionery and pastries; the poorer classes – in Cartagena, as in the other cities of the coast, Barranquilla, Santa Marta, understand good food, possess a pleasant, primitive sybaritism, and often indulge in Homeric culinary satisfactions undegraded by the excessive use of alcohol. The mass of people love easy, comfortable, abundant, gay living.

(7) THE CAUCA VALLEY

Jorge Isaacs, *María*

*The love-lost protagonist in this romance returns home to the
Cauca Valley not yet realizing that his María has died. 'Hula' is
a reference to the mountain Nevado de Huila (5750m).*

At four the next afternoon I reached the summit of the Cruces. There I dismounted to tread again the soil whence I had said farewell to my native country. Again I saw the valley of Cauca, a land as fair as I was unfortunate. So often had I dreamed of beholding it from that very mountain that even when I saw it before me in all its beauty I looked around to make sure that it was not a trick of sleep. My heart beat faster, as if it had a presentiment that María's head would soon rest upon it. My eyes were fixed on the hills at the foot of the afternoon sun – where my father's house was whitening.

Lorenzo had just caught up with me, leading by the halter a fine white horse which he had got in Tocotá for me to mount, the last three leagues of the day's ride . . .

The afternoon was expiring when I turned the last promontory of the Montañuelas. A rush of wind from the west was whistling about me among the rocks and thickets, and rumpling my horse's flowing mane. My father's house could no longer be seen on the edge of the horizon at my left; but on the right, far away, under a turquoise sky, was the glint of Huila's bulk, half covered by floating haze.

He who created that, I said to myself, cannot yet destroy the most beautiful of His creatures, whom He has permitted me to love so much. Again I forced back sobs that were choking me.

I had now passed on my left the pleasant and beautiful valley of Peñon, worthy of its lovely river. The city had gone to sleep upon its green and cushioned breast. Like a flock of great birds soaring in search of their nests, the foliage of the palms could be seen above it, lighted up by the moon.

(8) COLOMBIA: THE JUNGLE

José Eustacio Rivera, *The Vortex*

In his novel, Rivera describes the horror of the Colombian jungle that most of his countrymen never see, and that will in the end swallow alive his poet protagonist Arturo Cova and his pregnant mistress Alicia.

For the first time I saw the inhuman jungle in all its horror, saw the pitiless struggle for existence. Deformed trees were held imprisoned by creepers. Lianas bound them together in a death grip. Stretched from tree to palm in long elastic curves, like carelessly hung nets, they caught falling leaves, branches and fruits held them for years until they sagged and burst like rotten bags, scattering blind reptiles, rusty salamanders, hairy spiders and decayed vegetable matter over the underbrush.

Everywhere the *matapalo* – the pulpy creeper of the forests – sticks its tentacles on the tree trunks, twisting and strangling them, injecting itself into them, and fusing with them in a painful metempsychosis. The *bachaqueros* vomit forth trillions of devastating ants. These mow down the mantle of the jungle and return to their tunnels over the wide swaths they cut, carrying leaves aloft like the banners of an army of extinction. The *comejen* grub gnaws at the trees like quick-spreading syphilis, boring unseen from within, rotting tissue and pulverising bark, until the weight of the branches that are still living brings the giant crashing to the ground.

Here the aphrodisiac parasite that covers the ground with dead insects, the disgusting blooms that throb with sensual palpitations, their sticky smell intoxicating as a drug; the malignant liana, the hairs of which blind animals; the *pringamosa* that irritates the skin; the berry of the *curuju*, a rainbow-hued globe that holds only a caustic ash; the purging grape; the bitter nut of the corojo palm.

This sadistic and virgin jungle casts premonitions of coming danger over one's spirits. Vegetable life is a sensitive thing, the psychology of which we ignore. In these desolate places only our presentiments understand the language it speaks. Under its influence man's nerves become taut and ready to attack, are ready for treachery and ambush. Our senses confuse their tasks; the eye feels, the back sees, the nose explores, the legs calculate, and the blood cries out: 'Flee! Flee!'

And yet, it is civilised man who is the champion of destruction. There is something magnificent in the story of those pirates who enslave their peons, exploit the environment, and struggle with the jungle. Buffeted by misfortune, they leave the anonymity of cities to plunge into the wilderness, seeking a purpose for their sterile life. Delirious from malaria, they loose themselves of their conscience and adapt themselves to the environment; and with no arms but the rifle and the machete, they suffer the most atrocious needs, while longing for pleasures and plenty. They live exposed to the elements, always ravenous, even naked, for here clothes rot on one's body.

Then some day, on the rock of some river, they build their thatched hut and appoint themselves 'masters of the enterprise'. Although the jungle is their enemy, they don't know whom to fight; so they fall upon one another and kill and subdue their own kind during intervals in their onslaught on the forests; and at times their trail is like that left by an avalanche. Every year the rubber workers in Colombia destroy millions of trees, while in Venezuela the balata rubber tree has disappeared. In this way they defraud the coming generations.

(9) The Magdalena Estuary

Gabriel García Márquez,
The General in His Labyrinth

> The dying liberator Simón Bolívar, in this novel about his last days, reaches the estuary of Colombia's prime river, the Magdalena, and its swamps, the Ciénaga Grande.

The channels through Ciénaga Grande, the great swamp, were slow and hot and gave off fatal vapors, and so they traveled on the open sea, taking advantage of the first trade winds from the north, which were early and benign that year. A cabin was ready for him on the well-maintained square-sailed brigantine, which was clean and comfortable and had a lighthearted way in the water.

The General boarded in good spirits and wanted to remain on deck to see the estuary of the Great Magdalena River, whose mud gave an ashen color to the water for many leagues out to sea. He was wearing old corduroy trousers, the Andean cap, and an English sailor's jacket given him by the captain of the frigate, and his appearance improved in the sunlight and the vagabond breeze. In his honor the frigate's crew caught a gigantic shark, in whose belly they found a variety of metal objects, including a pair of spurs. He enjoyed everything with a tourist's pleasure until he was overcome by fatigue and sank down into his own soul. Then he signaled José Palacios to approach and whispered in his ear:

'Papa Molinares must be burning the mattress and burying the spoons by now.'

Towards midday they passed Ciénaga Grande, a vast extension of muddy waters where all the birds of the air fought over a school of golden mojarra. On the burning saltpeter plain between the swamp and the sea, where the light was clearer and the air was purer, there were fishing villages with tackle spread out to dry in the patios, and beyond them lay the mysterious town of La Ciénaga, whose diurnal phantoms had caused the disciples of Humboldt to doubt their science. On the other side of Ciénaga Grande rose the crown of eternal ice on the Sierra Nevada.

(10) Pedernales

Paul Bowles, *Call at Corazón*

Bowles's abstract intellectual American tourist watches women washing, and analyses his own mind, near Pedernales in Colombia's Magdalena delta. 'Call at Corazón' is in Collected Stories – see Booklist.

After he had bought the monkey and tied it to the metal post of the bunk in the cabin, he took a walk to explore the port. It was a town made of corrugated tin and barbed wire. The sun's heat was painful, even with the sky's low-lying cover of fog. It was the middle of the day and few people were in the streets. He came to the edge of the town almost immediately. Here between him and the forest lay a narrow, slow-moving stream, its water the color of black coffee. A few women were washing clothes; small children splashed. Gigantic gray crabs scuttled between the holes they had made in the mud along the bank. He sat down on some elaborately twisted roots at the foot of a tree and took out the notebook he always carried with him. The day before, in a bar at Pedernales, he had written: 'Recipe for dissolving the impression of hideousness made by a thing: Fix the attention upon the given object or situation so that the various elements, all familiar, will regroup themselves. Frightfulness is never more than an unfamiliar pattern.'

He lit a cigarette and watched the women's hopeless attempts to launder the ragged garments. Then he threw the burning stub at the nearest crab, and carefully wrote: 'More than anything else, woman requires strict ritualistic observance of the traditions of sexual behaviour. That is her definition of love.' He thought of the derision that would be called forth should he make such a statement to the girl back on the ship. After looking at his watch, he wrote hurriedly: 'Modern, that is, intellectual education, having being devised by males for males, inhibits and confuses her. She avenges . . .'

Two naked children, coming up from their play in the river, ran screaming past him, scattering drops of water over the paper. He called out to them, but they continued their chase without noticing him. He put his pencil and notebook into his pocket, smiling, and watched them patter after one another through the dust.

When he arrived back at the ship, the thunder was rolling down from the mountains around the harbor. The storm reached the height of its hysteria just as they got under way.

Biographies and plot summaries

BOWLES, Paul (see under Mexico). He was a short while in **Santa Marta**, Colombia in 1934, and set his short stories 'The Echo' and 'Call at Corazón' (Extract 10) there.

DIDION, Joan (see under El Salvador).

GARCIA MARQUEZ, Gabriel (1928–). García Márquez was born on 6 March 1928 in the tropical Caribbean coastal town of **Aracataca**, and brought up by his grandparents until he won a scholarship to a boarding school in **Bogotá** at the age of 8. He went on to the university, but left in 1948 after the *bogotazo* (the assassination of Gaitán and subsequent street violence). Back on the coast in **Cartagena** he began his career as a journalist, which he continued for

three years in Paris from 1957, and then for the Cuban press agency Prensa Latina in New York in 1961. He has lived most of his adult life abroad in exile since marrying in 1958, mainly in Mexico City, where from 1961 he wrote film scripts. He was a friend of Omar Torrijos of Panama, and remains close to Fidel Castro. In 1982 he won the Nobel prize for literature.

García Márquez began publishing short stories in 1947 (see his *Collected Stories*, 1984). His first novel *La hojarasca* came out in 1955 (*Leaf Storm and Other Stories*, 1972) after seven years of rejections. Like many of his later novels this was set in 'Macondo', a tropical backwater in the **banana plantation region**, where people barely survive in the lethargy induced by the heat and the oppressive politics, with a few rebels who come alive because of their vitality and humour. Here, as later, the geography and climate are determinants. In 1961 he published his own favourite, written in Paris in 1957, *El coronel no tiene quien le escriba* (*No One Writes to the Colonel and Other Stories*, 1968). Set in a tropical dump, under a petty ogre the mayor, it chronicles the old, honest colonel and his wife resisting their oppressive circumstances, and waiting both for a pension and the cock fight that will change their lives. In a laconic, and very visual prose we learn about their dead son, their poverty, the colonel's humour, the political background, and village life. The author is not interested in motivation or mental life, but depicts his characters through actions, visually, as if on a screen. It makes them very human, unpredictable and enigmatic.

In 1962 he published his third novel *La mala hora* (*In Evil Hour*, 1980) with vivid descriptions of village life in this forgotten, swampy area of Colombia, miles away from highland Bogotá, with the plot centring on mysterious posters appearing on the walls denouncing those in power. García Márquez's Caribbean roots and childhood continued to haunt him, and in 1965 he wrote *Cien años de soledad*; it was finally published in 1967 (*One Hundred Years of Solitude*, 1970 – Extract 4), for many his masterpiece and the book whose sales allowed García Márquez to live from his writings alone. It chronicles the rise and fall of a patriarchal family, the Buendías, cursed by a prediction, and searching for love and happiness, and only finding it at the end as the dynasty fades and Macondo is blown off the map. The novel is full of wonderful details that the author assures are true but that were read as magical, from priests levitating to beautiful girls flying off with the laundry. It is a compendium of Latin American history, where Macondo

Winner of the 1982 NOBEL PRIZE FOR LITERATURE

ONE HUNDRED YEARS OF SOLITUDE

GABRIEL GARCÍA MÁRQUEZ

PICADOR

stands for Colombia, and the rest of the continent. Here García Márquez perfects his dead-pan chronicler style, with lists and hyperbole, long descriptions and short, pithy dialogues. The novel is also an act of remembering, the unofficial recording of life on the coast up to the banana boom, fighting 'the state of idiocy without a sense of the past'.

García Márquez explored the loneliness of power developing the character of his memorable Colonel Buendía into a novel about a mother-obsessed dicator, narrated by the people in long sentences close to poetry – *El otoño del patriarca*, 1975 (*The Autumn of the Patriarch*, 1983). He returned to his more concise style with *Crónica de una muerte anunciada* in 1981 (*Chronicle of a Death Foretold*, 1982), about the passivity of people in **Cartagena** in not stopping the murder they all knew was going to happen. It is a marvellous exploration of machismo, honour, small-town mentality, and a puzzling over what really happened. He returned to the

The birthplace of García Márquez in Aracataca, now the Casa Museo
Gabriel García Márquez.

broad canvas in 1985 with *El amor en
los tiempos del cólera* (*Love in the Time
of Cholera*, 1988 – Extract 5), detail-
ing coastal life in a composite of
Cartagena, **Santa Marta** and **Barranquilla**, with its heat, insects and
smells, around an impossible love
affair at the turn of the century that
reaches fruition only when the two
lovers are in their seventies, after
living full lives (one as a happy wife to
a doctor, the other as a silent Don
Juan who remained faithfully in love
for 51 years, 9 months and 4 days,
despite his 622 love affairs), and sail
up the **Magdalena River** in a river-
boat making love. In 1989 García
Márquez published his eighth novel,
El general en su laberinto (*The General
in his Labyrinth*, 1990 – Extract 9)
based on the last months of South
America's great liberator Simón Bolívar as he sails down the **Magdalena** to
die. Here the style is held together by
historical research, exploring the
familiar Marquesian themes of love
and power.

García Márquez has published jour-
nalistic pieces (*The Story of a Shipwrecked Sailor*, 1982 and *Clandestine in

Chile: the Adventures of Miguel Littín,
1987), and is currently at work on his
memoirs. He has said that he is a
realist because in Latin America everything is possible, everything is
real.

ISAACS, Jorge (1837–1895). Although born in Colombia, Isaacs
came from English Jewish roots. He
studied medicine in **Bogotá** and London. Sent back home because his
father went bankrupt, he worked on
the construction of a road from **Calí**
to the sea. He was a poet; he became
editor of a newspaper, *La República*;
he took up the post of Consul in
Chile; and he fought in the civil wars.
Isaacs was particularly interested in
Indian life, and the countryside outside the large cities. He published
María, 1867 (*María: A South American Romance*, 1890 – Extract 7), a
romantic tale concerning María, an
orphan brought up by relatives, whose
son falls in love with her. He is sent
abroad to study, and she dies just as
he is about to reach home again. The
novel is set in the local countryside

that Isaacs knew well. The colonial *hacienda* **'El Paraíso'**, near **Palmira**, in the Departamento of Valle, Calí, where Isaacs wrote his novel, can be visited.

ISHERWOOD, Christopher (1904–1980). Isherwood was born at High Lane, Cheshire, and died in California. After graduating from Cambridge, he went as a teacher to Berlin, then emigrated to California in 1939 where he lived from writing scripts. In 1947 Isherwood travelled down the west coast of South America with the painter William Caskey, and kept a diary on which *The Condor and the Cows*, 1949 (Extract 3) is based. The pair travelled from **Cartagena** in Colombia to Lima in Peru (there are photos of the surrealist poet Emilio Adolfo Westphalen and the painter Fernando de Szylo) to Buenos Aires, where they met Victoria Ocampo (◊ Argentina) and Jorge Luis Borges (◊ Argentina) whose photograph appears in a light-hearted but observant travelogue.

RIVERA, José Eustacio (1889–1928). Born in **Neiva** on 19 February 1889, Rivera was fifth son of a landowning family. Expelled from boarding school in 1902, he started work as a clerk and then studied with a scholarship in **Bogotá** in 1906–09. He began writing poems in 1907. Protesting the separation of Panama from Colombia, Rivera was briefly imprisoned. He was appointed schools inspector in **Ibagué**, where he first learnt about the Amazon world, travelling around the country, especially the *llanos* (cattle plains). He graduated as a lawyer in **Bogotá** in 1917, got a job in the **Casanare** where he worked from 1918 to 1920. He published a book of 55 sonnets in 1921. He then served on a government commission to trace the boundaries between Colombia and Venezuela, where he got to know first hand the rough and violent life of the jungle rubber workers and Tomás Funes, the *cacique*. He campaigned on their behalf and wrote *La vorágine*, 1924 (*The Vortex*, 1935 – Extract 8), based on the lawless jungle, narrated by an unbalanced Romantic poet Arturo Cova, on the run with his pregnant mistress Alicia. The couple flee **Bogotá**, pass through the *llanos* and end up in the **jungle**, where Cova hears about and meets the rubber barons, especially a woman. The novel ends with the couple disappearing into the vortex. *The Vortex* suggests the uselessness of civilized values like love, or legality in the jungle where only survival matters. It is also a critique of machismo. In 1928 Rivera travelled to the USA via Cuba, hoping to sell the film rights, and died suddenly in New York on 1 December 1928.

SOLANO, Armando (1887–1953). Solano was born in **Paipa, Boyacá** on 17 December 1887, and died in **Bogotá**. He was a lawyer, diplomat, journalist and writer. His books included a study of his country, *Colombia*, and another on Colombia's cities, *País de ciudades*.

VENEZUELA

'This house, this pioneer
democracy, built / on
foundations, not of rock,
but blood as hard as rock.'
Robert Lowell, Notebook

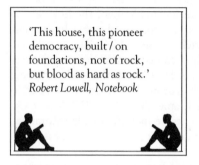

Venezuela, or the República de
Venezuela, was named by the
Florentine explorer Amérigo Ves-
pucci, who first called the New
World the 'New World' and who
lent his surname to it (America).
He called the country 'Little
Venice' when he saw Indian
fishermen's huts on stilts. Columbus had discovered Venezuela
on his third voyage in 1498.
Venezuela, with its 912 050 sq km, is the sixth largest country in South
America, and has borders with Colombia and Brazil and disputed ones
with Guyana, claiming some 150 000 sq km of territory. It has 2813
km of coastline, and lies entirely within the tropics with a climate
largely dependent on elevation. There are rainy and dry seasons. The
population reached some 19.7 million in 1990 with a large majority
(74%) living in urban areas. Venezuela is a *mestizo* country (70%) with
a white proportion of 20% partially from oil workers and limited
immigration in 1945. On the coasts, there are negroes (8%), and some
32 000 unassimilated Indians (2%) in remote areas. Spanish is spoken
by almost 95%. However, Venezuela is essentially an Andean country,
for 65% live in mountainous areas.

The country has every kind of climate and terrain, from snow-
covered peaks like the **Pico Bolívar** (5000 m), named after Simón
Bolívar the Caracas-born 'liberator', to tropical jungle and desert. Half
the land is forested, and the rest is native grass. This regional variety
probably allowed Joseph Conrad ◊ to make the Venezuela he barely
knew into Sulaco, representing all South America (see Extracts 5 and
11). The **Cordillera Oriental** of the Andes breaks into two lines with
the Cordillera of **Mérida** (Mérida is the Universidad de los Andes
campus town) containing most of Venezuela's towns and cities in fertile
basins, including **Caracas** at 910 m, with its population of nearly 4
million, and its port **La Guaira**. Caracas, founded in 1567 on an
earthquake fault, is today a sky-scraper, car-dominated city (see

Lowell's poem – Extract 1), based on oil revenue. It was the birthplace of **Simón Bolívar** whose reconstructed house is a **museum**, and whose body lies in the **Panteón Nacional**. The German explorer Alexandre von Humboldt ◊ lived in Caracas in 1800, and was the first to climb the nearby **Avila** mountain that today is a national park, with a cable car and a **Hotel Humboldt** on top.

Half of Venezuela comes under the name of the **Guyana Highlands**, an ancient mountainous formation virtually devoid of people (3% of population). In the sixteenth century it was near the source of the **Orinoco River** that greedy Europeans located Manao, the Eldorado of gold streets, near a non-existent Lake Parima, sought after by Raleigh ◊. However, in 1864 the world's richest mine, El Callao, was found there, with huge deposits of iron ore, linked to well-developed cities like **Ciudad Guayana** on the Orinoco. Here also is the world's highest waterfall, the **Angel Falls** with a 979 m drop, discovered in inaccessible country by an American pilot called James Angel in 1935. Just across the border in Guyana lies the jungle table mountain called **Roraima**, where Sir Arthur Conan Doyle (◊ Brazil) set his dinosaurs in his novel *The Lost World*, 1912.

The **Orinoco**, Latin America's third largest river, drains an enormous forested area. The river is about 2400 km long, and at one point the land is so flat that a tributary flows back, joins the Rio Negro, and flows out into the Amazon. This **Casiquiare** canal was first travelled along by Alexandre von Humboldt and his companion Aimé Bonpland, as recorded in wonderful detail in Humboldt's *Travels*, 1825 (Extract 2). In the 1950s, Alejo Carpentier ◊ travelled up the Orinoco while living in exile in **Caracas**, and based his quest novel *Los pasos perdidos*, 1953 (*The Lost Steps*, 1956 – Extract 6) on his excursion. More recently, Redmond O'Hanlon travelled in Humboldt's footsteps in *In Trouble Again. A Journey Between the Orinoco and the Amazon*, 1988. Rómulo Gallegos ◊ set his jungle novel *Canaima*, 1935 (*Canaima*, 1984 – Extract 9) near **Ciudad Bolívar** (earlier Angostura, giving its name to the 'bitters', a febrifuge bark). Henri Charrière (◊ French Guiana), on the run from Devil's Island, ended up in the Venezuelan jungle near this same city (Extract 3). It was in the Venezuelan jungle that W.H. Hudson ◊ set his romance *Green Mansions*, 1904 (Extract 12).

The *llanos* or natural treeless grass plains are cattle country, and are the scene for Gallegos's most famous novel *Doña Bárbara*, 1929 (*Doña Bárbara*, 1931), in which the city-born landowner challenges the amoral *cacica*, epitomizing the spirit of the wild plains, defeats her and marries her daughter in an allegory of Venezuela's racial and cultural future. Incidentally, Gallegos describes in detail the customs of the countryside south of the Apure River, a tributary of the Orinoco, with its canoes in canals, and rodeos. It is a novel-cum-tourist guide.

Alexandre von Humboldt

Colonialism, Tyranny and Democracy

Venezuela was the first part of South America to be colonized by Europeans. The first Spanish settlers founded **Nueva Cádiz** on Cubagua island collecting pearls, especially off Margarita island. **Cumaná** was founded in 1523, and served as centre for countless expeditions to locate Eldorado. When gold was not found the area became settled by farmers who planted cacao, tobacco, coffee, indigo and dried beef called *tasajo* (*charque* in Argentina) for export. Venezuela remained a backwater during its colonial days. In 1717 it became the viceroyalty of New Granada, and then its own Captaincy General. It was also where the first outbreak of independence took place in 1797. A revolutionary called Francisco Miranda (he lived in London for a while in what is today Miranda House, 58 Grafton Street, WC1) landed in 1806 and by

1810 had set up a revolutionary *junta*, became a dictator, and was then betrayed and died in a Spanish prison. The same *junta* appointed Bolívar who, after several battles, led the country to Independence in 1821 as the República de Gran Colombia. He died in Colombia, embittered about politics (see García Márquez, *The General in his Labyrinth*). Bolívar was renowned in his day as one of the great romantic men of action, an intellectual Rousseau-ist, and friend of Humboldt. Even Lord Byron named a boat 'Bolívar' in the man's honour, and dreamed of going to Venezuela to fight. One of Venezuela's most respected journalists and novelists (he won the Cervantes Prize in 1991), Arturo Uslar Pietri (1906–   ), has a historical novel *Las lanzas coloradas*, 1931 (*The Red Lances*, 1963) set in Bolívar's period with a racial and cultural clash between a mulatto and a white. Uslar Pietri is accurate on details. Venezuela's other crucial figure is the educator Andrés Bello (1781–1865), a patriot, monarchist and poet, who lived 20 years in exile in London (1810–29), an agent of Venezuela's revolutionary *junta*, but he returned to Chile in 1829, where he published his work on Castilian grammar.

In 1829 Venezuela broke away and became what it is today. From the late 1820s to 1935, the nation suffered the '*época de caudillos*', one tyrant after another devastating the country. Some have stood out, like General José Antonio Paéz, the *llanero* (wild man from the plains) whose biography was written by Cunninghame Graham (◊ Paraguay). During Guzmán Blanco's dictatorship Venezuela lost border territory to Britain, hence the unsolved dispute with Guyana. In 1908 Juan Vicente Gómez, *el brujo* (the sorcerer) came to power until his death in 1935 – one of the worst of all Latin American dictators. Pablo Neruda (◊ Chile) wrote: 'Gómez, Venezuela's quagmire, / slowly submerges faces, / intellects, in his crater'. Gómez built a personal fortune with black gold or oil, discovered in 1914 and exported from 1917 to take up 90% of Venezuela's exports and convert the country into the richest in Latin America in the 1950s. By 1928 it was the world's second largest producer. Revenue from oil made the rich richer and the poor poorer, although education flourished, and public health eliminated malaria by the 1960s. Gómez's life as recounted by Thomas Rourke, himself a novelist (*Gómez: Tyrant of the Andes*, 1936), reads like grotesque magical realism.

For a brief moment, after a civilian coup in 1945, Venezuela held its first open elections with universal suffrage. The novelist Rómulo Gallegos was elected president in 1948, but before he could put into practice his progressive ideas he was ousted in the same year by another dictator, Pérez Jiménez, who remained in power until 1958. Pérez Jiménez invented a slogan '*sembrar petróleo*', ('sow petrol'), but it did not affect the majority. The novelist Isabel Allende ◊, in exile in

Caracas in the 1970s, created an imaginary town 'Agua Santa', where people remained poor, while nearby the oil men lived in modern compounds, divorced from the reality of the country (Extract 13). It is a metaphor of what happened from the 1930s to 1980s. At last, one of Venezuela's most literate politicians, Rómulo Betancourt, returned to power until 1963. From then Venezuela overborrowed, the oil market slumped, and the country became indebted, although still democratic.

Of all Venezuela's writers it is ex-president Rómulo Gallegos who most effectively tried to incorporate his diverse country and its history into fiction that deliberately includes most geographical areas with debates about how to create a Venezuela of the future. His novels are set in the *llanos*, in the jungle, on the coast. They deal with white landowners, wild *llaneros*, Indians, and mulattos. But most of his old-fashioned novels remain untranslated (*La trepadora*, 1925, about a mulatto who rises out of his class and marries well; *Cantaclaro*, 1934, set on the *llanos* with a folk-singer; *Pobre negro*, 1937, about racial conflicts; etc).

Thanks to oil, Caracas has always been a cultural centre, with a flourishing state publishing house (Monte Avila), excellent newspapers and critics (Juan Liscano and Guillermo Sucre are both poet–critics of the highest order), with literary prizes (the Rómulo Gallegos one of the richest), and many good but untranslated novelists like Miguel Otero Silva (1908–81), Guillermo Meneses (1911–), José Balza (1939–), Salvador Garmendia (1928–), Luis Britto García (1940–) and José Napoleón Oropeza (1950–). There are many excellent poets, including Liscano (1915–) and Sucre (1933–), mentioned above, and José Antonio Ramos Sucre (1890–1929) and Juan Sánchez Pelaez (1922–). Of Venezuelan writers translated, there is Ramón Díaz Sánchez ◊, with work set on the coast near **Cumaná** (Extract 10), and Teresa de la Parra (1889–1936), whose *Las memorias de Mamá Blanca*, 1928 (*Mama Blanca's Souvenirs*, 1959) is set in a childhood sugar plantation. Lisa St Aubin de Terán's ◊ two Venezuelan novels provide a vivid account of Venezuelan country life (Extract 4). A Venezuelan essayist, Mariano Picón Salas, has had his *A Cultural History of Spanish America: From Conquest to Independence*, 1962, translated.

The following cultural centres and writers' houses can be visited: **Casa Andrés Eloy Blanco**, Calle Sucre 79, Cumaná; the **Instituto de Investigaciones Literarias Gonzalo Picón Febres** at Prolongación Av 1, Mérida; the **Casa de la Cultura Carlos Gauna**, Avenida Las Lágrimas, Araure, Acarigua; and the **Fundación Casa Nacional de la Poesía Pérez Bonalde**, Avenida Luis Roche, Centro Rómulo Gallegos, Altamira, Caracas.

BOOKLIST

The following selection includes all titles which are extracted in this chapter as well as those mentioned in the introduction which are available in English. In general, paperback editions are given when possible. The editions cited are not necessarily the only ones available. For most of the extracted works, the original publisher in English can be found in 'Acknowledgments and Citations' at the end of the volume, as can the exact location of the extracts and the editions from which they are taken. The date in square brackets is the original publication date of the work in its original language. Extract numbers are highlighted in bold for ease of reference.

Allende, Isabel, *Eva Luna* [1987], Margaret Sayers Peden, trans, Hamish Hamilton, London, 1989/Knopf, New York, 1988. **Extract 13.**

Carpentier, Alejo, *The Lost Steps* [1953], Harriet de Onís, trans, Penguin, London, 1968/Knopf, New York, 1956. **Extract 6.**

Charrière, Henri, *Papillon* [1969], Patrick O'Brien, trans, Grafton, London, 1980/Penguin Books, New York, 1983. **Extract 3.**

Conrad, Joseph, *Nostromo* [1904], Penguin, London, 1963. **Extracts 5 and 11.**

Díaz Sánchez, Ramón, *Cumboto* [1950], John Upton, trans, University of Texas Press, Austin, TX, 1969. **Extract 10.**

Gallegos, Rómulo, *Canaima* [1935], Jaime Tello, trans, North American Association of Venezuela, Caracas, 1984/Oklahoma University Press, Norman, OK, 1991. **Extract 9.**

Gallegos, Rómulo, *Doña Bárbara* [1929], Robert Malloy, trans, Pe-

ter Smith Books, Magnolia, MA, 1948.

Hudson, W.H., *Green Mansions* [1904], Robin Clark, London, 1990/Dover, New York, 1989. **Extract 12.**

Humboldt, Alexandre von, *Travels* [1834], Jason Wilson, trans, Penguin, London, 1993. **Extract 2.**

Lowell, Robert, *Notebook*, Faber and Faber, London, 1970/Farrar, Straus and Giroux, New York, 1970. **Extract 1.**

Neruda, Pablo, 'Canto General', in *Selected Poems*, Anthony Kerrigan, trans, Jonathan Cape, London, 1970/Delacorte Press, New York, 1972. **Extract 7.**

O'Hanlon, Redmond, *In Trouble Again: A Journey Between the Orinoco and the Amazon*, Hamish Hamilton, London, 1988.

Parra, Teresa de la, *Mama Blanca's Souvenirs* [1928], Harriet de Onís, trans, Pan American Union, Washington, DC, 1959.

Raleigh, Sir Walter, 'The Discovery of the Large, Rich and Beautiful Empire of Guiana', in *Selected Writings*, Gerald Hammond, ed, Penguin, London, 1986. **Extract 8.**

Rourke, Thomas, *Gómez: Tyrant of the Andes*, William Morrow, New York, 1936.

Salas, Mariano Picón, *A Cultural History of Spanish America: From Conquest to Independence*, University of California Press, Berkeley, CA, 1962.

St Aubin de Terán, Lisa, *Keepers of the House* [1982], Penguin, London, 1983. **Extract 4.**

Uslar Pietri, Arturo, *The Red Lances* [1931], Harriet de Onís, trans, Knopf, New York, 1963.

Extracts

(1) CARACAS

Robert Lowell, Notebook

The US poet Robert Lowell visited Caracas in 1967 for a cultural congress, and wrote this sonnet.

Through another of our cities without a center, as hideous
as Los Angeles, and with as many cars
per head, and past the 20-foot neon sign
for *Coppertone* on a church, past the population
earning $700 per capita
in jerry skyscraper living-slabs, and on to the White House
of El Presidente Leoni, his small men with 18-
inch repeating pistols, firing 45 bullets a minute,
the two armed guards petrified beside us, while we had champagne,
and someone bugging the President: 'Where are the girls?'
And the enclosed leader, quite a fellow, saying,
'I don't know where yours are, but I know where to find mine.' . . .
This house, this pioneer democracy, built
on foundations, not of rock, but blood as hard as rock.

(2) CUMANA

Alexandre von Humboldt, Travels

On 16 July 1799, Alexandre von Humboldt and his botanist companion Aimé Bonpland arrived in Cumaná, and lived there a year while they explored the area. Here he describes the elation of stepping on to the New World.

Our eyes were fixed on groups of coconut trees that bordered the river, whose more than sixty feet high trunks dominated the landscape. The plain was covered with thickets of *Cassia*, capers and arborescent mimosa which, similar to Italian pines, spread their branches out like parasols. The pinnated leaves of the palms stood out against the blue sky without a trace of mist. The sun was climbing rapidly towards its zenith; a dazzling light spread through the atmosphere over the whitish hills covered in cylindrical cacti, as well as the becalmed sea and the shores populated with pelicans (*Pelicanus fuscus*, Lin), flamingoes and herons. The intense luminosity of the day, the vivid colours and forms of the vegetation, the variegated plumage of the birds, all bore the grand seal of tropical nature.

The town of Cumaná, capital of New Andalusia, lies a mile from the landing stage of the Boca battery where we stepped ashore after crossing the bar of the river Manzanares. We had to traverse a vast plain (el Salado), between the Guaiquerí dwellings and the coast. The reverberation from the parched land increased the intense heat. The thermometer, plunged into the white sand, reached 37.7°C . . . The first plant we gathered from American soil was the *Avicennia tomentosa* (Mangle prieto) which scarcely reaches two feet high here. This shrub, with the *Sesuvium*, the yellow *Gomphrena*, and the cacti, covered a ground saturated with soda salts; they belong to the scant social plants like European heaths, and in the torrid zone thrive only on the sea shore and high in the Andean plateaux . . .

The Indian pilot led us across his garden, that seemed more a copse than cultivated land. As proof of the land's fertility he showed us a silk-cotton tree (*Bombax heptaphyllum*) whose trunk measured nearly two and a half feet in diameter after only four year's growth. However, I think the Indian's estimate of the tree's age was somewhat exaggerated . . . Still on the Cumaná beach, in the Guaiquerí's garden, we saw for the first time a *guama* (*Inga spuria*) loaded with flowers, remarkable for the length and silvery brilliance of their numerous stamen. We passed the neatly arranged streets of the Indian quarters, bordered with small, new houses of attractive design. This part of the town has just been rebuilt after the earthquake a year and a half before our arrival that destroyed Cumaná. Hardly had we crossed the wooden bridge over the Manzanares river, full of bavas or small crocodiles, than we saw traces of that terrible catastrophe everywhere; new buildings rose over the ruins of the old.

(3) GUIRIA AND EL DORADO

Henri Charrière, *Papillon*

Escaped convict Charrière describes the ironically named El Dorado prison after his landing at Guiria, opposite the island of Trinidad.

Two hours later we reached a big village, a seaport that aspired to be a town: its name was Guiria. The administrator handed us over to the district chief of police himself. They treated us fairly well in the police station, but we were closely questioned, and the stupid official in charge of the interrogation absolutely refused to believe that we had come from British Guiana, where we had been free. And on top of that, when he asked us to explain how we came to reach Venezuela so exhausted and in such a state of destitution after so short a voyage as that from Georgetown to the Gulf of Paria, and I told him about the cyclone, he said we were making game of him . . .

As I've said, the port of Guiria is on the Gulf of Paria, over against Trinidad. It also has the advantage of being on the mouth of a huge river, the Orinoco, which is almost as big as the Amazon.

There we were, the five of us chained and ten policemen to look after us, and we travelled in the direction of Ciudad Bolívar, a big town that was the capital of the state of Bolívar. On these earth roads the journey was very tiring; we were all of us, prisoners and police, jerked and flung about like so many sacks of potatoes in the back of the lurching, bounding lorry; and it lasted for five days on end. Every night we slept on the lorry and the next morning we set off on this mad rush towards God knows where.

At last, five or six hundred miles from the sea, we reached our journey's end: it was where the earth road through the virgin forest from Ciudad Bolívar to El Dorado came to a halt. Both guards and prisoners, we were utterly exhausted by the time we reached the village.

Let me tell you about this El Dorado. To begin with it was the great hope of the Spanish conquistadores who saw that the Indians from those parts possessed gold and who firmly believed that there was a mountain of gold there: or if not entirely of gold then at least half gold and half earth. Now El Dorado is a village on the bank of a river full of caribes, of piranhas, those carnivorous fish that can entirely devour a man or an animal in a few minutes, and of tembladores – electric eels that instantly knock their victim with an electric shock and then later suck his rotting carcass. In the middle of the river there is an island, and on this island there was a real genuine concentration camp. This was the Venezuelan penal settlement.

(4) La Caldera,
Sierra Nevada de Merida

Lisa St Aubin de Terán, *Keepers of the House*

Lydia, the English girl married to the Beltran family, and pregnant, is forced to abandon their history-soaked farm in the Venezuelan Andes (Sierra Nevada de Mérida region) and, with her dead husband in the jeep, heads for La Caldera.

Lydia drove on to the town of La Caldera, stopping only once to shoot down one of the troop of vultures to decoy its brothers from Diego and herself. She passed the Plaza Bolívar, and the other square with its statue of General Mario and its derelict mansions; and she passed street after deserted street of rubble and clay. Even the cathedral had broken doors and windows, and what looked like a sand dune in its open aisle. The covered market-place flapped shreds of coloured canvas and the looted stalls were overturned. There were pieces of bone and skull in the most unexpected places, and many of the doors on many of the houses were barricaded and marked with a black cross as though for plague. The whole place was desolate. Lydia left the town behind her, and the cemetery that hemmed its outskirts, overflowing in endless skimped additions. Then the road took her downhill, past a disused barracks, to a wide bridge across the dry bed of the River Momboy, and she climbed once more with the road, to the hill that lay outside the town of La Caldera. It was a suddenly high place in the slow descent to the sea, and because there had once been a prison there, it was known by the name of Calvary. Lydia shot down one more vulture, buying her own time with its death: and, keeping her engine running, she stepped down for a moment to take one last look at the valley she was about to leave.

As she faced the highlands, she could see, to her right, the stone wall of the barracks of Escuque where the Massacre had taken place, and high on a hill above it, outlined against the sky, was the skeleton of the magnolia tree that Diego's grandfather had planted there as a token of thanks to the people who had helped him. Then, to her left, she saw the tall flue of her own mill chimney in the sun. It was the tallest chimney of its time in the Andes, and it stood like a cenotaph to all those who had given their lives to the hacienda.

(5) THE LLANOS

Joseph Conrad, *Nostromo*

*In Conrad's fictional Costaguana, closely based on his experi-
ences of Venezuela, Mrs Gould, British wife of the mine owner,
takes her first trip into the interior beyond Sulaco, and discovers
the llanos (cattle plains).*

Men ploughed with wooden ploughs and yoked oxen, small on a
boundless expanse, as if attacking immensity itself. The mounted
figures of *vaqueros* galloped in the distance, and the great herds fed with
all their horned heads one way, in one single wavering line as far as eye
could reach across the broad *potreros*. A spreading cotton-wool tree
shaded a thatched *ranche* by the road; the trudging files of burdened
Indians, taking off their hats, would lift sad, muted eyes to the
cavalcade raising the dust of the crumbling *camino real* made by the
hands of their enslaved forefathers. And Mrs Gould, with each day's
journey, seemed to come nearer to the soul of the land in the
tremendous disclosure of this interior unaffected by the slight European
veneer of the coast towns, a great land of plain and mountain and
people, suffering and mute, waiting for the future in a pathetic
immobility of patience.

(6) LOS ALTOS

Alejo Carpentier, *The Lost Steps*

*Cuban novelist Carpentier's jaded New Yorker musicologist
returns to his native Venezuela with his mistress Mouche on their
way up the Orinoco to research into the origins of music in a
stone-age tribe. At the time of writing, Carpentier was in exile in
Caracas.*

We got to Los Altos shortly after noon, by a little narrow-guage train
that looked like an amusement-park railway. I liked the place so much
that for the third time that afternoon, with my elbows on the railing of
the waterfall, I was looking out over what I had acquainted myself with
on my earlier walks. Nothing that met the eye was monumental or
impressive. Nothing had been transferred to picture post-cards or been
mentioned in guide-books. And yet I found myself in this provincial
corner, where every nook, every nail-headed door, spoke of a peculiar
way of life, a charm that the museum cities, with their over-admired,
over-photographed stones, had lost.

Seen by night, the city became an illuminated strip of a city set upon
a mountainside, with visions of glory and visions of hell created out of

the darkness by the street-lights. Those fifteen lights, abuzz with insects, had the isolating function of picture-illumination or theatre spot-lights, bringing into full relief the stations of the winding road that led to the Calvary of the summit.

(7) THE ORINOCO
Pablo Neruda, *Canto General*

The Chilean poet Pablo Neruda enumerates the great rivers of Latin America (Orinoco, Amazon, Tequendama, Bío-Bío, but not the Paraná) in his song to the geography and history of the region, the Canto General, 1950. This extract is taken from the translation by Anthony Kerrigan – see Booklist.

> Orinoco, let me stay on the banks
> of your hour without hour;
> leave me to go naked as then,
> to go into your baptismal darkness.
> Orinoco of the scarlet water,
> let me sink my hands returning
> to your maternity, to your coursing,
> river of races, bedrock of roots
> your ample murmur, your savage sheen
> comes from where I come, from the spare
> exultant heights, from out of a secret
> like a blood-stock, from out of a silent
> mother-source of clay.

(8) THE ORINOCO
Sir Walter Raleigh

Sir Walter Raleigh, writing in 1596, describes South America's third largest river (some 1900 km long). This passage is from his essay 'The Discovery of the Large, Rich and Beautiful Empire of Guiana'.

The great river of *Orinoco* or *Baraguan* hath nine branches which fall out on the north side of his own main mouth: on the south side it hath seven other fallings into the sea, so it disembogueth by 16 arms in all, between Islands and broken ground, but the Islands are very great, many of them as big as the Isle of *Wight* and bigger, and many less: from the first branch on the north to the last of the south it is at least 100 leagues, so as the river's mouth is no less than 300 miles wide at his entrance into the sea, which I take to be far bigger than that of *Amazones*: all those that inhabit in the mouth of this river upon the several north branches are these *Tivitivas*, of which there are two chief Lords which have continual wars one with the other: the Islands which lie on the right hand are called *Pallamos*, and the land on the left *Hororotomaka*, and the river by which *John Douglas* returned within the land from *Amana* to *Capuri*, they call *Macuri*.

These *Tivitivas* are a very much goodly people and are very valiant, and have the most manly speech and most deliberate that ever I heard of what nation soever. In the summer they have houses on the ground as in other places: In the winter they dwell upon trees, where they build very artificial towns and villages, as it is written in the Spanish story of the *West Indies*, that those people do in the low lands near the gulf of *Uraba*: for between May and September the river of *Orinoco* riseth thirty foot upright, and then are those Islands overflown twenty foot high above the level of the ground, saving some few raised grounds in the middle of them: and for this cause they are enforced to live in this manner. They never eat of any thing that is set or sown, and as at home they use neither planting nor other manurance, so when they come abroad they refuse to feed of aught, but of that which nature without labour bringeth forth. They use the tops of *Palmitos* for bread, and kill deer, fish and porks for the rest of their sustenance, they have also many sorts of fruits that grow in the woods, and great variety of birds and fowl.

(9) The Orinoco Delta

Rómulo Gallegos, *Canaima*

Marcos, the protagonist of the novel, begins to learn about the special nature of Venezuela's Orinoco Delta.

It was there where he learned since childhood and with efficiency of a vigorous instinct applied to a given aim, the only knowledge he was interested in – the geography of the vast region, which later on would be the fugitive setting of his life of adventurer.

The course of the large Guayana rivers and the way to pass from one to the other through the labyrinth of the tributaries, *caños*, and canoe-towing paths connecting them, the scarcely passable roads through intricate forests and uninhabited savannas, the uncertain course, known only by the Indians and just marked by the *arestín* growing along the old friars' road to reach Rionegro, avoiding the great Orinoco rapids and all the courses the natives know how to draw across that immense wilderness, and who of those Indians were the best rubber tree tappers, who were good tapioca makers, and where they lived. Live geography, learned through rubber seekers' stories, while for the dead one, the one taught at school, he had no inclination whatsoever.

One day, when a Rionegrego had brought along with him a Makiritare Indian from the Padamu banks to show him Angostura – as Ciudad Bolívar is called by the natives for whom a century and a half of republican history has not taken place, noticing that his native was being cut off from the general conversation, and wishing to free him from the children's curiosity, told him:

'You going with Marcos, not being a bad fellow,' said the Rionegrero, using the Indian way of talking the general language. 'He being your guide, and you knowing Angostura'.

(10) Venezuela: A Coconut Estate, Near Puerto Cabello

Ramón Díaz Sánchez, *Cumboto*

The novelist evokes a coconut estate called Cumboto, near Puerto Cabello, the port for Valencia, and the origins of the port itself.

The plantation still bears the region's original name – Cumboto – and stretches from the seacoast on the north to the foot of the mountain range on the south. Within its original boundaries villages sprang up, with their little squares and churches. It is crisscrossed by roads and rivers. The railroad line runs east and west, parallel to the main highway, and every day the piercing whistle of the locomotive makes us turn our heads and blink.

Along the coast the vegetation is coarse and twisted, like a Negro's hair. It is made up mostly of cactus, acacia, and other hostile plants. But farther inland, where the rivers moisten and soften the earth, the soil is black and the trees grow luxuriantly, with immense, spreading foliage at the top. Almost the entire estate was planted with coconut trees by some ancestor of Don Federico's, and a battery of vats for boiling the coconut oil was installed not far from the main house.

Once, when Don Federico's parents were still alive and the house was filled with laughter and he and I were children, I heard his father tell a story I have never forgotten. It was a Sunday morning and some visitors from the city were there. I was drilling holes in green coconuts to get the sweet, white milk to make a refreshing drink for the guests that hot summer day, and Doña Beatriz was playing the piano – some piece of music that was as slow and dark as the river. All at once Don Guillermo flung his enormous arms above his head and called out in his trumpet-like voice: 'Listen everybody!' he said. 'I'm going to tell you about the settling of this country and the founding of this plantation.'

Don Guillermo had been drinking a great deal of beer that morning, and he was as red as a crab.

'Before Puerto Cabello was built, the nearest town was Borburata, on the coast between the savanna of Santa Lucía and the beach called Gañango. Although it was a prosperous village, it was destined to survive only a short time. When Lope de Aguirre invaded the country the townspeople moved out, and the whole area was almost completely deserted. Some time later the Guipuzcoana Company was formed; this was a Spanish investment firm interested in exploiting the agricultural riches of Venezuela. That was the beginning of Puerto Cabello; the company, to protect its interests, built warehouses, walls and forts, a church, and a shipyard there. As for the Indians, we know hardly anything about them. It is generally believed that the people of Borburata and the employees of the Guipuzcoana Company were the first settlers, but that is not true: the Negroes had arrived before them.'

(11) VENEZUELA: 'COSTAGUANA'

Joseph Conrad, *Nostromo*

Although Joseph Conrad deliberately packs all Latin America into his invented Costaguana, he admitted (see biographical entry) that its geography was mainly Venezuelan, where he had once stayed in Puerto Cabello, its Golfo Triste, near the mountain Higuerota, named after a coastal Venezuelan village called Higuerote.

Sulaco had found an inviolable sanctuary from the temptations of a trading world in the solemn hush of the deep Golfo Placido as if within an enormous semi-circular and unroofed temple open to the ocean, with its walls of lofty mountains hung with the morning draperies of cloud.

On one side of this broad curve in the straight seaboard of the Republic of Costaguana, the last spur of the coast range forms an insignificant cape whose name is Punta Mala. From the middle of the gulf the point of the land itself is not visible at all; but the shoulder of a steep hill at the back can be made out faintly like a shadow on the sky.

On the other side, what seems to be an isolated patch of blue mist floats lightly on the glare of the horizon. This is the peninsula of Azuera, a wild chaos of sharp rocks and stony levels cut about by vertical ravines. It lies far out to sea like a rough head of stone stretched from a green-clad coast at the end of a slender neck of sand covered with thickets of thorny scrub. Utterly waterless, for the rainfall runs off at once on all sides into the sea, it has not soil enough – it is said – to grow a single blade of grass, as if it were blighted by a curse. The poor, associating by an obscure instinct of consolation the ideas of evil and wealth, will tell you that it is deadly because of its forbidden treasures. The common folk of the neighbourhood, peons of the *estancias*, *vaqueros* of the seabord plains, tame Indians coming miles to market with a bundle of sugar-cane or a basket of maize worth about threepence, are well aware that heaps of shining gold lie in the gloom of the deep precipices cleaving the stony levels of Azuera.

(12) VENEZUELA: THE JUNGLE

W.H. Hudson, *Green Mansions*

Hudson's Venezuelan narrator describes his joy at escaping city life in Caracas and returning to the jungle, where he will meet Rima, and have to face up to her death. Hudson never visited Venezuela, though he lived for 32 years in Argentina.

I spent several hours in this wild paradise, which was so much more delightful than the extensive gloomier forests so often penetrated in Guayana; for here, if the trees did not attain to such majestic proportions, the variety of vegetable forms was even greater; as far as I went it was nowhere dark under the trees, and the number of lovely parasites everywhere illustrated the kindly influence of light and air. Even where the trees were largest the sunshine penetrated, subdued by the foliage to exquisite greenish–golden tints, filling the wide lower spaces with tender half-lights, and faint blue-and-grey shadows. Lying on my back and gazing up, I felt reluctant to rise and renew my ramble. For what a roof was that above my head! Roof I call it, just as the poets in their poverty sometimes describe the infinite ethereal sky by that word; but it was no more roof-like and hindering to the soaring spirit than the higher clouds that float in changing forms and tints, and like the foliage chasten the intolerable noonday beams. How far above me seemed that leafy cloudland into which I gazed! Nature, we know, first taught the architect to produce by long colonnades the illusion of distance; but the light-excluding roof prevents him from getting the same effect above. Here Nature is unapproachable with her green, airy canopy, a sun-impregnated cloud – cloud above cloud; and though the highest may be unreached by the eye, the beams yet filter through, illuming the wide spaces beneath – chamber succeeded by chamber, each with its own special light and shadows. Far above me, but not nearly so far as it seemed, the tender gloom of one such chamber or space is traversed now by a sudden shaft of light falling through some break in the upper foliage, giving a strange glory to everything it touches – projecting leaves, and beard-like tufts of moss, and snaky bush-rope. And in the most open part of that most open space, suspended on nothing to the eye, the shaft reveals a tangle of shining silver threads – the web of some large tree-spider.

(13) VENEZUELA: VILLAGE LIFE

Isabel Allende, *Eva Luna*

Chilean writer Isabel Allende, in exile in Venezuela, invents a typical backwater village and calls it 'Agua Santa'.

Agua Santa was a modest village, with adobe, wood, and reed houses lining the roadway; machetes defended it against a wild vegetation that would engulf it in an instant's inattention. The country's waves of immigrants had not washed as far as this backwater, nor had the uproar of modern life; people were affable, their pleasures simple, and if it had not been for the proximity of the penal colony on Santa María, Agua Santa would have been a hamlet like any other in that region. The presence of the *guardia* and the whorehouse, however, gave it a touch of cosmopolitanism. For six days of the week, life went along without incident, but on Saturday they changed the guard at the prison and the off-duty sentries came to town to amuse themselves, altering the routine of the villagers, who tried to ignore them, pretending that the racket they raised came from a sabbat of monkeys in the treetops, but nonetheless taking the precaution of bolting their doors and locking up their daughters. The Indians also came to town on Saturday, to beg a banana, a swig of alcohol, or bread. They came in single file, ragged, followed by a pack of dwarf dogs, the children naked, the old worn by time, the women pregnant – all with a faint expression of mockery in their eyes. The priest kept a coin from the tithe box for each of them, and Riad Halabí gave each a cigarette or a piece of candy.

Before the arrival of the Turk, as he became known, commerce had been limited to an occasional sale of produce to the truck drivers who passed on the highway. In the early morning, children would set up canvas tents to protect themselves from the sun, and on a box display vegetables, fruits, and cheese they fanned constantly to keep away the flies. If they were lucky, they would sell something and return home with a few coins. It was Riad Halabí's idea to make a formal agreement with the drivers, who hauled cargo to the oil camps and returned empty to the capital, to carry the produce of Agua Santa to the city . . . Without intending it, his store had become the center of the commercial life of Agua Santa; almost all the business of the area passed through his hands.

Biographies and plot summaries

ALLENDE, Isabel (see under Chile). Her novel *Eva Luna*, 1987 (*Eva Luna*, 1988 – Extract 13) describes the growing up of a natural story-teller. Set in Venezuela (where Allende was exiled) the novel follows two parallel, picaresque lives, and the development of Eva's romantic pulp-novel gifts, ending in happiness for the two lovers. The style is vivid, and humanly warm. She continued with this vein of a woman's oral tales with *Cuentos de Eva Luna*, 1990 (*The Stories of Eva Luna*, 1990) where we get examples of the stories she invents, all set in a Venezuelan backwater called 'Agua Santa', and dealing with local characters. The sad, erotic and sometimes violent stories are always intensely readable.

CARPENTIER, Alejo (1904–1980). Carpentier was born on 26 December 1904, son of a French architect and Russian school mistress. He was educated in Cuba, at a lycée in Paris for eight months in 1913, and then at the University of Havana, where he studied architecture and music. In 1921 he turned to journalism. In 1924 he edited *Carteles*, an avant-garde magazine. During that period he wrote Afro–Cuban poems. In 1927 Carpentier was imprisoned for six months for signing manifestos against the Cuban dictator Machado, and in prison he wrote his first novel *Ecué-Yamba-O*, published in Madrid in 1933, meaning 'God be praised' in *lucumí*, about Afro–Cuban subculture, with photographs. He got out of Cuba on a false passport, lent by the surrealist Robert Desnos, and lived in exile in Paris from 1928 to 1939, on the fringe of the surrealist movement. He wrote four musical scenarios for Amadeo Roldán, and one ballet in 1928. In 1946 he published his study *La música en Cuba*. He took part in the *négritude* movement, exploring voodoo and negro music, with Nicolás Guillén. In 1937 Carpentier was in Spain, attending the Writers' Congresses: he returned to Cuba in 1939. He visited Haiti in 1943 with Louis Jouvet, the source for his second novel *El reino de este mundo*, 1949 (*The Kingdom of this World*, 1957), based on the building of the Sans Souci Palace, voodoo, Henri Christophe, the black revolution, Pauline Bonaparte, and the shaman Mackandal, in a story dealing with the excesses of Haitian history as surrealist farce. From 1945 to 1959 Carpentier lived in **Caracas**, working as a journalist.

A trip up the **Orinoco** led to *Los pasos perdidos*, 1953 (*The Lost Steps*, 1956 – Extract 6), following the narrating musicologist in his disgust for New York, fleeing his stale marriage, and accompanied by Mouche his mistress, going up the Orinoco to seek musical instruments, and the origins of music. Carpentier has written a parable illustrating his theory of '*lo real maravilloso*', that Latin America is a surreal country with all stages of history co-existing, so that the narrator reaches the beginning of social life, with a new mistress Rosario, but cannot remain in this utopia as he runs out of ink and paper. He cannot retrace his lost steps. The artist cannot escape his time.

In 1957 Carpentier published the subtly constructed *El acoso* (*The Chase*, 1989) about gangster student politics in Havana under Machado. In 1959, on Castro's triumph, he returned to Cuba and published *El siglo de las luces* (Explosion in a Cathedral, 1963), dealing with the contradictory impact of the French Revolution in the Caribbean, with three main characters, all sentimentally involved. Carpentier uses real historical characters like Victor Hugues, in a vast historical tableau. In Cuba, Carpentier became Director of the state publishing house. In 1966 he was sent as cultural attaché to Paris, where he died in 1980. He also wrote an ironic novel about a cultured dictator, *El recurso del método*, 1974 (*Reason of State*, 1976); a mocking counter biography of Columbus, *El arpa y la sombra*, 1979 (*The Harp and the Shadow*, 1991), a historical pastiche about Vivaldi's opera on Moctezuma, *Concierto barroco*, 1974 (*Concierto Barroco*, 1988), as well as short stories. His journalism has been collected.

CHARRIERE, Henri (see under French Guyana).

CONRAD, Joseph (1857–1924). Jozef Teodor Konrad Korzeniowski, alias Joseph Conrad, was born in Podolia, Ukraine. He came from the Polish nobility. He went to sea early in his life, and spent 20 years as a sailor. He soon picked up a smattering of Spanish, gun-running for the Carlist pretenders to the Spanish throne. His life at sea with the British Merchant Navy led to the convincing background of many of his novels, including the night rowing scenes in *Nostromo*, 1904. He turned to fiction in 1895, married Jessie and settled in England in 1896 where he wrote his major works between 1897 and 1911. He spent three days at **La Guaira** (the port for Caracas), and twelve hours at **Puerto Cabello**. *Nostromo* (Extracts 5 and 11) refers to an Italian adrift in a continent of immigrants. Conrad deliberately packs in all Latin America. In a letter to Cunninghame Graham (◊ Paraguay), he explained: 'Costaguana is meant for a S. American state in general; thence the mixture of customs and expressions.' In 1918 to the critic Edmund Gosse, he also wrote that 'The geographical base is . . . mainly Venezuela . . .' with bits of Mexico and Chile. He sets the action of this dense novel in a town called 'Sulaco', capital of a province in a Republic called 'Costaguana', or 'Costa' ('coast') and 'Guano' (the bird droppings that created guano islands, and wealth off Peru), maybe Costa Rica. Nearby in the *sierra* there is a snow-covered peak called 'Higuerota' (there is a village called **Higuerote** in Venezuela), and a peninsula called 'Azuera'. Throughout the novel there are Spanish words that come from all over the continent. He places his action in a vividly defined geography. Sulaco, the port and capital of the province, like so many Latin American towns, is 'so isolated from the world'. Higuerota, the peak, which 'soared out of the shadows of rock and earth like a frozen bubble under the moon' always dominates. And there is

Joseph Conrad

also the great San Tomé mine, carved out of a mountain, like Potosí itself. Costaguana is a land haunted by violence, and corrupted by European gold-fever. Of the gallery of characters in the novel, each represents a point of view in the European–New World conflict. Captain Joseph Mitchell, who ends up retired in Great Britain, speaks for British sensibilities faced with Latin chaos. Another apparent British voice belongs to Charles or Carlos Gould, born in Costaguana but British-educated, trying to maintain British standards of behaviour in a vile republic. His father had tried to stem the Latin corruption, but had been defeated by circumstances. Gould takes on the risk of mining, with powerful American backers, and succeeds. The third expression of Englishness abroad is Mrs Gould herself. She was seduced by Gould's exotic foreignness: deeply in love with her husband she followed him out to Costaguana. Her character develops cool insights into the corruption of her husband's love, leading to her emotional dependence on Dr Monygham at the end. She is truly English, but being a woman displays none of the rigid prejudices condemning Latin America. The bitter, even cynical, Dr Monygham sees into Mrs Gould's heart, and her tragedy. He stands for the inner, suffering view.

Another version of adapting to local Latin American realities emerges through the eponymous Nostromo, the feared and respected womanizing foreman of dockers. In the first part of the novel the reader regards him from the outside, controlling events through his physical bravery. He is intimate with the Italian inn-keeper, and belittled by his bad-tempered wife. Nostromo, a hero of the people, comes to centre stage in the action-packed second part of the novel, as he is responsible for hiding the silver from the rebels – burying it on one of the nearby Isabel islands after a desperate night sea journey with the cowardly and treacherous Hirsch, and Decoud. The third section dramatizes Nostromo's confusions about which of the inn-keeper's two daughters to love, his dreadful mistakes, and the tragic unhappiness this awakens. At the same time Nostromo surreptitiously digs out silver bars to enrich

himself, and betray his roots and the people. He realizes this too late in a diatribe against the rich. Martin Decoud, the local Sulaco aristocrat, who helps Nostromo load the silver and hoard it on the Isabel islands, also lives out an impossible quest for happiness and love, and kills himself. Decoud changes from a Parisian dilettante and dandy journalist to a committed conspirator and revolutionist. Of the Latin Americans in the novel, Don José Avellano, diplomat, poet, and author of an invented history of Costaguana, is famous for his grandiloquent speeches preaching good sense: his analysis of Latin America is that 'militarism is the enemy'. Conrad is unsparing in his description of General Montero, a future dictator. However, the most intriguing character in Conrad's gallery of rogues is the embittered Dr Monygham. He first appears to the reader as a man who defied the 'conventionalities of Sulaco'. The doctor is finally revealed to the reader as the bitter hero of this novel.

In *Nostromo*, through a novel purportedly dealing with Latin American republics and their revolutions, Conrad has criticized his age for its slavery to silver and treasure above human compassions. In 1903 Conrad collaborated with Ford Madox Ford to write *Romance*, about an impecunious Englishman's love for mysterious Seraphina and 'far-off lawless adventures' in Jamaica, and, mainly, Cuba, and a pirate haven called 'Rio Medio', just after the wars of liberation in Mexico. 'A Romantic tale – Gaspar Ruiz' from *A Set of Six*, 1908, is narrated by old General Santierra, Chilean patriot, recalling events of some 50 years before about Gaspar Ruiz, a friendly giant forced to change sides in the violent revolutionary wars between the *criollos* and the Spaniards. Hiding with a Royalist family, he falls for the frigid Erminia, ending up as a guerrilla *cacique* against the new republican government until his wife and child are tricked and taken hostage. He surrounds the fort in the Andes, and loads a canon on to his back, which finally breaks. Only then does Erminia relent, and admit she loves him, as he dies. Conrad died in 1924 near Canterbury. See Ian Watt, *Joseph Conrad: Nostromo*, Cambridge University Press, 1988.

DIAZ SANCHEZ, Ramón (1903–1968). Díaz Sánchez was born in **Puerto Cabello** and died in **Caracas**. He worked in several jobs, was a reporter, then co-director of *El Tiempo* in **Caracas**, and Director of Culture and Fine Arts. He wrote several novels, including *Cumboto, cuento de siete leguas*, 1950 (*Cumboto*, 1969 – Extract 10) set on a coconut *hacienda* near his home town, dealing with the last in line of a powerful family fighting to keep his land, surrounded by the ex-slaves at the turn of the century. Federico's relationship with the narrator, black Natividad, is spoiled when Federico falls for a sexy black girl called Pascua. The novel explores the place, the lifestyle, the conflict between blacks and whites, social conventions, ending with the arrival of the fruit of their love, a mulatto boy who ends up as the new owner of the *hacienda*. The novel is simply and movingly told, a recreation of forgotten lives, and was chosen by the William Faulkner Foundation as the most notable novel written in Latin America between 1945 and 1962.

GALLEGOS, Rómulo (1884–1969). Gallegos was born in **Caracas** on 2 August 1884. He studied law, published a magazine in 1909, and short stories in 1910. He taught at several schools until 1930. *Doña Bárbara*, 1929, (*Doña Bárbara*, 1931) deals with the clash between civilization, progress and modernity and barbarism in the form of the amoral Doña Bárbara, a *cacica* from the *llanos* at war with Santos Luzardo, from the city. Gallegos describes the plains in detail. *Canaima*, 1935 (*Canaima*, 1984 – Extract 9) introduced the virgin, lawless jungles of the **Orinoco basin**. The title refers to the notion of a 'hidden enemy' of the Pemón Indians. Gallegos uses a poetic tone to evoke nature, with many lists of fauna and flora, almost a compendium. The plot is simple, and concerns Marcos Vargas and his dealings with rubber tappers, Indians and local adventurers. In all, Gallegos published ten novels. He entered politics in 1931 as a senator, but went into exile in Spain until the fall of Gómez in 1935. In 1936, he became Minister of Education, and in February 1948 was elected President of Venezuela for five months until toppled by a military coup. He lived in exile again until 1958. His house in Caracas has been converted into **CELARG**, an important Latin American cultural centre.

HUDSON, W.H. (1841–1922). See also under Argentina. In 1904 Hudson wrote the best-selling *Green Mansions: A Romance of the Tropical Forest*, which, added to his Civil List pension, finally assured financial security. This romance concerns Abel Guevez de Argensola, from **Caracas** who has to flee as a failed conspirator. He travels down the **Orinoco** to Angostura (now **Ciudad Bolívar**) and decides to hide himself in the 'almost unexplored' regions of Guyana. In **Manapuri** he falls ill and recuperates with the Maquiritari tribe near the **Queneveto** mountains. Wandering the jungles he becomes aware of 'a secret innocence and spirituality in nature' and decides to stay with the Indians. He hears an 'exquisite bird-melody' but cannot identify the bird. He roams an area that the Indians – 'naked, brown-skinned, lynx-eyed and noiseless' – fear, and spots a 'girl form'. Her skin is alabastrian, and she is all alertness, like an animal or a humming-bird. It is Rima, who laments her mother's death and yearns to return to her birthplace. Nuflo tells Rima's story; how he found her mother pregnant, and looked after the baby after she died in childbirth. In Riolama Abel discovers how mother and nature 'seemed one and the same thing'. On their return their huts are burnt down. Abel is desperate to find Rima, who had rushed on ahead. He meets his old Indian friend Kua-Kó, who tells him that Rima had been burnt alive as she was an evil spirit. They fight and Abel kills the Indian. He seeks out the exact tree where Rima died to rescue her bones, and comes across her skeleton. He goes mad, and wanders the jungle till he reaches Georgetown. By now he has reconciled himself to his loss and Rima has become a 'Rima of the mind, whose words when she spoke reflected my despair'. By 1977 *Green Mansions* had been through 70 editions, and it is enshrined in Epstein's sculpture to Rima and Hudson in Hyde Park, London. W.H. Hudson never visited the Venezuelan–Guyana jungle.

HUMBOLDT, Alexandre von (1769–1859). Humboldt was born on the family estate at Tegel in Berlin in 1769. With his elder brother Wilhelm, he was educated by tutors and then at Frankfurt, Göttingen and Hamburg universities where he studied botany, literature, archaeology, electricity, mineralogy and the natu-ral sciences. In 1790, he first travelled abroad, and published in botanical and chemical journals. He worked in the Prussian Mining Administration – and befriended Goethe at Jena – until his mother died in 1796. A large inheritance enabled Humboldt to travel. After a few frustrations he was allowed by Charles IV of Spain to travel in the Spanish American colonies, at his own expense, with his companion Aimé Bonpland. After five years in the New World (1799–1804), Humboldt settled in Paris to begin publishing his encyclopaedic *Voyage aux régions équinoxiales du Nouveau Continent*, finally completed in 30 volumes in 1834, of which the *Travels* (Extract 2) comprised volumes 27 to 30. Humboldt was not only a prominent figure in the Parisian scientific world, but also Chamberlain to Frederick Wilhelm III, and Councillor of State to Frederick Wilhelm IV. In 1829 he travelled to Russia and Central Asia, and published his account in French in 1843. In 1834 he began his comprehensive survey of creation, *Kosmos*, completed posthumously in 1862. He died in 1859, a bachelor, and was buried in the family vault at Tegel, honoured as one of the great speculative scientific travellers of the nineteenth century. Humboldt's way of including many kinds of insight and study into one volume inaugurated a new kind of travel writing which would lead to Darwin (◊ Uruguay), Bates (◊ Brazil), Hudson ◊, and up to Matthiessen (◊ Peru). See Jason Wilson, 'Introduction' to Humboldt's *Travels*, Penguin, London, 1993.

LOWELL, Robert (see under Argentina).

NERUDA, Pablo (see under Chile).

RALEIGH, Sir Walter (c1554–1618). Raleigh, who was beheaded for treason in the Tower of London in 1618, was a Renaissance scholar, poet, courtier and explorer. He twice sailed to seek El Dorado up the **Orinoco**, into the hinterlands of Venezuela, then called Guiana, belonging to Spain. He wrote *The Discovery of the Large, Rich and Beautiful Empire of Guiana* (Extract 8) in 1596. He returned there later, but failed to find any gold or riches and played down being lost in the labyrinth of rivers, the heat, lack of food, to speculate on Manoa and the Amazon women, with details on the Indians, their food, canoes, hammocks, turtle eggs, crocodiles and poisoned arrows.

ST AUBIN DE TERAN, Lisa (1953–). St Aubin de Terán was born in London. At sixteen she married an exiled Venezuelan and returned to help him run his sugar and avocado farm in the **Venezuelan Andes** for seven years. Her first novel *Keepers of the House*, 1982 (Extract 4), is a family saga of the winding down of the Beltrán dynasty, whose life stories are recorded by Lydia, a young English girl married to the last of the Beltráns, living in the *hacienda* La Bebella, in the Venezuelan Andes on the **Momboy River**, near **La Caldera**, with its heat, apathy, and marginalization. All the stories Lydia retells in the novel are oral, from her older husband and Benito, old retainer. The novel opens with a genealogical tree. This forgotten place, soon to be abandoned thanks to the oil boom, is a place of 'extremes'. Lydia's keen eyes, and research, 'chronicle our decline'. She had married the last of the line. When Diego is paralysed by a stroke she has to leave, pregnant. Preparing her escape in a battered jeep, she organizes her notes which comprise the novel we read. Her story begins in 1785 with the arrival of the Beltrán brothers in the valley. They marry two rich and noble spinster sisters waiting for some miracle. They discover gold buried under the tiles which buys them machinery, and power. Soon interbreeding leaves the whole valley related as vague cousins, full of genetic flaws. The background of this village slowly becoming a ghost town is present-day Venezuela 'systematically vandalizing and neglecting the land and destroying its natural resources', excited by 'transitory oil'. The novel ends with pregnant Lydia realizing that her future child is 'laden with history even before it was born'. Lisa St Aubin de Terán's second novel *The Slow Train to Milan*, 1983, follows South Americans in Europe, and her third, *The Tiger*, 1985, is a fictional biography of Lucien – a macho tyrant in Venezuela, brought up by a ferocious grandmother in the *llanos* who controls him like a 'tiger' all his life, through his outrageous lifestyle in **Caracas**, to his travels to Nazi Germany and Rio, and his final death as a traitor in Venezuela.

Lisa St Aubin de Terán

ECUADOR

'The city, like all Ecuador, produced a curiously baffling impression. Lee felt there was something going on here, some undercurrent of life that was hidden from him.'
William Burroughs, Queer

Ecuador, or the República del Ecuador, is so named because it is on the Equator. It is the second smallest country in South America, comprising 270 670 sq km, including 685 km of Pacific coast, and disputed borders with Peru and Colombia. The population reached 10.8 million in 1990. **Quito**, the capital, founded by Sebastián de Benalcázar in 1534, lies 2800 m up, with a population of 1 110 250 in 1982. The largest city in Ecuador is the coastal city of **Guayaquil** (see Burrough's description, Extract 5) at the mouth of the **Guayas River** with a population of 1 600 000, founded by Francisco de Orellana (first European to descend the Amazon in 1541) in 1537. The rivalry between these cities, and between the coast (46% of the population) and the highlands (51%) can also become a racial rivalry. Forty per cent of the people are pure-blooded Indians (with the head-shrinking Jívaros as the most renowned); 50% are *mestizo*. There is a white population of some 8%, and there are also negroes, brought over as slaves in the eighteenth century, on the coast. The fiction of Adalberto Ortiz ◊ deals with the black population (Extract 10), as does Moritz Thomsen ◊ in his autobiography of farming near **Esmeraldas** (Extract 9). Those living on the coast are called *cholos*. *Montuvios* are a mixture of negro and Indian. It is from this reality that Aguilar Malta ◊ writes his fiction (Extract 4). Fifty-four per cent of the people live in urban centres, and only 2% in the **Oriente** region (*east* of the Andes, in the Amazon forest). In Ecuador there are no racial categories, but cultural and linguistic differences. That is, 'whites' speak Spanish, relate to Spanish culture, wear Western clothes, and live in cities. In this sense, 60% of Ecuador is Indian. The religion is Roman Catholic. The official language is Spanish, though a majority speak Quechua, imposed on local tribes by the Incas. In the Oriente region, Jivaroan is the main language.

The economy has developed through different agricultural booms. At the turn of the century, Ecuador was the world's major producer of cocoa, until the crops were ravaged by the monilia disease, and competition from Africa. Later, Ecuador became the world's greatest banana exporter. Cotton, sugar cane, maize (the staple diet), barley, rice and coffee are also produced on the coast. In 1967 large oil-fields were discovered in Oriente around **Lago Agrio**, and from 1972 exported. Tourism has become important, with Indian weaving a main attraction, especially at the market of **Otavalo**, where Indians derived from the Cara tribe sell their wear. An important part of this tourist trade is the Panama hat, made mainly in **Montecristi**, so named because it was sold to US gold prospectors crossing the Panama canal in the 1840s. These hats are made from *toquilla*, a local palm-like fibre that has to be continuously moistened. Vonnegut ◊ quotes these facts in his novel *Galapagos* (Extract 7). The sale of imitation Jívaro heads is also famous. Old **Quito** was declared a world heritage site by UNESCO in 1978. There are balsa trees in the **Guayas valley**, and *tagua* – vegetable ivory – is also harvested. Only 5% of the land is agricultural.

The *sierra* with the Andes is a massive barrier to east–west movement. There are two distinct *cordilleras*, with a fertile valley between them, named by Alexandre von Humboldt (◊ Venezuela) as the **Avenue of Volcanoes**, where Quito lies along the route of the old Inca highway. In Ecuador there are about 20 active volcanoes, with **Cotopaxi** as the world's highest active one at 5900 m. **Pichincha**, visible from Quito, erupted in 1981. **Sangay** is one of the world's most active volcanoes. In all, there are 51 volcanic peaks, with **Chimborazo** at 6310 m the highest. Humboldt tried to climb it and failed, but held the world altitude record at the time. Walter James Turner's poem 'Romance' evokes Chimborazo and Cotopaxi as symbols of the golden land of dreams: it ends 'The houses, people, traffic seemed / Thin fading dreams by day, Chimborazo, Cotopaxi / They had stolen my soul away!'. Graham Greene knew this poem by heart.

The coast, known as *tierra caliente*, is where bananas, cocoa, fishing and logging are central to the way of life. There is rainforest around **Esmeraldas**, with swamps and mangroves along the coast. This is where Moritz Thomsen ◊ had his farm. **Oriente** is typical Amazonian forest, still largely unexplored but where oil was found.

A HISTORY OF TURMOIL

Before the Spanish conquest what is now Ecuador was made up of several tribes with *caciques*, at war with each other. Remains of stone age settlements date back to 9000 BC. The Caras tribe settled in the **Quito** area. They were sun worshippers. The Caras were followed by the Duchicel dynasty. These tribes lived on maize, beans and potatoes, and were already excellent weavers. They traded with the Amazon lowlands for *achiote* (a red dye), parrots and monkeys. By 1480 the Incas had conquered these tribes, and built a city at present-day **Cuenca**. They introduced the cocoa leaf, llamas, peanuts and sweet potatoes. They uprooted the local tribes, and imposed their language, Quechua. Just before the Spaniards arrived there was a civil war between Atahualpa from Quito and Huáscar from Cuzco over the Inca empire. Atahualpa won, but he was defeated and killed by Pizarro in 1533, who had landed near **Esmeraldas** in 1532. **Quito**, sacked by the Incas, was reconquered by Sebastián de Belalcázar, and refounded on 6 December 1534. In 1539 Pizarro placed his brother Gonzalo as first governor of Quito. He was ousted by the Spaniards in 1548.

Over the colonial period Ecuador was administered as a province in the viceroyalty of Peru, with **Quito** as a 'royal *audiencia*'. It lay on the trade road from Peru to Cartagena. The Spaniards imposed the *encomienda* system, where the Indian majority lived as serfs under the Spaniards. There were many revolts against Spain's domination, one led by Eugenio Espejo, who died in 1795, and after whom the **National Library** is named. The colonial period saw the province dominated by the Church: there are some 36 churches in Quito alone. This eccleciastical dominance can be seen in the founding of the Jesuit seminary of **San Luis** in 1594, and their university of **San Gregorio Magno** in 1622. The Dominicans founded another university, of **Santo Tomás de Aquino** in 1688. The wealth of the church is visible in many museums and churches today in Quito.

The first independence uprising against Spain took place in 1809, but all the leaders were executed. Another in 1810–12 was also put down. Sucre, once of Bolívar's generals, finally defeated Spain at the battle of Pichincha on 24 May 1822. A little later that year in **Guayaquil**, Bolívar met San Martín to discuss the future of the liberated states, but nothing came about and Ecuador became part of Gran Colombia until 1830, when it withdrew and became fully independent.

Ecuadorian history is of turmoil, a feud between the conservatives and liberals. The most colourful period was Gabriel García Moreno's theocratic dictatorship, 1861–65 and 1869 until his assassination in 1875. He was a fanatic Catholic, and accepted only practising Catholics as citizens. He introduced eucalyptus, improved roads, and began the railroads. He imposed severe censorship (with the intellectual Juan Montalvo as a bitter critic), ecclesiastic courts, and placed

Ecuador under the Jesuits. Nineteenth century life can be looked at as a feud between *costeños* and *serranos*, between anti-clerical **Guayaquil** and the more conservative **Quito**. Only in 1908 was the rail link between Quito and Guayaquil finished.

What most affected Ecuador in the twentieth century was the 1941 Peruvian invasion of the **Oriente** district, when Peru annexed two thirds of Ecuador's Amazonian territory, some 180 000 sq km in all. In 1832 Ecuador had lost around 324 000 sq km to Colombia, and in 1904 more to Brazil. The 1941 invasion saw Ecuador shrunk to *half* her original territory. The borders are still disputed, and there were skirmishes in 1981.

The later years have been dominated by one man, José María Velasco Ibarra, who was first elected in 1944, and again in 1952 and 1960 and in 1968. During his presidencies the railways were nationalized, and oil changed the agricultural economy. With the threat of Castroism, much needed land reform was carried out in 1964, which led to a surge of cooperative farms replacing the old *haciendas*.

The crucial factor in Ecuadorian life has been the position of the Indian and land. Icaza ◊ has dramatized the miserable *huasipungo* system (Extract 1). The main solutions proposed by intellectuals have been *acholamiento*, that is, integrating the highland and lowland Indians and negroes with the élites. The fight against disease and illiteracy was begun in 1945 under Benjamín Carrión and Jorge Carrera Andrade ◊ around the **Casa de la Cultura** (a politically active cultural centre in **Guayaquil**), but the problem remains.

See Victor Wolfgang von Hagen, *Ecuador: The Unknown*, 1989. For an idiosyncratic, and poetic view see Henri Michaux's ◊ *Ecuador* (Extract 8).

THE GALAPAGOS

The **Galápagos Islands**, tips of huge volcanoes sticking out from the ocean, lie some 950 to 1100 km off Ecuador. They were discovered by Europeans in 1535, but became part of Ecuador only in 1832. A penal colony was placed on **Floreana**. Apart from pirates and sailors calling at the strange 'Enchanted Islands' (see Melville ◊, Extract 3) to stock water and food, the Galápagos are famous for Charles Darwin's ◊ (Extract 2) solving of the problem of speciation back home, based on his study of local finches (which is why Vonnegut sets *Galápagos*, his novel about mutation, there). The islands are also renowned for the swimming iguanas and giant tortoises after whom they are named. In 1959 the islands were declared a national park, and the **Charles Darwin Research Station** opened.

BOOKLIST

The following selection includes all titles which are extracted in this chapter as well as those mentioned in the introduction which are available in English. In general, paperback editions are given when possible. The editions cited are not necessarily the only ones available. For most of the extracted works, the original publisher in English can be found in 'Acknowledgments and Citations' at the end of the volume, as can the exact location of the extracts and the editions from which they are taken. The date in square brackets is the original publication date of the work in its original language. Extract numbers are highlighted in bold for ease of reference.

Aguilar Malta, Demetrio, *Don Goyo* [1933], John and Carolyn Brushwood, trans, Humana Press, Clifton, NJ, 1980. **Extract 4.**

Burroughs, William, *Queer* [1984], Picador, London, 1986/Viking Penguin, New York, 1985. **Extract 5.**

Carrera Andrade, Jorge, *Selected Poems*, Hays, H.R., trans, State University of New York, Albany, NY, 1972. **Extract 6.**

Darwin, Charles, *Voyage of the Beagle* [1839], Penguin, London, 1989. **Extract 2.**

Icaza, Jorge, *Huasipungo* [1934], Mervyn Savill, trans, Dennis Dobson, London, 1962/*Huasipungo: The Villagers*, Bernard M. Dulsey, trans, Southern Illinois University Press, Carbondale, IL, 1964. **Extract 1.**

Melville, Herman, 'The Encantadas or Enchanted Isles', in *Billy Budd, Sailor and Other Stories*, Harold Beaver, ed, Penguin, London, 1967. **Extract 3.**

Michaux, Henri, 'Ecuador' [1929], in *Selected Writings: The Space Within*, Richard Ellman, trans and ed, Oxford University Press, Oxford, 1952/New Directions, New York, 1968. **Extract 8.** (Also *Ecuador*, Robin Magowan, trans, University of Washington Press, Seattle, WA, 1970.)

Ortiz, Adalberto, *Juyungo* [1943], Susan Hill and Jonathan Tittler, trans, Three Continents Press, Washington, DC, 1982. **Extract 10.**

Thomsen, Moritz, *The Saddest Pleasure* [1990], The Sumach Press, London, 1991/Graywolf, St Paul, MN, 1990. **Extract 9.**

von Hagen, Victor Wolfgang, *Ecuador: The Unknown*, University of Oklahoma Press, Norman, OK, 1939.

Vonnegut, Kurt, *Galápagos*, Grafton, London, 1987/Dell, New York, 1986. **Extract 7.**

Extracts

(1) ECUADORIAN ANDES

Jorge Icaza, *Huasipungo*

Icaza describes the miserable Indian village of Tomachi, high in the Ecuadorian Andes.

Dusk was falling as the little procession reached the village of Tomachi. The winter climate, the high altitude and the poverty reigning in Tomachi made it appear a village of mud, refuse and desolation. The low, rambling huts flanking the solitary muddy road were abject and their sole adornment was the middens. Abject, too, the children who squatted in the doorways of the huts, playing with lumps of filth, their teeth chattering from malaria. Abject the women who from morning to night stood at the stove, cooking *mazamorra*, a porridge of maize flour, salt and water, or preparing *locro*, a fricassé made of tripe. Abject, too, were the men who worked from six in the morning until six at night on their small plots of land, in the forest or carrying their wares on their mules to the neighbouring villages. The narrow street was tattooed with drains filled with turgid water, which served as a trough for the cattle. Here the pigs built their muddy sties where they wallowed to find relief from the great heat, and here the children crawled on all fours to quench their thirst.

A bitterly cold wind was blowing; the valley below was enveloped in silence and the twilight made the stark outlines of the Indians' huts appear even smaller. These pathetic hovels consisted of only a single room; the floor was made of beaten earth and the thatched roof had turned black from the rain and smoke. Since there was no outlet for the smoke, it seeped through every crack and crevice into the open air. Jacinto's house was closed. The owners were probably on the way to Sangolquí. The only signs of life were two black pigs wallowing in the mud, and rooting among a few old tin cans. Some distance away, two dogs were quarrelling over a bone.

(2) Galapagos Islands

Charles Darwin, *Voyage of the Beagle*

Darwin sailed into the Galápagos Islands on the Beagle in September 1835, but it was not until he was going over his notes back in London that he realized the importance of Galápagos finches to his theory of speciation.

In the morning we landed on Chatham Island, which, like the others, rises with a tame and rounded outline, interrupted only here and there by scattered hillocks – the remains of former craters. Nothing could be less inviting than the first appearance. A broken field of black basaltic lava is every where covered by a stunted brushwood, which shows little signs of life. The dry and parched surface, having been heated by the noonday sun, gave the air a close and sultry feeling, like that from a stove: we fancied even the bushes smelt unpleasantly. Although I diligently tried to collect as many plants as possible, I succeeded in getting only ten kinds; and such wretched-looking little weeds would have better become an arctic, than an equatorial Flora.

The thin woods, which cover the lower parts of all the islands, excepting where the lava has recently flowed, appear from a short distance quite leafless, like the deciduous trees of the northern hemisphere in winter. It was some time before I discovered, that not only almost every plant was in full leaf, but that the greater number were now in flower. After the period of heavy rains, the islands are said to appear for a short time partially green . . .

The natural history of this archipelago is very remarkable: it seems to be a little world within itself; the greater number of its inhabitants, both vegetable and animal, being found nowhere else. As I shall refer to this subject again, I will only here remark, as forming a striking character on first landing, that the birds are strangers to men. So tame and unsuspecting were they, that they did not even understand what was meant by stones being thrown at them; and quite regardless of us, they approached so close that any number might have been killed with a stick.

The *Beagle* sailed round Chatham Island, and anchored in several bays. One night I slept on shore, on a part of the island where some black cones – the former chimneys of the subterranean heated fluids – were extraordinarily numerous. From one small eminence, I counted sixty of these truncated hillocks, which were all surmounted by a more or less perfect crater . . . From their regular form, they gave the country a *workshop* appearance, which strongly reminded me of those parts of Staffordshire where the great iron-foundaries are most numerous.

(3) GALAPAGOS ISLANDS

Herman Melville, *The Encantadas*

In his sketches about the life he had glimpsed on the Galápagos, Melville first defines the geography carefully before launching into the human tale. 'The Encantadas or Enchanted Isles' is included in Billy Budd and Other Stories – see Booklist.

Take five and twenty heaps of cinders dumped here and there in an outside city lot; imagine some of them magnified into mountains, and the vacant lot the sea; and you will have a fit idea of the general aspect of the Encantadas, or Enchanted Isles. A group rather of extinct volcanoes than of isles; looking much as the world at large might, after a penal conflagration.

It is to be doubted whether any spot of earth can, in desolateness, furnish a parallel to this group. Abandoned cemeteries of long ago, old cities by piecemeal tumbling to their ruin, these are melancholy enough; but, like all else which has but once been associated with humanity, they still awaken in us some thoughts of sympathy, however sad. Hence, even the Dead Sea, along with whatever other emotions it may at times inspire, does not fail to touch in the pilgrim some of his less unpleasurable feelings . . .

But the special curse, as one may call it, of the Encantadas, that which exalts them in desolation above Idumea and the Pole, is, that to them change never comes; neither the change of seasons nor of sorrows. Cut by the Equator, they know not autumn, and they know not spring; while already reduced to the lees of fire, ruin itself can work little more upon them. The showers refresh the deserts; but in these isles, rain never falls. Like split Syrian gourds left withering in the sun, they are cracked by an everlasting drought beneath a torrid sky . . .

Another feature in these isles is their emphatic uninhabitableness. It is deemed a fit type of all-forsaken overthrow, that the jackal should den in the wastes of weedy Babylon; but the Encantadas refuse to harbor even the outcasts of the beasts. Man and wolf alike disown them. Little but reptile life is here found: tortoises, lizards, immense spiders, snakes, and that strangest anomaly of outlandish nature, the *aguano*. No voice, no low, no howl is heard; the chief sound of life here is a hiss.

(4) GUAYAQUIL

Demetrio Aguilar Malta, *Don Goyo*

In Aguilar Malta's novel, the Guayas River delta fishermen and islanders reach the shockingly modern port of Guayaquil, now the largest city in Ecuador.

They reached Guayaquil via the Estero Salado. Put in at Puerto Duarte, not far from American Park, which they could see in the distance, full of bathers.

Guayaquil was awakening into the full swing of daily life. A distant hivelike buzzing reached their ears. Smoke from dozens of small coal ovens arose from the outskirts of the city, plumed the shore. As the growing light swept away dawn, the streets yawned and stretched, and the houses opened the eyelids of their windows.

They tied the canoe to the first dock. Emptied out the fish for the street hawkers who were waiting. Then they half washed the canoe. And after that, with difficulty, by exercising superhuman effort, they put on their shoes, put on clean shirts, dabbed a few drops of water on their faces, and went ashore.

One of them grumbled:

– Let's go in. And take the streetcar.

– No. let's walk. It's better.

– Don't act so dumb. Let's get the streetcar. It's a long way!

– The other shore. We have some business over there.

They went through the middle of the slums on the outskirts of the city, all wooden houses. Traveled over the dirty and neglected streets, breathing the noxious putrid air around them.

– They ought to call this place Puerto Stink.

– For sure.

They reached the curve made by the Sucre–Vélez streetcar. Waited a few minutes. Soon they heard the growling of the motor, and a little later the vehicle they wanted came into view.

– It looks like a palm worm.

It came to a halt, half trembling, and they got on and paid their fare. The streetcare started moving again.

Cusumbo felt uncomfortable. He twisted around nervously in his seat. Looked all around him. Sweated. Felt hostile toward everything he saw.

(5) GUAYAQUIL

William Burroughs, *Queer*

Burroughs's morphine addict Lee reaches Guayaquil, and is about to set off on his disastrous trip into the jungle to find yage.

Guayaquil is built along a river, a city with many parks and squares and statues. The parks are full of tropical trees and shrubs and vines. A tree that fans out like an umbrella, as wide as it is tall, shades the stone benches. The people do a great deal of sitting.

One day Lee got up early and went to the market. The place was crowded. A curiously mixed populace: Negro, Chinese, Indian, European, Arab, characters difficult to classify. Lee saw some beautiful boys of mixed Chinese and Negro stock, slender and graceful with beautiful white teeth.

A hunchback with withered legs was playing crude bamboo pan-pipes, a mournful Oriental music with the sadness of the high mountains. In deep sadness there is no place for sentimentality. It is as final as the mountains: a fact. There it is. When you realize it, you cannot complain.

People crowded around the musician, listened a few minutes, and walked on. Lee noticed a young man with the skin tight over his small face, looking exactly like a shrunken head. He could not have weighed more than ninety pounds.

The musician coughed from time to time. Once he snarled when someone touched his hump, showing his black rotten teeth. Lee gave the man a few coins. He walked on, looking at every face he passed, looking into doorways and up at the windows of cheap hotels. An iron bedstead painted light pink, a shirt out to dry . . . scraps of life. Lee snapped at them hungrily, like a predatory fish cut off from his prey by a glass wall. He could not stop ramming his nose against the glass in the nightmare search of his dream. And at the end he was standing in a dusty room in the late afternoon sun, with an old shoe in his hand.

The city, like all Ecuador, produced a curiously baffling impression. Lee felt there was something going on here, some undercurrent of life that was hidden from him. This was the area of the ancient Chimu pottery, where salt shakers and water pitchers were nameless obscenities: two men on all fours engaged in sodomy formed the handle for the top of a kitchen pot.

(6) GUAYAQUIL

Jorge Carrera Andrade

*Carrera Andrade writes a brief, impressionistic poem on Guaya-
quil. From Selected Poems – see Booklist.*

The vestibules,
The canoes in the estuary
And the empty shipyard speak of sun.

Only a white shadow
Releases its street cry in the wind.
Light paints the windowblinds.

(7) GUAYAQUIL

Kurt Vonnegut, *Galápagos*

*The people who are meant to take the cruise to the Galápagos
meet in a hotel in Guayaquil as war breaks out, and only a few
escape into the isolation of the Islands.*

The Hotel El Dorado was a brand-new, five-storey tourist accommoda-
tion – built of unadorned cement block. It had the proportions and
mood of a glass-front bookcase, high and wide and shallow. Each
bedroom had a floor-to-ceiling wall of glass looking westward – towards
the waterfront for deep-draught vessels dredged in the delta three
kilometres away.

In the past, that waterfront had teemed with commerce, and ships
from all over the planet delivered meat and grain and vegetables and
fruit and vehicles and clothing and machinery and household ap-
pliances, and so on, and carried away in fair exchange, Ecuadorian
coffee and cocoa and sugar and petroleum and gold, and Indian arts and
crafts, including 'Panama' hats, which had always come from Ecuador
and not from Panama.

But there were only two ships out there now, as James Wait sat in the
bar, nursing a rum and Coca-Cola. He was not a drinker, actually,
since he lived by his wits, and could not afford to have the delicate
switches of the big computer in his skull short-circuited by alcohol. His
drink was a theatrical prop – like the price tag on his ridiculous shirt.

He was in no position to judge whether the state of affairs at the
waterfront was normal or not. Until two days before, he had never even
heard of Guayaquil, and this was the first time in his life he had ever
been below the equator. As far as he was concerned, the El Dorado was

no different from all the other characterless hostelries he had used as hideouts in the past – in Moose Jaw, Saskatchewan, in San Ignacio, Mexico, in Waterviliet, New York, and on and on.

He had picked the name of the city where he was now from an arrivals-and-departures board at Kennedy International Airport in New York City. He had just pauperized and deserted his seventeenth wife – a seventy-year-old widow in Skokie, Illinois, right outside Chicago. Guayaquil sounded to him like the last place she would ever think of looking for him.

(8) Quito

Henri Michaux, *Ecuador*

Belgian poet and painter Henri Michaux describes Quito, at 2850 m, in his laconic and stimulating travel book Ecuador:. This passage, 'La Cordillera de Los Andes', is extracted from Selected Writings – see Booklist.

The first impression is terrifying and close to despair.
First the horizon disappears.
Not all the clouds are higher than we are.
Endlessly and without accidents – these are, where we are,
The high plateaus of the Andes which stretch far out, which stretch far
    out.
The soil is black and without attachments.
A soil that has come from within.
It takes no interest in plants.
This is a volcanic earth.
Naked! and the black houses above
Let it keep all its nakedness;
The black nakedness of the foul.

Let the man who does not like clouds
Stay away from the Equator.
They are the faithful dogs of the mountain,
Big faithful dogs;
Crown the horizon proudly;
The altitude of the place is 3,000 meters and over, they say,
Is dangerous, they say, for the heart, for the breathing, for the stomach
And for the whole body of the stranger.

Squat, brachycephalic, short-stepping,
Heavily-loaded Indians walk about this city, stuck in a crater of clouds.

Where is it going this stooping pilgrimage?
It crosses and crosses back and forth and climbs; nothing more; it's the daily life.
Quito and its mountains.
They fall on it, then marvel, draw back, quiet their tongues! everything becomes path; whereupon they are paved.
All of us smoke the opium of high altitude here, with low voices, short steps, short breaths.
The dogs rarely quarrel, the children rarely, rarely laugh.

(9) QUITO

Moritz Thomsen, *The Saddest Pleasure*

Thomsen is seen off at Quito airport by Ramón, his black farming partner from Esmeraldas.

Ramón doesn't want a despedida any more than I do. He is still a country type, nervous in the city traffic, and he wants to get back to the empty country roads. He drives me out to the airport a couple of hours before I want to arrive, with the intention of simply dropping me off at the door and fleeing back to the jungle. But at the airport the children, who have never seen jets and in fact have scarcely ever seen Quito, beg and pester and finally Ramón, who secretly loves jets with a terrible passion, gives in. We park the car and all of us go up on top of the building and watch the planes coming in and taking off. Ester's eyes begin to water.

We stand at the railing of the observation deck facing into the sun, our backs to Pichincha, which is cut and quartered into small, brilliantly green Indian fields of corn or alfalfa, beans and potatoes. On the lower slopes the duller, larger plantings of eucalyptus glow like groves of olives, and up near the peak smashed against the mountain lies a great silver cross, an army plane that had got lost in the fog. In front of us lies the runway with a hump in its center like a humping dog's back.

It is the howling of jets that now defines the beginnings of journeys and announces with a sneer the mediocritization of the world's cities to which one must now travel with diminishing anticipations.

(10) Santo Domingo de los Colorados

Adalberto Ortiz, *Juyungo*

Ecuadorian novelist Ortiz describes the jungle village Danto Domingo de los Colorados, where his black Ecuadorians live out their struggle.

Don Valerio Veduga Barberán combed his fingers through his dull disheveled hair, and it seemed to him that the mist falling that morning on the village of Santo Domingo de los Colorados was a fine-gauze mosquito netting. He let his gaze run over the straw roofs which, across from his house of zinc, streamed straight as Indian hair. They reminded him of the grave and silent vultures which flapped their black, open wings, as if to say: 'Tomorrow I make a home, tomorrow I make a home.'

The noisy overflow of the crystalline torrent reached his ears. It snaked through the underbrush, from where unkempt and diligent women, each with a gourd, carried water. Meanwhile, children and adolescents, greenish as the pulp of tender papayas, played with coconuts and glass marbles beneath the hovels that partially surrounded the dilapidated square. The plaza was carpeted with brush and weeds, and rent, in its tremulous and humid verdor, by the diagonal wounds of the familiar little paths.

And that unhealthy dampness, which seemed to take concrete form in almost every face, revealed past fevers and hidden parasites. All human life was reduced by the preponderant jungle setting that surrounded it.

For all the inhabitants of the village, except Don Valerio, holidays and Sundays were always cause for uneasiness and turmoil because the Blacks, tired of their chores, their faces sweaty and happy, came from the Quinindé highway project looking for fun. They would drink until the bars ran dry and would take women by force, creating outrageous scandals which endangered the virginity of all the pale damsels and the honor of the husbands of all the other women.

Biographies and plot summaries

AGUILAR MALTA, Demetrio (1909–1981). Born on 24 May 1909 in **Guayaquil**, Aguilar Malta was self-taught, worked as a journalist, wrote and directed films, was a painter, and also became Ambassador to Mexico. All his work has oscillated between bitter denunciation, and mythical re-creation of alien, Indian minds and lives. As a member of the '*Grupo de Guayaquil*' he published jointly with Joaquín Gallegos Lara and Enrique Gil Albert in 1930 short stories protesting the treatment of coastal *mestizos* and negroes. His first novel *Don Goyo*, 1933 (*Don Goyo*, 1980 – Extract 4), deals mythically with the *cholos* (*mestizo* coastal dwellers, as opposed to *montuvios*, from the mountains) who inhabit the coastal islands in the **Gulf of Guayaquil**, and who fish from the mangrove swamps. Their patriarch and founder is Don Goyo, who, rather than give in to demands from the hated whites to give up his islands and cut down all the mangroves, is metamorphosed into the nature around him. The novel is social protest, with realistic central characters like Cusumbo, whose life we follow, as well as mythically described scenes involving Goyo. Aguilar Malta, in Spain when the civil war broke out, wrote two books concerning his experiences there: ¡*Madrid!* and *España leal*. Three other of his novels have been translated: *La caballeresa del sol*, 1964 (*Manuela, la caballeresa del sol*, 1967); *Siete lunas y siete serpientes*, 1970 (*Seven Serpents and Seven Moons*, 1979), set in the mythical South American country of Santorontón in a jungle village – a tropical, magical

allegory of the fight between good and evil; and *Babelandia*, 1985. Aguilar Malta saw himself as a chronicler of Ecuadorian life, collecting his fiction and theatre as *Episodios americanos*. See Clementine Christos Rabassa, *Demetrio Aguilar-Malta and Social Justice*, Fairleigh Dickinson University Press, Cranbury, NJ, 1990.

BURROUGHS, William (see under Mexico).

CARRERA ANDRADE, Jorge (1903–1978). Carrera Andrade was born in **Quito** on 28 September 1903 and also died there. He published his first book of poems in 1922, siding with the Ecuadorian Indians, and was briefly imprisoned before leaving for Europe in 1933. From 1934 he took up diplomatic posts, representing Ecuador at UNESCO, as Consul General in Japan in 1940, and after the war years in the USA. He was subsequently ambassador in Venezuela, in the UK, and in France in 1964. As a poet he is an 'American-ist', dealing with Latin American realities, especially the exuberant nature and the Indians, in sensual lines and images, close to surrealism. He has also written a history of Ecuador. In English, we have *To the Bay Bridge*, 1941; *Secret Country*, 1946; *Visitor of Mist*, 1950; a *Selected Poems*, 1972 (Extract 6); and his *Reflections on Spanish American Poetry*, 1973.

DARWIN, Charles (see under Uruguay).

ICAZA, Jorge (1906–1978). Icaza was born in **Quito** on 10 July 1906 and also died there. He worked as a civil servant, and became director of Quito's **National Library**. He began by writing plays, and then a collection of stories in 1933, before publishing his novel *Huasipungo*, 1934 (*Huasipungo*, 1962 – Extract 1; and *Huasipungo: The Villagers*, 1964) which exposed the raw racist deal that mountain Indians living in a village called Tomachi received from the rich, stupid landowners, and *cholos* in the early 1930s as they were forced to build a road after oil had been discovered. There are scenes of rape, of starvation, of killing hard work. A rebellion over the loss of their ancestral land and huts – *huasipungos* – leads to the mutiny being ruthlessly put down by the army, in the interests of progress and wealth for the few. The novel ends with the rebels' Quechua battle-cry '*Nucanchic huasipungo*' ('Our plot of land') echoing in the empty valley, a reminder of the long history of Indian exploitation, of being treated like slaves, or animals. Icaza wrote several other untranslated novels.

MELVILLE, Herman (1819–1891). Melville was born on 1 August 1819 in New York. In 1841 he worked on a whaler, bound for the Pacific. He deserted ship in the Marquesas, and returned to the USA, where he was discharged in 1844. He wrote his stories about the **Galápagos** and Chile on the estate where he lived near Pittsfield, MA. 'The Encantadas' (Extract 3) comprises retold sketches associated with the Galápagos Islands. One recalls the '*chola*' widow whose husband and brother drowned, left alone hunting tortoise, with her dogs, and possibly raped by visiting whalers, until she is taken on board.

'Benito Cereno' tells of a ship anchored off St Maria, southern Chile, and a meeting with a slaver full of black slaves. Melville is not precise about the background he used for his fictions.

MICHAUX, Henri (1899–1987). Michaux was born in Namur, Belgium and died in Paris. In 1927–28 he travelled to Ecuador with Ecuadorian poet friend Alfredo Gangotena. Their experiences were published as *Ecuador: Journal de Voyage*, 1929 (*Ecuador*, 1970) – see Extract 8. Its diary jottings, poems and impressions, already reveal Michaux's attraction to other mentalities, mysticism and intense religious and drug-induced experiences. See Henri Michaux, *Selected Writings*, Richard Ellman, ed and trans, New Directions, New York, 1952.

ORTIZ, Adalberto (1914–). Born in **Esmeraldas**, Ortiz was secretary for the **Casa de la Cultura Ecuatoriana**, and delegate for Ecuador at a World Peace Council in 1953. He has been a teacher and diplomat. His novel *Juyungo*, 1943 (*Juyungo*, 1982 – Extract 10) – its title is a pejorative term for blacks that means 'monkey' or 'devil' – won first prize for the best novel in Ecuador for 1942. It is a realistic account of the life of a proud coastal *zambo* (part-black and part-Indian) who kills two whites defending his family. All his life he looks for racial and social equality, and ends up as a patriot fighting the invading Peruvians. Local historical events, the way of life, the food, houses, beliefs of the main character Ascensión Lastre, nicknamed Juyungo, and his world around tropical coastal **Esmeraldas** are interesting for their local colour. Adalberto Ortiz is also a poet.

THOMSEN, Moritz (1915–1991). Thomsen was born in Hollywood, CA, and died of cholera in **Guayaquil** on 28 August 1991. Halfway through his life, he joined the American Peace Corps and began farming in Ecuador. He wrote about his farm near **Esmeraldas** in *Living Poor*, 1971, and later of how he was duped by his partner in *The Farm on the River of Esmeraldas*, 1978. In 1990 he published *The Saddest Pleasure: A Journey on Two Rivers* (Extract 9), in which his rebellion against middle-class American values, and his experience of 12 years living poor in Ecuador, form a background of memories against a trip up the Amazon. He is an acute, honest observer of Latin American life, and of himself. As well as a travel book, this is about how Thomsen discovered himself, late, as a writer.

VONNEGUT, Kurt (1922–). Born in Indianapolis, IN, Vonnegut graduated at Cornell University, New York. His experiences in the second world war served as the basis for *Slaughterhouse Five*, 1969. He has written science fiction, and a biting satire set in **Guayaquil** and the **Galápagos Islands** called *Galápagos*, 1987 (Extract 7). The novel is packed with ideas, viewing the extinction of the human race and its survival as sea creatures mutated from passengers on a cruise thousands of years back in our times. *Cat's Cradle*, 1963, is set on the fictional Latin American island nation of 'San Lorenzo'.

PERU

'He loved the broad spaces and the magnificent grandeur of the Andes . . . The Indian Rosendo attributed to them all the shapes and characters imaginable, and he spent long hours watching them. Deep within him, he believed that the Andes held the baffling secret of life.'
Ciro Alegría,
Broad and Alien is the World

Peru, or the República de Peru, is possibly derived from the name of a river 'Piru' or from the name of a chieftain 'Birú' who became synonymous with gold (for Pizarro sailed for 'Birú' in 1524). It is the third largest country in South America with 1 285 215 sq km, a coast of 2250 km along the cold Humboldt (or Peru) current and disputed borders with Chile, Ecuador and Bolivia, and with Brazil and Colombia. The country is divided into three natural zones that become cultural frontiers. The Pacific Ocean coast along the cold current is very dry, cloudy half the year with garúa (mist), and lies on an earthquake belt. During Incan times this dry coastal zone was well irrigated and terraced, but now only the oases give cotton and sugar. The ports are for fishing boats in the fish-rich sea. It is here that **Lima** was founded in 1535. The capital city reached a population of 4 605 000 in 1989 (including its port **Callao**). Lima was rebuilt in 1746, and its university **San Marcos** dates back to 1551. Its site is not ideal: a famous essay by Salazar Bondy is entitled Lima, la horrible. Mario Vargas Llosa's ◊ first novel La ciudad y los perros, 1962 (The Time of the Hero, 1966 – Extract 4) refers in its Spanish title to the 'city' Lima. The novel deals with the city's middle-class **Miraflores** families, and its military and working class in a drama of urban alienation. His later Conversación en La Catedral, 1970 (Conversation in the Cathedral, 1975) recreates city life in a bar during Odría's dictatorship. The coast is essentially mestizo, some 40% of the population. There are also negroes and Asians (1%). Less than 15% call themselves white or European, but these so-called '40' families, or 2% of the population, control the wealth of the nation.

The second natural region, often quite separate from the coast, is the **Andes**, with deep canyons, or *quebradas*, and *páramos*, and higher up *puna* (short grass). It is here that the majority of Indians live as subsistence farmers, or as miners in silver and copper mines. Fifty per cent of the country remains rural. Peru is officially a bilingual culture, with Spanish as the commercial language, spoken by 67%, and Quechua by 27%. There are also pockets of Aymará (3%). Of a total population of 21 792 000 in 1989, 46% were Indian from the *sierra*. This proportion has created enormous problems for Peruvian identity. The clash of cultures is the theme of much of José Maria Arguedas's ◊ fiction. There is a tradition of protest novels describing the unchanged misery of Indians, especially in Ciro Alegría ◊ and Manuel Scorza (1928–83) in his novel *Redoble por Rancas*, 1970 (*Drum for Rancas*, 1977). One of Peru's most powerful political movements, founded by Victor Raúl Haya de la Torre – APRA (Alianza Popular Revolucionaria Americana) – began as a revindication of Indian *ayllu* or community rights. José Carlos Mariátegui was an early follower, and his influential essay *Siete ensayos de interpretación de la realidad peruana*, 1928 (*Seven Interpretive Essays on Peruvian Reality*, 1971) reflects this interest. César Vallejo's ◊ earlier poems from *Los heraldos negros*, 1919, and *Trilce*, 1922, are often set in his *sierra* home town of **Santiago de Chuco**, and packed with literal references to place. His birthplace is today the **Casa-Museo Poeta César Vallejo Mendoza** (Calle César Vallejo, Santiago de Chuco, La Libertad).

The third region is the *montaña*, or **Amazonian jungle** that is thinly populated, and with oil. Some 350 000 jungle Indians live in this area, which takes up three-fifths of Peru. It is a frontier zone that has fascinated Vargas Llosa who has partially set three of his well documented, realistic novels here: *La casa verde* 1965 (*The Green House*, 1968), *Pantaleón y las visitadoras*, 1973 (*Captain Pantoja and the Special Service*, 1978) and *El hablador*, 1987, (*The Storyteller*, 1989). It is here also near **Pucallpa** that Peter Matthiessen ◊ set his drama of visionary change, *At Play in the Fields of the Lord* (Extract 8), based on his travels (Extract 9).

INCAS AND SPANIARDS

Before the Spaniards arrived, Peru had seen several mysterious but advanced civilizations that left the Nazca lines, Paracas weaving, Moche ceramics, the Chimu adobe city **Chan Chan** near **Trujillo**, and **Tiahuanaco** up near **Lake Titicaca**. By 1438 the Inca dynasty had united an empire of some 25 million over lands that today include Bolivia, Ecuador, northern Argentina and Chile in a totalitarian state. The Incas ('children of the sun') called this empire Tawantinsuyo.

César Vallejo's house in Santiago de Chuco, now a museum

They built a network of roads, terraces, wonderful irrigation, but had no writing. They used *quipu* (knotted string, a mnemonic device for keeping records and sending messages) and sent *chasquis* (long-distance runners) along their roads to keep their empire in control. **Cuzco** (meaning 'navel of the world') was their capital and still retains its beautiful stones which bewitched the boy in Arguedas's ◊ novel *Deep Rivers* (Extract 3).

The Spaniards arrived just after Atahualpa (13th Inca emperor) had won a five-year civil war with his brother. An illiterate peasant, Francisco Pizarro, heard reports about Peruvian splendour after he had crossed to the Pacific with Balboa in 1524. He returned to Spain and obtained permission to conquer. He landed with four of his illiterate brothers and Diego de Almagro, and 180 men and horses in 1531, crossed the mountains and met Atahualpa at **Cajamarca**. He slaughtered the Incas, kidnapped Atahualpa, ransomed him for a room of gold and murdered him. It is said that the reason for the murder was Atahualpa's throwing the Bible to the ground when it was handed to him.

How the outnumbered Spaniards defeated such an organized military empire has long impressed people. Partly it was due to the horse: 'After God, we owed our victory to the horses' (R. Cunninghame Graham, *The Horses of the Conquest*, 1930); partly to the Incan legend of Viracocha, fair and with beard (the creator-god in human form who disappeared across the Pacific Ocean but whose return was prophesized); partly to gunpowder; and very much to cunning and ruthlessness. Pizarro entered **Cuzco** in 1535. The Incas tried to rebel under Manco Capac in 1536. Worse, Pizarro had humiliated Almagro who rose against him but was executed in 1538. Pizarro was then assassinated by Almagro's followers in 1541 (his corpse can be seen in **Lima's Cathedral**), so Gonzalo Pizarro became the ruler. He killed a Spanish Viceroy bringing over the New Laws, and was in turn executed in 1548. Only then did the Spaniards settle down in their vast *haciendas* with *encomienda*-owned Indian serfs. This bloody period, with Spanish cut-throats, gave rise to the Black Legend (*leyenda negra*, created by Spain's reputation for cruelty and intransigence in the New World towards the Indians), and elicited lasting European sympathy for the Incas in plays like William Davenant's *The Cruelty of the Spaniards in Peru*, 1658, Marmontel's *Les Incas*, Richard Brinsley Sheridan's, *Pizarro*, 1799, and Peter Shaffer's, *The Royal Hunt of the Sun*, 1964. William H. Prescott's *The Conquest of Peru*, 1847 brought the events vividly to the nineteenth century public's attention, leading to romances like Kingston's *Manco the Peruvian Chief*. Peruvians themselves have glamourized their past – for example, César Vallejo in *The Black Heralds*, and Abraham Valdelomar (1888–1919) in *Los hijos del sol*, 1920 (*The Children of the Sun: A Suite of Inca Legends from Peru*, 1968).

COLONIALISM AND INDEPENDENCE

Over the years 1561 to 1581, order was imposed through the Viceroyalty which governed the whole of South America from **Lima** where court

Notes to map (facing page): [a]*The setting for the novels The Time of the Hero, 1962, The Real Life of Alejandro Mayta, 1984, Aunt Julia and the Scriptwriter, 1977, and Conversation in the Cathedral, 1970;* [b]*See novels The Green House, 1965, and Who Killed Palomino Molero?, 1986;* [c]*See The Green House, and also Nicholas Shakespeare's novel The Vision of Elena Silves, 1989;* [d]*César Vallejo's Andean birthplace, now a museum;* [e]*See Pablo Neruda, Extract 6;* [f]*See Captain Pantoja and the Special Service, 1973;* [g]*See Peter Matthiessen's novel At Play in the Fields of The Lord, 1965, and travel book The Cloud Forest: A Chronicle of the South American Wilderness, 1960;* [h]*Mario Vargas Llosa's birthplace.*
Hollow circle = capital city; ruled area = mountainous region.

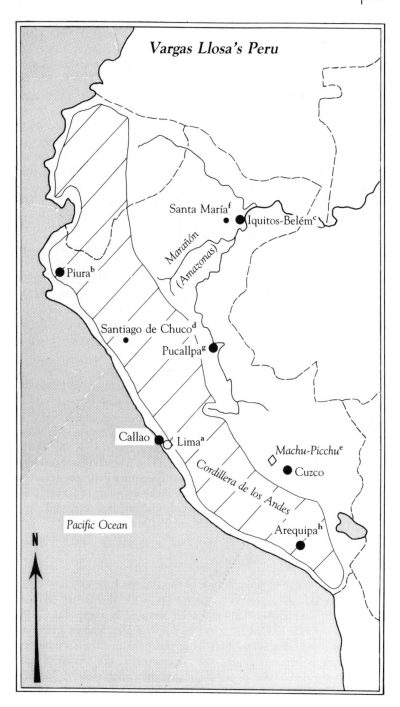

Vargas Llosa's Peru

Santa María[f]

Iquitos-Belém[c]

Marañón
(Amazonas)

Piura[b]

Santiago de Chuco[d]

Pucallpa[g]

Callao

Lima[a]

Machu-Picchu[e]

Cuzco

Cordillera de los Andes

Pacific Ocean

Arequipa[h]

N

life became sumptuous, as the city had a monopoly of trade via **Callao** to Balboa, then on mule to Porto Bello and Spain. Thornton Wilder's ⟨? novel *The Bridge of San Luis Rey* is set in colonial times, and one section refers to a famous love-story where an ageing Viceroy falls for Pericholi, a singer given her nickname from his curse of '*perra chola*' ('Peruvian bitch'). Verdi also wrote an opera about her (*La Perichole*).

Spain ruled South America through the church and the Inquisition that ran from 1570 to 1761. The **Inquisition Museum** in Lima should be visited, as it is by a character in Vargas Llosa's novel *Historia de Mayta*, 1984 (*The Real Life of Alejandro Mayta*, 1986). During this colonial period there were occasional rebellions, like the one by Tupac Amaru II in 1780, but they were quelled. The best account of Incan life is by a *mestizo* called Inca Garcilasso de la Vega whose *Royal Commentaries* appeared in Lisbon in 1609 and in English in 1688. There is a **Casa Museo Inca Garcilasso de la Vega** in **Cuzco** (Calle Garcilasso de la Vega). Later, Ricardo Palma (1833–1919) collected what he called *Las tradiciones peruanas* from 1872 to 1910 (*The Knights of the Cape and 37 Other Selections from the Tradiciones peruanas*, 1945). One extraordinary discovery in 1911 by the American archaeologist Hiram Bingham was the jungle fortress of **Machu-Picchu** (see Pablo Neruda's poem, Extract 6), which was never discovered by the Spaniards.

Lima had been a very conservative city, loyal to Spain, and was slow to take up Independence after Napoleon's 1808 invasion of Spain. It was thanks to Argentine General San Martín, and then Bolívar and his general Sucre, that on 28 July 1821 Independence was established. For a while Bolívar was dictator, then there was a Peruvian–Bolivian Confederation, until General Castilla ruled from 1844 to 1862, enriching Peru with the *guano* monopoly. The first civilian president was not elected until 1872. But nineteenth-century Peru was devasted by the War of the Pacific, and the Chilean invasion of Lima (they stayed three years). Economic and political stability emerged only under Leguía, in power in 1908–12 and 1919–31.

THE LOT OF THE INDIANS

During these hundred years the lot of the Indians had not changed at all. Indian reform movements sprang up, with the writer Manuel González Prada (1844–1918), and then Haya de la Torre and Carlos Mariátegui (1895–1930) basing radical political programmes on Indian integration and education. Mariátegui later joined the Communist Party. Their policies continued to be relevant over the following years of dictators like Odría in 1948 or the left-wing general Velasco Alvarado in 1968, and the Belaúnde presidencies. Behind APRA's

Alan García, elected in 1985, and his nationalizing of the banks and refusal to pay interests to the International Monetary Fund (leading to 4329% inflation in April 1989), and then the campaign for presidency between novelist Vargas Llosa and Fujimori in 1990, there have been active guerrilla movements, from those originally inspired by Guevara and Cuba where a young poet Javier Heraud (1942–64) – 'He said goodbye and left / and one day he was up there on top / alongside the guerillas' – was killed, to the ominous Maoist movement, Sendero Luminoso, whose leader Abimael Guzmán was surprisingly caught and tried in September 1992. The lot of the Quechua-speaking Indians has become crucial as the *barriadas* (shanty-towns) swell in **Lima**. Investigating the guerrillas is the motive behind novels by Mario Vargas Llosa, *The Real Life of Alejandro Mayta*, 1986 (Extract 5) and Nicholas Shakespeare ◊ (Extract 2).

Apart from Vallejo's poetry there are two anthologies that give a good sense of the variety of contemporary Peruvian poetry: *Peru: the New Poetry*, 1970 and 1977 and *The Newest Peruvian Poetry in Translation*, 1979. Good fiction writers like Julio Ramón Ribeyro (1929–) and Alfredo Bryce Echenique (1939–) await translation.

The following writers' houses may be visited: **Casa-Museo del Poeta José María Eguren** (Calle Colón 300 y/o, Plazuela San Francisco de Asís s/n, Barranco-Lima); **Casa-Museo del Novelista Martín Adán** (Calle Sánchez Carrión, Cuadra 1, Barranco-Lima – cf his novel *The Cardboard House*, 1990); and **Casa-Museo Doctor Raúl Porras Barrenechea** (Calle Narciso de la Colina 398, Miraflores, Lima).

BOOKLIST

The following selection includes all titles which are extracted in this chapter as well as those mentioned in the introduction which are available in English. In general, paperback editions are given when possible. The editions cited are not necessarily the only ones available. For most of the extracted works, the original publisher in English can be found in 'Acknowledgments and Citations' at the end of the volume, as can the exact location of the extracts and the editions from which they are taken. The date in square brackets is the original publica- tion date of the work in its original language. Extract numbers are highlighted in bold for ease of reference.

Adán, Martín, *The Cardboard House* [1928], Katherine Silver, trans, Graywolf Press, St Paul, MN, 1990.

Alegría, Ciro, *Broad and Alien is the World* [1941], Harriet de Onís, trans, Merlin, London, 1983/ Holt, Rinehart and Winston, New York, 1963. **Extract 11.**

Arguedas, José María, *Deep Rivers*

[1958], Frances Horning Barraclough, trans, University of Texas Press, Austin, TX, 1978. **Extract 3.**

Cisneros, Antonio, 'Paracas', in *Peru: The New Poetry*, Maureen Ahern and David Tipton, eds, London Magazine Editions, London, 1970/Red Dust, New York, 1977. **Extract 7.**

Kingston, William, *Manco the Peruvian Chief*, Collins, London, undated.

Mariátegui, José Carlos, *Seven Interpretive Essays on Peruvian Reality* [1928], University of Texas Press, Austin, TX, 1971.

Matthiessen, Peter, *At Play in the Fields of the Lord* [1965], Collins Harvill, London, 1988/Random House, New York, 1987. **Extract 8.**

Matthiessen, Peter, *The Cloud Forest: A Chronicle of the South American Wilderness* [1960], Collins Harvill, London, 1988/ Viking, New York, 1961. **Extract 9.**

Neruda, Pablo, *The Heights of Macchu Picchu* [1945], Nathaniel Tern, trans, Jonathan Cape, London, 1966/Farrar, Straus and Giroux, New York, 1967. **Extract 6.**

The Newest Peruvian Poetry in Translation, Luis A. Ramos-García and Edgar O'Hara, eds, Studia Hispanica Editions, Austin, TX, 1979.

Palma, Ricardo, *The Knights of the Cape and 37 Other Selections from the Tradiciones peruanas*, Harriet de Onís, trans, Knopf, New York, 1945.

Peru: The New Poetry, Maureen Ahern and David Tipton, eds, London Magazine Editions, London, 1970/Red Dust, New York, 1977 (revised ed).

Prescott, William H., *The Conquest of Peru*, R. Bentley, London, 1847/Random House, New York, 1979.

Scorza, Manuel, *Drum for Rancas* [1970], Edith Grossman, trans, Secker and Warburg, London, 1977/Harper and Row, New York, 1977.

Shaffer, Peter, *The Royal Hunt of the Sun* [1964], Penguin, London, 1981.

Shakespeare, Nicholas, *The Vision of Elena Silves* [1989], Penguin, London, 1990. **Extract 2.**

Sheridan, Richard Brinsley, *Pizarro* [1799], J. Ridgway, London, undated.

Valdelomar, Abraham, *The Children of the Sun: A Suite of Inca Legends from Peru* [1920], Southern Illinois University Press, Carbondale, IL, 1968.

Vallejo César, *The Black Heralds* [1919], Richard Schaaf and Kathleen Ross, trans, Latin American Literary Review Press, Pittsburg, PA, 1990.

Vallejo, César, 'On the Other Side of Life and Death', Hardie St Martin and Robert Mezey, trans, in the anthology *The Eye of the Heart*, Barbara Howes, ed, Allison and Busby, London, 1987/ Bobbs-Merril, New York, 1972. **Extract 10.**

Vallejo, César, *Trilce* [1922], David Smith, trans, Grossman, New York, 1973.

Vargas Llosa, Mario, *Captain Pantoja and the Special Service* [1973], Gregory Kolovakos and Ronald Christ, trans, Faber and Faber, London, 1987/Harper and Row, New York, 1978.

Vargas Llosa, Mario, *Conversation in the Cathedral* [1970], Gregory Rabassa, trans, Harper and Row, New York, 1975.

Vargas Llosa, Mario, *The Green House* [1965], Gregory Rabassa, trans, Picador, London, 1986/ Harper and Row, New York, 1968.

Vargas Llosa, Mario, *The Real Life of Alejandro Mayta* [1984], Alfred

MacAdam, trans, Faber and Faber, London, 1986/Farrar, Straus and Giroux, New York, 1986.
Extract 5.
Vargas Llosa, Mario, *The Storyteller* [1987], Helen Lane, trans, Faber and Faber, London, 1990/Farrar, Straus and Giroux, New York, 1989.
Vargas Llosa, Mario, *The Time of the Hero* [1962], Lysander Kemp, trans, Picador, London, 1986/

Grove Press, New York, 1966.
Extract 4.
Vargas Llosa, Mario, *Who Killed Palomino Molero?* [1986], Alfred MacAdam, trans, Faber and Faber, London, 1988/Farrar, Straus and Giroux, New York, 1987.
Extract 1.
Wilder, Thornton, *The Bridge of San Luis Rey* [1927], Penguin, London, 1989/Harpercollins, New York, 1986.

Extracts

(1) Amotape

Mario Vargas Llosa,
Who Killed Palomino Molero?

Amotape, a village in the far north of Peru, is where Vargas Llosa's bolero singer hid with his runaway bride before being found out and murdered. The two policemen go there for clues.

Amotape is thirty miles south of Talara, surrounded by sun-parched rocks and scorching sand dunes. There are dry bushes, carob thickets, and here and there a eucalyptus tree – pale green patches that brighten the otherwise monotonous gray of the arid landscape. The trees bend over, stretch out and twist around to absorb whatever moisture might be in the air; in the distance they look like dancing witches. In their benevolent shade, herds of squalid goats are always nibbling the crunchy pods that fall off their branches; there are also some sleepy mules and a shepherd, usually a small boy or girl, sunburnt, with bright eyes.

'Do you think that old story about Amotape with the priest and his maid is the truth, Doña Lupe?'

The hamlet is a confusion of adobe huts and little corrals made from wooden stakes. It has a few aristocratic houses clustered around an old plaza with a wooden gazebo. There are almond trees, bougainvilleas, and a stone monument to Simón Rodríguez, Simón Bolívar's teacher, who died in this solitary place. The citizens of Amotape, poor, dusty folks, live off their goats, their cotton fields, and the truck and bus drivers who detour between Talara and Sullana in order to drink some *chicha*, the local corn beer, or have a snack.

The name of the town, according to local legend, comes from colonial times, when Amotape, a rich town then, had a greedy parish priest who hated to feed visitors. His maid abetted him in this by warning him whenever she saw a traveller approaching. She would call out, 'Amo, tape, tape la olla, que viene gente' (Master, cover, cover the pot, people are coming). Could it be true?

(2) BELEN

Nicholas Shakespeare, *The Vision of Elena Silves*

Nicholas Shakespeare sets his novel about the love between a nun and a guerrillero in the Peru of the 1980s, with war being waged between the Maoist Sendero Luminoso and the government. It opens in Belén, the river port for Iquitos, describing Don Leopoldo, the local sage.

He wears no hat and his face is lined, as if he has walked into a spider's web and forgotten to wipe it away. His love of precise dates and proven facts has earned him a reputation for being a little pedantic. He knows more than is necessarily interesting about the yellow cathedral, its cartridge-shaped windows, its Swiss-made clock; about the origin of the tiles on the old Palace Hotel and about Admiral Grau, the man in whom Peru had once put all her hope, whose bronze whiskers bristle defiantly as if he is still on the deck of the *Huáscar*.

This morning, the flies on the Admiral's head and epaulettes have the appearance of laurel leaves.

Don Leopoldo looks beyond the statue to the metal house opposite, its roof stained with the sun. He can tell anyone who cares to listen – fewer and fewer nowadays – about this house, constructed by Eiffel for the Paris Exhibition of 1896, dismantled for its voyage to another continent altogether, and then transported two thousand miles upriver from Pará to be reassembled, bolt by bolt, for an absentee rubber lord.

The Club de Leones has since moved its premises to a floor above the Banco Industrial, but Don Leopoldo remembers when the members played their poker in Eiffel's folly, drinking bottles of Allsopp's Pale Ale in a hot metal room like an oven.

El Club de los Pájaros Muertos, they called it.

He gazes at Eiffel's house and the buckled pillar into which a car has crashed. It upsets him no one has repaired it. These days he finds it easy to be upset. That's what happens when you are a dead parrot with long memories. Don Leopoldo can remember a time when there was no cathedral and women walked beside the open drains holding geranium-scented handkerchiefs to their noses. He remembers the town in the days when you bought your clothes from Don Ramur – Scotch tweed, alpaca, boaters; when the ice-cream you ate in the Booth supermarket came all the way from Liverpool; when the port you drank with Orestes Minero in the café Nanay was Taylor's finest, shipped from Pinhão.

Now the river is silting up and no boats come from Europe. Now you bought your shirts off the pavement and they had crocodiles on the pockets. Now in the café they hold aerobics classes.

(3) LIMA

José María Arguedas, *Deep Rivers*

The wandering judge and his sensitive son, the novel's narrator, arrive in Lima for the first time from the Andean provinces.

We walked down the street, crossed another very wide one, and then went along an alley which came out into the Plaza de Armas. We saw the domes of the cathedral. My father took me by the arm. The portico with its white arches came into view. We were in the shadow of the church.

'There's no one in the plaza now,' my father said.

It was the largest one I had ever seen. It was as if the arches were on the distant perimeter of some silent plain in the icy highlands. What if we suddenly heard the call of a *yanawiku*, one of the wild ducks that forage around the ponds of those plains!

We entered the plaza. The little trees that had been planted in the park and the arches seemed intentionally dwarfed in the presence of the cathedral and the Jesuit church.

'They must not have been able to grow,' I said. 'They couldn't, in front of the cathedral.'

My father led me up the steps to the terrace at the entrance of the cathedral and removed his hat as we neared the large central door. It took us a long time to cross the terrace. Our footsteps resounded on the stone. My father prayed as we walked along, not repeating the usual prayers, but talking freely to God. We were in the shadow of the façade. He did not tell me to pray; I just stood with my head uncovered, completely exhausted. It was an immense façade; it seemed to be as wide as the base of the mountains that rise up from the shores of some highland lakes. In the silence, the towers and the terrace echoed the smallest sound, like the rocky mountains that border the icy lakes. The rocks send back deep echoes of the cry of the ducks or of the human voice. The echo is diffused, and seems to spring from the very breast of the traveler, who is alert to the silence and oppressed by it.

(4) LIMA

Mario Vargas Llosa, *The Time of the Hero*

Alberto is the coward poet in Vargas Llosa's novel, set in Lima's Leoncio Prado Military Academy. Alberto wants to initiate himself sexually in the Victoria district of the city.

He got off at the corner of Wilson and the 28th of July. I'm fifteen but I look older, he thought. I haven't got any reason to be nervous. He lit a cigarette, then threw it away after only two puffs. As he went down the 28th of July, the avenue grew more and more crowded, and after he crossed the tracks of the Lima–Chorrillos streetcar he found himself in the midst of a swarm of workers, housemaids, mestizos with lank hair, mixed Chinese who walked as if they were dancing, copper-colored Indians, smiling half-breeds. He could tell he was in the Victoria district by the smell of native food and drink that filled the air, an almost visible smell of fried porkskin and pisco, of ham rolls and sweat, of beer and dirty feet.

As he crossed the Victoria Plaza, which was huge and crowded, the stone Inca that loomed against the sky reminded him of the hero's statue at the Academy, and also of what Vallano said once: 'Manco Cápac is a pimp, he's pointing the way to Huatica Street.' The crowd forced him to walk slowly, and he almost suffocated. The lights on the avenue seemed deliberately weak and far apart, thus accentuating the profiles of the men who walked by looking in the windows of the identical little houses lined up along the sidewalks. At the corner of Huatica and the 28th July, Alberto heard a chorus of abuse from inside a restaurant run by a Japanese dwarf. He saw a group of men and women arguing viciously around a bottle-covered table. He lingered a few moments on the corner. He had his hands in his pockets and he stole glances at the people around him. Some of the men were glassy-eyed, others seemed deliriously happy.

He straightened his jacket and went into the fourth block, the narrowest. There was an attempt at a superior smile on his lips but his eyes were full of anxiety. He only had to walk a few yards; he knew by heart that Golden Toes lived in the second house. There were three men at the door of it, one behind another. Alberto peered in the window: there was a tiny sitting room lighted by a red bulb, with a chair, a yellowed and unrecognizable photograph on the wall, and a small bench under the window. She must be short, he thought, disappointed. A hand took him by the shoulder.

(5) LIMA

Mario Vargas Llosa,
The Real Life of Alejandro Mayta

Vargas Llosa, fascinated by the early guerrilla uprising in Peru in the 1960s, describes one of the slums in Lima.

To get there from Barranco, you have to go to downtown Lima, cross the Rímac – a squalid creek this time of year – at the Ricardo Palma bridge, go along Piedra Liza and skirt the San Cristóbal hills. It's a long, risky, and at certain times of the day extremely slow route because of all the traffic. It also charts the gradual impoverishment of Lima: the prosperity of Miraflores and San Isidro progressively decays and grows ugly in Lince and La Victoria, then resurges illusively in the downtown area, with the tedious towers of banks, mutual-fund and insurance companies – among which nevertheless there proliferate promiscuous tenements and old houses that stay upright only by a miracle. But immediately after you cross the river, in the so-called Bajo el Puente sector, the city decomposes into vacant lots, where huts thrown together out of matting and rubble have sprung up, slums mixed in with garbage dumps that go on for miles. Once this marginal Lima was only poor, but now it's a place of blood and terror as well.

When you come to Avenida de los Chasquis, the asphalt gives out and the potholes take over, but a car can still bounce along a few more yards, fenced-in lots on either side, and broken street-lights – the kids smash the bulbs with slingshots.

(6) Machu-Picchu

Pablo Neruda, *The Heights of Macchu Picchu*

Chilean poet Neruda visited the imposing ruins of Machu-Picchu (not discovered until 1911) on his way back from Mexico to Chile in 1943. He wrote the poem extracted here in 1946, and it became a section in Canto General, 1950, his counter-history of Latin America.

Then up the ladder of the earth I climbed
through the barbed jungle's thickets
until I reached you Macchu Picchu.
Tall city of stepped stone,
home at long last of whatever earth
had never hidden in her sleeping clothes.
In you two lineages that had run parallel
met where the cradle both of man and light
rocked in a wind of thorns.
Mother of stone and sperm of condors.

High reef of the human dawn.
Spade buried in primordial sand.
This was the habitation, this is the site:
here the fat grains of maize grew high
to fall again like red hail.
The fleece of the vicuña was carded here
to clothe men's loves in gold, their tombs and mothers,
the king, the prayers, the warriors.
Up here men's feet found rest at night
near eagles' talons in the high
meat-stuffed eyries. And in the dawn
with thunder steps they trod the thinning mists,
touching the earth and stones that they might recognize
that touch come night, come death.

(7) PERU: BEFORE THE INCAS

Antonio Cisneros, *Paracas*

*Cisneros evokes a pre-Incaic coastal civilization in his poem
'Paracas'. The poem is included in Peru: The New Poetry – see
Booklist.*

Since early morning
the water has been rising between the red backs
of the shells

& fragile-footed gulls
chewing the small tidal animals
until they're swollen like boats
spread out beneath the sun.

Only rags
& skulls of the dead tell us

that beneath these sands
our ancestors were buried in droves.

(8) PERU: A JUNGLE TOWN

Peter Matthiessen, *At Play in the Fields of the Lord*

*Matthiessen describes Remate de Males, a frontier town on the
border with Brazil, today renamed Benjamin Constant. Translated, 'Remate de Males' means 'culmination of evils'.*

From where they stood, all of Remate could be seen; how dared they
put it on the maps at all! Its dispirited clearing was surrounded on three
sides by low thatched huts, like a debased caricature of a colonial plaza;
the fourth side faced the Río Espíritu. In the mud of the clearing, thin
dirty chickens picked and small hogs sighed.

To Quarrier, as to everyone who came there, the name 'Culmination
of Evils' caught the spirit of the place exactly. The clearing scarred a
wall of jungle which could not be held in check; the green absorbed
both fire and machete, flowing back across the tangle of ugly blackened
stumps to close the wound. The huts fought off rank weeds and thick
lianas which crept up from behind, and the interiors were infiltrated by
pale tentacles, squalid liverwort and creeping fungi. The plaza itself,
worn bare by feet and pigs, and beaten flat by heavy rains, had been a
quagmire for half a century; its soil was a sterile orange–red, as slick as
grease.

Through the prism of the mist, the heat of the low jungle sky seemed to focus on this wretched spot, where tarantulas and scorpions and stinging ants accompanied the mosquito and the biting fly into the huts, where the vampire bats, defecating even as they fed, would fasten on exposed toes at night, where one could never be certain that a bushmaster or fer-de-lance had not formed its cold coil in a dark corner. In the river, piranhas swam among the stingrays and candirus and the large crocodilians called lagartos; in adjacent swamps and forests lived the anaconda and the jaguar. But at Remate de Males such creatures were but irritants; the true enemies were the heat and the biting insects, the mud and the nagging fear, more like an ague, of the silent hostile people of the rain forest.

(9) Pucallpa

Peter Matthiessen, *The Cloud Forest*

Pucallpa (on the River Ucayali, capital of the department of Ucayali, with a population of some 95 000), is the source for Matthiessen's fictional Amazonian towns. It was also where he set off to find the prehistoric bones and where he was visited by Allen Ginsberg, who, like Burroughs (◊ Mexico), was in search of the drug yage. The Hotel Mercedes still exists.

With its mud streets, thatch roofs, and raffish waterfront, and its barefoot Shipibos with their nose ornaments and bright clothing, the Peruvian river town of Pucallpa is as colorful as it is hideous. The trading post for thousands of square miles of wilderness, it attracts a motley fleet of cargo craft and long canoes: these swarm like a hatch of flies on the broad Ucayali, drawn out of the water courses of the vast *selva* or Amazon jungle, which, lying there in steaming silence across the river, stretches away for twenty-five hundred miles to the Atlantic coast.

The cultural center of Pucallpa is the bar of the Gran Hotel Mercedes, which serves coffee and liquor and *gaseosas*, or soft drinks, from dawn until after midnight. From its open doors and windows a splendid view may be obtained of the hogs and vultures which pick over the orange quagmire of the street.

(10) SANTIAGO DE CHUCO

César Vallejo, *On The Other Side of Life and Death*

In this autobiographical story published in 1923, poet César Vallejo's narrator returns to his home town, Santiago de Chuco, in the province of Libertad, after the death of his mother. In reality, Vallejo had been studying in Lima when his mother died. The house he describes is a museum – see his biographical entry. This story is included in the anthology The Eye of the Heart – see Booklist.

It was not two years since my mother had died. I had had the news of her death in Lima, where I also learned that papa and my brothers had set out for a distant hacienda owned by an uncle, to do whatever they could to dull the pain of such an overwhelming loss. The estate was in a very remote area in the jungle, on the other side of the Marañon River. From Santiago I would continue in that direction, eating up endless paths through steep highlands and unfamiliar, scorching jungles.

My horse snorted suddenly. Chaff blew thickly on the light breeze, almost blinding me. A mound of barley. And then Santiago slid into view on its rugged mesa, with its burnt roofs under the setting sun. And eastwards on the abutment of a reddish yellow promontory, I could still see the graveyard, retouched at the hour by the sixth color of the afternoon; and it was more than I could take, and a vast inconsolable sorrow made me numb.

I got to the village as night fell. I turned the last corner, and as I entered the street my house was on, I made out a figure sitting alone on the stone bench by the door. Alone. Very much alone – so much so that it frightened me, drowning out the deep grief in my soul. Perhaps it was also because of the almost frozen peace with which the silhouette, stiffened by the wavering half-light, clung to the whitewashed face of my tears. A unique attack of nerves dried my tears. I went forward. My older brother Angel jumped up from the seat and embraced me. He had come in from the hacienda on business a few days before.

That night, after a frugal meal, we mounted a vigil until dawn. I visited all the rooms in the house, the corridors and stables, and although he made obvious efforts to turn aside my eagerness to explore the rambling old house we loved so well, Angel himself seemed to enjoy this torture of going through the hallucinating domain of life's deepest past.

During the few days of his stay in Santiago, Angel had lived alone in the house, where, he said, everything was as it had been left at Mama's death. He also gave me an account of her last healthy days before the fatal illness, and of her final moments. How often then did our brotherly embraces pierce us to the heart!

As in all rural houses of the Peruvian sierras, that almost always have a stone seat built-in next to the door, there was one leaning back by the threshold I had just crossed, doubtless the same ancient bench of my childhood, filled in and plastered innumerable times. With the shabby door open, we sat on the bench and there too we placed the sad-eyed lantern we carried with us. Its light fell squarely on Angel's face, which went paler moment by moment, as the night slipped by, until his face seemed nearly transparent. Once, seeing him like that, I kissed his grave, bearded cheek.

A flash of lightning, the kind that comes in summer in the sierras, from far off, with its thunder already spent, turned the night inside out. Rubbing my eyelids, I faced Angel. And there was nothing there – neither he nor the lantern nor the seat – nothing. And I heard nothing, I felt as if I were in a grave . . .

(11) Tumi, in the Andes

Cirio Alegría, *Broad and Alien is the World*

Through his protagonist Rosendo Maqui, Alegría describes the Andean village of Tumi, under the mountain Rumi.

Rumi was both forbidding and gentle, stern and friendly, solemn and benign. The Indian Rosendo believed that he understood its physical and spiritual secrets as though they were his own. Or rather, those of his wife, for love is a stimulus to knowledge and possession. Except that his wife had grown old and sick, while Rumi was always the same, haloed by the prestige of immortality.

'Which is better,' Rosendo tried to decide, 'the earth or woman?'

He had never thought it through clearly, but he loved the earth very much . . .

From where he was sitting at the moment he could see the village, the modest and strong centre of the community of Rumi, owner of much land and cattle. The road dropped down into a hollow to enter the town through a double row of little houses pompously called the Calle Real. About the middle the street opened on one side into what was also known pompously as the Village Square. In the centre of the square, shaded by an occasional tree, rose a sturdy little church. The houses had roofs of red tile or grey thatch, and the walls were yellow or violet or red, depending on the color of the clay with which they had been stuccoed. Each had its own garden patch in the back, sown in lima beans, cowpeas, vegetables, and bordered with leafy trees, prickly pears and magueys. It was a delight to see the gay picture the village made, and still more delightful to live there. What does civilization know? Of course, it can deny or affirm the excellence of this kind of life. Those who had made it their business to live here had known, for centuries, that happiness comes from justice, and justice from the common good. This had been established by time, force of tradition, man's will, and the unfailing gifts of the earth. The villagers of Tumi were content with their lot.

Biographies and plot summaries

ALEGRÍA, Ciro (1909–1967). Alegría was born in **Huamachuco**, in the north of Peru on 4 November 1909. He lived for a time in the Amazonian area with a grandfather, and then went to school in **Trujillo**. He joined Haya de la Torre's radical APRA (see introduction) that aimed to integrate the Indians into Peruvian society. He was twice imprisoned, in 1931 spending 14 months in **Lima prison**. In 1934, in exile in Chile, he became paralysed after a severe attack of TB. In 1935 he published his first protest novel *La serpiente de oro* (*The Golden Serpent*, 1943) about village Indians in the jungle on the **River Marañón** (further down becoming the Amazon), which is the golden serpent, and their rafts. In 1939 Alegría published his novel about Indian exploitation in the *sierra*, *Los perros hambrientos*, condemning the white landowners. In 1941 he published *El mundo es ancho y ajeno* (*Broad and Alien is the World*, 1941 – Extract 11) about Indian resistance to being ejected from their traditional Andean lands, led by their mayor Rosendo Maqui in Rumi, northern Peru in the 1920s. Despite the anthropological care with which the Rumi community is described, it is a pessimistic novel about how they are unable to fight

capitalism. Alegría spent the war in New York, and lived in Cuba in the 1950s. A book on the Cuban revolution was published posthumously in 1971.

ARGUEDAS, José María (1911–1969). Arguedas was born on 18 January 1911 in **Andahuaylas**, highland Peru. He committed suicide in **Lima** in 1969. Son of a travelling provincial judge, he was brought up by the Quechua-speaking Indian servants in his step-mother's large house, and early learnt about the deep racial divisions in Peruvian society between whites like himself and Indians. From 1953 he worked as a museum curator, university professor and ethnographer. From his earliest published story in 1935, Arguedas has tried to combine his knowledge of Quechua and Spanish, moulding Spanish to Quechuan syntax in original and moving ways. His novel *Los ríos profundos*, 1958 (*Deep Rivers*, 1978 – Extract 3) beautifully evokes the landscape of Peru accompanying Ernesto's painful awakening to the suffering of the Indians as he grows up with his wandering father, and then is sent to a boarding school in **Abancay** (high up on the road to Cuzco). The boy narrator is a loner and outsider who relates emotionally to nature, trees, insects and Indian artifacts. At the end he sides with the market-women as they revolt against the white landowners. An earlier novel, *Yawar Fiesta*, 1941 (*Yawar Fiesta*, 1984), deals with a community of Indians ejected from their ancestral lands (the title refers to the Indian version of bull-fighting). Arguedas wrote poetry in Quechua, translated as *The Singing Mountains: Songs and Tales of the Quechua People*, 1971. Several other works dealing with his profound and intimate knowledge of Indian culture remain untranslated, like *El sexto*, 1961, about prison life (from Arguedas's own year in the El Sexto prison in 1937 for organizing a demonstration); *Todas las sangres*, 1964; and *El zorro de arriba y el zorro de abajo*, posthumous, 1969, in which two foxes discuss the two Perus split between the mountains and the coastal town of **Chimbote**, laying bare the sickness in the country. The diary sections written by Arguedas himself reveal his despair about Indians in Peru.

CISNEROS, Antonio (1942–). Born in **Lima**, Cisneros has travelled widely, as can be seen in his poems. He spent some ten years abroad, staying at Southampton University, Nice, and Budapest. His first of eight books of poems appeared in 1961, much influenced by Ezra Pound's cantos, and Pound's way of blending history with quotations, as well as by the American Beats. *Comentarios reales*, 1964, won the National Poetry Prize; *Canto ceremonial contra un oso hormiguero*, 1968, the Cuban Casa de las Américas prize; and *La crónica del niño Jesús*, 1981, the Rubén Darío prize. His first selection in English was *The Spider Hangs Too Far from the*

Ground, 1970, and a selection of his poetry from 1964 to 1981 appeared as *At Night the Cats*, 1985, in which his move away from sarcasm and irony to ecological commitment is clear. Cisneros is currently a professor of literature at the University of San Marcos, Lima. He is also a journalist. He wrote: 'It is becoming increasingly difficult to live in such a poor, sad, violent country. Nonetheless here I reside between fear and hope!'

MATTHIESSEN, Peter (1927–). Matthiessen was born in New York on 22 May 1927, and was educated at Hotchkiss, Yale, where he obtained his BA in 1950, and the Sorbonne. He married and lived as an expatriate in Paris where he co-founded the *Paris Review*. He is a well known travel writer, formed by the Beat generation, with interests in Buddhism (see *The Snow Leopard*, 1978); Red Indian rights (cf *Indian Country*, 1985); immigrants' rights (a profile of Cesar Chavez, *Sal Si Puedes*, 1970); and ecology. He has written four novels, and short stories.

At Play in the Fields of the Lord, 1965 (Extract 8), is a thesis novel dealing with issues from drugs and visions, to missionaries and Indians, framed by the epilogue from Herman Hesse about the best way to God. The hero Lewis Moon is a Beat on the road, on a spiritual quest. He is a tough bum who finds himself in the jungles of Peru and Bolivia (but unnamed), at the edge of the civilized world. He seeks a return to a primordial and instinctual way of living in the blank spaces of the maps. The plot of the novel involves Moon and his adventuring buddy Wolfie using their plane as mercenaries to bomb intractable jungle Indians, called the Niaruna. Moon's ambivalence about this job emerges from the fact that he

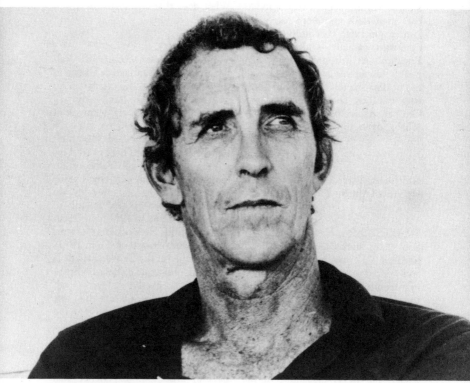

Peter Matthiessen

is part American Indian, rebelling against what the Americans have done with their Indians. He hates clean, white America, represented by the missionaries in the novel. After a violent, drunken fight, Moon drinks the local Indian vision-inducing drug *ayahuasca* (*yage*), steals the plane, and parachutes into the Niaruna tribe, to learn painfully their way of life. To the missionaries Moon had crashed, and died in the jungle until one of the missionary wives bathes naked, and is approached by Moon in tribal warrior outfit. From this erotic encounter he catches influenza, and contaminates his tribe. It is here that Moon begs for Western medicines from his rival, Quarrier the missionary. The mis-

sionaries stand for another view of South American Indians. The novel opens with Martin Quarrier, his big, mid-western wife Hazel and their son Billy landing at Madre de Dios in a DC3 from North Dakota. Matthiessen has depicted Quarrier as a proto-anthropologist, who understands the Indians' otherness, but is split by his fundamentalist drive, and divided by lust and his supposed spiritual love. At the novel's end he changes sides, and warns the Indians that the Peruvian army is approaching. He is ironically hacked to death by an informer Indian.

In *The Cloud Forest: A Chronicle of the South American Wilderness*, 1961 (Extract 9), Matthiessen is an amateur ornithologist who wanders the 'mysterious continent' of South America in 1960. He admits to taking *ayahuasca*, casually, while waiting in **Pucallpa**. At the end of the book, unable to take his giant fossil jaw out of Pucallpa, he tells how Allen Ginsberg was there and also saw the jaw. Ginsberg had corresponded with Burroughs about *yage* (*The Yage Letters*, 1963).

NERUDA, Pablo (see under Chile). He visited **Machu-Picchu** in 1943.

SHAKESPEARE, Nicholas (1957–). Son of an ambassador, Shakespeare lived some 25 years in Latin America, and worked as a *gaucho* on an *estancia* in Argentina. He is literary editor for the *Daily Telegraph*. His first novel *The Vision of Elena Silves*, 1989, focuses on Peru's revolutionary Maoist Sendero Luminoso. In *Granta* (Spring, 1988), Shakespeare wrote about Abimael Guzmán, its enigmatic leader, but never met him. In the novel Guzmán appears as a university lecturer, fanatical Maoist, and secret lover of Frank Sinatra's music. He has a skin disease covering his face with pustules, hates Fidel Castro, and sees the future of Peru as purely Quechua-speaking and Indian. The novel is also a love story set in **Belén** in Amazonian Peru where Gabriel Lung, part-Chinese, a revolutionary who turns to the Sendero Luminoso, falls for Elena Silves of Portuguese stock who has a vision that embarrasses the local bishop. In fact, her vision was of her lover, not the Virgin Mary. Finally, after twenty years, they meet up and are killed, or live far away in the jungle. Incidental details include Gabriel escaping a massacre in prison. The novel echoes the words of one of its characters: 'To be a Peruvian.

What does that signify to the world outside? Nothing.'

VALLEJO, César (1892–1938). Vallejo was born in **Santiago de Chuco** in the province of Libertad, Peru, 3115 m up in the Andes, on 15 March 1892. He was the youngest of 11 children, from a religious family, a *mestizo* with Indian blood. His childhood was intense and happy, until his mother died in 1918. Some of his most moving poems deal emotionally with the break-up of family life. In 1905 Vallejo went to school in **Humachuco**, and in 1911 to university in **Trujillo**. He worked as a tutor, and a cashier's assistant. From 1913–17 he studied at the **Universidad de la Libertad**, and wrote a thesis on Spanish Romantic poetry.

In 1913 Vallejo wrote his first poems, and in 1919 published *Los heraldos negros* (*The Black Heralds*, 1990), trying out several styles, fused by his intense sincerity. Back home he was falsely arrested, spending 112 days in prison, an experience that entered *Trilce*, 1922 (*Trilce*, 1973), 77 avant-garde poems moving from childlike cries about loss, to erotic and sexual disasters to hermetic experiments, one of the greatest books of poems written in Spanish. He published his short stories (Extract 10) in 1922. In 1923 he left for Paris, never to return to Peru, living as a journalist, always on the breadline, and ill. By 1928 he had awoken to the suffering of the people, and he visited Moscow, the first of three journeys, and wrote two books, interviewing the revolutionary poet Mayakovsky. He married Georgette in 1929. In 1931 he published *El Tungsteno* (*Tungsten: a Novel*, 1988). He did not publish any further poetry. In 1930 he visited Spain, and became a founder member of the Spanish Communist

Party. He was expelled from France in 1932, then allowed back. During the Spanish Civil War he was too ill to fight, but took part in the Writers' Congresses.

Just before he died in Paris on 15 April 1938, Vallejo had prepared a sequence of moving poems about the fall of Spain, with names and places, *España, aparta de mí este cáliz* (Spain, Let This Cup Pass From Me, 1977). After his death his *Poemas humanos* were published (1940), combining his earlier literary experiments with complex emotional responses to the crises of his times (*The Complete Posthumous Poems*, 1978). Several anthologies of his moving and influential poetry exist in English (*Selected Poems*, 1976; *Selected Poems*, 1981; *César Vallejo: A Selection of his Poetry*, 1987). His example and sincerity have been an enormous influence on Latin America's politicized poetry. See J. Franco, *César Vallejo: The Dialectics of Poetry and Silence*, Cambridge University Press, 1976.

VARGAS LLOSA, Mario (1936–). Born in **Arequipa**, Vargas Llosa was educated in Cochabamba, Bolivia, where he lived with his family from 1937 to 1945. He then moved to **Piura**. He graduated from **San Marcos de Lima** university in law and literature. In 1958 he won a scholarship to do a doctorate at Madrid University on the fiction of his friend Gabriel García Márquez, and the work was published in 1971. He moved to Paris, and then London, where he lived for many years working as a journalist, broadcaster and university teacher. In 1976 he became president of International PEN club. His first short story appeared in 1956, and a book of stories, *Los jefes*, in 1958 (*The Cubs and Other Stories*, 1980).

Vargas Llosa's first novel, *La ciudad y los perros*, 1962 (*The Time of the Hero*, 1966 – Extract 4), recreated his boarding-school days in the **Leoncio Prado** military academy in **Lima** where the pupils were called *'perros'* ('dogs'). The plot involves someone stealing exam papers, and being murdered. There are tough characters from all social classes, from a budding poet to El Jaguar, the slum kid turned leader. Carefully constructed, and brilliantly realistic, the novel has a sting in its tail in the form of an unidentified monologue. The rites of *machismo* in Lima society and exposure of the corrupt military led to 1000 copies of the novel being publicly burned. It won the Biblioteca Breve Prize in Barcelona in 1962. The first edition had a map of Peru, and a photograph of the actual school. His second novel, *La casa verde*, 1965 (*The Green House*, 1968) is a complex account of the setting up of a brothel – the green house – in **Piura**, with sections in the Peruvian jungle. The novel has an overlapping time-scheme that throws characters back and forward, in an unidentifiable way so that an Indian girl becomes a whore, and a Japanese trader in Indians a leper. It won the Rómulo Gallegos prize in 1967. He then published a long, pessimistic novel set in **Lima**, in a bar (the Cathedral), during the Odría dictatorship, *Conversación en La Catedral*, 1970 (*Conversation in the Cathedral*, 1975) about political corruption and degradation. This was followed by a comedy located in the jungle near **Iquitos** called *Pantaleón y las visitadoras*, 1973 (*Captain Pantoja and the Special Service*, 1978), about furnishing whores for sex-starved soldiers.

In 1983 Vargas Llosa based *La tía Julia y el escribidor*, 1977 (*Aunt Julia and the Scriptwriter*, 1982) on his own affair when 18 with his 32-year-old

Mario Vargas Llosa

aunt, and later marriage to a cousin, Patricia, still his wife (they have three children). It is a change in tone from the more earnest novels criticizing aspects of Peruvian history, for it is light and funny. It concerns a soap opera broadcaster, with samples of his mad plots, and Vargas Llosa's affair. He then wrote an epic about an incident in nineteenth century Brazilian history (the only non-Peruvian novel), called *La guerra del fin del mundo*, 1981 (*The War of the End of the World*, 1984), in which he orchestrates brilliant battle scenes around **Canudos** (in the *sertão*), and the Christ-like rebel Conselheiro, (in the wake of Brazilian journalist Da Cunha's (◊ Brazil) account in 1902). In *Historia de Mayta*, 1984 (*The Real Life of Alejandro Mayta*, 1986 – Extract 5) Vargas Llosa returns to revolutionary politics, and the first failed guerrilla uprising in Peru in the

late 1950s. Vividly realistic, with dialogues that match the varied characters, it is structured like an investigation into Mayta's complex motives, from his poverty, his intellectualism, to his homosexuality. The author continues to be fascinated by fanatics. In 1986, he wrote a short complex novel *¿Quién mató a Palomino Molero?* (*Who Killed Palomino Molero?*, 1987 – Extract 1) about two local **Piura** cops trying to solve the sadistic murder of a *cholo* (half-caste) bolero singer. The sordidity of coastal life in **Talera**, and the racism of Peruvian society are finely evoked. Vargas Llosa recreates the Peruvian jungle again in *El hablador*, 1987 (*The Storyteller*, 1989) in the context of the evangelical invasion of Amazon Indians and a Jewish friend of the named author turning himself into an oral storyteller recreating Machiguenga myths (and Kafka). Most recently Vargas Llosa has published *Elogio de la madrastra*, 1988 (*In Praise of the Stepmother*, 1990), about a boy who seduces his

step-mother and destroys her relationship with his father, told with full accounts of their fantasy lives.

Despite this prolific fiction, Vargas Llosa has kept up voluminous critical and newspaper writing, not yet collected in English, apart from a study on Flaubert (*The Perpetual Orgy*, 1986). Vargas Llosa carefully researches the background to his fiction: for example, he several times visited Amazonian Peru between 1958 and 1981, and his work can be seen as a chronicle of Peruvian life and history from the early 1950s in a realistic mode. In 1987, when Peruvian president Alan García nationalized the banks, Vargas Llosa was stirred into politics, becoming the conservative alliance candidate. He was defeated in the presidential elections by Alberto Fujimuri in 1990 (see Vargas Llosa's account in *Granta*, No 36, 1991). He speaks his mind, and cares little about being ostracized by the left. Vargas Llosa is also a playwright, with plays produced in English like *Kathy and the Hippopotamus*, 1990. He now lives in London. See Charles Rossna (ed), *Mario Vargas Llosa: A Collection of Critical Essays*, University of Texas Press, Austin, TX, 1978.

WILDER, Thornton (1897–1975). See also under Chile. Wilder's second Pulitzer Prize winning novel, *The Bridge of San Luis Rey*, 1927, is set in viceregal Peru. An Incan bridge between Lima and Cuzco collapses so that five people are killed. A priest investigates the lives of these five to see if their deaths were accidental or planned. Wilder concentrates on 'inner life'. There are references to the viceroy's intricate court life – 'a ceremonial so complicated that it could only be remembered by a society that had nothing else to think about'; the acting of Spanish plays; an Abbess who was a proto feminist fighting the tendency for women in Peru to blame their own ugliness for all that befell them, and doing anything for a caress. Behind the mock letters and incidents, Wilder touches on the meaninglessness of life. The Peruvian setting is not detailed, as this novel is about universals like the lack of love, the ironies of fate, and the impotence of living in distant provinces. The bridge of the title lies on the **road to Cuzco** and was called the Huaca-chaca – the Holy Bridge – which crossed the **River Purimac** below the town of **Curubamba**. It was the longest continuously used bridge in the Americas (1350 until 1890), and was 45 m long, hanging 42 m above the roaring river.

BOLIVIA

'A roof here does not give a view of rooftop life, as in Southern Spain or Greece; the view here is of a whole mythology. To scan the horizons from up here is to attend a silent conference in immensity and solitude. To feel caught in a solid noose of colossal forces.'
Gordon Meyer,
Summer at High Altitude

Bolivia, or the República de Bolivia, is named after the liberator Simón Bolívar. It is an inland republic bounded by Brazil, Paraguay, Argentina, Chile and Peru. Bolivia is the fifth largest country in Latin America, with 1 098 581 sq km of territory. By 1990 the population reached some 7.3 million divided roughly into 30% *mestizo*, 25% Quechua-speaking (the language of the Incas), 17% Aymará, and 14% European. The *mestizos* are called *cholos* and include Indians who speak Spanish. All the whites also speak Quechua or Aymará, because during colonial times the Indians were not allowed to learn Spanish. From statistics, its clear that some 36% of the country does not speak Spanish. The population of Bolivia remains essentially rural, with little migration to the cities, and little immigration from Europe. Most of the people live densely in the highlands above 3000 m. The legal capital is **Sucre**, and the actual seat of government is **La Paz**, founded in 1548 by a Spanish monk Pedro de la Gasca. It is built in a gorge at 3800 m high, under towering mount **Illimani** (6800 m).

Bolivia is a country where geography determines many aspects of cultural life. The whole country lies within the tropics, but different heights mean very different climatic zones. Bolivia can be divided into three regions. The first is the *altiplano* on the west, lying between 3000 m and 4300 m. Cold, barren and windswept, this region is home for 55% of the population, and includes the cities of **La Paz**, **Oruro**, most of the mines and two famous lakes. The first of the lakes is **Lake Titicaca**, some 180 km long and 75 km wide, and with a 3809 m high frontier with Peru. To its south are the remains of the mysterious

Tiahuanaco civilization. Lake Titicaca drains into **Lake Poopó**. At this altitude potatoes, broad beans, oca and quinoa are grown, and until 1952 most of the land was owned by large landowners who developed out of the *encomienda* system of the colonial period. The mines produced white gold, silver, copper, tungsten, lead, zinc and especially tin, with the world's largest tin mine at **Llallagua**. Christopher Isherwood (◊ Colombia) passed through **La Paz** in 1948, and witnessed Indian festivals.

The next area is the **Valles** or the Andes, deep valleys with high mountains, holding some 30% of the country's population, where most of the coca farming takes place. Chewing green coca leaves was the main way the Indians supported hard work at such high altitudes. Coca production was an Incan monopoly, and coca leaves were given as favours, even used as money. Only recently has the production of cocaine given another connotation to what is a common and mild drug, used, for example, as a tea – *mate de coca* – to counteract altitude sickness or *soroche*. The coca-leaf was an ingredient in the original formula for coca-cola.

The third area, the most remote, covers three-fifths of Bolivia and is known as **Oriente** (East). This area comprises lowland plains, ranging from the *yungas* of the upper Beni with tropical rainforest to swamps and the Bolivian Chaco with scrub forest. **Santa Cruz** is the main town of this area which only in 1954 was linked by an all-weather road to La Paz. Gordon Meyer (◊ Argentina and Uruguay) travelled to Santa Cruz to work on archives dealing with the expulsion of the Jesuits, and he gives a fine description of the isolated city in the 1960s (Extract 5). Less than 15% of Bolivia's population live in the Oriente, yet it could support much more agriculture. There are wild rubber trees in the **Beni**, an isolated, dangerous area where C.H. Prodgers went in 1901 to check on rubber tappers and wrote *Adventures in Bolivia*, 1922. In the Beni there is a beginning of cattle farming, and rice. In the **Chaco** petrol was discovered – it led to a war with Paraguay – with the Camiri field as the largest in Bolivia, a country that exports its oil and natural gas. Julian Duguid ◊ travelled round the Bolivian Chaco in the 1920s and called it *Green Hell: A Chronicle of Travel in the Forests of Eastern Bolivia*, 1931 (Extract 4).

INDIANS, INCAS AND SPANIARDS

Before the Incan conquest in the fifteenth century, what is today Bolivia was the site of a civilization only recently studied, the Tiahuanaco, whose hieroglyphs are still undeciphered. During Incan times Bolivia was known as Kollasuyu, and the Indians were exceptionally allowed to keep their own Aymará language. In 1532 the Incan

Gordon Meyer

empire crumbled under the assault from Francisco Pizarro and Diego de Almagro. In 1559 this region became an *audiencia*. Within a relatively short time the owners of the land had changed from Incan to Spaniard, so that the Indians had simply changed masters. They were drafted into conscripted labour – the Mita – and were virtual vassals in the *encomiendas*. They worked the mines, and remained subsistence farmers.

During Spanish rule in 1545 the *cerro rico* (rich mountain) was found at **Potosí** in the *altiplano*. During the seventeenth and eighteenth centuries Potosí at 4020 m became the most important and richest city in South America, with more people living there than in London. In 1650, its population was 160 000, yet today it has been forgotten. Apart from some Indian insurrections, all called Tupac Amaru (**La Paz** was beseiged for nearly a year in 1781), it was not until the French invasion of Spain that the *criollos* tried to attain independence. At the **University of St Francis Xavier** in **Chusquisaca** on 25 May 1809 some *criollos* refused to swear allegiance to the King, and their leader was hanged. But the Spaniards were not finally defeated until 1825. On 6 August, what had been known as Alto Peru became Bolivia, and Simón Bolívar actually drafted a constitution. For a while there was the possibility of a Bolivian–Peruvian federation, but the reality was 40 years of civil war. Between 1825 and 1967 there were 179 'revolutions', meaning 'palace coups'. Pablo Neruda (◊ Chile) has a bitter poem about one of the presidents, called Melgarejo (in power 1864–71): 'His life fragment / of blind force and opera unleashed / above the craters and mesetas'.

THE GUANO AND CHACO WARS

Bolivia fought two disastrous wars. The first was over *guano* – the sea bird droppings fertilizer – when Chile first blockaded **Antofagasta**, officially Bolivian, but peopled by Chileans, to take Bolivia's coast away, compensating it with a rail link from Arica to La Paz, and free transit of Bolivian goods. This was the War of the Pacific. Peru also lost land to Chile. The second war was over oil in the **Chaco**. Border clashes with Paraguay began in 1927 and war was declared in 1932, reaching stalemate in 1935. Bolivia, trained and armed by Germans, could not match the Paraguayans down in the lowlands. The Chaco war seen from the Paraguayan side emerges in Roa Bastos's (◊ Paraguay) novel *Son of Man*, 1965. Augusto Céspedes's untranslated novel *Sangre de mestizos: Relatos de la guerra del Chaco*, 1936, acts as reportage of the horrors of a war fought in a hostile natural environment, where thirst was one of the enemies. Bolivia lost 233 100 sq km of territory. Earlier, in 1900, the isolated jungle state of Acre had declared its independence from Bolivia, based on its rubber wealth, and Bolivia sold it for cash to Brazil.

RECENT COUPS

The Chaco war, and conscription, led to an awareness of Bolivia's stratified society, with the majority of Indians at the bottom, stuck in poverty. The Indian problem had long antagonized Bolivian intellec-tuals. Alcides Arguedas's (1879–1946) untranslated protest novel *Raza de bronce*, 1919, dramatized the conflict between Indians and landowners (Arguedas himself was one) near **Lake Titicaca**. He had earlier written a pessimistic study of Bolivia's stratification in *Pueblo enfermo*, 1909. Some Bolivian intellectuals, like Franz Tamayo, argued that Bolivia's future lay with its overwhelming Indian heritage. Although there was a first socialist coup in 1936, nothing really happened concerning the poverty of the Indians until 1952 when Victor Paz Estenssoro came to power with his MNR party. The origins of this party were fascist, and close to Peronism, which Paz Estenssoro in exile in Buenos Aires admired. But he found allies in the mining unions, with Juan Lechín as their leader. There was a short bloody coup and Paz Estenssoro began the Bolivian revolution with land reform, educating Indians, universal suffrage, abolishing *pongueaje* (where Indians had to give three to four days free labour on estates) and nationalizing the mines. Patiño, the tin baron of Bolivia, had become one of the world's five richest men, his family had married into European aristocracy, and all his wealth had been taken out of Bolivia. Nationalization was a popular move, although tin prices fell, and the state tin industry barely made a profit over the following decades. Augusto Céspedes novelized the inhuman working conditions of the miners in his untranslated *Metal del diablo,* 1946.

Paz Estenssoro was in power from 1952 to 1964, slowly moving to the right until guerrilla movements ushered in another coup, with the popular Quechua-speaking General Barrientos as co-president. It was under Barrientos that Régis Debray was caught and imprisoned for 30 years in 1965, and that Che Guevara was cornered in **La Higuera**, and murdered in October 1967. This period forms the background to Jon Cleary's ◊ novel *The Mask of the Andes*, 1971 (Extract 3). Barrientos did not scrap the 1952 legislation, but was killed in a helicopter crash in 1969. Absurdly, after a period of incredible inflation, a 77-year-old Paz Estensorro was recalled to presidency in 1985, followed in 1989 by Jaime Paz Zamora.

Throughout these years the lot of the Indians has not changed. Life expectancy is still around 35 years, and their standard of living is about the lowest in South America. R. C. Hutchinson's ◊ novel *Rising*, 1982 (Extract 1) movingly incorporates the Indian problems in Bolivia into his drama of redemption through love. His novel refutes the oft-told story of Queen Victoria's tantrum after one of her ministers was made to ride round La Paz on a donkey for refusing to attend a local function, with her 'Bolivia no longer exists' as she pencilled it off her map.

Bolivia's Renato Prada Oropeza (1937–) wrote *Los fundadores del alba*, 1969 (*The Breach*, 1971) which gives a moving picture of a Bolivia wracked by poverty, guerrilla wars, illiterate peasants, and personal tragedies without lapsing into propaganda or simplistic solutions.

BOOKLIST

The following selection includes all titles which are extracted in this chapter as well as those mentioned in the introduction which are available in English. In general, paperback editions are given when possible. The editions cited are not necessarily the only ones available. For most of the extracted works, the original publisher in English can be found in 'Acknowledgments and Citations' at the end of the volume, as can the exact location of the extracts and the editions from which they are taken. The date in square brackets is the original publication date of the work in its original language. Extract numbers are highlighted in bold type for ease of reference.

Cleary, Jon, *Mask of the Andes* [1971], Collins, London, 1982. **Extract 3.**

Duguid, Julian, *Green Hell: A Chronicle of Travel in the Forests of Eastern Bolivia*, Jonathan Cape, London, 1931. **Extract 4.**

Hutchinson, R.C., *Rising* [1976], Penguin, London, 1982. **Extract 1.**

Matthiessen, Peter, *The Cloud Forest: A Chronicle of the South American Wilderness* [1960], Collins Harvill, London, 1983/ Viking, New York, 1961. **Extract 7.**

Meyer, Gordon, *Summer at High Altitude*, Alan Ross, London, 1968. **Extracts 2, 5 and 6.**

Prada Oropeza, Renato, *The Breach* [1969], Walter Redmond, trans, Doubleday, Garden City, NJ, 1971.

Prodgers, C.H., *Adventures in Bolivia*, The Bodley Head, London, 1922.

Roa Bastos, Augusto, *Son of Man* [1961], Rachel Caffyn, trans, Gollancz, London, 1965.

Extracts

(1) Bolivia: An Andean Town

R.C. Hutchinson, *Rising*

Hutchinson places his novel about the tensions in Bolivia between class and race, landowners and peasants, up in the sierra in the fictional town of San Carlos, where two powerful brothers are forced to employ a poor half-caste cousin to help them get rid of rebellious Indians.

From the third floor of the Hotel Los Andes, at which most visitors to San Carlos find themselves, you see the whole length of the Avenida Mendoza to where, in the Plaza de Armas, the romanesque façade of the Cathedral of San Vicente overtops an exuberance of eucalypti and royal palms. The south side of this avenue seems always to be under improvement: already the line of decrepit timber houses and single-storey workshops is broken by a buxom supermercado, and farther on, where a sprawl of Indio habitations has been decently levelled, a random scaffolding of pine-trunks marks the intention to erect a smart, square building which will house a dentist's surgery as well as a new branch of the Banco Industrial. The casual observer may wonder whether this incoherent thoroughfare is in process of construction or of final dismantlement, but the aspect of the farther side, where the colonial houses extend with hardly a break as far as the second intersection, should resolve such doubts. Many of those buildings have been turned to modern uses – the old prefectorial Residencia, for example, now houses a Bata shop with lawyers' offices above – but their basic structure is little changed; most of them have kept their fine studded doors, the intricate structure of the original balconies. Here is stability and the forthright reminders of Philips Radio and Coca Cola which bombard the eye from every point of vantage may be taken as the signature of advancing civilization.

Mask your eyes against the garnish of modernity, the florid shop signs, the motor cars, and you will find it easy to imagine the street as it was at the turn of the century. The cobbled roadway could not have been rougher then. Among the vehicles on view there are some – a springless cart drawn by a spavined mule, the box on perambulator wheels attached to a boy's bicycle – which could well be survivals from the throng that squeezed and jockeyed through the meagre channel three quarters of a century ago. The clothes of course have changed: the enormous hats and trailing skirts of the European ladies are gone, you no longer see clerks in formal jackets and hard headgear. But the 'bowlers', brilliant shawls and lavish petticoats of the Indio women are timeless, the horseman with his short jerkin and tight trousers who rides nonchalantly between the Citroens and Chevrolets is a photo-copy of his grandfather making the same journey. The younger street you are contemplating has a makeshift quality, it suggests a bare and backward land pretending to a nineteenth century aggrandizement, a European sophistication. So early as this there are lamp standards, which serve as props for ragged idlers; the pavements, already holed and broken, with their freight of men and women doubled under monstrous loads, could almost belong to the lowlier streets of any town in Southern Europe, except that the faces are printed less with anxious poverty than with a settled dullness, an air of disconnection with the traffic clattering past them.

(2) BOLIVIA: COCA

Gordon Meyer, *Summer at High Altitude*

Meyer describes the Andean village of Tarabuco (3295 m up, some 64 km from Sucre), and explains coca culture.

Tarabuco lies some sixty kilometres south-east of Sucre. The insignifi-cant looking watershed we passed on the way is one of the world's great disjunctions; the water flowing north from it finishes in the Amazon's mouth; that flowing south, in the Río de la Plata. There were distant views of the young Pilcomayo, which has run of some 1000 miles to its outlet in the River Paraguay.

The pueblo of Tarabuco is red: from the Indians, their ponchos, the steaming cauldrons of chicken and peppers. It was the day of the weekly fair. On sale were utensils, food, trinkets, quena pipes and coca leaves. Every Indian in these altitudes takes the drug.

The leaves come from the shrub Erythroxylon coca, Lam., which is about six feet high, with bright green leaves and white blossoms. The blossoms are followed by small scarlet berries. It is raised from the seed, on beds called almazigas. When the young shoots are 1½–2 feet high, they are planted out in coca fields (cocales). When the leaves, on being bent, crack or break off, they are stripped off carefully to avoid injury, and dried in the sun on cloths. They dry a pale green, and the important thing now is to keep them dry.

The drug-takers carry a leather pouch and small gourd. The pouch contains the supply of leaves, the gourd pulverised unslaked lime. A few leaves, the stalks having been carefully picked off, are masticated into a small ball. At this stage a very slight admixture of the powdered lime is made; this draws out the taste, and the saliva flows. Part of the saliva is expectorated, part swallowed. If you don't do it properly, you burn your lips. The flavour is slightly bitter and aromatic, like poor green tea. Habitués have bad breath, pale lips and gums, greenish stumpy teeth, and an ugly black mark at the angles of the mouth. One far gone will have an unsteady gait, yellow skin, dim and sunken eyes with purple rings, quivering lips and general apathy.

Unharmful in small doses, it may even be beneficial. Chewing it, one can go without food for days, and this is one reason why it is chewed so much.

(3) BOLIVIA: THE INDIANS

Jon Cleary, Mask of the Andes

Cleary's topical adventure novel about foreigners in Bolivia, Bolivian struggles between altiplano Indians and the ruling oligarchy, and revolution, ends with Taber burying his American priest friend, and dealing with the Indians' stare.

The gravediggers, both Indians, began to toss earth in on the coffin. One of them looked up and caught Taber's eye. The man's face was the same mask Taber had been seeing ever since he had arrived in Bolivia, but there was something in the dark eyes that hinted at a message in the cocaine-dulled mind behind them. Taber tried desperately to read it, but it was too vague, like an echo of a whisper in a long-forgotten tongue, to catch and translate. It could have been a message of hate or pity or just plain careless indifference. Then it struck him that since the time of Pizarro it would have been the Indians who would have been digging the graves and tossing the earth in on the Spaniards, the criollos, the Americans, the British, the Germans, on all outsiders. For a people for whom time had stood still for centuries, whose patience rivalled that of the earth itself, perhaps that was revenge enough.

(4) THE CHACO

Julian Duguid, Green Hell

San Lorenzo in the Bolivian state of Nuflo de Chavez is too small to figure in the map novelist and traveller Julian Duguid provides for his reader.

On the bright blue official map of Eastern Bolivia a little row of dots runs away into the distance. They are a pompous high-sounding brood called after saints or some natural peculiarity, and would cause a stranger to think that the country is highly populated. To one such dot we made our entry in the cool of an evening and there resolved to await Tiger-Man. The dinner bell clanked dolefully on the neck of the old white horse, the procession wound its way through the wooded parkland and the inhabitants of the boldly marked San Lorenzo turned out to welcome us.

'What do you think of our first town?' asked Urrio.

I stared, uncomprehending, at the single rickety house that stood by a broken down cattle corral.

'When do we come to it?'

Urrio laughed.

'You must adjust your scale of values. That shack is San Lorenzo.'

'Good Lord!' said Bee-Mason. 'Your map makers *have* got nerve.'

'One must fill in the country somehow,' said Urrio.

San Lorenzo had a population of nine and a falling birth rate. A man and a woman with five girl children, a servant and his barren wife. That was all. The father was a gnarled old Indian in a pair of blue cotton trousers and a shirt. A few long hairs, separate and wiry, like cat's whiskers, stuck out from his yellow face: and his high cheek bones and narrow slanting eyes had more than a touch of the Mongolian.

His arm was passed affectionately about the scraggy waist of his wife, who, bony and cheerful, grinned out of a forest of coarse black hair that fell around her shoulders. Of the five children, two were blind.

The house was a gem. It stood in the midst of palm trees of the tall, thin variety that is topped by a rustling crest. This tree is peculiar in that it has an intensely hard fibrous rim and a hollow interior. Consequently when sliced up the centre it provides two durable curved logs which are invaluable for building purposes. San Lorenzo was fashioned entirely of palm, and looked more like a thatched stockade than a dwelling, for the posts had been driven into the ground at regular distances and were not joined together. The roof was made from the leaves of another brand of palm, a gigantic affair which grew the wrong way up, like an inverted shuttlecock.

(5) SANTA CRUZ

Gordon Meyer, *Summer at High Altitude*

In 1965 novelist Gordon Meyer travelled overland with Mara Rincón through Uruguay to Corumbá, and stayed in sleepy Santa Cruz (founded in 1561, now booming with a population of over 600 000, thanks to oil and drugs) to study the expulsion of the Jesuits. He published his account months before dying in London.

The wind blows hard from the sierras, which from here begin their multiplication until they compose the Andean backbone. When it is dry, the dust flies, miniature sandstorms rage at street corners. When it rains the red earth roads invent a Flanders nightmare.

No cars. Jeeps, lorries, buses, names of film stars compose the pretence of the 20th century; the fingerprints are the conquistadores. Houses are low and pillared; sometimes two-storeyed, when the pillars form a balcony above, a gallery below. Red tiles undulating with age and debility, fertile with growths. The many additions and alterations to the twin-towered cathedral do not show as such. The final termination, dating from 1946, cannot change the fact that everything in Santa Cruz stopped long ago; the style is convincingly 18th century baroque. A door opening on to a street gives a glimpse of patios and gardens, a life that from everywhere else has vanished. The city is unique, living in its own uneroded epoch – Santa Cruz de la Sierra, capital of the old Jesuit theocracy, the old colonial province of Chiquitos. This strange attraction the Jesuits have for *me*!

(6) SUCRE

Gordon Meyer, *Summer at High Altitude*

Meyer and his travelling companion reach isolated Sucre, Bolivia's official capital which lies 2790 m up, with a population of 87 000.

Here, in the deepest section of a mountain system spreadeagling some 150° of latitude, on the site of the Inca settlement called The Golden Bridge, the Spaniards built this city of Charcas, now called after Marshall Sucre.

A city cut off as the cities of Tibet, minute, and known all over South America. Even today it still has only 72,000 inhabitants, is still the legal capital, and distills the air of a national capital. It is a memory distilled, become atmospheric.

It has had four names: Chuquisaca (name of the province), La Plata,

Charcas, Sucre. ('Five' said Gunnar Mendoza, head of the Archives, to me, 'because it is also called The City of the Four Names').

From the tall red cerro, Sica-Sica, at the northern extremity of the city a wash of red-tiled roofs flows up to this college. From this curvilinear roof of glass bricks you look as into wells into the otherwise hidden patios, with their inner balconies and staircases. The right angle dominates, the whole possesses a geometrical neatness. The angles of the roofs are finished off in chalk; which gives the city another name. The White City. A university on a mountain top. Neat, clean, minute, Sucre seems a plaything carefully positioned only yesterday.

Whence its look of perfection? It was a sub-product of Potosí, the Spanish–American treasure house at over 13,000 feet; too high for the rapidly increasing millionaires. They came down here to build their palaces, Sucre began with its social development, design, culture and immense wealth already accomplished. The phrase 'as rich as Potosí' had already appeared in English as well as Spanish literature.

A roof here does not give a view of a rooftop life, as in Southern Spain or Greece; the view here is of a whole mythology. To scan the horizons from up here is to attend a silent conference in immensity and solitude. To feel caught in a solid noose of colossal forces.

(7) Tiahuanco

Peter Matthiessen, *The Cloud Forest*

Matthiessen describes the ancient, mysterious ruins of Tiahuan-co, just off Lake Titicaca which he passed in the late 1950s on his way down to La Paz.

We debarked at Guaqui, in Bolivia, while the day was early, and I was offered a ride in their hired limousine by an affable South African and his wife. On the way to La Paz we stopped for a time at the pre-Inca ruins at Tiahuanaco. The modern village of this name is only a few miles from Guaqui, and its foundations are largely of stone taken from the ruins; the church itself was constructed in this manner and two of the great stone idols for which these ruins are best known, standing like sentinels at the gateway of the House of God.

The ruins are spread over a wide area of the *puna*, beyond the village. Excavation has been limited, and probably much remains to be discovered. Walls, storerooms, aqueducts, and an imposing 'Gate of the Sun' have been unearthed, in addition to a number of the figures sometimes referred to, due to their woeful expression and for want of more exact archaeological information, as 'crying gods'. . . . The road from Tiahuanaco to La Paz leads across an *altiplano* far more desolate in aspect than its counterpart in southern Peru; it is higher and is brown rather than green. The adobe walls of the Quechuas (actually, the Indians of this region are called Aymaras, though the two groups are closely related; farther south and east, in the region of Cochabamba, they are called Quechuas again) seem poorer than those in Peru, and there is an increased number of the strange wandering black dogs. The Indians themselves, on the other hand, look cleaner and more active and have been known to smile, possibly in consequence of a heightened morale induced by Bolivia's agricultural reforms; they are not so colorful as their cousins in Peru, though the most apparent difference in their dress is the brown derby hat worn by the women. At one point the car passed a funeral procession, and the file of Indians was reflected in long rain puddles as they shambled over the plain toward the road; the corpse was draped in a shiny black material and was carried on a sort of thin stretcher which sagged sadly between the four pall-bearers.

La Paz is situated in a canyon, and one comes upon it very suddenly: the plateau terminates abruptly, and there is the city, flowing down the steep slope below. From its highest point to its outskirts, on the floor of the canyon, there is a fall of nearly two thousand feet. It is a pretty, light, airy city, and its setting is enhanced by the towering snowfields of Mount Illimani, rising beyond out of the clouds which shroud its base.

Biographies and plot summaries

CLEARY, Jon (1917–). Cleary was born in Sydney, Australia on 22 November 1917. Since 1945 he has lived as a full-time writer and journalist, publishing over 19 novels, including *Mask of the Andes*, 1971 (Extract 3), known as *The Liberators* in the USA. In a small *pueblo* high in the **Bolivian Andes** called **Altea**, near the cathedral town of **San Sebastian**, down from La Paz, and near a lake, an American priest called Padre Terence McKenna, his sister, and a British agronomist from the UN Food and Agriculture Organisation called Harry Taber get involved in the post-1952 revolutionary politics of Bolivia, the oppressed Quechua-speaking *campesi-* *nos* or Indians, and upper-class *criollos* during Che Guevara's attempted uprising (McKenna hears a confession of murder from a revolutionary), in the late 1960s. In the wake of Greene, Cleary writes both to entertain and inform readers about the world they live in.

DUGUID, Julian (1902–). Duguid was born on 24 May 1902 at Birkenhead, Cheshire. He has been a BBC reporter. He travelled with Mamerto Urriolagoitia, who was Bolivian Consul General in London, and Bee Mason, a photographer, from Buenos Aires up to Corumbá, and then across the unexplored Bolivian **Chaco** that a few years later was the scene of a war between Bolivia and Paraguay over oil (see Roa Bastos ◊ Paraguay). His witty and accurate account of this treck became a best-seller when published as *Green Hell: A Chronicle of Travel in the Forests of Eastern Bolivia* in 1931 (Extract 4). He wrote a biography, *Tiger Man, An Odyssey of Freedom: A Biography of Sacha Siemel*, 1932, based on their colourful guide, and two novels set in the Bolivian jungle, *A Cloak of Monkey Fur*, 1936, and *Father Coldstream*, 1938.

HUTCHINSON, R. C. (1907–1975). Born in Watford, UK, on 23 January 1907, Hutchinson was educated at Monkton Combe School and Oriel College, Oxford. He liked placing his well researched, long, realistic novels (17 in all) in exotic locations. He set his unfinished last novel *Rising*, 1976 (Extract 1), in Bolivia. The novel opens in a Bolivian city with two powerful and wealthy upper-class brothers meeting the mayor to decide how to protect their mine from revolutionary saboteurs. They are forced to employ their poor cousin

Colonel Sabino de Juanos, known as the butcher of **Cubiquite**. Then follows a dense but always gripping investigation into their various lives up on the Andes *estancia*. The massacre at Cubiquite was the colonel's revenge on his Indian mistress who had run off with Papac, a *curandero* (witch-doctor or faith-healer). We get quite believable clashes between the church and army, between rich Creoles and the Indians, between men and women. The characters are rounded, yet fit into a historical unfolding that limits them. The curse of the rocky, aggressive land on the people, and the question of who really owns the land are the themes. Colonel Sabino finally learns brotherly love – a man who has 'overcome the monstrous barricades which keep us estranged from each other'. The novel is almost an allegory of the soul's journey, set in Bolivia.

MATTHIESSEN, Peter (see under Peru).

MEYER, Gordon (see under Argentina and Uruguay).

GUYANA

'Next day they arrived at the
mouth of the Demerara . . .
Small shipping of all kinds lay
round them; on the farther
bank a low green fringe of
mangrove; behind, the tin
roofs of the town were visible
among feathery palm trees;
everything steamed from the
recent rain.'
Evelyn Waugh,
A Handful of Dust

Guyana, formerly British Guiana,
is derived from a word meaning
'land of waters'. It is a Cooperative Republic, with a land area of
215 000 sq km, and 370 km of
Atlantic coast. Its population
reached one million in 1990.
Over 80% of the people live on
the coastal plain. **Georgetown** is
the capital with a population of
188 000 in 1983. Amerindians
(Indians, also known as 'bucks')
have increased since the 1930s,
and numbered 29 500 in the
1960s, from Warraws, Arawaks,
Caribs and Makusi. Africans were
brought over as slaves for the
plantations and represent about 31% of the population ('Creoles').
Indentured labour brought out Indians from East India (known as East
Indians), who represent 50% of the population. There are also
Chinese, Portuguese and a small proportion of other Europeans. The
racial divisions mean that 57% of the people are Christian, 33%
Hindu, and 9% Sunni Muslim.

Roy Heath's ◊ autobiography *Shadows Round the Moon: Caribbean
Memoirs,* 1990, of growing up in **Georgetown** in the 1930s, as a
middle-class schoolteacher's son, gives a fine picture of Guyana's
colonial and racial divisions, while the novel *Orealla* (Extracts 3 and 4)
evokes the conflicts between a Macusi, a Creole and his boss. Wilson
Harris's ◊ *Tumatumari* (Extract 11) also recreates the masks of fear worn
by the different classes and races under British colonialism. The poet
Martin Carter, imprisoned by the British, spoke for those oppressed by
colonialism in his *Poems of Resistance,* 1954. The official language of
Guyana is English, with Hindi and pidgin also spoken.

Inland, it is mainly jungle (85% of the land is selva) and a little savannah, crossed by rivers like the **Essequibo**, the **Berbice** and the **Demerara**. **Lake Amuku** is probably the site of Manoa, the fabled City of Eldorado that attracted Ralegh (◊ Venezuela) and many others. Guyana is equatorial lowland, with high humidity and heavy rainfall. The wet season lasts from April to August. The selva contains the *balata* (latex tree) among its many species. Sugar-cane – once mostly owned by one firm, Booker McConnell – is the main crop, followed by rice, and bauxite which is dug from open mines. Travel accounts of this jungle include Evelyn Waugh's ◊ *A Handful of Dust* (Extracts 7 and 10), while many novels are set inland – see Harris and Mittelholzer ◊. In 1859 Anthony Trollope, the eminent Victorian novelist, and inventor of the British red pillar-box, visited Guyana, 'the Elysium of the tropics . . . the Transatlantic Eden', as recorded in his travel book *The West Indies and the Spanish Main*, 1859.

Guyana was sighted by Columbus, but not occupied by the Spanish. Sir Walter Raleigh alerted Europe to this Eldorado land. The first settlers were the Dutch in 1616. By 1621, Guyana was part of the Dutch West Indian Co, and slaves were brought in as land was cultivated, and the swamps drained. The French occupied Georgetown, and then the Dutch reclaimed it, and renamed the capital Stabroek (meaning 'standing brook') as it appears in Waterton ◊ (see Extract 6). The British took over in 1796. In 1812, they renamed the capital Georgetown. This colonization by Western European powers makes Guyana very different from its Spanish American neighbours. Sir Robert Schomburgk (1804–65), discoverer of the giant water lily *Victoria regia*, surveyed British Guiana in 1841, following his *Description of British Guiana* in 1840. After slavery was abolished in 1807 (there were an estimated 100 000 slaves), East Indians were brought in to work the plantations. There was a gold boom in the 1890s. There have been border problems with Venezuela, which claims the North Western District. The Jonestown (now **Agricola**) commune massacre caught the world's headlines in the 1960s (see Shiva Naipaul ◊).

Political and cultural life has been dominated by the colonial struggle and by the rivalry between the East Indians led by Cheddi Jagan, who became more and more pro-communist, and the Africans led by Forbes Burnham, equally Marxist. During 1961–64 there was rioting, and British troops were brought in. In 1966 Independence was granted under Forbes Burnham. In 1985 Burnham died, and was succeeded by Desmond Hoyte. In 1992 Jagan won the elections. Both Shiva Naipaul's novel *A Hot Country* (Extract 9) and his essays explore these politics and culture, as do essays by his brother V. S. Naipaul (◊ Belize) – Extract 5. Jamaican novelist Andrew Salkey (1928–) also visited in the late 1960s. One consequence of these years has been exile for writers. Apart from those included here in the biographies, like Wilson

Harris and Edgar Mittelholzer, the novelist Jan Carew (1925–) has several novels placed in his homeland, including *Black Midas*, 1958. Excellent poets live in England whose work evokes Guyanese childhoods, like Fred D'Aguiar's *Airy Hall*, 1989, named after the village where he grew up in what he called a 'fowl-coop Republic'; Mark McWatt, *Interiors*, 1988 (he is also a critic); David Dabydeen's *Coolie Odyssey*, 1988; and Grace Nichols with her novel *Whole of a Morning Sky*, 1987, and poems *The Fat Black Woman's Poems*. See also the anthology *From the Green Antilles*, 1966.

BOOKLIST

The following selection includes all titles which are extracted in this chapter as well as those mentioned in the introduction which are available in English. In general, paperback editions are given when possible. The editions cited are not necessarily the only ones available. For most of the extracted works, the original publisher in English can be found in 'Acknowledgments and Citations' at the end of the volume, as can the exact location of the extracts and the editions from which they are taken. The date in square brackets is the original publication date of the work in its original language. Extract numbers are highlighted in bold for ease of reference.

Carew, Jan, *Black Midas*, Secker and Warburg, London, 1958/Kraus, New York, 1958.

Carter, Martin, *Poems of Resistance*, Lawrence and Wishart, London, 1954.

Dabydeen, David, *Coolie Odyssey*, Dangaroo Press, Mundelstrup, Denmark, 1988.

D'Aguiar, Fred, *Airy Hall*, Chatto and Windus, London, 1989.

From the Green Antilles, Barbara Howes, ed, Macmillan, New York, 1966.

Harris, Wilson, *The Eye of the Scarecrow*, Faber and Faber, London, 1970. **Extract 2.**

Harris, Wilson, *Tumatumari*, Faber and Faber, London, 1968. **Extract 11.**

Heath, Roy, *Orealla* [1980], Flamingo, London, 1986/Schoken, New York, 1987. **Extracts 3 and 4.**

Heath, Roy, *Shadows Round the Moon: Caribbean Memoirs*, Flamingo, London, 1991.

McWatt, Mark, *Interiors*, Dangaroo Press, Mundelstrup, Denmark, 1988.

Mittelholzer, Edgar, *My Bones and My Flute* [1955], Longman, London, 1991. **Extract 1.**

Naipaul, Shiva, *A Hot Country*, Hamish Hamilton, London, 1983. **Extract 9.**

Naipaul, V.S., 'A Handful of Dust: Return to Guiana', in *New York Review of Books*, 11 April 1991. **Extract 5.**

Naipaul, V.S., *The Middle Passage. Impressions of Five Societies – British, French and Dutch – in the West Indies and South America*, André Deutsch, London, 1962.

Nichols, Grace, *The Fat Black Woman's Poems*, Virago, London, 1984.

Nichols, Grace, *Whole of a Morning Sky*, Virago, London, 1987.

Salkey, Andrew, *Georgetown Journal: A Caribbean Writer's Journal*, New Beacon Books, London, 1972.

Trollope, Anthony, *The West Indies and the Spanish Main* [1859], Sut-ton, London, 1989.

Waterton, Charles, *Wanderings in South America* [1825], Century, London, 1985.

Waugh, Evelyn, *A Handful of Dust* [1934], Penguin, London, 1951/ Little, Brown Inc, Boston, MA, 1977. **Extracts 7 and 10.**

Extracts

(1) THE BERBICE RIVER

Edgar Mittelholzer, *My Bones and My Flute*

Milton, a rebel painter from British Guiana's middle class, narrates Mittelholzer's story of a cursed eighteenth century Dutch manuscript, and a search to exorcize evil spirits on a station up the Berbice river.

At the time of these events – the early nineteen-thirties – the steamer made the trip up the Berbice River only once a week. It left New Amsterdam, the little town at the mouth of the river, every Wednesday morning, arrived at Paradise, the terminus, a hundred and ten miles up, anytime between seven and half past seven in the evening, setting out on the return trip for New Amsterdam on the following morning. This meant that once you missed this Thursday morning opportunity you were committed irrevocably to jungle life for at least one full week. Knowing the Nevinsons as I did, however, I had no qualms about this fortnight we had planned to pass at Goed de Vries where the Berbice Timber and Balata Company have their up-river station.

(2) GEORGETOWN

Wilson Harris, *The Eye of the Scarecrow*

Harris's narrator recalls his friend 'L' in Georgetown.

L–'s room stood at the top of two storeys whose windows glanced in the sunlight across Water Street towards the burning estuary of the Demerara river where the crest of a wave occasionally flickered as if it sought a pencil of relief (or was it extinction?) beneath the shadow of pavement on the sea wall withstanding the Atlantic . . .

It is this frail visionary organization of memory – one thing against another, and everything apparently laying siege to nothing (while nothing seems to extend into the immaterial capacity and absorption of everything), which highlights the transient figures of the insensible past into ideal erections against chaos, standing within a measureless ground plan of spiritual recognitions, intimacies and identities . . .

As a child of eight, nineteen years before the great Strike, I climbed the mound – at the northern extremity of Water Street – towards the wall overlooking the river's mouth in the Atlantic. That was long before the Municipal Authority had thought of erecting a bath-hut and converting the desolate foreshore into an open swimming pool. No one was around (or if there was I have now forgotten) but I still remember clearly the spirit which moved in that place; and the dislocated image which returns seems strangely to address me within the beckoning associations not only of 1948 but of 1964 when this late entry in time is being made. The air over the foreshore was filled with a tumultuous cloud of palm flies, flying wires of insects with gauze-like wings which seemed, in their cloud-like angelic transparency, like the subtlest dispersal in nature of a nameless fear of demons: the flying wisp of a bandage torn from the blank compulsive heart of sickness and death, the crippled self-deception of beggars – stationed in the shadow of the commercial houses of Water Street as in a depression in a mental landscape (that world-wide depression of the 1920s and 30s) – protesting with the greatest unconscious eloquence, born of a kind of degrading hollow silence, to be rarefied and uplifted from being mere chains upon themselves and rooted stumps and imprisoned castaways.

(3) GEORGETOWN

Roy Heath, *Orealla*

Ben, a rebel Creole servant in Georgetown in charge of the stable and horses, befriends Carl, the Amerindian, and intuitively understands the differences between them.

With the hot sun raining down on him, Ben set out for the Public Buildings along the pitch road, thinking of visionary journeys, the lairs of jaguars, black-water creeks and whistling anacondas dragging themselves along the beds of dried-up rivers. Carl's world, at once real and legendary, possessed the quality of a projected vision that one saw on the white screens in the new picture-houses of Robb Street and Middle Street, moving images that rivalled life itself. He could be there next week, but now he was here in Georgetown, which paraded its precisely measured avenues, where animals were harnessed and people no longer needed to be harnessed, being so docile, where nakedness was a vision of conquest or immorality. Ben's heart pounded at the thought that Carl's world really existed, that the stuffed alligators in shop windows, with varnished skins and gaping red mouths, were real tokens of a dripping forest.

(4) GEORGETOWN

Roy Heath, *Orealla*

Ben summarizes Georgetown's dismal history, in opposition to Carl's paradise.

Henceforth, if his life was to be worthwhile, he must begin at the beginning. Orealla was doomed to be trodden into extinction by the horsemen of progress; and Carl, who had no stomach for life in town, was destined to drink from the same bitter cup as his father. The beginning was Georgetown itself with its inequalities, its prison, its avenues of jacaranda and flamboyant, its stretch of river and ocean, its fishing boats laid up in channels along stone jetties, its secret back yards, its sugar wharves, ships sinking below the street at ebb-tide and floating out to sea on flood-tide, its hundred churches bearing the cross of an alien martyr who had taken root in their hearts, and administrative buildings conceived for permanence of an alien rule, its elegant houses inspired in the dream-time of slavery, its stray dogs, said to be descendants of a pair of mongrels escaped from a governor's yard; its beggars deformed by continual stooping and its drummers, who had never lost the art of summoning up the spirits of departed ancestors.

(5) GEORGETOWN

V.S. Naipaul, *A Handful of Dust: Return to Guiana*

Trinidadian novelist V.S. Naipaul visited Georgetown in 1991.
This extract is taken from the New York Review of Books – see
Booklist.

Georgetown, the capital, once one of the most beautiful wood-built cities of the world (with the great hardwood forests just a few miles inland), weathered and decayed. Over the run-down city there now rises, at the end of one of the principal avenues, an extraordinary, mocking monument of the Cooperative Republic: a giant African-like figure, long-armed and apparently dancing, with what looks like cabalistic emblems on its limbs. This figure of African reawakening is said to honor Cuffy, the leader of a slave revolt in Guyana in 1763; but there are black people who believe that – whatever the sculptor intended – the figure was also connected with some kind of obeah working on behalf of Forbes Burnham, the Guyanese African leader. Mr Burnham is believed to have, in the end, mixed his Marxism with obeah, and to have had an obeah consultant.

In the Georgetown Botanical Gardens – one of the many such gardens, of experiment and scholarship, established by the British in various parts of the empire in the eighteenth and nineteenth centuries – there is another, complimentary monument of Mr Burnham's rule. It is the mausoleum that was put up for Mr Burnham after his death in 1984. It is a spiderlike structure, with a low central pavilion with an outer colonnade of concrete brackets that look like spider's legs. The intention was that the founder of the Cooperative Republic should be embalmed and displayed for ever, like Lenin; but something went wrong and the body decomposed before it could be treated.

(6) GEORGETOWN

Charles Waterton, *Wanderings in South America*

Waterton describes Stabroek, later Georgetown, at the begin-
ning of the nineteenth century.

Stabroek, the capital of Demerara, has been rapidly increasing for some years back; and if prosperity go in hand with the present enterprising spirit, Stabroek ere long will be of the first colonial consideration. It stands on the eastern bank at the mouth of the Demerara, and enjoys all the advantages of the refreshing sea-breeze; the streets are spacious, well bricked, and elevated, the trenches clean, the bridges excellent,

and the houses handsome. Almost every commodity and luxury of
London may be bought in the shops at Stabroek; its market wants
better regulations. The hotels are commodious, clean, and well
attended. Demerara boasts as fine and well-disciplined militia as any
colony in the western world.

The plantations have an appearance of high cultivation; a tolerable
idea may be formed of their value when you know that last year
Demerara numbered seventy-two thousand nine hundred and ninety-
nine slaves. They made above forty-four million pounds of sugar, near
two million gallons of rum, above eleven million pounds of coffee, and
three million eight hundred and nineteen thousand five hundred and
twelve pounds of cotton; the receipt into the public chest was five
hundred and fifty-three thousand nine hundred and fifty-six guilders
. . .

(7) GEORGETOWN

Evelyn Waugh, *A Handful of Dust*

*Waugh's Tony Last, turned explorer because of his disastrous
marriage and the death of his son and heir, arrives at the
Demerara river and Georgetown with the cranky Dr Messinger.*

Next day they arrived at the mouth of the Demerara. The customs
sheds were heavy with the reek of sugar and loud with the buzzing of
bees. There were lengthy formalities in disembarking their stores. Dr
Messinger saw to it while Tony lit a cigar and strayed out on to the
quay. Small shipping of all kinds lay round them: on the farther bank a
low green fringe of mangrove; behind, the tin roofs of the town were
visible among feathery palm trees; everything steamed from the recent
rain. Black stevedores grunted rhythmically at their work; West Indians
trotted busily to and fro with invoices and bills of lading . . .

(8) GUYANA: THE AMERINDIANS

Charles Waterton, *Wanderings in South America*

*Waterton evokes the Amerindians he came into contact with,
and describes their lifestyle in British Guiana in the early years of
the nineteenth century.*

There are five principal nations or tribes of Indians commonly known
by the name of Warow, Arowack, Acoway, Carib, and Macoushi.
They live in small hamlets, which consist of a few huts, never

exceeding twelve in number. These huts are always in the forest, near a river or some creek. They are open on all sides (except those of the Macoushi) and covered with a species of palm leaf.

Their principal furniture is the hammock. It serves them both for chair and bed. It is commonly made of cotton, though those of the Warows are formed from the aeta tree. At night they always make a fire close to it. The heat keeps them warm, and the smoke drives away the mosquitoes and sandflies . . .

They cut down about an acre or two of the trees which surround the huts, and there plant pepper, papaws, sweet and bitter cassava, plantains, sweet potatoes, yams, pine-apples, and silk-grass. Besides these, they generally have a few acres in some fertile part of the forest for their cassava, which is as bread to them. They make earthen pots to boil their provisions in. They have to grate the cassava before it is pressed, preparatory to baking . . . They have no cows, horses, mules, goats, sheep, or asses. The men hunt and fish, and the women work in the provision ground, and cook their victuals.

In each hamlet there is the trunk of a large tree hollowed out like a trough. In this, from their cassava, they make an abominable ill-tasted and sour kind of fermented liquor, called piwarri. They are very fond of it, and never fail to get drunk after brewing. The frequency of the brewing depends upon the superabundance of cassava.

Both men and women go without clothes. The men have a cotton wrapper, and the women a bead-ornamented square piece of cotton about the size of your hand, for the fig-leaf. Those far away in the interior use the bark of a tree for this purpose. They are very clean people, and wash in the river or creek at least twice every day. They paint themselves with the roucou, sweetly perfumed with hayawa or accaiari. Their hair is black and lank, and never curled. The women braid it up fancifully, something in the shape of Diana's head-dress in ancient pictures. They have very few diseases . . .

They have a kind of priest called a pee-ay-man, who is an enchanter. He finds out lost things. He mutters prayers to the evil spirit over them and their children when they are sick. If a fever be in the village, the pee-ay-man goes about all night long, howling and making dreadful noises, and begs the bad spirit to depart.

I could find no monuments or marks of antiquity amongst these Indians; so that after penetrating to the Rio Branco, from the shores of the Western ocean, had anybody questioned me on this subject, I should have answered, I have seen nothing amongst these Indians which tells me that they have existed here for a century, though, for aught I know to the contrary, they may have been here before the Redemption, but their total want of civilization has assimilated them to the forests in which they wander . . .

They are very jealous of their liberty, and much attached to their own mode of living. Though those in the neighbourhood of the European settlements have constant communication with the whites, they have no inclination to become civilized. Some Indians who have accompanied white men to Europe, on returning to their own land have thrown off their clothes, and gone back into the forests.

In George Town, the capital of Demerara, there is a large shed, open on all sides, built for them by order of the government. Hither the Indians come with monkeys, parrots, bows and arrows, and pegalls. They sell these to the white men for money, and too often purchase rum with it, to which they are wonderfully addicted.

(9) GUYANA: 'CUYAMA'

Shiva Naipaul, *A Hot Country*

Naipaul's satire of intellectual life in the 'Co-operative Republic of Cuyama' (Guyana) and 'Charlestown' (Georgetown) opens with a girl remembering her school history lessons. Through his account of her recollections, Naipaul passes on to the reader necessary information.

Sitting on the windy veranda of the school-house, she grew sleepy in the afternoon heat. Dust rose in swirls from the stony playground, powdering the feathery leaves of the tamarind tree that grew there. How old was she? Probably nine or ten. A meagre, brown-skinned girl with plaited hair tied with red ribbons.

Far away, on the spacious plains of Central Asia (so she learned from another of her books), the Kirghiz were living in tents of hide. In the spring, when the snows had begun to melt, they would take their flocks up to the high pastures where the spring flowers would be coming into bloom.

Snow.

Spring flowers.

Rich pastures.

A pinch on the arm restored her to attention.

– What is the population of Cuyama?

– Just over one million.

Where do the vast majority of the Cuyamese people live?

– On the coastal plains.

– What is the main cash crop of Cuyama?

– Sugar-cane.

She watched the clouds of golden dust swirling up from the playground, settling on the leaves of the tamarind tree.

The jungle at their backs . . . and, in between it and the brown ocean – the endless, waving fields of sugar-cane.
– After the Spaniards, which nation ruled Cuyama?
– The Dutch.
– That is so. For nearly one hundred years the Dutch ruled Cuyama. Their legacy persists in the names of many of our towns and villages. Can you name any of these towns and villages?
– New Utrecht.
– Alkmaar.
– Gronginen.
Teacher hitched up the sleeves of his cream-coloured shirt, stained with circles of sweat at the arm-pits.
– It was the Dutch who first drained the coastal swamps of our country and who first built dykes to protect us from the high tides of the Atlantic. It was a task for which they were particularly well suited because their own country was very low-lying and flat, some of it below sea-level. On the reclaimed lands and along the banks of the rivers, they established their plantations. The remains of some of those early plantations can still be seen. In those days they did not only grow sugar-cane. Cotton, tobacco and indigo were also cultivated. But what did the establishment of these plantations mean? Can anyone tell me?
– Slavery.

(10) Guyana: A Journey Upriver

Evelyn Waugh, *A Handful of Dust*

Tony Last and Dr Messinger begin their journey upriver into the virgin forested interior.

Bats like blighted fruit hung in clusters from the thatch and great spiders rode across it astride their shadows. This place had once been a balata station. It was the farthest point of commercial penetration from the coast. Dr Messinger marked it on his map with a triangle and named it in red 'First Base Camp'.

The first stage of the journey was over. For ten days they had been chugging upstream in a broad, shallow boat. Once or twice they had passed rapids (there the outboard engine had been reinforced by paddles; the men strained in time to the captain's count; the bo'sun stood in the bows with a long pole warding off the rocks). They had camped at sundown on patches of sandbank or in clearings cut from the surrounding bush. Once or twice they came to a 'house' left behind by balata bleeders or gold washers . . .

Since they had left Georgetown there had not been any part of his

body that was ever wholly at ease. His face and neck were burned by
the sun reflected from the water; the skin was flaking off them so that
he was unable to shave. The stiff growth of beard pricked him between
chin and throat. Every exposed part of his skin was bitten by cabouri
fly. They had found a way into the buttonholes of his shirt and the laces
of his breeches; mosquitoes had got him at the ankles when he changed
into slacks for the evening. He had picked up bêtes rouges in the bush
and they were crawling and burrowing under his skin; the bitter oil
which Dr Messinger had given him as protection had set up a rash of its
own wherever he had applied it. Every evening after washing he had
burned off a few ticks with a cigarette-end but they had left irritable
little scars behind them; so had the djiggas which one of the black boys
had dug out from under his toe-nails and the horny skin on his heals
and the balls of his feet. A marabunta had left a painful swelling on his
left hand.

As Tony scratched, he shook the framework from which the
hammocks hung. Dr Messinger turned over and said, 'Oh, for God's
sake.' He tried not to scratch; then he tried to scratch quietly; then in a
frenzy he scratched as hard as he could, breaking the skin in a dozen
places.

(11) TUMATUMARI

Wilson Harris, *Tumatumari*

*Prudence describes her first visit inland at Tumatumari after the
death of her child and husband in this novel about memory and
identity.*

Prudence recalled how she had greeted the sight of the house the first
time she came to it thirteen and a half months ago after her long boat
journey upriver from the coast. It had seemed to her grotesque at first
upon its stilts on the hill. But upon closer inspection of the site on which
it stood she realized how abnormally consistent it was with the peculiar
rhythm and abruptness of the terrain. Rain as well as sun. This rhythm
of landfall and waterfall struck her as she recalled each leg of the
journey into the interior – the footfall of the bush, sleeping mile after
mile, somersault and flame. Lightning fauna. Flora. The dance of place.
She craned her neck . . . orchid . . . wing . . . topmost branch . . .

She remembered how the dark seal of the riverbank would smoulder:
subterranean impress, cracks of light, skeleton plumage. The golden
sand banks which rose out of the bed of the river ceased without
warning at the foot of Tumatumari and turned white as snow over the
rapids above. The metamorphosis was so remarkable it seemed to her

fresh ammunition of wilderness. As if every given state of things began to alter – the fertility of the rainforest and the barren reaches of poles of desert were ignited by an element far older, though frailer, than uniformity or persuasion, the hairspring of life . . . The stilts of earth danced within this refractive sun.

Biographies and plot summaries

HARRIS, Wilson (1921–). Harris was born on 24 March 1921 in **New Amsterdam**, Berbice. As a senior government land surveyor, he led many surveying and engineering trips into the Guyanese jungle and savannahs between 1955 and 1958. Since 1959 he has lived in England. He began as a poet, and has published many dense novels clearly set in Guyana, but exploring through metaphor and analogy his characters' inner depths – like the four novels that make up *The Guyana Quartet*, 1985 (*Palace of the Peacock*, 1960; *The Far Journey of Oudin*, 1961; *The Whole Armour*, 1962; *The Secret Ladder*, 1963). Later novels continue to be set in jungly, multiracial Guyana, like

Wilson Harris

The Eye of the Scarecrow, 1965 (Extract 2), in which the narrator recalls a childhood friend 'L', a mining expedition into the interior, an aeroplane crash, and the 1948 Georgetown strike, in a difficult, dislocated technique invoking the past. *Tumatumari*, 1968 (Extract 11) refers to some mystical waterfalls in the interior where Prudence comes to terms with her dead engineer husband and dead foetus, living in the jungle with 'blind' Indians nearby, as she delves into her own Guyanese past, family, racism, tellurism, and visions. Harris's characters are forced to recast their fixed pasts. He is difficult to read, but has thought out his richly mythic and symbolic style with correspondences between personal events and nature and history. His most recent novel, *The Four Banks of the River of Space*, 1990, is also set in Guyana in the form of a dialogue within the narrator among hostile selves, involving Macousi Indians, 'living dreamers', masks, and myths. He has also set a novel in Mexico (*Companions of the Day and Night*, 1975) and has published criticism. See Hena Maes-Jelinek, *Wilson Harris*, Twayne, Boston, MA, 1982.

HEATH, Roy (1926–). Born in Guyana on 13 August 1926, Heath now lives in London. His school-teaching father died early, and he grew up in Jonestown (renamed **Agricola**) and from the age of eight, in **Georgetown**. He joined the civil service, but in 1945 left for England where he worked as a schoolteacher. He obtained a degree at the University of London in French in 1956. Heath is a lawyer and a teacher. His first novel came out in 1974 (*A Man Come Home*), followed by the Georgetown trilogy with *From the Heat of the Day*, 1979, *One Generation*, 1981, and *Genetta*, 1981, relating the tragedy of the Armstrong family and middle-class values in twentieth century Guyana. He followed these with *The Murderer*, 1981 (it won the *Guardian* fiction prize) and most recently *Orealla*, 1984 (Extracts 3 and 4). 'Orealla' is a mythic Macusi Indian place away from Georgetown, work, class and wage-slavery. The novel chronicles the rise and fall of Ben, small-time thief, black, ugly and a writer who looks after houses, lives with a barren wife, and has a mistress with three kids. He befriends the aboriginal Carl who sleeps on the floor. Heath is accurate about place. The novel is set at the turn of the century and is acute about the bucks or Indians, the upper-class, markets, horse taming, etc. Finally Ben is hanged for murdering his master. Heath approves of rebels, and views himself as a 'chronicler' of Guyanese life. His *Shadows Round the Moon: Caribbean Memoirs*, 1990, is a rite-of-passage study of himself from infancy through adolescence, school, friends and work, around family life, godfathers, older friends, neighbours, and class and race prejudices, until his self-exile in England.

MITTELHOLZER, Edgar (1909–1965). Mittelholzer was born in **New Amsterdam** on 16 December 1909, and committed suicide by setting fire to himself in an English field in April 1965. He came from a Swiss–German family, but had coloured blood, which he explored as a conflict in his autobiography *A Swarthy Boy*, 1963. He left Guyana in 1941, lived in Trinidad and Montreal and settled in Britain. His first novel, *Corentyne Thunder*, came out in 1941 and follows the life of Rangolall, a poor East Indian indentured labourer, up to his death. Mittelholzer published 23 further novels (with eight set in Guyana), including the *Kaywana Trilogy* which outlines the history of British Guiana from 1616 to 1953 through the Van Groenwegel family, concentrating on their 'sexual urge'. The novel *My Bones and My Flute*, 1955 (Extract 1), is a possession story narrated by a middle-class coloured painter rebel, Milton. Milton is invited by a historian businessman ostensibly to paint upriver, but in fact to help deal with a curse that whoever touched an eighteenth century manuscript would be possessed. The Nevison family, and Milton, then live through different stages of this curse at a saw-mill up the **Berbice River**. The novel ends when the Dutchman massacred during a slave revolt in 1763 is properly buried, and his spirit laid to rest. The atmosphere is good and the tale well told. The British Guiana of the 1930s, with its racism between 'swarthy' families and blacks, with its differences between the coast and the interior of 'bucks' and legends, is realistic.

NAIPAUL, Shiva (1945–1980). Born in Port of Spain, Trinidad, Shiva Naipaul was the younger brother of V. S. Naipaul (◊ Belize). He first went to Guyana in 1966, and returned in 1968. His third novel, *A*

Hot Country, 1983 (Extract 9), mocks the vacancy and futility of post-colonial life in Guyana, thinly disguised as 'Cuyama', under a populist dictatorship. Aubrey Saint-Pierre is a liberal, pedantic intellectual, scion of one of the great families, and owner of a bookshop, who marries an Indian girl whose family have Christianized themselves, uprooted from their Indian past. Dina is bright, but slowly dies spiritually in the mindless atmosphere of Cuyama. An old university friend, now a journalist, arrives from Britain, and sees the sights of the ex-colony. The novel ends with Aubrey realizing his own futility. Dina voices the theme of the novel: 'How passionately she hated this tropical sun, the never-ending succession of yellow afternoons, the foaming ugliness of the silted ocean. With what passion she hated the meanness, the ugliness, the brutishness of their lives. There was no sense to their existences. Nothing worthwhile had ever been created on this sterile patch of earth perched on the edge of a cruel continent . . .'. Naipaul investigated the Jonestown mass suicide in Guyana in *Black and White*, 1980.

NAIPAUL, V. S. (see under Belize).

WATERTON, Charles (1782–1865). Waterton was born on 3 June 1782. This Catholic aristocrat, who never took science seriously, journeyed out to British and Dutch Guiana to manage his family sugar mill in Demarara in 1812. He returned three more times (1816, 1820, 1824), and published his 'concise, unadorned account', *Wanderings in South America* (Extracts 6 and 8), in 1826. He was an eccentric traveller, always walking barefoot and curious to investigate all animate matter, letting bats suck blood from his toes, or experimenting on himself with the Indian paralysing poison *curare*. He is acute on the toucan's bill, on humming birds, on the jungle Indians' skills. He read *Don Quixote* everyday. When he returned to his stately home, Walton Hall in the West Riding, he set up a zoo. See Julia Blackburn, *Charles Waterton: Traveller and Conservationist*, The Bodley Head, London, 1989.

WAUGH, Evelyn (1902–1966). Born in Hampstead, London, Waugh was educated at Lancing, and then Oxford. He became a schoolteacher, and later worked as a journalist. In 1930 he converted to Catholicism. His fourth novel, *A Handful of Dust*, 1934 (Extracts 7 and 10), tells of adultery among the embattled aristocracy of the 1920s, and ends in 'Amazonas', an unexplored blank on the map between Brazil and Guyana. Tony Last spends his last pennies on refurbishing and preserving Hetton, his property and identity. Brenda, his empty, flighty wife, has an affair with mumsy-dominated Beaver. The novel is scattered with sharp cameos of ridiculous socialites and club-land addicts. Tony Last, after a vain and gallant effort to pretend to commit adultery in Brighton, sets off for South America as an explorer with Dr Messinger. In the last section Waugh compresses all the discomforts and tortures of jungle travel into a few pages. Ostensibly the two 'heroic' men are in search of a fabulous, forgotten city, an Eldorado of Incas in the tropical rainforest. Dr Messinger leads Last into a fateful trap where he drowns and Tony Last reads Dickens endlessly to an illiterate half-caste in an oasis in the jungle. From 2 January to 5 April 1933, Waugh travelled inland to British Guiana and Brazil and wrote his 'direct' and 'accurate day-to-day chronicle' entitled *Ninety-Two Days*, 1934, from which the South American details of his novel emerge. Waugh's travel book is a debunking of romantic travel. In 1939 he wrote *Robbery Under Law:* *The Mexican Object-Lesson*, a diatribe against Lázaro Cárdenas's expropriation of oil, and Marxist government. Mexico City is a 'huge, crowded, cosmopolitan, infernally noisy place'.

SURINAM

'In Suriname it rains a lot. Sometimes you're simply scared that you'll get up one morning and notice that your house has been washed away and is floating in the middle of a kwie-kwie swamp.'
Paul Marlee, Guinea-Pig

Surinam (in English) or the Republic of Suriname, lies between Guyana and Cayenne, with a land area of 163 820 sq km, and 315 km of Atlantic Coast. Its population reached 400 000 in 1989, with some 26 000 Amerindians. Its capital **Paramaribo** had 193 000 inhabitants in 1980. In 1738 the Dutch opened the colony to any immigrants, including a Jewish settlement (see Extract 6 by Paul Marlee). Between 1650 and 1820, some 300 000 African slaves were brought over. Voltaire's (◊ Paraguay) Candide reacts shockedly to this trade in slaves (Extract 5). Carpentier's (◊ Venezuela) character Esteban is equally nauseated by the cool Dutch way of dealing with slaves (Extract 1). John Stedman's five years in Surinam (1773–78) led to his vivid account of slave life and his affair with the slave Joanna (see Booklist). Runaway slaves became known as 'Bush Negroes', returning to jungle lifestyles abandoned in Africa, and now form 8% of the population (see Extract 3 by Shiva Naipaul). In 1863, slavery was abolished, and from 1873 indentured labourers were brought over. By 1917 some 34 300 had come from India, though a third returned. They are known as 'Hindustanis'. Later Javanese immigrants came over, and brought their rice culture with them. Amerindians form only 2% of the population. Dutch and English are the official languages (and you drive on the left), though most people speak the local pidgin called 'Talkie-talkie'. The coast is swampy, with mangrove and sand dunes, and its interior is a tropical, forested plateau. Rice, and open-mined bauxite, are the main products. The Surinamese writer Paul Marlee ◊ describes the country well in his novel *Guinea-Pig* (Extracts 2, 4 and 6).

Surinam was occupied by the Dutch in 1616, and formed part of the Dutch West indies, ruled from **Paramaribo**. In 1667 the territory, occupied by the British and called Willoughbyland, was given to Holland in exchange for Nieuw Amsterdam (New York), captured by the British three years earlier. It was during this period that Aphra Behn (1640–89), married to a Dutch merchant, set her prose romance *Oroonoko or the Royal Slave*, 1688, in which Oroonoko, and his beloved Imoinda end up as slaves in Surinam, try to rebel, are caught and flogged so that he decides to kill the governor, and is finally executed. By 1954 Surinam was a self-governing part of the Netherlands. In 1975 it was granted full independence, and has been in the grip of a civil war that drained the population after 15 opposition leaders were murdered in 1982, and most of the middle class fled. Some 200 000 Surinamese live in Holland. Dutch influence is evident in drainage, dyke work and architecture. In 1961 V.S. Naipaul (◊ Belize) visited Surinam and wrote about it. The US poet Selden Rodman visited in 1970 and wrote, 'poets and novelists are rare in Surinam'. For stories and poems by Dutch writers from Surinam, see Barbara Howes's anthology *From the Green Antilles*, 1966.

BOOKLIST

The following selection includes all titles which are extracted in this chapter as well as those mentioned in the introduction which are available in English. In general, paperback editions are given when possible. The editions cited are not necessarily the only ones available. For most of the extracted works, the original publisher in English can be found in 'Acknowledgments and Citations' at the end of the volume, as can the exact location of the extracts and the editions from which they are taken. The date in square brackets is the original publication date of the work in its original language. Extract numbers are highlighted in bold for ease of reference.

Behn, Aphra, *Oroonoko or the Royal Slave* [1688], W. W. Norton, New York and London, 1973.

Carpentier, Alejo, *Explosion in a*

Cathedral [1962], John Sturrock, trans, Minerva, London, 1991/ Little Brown, Boston, MA, 1963. **Extract 1**.

From the Green Antilles, Barbara Howes, ed, Macmillan, New York, 1966.

Marlee, Paul, *Guinea-Pig*, Karnak House, London, 1990. **Extracts 2, 4 and 6**.

Naipaul, Shiva, *Beyond the Dragon's Mouth: Stories and Pieces*, Hamish Hamilton, London, 1984. **Extract 3**.

Naipaul, V.S., *The Middle Passage. Impressions of Five Societies – British, French and Dutch – in the West Indies and South America*, André Deutsch, London, 1962.

Rodman, Selden, *South America of the Poets*, Hawthorn Books, New York, 1970.

Stedman, John, *Narrative of a Five Years' Expedition against the Revolted Negroes of Surinam* [1796], Johns Hopkins University Press, Baltimore, MD, 1988.

Voltaire, *Candide* [1759], John Butt, trans, Penguin, London, 1947/R. Bruce Baswell, trans, Tudor Publishing Co, New York, 1934. **Extract 5.**

Extracts

(1) PARAMARIBO

Alejo Carpentier, **Explosion in a Cathedral**

Esteban, the dreamer, and secret lover of Sofía, in Carpentier's saga of the Caribbean during the aftermath of the French Revolution, reaches Paramaribo.

Esteban's stay in Paramaribo – after the departure of *L'Italie Conquise* – ended with the arrival of the *Amazon*, a merchantman from Baltimore, returning from the River Plate. During the interval of waiting he had enjoyed the favours of a mature lady, who read novels which she considered to be still contemporary, such as Richardson's *Clarissa Harlowe* and *Pamela*, but whose body was cool and sweet-smelling, and always smothered with rice powder, which she applied with magnificent prodigality. She entertained him with Portuguese wines, while her husband slept out at his hacienda 'Egmont', for reasons already established.

Two hours before carrying his baggage aboard the *Amazon*, Esteban went to the hospital in the town, to get the senior physician, Greuber, to confirm that a certain small swelling under the left arm, which was troubling him, was benign. After an emollient had been applied to the painful spot, the worthy doctor took leave of him in an ante-room, where nine negroes under armed guard were quietly smoking a bitter, fermented tobacco smelling of vinegar, in clay pipes whose stems were so eroded that the bowls touched their teeth. The young man learned with horror that these slaves, convicted of attempted flight and desertion, had been condemned by the Courts of Justice in Surinam to have their left legs amputated. And since the sentence must be cleanly and scientifically carried out, without resort to archaic methods belonging to the age of barbarism and which might cause excessive suffering or endanger the prisoners' lives, the nine slaves had been brought to the best surgeon in Paramaribo, so that he could carry out the court's verdict, saw in hand.

'They cut off the arms as well,' said Doctor Greuber, 'when a slave lifts his hand against his master.' And the surgeon turned to the men who were waiting: 'Who's first?'

When he saw a tall negro with a determined forehead and powerful muscles stand up in silence, Esteban ran out to the nearest tavern, on the point of fainting, and shouted for brandy to overcome his horror.

(2) PARAMARIBO

Paul Marlee, *Guinea-Pig*

Marlee's narrator returns to his home town Paramaribo from the Netherlands.

Early Sunday morning at Government Square close by the Suriname river. No one yet in the streets. He stands there fascinated. He has only been back a few days in the tropical sun after a long stay in the Netherlands. The two little dinosaurs roll back and forth in the grass, their jaws locked like two tongs. Then they let go of each other; stand glaring; and suddenly go at one another again. *Everything seems to be so confusing. His mind races like a defective projector. The confusion turns into chaos. Images appear, disappear again. It is as if he experiences everything simultaneously.* Before you go into the battle you marry Helen of Troy. Together with her you will now wage battle against her own people. Finally, utterly frustrated and realizing the futility of the whole affair, you book one way for Paramaribo. There, now, you present yourself as nationalist, artist, would be senator. Fuck the Dutchman. Fuck Helen. Here in Paramaribo you are now a great writer, here in your own fatherland a great stage-director. You never failed in Amsterdam; you simply never had equal chances. By accident, or by habit, you still walk around with 'het parool'[1] in the pocket. You're going to reeducate your own people now, and show them that you are their artist; that you're the one they should make a monument for later. Then, of course, you've got the literary burps of the great, mediocre, political–poetical stuntman . . . Soon another artistic genius or professor from Holland will appear again on t.v. to help alleviate the boredom of our small city. Hybridized Portuguese Jews, Chinese, Mulattoes, Africans, Whites, Amerindians, East Indians, Lebanese, Indonesians: an unbelievable combination, seemingly thrown together by the inscrutable forces of history. A capricious concurrence of circumstances? A new experiment of the Cosmic laboratory? A unique chance? The world in miniature as can be read from our tourist folders. We Caribbeans of mixed race, we are a remarkable and interesting phenomenon in the universe.

[1]Author's note: a Dutch newspaper.

(3) SURINAM: THE BUSH NEGROES
Shiva Naipaul, *Beyond the Dragon's Mouth*

Shiva Naipaul reports on the Bush Negroes of Surinam in 1981.

Bush Negro country is forbidding – even from the air. At five or six thousand feet, broken only by the dark ribbons of the meandering rivers and creeks, the Amazonian jungles of Surinam look like broccoli gone mad. At that height the outlines of massive rock outcrops can be glimpsed in the depths of the rivers. Jungle and rapid-fomenting rocks: together they had guaranteed the safety and isolation of these men who had fled the slave plantations of Holland's only South American colony. The white men, however, have never quite been able to stop pursuing them. Originally, they did so as missionaries – and still do. Latterly, and with increasing frequency, they have begun to come among them as tourists. I was sharing the small, propeller-driven Surinam Airways plane with a noisy party of Dutch travellers, skins shining with insect repellent, in search of an adventurous weekend in the Bush. The little plane droned on, shuddering through the cloudy vapours exhaled by the jungle below us. We were heavily loaded with medicines, food and equipment for the mission hospital at Stoelman's Island on the Marowijne River. From Stoelman's Island I would make my way up the Tapanahony River, a tributary stream of the Marowijne, to the village of Drietabbetje, the residence of the paramount chief of the Ndjuka tribe of Bush Negroes.

(4) SURINAM: THE RAIN
Paul Marlee, *Guinea-Pig*

Marlee, writing in exile, describes the tropical Surinamese weather.

In Suriname it rains a lot. Sometimes you're simply scared that you'll get up one morning and notice that your house has been washed away and is floating in the middle of a kwie-kwie swamp.[1] You could be standing there under a balcony alongside the street, waiting for hours for the rain to stop. Others, whom the same fate befell, will be standing next to you. A car may be passing now and then. Everyone looks after the car and then gazes back into the rain.

[1]Authors note: The many swamps and low lying coastal areas of Suriname formerly abounded with kwie-kwie, a pantzer-like (thick shells run from back to belly), small, freshwater fish; regarded as a delicacy by the population. Today most swamps have been depleted because of over-fishing; or have been converted into rice-polders.

(5) SURINAM: SLAVERY

Voltaire, *Candide*

After leaving Paraguay, with its Jesuit missions, Candide travels to Dutch Surinam to discover the horrors of slavery.

'. . . and in the distance I see a town which I think must be Surinam. It belongs to the Dutch, you know. Our troubles are over, and happiness lies before us.'

As they were approaching the town, they noticed a negro lying full length at the side of the road and wearing nothing but a pair of blue canvas drawers. The poor fellow had no left leg and no right hand. Candide addressed him in Dutch:

'What are you doing here, my friend?' he asked. 'And what a dreadful state you are in!'

'I am waiting for my master, Mr Vanderdendur, who owns the famous sugarworks,' replied the negro.

'Did Mr Vanderdendur treat you like this?' asked Candide.

'Yes, Sir,' said the negro, 'it's the custom. For clothing, we are given a pair of canvas drawers twice a year. Those of us who work in the factories and happen to catch a finger in the grindstone have a hand chopped off; if we try to escape, they cut off one leg. Both accidents happened to me. That's the price of your eating sugar in Europe. My mother sold me on the coast of Guiana for fifty Spanish shillings. When she parted with me, she said: 'Always honour and adore your fetishes, my dear boy, and they will make you happy; you have the honour of being a slave for milords the white men, and that is how you will make your parents' fortune.' I don't know whether I made that fortune,' he continued, with a shake of his head, 'but they certainly did not make mine. Dogs, monkeys, and parrots are much less miserable than we are. The Dutch fetishes, who converted me, tell me every Sunday that we are all children of Adam, black and white alike. I am no genealogist; but if these preachers speak the truth, we must all be cousins. Now, you will surely agree that relatives could not be treated more horribly.'

'Oh, Pangloss!' cried Candide. 'A scandal like this never occurred to you! But it's the truth, and I shall have to renounce that optimism of yours in the end.'

'What is optimism?' asked Cacambo.

'It's the passion for maintaining that all is right when all goes wrong with us,' replied Candide, weeping as he looked at the negro. And with tears in his eyes, he pursued his way to Surinam.

(6) TORARICA

Paul Marlee, *Guinea-Pig*

Marlee tells of Torarica, the Jewish settlement in Surinam.

The old capital of Suriname, founded around the middle of the seventeenth century alongside the Para river by Jews and Englishmen. The later extensive settlement of the Jews named Jodensavanne (Jewish Savanna) upstream the Suriname river was, because of different factors, reclaimed from the settlers by the indomitable jungle. The main of these factors is the fact that the settlers (for those times) built their settlement too far in the interior. Placed in a humid, tropical climate, outnumbered by slaves and Amerindians, surrounded by an immense, unfathomable jungle; and isolated from any form of familiar civilization, they slowly started losing heart, and a process of disintegration ensued. The ruins of their synagogue – the oldest of the Americas – and their grave sites have been declared a national monument. Their congregation, which is also regarded as the oldest Jewish congregation in the Americas, is still extant in Paramaribo.

Biographies and plot summaries

CARPENTIER, Alejo (see under Venezuela).

MARLEE, Paul (1947–). Marlee currently teaches in Surinam. He set his novel *Guinea-Pig*, 1990 (Extracts 2, 4 and 6), written in English, in the Surinam of his childhood, and describes the habitat, nature (especially the rain, and the Kwie-Kwie swamps) and historical curiosities of the country well. The plot of *Guinea-Pig* has a Portuguese Jewish descendant on a scholarship in Puerto Rico reliving his life, ending with an initiation dream that confirms he is a writer. Paul Marlee has written further fiction in Dutch.

NAIPAUL, Shiva (see under Guyana).

VOLTAIRE (see under Paraguay).

FRENCH GUIANA

'As you pass the islands, the stately hills on the main, ornamented with ever-verdant foliage, show you that this is by far the sublimest scenery on the sea-coast from the Amazons to the Orinoco.
Charles Waterton,
Wanderings in South America

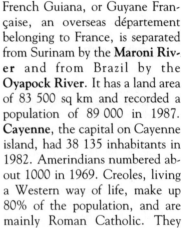

French Guiana, or Guyane Fran-çaise, an overseas département belonging to France, is separated from Surinam by the **Maroni River** and from Brazil by the **Oyapock River**. It has a land area of 83 500 sq km and recorded a population of 89 000 in 1987. **Cayenne**, the capital on Cayenne island, had 38 135 inhabitants in 1982. Amerindians numbered about 1000 in 1969. Creoles, living a Western way of life, make up 80% of the population, and are mainly Roman Catholic. They speak a West Indian French dialect called 'Créole', and French and Amerindian languages. The country is divided between foothills rising to the **Guiana Highlands** and a coastal strip where the majority of people live. The climate is equatorial, with heavy rainfall on the east coast, a short rainy season, and high humidity. Almost 90% of the country is covered by tropical selva.

Settled by France in 1604, in Guiana's early years there were few plantations and thus little slavery, and little indentured labour from the East Indies.

France acquired Guiana in 1667. After occupation by Portuguese forces, the country was restored to France in 1817. In 1852 a penal settlement was established at **Saint Laurent du Maroni**, and later at **Devil's Island** on the Iles du Salut off Cayenne, finally abolished in 1945: it housed famous prisoners like Dreyfus, and later Henri Charrière ◊. There was a gold rush in 1855. Lafcadio Hearn (1850–1904), born on the Greek island of Lefkas but accepted as a US novelist and critic, visited French Guiana and wrote about it in his journal *Two Years in the French West Indies*, 1890. Inhabitants are full French citizens, can vote, and have been represented in the French Parliament since 1877. In 1967, France established a Eurospace centre at **Kourou**, now a town of some 50 000.

The explorer Charles Waterton (◊ Guyana) wrote perceptively about **Cayenne** in the early nineteenth century (Extract 1). Alejo Carpentier (◊ Venezuela) sets his historical novel *El siglo de las luces*, 1959 (*Explosion in a Cathedral*, 1963) in the same period – Carpentier has the real-life character Victor Hugues, erstwhile revolutionary, become a dictator as governor of **Cayenne**.

BOOKLIST

The following selection includes all titles which are extracted in this chapter as well as those mentioned in the introduction which are available in English. In general, paperback editions are given when possible. The editions cited are not necessarily the only ones available. For most of the extracted works, the original publisher in English can be found in 'Acknowledgments and Citations' at the end of the volume, as can the exact location of the extracts and the editions from which they are taken. The date in square brackets is the original publication date of the work in its original language. Extract numbers are highlighted in bold for ease of reference.

Carpentier, Alejo, *Explosion in a Cathedral* [1962], John Sturrock, trans, Minerva, London, 1991, London, 1971/Little Brown, Boston, MA, 1963.

Charrière, Henri, *Papillon* [1970], Patrick O'Brien, trans, Grafton, London, 1986/Penguin Books, New York, 1983. **Extracts 2 and 3**.

Hearn, Lafcadio, *Two Years in the French West Indies*, Harper, New York, 1890.

Waterton, Charles, *Wanderings in South America* [1825], Century Hutchinson, London, 1985. **Extract 1**.

Extracts

(1) CAYENNE

Charles Waterton, *Wanderings in South America*

Waterton passed through Cayenne in the 1820s, describing it with his idiosyncratic naturalist's eye. He refers to its governor Victor Hugues, a real-life character in Carpentier's Explosion in a Cathedral.

On the fourteenth day after leaving Pernambuco the brig cast anchor off the island of Cayenne. The entrance is beautiful. To windward, not far off, there are two bold wooded islands, called the Father and Mother; and near them are others, their children, smaller, though as beautiful as their parents. Another is seen a long way to leeward of the family, and seems as if it had strayed from home and cannot find its way back. The French call it *l'enfant perdu*. As you pass the islands, the stately hills on the main, ornamented with ever-verdant foliage, show you that this is by far the sublimest scenery on the sea-coast from the Amazons to the Orinoco. On casting your eye towards Dutch Guiana, you will see that the mountains become unconnected and few in number, and long before you reach Surinam the Atlantic wave washes a flat and muddy shore.

Considerably to windward of Cayenne, and about twelve leagues from land, stands a stately and towering rock, called the Constable. As nothing grows on it to tempt greedy and aspiring man to claim it as his own, the sea-fowl rest and raise their off-spring there . . .

Cayenne is capable of being a noble and productive colony. At present it is thought to be the poorest on the coast of Guiana. Its estates are too much separated one from the other by immense tracts of forest; and the revolutionary war, like a cold eastern wind, has chilled their zeal and blasted their best expectations.

The clove-tree, the cinnamon, pepper, and nutmeg, and many other choice spices and fruits of the eastern and Asiatic regions, produce abundantly in Cayenne.

The town itself is prettily laid out, and was once well fortified. They tell you it might easily have been defended against the invading force of the two united nations; but Victor Hugues, its governor, ordered the tri-coloured flag to be struck, and ever since that day the standard of Braganza has waved on the ramparts of Cayenne.

He who has received humiliations from the hand of this haughty, iron-hearted governor may see him now in Cayenne, stripped of all his revolutionary honours, broken down and ruined, and under arrest in his own house. He has four accomplished daughters, respected by the whole town. Towards the close of day, when the sun's rays are no longer oppressive, these much-pitied ladies are seen walking up and down the balcony with their aged parent, trying, by their kind and filial attention, to remove the settled gloom from his too guilty brow.

This was not the time for a traveller to enjoy Cayenne. The hospitality of the inhabitants was the same as ever, but they had lost their wonted gaiety in public, and the stranger might read in their countenances, as the recollection of recent humiliations and misfortunes every now and then kept breaking in upon them, that they were still in sorrow for their fallen country . . .

About a day's journey in the interior is the celebrated national plantation. This spot was judiciously chosen, for it is out of reach of enemies' cruisers. It is called La Gabrielle. No plantation in the western world can vie with La Gabrielle. Its spices are of the choicest kind; its soil particularly favourable to them: its arrangements beautiful; and its director, Monsieur Martin, a botanist of first-rate abilities. This indefatigable naturalist ranged through the East, under a royal commission, in quest of botanical knowledge; and during his stay in the western regions has sent over to Europe from twenty to twenty-five thousand specimens in botany and zoology. La Gabrielle is on a far-extending range of wooded hills. Figure yourself a hill in the shape of a bowl reversed, with the buildings on the top of it, and you will have an idea of the appearance of La Gabrielle. You approach the house through a noble avenue, five hundred toises long, of the choicest tropical fruit-trees, planted with the greatest care and judgement; and should you chance to stray through it after sunset when the clove trees are in blossom, you would fancy yourself in the Idalian groves, or near the banks of the Nile . . .

Not far from the banks of the river Oyapoc, to windward of Cayenne, is a mountain which contains an immense cavern. Here the cock of the rock is plentiful. He is about the size of a fantail pigeon, his colour a bright orange, and his wings and tail appear as though fringed; his head is ornamented with a superb double-feathery crest, edged with purple. He passes the day amidst gloomy damps and silence, and only issues out for food a short time at sunrise and sunset. He is of the gallinaceous tribe. The South American Spaniards call him *gallo de Rio Negro*, and suppose that he is only to be met with in the vicinity of that far-inland stream; but he is common in the interior of Demerara, amongst the huge rocks in the forests of Macoushia, and he has been shot south on the line, in the captainship of Para.

(2) Devil's Island

Henri Charrière, Papillon

'Papillon' is precise in his description of his island prison.

This was the smallest of the three Iles du Salut. The most northerly, too, and the most directly in the path of the wind and the waves. First there was a narrow strip that ran right round the island at sea level, and then the ground rose steeply to a little plain with the warders' guard-house and a single block for the convicts – about ten of them. Convicts sentenced for common-law offences were not officially supposed to be sent to Devil's Island; it was reserved for political offenders, each of whom lived in his own little house with a corrugated-iron roof. On Mondays they were given their rations for the week, uncooked, and every day a loaf of bread. There were perhaps thirty of them. The medical attendant was Dr Léger, who had poisoned his whole family in Lyons or thereabouts. The political prisoners would have nothing to do with the convicts and sometimes they would write to Cayenne, complaining about some transportee or other. When that happened he'd be taken away and sent back to Royale.

There was a cable, a wire rope, between Royale and Devil's Island, because quite often the sea was too rough for the boat from Royale to come over to the little concrete landing-stage.

(3) Saint-Laurent-Du-Maroni

Henri Charrière, Papillon

Charrière's gripping account of life as an escaping prisoner on Devil's Island opens with his arrival from France at Saint-Laurent-Du-Maroni.

The warders had gone off in relays to change. Each in turn came back dressed in white with a sun-helmet instead of a képi. Julot said. 'We're almost there.' It was appallingly hot, for they had shut the port-holes. Through the glass you could see the bush. So we were in the Maroni. The water was muddy. Untouched virgin forest, green and impressive. Disturbed by the ship's siren, birds rose and flew across the sky. We went very slowly, and that allowed us to pay close attention to the thick dark-green, overflowing vegetation. We saw the first wooden houses, with their corrugated iron roofs. Black men and women stood at their doors, watching the ship go by. They were quite used to seeing it unload its human cargo, and so they never bothered to wave as it passed.

Biographies and plot summaries

CHARRIERE, Henri (1906–1973). Charrière was born in the Ardèche in France. As a criminal he was nick-named 'Papillon' ('Butterfly'). He was convicted of a murder he had not committed, and sent out to French Guiana, France's penal colony. In 13 years, between 1931 and 1943, Papillon tried to escape nine times from **Devil's Island** and other places, until he made it to the haven of Venezuela, where he died in 1973. His auto-biography *Papillon* (Extracts 2 and 3) reads like an adventure story, packed with graphic details, from how sharks devoured his best friend's corpse, to camp murders, to an escapee sinking in mud after a desperate drift from Devil's Island. He wrote his account of his years in the tropical penal colonies quickly in exercise books, and published it in 1970 when it became a literary sensation. It was made into a film in 1973.

WATERTON, Charles (see under Guyana).

BRAZIL

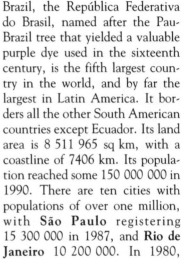

'The day was wildly, shockingly beautiful, a sort of glaring, surrealistic Swiss landscape: Corcovado, with its purple stone and blue woods; the cliff across the lake crowned with shacks; black children playing stick ball around the lagoa; expensive cars winking in the sun.'
Antônio Callado,
Don Juan's Bar

Brazil, the República Federativa do Brasil, named after the Pau-Brazil tree that yielded a valuable purple dye used in the sixteenth century, is the fifth largest country in the world, and by far the largest in Latin America. It borders all the other South American countries except Ecuador. Its land area is 8 511 965 sq km, with a coastline of 7406 km. Its population reached some 150 000 000 in 1990. There are ten cities with populations of over one million, with **São Paulo** registering 15 300 000 in 1987, and **Rio de Janeiro** 10 200 000. In 1980, 66.7% of the population was urban. A consequence of this urban explosion was the shanty town, known as *favela*, which means euphemistically 'little bean field' from a small yellow flower. Urban problems like rootlessness, isolation, and class and race differences are recreated in the novels of Machado de Assis ◊ written under the Empire about a **Rio** with elegant houses, and servants. Later, Clarice Lispector ◊ explored the inner lives of women in **São Paulo**, and young writer Caio Abreu ◊ captures the modern stresses of a great industrialized city. In 1920 Brazilian modernism, situated in **São Paulo** and epitomized by the writer Mário de Andrade ◊, competed with European avant-garde art movements with a week of modern art in 1922, 'cannibalist' theories about culture (trying to avoid imitating Europe), and led to the famous São Paulo Bienale (an art show with a prestigious prize), fine buildings and museums, and modernist works that include Oswald de Andrade's (1880–1954) novels *Serafim Ponte Grande*, 1933 (*Seraphim Grosse Pointe*, 1979), *A morta*, 1937 (*The Dead Woman*, 1980), and *Memórias sentimentais de João Miramar*, 1923 (*The Sentimental Memoirs* *of John Seaborne*, 1979) and the poems of Manuel Bandeira (1886–1968), of which there is a selection in English entitled *This Earth, That Sky*, 1988 (see also his essay *A Brief History of Brazilian Literature*, 1964).

CITIES, RIVERS AND FORESTSS

The triangle formed by **Rio, São Paulo** and **Belo Horizonte** accounts for four out of every ten Brazilians, and most of the industry. For example, 40% of Brazil's industrial output is centred in São Paulo. But **Brasília** has been the capital since it was built 1960, with a population of 1.6 million. One of Brazil's most committed modernists, João Guimarães Rosa (1908–67) set his anthologized short story 'The Thin Edge of Happiness' around the building of Brasília.

Amerindians number about 200 000, and try to live in the **Amazon Basin**. Negroes constitute some 11% of the population. The rest of the population are *mestizos* from the Portuguese, with nineteenth century immigration from Italy, Germany and Japan. Between 1874 and 1949, 4 546 560 immigrants arrived in Brazil, which explains why in the 1950 census 62% were white, and only 26% *pardo* (brown), of mixed race. The language is Portuguese (with some 120 Indian languages), and the religion Roman Catholicism.

Most of the country is made up of hilly uplands, with few plains. Ninety per cent of Brazil lies within the tropics. Three great river systems dominate Brazil. The **Amazon** (so named after naked warrior women were seen by early explorers) in the region of **Amazonia** (60% of Brazil) holds one-fifth of all the world's fresh water. From its Andean source to its 320 km wide mouth, the Amazon runs slowly for some 6500 km. Ships drawing 4 m of water can reach Iquitos in Peru. The Amazon has over 500 tributaries. Many works explore this mighty river, from those of naturalists like A.R. Wallace, and Henry Bates ◊ to travellers and fiction writers like V.S. Pritchett ◊, Moritz Thomsen (◊ Ecuador), H.M. Tomlinson ◊, and James Hamilton-Paterson ◊. The Amazon is the main thoroughfare into the interior. Then there is the **Paraguay/Paraná/Plata** river system, where in 1973 Brazil constructed the huge **Itaipu dam** (the largest hydro-electrical plant in the world), and thirdly the **Rio São Francisco**, entirely within Brazil.

Of the major vegetation zones, the tropical rainforests lie at the heart of today's ecological worries, and attempts to preserve the Indian way of life. Norman Lewis (◊ Guatemala) protested the genocide of jungle Indians in 1968, dramatized in Christopher Hampton's play *Savages*, 1974. The forest forms the background to many adventures, from H.M. Tomlinson to Conan Doyle ◊, Fleming ◊, Souza ◊ and Darcy Ribeiro ◊.

The next well defined region is the *sertão* of the North East, with its droughts and *caatinga* or scrubby thorn woodlands, and poverty. The lifestyle is based on cattle, *vaqueiros* (cowboys) and *cangaceiros* (bandits like the legendary Lampião). It was in the *sertão* that the mystic Antonio Conselheiro rebelled, and was finally killed in **Canudos** in 1897 – see Extract 10 by da Cunha ◊, a study by Cunningham Grahame (◊ Paraguay) and Mario Vargas Llosa's (◊ Peru) epic novel *The War of the End of the World*, 1981. The *sertão* has been explored by many excellent writers from Ramos ◊, Rachel de Queiroz, João Ubaldo Ribeiro ◊, Torres ◊, and Chatwin ◊.

A final geographical zone that has entered literature is the surgarcane region round **Bahia (Salvador)**, chronicled by Jorge Amado ◊ and José Almeida (1887–1980) in *A bagaceira*, 1928 (*Trash*, 1978). Poet Manuel Bandeira sums up Brazil's nature as '*esta terra de feracidades excepcionais*' ('this land so monstrously fertile').

EARLY HISTORY

In 1494 Pope Alexander VI gave Portugal all land 370 leagues west of the Cape Verde (48 W) Islands in a treaty called Tordesillas. On 22 April 1500, Pedro Alves Cabral sighted land and called it Vera Cruz. By January 1502 **Rio de Janeiro** was named. For the next 25 years it remained a no-man's land. By 1534 the Portuguese began to colonize this new land, setting their first capital in São Salvador da Bahia, today known as **Salvador** (and sometimes **Bahia**), with their first Governor General in 1549. Salvador remained the capital for 214 years.

The early years of the colony were based on the sugarcane boom, supplying nearly all of Europe's sugar in the seventeenth century. The mills were run by white Portuguese who, from 1538, imported slaves from Africa (mainly Guinea and Sudan) to run the mills and cut the cane as the local Indians virtually died out after catching European diseases. Amado has fictionalized this area, as has Lins do Rego (1901–1957) with his *Menino do engenho*, 1932, *Doidinho*, 1933 and *Bangüe*, 1934 (collected as *Plantation Boy*, 1966). Brazil's great essayist, Gilberto Freyre, begins with the sugar plantation owners in his *The Masters and the Slaves – a Study in the Development of Brazilian Civilization*, 1933, to define Brazilian culture itself. The African influence in Brazil arose from this need for a workforce. Some 3.5 million black slaves were brought over until the slave trade was suppressed in 1853, and slavery finally abolished in 1888. The African influence is very marked in the **Bahia** region, in the celebrated carnivals, and the African religious cults known as *Candomblé* in Bahia and *Macumba* in the rest of Brazil, vividly portrayed by Jorge Amado ◊.

When the Portuguese had expelled the invading French, and then Dutch, they set about opening up the interior of their vast colony, pushing well beyond the Tordesillas line. This penetration was carried out by the *bandeirantes* and the Jesuit missionaries. The *bandeirantes* were pioneers or gangs of explorers looking for gold and are named after their flag or *bandeira*. Gold had been found in **Minas Gerais** (meaning general mines) in 1693, initiating the second boom in Brazilian history (1696–1800). In 1933 the city **Ouro Prêto** was declared a museum to the gold boom. The missionaries tamed and Christianized the Indians until the Marquis of Pombal expelled the Jesuits in 1759.

THE AMERINDIANS

The fate of the aboriginal Indians (or Amerindians) has given Brazil notoriety since Norman Lewis's 1968 exposure in the *Sunday Times* of Amazonian Indian genocide. When Brazil was discovered the whole of what is Brazil today held some one million Indians. By 1950 the number had shrunk to 150 000. By 1987, all the Kreen-Akrore had gone. First the *bandeirantes* looking for gold, then the rubber tappers (called *seringueiros*), then migrants from *favelas* (shanties or slums) along the new jungle highways, and gold prospectors (called *garimpeiros*) – recently 45 000 invaded Yanomani territory – have persecuted these Indians. When Brazil was discovered the Indians worked as slaves; their language Tupi-Guaraní was used as the *lingua franca* by missionaries. Words from their language even passed into English, like tapioca and cashew. The name given to the cross-breeding between Portuguese and Indians was *mameluco*; the *caboclo* is also half-Indian and half-Portuguese. In 1910 the SPI (Indian Protection Service) was set up and run by Marshal C.M. da Silva Rondon who protected the Amazonian Indians while developing a telegraph link. Rondon led Theodore Roosevelt into the Amazon jungle, and he appears in Roosevelt's classic *Through the Brazilian Wilderness*, 1914. **Rondonia** was named after this Indian benefactor. When a government inquiry revealed such corruption that the IPS was closed, another agency, FUNAI, was set up in 1968. The **Xingu National Park** was set aside for displaced Indians in 1961 and run by the Villas Boas brothers.

The most famous study of Brazilian Indians is by the French anthropologist Claude Lévi-Strauss, *Tristes Tropiques*, 1955. For further reading, see John Hemming, *Amazon Frontier: The Defeat of the Brazilian Indians*, 1987 and Alex Shoumatoff's quirky and vivid travels in *The Rivers Amazon*, 1978 (Century, 1986).

THE 19TH CENTURY – RUBBER AND COFFEE

Brazil had no wars of independence like the rest of Spanish America. In 1807 the Portuguese royal family, with all their retainers and gold,

Jorge Amado

escaped the French invasion of Lisbon aided by the British fleet, and set off for their colony Brazil. They reached **Rio de Janeiro** in January 1821 and set up court. In 1821 the King João VI returned to Portugal, leaving his son Pedro as regent. Dom Pedro was ordered to return to Portugal, refused, defying the Cortes, and proclaimed independence, bloodlessly on 7 September 1822. (The Cortes was the historic assembly of nobility, prelates and commoners which met and ordered Dom Pedro back to Portugal in order to prevent Brazilian independence.) The house of Braganza (Bragança) ruled for 67 years, for Dom Pedro II continued the empire until 1889. Brazil had no university or printing presses until the nineteenth century. A meticulously detailed history of Brazil from 1500 to 1808 was written by the Romantic poet Robert Southey (1774–1843), who knew Spanish and Portuguese well, living in Portugal in 1795 and in 1800. His three quarto volumed *The History of Brazil* appeared in 1810, 1817 and 1819.

The nineteenth century saw two further booms affecting Brazil's everyday life and economy. The first was the rubber boom based on the *hevea brasiliensis* tree, and the rubber-tappers who worked the isolated trees in the jungle. In 1876 a British resident named Sir Henry Wickham sent hevea seeds to London, and these were then sent out to the Far East and planted in rows. By 1913 Asia had outstripped Brazil in rubber production. The rise and fall of the rubber boom is symbolized by **Manaus's Opera House** that once had Caruso singing in it: today Manaus (Manáos in Brazilian) is a free-port (see Hamilton-Paterson, Extract 13). In 1927 Henry Ford tried to industrialize rubber production on a mammoth scale, set up a one million hectare farm (Fordlandia) but failed because he could not recruit enough workers. One side-product of the rubber boom was the opening up of Amazonia, with all the ecological disasters involved in converting jungle to cattle ranges. The yearly loss of rainforest has been calculated as between 1.7 and 8 million hectares.

The second nineteenth century boom was coffee, smuggled out of French Guiana in 1727 and introduced in **São Paulo** around 1830. Brazil is the world's greatest coffee exporter. Coffee was the basis of São Paulo's industrialization, for coffee needed rail links, a port and a labour force, *colonos*, and this ushered in immigration from Europe. Most of these immigrants settled in the southern states.

20TH CENTURY PRESIDENTS

Since the fall of the Braganza family in 1889, Brazil has not known many democratically elected governments. Between 1906 and 1930

Notes to map (facing page): [a]*There are vivid descriptions of Manaus in James Hamilton-Paterson's novel* Gerontius, *1989, and in Moritz Thomsen's travel account* The Saddest Pleasure, *1990;* [b]*There are classic accounts of travels along this river by Alexandre von Humboldt (who reached it from the Orinoco, via the Casiquiare), Henry Bates and A. R. Wallace;* [c]*Henry Bates lived here for three and a half years in 1851;* [d]*Sir Arthur Conan Doyle sets his novel* The Lost World, *1912, here;* [e]*H. M. Tomlinson travelled up the Madeira river to Pôrto Velho in his* The Sea and the Jungle, *1912;* [f]*See James Hamilton-Paterson's extract (2) and Moritz Thomsen for a modern view.*

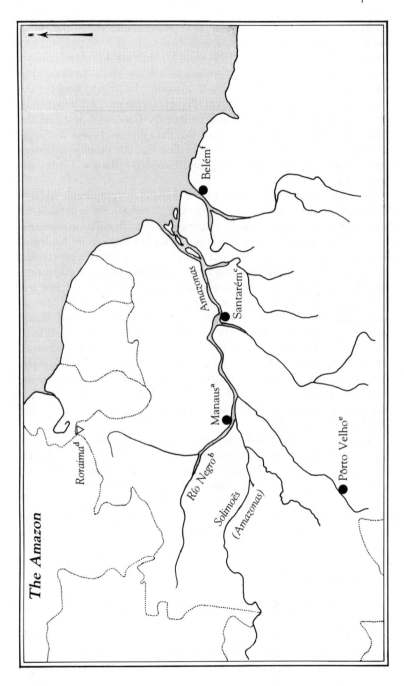

The Amazon

Belém[f]

Amazonas

Santarém[c]

Manaus[a]

Roraima[d]

Río Negro[b]

Solimoẽs
(Amazonas)

Pôrto Velho[e]

there were eight presidents. The next phase stands out – the dictatorship of Getúlio Vargas – the Estado Novo – from 1930 to 1945, and his re-election from 1951 to 1954 until he shot himself. Vargas was a populist, similar to Perón in Argentina who defended the working class (minimum wages, paid holidays). Among the fringe benefits he brought was the invitation of the French architect Le Corbusier to Brazil in 1936, who laid out the **University City**, and designed the **Ministry of Education**, and formed Brazilian architects like Niemeyer and Costa, who later built the futuristic **Brasília**. But many writers were against him, like Jorge Amado ◊, and Graciliano Ramos ◊, who was imprisoned.

Between Vargas's fall and 1964 came three leftish presidents. In 1955 Kubitschek was voted in on a nationalistic ticket. He is famous for moving the capital from **Rio** (created in 1763) to **Brasília**, inaugurated in 1960. US novelist John Dos Passos describes this city in his travel book *Brazil on the Move*, 1963. By the 1960s the military were turning ferociously anti-communist, and toppled Goulart who had taken over in 1961, in what they called a revolution in 1964. Between 1964 and 1985 (21 years) the military were in power. These were the years of urban guerrillas, with theorists like Carlos Marighela, Third World priests, and writers dealing with these issues, like Antônio Callado ◊. In 1985, after the president-elect died, the writer José Sarney (1931–), author of *Noites das águas*, 1969 (*Tales of Rain and Sunlight*, 1986), became president. In 1989 he was succeeded by the young Fernando Collor de Mello, who subsequently became embroiled in a major corruption scandal and was impeached and replaced in October 1992 by Itamar Franco.

Whoever runs Brazil will encounter awesome problems in a country that is partially advanced and modern, and partially very Third World. The problems include a foreign debt of over $100 billion; the Amazon degradation; the Indian problem; inflation (2000% when Fernando Collor de Mello took over). There is a need for agrarian reform: in 1987 5% of the population owned 80% of the land. There is terrifying poverty in the *favelas* of **Rio de Janeiro** and **São Paulo**, and in the *sertão*.

LITERARY DIVISIONS

Brazilian literature has recreated the disparity between north and south, between city and country. Deliberately nationalistic, Brazilian authors have adopted European models by 'Brazilianizing' them. In a country of well defined regions, and vast territories, *minha terra* is crucial, so that Machado de Assis is linked with **Rio de Janeiro**, a *carioca* (an inhabitant of Rio), and Jorge Amado with **Bahia**. Brazilian culture has vivid popular bases in carnival, in music, from bossa-nova to Villa-Lobos, in art and architecture.

There is also the foreigner's Brazil, the lawless land where the Nazis hid (see George Steiner's novel about Hitler in the Mato Grosso, *The Portage to San Cristobal of A.H.*, 1981); or where petty criminals, artists and bohemians feel at home (see Frank Tuohy's ◊ fiction); where Elizabeth Bishop ◊ and Stefan Zweig lived. Brazil has also figured as every tourist's dream, from Darwin's (◊ Uruguay) first entry into **Rio**, to Kipling's ◊ (see Extract 18).

Finally, Brazil has produced writers whose work does not fit into categories, from Rubem Fonseca's (1925–) hilarious *Bufo & Spallanzani*, 1985, to Nélida Piñon's (1936–) feminist saga of immigration and men in power, *A república dos sonhos*, 1984 (*The Republic of Dreams*, 1989), and very varied poets, from the politically committed to concrete ones best seen in anthologies like *Brazilian Poetry, 1950–1980*, 1983, and *An Anthology of Twentieth Century Brazilian Poetry*, 1972. Excellent Brazilian short stories can be read in Thomas Colchie's *The Penguin Book of Latin American Short Stories*, 1992. The Pakistan-born writer Zulfikar Ghose has written a trilogy called *The Incredible Brazilian*, 1972, *The Beautiful Empire*, 1975, and *A Different World*, 1978, narrated by Gregorio Peixoto da Silva Xavier, a novelistic recreation of twentieth century Brazilian culture. Anita Mason sets her thriller *The Racket*, 1990, in **Florianópolis**, observing Brazilian corruption through her upright history teacher. US poet Elizabeth Bishop wrote an excellent introduction to Brazilian culture and history in her *Brazil*, 1962.

The following museums and writers' houses can be visited: the home of literate ex-president of Brazil Rui Barbosa (1849–1923), a cultural centre with a huge library, called the **Fundação Casa de Rui Barbosa**, Rua São Clemente 134, Botafogo, Rio; the **Museu Casa de Rui Barbosa** in the Rua Rui Barbosa 12, Salvador; writer José Bento Monteiro's (1882–1948) house, now the **Museu Histórico de Cultura e Pedagogia Monteiro Lobato** at Taubaté, São Paulo (Monteiro Lobato wrote *Urupés* in 1918, provocative stories about the poor in the *sertão* translated as *Brazilian Short Stories*, 1925); poet Castro Alves's house, **Museu Castro Alves**, at Colégio Ipiranga, Rua do Sodré, Salvador; and the reconstruction of another of his houses, the **Museu do Parque Histórico Castro Alves**, Casa Muritiba, Bahia; and Afrânio Peixoto's house, the **Casa de Cultura Afrânio Peixoto**, at Praça Afrânio Peixoto, Lençóis, Bahia.

BOOKLIST

The following selection includes all titles which are extracted in this chapter as well as those mentioned in the introduction which are available in English. In general, paperback editions are given when possible. The editions cited are not necessarily the only ones available. For most of the extracted works, the original publisher in English can be found in 'Acknowledgments and Citations' at the end of the volume, as can the exact location of the extracts and the editions from which they are taken. The date in square brackets is the original publication date of the work in its original language. Extract numbers are highlighted in bold for ease of reference.

Abreu, Caio, Dragons [1988], David Treece, trans, Boulevard, London, 1990. Extract 22.

Almeida, José, Trash [1928], Robert Scott-Buccleuch, trans, Peter Owen, London, 1978.

Amado, Jorge, Shepherds of the Night [1964], Harriet de Onís, trans, Collins Harvill, London, 1989/ Knopf, New York, 1967. Extract 23.

Amado, Jorge, Tent of Miracles [1969], Barbara Shelby, trans, Collins Harvill, London, 1989/ Knopf, New York, 1971. Extract 24.

Andrade, Mário de, Macunaíma [1928], E.A. Goodland, trans, Quartet, London, 1984/Random House, New York, 1984. Extract 27.

Andrade, Oswald de, Seraphim Grosse Pointe [1933], Kenneth D. Jackson and Albert Bork, trans, Nefertiti Head Press, Austin, TX, 1979.

Andrade, Oswald de, The Sentimental Memoirs of John Seaborne [1923], Nefertiti Head Press, Austin, TX, 1979.

Anjos, Cyro dos, Diary of a Civil Servant [1937], Arthur Brakel, trans, Fairleigh Dickinson University Press, Cranbury, NJ, 1988. Extract 3.

An Anthology of Twentieth Century Brazilian Literature, Elizabeth Bishop and Emmanuel Brasil, eds, Wesleyan University Press, Middletown, CT, 1972.

Bandeira, Manuel, A Brief History of Brazilian Literature [1938], Ralph Dimmick, trans, Pan American Union, Washington, DC, 1958.

Bandeira, Manuel, This Earth, That Sky: Poems by Manuel Bandeira, Candace Slater, trans, University of California Press, Berkeley, CA, 1988.

Bates, Henry, The Naturalist on the Amazons, J.M. Dent, London, 1863. Extract 26.

Bishop, Elizabeth, Brazil, The Sunday Times, London, 1962.

Bishop, Elizabeth, 'The Burglar of Babylon', in The Complete Poems, 1927–1979, Chatto and Windus, London, 1983/Farrar, Straus and Giroux, New York, 1983. Extract 15.

Brazilian Poetry, 1950–1980, Emmanuel Brasil and William Jay Smith, eds, Wesleyan University Press, Middletown, CT, 1983.

Callado, Antônio, Don Juan's Bar [1971], Barbara Shelby, trans, Knopf, New York, 1972. Extracts 14 and 16.

Chatwin, Bruce, The Viceroy of Ouida, Jonathan Cape, London, 1980. Extract 29.

Cunha, Euclides da, Rebellion in the Backlands [1902], Samuel Putnam, trans, University of Chicago Press, Chicago, IL, 1957. Extract 10.

Dos Passos, John, Brazil on the Move, Sidgwick and Jackson, London,

1963/Paragon House, New York, 1991.

Doyle, Sir Arthur Conan, *The Lost World* [1912], John Murray, London, 1960. **Extract 9.**

Fleming, Peter, *Brazilian Adventure* [1933], Penguin, London, 1957. **Extract 17.**

Freyre, Gilberto, *The Masters and the Slaves – a Study in the Development of Brazilian Civilization* [1933], S. Putnam, trans, Knopf, New York, 1956.

Ghose, Zulfikar, *The Incredible Brazilian*, 1972, *The Beautiful Empire*, 1975, *A Different World*, 1978, Macmillan, London.

Guimarães Rosa, João, *The Third Bank of the River and Other Stories* [1962], Barbara Shelby, trans, Knopf, New York, 1968.

Hamilton-Paterson, James, *Gerontius* [1989], Vintage, London, 1990/ Soho Press, New York, 1991. **Extracts 2 and 13.**

Hampton, Christopher, *Savages*, Faber and Faber, London, 1974.

Hemming, John, *Amazon Frontier: The Defeat of the Brazilian Indians*, Macmillan, London, 1987.

Kipling, Rudyard, 'Brazilian Sketches', in *Journeys in Time*, Blair Niles, ed, Coward-McCann, New York, 1946. **Extract 18.**

Lévi-Strauss, Claude, *Tristes Tropiques* [1955], John and Doreen Weightman, trans, Picador, London, 1989.

Lins do Rego, José, *Plantation Boy* [1932–34], Emmi Baum, trans, Knopf, New York, 1966.

Lispector, Clarice, *The Apple in the Dark* [1961], Gregory Rabassa, trans, Virago, London, 1985/ Knopf, New York, 1967. **Extract 32.**

Lobato, José Bento Monteiro, *Brazilian Short Stories*, Haldeman-Julius, Girard, KS, 1925.

Machado de Assis, Joaquim Maria, *Epitaph of a Small Winner* [1881], William Grossman, trans, Penguin, London, 1968/Noonday, New York, 1952. **Extract 19.**

Magalhães Júnior, R., 'The Immunizer', William Grossman, trans, in *Modern Brazilian Short Stories*, University of California Press, Berkeley, CA, and London, 1967. **Extract 30.**

Mason, Anita, *The Racket*, Constable, London, 1990.

Neruda, Pablo, 'Canto General' in *Selected Poems*, Anthony Kerrigan, trans, Jonathan Cape, London, 1970/Delacorte Press, New York, 1972.

The Penguin Book of Latin American Short Stories, Thomas Colchie, ed, Penguin, London, 1992.

Piñon, Nélida, *The Republic of Dreams* [1984], Helen Lane, trans, Knopf, New York, 1989.

Pritchett, V.S., *Dead Man Leading*, Chatto and Windus, London, 1937/Oxford University Press, New York, 1984. **Extract 1.**

Ramos, Graciliano, *Childhood* [1945], Celso de Oliveira, trans, Peter Owen, London, 1979. **Extract 5.**

Ribeiro, Darcy, *Maíra* [1978], E.H. Goodland and Thomas Colchie, trans, Picador, London, 1984/ Random House, New York, 1984. **Extract 6.**

Ribeiro, João Ubaldo, *Sergeant Getúlio* [1971], translated by the author, André Deutsch, London, 1980/Houghton Mifflin, Boston, MA, 1978. **Extract 31.**

Sarney, José, *Tales of Rain and Sunlight* [1969], Vera Hallam, trans, Wyvern-Sel, Bringsty, Worcestershire, 1986.

Southey, Robert, *The History of Brazil* [1810, 1817, 1819], Longman, London. Reprint of early edition published by Greenwood Press, Westport, CT.

Souza, Márcio, *Mad Maria* [1980], Thomas Colchie, trans, Avon Books, New York, 1985. **Extract 7.**

Steiner, George, *The Portage to San Cristobal of A.H.*, Faber and Faber, London, 1981.

Thomsen, Moritz, *The Saddest Pleasure* [1990], The Sumach Press, London, 1991/Graywolf, St Paul, MN, 1990. **Extracts 20 and 25.**

Tomlinson, H.M., *The Sea and the Jungle*, Duckworth, London, 1912/The Marlboro Press, Vermont, 1989. **Extract 8.**

Torres, Antônio, *The Land* [1976], Margaret A. Neves, trans, Readers International, London, 1987. **Extract 12.**

Trevisan, Dalton, 'Death on the Square', in *The Vampire of Curitiba and Other Stories*, Gregory Rabassa, trans, Knopf, New York, 1972. **Extract 11.**

Tuohy, Frank, *The Animal Game*, Macmillan, London, 1957. **Extract 28.**

Tuohy, Frank, 'A Survivor in Salvador', in *The Collected Stories*, Macmillan, London, 1984/Holt, Rinehart and Winston, New York, 1984.

Tuohy, Frank, *The Warm Nights of January*, Macmillan, London, 1960. **Extract 4.**

Vargas Llosa, Mario, *The War of the End of the World* [1981], Helen Lane, trans, Faber and Faber, London, 1986/Farrar, Straus and Giroux, New York, 1986.

Veríssimo, Erico, in *The Green Continent*, Harriet de Onís, trans, Poetry London Editions, 1947. **Extract 21.**

Extracts

(1) THE AMAZON

V.S. Pritchett, *Dead Man Leading*

Pritchett sets his quest-for-a-missing-father novel on a tributary of the Amazon.

This was the second day on the river. The sights around them never changed. They unwound like a repeated panorama on a reel. There was the screen of continuing and continuing green on the banks, a flow of brown water like strong tea, bark-stained and root-stained by the drainage of the forest, and a sky like the wall of a huge blue house, quite immovable. Sometimes they were in narrow waters and sometimes in wide – this was the only change. At the estuary and in those places where the river widened into an inland sea, the far bank became dimmed to a lean, hot blur of forest, faint as a distant fence in a flat country. In the hours when the river was narrow, the water light was suspended in the hollows of the foliage and the launch appeared like a fly fixed in flight between sky and sky-reflecting water. In channels narrower still, where the branches of the trees almost met overhead, one seemed to be passing show cases of fantastic drapery and millinery, in an overheated shop, green unfolding upon green, in the absolute silence. Sometimes there was a break where the cases had been smashed and the trees apparently grabbed out with their rigging of liana trailing after them; and sometimes there were muddy coves where tree ferns made a shade of ospreys. A thatched hut built upon a platform of piles, whitened now the water was sinking in the dry weather, would be in these hollows; and on the platform brown people sat like grubs, half naked, watching the wash of the launch chuckle along the banks of mud. The people made no sign with their hands, nor was there any expression of curiosity in their eyes, nor recognition. They sat fixed and still with the water light wavering over their bodies in their aquarium of soundless shade.

(2) BELEM

James Hamilton-Paterson, *Gerontius*

Hamilton-Paterson describes Pará, founded in 1616, on the way upriver. Pará is now Belém, with a population of over one million. The novel is set in the 1920s.

An infrequent tram screeched slowly past trailing an electrical smell of ozone and the scent of whetted knives from binding brake shoes. At the glassless windows (fitted, however, with oilskin blinds which could be lowered in downpours) were men in brilliant white shirt-sleeves on their way from their suburbs to banks and offices and godowns, many holding folded handkerchiefs delicately to their moustaches to keep out the dust, others lightly fanning themselves with newspapers. Several of them disembarked at an imposing bank or bourse from whose pediment a lopsided spray of flame-coloured blossoms trailed from the cleft in which it had taken root. The effect of this brilliant weed was artlessly to add a seductiveness to the cracked temple of mammon which dominated the mango-lined boulevard as coquettishly as any Latin beauty with a carnation over one ear. It served also to remind that this was a *vegetable* town, a town owing its existence and prosperity to sap and lignum, to nuts and fruits and juices.

(3) BELO HORIZONTE

Cyro dos Anjos, *Diary of a Civil Servant*

The narrating civil servant in this novel set in Belo Horizonte (Brazil's third city, capital of Minas Gerais) reflects on his home town.

In truth, it was a beautiful adventure. Going to bed very early, contrary to my habits, I woke up at four o'clock in the morning, and could not get back to sleep. I tried as best I could for an hour, but stayed in the Proustian dominion of insomnia, where thoughts have no clear outline, and one's consciousness becomes confused. Then, as the streetcars had begun to go down Erê Street, and the roosters had initiated their concert, and, finally, as the factory had made some indications of being alive, I became aware of the uselessness of my attempts and got up, resigned to my fate. What a beautiful foredawn!

Going up Erê Street, I turned left on Diábase, which, farther up, has its name changed to Esmeralda. I followed it to the end, and going up the highway from there, I got to Pintos's Hill. From the top of the promontory, I contemplated Belo Horizonte that was just awakening. The colors of the sky, vivid by then, and the luminous beauty of the city hurt my eyes. The sumptuous buildings, the fine public gardens, and the straight avenues situate Belo Horizonte outside the normal patterns of Minas Gerais. In all the houses, nonetheless, resides the same venerable spirit of Sabarabuçu, Tejuco, Ouro Preto, and all the other hallowed hamlets. I think about the man from Minas, the Mineiro, who is getting up, who reads his *Minas Gerais*, who feeds his birds, and who gets ready, calmly, for the daily grind. His wife is hurriedly mending a pair of socks for him, and she asks him not to forget to leave some money for her shopping. He leaves on the sly, however. Do the shopping tomorrow. You're too eager to spend money. The kids have clothes on their backs, there is food in the pantry, what more do we need?

My eyes leave the city, however, and become lost in the horizon. Its majesty, the fine morning air, and the intensity of the light drive the amanuensis into ecstasy – a nocturnal bird caught by the dawn.

(4) BRAZIL: A FESTIVAL NIGHT

Frank Tuohy, *The Warm Nights of January*

The French expatriate painter Bella, and a gay cosmopolitan friend, Alix, make their way out of Rio to a Candomblé session.

It was later and they were far away. They had crossed the ferry, slipped through a suburb and emerged on to a federal highway.

Now the tropic night was pale at the edges, as if a lid had been slightly raised off the surface of the world. The road climbed through patches of mist and low cloud; there were masses of brown foliage, strands of wire; occasionally a mud and straw hut with a flickering light inside it, like a hallowe'en mask.

For half an hour it had been the deadest of worlds, the salt beds following one another along the shore of the lagoon. Now, after the first houses, the car heaved and swayed into a central square, with a row of cafés, a Portuguese baroque church and the town jail. The moon was obliterated among a mass of lights.

It was a festival night, with strings of electric bulbs sagging between palm-trees and lamp-posts. Loud-speakers pumped music. There were stalls of cheap toys, gambling games, air-rifles. The crowd was an easy one to push your way through: coloured shirts or smock-like dresses hung on the gaunt soap-smelling bodies, and nothing seemed really solid except an occasional pregnant belly. They were a gentle, undernourished race of country people, so mixed in blood that they were beginning to turn out all the same.

Bella and Alix made their way towards a bar constructed of bamboo and planks and thatched with palm-leaves. A bench and an iron table were cleared for them and a boy brought glasses of *aguardente* mixed with coconut-milk.

(5) BRAZIL: FROM THE SERTAO TO VICOSA

Graciliano Ramos, *Childhood*

Ramos's child narrator describes a family move from the sertão backlands to Vicosa.

We relaxed one afternoon in the house of the popular poet Cordeiro Manso. Afterwards we spent the night near a muddy dam where ducks swam. A tent was constructed out of bundles, boxes and tarpaulins, and there I stretched out on rolls of cast-off cotton; I was cold, illuminated by candles of carnauba wax. My ribs rubbed against the stakes of a fence; I was interrupted in my sleep by the cry of the wind, the talk of the mule drivers quartered in the vicinity, and the almost human moans of a sick sheep.

Other stopping places escaped my memory. José Leonardo and Antônio Vale said goodbye – and with them the backlands disappeared. Cactus and cereus trees were replaced by a dense and very green vegetation; on the dark paths the cattle bells became silent; brooks appeared, grew larger; transformed into rivers, they delayed our journey.

Unknown figures came to meet us, amiable and laughing, cousins of various degrees, who were so familiar that it seemed as if we had always lived together. Evidently my father's economic situation was not serious. He had migrated and run into debt, but he had pulled himself together, and, thanks to the production of the farm, he reassured his relatives. The older ones perceived him from a distance; the younger ones would come up to him, tender and full of praise. And so, tolerated by some, flattered by others, he would plant his severed roots again in the old lands . . .

I made the rest of the trip with a happy young man, who tried to explain to me the chimneys of the sugar mills, the fields under cultivation, and the robust trees clustered together which obstructed the landscape. The great deserted whitish spaces of sand and gravel, the scattered woods, benches made from the macambira tree, stone fences, pens and corrals, luminous days streaked by the flight of migratory birds – all disappeared. By-paths would ascend, descend, and twist, and beside them houses and flower and vegetable gardens were arranged. Those who passed by didn't wear leather. At almost any point I found myself in a hole between hills. Abundant and noisy water, immense pastures, foggy mornings.

We reached the district of Viçosa in Alagoas. Before establishing himself in the city, my father was a guest in a mill whose fire was dead.

(6) Brazil: A Jungle Village

Darcy Ribeiro, *Maíra*

In Ribeiro's novel, the priest-educated Indian returns to his home Indian village in the Amazonian jungle.

From up here, withdrawn in my void, I see my Mairun village through the haze of a sunny afternoon. It is a circle of houses ringed by two roads of beaten earth. One passes in front of the houses: that's the inner road. The other, passing behind, is the outer one. From each house runs a little path to the dancing ground where the Great House of Men is situated.

The whole village has the form of an enormous cartwheel with its axis at the Great House. The spokes are the paths from the houses, and the studded rim, the two circular roads with the houses in between. From up here, flying toward it, I see, engraved in the earth, protruding from the forest surrounded by tiny plots of land, the village where I was born. The houses are enormous baskets woven with branches still green and flexible, that are then covered with satin-tail grass. The largest of them, the Great House of Men, was for many years the point of reference for Father Vecchio who never rested until he built a chapel even larger. But the Cross could never compete in grandeur with the ornament of the Great House: two tree trunks, whole and dried, with their roots outside, attached to the summit.

Now it must be darkest night in my village. In the houses everyone is asleep in hammocks slung between poles in the walls and in the central masts, forming the little groups of each family. The hammock of the man is lowest; above it is the woman's; and above hers, the children's. Below them, and to combat the chill of early dawn, burns a little fire of twigs that barely illuminates the ground.

(7) Brazil: The Jungle

Márcio Souza, *Mad Maria*

Souza's novel opens with a portrait of the British engineer, and the Amazonian jungle through which they will struggle inch by inch as they try to lay down rail track.

The mist was heaviest nearer to the ground. The great, sweated bulk advanced laboriously, panting its vapors, squealing. This was somewhere along the Rio Abunã, on no particular morning, in the summer of 1911. In the Cambrian period it must have been so.

Stephan Collier, construction engineer, was about to face the worst moments of what technically would have appeared to be a simple undertaking – were it not for thirty miles of marsh and swamps. Or the unthinkable working conditions his men were forced to endure. In fact, most of them would not survive, because the task was too difficult, because you could not make men adapt to so hostile a terrain. Collier would have liked to have been somewhere far, far away from it all, for he had no particular inclination to risk himself in this way. He knew he was not immune to every disease around, and whoever felt sick in the Abunã was a dead man. Working conditions were hardly the bloody forte of this insane project!

Collier could make out a gang of nine Barbadians carrying a rail through the swamp. The day was beginning to grow light. Soon the sun would burn its way across a cloudless sky.

The Barbadians had already begun to sweat heavily, their black muscles gleaming as they worked, wading through waters up to their knees. Collier had all together a hundred and fifty men there, under his direct orders. The job was to cut a railway through the marshy terrain of the Rio Abunã; seemingly not an impossible operation. After all, hadn't six Barbadians just lugged a rail over to where still others were hard at work opening trenches with picks and spades?

Our Collier was thirsty and his arms were lumped with swellings. Each time he would run his hand over his forearm, it felt as though he was touching the thick hide of a Saurian reptile. Actually, both arms had been savaged by mosquitoes, because Collier could not be bothered wearing a long-sleeved shirt. Unfortunately work had taken him some twenty meters into virgin jungle, where he was soon set upon and sucked at by swarms of insects. His left elbow had quickly turned into a ripe cherry, while the right one looked more like a spongy, bloodied apple.

(8) Brazil: The Jungle

H.M. Tomlinson, *The Sea and the Jungle*

The novelist H.M. Tomlinson escaped a London winter in 1911 and travelled up the Amazon, then a tributary, to Porto Velho to deliver coal to a railway line up the jungle.

After crossing the Igaripe the character of the forest changed. It was now a growth of wild cacao trees. Nothing grew beneath them. The floor was a black paste, littered with dead sticks. The woods were more open, but darker and more dank than before. The sooty limbs of the cacao trees grew low, and filled the view ahead with a perplexity of leafless and tortured boughs. They were hung with fruit, pendent lamps lit with a pale greenish light. We saw nothing move there but two delicate butterflies, which had wings as transparent as mica though spotted with rose, such as might have been served Titania herself; yet the gloom and black *ooze*, and the eerie globes with their illusion of light hung upon distorted shapes, was more the home of the fabulous sucuruja, the serpent which is forty feet long.

In the clearing were the huts of an Indian village. Only the roofs could be seen, through some plantations of bananas. Around the clearing, a side of which was cut off by a stream, was the overshadowing green presence. Some chocolate babies, as serious as gnomes, looked up as we came into daylight, opened their eyes wide, and fled up the path between the plantains.

If I could sing, I would sing the banana. It has the loveliest leaf I know. I feel intemperate about it, because I came upon it after our passage through a wood which could have been underground, a tangle of bare roots joining floor and ceiling in limitless caverns. We stood looking at the banana plant till our mind was fed with grace and light. The plantain jets upwards with a copious stem, and the fountain returns in broad rippled pennants, falling outwardly, refined to points, when the impulse is lost. A world could not be old on which such a plant grows.

(9) BRAZIL: 'MAPLE-WHITE LAND'

Sir Arthur Conan Doyle, *The Lost World*

Malone, Professors Challenger and Summerlee, and Lord John Roxton have climbed a pinnacle and can look into the Lost World, or Maple-White Land, with its stegosaurus, pterodactyl, ape-men ('missing-links') and iguanodons still thriving.

The first impression which I received when I had recovered my breath was the extraordinary view over the country which we traversed. The whole Brazilian plain seemed to lie beneath us, extending away and away until it ended in dim blue mists upon the farthest sky-line. In the foreground was the long slope, strewn with rocks and dotted with tree-ferns; farther off in the middle distance, looking over the saddle-back hill, I could just see the yellow and green mass of bamboos through which we had passed; and then, gradually, the vegetation increased until it formed the huge forest which extended as far as the eyes could reach, and for a good two thousand miles beyond.

I was still drinking in this wonderful panorama when the heavy hand of the Professor fell upon my shoulder.

'This way, my young friend,' said he; '*vestigia nulla restrorsum*. Never look rearwards, but always to our glorious goal.'

The level of the plateau, when I turned, was exactly that on which we stood, and the green bank of bushes, with occasional trees, was so near that it was difficult to realize how inaccesible it remained. At a rough guess the gulf was forty feet across, but, so far as I could see, it might as well have been forty miles. I placed one arm around the trunk of the tree and leaned over the abyss. Far down were the small dark figures of our servants, looking up at us. The wall was absolutely precipitous, as was that which faced me.

(10) CANUDOS

Euclides da Cunha, *Rebellion in the Backlands*

Canudos, north of Salvador in the sertão, is the town of Antonio
Conselheiro's heroic resistance, here described by da Cunha in
his classic reportage of the mystic's defiance.

The next morning their fears were gone, and they were once more the
impatient heroes of old. Marching rapidly and with no further qualms,
they made their way down the trench that is known as the Sargento
River, which now of a sudden overflowed with uniforms. Then they
climbed the barren hill whose slopes on the opposite side descend
abruptly into the Umburanas Valley. There, they were surprised to see,
directly ahead of them and down below, a mile and a quarter away – the
village of Canudos.

This was a relief. There were the two ruined churches, facing each
other across that legendary square – the new church, its towers gone, its
main walls crumbled, split from top to bottom, a veritable rubbish
heap; the old one, likewise ruined and blackened, its façade missing,
but a bit of shattered belfry still standing, the belfry where that fantastic
sexton so many times summoned the faithful to prayers and to the
battle. Round about was the compact mass of huts. They were in time;
they were not to be deprived, after all, of those half-rations of glory
about which they were so concerned. And so they made their
triumphal entrance into camp, with the mien of those who are destined
to go down in history but who in reality had come there in search of a
bloody but an easy victory.

The appearance of the camp had changed; it no longer presented the
turbulent aspect of former days. It was now like another village
alongside Canudos. Crossing the dry bed of the Vasa-Barris, the new
comers made their way through a winding gully. Halfway down this
gully, in a wide concavity to the right, there was a huge leather-covered
shed, the field hospital; and, a short distance farther on, they came to
the tent of the commander-in-chief.

Meanwhile, they had the impression of being in a newly built town.
Scattered over the slopes on either side or clustered in tiny valleys,
their colors standing out against the grayish hue of the tents, were
numerous houses of a novel kind and with a festive air, being wholly
constructed of foliage, the roofs and walls green with the boughs of the
joaz tree. These dwellings appeared to be singularly inappropriate to
those who inhabited them, but they were as a matter of fact the only
ones suitable to this region. It was the burning heat, transforming the
tents into flaming furnaces, which had inspired this primitive, bucolic
architecture.

(11) CURITIBA

Dalton Trevisan, *Death on the Square*

Trevisan sets all his stories in his home town of Curitiba, where Angel Clare in Thomas Hardy's Tess of the D'Urbevilles goes to farm. It is capital of Paraná state. 'Death on the Square' is included in The Vampire of Curitiba and Other Stories *– see Booklist.*

The town was proud of its square, with a church, a hospital, a pharmacy, a dry-goods store, a photographer, two taxis, and, in the middle of the rose beds, the bust of the hero. There were old houses with fluted tiles, their street doors opening into dark hallways where at night a bulb flickered under a colored silk shade. Next to the church, brightening a patch of the square, the two illuminated doors of the Santo Expedito pharmacy lingered.

Jonas had prospected for diamonds, had been a professional gambler, and it was known that he had stood trial for a man's death. He had finally returned to our town with that woman. Her gentleman friend had mistreated her and abandoned her. Jonas found her dancing in a cabaret; they got married and had three children. The old druggist died and Jonas bought the pharmacy from his widow.

In the small room in back, with a window on the alley, he set up his laboratory, where he filled prescriptions, gave injections, and even invented a wax for toothaches. And he would saw rings off the swollen fingers of pregnant women who could not loosen them. Poor people preferred him to the doctor: he got rid of worms in children, conjured away warts, and settlers came to have him put a curse on the vermin in horses and cows. He would mumble his prayers and stroke the sign of the cross on the sick animal with a piece of kindling wood – the worms fell off like the ripe fruit of a jaboticaba tree.

(12) JUNCO, IN THE SERTAO

Antônio Torres, *The Land*

Junco is a village in the sertão, where the narrator was born, and from which most people dream of escaping. Lampião was one of Brazil's most notorious bandits.

So it was that a place forgotten in time awoke from its stupor to make the sign of the cross. Junco: a scarlet bird called Sofre, which learned to sing the national anthem. A speckled hen called Sophie, which learned to hide her nests. An ox named Sufferer. A yoke: winter begins, summer ends. The most beautiful sunrise in the world and the longest sunset. The smell of rosemary and the words lily-of-the-valley. I never saw a lily-of-the-valley. Shards: of red tile, of glass. The sound of hoes being sharpened, of cattle-drivers' mournful calls along the road, of men scratching a living from the land. My mother's black tobacco-juice spittle, my father's mute complaints. My grand-mother's red and white roses. Roses of love: I'll love you till I die.'

This is the land that spawned me.

'Lampião the bandit passed over here.'

'No he didn't. He sent a message saying he was coming but he didn't actually come.'

'Why not?'

'Why should Lampião waste his time coming here? This is the end of the world.'

Girls looking out of windows at the road seem to say – yes, it is the end of the world. They are dreaming of the boys who went to São Paulo and never came back to fetch them. They are waiting for the bank clerks from Alagoinhas and the oil workers from Petrobrás. They are waiting, but not for country hicks. City boys only.

(13) MANAUS

James Hamilton-Paterson, *Gerontius*

Elgar, the ageing composer on a cruise up the Amazon in 1923, recreated in this novel, reaches Manaus, once glamorous capital of the rubber-boom jungle.

Suddenly in sunlight across an expanse of water Manaos rose up as a sizeable town, all white houses and towers. The trees and vegetation which split up the red of its tiled roofs appeared by contrast a brighter green than the surrounding forest. As they approached with a blare of C which lost itself over the waters and rebounded feebly from the low red earth cliffs the passengers lining the *Hildebrand*'s decks could make out individual features. Dominating everything with civic extravagance was the dome of the Opera House glittering in its topee of blue and gold Alsatian tiles. On the foreshore a series of floating wharves supported an extensive shanty-town of dilapidated huts in addition to cranes and the monster hardware associated with modern commerce. It seemed altogether extraordinary to find a city of this size so remotely situated; the decrepit dwellings merely emphasised the mercantile solidity of the buildings behind.

And now the movement of people became apparent on the distant dockside: men in white shirts, women with parasols, gathering to wait in the shade of sheds and godowns for these visitors from another world. Edward stood largely unmoved watching the frenzied muster of tattered children with trays around their necks, the silver winking of ice-cream carts. Drifting round the thermals over the town the inevitable cloud of *urubus* circled, sifting with their slitted nostrils the rich boiling of metropolitan odours for the delirious perfume of carrion.

(14) MIRANDA

Antônio Callado, *Don Juan's Bar*

João, one of the carioca rebels, arrives in Miranda on his way to Corumbá on the Bolivian border, separated by a century in time from Rio.

João sat in the dining car aboard the Brazilian Northwest train which was carrying the group, distributed throughout the cars, all bound for Corumbá. Before his eyes were a hundred visions of Salvador – policeman, torturer, and purchaser of snares and of Joelmir, ex-Army sergeant dishonorably discharged from the ranks. First, they passed the well-ordered landscape of São Paulo with its factories and farms, its yellow tractors, its cotton and coffee fields through which the scarlet locomotive made its way as cleanly as a plow. Then came the pepper trees, fruit trees, amaranths of Mato Grosso; and Zebu cattle dotting the Pantanal; buffalos up to their necks in pools of clear water; and rustics in the fields who stopped what they were doing to gape at the train or climbed into the second class cars with their bundles of belongings when it pulled into a station. It was an opulent landscape, and the cowboys and farmhands who peopled it seemed to be willing to wait for centuries until some part of the wealth found its way into their bundles tied onto sticks. João leaned back in his dining-car chair, occasionally steadying the cup or coffee-pot as they slid along the table with the motion of the train, and gazed out at the men in the fields and on the station platforms, dividing them arbitrarily into Salvadors and Joelmirs.

He got off the train in Miranda, suitcase in hand. The stationmaster directed him to Agenor Carrilho Plaza, the main square in the middle of town, where he would find hotels and the Penguin Bar. João took a room in the Travelers' Hotel. Before going to the Penguin, he walked round the square, and then down the Rua do Carmo to the bridge over the Miranda River, soaking up the atmosphere of the peaceful, pleasant little town with its pharmacies, its rooming houses, its Ivone's Garden Beauty Salon.

(15) Rio de Janeiro

Elizabeth Bishop, *The Burglar of Babylon*

From 1952 onwards the US poet Elizabeth Bishop lived in Rio.
'The Burglar of Babylon', from which these stanzas are taken, is
in The Complete Poems – see Booklist.

On the fair green hills of Rio
    There grows a fearful stain:
The poor who come to Rio
    And can't go home again.

On the hills a million people,
    A million sparrows, nest,
Like a confused migration
    That's had to light and rest,

Building its nests, or houses,
    Out of nothing at all, or air
You'd think a breath would end them,
    They perch so lightly there.

But they cling and spread like lichen,
    And the people come and come.
There's one hill called the Chicken,
    And one called Catacomb;

There's the hill of Kerosene,
    And the hill of the Skeleton,
The hill of Astonishment,
    And the hill of Babylon.

Micuçú was a burglar and killer,
    An enemy of society.
He had escaped three times
    From the worst penitentiary . . .

(16) Rio de Janeiro

Antônio Callado, *Don Juan's Bar*

Callado catches the bizarre collision between beauty and death in Rio through Karin, in his novel about guerrillas who go off to Corumbá (on the Bolivian border) to fight.

She washed her face and brushed her hair, then opened the living room window to purify the air.

The day was wildly, shockingly beautiful, a sort of glaring, surrealistic Swiss landscape: Corcovado, with its purple stone and blue woods; the cliff across the lake crowned with shacks; black children playing stick ball around the Lagoa, expensive cars winking in the sun. And the lake, Lagoa Rodrigo de Freitas, glittering as Karin had never seen it glitter. She rubbed her eyes. The lake was covered with silver, a silver coat of mail glancing with rays of silver light. A layer of silver lay on each crest of each wavelet modeled by the breeze. The whole lake was curdled with silver clabber. Hovering over the shameless beauty of it all was the stink.

Karin put on a pair of shorts and a blouse and crossed the street to the shore of the Lagoa. Then she saw that the solid silver shield on the lagoon was made of dead fish – dozens, hundreds, millions of small dead fish whose scales sparkled in the sun. It looked like a European lake in winter, but it was solid with death, frozen with lifeless fish.

(17) Rio de Janeiro

Peter Fleming, *Brazilian Adventure*

Fleming, on his way to discover what had happened to Colonel P.H. Fawcett in 1925 (he had just disappeared), arrived in Rio in 1932.

We came into Rio at sunset. This must surely be the best time to do it.

For some hours Brazil had been in sight, a dark-green formidable outline, a coast (a far as we could see) almost unscathed by man. The huge cliffs slanted a little backwards, as if the land had been reined in sharply on the brink of salt perdition. The charging jungle stopped short only at the sea. I got the impression of a sub-continent with imperfect self-control.

We were passing a little island in the harbour's mouth. Against a tawny sunset the hills behind the city stood up fiercely. On their crests the tiny black silhouettes of trees showed with more than their share of detail and prominence. Some frigate birds went out past us to the darkening sea, flying low. The water front, still some way ahead of us, flaunted a solitary skyscraper. All sky-scrapers look foolish and unnatural when isolated from their kind. It is only in the mass, huddled and strenuously craning, that they achieve a sort of quaint crude dignity. Alone, cut off from their native background of competition and emergency, they appear gauche and rather forlorn. With this one it was particularly so. Ridiculously at variance with all that we could see, hopelessly irrelevant to all that we imagined, it had the pathos of the boor. It domineered without conviction, the totem of another tribe. It knew itself for a mistake, an oversight, an intrusion. It was like a bag of tools left behind, when the curtain rises, on a stage set for romance.

Later I was told that during the last revolution they threw a full-sized billiard table out of a window on its fourteenth floor. Then I forgave it. Where that sort of thing can happen to them, there is a place for sky-scrapers.

(18) Rio de Janeiro

Rudyard Kipling, *Brazilian Sketches*

Kipling arrived at Rio by boat in 1926.

Then men came aboard, ready – as men are the world over – to show a stranger the place they love. In two minutes the shadowy lines of the crowded wharves vanished, and the car was sweeping down a blazing perspective, chequered strongly with double lines of tree-foliage and flanked with lit and packed clubs, shops, and cafés. This world of light gave of a sudden, between the shoulders of gigantic buildings, on to even vaster spaces of single way avenues, between trees, with the harbour on one side, fringed by electric lights that raced forward, it seemed for ever, and renewed themselves in strings of pearl flung round invisible corners; while, above everything, one saw and felt the outlines of forested mountains. All the world was with us in cars, all filled with bare-headed folk, all going at top speed, but not more swiftly than certain devils of motor-buses, whose workaday tones I later mistook for the thunder of an aeroplane outside my eighth-floor window. Somewhere to our right rose a hill up which the lavish lights climbed and broke, on half-indicated twists of road. One knew enough from old novels to be aware that this must be Santa Thereza, the quarter where the virtuous clerk, and the lover exiled by Fate, used to live while they were making their fortunes. It is to-day, as it always has been, a place of pleasant residences. It looks out at the very jaws of the harbour mouth – two smooth crocodile teeth of stripped rock that many eyes must have watched barring the way home in the days when men died between noon and dusk. There were glimpses of pink and white houses here, with plumes of palm upspringing, or, more intimate still, friezes of quiet banana-fronds behind ivory walls. But we kept to the water-front with the multitude who were taking the air.

The night was reasonably – that is to say, tropically – warm. Hats, coats, hurry, time, and the other trifles had been dropped on the far side of the Line. The only trouble that remained was lest this dream-city of shell-white palaces, intensely lighted green foliage, arrogant statuary, silvered waters, and brooding mountains, would vanish if one dared look aside. But it held on, as one enormous loop of road slid into the next; still skirting water, still lit by the insolent, all-powerful lights, but – one must pay something to the Gods – perfumed throughout by the flying cars. (Note here, the Brazilian as a driver can paralyse any Place de la Concorde taxi-man. But jealous Southerners say that an Argentine 'all out' gives him points.)

(19) RIO DE JANEIRO

Joaquim Maria Machado de Assis,
Epitaph of a Small Winner

The novel's rich bachelor narrator in Rio meets a man called Damasceno from the North and catches his vulgarity.

Never fear, I shall soon have done with extraordinary things, and we shall then resume the narrative proper.

The bearer of the note was married to a sister of Cotrim, had arrived from the North a few days earlier, was named Damasceno, and had taken part in the bloodless revolution of 1831. He told me all this in the first five minutes. He had left Rio de Janeiro because he disagreed with the policies established by the regent, who was an ass, almost as big an ass as the ministers that served under him. Besides, another revolution was on its way.

At this point, although the political ideas he expressed were somewhat tangled, I managed to formulate a notion of the sort of government he desired: it was a dictatorship tempered – not, as some would have it, by the spirit of the people – but by the rifles of the National Guard. I was unable to discover whether he preferred a single dictator or an oligarchy.

He expressed opinions about various matters, among them the development of the slave trade and the expulsion of the English. He greatly enjoyed the theatre; upon his arrival, he had gone immediately to the São Pedro Theatre, where he had seen an excellent drama, *Maria Joanna*, and a very interesting comedy, *Kettly, or the Return to*

Switzerland. Also, he had liked Deperini very much, in *Sappho* or in *Anne Boleyn*, he did not exactly remember which. But Candiana! Yes, sir, she was really hunky-dory. Now he wanted to hear *Ernani*, which his daughter often sang at the piano. '*Ernani, Ernani, involami* . . .,' he trilled, and rose to his feet. In the North, all these things were just echoes. His daughter was dying to hear all the operas. She had a very sweet little voice. And wonderful taste in music. Oh, he had been so anxious to come back to Rio de Janeiro. He had already wandered through the whole city, remembering this place and that, sometimes feeling as if he was going to cry. He would never go away again. He had been very seasick during the trip as, indeed, had been all the passengers except an Englishman . . . the devil take the English! This country would never be right until every last one of them had been thrown out.

(20) Rio de Janeiro

Moritz Thomsen, *The Saddest Pleasure*

On his journey to Manaus in 1978, Thomsen stopped in Rio.

Now, like a stone thrown into a whirlpool I am dropped into the heart of Rio. The place jumps to an awful rhythm; cars and people rush through the streets. Noises (though car horns are forbidden), excremental smells, dust, blaring music, torn up avenues, whole torn up sections of town. Excavations, board walks, blocks of streets with leaky water pipes and the gutters gushing full; thousands of men in red and yellow plastic construction hats stand in hundreds of holes dug into the streets and fuss with a wild tangle of plastic piping and electric cable. (The patient is not going to recover.) Rio, like New York or Chicago, like Calcutta or Paris, is plainly a city that no longer works very well, but observing the frenzy it looks as though they were trying to fix it in a single day.

(21) Rio de Janeiro

Erico Veríssimo

Veríssimo, a native of Pôrto Alegre and a prolific novelist of his region, was also a travel writer, with a good book on Mexico. Here, he writes about Rio. This passage is taken from the anthology The Green Continent – see Booklist.

The natural setting of Rio is really breathtaking. The city stretches out lazily in all directions, between the mountains and the sea, winding about the hills, skirting the bay, at whose entrance Sugar Loaf Mountain stands guard. It almost always has a festive, holiday air. If it were painted scenery, one could say that the artist had overdone the colour and decorative effects and had deliberately assembled in a single landscape all the varied beauty that God had scattered with thrifty hand over the whole surface of the globe.

The waters of the bay are a smooth green dotted with islands, boats, beacons, buoys, sails . . . Over it gulls and airplanes trace their flight; often bands of strident-voiced green parrots cross the sky. The spendthrift sun flings handfuls of golden coins over the waters. And on certain days a luminous blue mist, lightly tinged with rose, hovers in the air, giving the city the appearance of a toy wrapped up in cellophane.

How can one remember the names of the countless mountains, or describe their appearance? The light plays tricks with the shape and the colour of these hills. We go to bed at night certain that we know the name of the stone walls, and we wake up the next day to discover a new peak, a new chain of mountains, to find that during the night some mischievous invisible sculptor has stayed up working for the sole purpose of changing the landscape or to invent some new wonder. There are days on which the clouds hide the peaks or invent plumes, wigs, and veils for the mountains' heads. The air smells of sun, sea, and forest. The visitor to Rio is immediately infected by this holiday spirit, by an almost pagan attitude to life, as though suddenly all his inner gloom had been dissipated under the influence of this blazing sun, these fragrant perfumes. For there is magic and music in the air, a caress in the wind, a bright mystery in this luminous city of São Sebastião do Rio de Janeiro.

On the summit of Corcovado, His arms extended toward the sinful city, stands the statue of Christ the Saviour. As one stands at the base of the monument and looks out over the city and the sea, one gasps, as though wounded by so much beauty. Gasps and almost blushes. The scenery is overpowering, almost indecent in its beauty. Those who have a sense of economy are somewhat irked at such a riotous excess of colours. Those whose aesthetic sense leans toward restraint and the golden mean feel almost offended by this lavish display of colours and forms. An ascetic would be inclined to close his eyes, as though he had suddenly come face to face with a naked woman.

The first time I looked down upon Rio from the heights of Corcovado the beauty of the landscape hit me like a blow in the solar plexus.

(22) Rio Grande do Sul

Caio Abreu, *Dragons*

Abreu's story is told by a man talking to Dudu, who we discover he has killed back in his home town of Passo da Guanxuma, a fictionalized name for a town in Rio Grande do Sul, near the Uruguayan border.

It was exactly seven years ago today that I ran away forever from Passo da Guanxuma, Dudu. It's September, the month of your birthday, but I can't remember which day.

This just came back to me now while I was looking at my face in the mirror trying to decide whether or not to shave. You know what my beard is like, so stiff and thick. If I shave every day my face gets covered in cuts, ingrowing bristles, red patches. If I don't shave my face starts to look dirty. I couldn't make up my mind. But it was when I looked in the mirror that I saw the calendar next to it and then I got that heavy feeling in my heart, that memory of Passo, of *September* and you. When I thought of September, I thought of some dumb things too, like little butterflies fluttering about, little flowers breaking through the soil, winds blowing, a sky as blue as if it had been painted by hand. My God, there were so many idiotic things about that town. Still are, right?

Then I looked out of the window. The window in my room looks out onto the back of another building, there's always this grey fug hanging there. A thick, oily fug. If you were here, and you looked straight out you'd see a lot of little bathroom windows but they're too small to get even a glimpse of all the hanky-panky that must be going on behind them. If you looked down you'd see trashcans all piled up in the yard. You'd only see a little patch of sky if you looked up – and when I wrote *little patch of sky* I remembered that old tune you liked so much, wasn't it a *chorinho*? I always look up, to see the grey air between my window and the side of the other building stretch up until it merges with the sky; a thick cloak of soot cast over this town that's so far from Passo and everything that's clear, even if it is a bit dumb.

When I think like that, here in this town Dudu, you've no idea what a crazy, crazy longing I get to go back. But I'm not going back. You know better than absolutely anyone that I can never go back.

(23) SALVADOR (BAHIA)

Jorge Amado, *Shepherds of the Night*

*Salvador, also known as Bahia, is the city where Amado sets his
gang of negroes and mulattos, and their Candomblé rituals and
processions.*

They got off the street car at Baixa do Sapateiro and set out for
Pelourinho Square. It was a small conglomeration in bright hues,
swelled by the curious and passersby.

The streetcar was left standing there on the rails, empty, for both the
conductor and the motorman, as though by common consent, had
deserted the vehicle and joined the throng. This gave rise to the traffic
tie-up which caused so much confusion in the city, upsetting commerce
and industry. Several truck drivers at the same time and without
previous agreement left their big trucks in Sete Portas, in front of the
Lacerda elevator, on the docks, at the Calçada Station, at the bus stop
of Amaralina, at Pitangueiras, and in Brotas, and all set out for the
Church of the Rosary of the Negroes. Three buses full of workers
decided by a quick vote to call a holiday and went to the festival.

The *orixá* ascended Pelourinho slope amid the greatest turmoil,
disobedient, attempting to jerk loose from Doninha's hands, trying out
dance steps in the street. From time to time he let out a loud guffaw,
which nobody could resist, and they all laughed with him. 'Where were
his solemn promises?' Doninha asked, but he paid no attention, he was
the master of the city.

At the square, the two corteges met, that of Ogun coming from
Baixa do Sapateiro, that of Vevéva from Terreiro de Jesus.

(24) SALVADOR (BAHIA)

Jorge Amado, *Tent of Miracles*

*Amado's populist novels pose the negro working class with their
vital culture and lifestyles against the official culture in Salvador
(or Bahia), the state capital and Brazil's fifth city.*

In the neighborhood of Pelourinho in the heart of Bahia, the whole
world teaches and learns. A vast university branches out into Tabuão,
the Carmo Gates, and Santo-Antônio-Beyond-Carmo, into Shoemak-
ers' Hollow, the markets, Maciel, Lapinha, Cathedral Square, Tororó,
Barroquinha, Sete Portas, and Rio Vermelho, wherever there are men
and women who work. And from the working of metal and wood, the
blending of medicines from herbs and roots, and the cadence of

quick-blooded rhythms, is created a fresh, original image of novel colors and sounds.

Listen to the wood and leather drums, the twanging bow, the beaded gourds and rattles, the tambourines and coconuts, the metal bells and gongs, atabaque, berimbau, ganzá, adufe, caxixí, agogô: musical instruments of the poor, rich in melody and rhythm. Music and dance were born on the common man's campus:

Camaradinho ê

Camaradinho, camará

Next door to the Slave's Church of Our Lady of the Rosary, on a second floor with five windows opening out into Pelourinho, Master Budião set up his Angola Capoeira Academy. His pupils begin to arrive in the late afternoon and early evening, weary from the day's work but still ready for fun . . .

The Tent of Miracles, Ladeira do Tabuão No 60, is the main building of this popular university. There's Master Lídio Corró painting miracles, casting magic shadows, cutting rough engravings in wood; there's Pedro Archanjo, who might be called the chancellor of the university himself. Bent over the old worn-out type and temperamental printing press in the ancient, poorly furnished shop, the two men are setting type for a book about life in Bahia.

Not far away on the Tereiro de Jesus is the School of Medicine, where students learn other cures for illness and other ways to care for the sick. And they learn other things as well – bad rhetoric, and how to spout sonnets, and theories of dubious value.

(25) SALVADOR (BAHIA)

Moritz Thomsen, *The Saddest Pleasure*

Thomsen finds himself alone in Salvador where he evokes Jorge Amado ◊ and meets the writer Darcy Ribeiro ◊.

From the window of my room at the back of the hotel where I lie in bed for almost a week, I can look down into the lower, older part of the city: to the sixteenth-century harbor, the great bay that turns gold and bronze in the late afternoons, and across the water to the island of Itaparica. The town belongs to Jorge Amado, that romantic who had made truth out of a lying vision, who has superimposed over the squalor of an incredible poverty the soul of a new race. Everything is bouyant, mildly glittering, strangely silenced and distanced, suspended in the sea air of the deep tropics; everything floats, matching my own delirium. Although I have scarcely stepped into its streets and have already seen terrible signs of decay, overcrowding, widespread poverty, and public corruption, I have been seduced by this city. I gaze down into the tiny harbor with its star-shaped stone fort or sit in the meltingly beautiful evening light thinking with amazement, 'It's the most beautiful city in the world, the realest city in the world, the only city I could learn to love.' Later when I have seen its narrow back streets blocked with garbage; walked through the barrios where the prostitutes call to you out of dark doorways – sections of town so collapsed and stinking that only Amado with his obsessions could have reinvented them into places of passion and the possibility of finding love; talked to some of its hordes of little shoe-shine boys who are twisted with hunger – after all this and more, Bahia will still remain that magic city, that mysterious, throbbing, and sensual place for which, against all common sense, one feels a kind of tragic urban passion.

(26) SANTAREM

Henry Bates, *The Naturalist on the Amazons*

In 1851 Henry Bates established his headquarters at Santarém, in the state of Pará, founded in 1661, with a population today of 250 000. He was there for 3½ years, travelling up the Tapajos River. He lived near the beach and the aldeia or Indian part of town.

Although containing no more than 2500 inhabitants Santarem is the most civilised and important settlement on the banks of the main river from Peru to the Atlantic. The pretty little town, or city as it is called, with its rows of tolerably uniform, white-washed and red-tiled houses surrounded by green gardens and woods, stands on gently sloping ground on the eastern side of the Tapajos, close to its point of junction with the Amazons. A small eminence on which a fort has been erected, but which is now in a dilapidated condition, overlooks the streets, and forms the eastern limit of the mouth of the tributary. The Tapajos at Santarem is contracted to a breadth of about a mile and a half by an accretion of low alluvial land, which forms a kind of delta on the western side; fifteen miles further up the river is seen at its full width of ten or a dozen miles, and the magnificent hilly country, through which it flows from the south, is then visible on both shores. The scenery as well as the soil, vegetation and animal tenants of this region, are widely different from those of the flat and uniform country which borders the Amazons along most part of its course. After travelling week after week on the main river, the aspect of Santarem with its broad white sandy beach, limpid dark-green waters, and line of picturesque hills rising behind the fringe of green forest, affords an agreeable surprise. On the main Amazons, the prospect is monotonous unless the vessel runs near the shore, when the wonderful diversity and beauty of the vegetation affords constant entertainment.

(27) SAO PAULO

Mário de Andrade, *Macunaíma*

Macunaíma arrives at São Paulo and deals with its corruption in terms of his mythical, Amazonian background so that all that is modern seems ridiculous.

São Paulo is built on seven hills, the traditional feature of Rome, City of the Caesars, Capital of Latinity, from which we sprang; their feet are kissed by the slender and restless lymph of the river Tietê. The supply of water is magnificent, and the climate equable to that of Aquisgrana or of Anverres; and the soil matches them in salubrity and abundance, so that it may well be as the historians lay down in fine style that from this earth, this air and this water an urban fauna was spontaneously generated.

The city is most beautiful and it is delightful in its conviviality. It is intersected by roads cleverly made narrow and adorned with the most graceful statuary and finely wrought lampposts, astutely diminishing the available space in such a way as to render these arteries incapable of letting the populace through. Thus, the effect is obtained of great crowds whose estimated number can be increased at will so as to be favorable to the elections which are the inventions of the inimitable Mineiros, at which times the aldermen and councillors dispose of great matters which gain them honored days and the admiration of all, accompanied by outbursts of oratorical eloquence in the purest style and with the most sublime embellishments of rhetoric.

The arteries of which we spoke are all littered with fluttering scraps of paper and fruit peelings sailing along, with a foundation of the finest whirling dust where a thousand and one macrobes are dispersed that decimate the population. For this is the way our elders and betters have solved the problem of circulation: these insects devour the wretched life of the rabble and prevent the undue accumulation of unemployed and laborers, thus keeping the total number of people constant. Not content with that dust stirred up by the feet of the pedestrians and by those roaring machine contraptions called automobiles and electric trolley buses (also called 'cars' and 'trams', barbarisms coming certainly from the English), the diligent City Council charters some enormous anthropoid hippocentaurs, dull-blue in color, collectively called Public Sanitations which, *per amica silencia lunae*, when traffic in the streets has ceased and dust falls harmless to the ground issue from their dens, and with huge rakes like cylindrical brooms pulled by mules lift the dust from the asphalt and rouse the insects from their sleep, stirring them into activity. These nocturnal activities are discreetly conducted by the light of small lamps situated at huge intervals so as to maintain an almost total darkness, allowing the depredations of crooks and thieves to proceed undisturbed.

(28) SAO PAULO

Frank Tuohy, *The Animal Game*

Celina drives out of São Paulo. She is victim of a passionate affair with a petty British criminal. Trying to take control of her own life she discovers humiliation.

Celina turned down a long avenue into the suburbs. Her throat hurt and her arms were trembling. She passed silent factories, twice bumped over railway lines, and crossed the river, whose warm stink rose up through the darkness. Now the car slid out into the empty night, into the interior of the state. Driving always calmed her; her few tears had gone, leaving only a dry stiffness round the eyes. She had looked back only once, when the car swooped first on to the wide concrete highway. Then the red glare of the city took up half the sky. She would drive on until the glare was gone, and then she would feel that she had escaped from all of it.

Much later, Celina stopped. She had only seen night wanderers, wild dogs and stumbling men. She thought she had been driving for about four hours. She had no idea of the time, for the car clock was not working, and when her life was running fast she did not wind her watch. Whenever she turned round, though, the light was still there. At last she realised that it was no longer the city; it was the morning.

The Packard bumped on to the unmade side of the road, and she stopped the engine. Silence surrounded her. Almost immediately she fell asleep. When she awoke, the light had advanced and a chain of hills planted with eucalyptus had sprung up in front of her. Cocks were crowing at various distances. On the banks of red earth beside the car, the tussocks of grass were wet with dew and heavily scented – *capim*: it was one of the smells of her childhood. But, in this sad remote continent, the morning brought only a few moments of freshness. The coils of mist along the road died away and the woods of eucalyptus were completely silent, for no insect can live in them, and thus they are deserted by the few singing birds that remain.

(29) THE SERTAO

Bruce Chatwin, *The Viceroy of Ouida*

Chatwin goes back in time to the story of Francisco Manoel da Silva, who left Brazil for Ouidah in Dahomey, now Benin, in 1812.

The man who landed at Ouidah in 1812 was born, twenty-seven years earlier, near Jaicos in the Sertão, the dry scrubby cattle country of the Brazilian North-East.

The Sertanistas are wild and poor. They have tight faces, sleek hair and sometimes the green eyes of a Dutch or Celtic ancestor. They hate negroes. They believe in miraculous cures, and their legends tell of a phantom king called Dom Sebastião, who will rid the earth of Antichrist.

Like all people born in thorny places, they dream of green fields and a life of ease. Sometimes, with light hearts, they set out south for San Salvador da Bahia, but when they see the sea and the city, they panic and turn back to the badlands.

Francisco Manoel's father, a hired hand on a ranch, was killed while driving steers at a round-up . . .

(30) THE SERTAO

R. Magalhães Júnior, *The Immunizer*

This short story opens with a description of the arid sertão in northwest Brazil. 'The Immunizer' is included in the anthology Modern Brazilian Short Stories – see Booklist.

The lowland extended, broad and level, from Carnotim Range to the Jaibara River. Only the termite mounds interrupted its flatness. It was an enormous picture of desolation. The lowing of the oxen sounded like a death rattle as they gnawed at the remaining grass roots. The grass itself had been pitilessly scorched by the drought and then swept away by the fury of the whirlwinds. Indeed, virtually all the vegetation had disappeared. In the distance one could see the lone, spectral figure of a leafless tree on whose branches a flock of black vultures had settled, lending a note of mourning to the countryside.

In the midst of the plain, the sole survivor of the tragedy, a jujube tree spread its green, hospitable foliage over the exhausted traveler. The drought had transformed the fertile, generous backlands into a great Sahara, and the tree was a tiny oasis. It was here that Pedro Macambira rested, setting down his cans of creosote around the ancient tree trunk. He had brought them to cure the mange sores from which several of his cattle were suffering . . .

(31) THE SERTAO

João Ubaldo Ribeiro, Sergeant Getúlio

The novel opens with a monologue by the hired thug who tells about corruption, petty bosses and the poor sertão.

The great pox is like this, it's always on the move. If you leave it alone it shrinks you up and turns itself into all kinds of other distempers, so that one should always guard against women on the road. First rule. From Paulo Afonso to there, a long stretch, especially by night under these conditions. An oxcart road, dammit. There are all those villages and towns out there, Canindé de Sâo Francisco and Monte Alegre de Sergipe and Nossa Senhora das Dores and Siriri and Capela and other such scattered places, God knows how many. Propriá and Maruim, you know what they're like, dust and cotton bales up on the trucks and the raw dryness out there. And rough country, cactus and catchweed, everything stinging, thorns underfoot, a nightmare. The plants and the women equally disease-bearing, you could get skin sores from them, all kinds of treacherous creatures, ticks, scorpions, chiggers, think of it. Back there I killed three wretched characters on top of some low thornbushes; one of them fell to the ground slowly, worrying about the thorns, no doubt. Now there's a question, whether someone who is about to die worries about comfort? If I were a knifeman I would have finished him with the steel blade, but it makes a strange sound and is untidy because of all the blood that comes spurting out. And so I shot him in the back of the head from a special position I knew that doesn't waste ammunition. And I called him names on top of that for making me go hunting in these badlands, running around in this white heat and hashing up my brand-new boots in these knotted vines. Nothing to see but melon cactus and brown bushes and rough grass and buzzards. He didn't even hear me, he just folded up and went cold. A routine job. How far would he have made me go? Itapicuru? Vitória da Conquista? I don't know. There are no limits to the weakness that makes a man bolt, turning his soul loose in the world, running from his destiny.

(32) VILA BAIXA

Clarice Lispector, *The Apple in the Dark*

Lispector's protagonist Martim reaches the farm outside Vila Baixa (near São Paulo), and is hired by the two women owners as an odd-job worker, while he comes to terms with himself in this empty landscape.

On that afternoon when Martim and Vitória rode out so that the mistress of the farm could show him where the irrigation ditches should be dug – on that afternoon when they rode up the same slope down which the man had come alone – then he stood out MATURE from the darkness of the cows.

High up on the crest the woman was looking over the ground. Then suddenly, innocent and unwarned, he recognized the landscape that he had seen when he had first come to the farm – that first time, when drunk with flight and exhausted, he had relied upon that vague thing which is the promise made to a baby at birth.

On horseback, with a flash of incomprehension worthy of a genius, he saw the countryside. Stupefied and attentive he saw that at the top of the rise there was that same freedom as if something had been unfurled in the wind. And like that first time the glory of the open air brought something to him that hit him hard on the chest and pained him with the extreme upset of happiness that one sometimes feels.

But with a new and unexpected hunger he wanted to give it a name this time.

The idea of wanting something more than just a feeling seemed to afflict Martim; that confused sign of a transition toward the unknown bothered him, and his unrest was passed along to the horse that kicked up as if he had been touched somehow and had the dazzled look that horses have.

As he faced that enormous extension of empty land Martim made a suffocated effort at painful approach. With the difficulty of someone who is never going to arrive he was approaching something that a man on foot might humbly call the desire of a man, but which a man on horseback could not resist the temptation to call the mission of a man. And the birth of that strange anxiety was now provoked by the vision of an enormous world which seemed to be asking a question, as it had been when he first walked upon the slope.

Biographies and plot summaries

ABREU, Caio Fernando (1948–   ). Abreu was born in **Rio Grande do Sul** state in Southern Brazil, near the Uruguayan border in a small town he fictionalizes as 'Passo de Guanxuma'. He published *Os dragões não conhecem o Paraíso* in 1988 (*Dragons*, 1990 – Extract 22). Abreu has won several prizes, including a Prix Molière for his play *The Curse of the Black Valley*. He lives in **São Paulo**, and works as a journalist. He made a documentary about Aids that won a prize in the Turin Film festival. Abreu's fiction and stories are colloquial, modern, and funny, dealing with 'urban excesses'. His Brazil is not exotic, Amazonian: it is poor but modish. **São Paulo** is contemporary with New York and Paris, where people have Jungian therapy, jog, do Tai Chi, I Ching and the Tarot. They are single, lonely, promiscuous and nostalgic. His literary influences are Clarice Lispector ◊, Borges (◊ Argentina) and Kafka, and his tone swings from despair to satire, with many references to popular Brazilian music.

AMADO, Jorge (1912–   ). Born in **Ilhéus, Bahia** on 10 August 1912, Amado was the son of a coffee planter. He studied law, worked as a journalist, and published his first novel in 1931, followed by a propagandist novel in 1934. Amado was elected to Congress in 1946 as a member of the Brazilian Communist Party and was a political activist until 1955 (he virtually gave up writing fiction). He has several times been imprisoned, and has lived in exile in Buenos Aires and France. He left the party in 1965. His early fiction exploited a denunciatory realism, highlighting social problems like those of black sugar-cane workers in *Jubiabá*, 1935 (*Jubiabá*, 1984) and fishermen in *Mar morto*, 1936 (*Sea of Death*, 1984). Slowly he came to an awareness that his Marxist beliefs need not constrict his style, and though his subject matter remained the poor black of **Bahia**, the style began to reflect their exuberance and sensuality, beginning with *Terras do sem fin*, 1942 (*The Violent Land*, 1945) and including *Os pastores da noite*, 1964 (*Shepherds of the Night*, 1967 – Extract 23), about a gang of mulattos at odds with the police, and corrupt Bahian politicians, who live their lives in trances and dances and *Candomblé*. *A tenda dos milagres*, 1969 (*Tent of Miracles*, 1971 – Extract 24) is written as the biography of a street philosopher in Bahia called Archanjo, based on hearsay, and full of mocking details about 'white' doctors. The novels are always well situated in Bahia, and are Amado's alternative history of his Afro–Brazilian tropical region. At times his style of exaggeration grates, and he is prolific and monotonous. Other novels in English are *Os velhos marinheiros*, 1961 (*Home is the Sailor*, 1964), narrated by a local archives historian in 1929 about a retired sailor in the Brazilian village of **Periperi**, a hero unmasked as a fraud who had never sailed; *Gabriela, cravo e canela*, 1958 (*Gabriela, Clove and Cinnamon*, 1962); *Dona Flor e seus dois maridos*, 1966 (*Dona Flor and Her Two Husbands*, 1969); and *Tiêta do Agreste*, 1977 (*Tieta*, 1979). Amado wrote a biography of Prestes, the Communist party leader, in 1947. His house in the **Largo do Pelourinho, Salvador** is today a museum. His memoirs have recently been published. See B.J. Chamberlain, *Jorge Amado*, Twayne, Boston, MA, 1990.

ANDRADE, Mário de (1892–1945). Andrade was born on 9 October 1892 in São Paulo where he also died. He studied music and drama, was an art critic, and in 1922 became a professor of musicology at the Conservatory. With Oswald de Andrade he helped organize the famous Semana de Arte Moderno in his home city that founded Brazil's modernist movement. In 1934 he became director of São Paulo's Department of Culture, and in 1937 founded Brazil's Society of Ethnography. He travelled round Brazil in this capacity. He was a poet and wrote short stories and novels. Mário de Andrade's most famous novel, *Macunaíma o herói sem nenhum carater (Rapsodia)*, 1928 (*Macunaíma*, 1984 – Extract 27), tells the story in a mocking, modernistic way of a popular folk hero, Macunaíma, seeking a lost amulet on a picaresque, Candide-like trip around Brazil's main regions, encountering different spirits and monsters in a continuous series of Ovidian metamorphoses that are erotic, funny, and a critique from the Indian angle of Brazil's quest for modernity and its lack of a 'genuine tradition'. The novel was written for fun on a farm at **Araraquara** in 1926. In 1927 he published *Amar, verbo intransitivo* (*Fräulein*, 1933), mocking Brazil's attraction for European fashions. His poems about **São Paulo**, *Pauluicéia desvairada* 1922, have been translated (*Hallucinated City*, 1969). He published several books on Brazilian music and musicology.

ANJOS, Cyro dos (1906–). Born on 5 October 1906 in **Montes Claros**

in the northern part of **Minas Gerais**, Cyro dos Anjos went to **Belo Horizonte** at 18, and graduated as a lawyer in 1932. He became a journalist, editor of the state press, and joined the civil service. In 1946 he moved to **Rio**. He has taught in the USA and at the University of Brasília. His novel *O amanuense Belmiro*, 1937 (*Diary of a Civil Servant*, 1986 – Extract 3) takes the form of diary jottings of a bachelor Civil Servant called Belmiro Borba living in **Belo Horizonte** in 1935, a skeptic and a day-dreamer harking back to his rural past, with literary ambitions. The light tone, with quotations from poets, and daily dramas, is reminiscent of Machado de Assis ◊. The political background is only alluded to, though one of Belmiro's café friends is a persecuted communist.

BATES, Henry (1825–1892). Bates was born in Leicester, UK. In 1848 he left England with A.R. Wallace to travel up the Amazon and study the abundant natural history as an entomologist. Wallace returned after four years (and wrote *Travels on the Amazon*, 1853) while Bates remained another seven years, and returned to the UK in 1859. He brought back some 8000 new species, mainly insect. Over the eleven years in the Amazon basin, Bates studied at **Pará**, up the **Tocantins River**, at **Santarém** for three and a half years and **Solimoens** on the **upper Amazon** for four. Encouraged by Darwin (◊ Uruguay) he published *The Naturalist on the Amazons*, 1863 (Extract 26), in which his meticulous prose conveys his wonder and the dangers he underwent.

BISHOP, Elizabeth (1911–1979). Born in Worcester, MA, on 8 February 1911, Bishop died in Brazil. She was brought up by her grandparents and studied at Vassar (she was pictured in Mary McCarthy's novel *The Group*, 1963). In 1943 she lived a year in Mexico where she met Pablo Neruda (◊ Chile) on top of a pyramid at Chichén-Itza. She published her first book of poems *North and South* in 1946. She travelled to **Rio de Janeiro** in 1951, fell ill and decided to stay on, sharing a flat in Rio and a house in the mountains in **Petrópolis** with her friend Lota Costellet de Macedo Soares from 1952 until her death. She travelled into the **Mato Grosso** jungles and up the **Amazon** in 1961 with Aldous Huxley (◊ Mexico). In 1967, after a trip down the **São Francisco River**, she restored an old colonial house she had bought in 1965 in **Ouro Prêto** called 'Mariana' (after the US poet Marianne Moore, and on the way to a village called Mariana).

Bishop's poems can be read as a diary of her fascination with the history and landscape (eg Extract 15). She became a close friend to Robert Lowell (◊ Argentina). In 1963 she published *Questions of Travel* and in 1976 *Geography III*. Her poem 'Arrival at Santos' describes the 'tourist' arriving at the port for **São Paulo**. She notices the Brazilian flag, 'a strange and brilliant rag', and captures the tropical nature as she goes back in time in 'Brazil, January 1, 1502' to show that little has changed since the discovery and her arrival. Brazil with its 'too many waterfalls', its 'exaggerated' beauties and mountains 'like the hulls of capsized ships,/ slime-hung and barnacled' is the 'strangest of theatres'. The most tender and amusing poem is about her gardener 'Manuelzinho'. Where Bishop lived there are sudden storms with hail ('the biggest size of artificial pearls'), owls count to five every night, and fireflies drift around like jellyfish, and there are bookworms, moths, tiny green hummingbirds and mildew that invades her house with its 'ignorant map'.

Elizabeth Bishop translated *The Diary of Helena Morley*, 1956, from the Brazilian, about a young girl growing up at the end of the last century in a forgotten village called **Diamantina** 200 miles northeast of **Belo Horizonte**, which Bishop visited and wrote about at length in the prologue to her translation. Bishop met the aged Helena Morley in **Rio**. She also translated and edited *An Anthology of Twentieth Century Brazilian Poetry*, 1972, and wrote the Sunday Times World Library book *Brazil*, 1963.

CALLADO, Antônio (1917–). Callado was born in **Niterói**, capital of the state of **Rio de Janeiro**. From 1937 he worked as a journalist, including war years in London for the BBC, and Paris, and from 1963 editing *O Jornal do Brasil*. He has travelled to Cuba, and was jailed for protesting against the military. He has written plays as well as novels. His novel *Quarup*, 1967 (*Quarup*, 1970), refers to an Indian ritual of death and resurrection and concerns a priest who, setting out to Christianize Indians, discovers himself sexually and politically, and becomes a revolutionary. Callado's novel *Bar Don Juan*, 1971 (*Don Juan's Bar*, 1972 – Extracts 14 and 16) follows a group of trendy lefties seduced into guerrilla war by Che Guevara's example. They are tortured, fall in and out of love, and travel off to **Corumbá** on the Bolivian border to join up. The novel ends with their decimation and a widow trying to make sense of 1960s radical politics.

CHATWIN, Bruce (1940–1989). Born in England on 13 May 1940,

Chatwin worked at Sotheby's and subsequently as a journalist for the *Sunday Times Magazine*. In 1977, his original and carefully written travel book *In Patagonia* was published. He describes a journey down to Tierra del Fuego in search of ancestors. In 1985, with Paul Theroux (◊ Honduras), he wrote *Patagonia Revisited*. His first novel *The Viceroy of Ouidah*, 1980 (Extract 29), was a failed biography about a slaver De Souza in Dahomey that turned into a self-conscious novel tracing the life of Francisco Manoel from Brazil to Africa, where he was made Viceroy of Ouidah. Always homesick for **Bahia** but never accepted by the upper-class, he married late, his white wife was poisoned, his twins became whores and all his fabulous riches faded. Werner Herzog's 1988 film *Cobra Verde* is based on *The Viceroy of Ouidah*. Chatwin wrote three further novels and died of Aids in 1989.

CUNHA, Euclides da (1866–1909). Born in **Rio de Janeiro** province, Euclides da Cunha started training as an engineer and in 1886 joined a military school, but he left to become a journalist in **São Paulo**. He rejoined the army after graduating as a civil engineer in 1891. When the **Canudos** revolt burst out in 1896, da Cunha was sent to cover the campaign, and the result is his masterpiece of socioeconomic, and anthropological–historical research *Os Sertões* 1902 (*Rebellion in the Backlands*, 1957 – Extract 10). In its attempt to situate Antônio Conselheiro's strange defiance, his work crosses many genres. It immediately became an explanation of a certain kind of Brazilian, formed by particular geographic forces, in this case the arid North-Eastern *sertão*, as opposed to the more Europeanized cities. The book can be read with much interest today for its topographical accuracy. The writers Cunninghame Graham (◊ Paraguay) and later Mario Vargas Llosa (◊ Peru) worked from da Cunha's treatise. Particularly moving is his outrage at what is done to the messianic prophet and his people in the name of progress. Euclides da Cunha was shot dead in a duel in 1909. His house can be visited: **Museu Euclides da Cunha**, Casa Euclidiana, Rua Marechal Floriano 105, São José do Rio Pardo, São Paulo.

DOYLE, Sir Arthur Conan (1859–1930). Conan Doyle was born in Edinburgh on 22 May 1859. He was a doctor, creator of Sherlock Holmes and Dr Watson, wrote historical novels, histories of the Boer war, and was interested in spiritualism. He wrote *The Lost World* in 1912 (Extract 9), narrated by journalist Malone off on an expedition with Professor Challenger and the man checking his theories, Professor Summerlee, together with explorer Sir John Roxton. They arrive in **Pará**, and proceed upriver through a gap into unexplored country. They manage to climb into the tabletop 'lost world', are attacked by pterodactyls and by ape-men, shoot and kill their way into an Indian camp, and escape back to civilization via a cave. There are maps, references to Darwin (◊ Uruguay), Wallace, Bates ◊ and Burton (◊ Uruguay). Doyle himself never actually went to the remote Brazilian jungle hills. He got his facts from Colonel Fawcett, who wrote 'Above us towered the Ricardo Franco Hills, flat-topped and mysterious, their flanks scarred by deep *quebradas*. Time and the foot of man has not touched those summits. They stood like a lost world, forested to their tops, and the imagination could picture the last vestiges there of an age long vanished. Isolated from the battle with changing conditions, monsters from the dawn of man's existence might still roam those heights unchallenged, imprisoned and protected by unscalable cliffs. So thought Conan Doyle when later in London I spoke of these hills and showed photographs of them' (see Colonel P.H. Fawcett, *Exploration Fawcett*, Century Hutchinson, London, 1988).

FLEMING, Peter (1907–1971). Born on 31 May 1907, Fleming was educated at Eton and Oxford. He was brother of the James Bond creator, Ian. In April 1934, he noticed an advertisement in *The Times* which set him off on his explorations in Brazil looking for the lost explorer Colonel Fawcett, who had gone missing in mysterious circumstances in 1925. In 1933, Fleming published his gripping, if at times facetious *Brazilian Adventure* (Extract 17), with a map and a glossary, and vivid descriptions. Fleming married the actress Celia Johnson, travelled as a journalist to China, fought in Norway and Greece during the war, and wrote several further books on travel and war history before he died.

HAMILTON-PATERSON, James (1941–   ). Hamilton-Paterson was born on 7 November 1941. He was educated at Oxford (winning the Newdigate Prize), and has been a journalist. He places his novel *Gerontius* (Extracts 2 and 13) in Brazil as the famous ageing composer Elgar takes an **Amazon** river trip to **Manaus** in 1923, and surprisingly re-meets a jilted German musician. The plot is not as good as the descriptive parts, for Hamilton-Paterson is fastidious in the way he evokes clouds, insects and

James Hamilton-Paterson

jungle. There are interesting diary entries with jottings on creativity, ageing, fame, the other passengers, and many references to local habits and soft drinks like Guaraná, made from the tropical jungle fruit of the same name. Hamilton-Paterson worked his way up the same river on a German tramp steamer to Manaus in 1974. He has also written short stories and poems, and an idiosyncratic study of different aspects of sea-life in *Seven-Tenths: The Sea and its Thresholds*, 1992. He lives in Italy and the Far East.

KIPLING, Rudyard (1865–1936). Born in Bombay, India, Kipling began as a journalist in Lahore, left India in 1889, and made his mark in literary London as a poet and short story writer. In 1892 he married and lived in the USA from 1892 to 1896, then settled in Sussex in 1902, and visited South Africa regularly from 1898. He won the Nobel prize for

Rudyard Kipling

literature in 1907. In 1927, his doctor recommended a sea voyage after an illness so Kipling went to Brazil and recorded his impressions for the **Morning Post**. He visited **Bahia, Rio**, a snake farm, a power factory, a coffee plantation, and the **Botanical Gardens** to see the Victoria Regia lily. *Brazilian Sketches* was published in 1927.

LISPECTOR, Clarice (1925–1977). Lispector was born on 10 December 1925 in Tchetchelnik in the Ukraine and emigrated with her Russian parents to Brazil as a baby. She was brought up in **Recife**, and moved to **Rio** when she was twelve. By 1944 she had graduated from university in law, worked as a journalist, published her first novel, and married a diplomat. She lived in Europe and then for eight years in the USA. She divorced, and returned to **Rio** with her two children, where she died in 1977. Her fiction deals with women and subjectivity, sensitivity, isolation and

suffering, with a clear existentialist bias. She is at odds with the regionalist writers of her day in that she delves into inner life and dramas in the city. *A maçã no escuro*, 1961 (*The Apple in the Dark*, 1967 – Extract 32) is an analytical novel about a guilty man Martim, on the run, who reaches a farm near **Vila Baixa** in an empty land. The farm is run by two women, Vitória and Ermelinda, and the threesome are locked into their mental lives, indifferent to communication, waiting for something to happen. The novel ends with Martim's arrest for some crime, but he has also come to terms with his fundamental self, his inner freedom in an existentialist sense. Further work in English includes *Laços de família*, 1960 (*Family Ties*, 1972); *A Legião estrangeira*, 1964 (*The Foreign Legion: Stories and Chronicles*, 1986); *A hora da estrela*, 1977 (*The Hour of the Star*, 1986); *Uma aprendizagem ou O livro dos prazeres*, 1969 (*An Apprenticeship or the Book of Delights*, 1986); *A paixão segundo G.H.*, 1964 (*The Passion according to G.H.*, 1988); a collection of stories from 1974 published as *Soulstorm*, 1989; and *Perto do coração selvagem*, 1949 (*Close to the Wild Heart*, 1990).

MACHADO DE ASSIS, Joaquim Maria (1839–1908). Machado de Assis was born poor on a hill in **Rio de Janeiro** in 1839. A mulatto and an epileptic, he was early orphaned, but despite these drawbacks he came to be the greatest fiction writer in nineteenth-century Latin America. He began work as a printer, took up journalism, and finally obtained a post in Brazil's civil service. He was self-taught, and a ruthless social climber, ending up first director of Brazil's Academy.

His early fiction is romantic and

ironic, dealing with the well-off and idle in his home town during Brazil's Second Empire. *Iaiá García*, 1878 (*Yayá García*, 1976, and retranslated in 1977) is a complicated love story in a secluded setting on a hill above **Rio**, involving widows, arranged marriages, and pretences, that finally ends well. It is like a formal dance, or a game of chess, as one of the characters observes about social life in Brazil. Machado de Assis's later work changes in tone, to become more savage in its satire, and far freer with the form of the novel, developing an acute wit. *Memórias póstumas de Brás Cubas*, 1881 (*Epitaph for a Small Winner*, 1952 – Extract 19) is his masterpiece in the *Tristram Shandy* tradition narrated from the tomb. It is a review of a mediocre sensualist's life in **Botafogo** and **Tijuca** in the slave-owning days before Independence, a kind of Brazilian *Candide*, refusing to look at life pessimistically, and showing no remorse. Machado de Assis reveals his own self-conscious art, with empty and disposable chapters, and a section called 'The defect of this book'. The upper-class bachelor dilletante is a sterile man, with affairs that mean nothing to him. People die suddenly, years flash past painfully. One character who leaps from being a tramp to a dandy philosopher is called Quincas Borba (he appears in a novel of 1891, *Quincas Borba*, translated as *Philosopher or Dog*, 1954). *Dom Casmurro*, 1899 (*Dom Casmurro*, 1953 and retranslated in 1992), is a study in male jealousy as rich as *Othello* as Bento recalls a childhood romance with Capitú and is tormented by his son's resemblance to his best friend. It is a bleak portrait of desire and love, which is continued in *Esaú e Jacó*, 1904 (*Esau and Jacob*, 1965) in which the eponymous twins reflect Brazilian history's in-fighting during the new Republic.

Machado de Assis wrote over 200 short stories, some collected in *The Devil's Church and Other Stories*, 1977, that delve into his ironic view of how social life deforms inner life, and how idealism is a mask for greed, self-seeking, and indifference. His later work is a condemnation of Brazil's idle ruling class. See Helen Caldwell, *Machado de Assis: The Brazilian Master and his Novels*, University of California Press, Berkeley, CA, 1970.

MAGALHAES Júnior, R. (1907–). Magalhães was born in **Ubajara** in the state of **Ceará**. He settled in **Rio**, wrote plays, novels, short stories, and a three-volumed study of Machado de Assis. In 1940 and 1942 he lived in New York, and in 1956 he was elected to the Brazilian Academy of Letters. He has held various official positions, and edited the magazine *Manchete*.

PRITCHETT, V.S. (1900–). Pritchett was born in Ipswich and educated in London. He worked as a journalist and is a master of the short story (see *The Complete Short Stories*, 1990). He has also written well on Spain, from *Marching Orders*, 1928, to *The Spanish Temper*, 1955. He published his novel *Dead Man Leading* in 1937 (Extract 1). It concerns a son travelling up a Brazilian tributary of the **Amazon**, in search of why his anguished father, the Rev Johnson, died. Pritchett has written critical reviews on Brazilian literature: see his *Collected Essays*, 1922.

RAMOS, Graciliano (1892–1953). Ramos was born on 27 December 1892 in **Quebrângulo** and brought up in the *sertão*, in the state of **Alagoas**, the eldest of 15 children of a

Graciliano Ramos

chapters, almost short stories. In 1945 Ramos published short stories, *Infância* (*Childhood*, 1979 – Extract 5), and joined the Brazilian Communist party. In 1952 he visited Russia. In 1953, his posthumous *Memórias do cárcere* (*Jail Prison Memoirs*, 1974) appeared, dealing with his imprisonment during Getulio Vargas's dictatorship in March 1936 for about ten months. Ramos's house can be visited: **Casa de Graciliano Ramos**, Palmeira dos Indios, Alagoas.

RIBEIRO, Darcy (1922–). Born in Brazil, Ribeiro is an anthropologist. He became Deputy Governor of the **State of Rio de Janeiro** and Education Minister under Goulart. He was **Brasília University's** first Rector, and has lived in exile in Mexico and Chile. His novel *Maíra*, 1978 (*Maíra*, 1984 – Extract 6) is about a Brazilian Indian brought up as a priest in Rome who returns educated to help his tribesmen in the **Amazon**. Ribeiro has written a history of Brazil, As *Américas e a civilização*, 1970 (*The Americas and Civilization*, 1971).

storekeeper who ended up as prefect in **Palmeira dos Indios**. In 1914 Ramos went to **Rio** and worked as a proofreader. Back in Palmeira dos Indios his wife died, leaving him with four children. His first novel appeared in 1933. Ramos situated his characters in this hostile environment. He liked working psychologically, from within his characters. His second novel *São Bernardo*, 1934 (*Sao Bernardo*, 1975) is narrated by Paulo Honorio, a landowner in collision with his spiritual, schoolteacher wife, who finally kills herself. In *Angústia*, 1936 (*Anguish*, 1946) he explores an uprooted *sertanejo* in the alienating city who kills a neighbouring girl he has been spying on. *Vidas secas*, 1938 (*Barren Lives*, 1961), as the title proclaims, is again set in the *sertão*, and focuses on a family trying to survive and revolt, and emigrating to the city – it takes the form of 13 independent

RIBEIRO, João Ubaldo (1940–). Ribeiro was born in 1940 in Brazil, and lives in **Salvador**, Bahia, where he edits the newspaper *Tribuna da Bahia*. He has a masters degree in Political Science from the University of Southern California, and in 1972–73 was a guest at the University of Iowa International Writing Program. *Sargento Getúlio*, 1971 (*Sergeant Getúlio*, 1980 – Extract 31) is narrated by a rough hired gunman travelling in the *sertão* towards **Aracajú**, on a mission to trap his boss's political enemy. When he is betrayed, he tries to shoot him, is caught by federal troops, but stubbornly fights. We learn about the harsh countryside and Getúlio's violent, sometimes funny view on life and himself. *O povo brasileiro*, 1984 (*An Invincible Memory*, 1989) is an ambitious novel, rewriting the history of Brazil seen through two interlocked families, one from Portugal, and the other from Africa, with leaps in time. Ribeiro translates his own work into English.

SOUZA, Márcio (1946–). Born in **Manaus**, Souza graduated from the **University of São Paulo** in the social sciences, and turned to film-making and theatre. He works with the Teatro Experimental do Sesc Amazonas, struggling to preserve the Amazon jungle. He published a best-selling comedy set in the jungle frontiers, *Galvez, Imperador do Acre*, 1976 (*The Emperor of the Amazon*, 1977), followed by *Mad Maria*, 1980 (*Mad Maria*, 1985 – Extract 7), centred on an English engineer determined to run a train called Mad Maria through the hell of the jungle at the turn of the century. The project is pointless, as the tracks lead nowhere, but Souza turns it into black humour. He has written a mock science fiction novel, with political undertones, *A ordem do dia*, 1983 (*The Order of the Day: An Unidentified Flying Object*, 1986). He lives in **Rio de Janeiro** and runs a publishing house.

THOMSEN, Moritz (see under Ecuador).

TOMLINSON, H.M. (1873–1958). Tomlinson was born in the East End of London and started working at the age of 12. He became a journalist. In 1912 he decided to travel on ship to deliver coal to **Pôrto Velho** in Brazil. He reads Bates ◊ and Humboldt (◊ Venezuela), travels past **Pará**, and

takes excursions into the jungle. The result is *The Sea and the Jungle*, 1912 (Extract 8), a delightful and honest book by a writer who published many novels, including *All Our Yesterdays*, 1930, an anti-war story.

TORRES, Antônio (1940–). Torres was born in **Junco** in Brazil's *sertão* in 1940. He went to school in **Alagoinhas**, and then in **Salvador**. He worked as a crime reporter, moved into advertising, travelled round Europe and settled in **Rio**. His third novel *Essa terra*, 1976 (*The Land*, 1987 – Extract 12) reports in a poetic and evocative way on the backwardness of his home village **Junco**. A man returns to his large family from **São Paulo**, and kills himself. His brother recalls his life in the village. *Balada da infância perdida*, 1908 has also been translated (*Blues for a Lost Childhood: A Novel of Brazil*, 1989).

TREVISAN, Dalton (1925–). Born on 14 June 1925 in **Curitiba**, Trevisan, after studying law, worked for his father in a ceramics factory. An accident in 1945 turned him into a police reporter and film critic in Curitiba newspapers. His short stories chronicle life in **Curitiba**, written from the viewpoint of an observer who is one of the knowing locals. He published his first book of stories, *Novelas Nada Exemplares* in 1959, followed by *Cemitério de Elefantes*, 1964, *O Vampiro de Curitiba*, 1965, and *A Guerra Conjugal*, 1969. A selection in English appeared as *The Vampire of Curitiba*, 1972 (Extract 11). He sketches out the background to his stories of human foibles, giving a clear picture of Curitiban life. The opening story, 'The Corpse in the Parlor' shows in a laconic way an authoritarian father who does not believe that thirteen-year-old Ivette is his daughter, and tortures her with cigarette burns until he dies. As he lies in his coffin, she approaches, lights a cigarette and burns his dead flesh. 'Death on the Square' follows Jonas who discovers that his wife is unfaithful to him, and only accepts her back on condition that she remain indoors. After his death she tries to attract her lover back, and fails.

TUOHY, Frank (1925–). Tuohy was born on 2 May 1925 in England. He graduated from King's College, Cambridge, and lectured at Turku University in Finland from 1947 to 1948; at the **University of São Paulo** from 1950 to 1956; and then in Krakow, Poland, to 1962, followed by a spell in Japan. He has published several collections of short stories (*The Collected Stories*, 1984), three novels, a book on Portugal, and a biography of W.B. Yeats. He has won the Katherine Mansfield, and the Faber memorial prizes. *The Animal Game*, 1957 (Extract 8), evokes Brazil, **São Paulo** and its sea coast, around a cluster of characters who relate to the country as outsiders or exiles. The novel describes Robert Morris's education in sensuality. The Brazil Tuohy captures is not the place in tourist brochures. The title refers to a lottery and to animal sensuality. Most of the characters are unhappy, but passionate, driven by forces beyond them, represented by the Brazilian Celina's humiliation through sexual passion. Tuohy presents a country with a crazy immigration mix-up, far from any glamorous melting pot. The novel satirizes the British abroad. Tuohy's second Brazilian novel, *The Warm Nights of January*, 1960 (Extract 4), refers to summer (January), and **Rio de Janeiro**, and defends the Brazilian way of life

through **Bella**, a bohemian French painter in **Copacabana**, and her black lover Hadriano. The plot is weak, with carnival scenes and a *macumba* trance, but Tuohy continues his investigation into exiles, this time predominantly French and cosmopolitan. His early short stories (*The Admiral and the Nun*, 1962) describe exiles, the British abroad and misfits in Brazil. The best is 'A Survivor in Salvador', about a Pole on the run from Poland and Wandsworth Scrubs to **Salvador** in Brazil, the land of petty criminals, and a last-ditch, and failed, attempt to survive by selling cocaine. At present Tuohy lives in Somerset in England.

VERISSIMO, Erico (1905–1975). Veríssimo was born in **Cruz Alta** in the state of *Rio Grande do Sul* on 17 December 1905, and died in **Pôrto Alegre**. He moved to Pôrto Alegre in 1930, where he published his first stories in 1933. He taught at many different universities, and travelled as a diplomat. In 1957 he published a readable history of Mexico – *Mexico, história duma viagem* (*Mexico*, 1960). Six of his modernistic novels have been translated into English and feature **Pôrto Alegre** and its specific geography. In *Caminhos cruzados*, 1935 (*Crossroads*, 1943), we follow the confused destiny of several characters in sensitive psychological probings, over a five-day period in the city. Others include *O resto é silencio*, 1943 (*The Rest is Silence*, 1946); *Olhai os lírios do campo*, 1938 (*Consider the Lilies of the Field*, 1947); *O tempo e o vento*, 1949 (*Time and the Wind*, 1951), part of a family dynasty trilogy in Pôrto Alegre; *Noite*, 1954 (*Night*, 1956); and *O senhor embaixador*, 1965 (*His Excellency, the Ambassador*, 1967). He also wrote *Brazilian Literature*, 1945.

Frank Tuohy

PARAGUAY

'Asunción . . . looks over the Chaco at the great desert, still an unknown wilderness of swamps and forests, then the river narrows and all traces of civilization are left behind.'
R.B. *Cunninghame Graham, South American Sketches*

Paraguay, or the República del Paraguay, is derived from a Guaraní word meaning 'a place with a great river' or 'the river of the Paraguá tribe' – Sir Richard Burton (◊ Uruguay) lists nine possible derivations. This land-locked country has river borders with Bolivia, Brazil and Argentina, and a land area of 406 750 sq km. Its population reached 4 518 000 in 1989. The capital city **Asunción**, founded by Martínez de Irala in 1537 on the River Paraguay, had a population of 729 000 in 1984 (see Greene and Meyer on Asunción, Extracts 1 and 2), with **Villarica**, **Ciudad del Este** (formerly Puerto Presidente Stroessner) and **Encarnación** as the principal cities. As in the rest of the continent there has been a vast migration to the urban areas, and also abroad, especially to Argentina.

The people are *mestizo*, with an Indian predominance. There is a large Mennonite colony of 5400 sq km in the hostile **Chaco** (from a Quechua word *chuco* meaning 'hunting ground') founded in 1927 with **Filadelfia** and **Colonia Neuland** as its centres, and with its own law, banks, schools, hospitals. The Mennonites are Protestants, pacifist, self-supporting, essentially German-speaking, and dress in nineteenth-century styles. There are also pockets of German (once hiding fugitive Nazis) and Japanese immigrants. Paraguay is the most bilingual of the South American countries, between Guaraní and Spanish, with 95% speaking Guaraní, and Spanish being the business and school language. This bilingualism is used by Augusto Roa Bastos ◊ in his novels, and even Horacio Quiroga's (◊ Argentina) Misiones based stories incorporate Guaraní terms. That so many of the people are Guaraní-speaking makes it hard for a writer to reach any audience in Paraguay itself, especially as 60% of the population lives rurally, even feudally. Some 20 000 Indians (Guayanas, Guayakis, etc) live in the forest. Only 2% of the population is white.

The economy is essentially rural, with huge *latifundios* (estates) and small *chacras* (smallholdings) where manioc (cassava), maize, cotton, leather, *yerba mate* (*Ilex paraguayensis*, the typical green tea, drunk strong and bitter – or with sugar – from a straw out of a gourd) are grown, and cattle are herded. In the Chaco *quebracho* (the Spanish means 'break axe') trees are felled for their red tanning dye. In 1988 **Itaipú**, the world's largest hydroelectric dam, was built in a joint Brazilian–Paraguayan venture (drowning the Guairá Falls as a consequence). Smuggling accounts for a high percentage of unrecorded economic activity, and recently banking has become important in Asunción.

The land is a rich, red sandstone and alluvial soil. In the east there are semi-deciduous forests, with hardwoods, and in the west luxuriant grasses. The **Chaco** takes up 237 800 sq km, and is known as 'Green Hell' (cf Julian Duguid ◊ Bolivia) with a mixture of dense jungle, grasslands, palm groves and swamp. It is here the Spaniards let cattle run wild in 1564, and they multiplied, where the Mennonites settled, and where a terrible, pointless war over oil was fought with over 36 000 Paraguayan deaths (Roa Bastos fought as a stretcher bearer, and the war enters his novel *Son of Man* – Extract 6). The Paraguayan climate is temperate, and subtropical.

THE JESUITS

The Guaraní-speaking Indians who inhabited Paraguay before the arrival of the Spaniards were semi-nomadic, and became natural allies with the Spaniards against the Inca Empire. The first Spanish settlement was at **Asunción** from 1536 to 1566, so that the city became the hub of the empire until the end of the sixteenth century, when Buenos Aires took over. The early history of the land was dominated by the Jesuits. They arrived in Lima in 1568, and moved into Paraguay in 1610, setting up 32 communistic settlements called *reducciones*. These communities were run paternalistically by the Jesuits as autonomous units. They were fortified against Brazilian slave raiders. The intention was to isolate and protect the Indians. They were lodged, made to go to church, taught music, shoemaking, clockmaking and other trades, and allowed to keep their Guaraní language (as a *lingua franca*), and everybody shared everything. Every *reducción* was centred round a grassy plaza, a church, and long building where the Indians lived.

Over 100 000 lived in these communes until this 'empire within an empire' aroused the jealousy of Spain, and in 1767 Charles III decreed the expulsion of the Jesuits from all the Spanish Empire. The ruins in Paraguay and northern Argentina are today tourist attractions. The Jesuit experiment fascinated many Europeans, including Voltaire ◊, Montesquieu, Robert Southey (A *Tale of Paraguay*, 1825, and Vol 2, 1817, of his *History of Brazil*), R.B. Cunninghame Graham ◊, Herbert Read ◊, and Gordon Meyer (◊ Argentina). The film *The Mission* (1986, directed by Roland Joffe, with Jeremy Irons and Robert de Niro), and Robert Bolt's novel of the film were based on the Jesuit experiment.

THE FIRST DICTATORS

Paraguay gained its independence from Spain on 14 May 1811, thanks to the astute lawyer Dr José Gaspar Rodríguez Francia, 'El Supremo', who immediately became Paraguay's dictator for life, from 1816 to 1840. He maintained Paraguay in total isolation from the rest of the world, refusing diplomatic and commercial relations, banning foreigners, and forcing bachelors, even priests, to marry. He hated the church. In his later years he forbade people to look at him, and shot all the dogs in **Asunción**. His dream was of complete self-sufficiency. This fanatic admirer of Robespierre and Napoleon shot his sister because she married without his approval. He caused an international scandal when he imprisoned the French botanist Aimé Bonpland for 10 years. Carlyle wrote an admiring essay on Francia in 1843. Edward Lucas White wrote of the dictator in his *El Supremo: A Romance of the Great Dictator of Paraguay*, 1916. And Augusto Roa Bastos has a recent novel narrated by Francia himself (*I the Supreme*, 1986 – Extract 5).

Francia was followed by another dictator, Carlos Antonio López, from 1840 to 1862, who, after the Argentine dictator Rosas's blockade, decided to build a strong, German-trained army. López was succeed by his son Federico Solano López from 1862 to 1870, who led Paraguay into a disastrous defensive war against Brazil, Argentina and Uruguay, known as the War of the Triple Alliance (1865–70). López tried to force Brazil out of Uruguay, and crossed the Argentine state of Corrientes without permission, thus setting off the war. This war ended with López's death in the battle of Cero Cora. Over a million Paraguayans died in battle or from cholera. The country was reduced to 300 000, with only 13% of them men. It also lost land. The bloody seige of **Humaitá** in 1869 was recorded by Sir Richard Burton. Solano López was a romantic, who planted a tree at Alfred de Musset's grave in France, and was outlived by his Irish mistress Eliza Lynch. Cunninghame Graham wrote a biography of his life, and Gordon Meyer recreated their last days. See also William Barret, *Woman on Horseback: The Biography of Francisco Lopez and Eliza Lynch*, 1938; and Henry Lyon Young, *Eliza Lynch Regent of Paraguay*, 1966. Just after this,

Paraguay decided to let in an Australian anarchist community (see Extract 3 by Michael Wilding ◊).

Nietzsche's sister Elisabeth emigrated to Paraguay in 1886 to set up a racially pure community called Nueva Germania (see Ben Macintyre, *Forgotten Fatherland: The Search for Elisabeth Nietzsche*, Macmillan, London, 1992). Richard Gott's *Land Without Evil: Utopian Journeys Across the South American Watershed* (Verso, London, 1993) combines a personal journey across Paraguay and Bolivia, with historical research into earlier travellers, and Jesuit missions.

THE TWENTIETH CENTURY

After this devastation, political life in Paraguay was fought out between the *azules* (liberals) and the *colorados* (land-owners), and in a period of 31 years there were 22 presidents. This led to Paraguay's second catastrophic war, called the 'Chaco war', from 1932 to 1935, supposedly over boundary disputes between Bolivia and Paraguay, but really over oil exploration between Standard Oil and Royal Dutch. The Paraguayans were vastly outnumbered by the Bolivians, but a mixture of the Chaco terrain, the Andean Indians fighting in the low-lying jungle, and the guerrilla tactics of Colonel Estigarribia led to Paraguay threatening to invade Bolivia, until a peace was forced on the two sides in 1935. In this war, Bolivia lost 80 000 men and Paraguay 50 000, many of whom died by just getting lost in the Green Hell. Finally, it was declared that there was no oil in the area. A captured Bolivian tank stands on display in **Asunción** today.

There were further coups and dictators (including a poet as president, Natalicio González) until 1954, when General Alfredo Stroessner took over. He was elected seven times (though in fact a dictator) until he was finally ousted in 1989 by Andrés Rodríguez, who lifted the curfew, freed the press, and let many dissidents back into Paraguay.

The dominant presence in Paraguayan literature is the novelist Augusto Roa Bastos, who spent most of his writer's life in exile, first in Argentina, then France. His theme is Paraguayan history itself, where fiction rewrites history. He is also concerned with Paraguayan identity in a country of predominantly Guaraní-speaking Indians. He seeks to unmask the official view, and counter censorship. The same position informs most of the poets in *Beyond the Rivers: An Anthology of Twentieth Century Paraguayan Poetry*, 1977, especially Elvio Romero and Josefina Pla. For recent journeys to Paraguay, see Norman Lewis's ◊ *The Missionaries*, 1988 (Extract 4) and Gerald Durrell's *The Drunken Forest*, 1956.

BOOKLIST

The following selection includes all titles which are extracted in this chapter as well as those mentioned in the introduction which are available in English. In general, paperback editions are given when possible. The editions cited are not necessarily the only ones available. For most of the extracted works, the original publisher in English can be found in 'Acknowledgments and Citations' at the end of the volume, as can the exact location of the extracts and the editions from which they are taken. The date in square brackets is the original publication date of the work in its original language. Extract numbers are highlighted in bold for ease of reference.

Barret, William, *Woman on Horseback: The Biography of Francisco Lopez and Eliza Lynch*, Peter Davies, London, 1938/Stokes, New York, 1938.

Beyond the Rivers: An Anthology of Twentieth Century Paraguayan Poetry, Charles Richard Carlisle, ed, Thorp Springs Press, Berkeley, CA, 1977.

Cunninghame Graham, R.B., *South American Sketches*, John Walker, ed, University of Oklahoma Press, Norman, OK, 1978. **Extract 7**.

Durrell, Gerald, *The Drunken Forest* [1956], Penguin, London, 1958.

Greene, Graham, *Travels with My Aunt* [1969], Penguin, London, 1971/Viking Penguin, New York, 1977. **Extract 1**.

Lewis, Norman, *The Missionaries*, Vintage Books, London, 1992/ Viking Penguin, New York, 1989. **Extract 4**.

Meyer, Gordon, *The River and the People*, Methuen, London, 1963. **Extract 2**.

Read, Herbert, *The Green Child* [1935], Robin Clark, London, 1989. **Extract 8**.

Roa Bastos, Augusto, *I the Supreme* [1974], Helen Lane, trans, Faber and Faber, London, 1987/Knopf, New York, 1986. **Extract 5**.

Roa Bastos, Augusto, *Son of Man* [1961], Rachel Caffyn, trans, Gollancz, London, 1965. **Extract 6**.

Southey, Robert, *The History of Brazil, Vol 2* [1817], Longman, London. Reprint of early edition published by Greenwood Press, St Paul, MN.

Southey, Robert, *A Tale of Paraguay* [1825].

White, Edward Lucas, *El Supremo: A Romance of the Great Dictator of Paraguay*, E.P. Dutton, New York, 1916.

Wilding, Michael, *The Paraguayan Experiment: A Documentary Novel*, Penguin, Sydney, 1985. **Extract 3**.

Voltaire, *Candide*, John Butt, trans, Penguin, London 1947/R. Bruce Baswell, trans, Tudor Publishing Company, New York, 1934. **Extract 9**.

Young, Henry Lyon, *Eliza Lynch, Regent of Paraguay*, Anthony Blond, London, 1966.

Extracts

(1) ASUNCION

Graham Greene, *Travels With My Aunt*

Greene's timid British narrator Henry Pulling, chasing his eccentric aunt Augusta, finds himself in Stroessner's Asunción. Greene was there in 1967, on National Day, and found himself in a street called Benjamin Constant, just like his character.

When I went up on deck after breakfast we were already approaching Asunción. Red cliffs were honeycombed with caves. Half-ruined huts stood at the very edge of the cliff and naked children with the pot-bellies of malnutrition stared down on us as the boat passed, moving like an overfed man who picks his way home after a heavy meal, giving little belches on the siren. Above the huts, like a medieval castle dominating some wretched village of mud and wattle, stood the great white bastions of Shell . . .

When at last the formalities were over and I stood beside my luggage on the corner of a street named after Benjamin Constant, I looked around awhile in vain for Wordsworth. Families exchanged greetings and drove away in cars. The Czech plastics manufacturer offered me a lift in his taxi. A small boy wanted to clean my shoes and another tried to sell me American cigarettes. A long colonnaded street, which sloped uphill in front of me, was full of liquor shops, and old women sat against the wall with baskets of bread and fruit. In spite of the dirt and fumes of old cars the air was sweet with orange blossom . . .

Soldiers were goose-stepping in front of the cathedral, and a very early tank stood on a plinth up on the green sward. The orange trees were everywhere, some in fruit and some in blossom . . .

Except for the skyscraper of a new hotel it was a very Victorian town. One soon ceased to notice the cars – they were an anachronism; there was a little white castellated Baptist church, a college built like a neo-Gothic abbey, and when we reached the residential quarter I saw big stone houses with bosky gardens and pillared porticos above stone steps which reminded me of the oldest part of Southwood, but in Southwood the houses would have been split into flats and the grey stone would have been whitewashed and the roofs would have bristled with television masts. In place of the orange and banana trees, I would have seen neglected rhododendrons and threadbare lawns.

(2) Asuncion

Gordon Meyer, *The River and the People*

In 1964, writer Gordon Meyer lodged in Asunción, after a trip
upriver from Buenos Aires searching for material for a biography
he never wrote on dictator Solano López and described what he
found unique about the city.

One might go out into the street now, into this early spring Asunción morning.

The clouds dispersing, the sun at once strikes through the gaps, illuminating the grass-grown cobbles, the old Spanish-colonial houses, some with their overhanging Andalucian-style balconies and rejas. White, pillared, porticoed, their roofs tiled or balconied, owning half or a whole block of ground, set with level lawns, and trees, they stand back from the street, protected by their iron and stone, muffled in shade, shutters down, silent. Somewhere inside, in those enormous dark rooms a serene and vanishing mode of life is being lived out. The palms rustle harshly, the mango trees let down their thick shadows; from a hidden patio brooms whisper, and from behind an iron reja women's voices fall softly on the silence.

Trees everywhere, as if the city were a brief interruption to the forest; and everywhere flowers: brilliant scarlet estrellas federales, detonating against the sky; violet Santa Rita spilling luxuriously over white walls.

Crossing the cobbled Avenida de España, down which the ancient claret-coloured trams batter their way to the centre, one can make for the Parque Caballero, once private residence of the General Caballero who survived the war.

It is a pleasant park, overlooking the immense river and forest. Its beautiful ornamental swimming-pool, with six flights of steps, is choked with litter, rotting leaves, everyone's rubbish. Near by moulders the ancient railway. Paraguay was once first in the South American race for civilization; possessing before the war the first shipyard, arsenal, telegraph system, railway (in the southern half of the continent), and a Navy of fifteen ships. And no beggars. Now she seems a country where civilization never really came off. Now, as spring's warmth grows, she seems to settle back into what might be her most coveted state, that of perfumed stupor. There are hints that one might discover Arcadian qualities. For one thing, apart from the busy centre of the capital, most noise seems to come from the birds.

Here, below the park, where the ground falls steeply to the river, are the shacks of the poor. By every falling stream-trickle squat women and girls, washing clothes; some of them are drying on the red earth. No noise, no disturbance; the quiet harmonizes with the noiseless river.

In the distance the government palace describes an indifferent antithesis to this squalor, although the shack area concludes its boundaries almost at the Palace walls, like a scene of feudal Europe.

(3) Asuncion

Michael Wilding, *The Paraguayan Experiment*

Wilding's documentary novel about a group of Australian anarchists here has them arriving in Asunción, and then taking a train to their commune 'New Australia'.

The married folk spent the night in the opera house. President Lopez had commissioned it on the model of Paris. It was to have been the greatest opera house of the southern hemisphere, but the war of the Triple Alliance broke out; Argentina, Brazil, and Uruguay all united against Paraguay and the building was never completed. It stood there, only partially roofed, filling an entire city block. This was our temporary shelter. And a company of Paraguayan soldiers was assigned to carry us wood and cook us food. They brought two huge military crocks into the centre of the opera house and fed us eggs and bread and quarters of beef. And they kept guard at the entrances, keeping out the onlookers and anyone else who had no business to transact. We never knew if this was just a courtesy of the government or a way of keeping us locked up or even one of Billy's schemes to keep us isolated from contamination . . .

There is only one railway line in Paraguay, and this was it. It was begun in 1859, the oldest in South America. It goes south-east from Asuncion past Villa Rica, where we were going, to Cazapa, 150 miles in all. It was built of Crimean War surplus, reassembled from the railway built by British troops from the coast to the battle lines. Dr Stewart persuaded President Lopez to buy the surplus up cheap and engage a British company to lay the track. And in 1889 a British company bought it off the government for £420 000. The Paraguayan Central Railway Co.

The wood-burning trains were unbelievably slow. It took ten hours to do ninety miles. But we watched the parrots and butterflies, the wild oranges, the pineapples. Occasionally we'd get out and pick oranges from beside the track and catch up with the train with no trouble at all. The track was unfenced and the grass spread right up to it and around it, the rails just peeping out through the green. And the Indians brought oranges and threw flowers and cigars to us as we past.

We couldn't have felt more tired if we'd done the journey on foot. The train went on through Villa Rica station and pulled up at a sawmill siding where we were to camp for the night.

(4) CAAZAPA

Norman Lewis, *The Missionaries*

In Stroessner's Paraguay, Norman Lewis is taken by a Lorcareciting 'spy' to his home town of Caazapá.

Caazapá, reached at sundown – after pushing the Citroën through miles, it seemed to us, of slippery mud – was at the end of the road, and if there was any place in the world to get away from it all, this was it.

Ghostly, once opulent houses, built in florid Victorian style, stood in gardens that had turned to beautiful thickets. Both the streets and the railway line had become meadows, and a line of trucks abandoned thirty years ago were brightly ornamented with convolvulus. There were slow-moving indulgent cows everywhere, and girls in long, immaculate white dresses milking them. The rain had stopped and we found harpists offering their services as serenaders in the small square, and among them a number of dignified men playing with tops. Girls sat in armchairs in the shallows of the river washing clothes among blue aquatic flowers. The velvet silence of this town was broken by the sweet tinplate hammering of a mission-church bell. In Caazapá the women dealt with the small-scale commerce and Julio introduced us to a girl seated at a nearby stall. Interbreeding was enforced upon Paraguayan survivors and most people in such small towns were related. This was Francisca, his cousin, who spoke freely, even with relish about her life. 'I'm seventeen years old, and sell eggs and honey. One child, as you see, but no husband. Our menfolk are incurably lazy. Why should I work to keep a man?'

Julio's house was in a nameless street in the outskirts of the town; a maroon-painted mansion enclosing three sides of a large patio in which bananas and pawpaws grew among the dense foliage of tropical plants, all of it coated with dew. The house was empty, serving as a pied-à-tierre for members of the family who happened to be in the area. It was glutted with solid, dark, well-made Victorian furniture. There appeared to be no locks on the doors. In Caazapá there was no longer electric light nor running water, although all the light fittings and the piping and taps were still in place, so the first task on arrival was to light the lamps, and draw water from the well. The English conception of privacy was unknown. While I was cleansing myself of red mud, people who seemed to be passing neighbours dropped in with a word of welcome, handled my personal belongings with good-natured curiosity, and went on their way . . .

We walked a few hundred yards to the town's centre for the evening meal, and I could only suppose that in Caazapá one stayed at home in the evening unless heavily armed. Nothing could have been calmer and more decorous than the atmosphere of the restaurant. The service was instantaneous, the waitress beautiful, and the food like most things in this country, a little bizarre, featuring as it did a strapping water-hen, complete with head and enormously splayed-out feet, but otherwise delectable.

(5) THE CHACO

Augusto Roa Bastos, *I the Supreme*

Dr Francia, amateur astonomer and intelligent dictator of Paraguay, tells how he brought an aerolith to Asunción.

When at the beginning of the Perpetual Dictatorship I saw the aerolith fall a hundred leagues away from Asunción, I ordered that it be taken captive. Nobody understood then, nobody will ever understand the meaning of this capture of the migrant meteor. Runaway-renegade from the cosmos, I ordered it brought in as a prisoner. For months a small army dragged it over the plains of the Chaco. They had to dig down more than a hundred varas before they found it. Its magnetic field extended all around it. Impassable barrier on the only route, that of the Northern Chaco, offering any probability of its sneaking out of the country. It was via that route that the French merchant Escoffier, shut up for years in prison with other foreign swindlers, tried to make his escape. Accompanied by a number of freed black slaves, he crossed the river and entered the Gran Chaco. A black slave woman who was pregnant tried to follow them, so as not to be separated from her lover. Bitten by snakes, wounded by Indian arrows, sick from fevers, the blacks died one by one until only Escoffier and the slave woman were left. The field of attraction of the meteor sucked them to the trench where some hundred sappers were excavating. The Frenchman was left no other recourse than to begin working with the others as long as his strength held out. Then he was shot to death and thrown into the hole. The slave woman gave birth to a son and went on cooking for the sappers. I might have left the meteor there in that spot; it would have been a good lookout post in that wasteland. But I preferred to have it in a safe place. It was no easy task. It cost me more than a hundred men to transport it, what with the continual struggle against savage tribes, the elements, predators, the terrible mystery of chance that refused to be reduced.

(6) Itape

Augusto Roa Bastos, *Son of Man*

*Roa Bastos's first novel opens with a description of the changes
that have overtaken the town of Itapé.*

At that time the village of Itapé was not at all like what it is to-day. For
more than three centuries after its foundation by a viceroy in far-away
Lima, it had remained a primitive hamlet buried in the red soil of the
Guairá. The wretched viceroy was only interested in taking possession
of that vast, unknown territory so that he could divide it up among his
officers as a reward for subduing the Indians. He did not care about the
poverty and misery to which his actions gave rise.

After a time all that remained of the village were a few stone and
adobe houses round the church. Wild ferns sprouted among the ruined
walls, and *amambay*, and here and there one of the wooden pillars was
putting out green shoots of its own. In the little square, by the wooden
belfry, the dry, withered plumes of the coco-palms seemed to burn like
flames in the sun, crackling in the heat with a sound like the chirping
of thirsty pigeons.

Then the railways came. Work began on the line to Encarnación,
giving employment to the villagers. Many of them were buried under
the *quebracho* sleepers which rang like metal ingots against their spades.

After the railway was finished, the village began to stretch itself.
There was a constant coming and going of naked feet on the earth
platform, from which rose clouds of dust. The same red dust formed a
downy film on the copper-coloured cheeks and ragged clothes of the
women who came to sell *chipás* and *aloja* to the passengers on the
weekly train.

Nowadays the trains are more frequent. There is a new station with a
concrete platform which has become as red as the old one. A branch
line goes to the sugar-refinery which has been built on the river-bank
near the village. Opposite the station there is a wine-vault, and the
shops of the Turks dazzle the eyes. Their walls seem to have been
bathed in quick-lime. The new church stands on the ruins of the old.
The lamp-shaped coco-palms have been cut down, and the belfry razed
to the ground. In their place has been erected an open-air theatre for
the celebrations which take place on Saint Clara's day.

Now there is noise and bustle, where before there was nothing –
nothing but the dusty ribbon of road leading to Borja and Villarica,
empty except for a few huts scattered at intervals along its length, and
for some ghostly cart, floating in the heat-haze which lay over the
plain.

But one relic of former times remains. About half a league from the village rises the hill of Itapé. The high-road passes the foot of it, crossed by a stream formed by the spring which rises on the hill. At certain hours of the day, when the light is right, it is possible to see, silhouetted against the rosy incandescence of the sky, the shelter which protects the figure of Christ on the top of the hill.

That is where mass used to be celebrated on Good Friday, the people of Itapé had their own liturgy, and the tradition soon became a legend.

(7) PARAGUAY: THE JESUITS
R.B. Cunninghame Graham, *A Jesuit*

In the sketch 'A Jesuit' (1896), Cunninghame Graham packs in information about Paraguay, and the ironic return of a Jesuit to the land from which the Jesuits had been expelled in 1767. 'A Jesuit' is included in the collection South American Sketches – see Booklist.

We left Asunción with its towers and houses hidden in orange gardens, and the great palace, in the style of Palladio, by the river's edge. Asunción, the capital of the viceroyalty of Paraguay – in the Spanish times a territory about as large as Europe, and now a sleepy, semi-Indian village, after having endured the three successive tyrannies of Francia and the two López – looks over the Chaco at the great desert, still an unknown wilderness of swamps and forests. Then the river narrows and all traces of civilisation are left behind. Here the Jesuit, for all had now begun to call him nothing else, seemed to brighten up as if he expected something, and his stories of the Jesuits of old times became more frequent. Little by little his own history came out, for he was not communicative, at least about himself. Near the Laguna de los Xarayes it appeared that the Company of Jesus had secretly started a mission amongst the Guasarapos, and he was of it. Never since the days of the Jesuits' glory in America had any missionary been bold enough to make the experiment. Fernández and Alvar Núñez, in times past, had written of their fierceness and intractability. Nuflo de Chaves, the bold adventurer, who founded the town of Sta Cruz de la Sierra, had met his death close to their territory. At long intervals they had been known to come to the mission of El Santo Corazón, or sometimes to wander even as far as that of Reyes in the district of the Moxos, while through the region of the upper Paraguay, stories of their outrages and murders were rife. In the long hot nights, as the vessel drew near to Corumbá, the passengers would sit and listen to the tales the Jesuit told. Seated in a cane chair, dressed in rusty black, a *jipijapa* hat, nothing about him priestly but his breviary and *alzacuello*, without an atom of pose, he held us spellbound. Even the Catalonian captain, nurtured to show his Liberalism by hating priests of all degrees, Catholic and Protestant, grew quite friendly with the 'little crow', as he called him, and promised to put him ashore as near the mission as he could. 'Mission, señor Captain! There is no mission, that is, now. I am the mission, that is, all that now remains of it.'

(8) PARAGUAY: THE JESUITS

Herbert Read, *The Green Child*

Olivero, mistaken for a spy in Buenos Aires, is sent to the Republic of Roncador (Paraguay – see Read's biographical entry) by horse with a gaucho. He ends up liberating the people from a tyrant in the capital, also called Roncador.

My fund of knowledge amounted to this: The country of Roncador was one of the smallest of the former Spanish provinces. It consisted of a high upland plateau, about the same size as Ireland. It was entirely pastoral in character, and only its geographical frontiers preserved its economic and political identity. That identity would never have existed but for the activities of the Jesuits, who early in the seventeenth century had penetrated into this fertile district, established a mission there, converted and organised the Guarani Indians who had previously led a more or less nomadic existence, taught them the principles of agriculture and trading, and some of the mechanical arts, such as shoe-making, carpentry and building. For a hundred and fifty years they had guided the destinies of the community they had been instrumental in creating, and though there is no doubt that they had exploited the Indians for the wordly glory of their priesthood, yet the system was designed for the general good, and if they had not made themselves objects of envy to the temporal powers, they might have succeeded in establishing a rational and truly Christian order of society which would have been an example to the whole world.

(9) PARAGUAY: THE JESUITS

Voltaire, *Candide*

Candide finds himself in the New World, and hears about the Jesuits from Cacambo, his guide.

'So you have already been to Paraguay?' said Candide.
'Indeed I have,' replied Cacambo. 'I was once a servant in the

College of the Assumption, so I know how the reverend fathers govern as well as I know the streets of Cadiz. It's a wonderful system they have. There are thirty provinces in their kingdom, and it is more than three hundred leagues across. The reverend fathers own the whole lot, and the people own nothing: that's what I call a masterpiece of reason and justice. I don't think I have ever seen such godlike creatures as the reverend fathers. They fight the Kings of Spain and Portugal over here and give them absolution in Europe. In this country they kill Spaniards, and in Madrid they send them to Heaven.

Biographies and plot summaries

CUNNINGHAME GRAHAM, Robert Bontine (1852–1936). Cunninghame Graham was born in London on 24 May 1852, and died in Buenos Aires on 20 March 1936 (but is buried on an island in Lake Menteith in Scotland). He was the son of a Scottish laird, and a half-Spanish mother. In 1878 he eloped with Gabriela, partly Chilean. His adventures began in South America at the age of 17, when from 1870 to 1872 he worked on an *estancia* in Gualeguaychú, Entre Ríos, during the civil wars, and met Urquiza, the general who ousted Argentine dictator Rosas at the battle of Caseros to become President himself from 1854 to 1860, and then retired in splendour to his palace in San José, Entre Ríos where he was murdered – the palace is well worth visiting. (Entre Ríos is the Mesopotamia of Argentina, 'between the rivers' Paraná and Uruguay.) Cunninghame Graham drove horses 300 miles to Córdoba. In 1873 he went out again to Paraguay, to start a *yerba mate* project. In 1876–77 he was back a third time trying to farm in **Bahía Blanca** at **Sauce Chico**, near **Sierra de la Ventana**, Indian territory. He also tried to drive horses to sell them

in Brazil and failed. After his marriage he went to Mexico in 1880. From 1914 to 1915 he was in Uruguay buying horses, and in 1917 was sent to Cartagena, Colombia, to buy beef during the first world war (and wrote a travelogue, *Cartagena and the Banks of the Sinú*, 1920). His last visit was to Buenos Aires in 1936 (visiting the Hudson museum). He had become a skilled rider with his Argentine horses, an MP, then a socialist, then a Scottish Nationalist, and he was imprisoned in Pentonville after 'Bloody Sunday'.

Cunninghame Graham has written many short sketches based on his experiences in South America, collected in John Walker's edition, *South American Sketches*, 1978 (Extract 7), taken from *Charity*, 1912; *Faith*, 1909; *Hope*, 1910; *Mirages*, 1936; *Success*, 1902; *Brought Forward*, 1916; and many others. Cunninghame Graham ran *estancias*, herded horses and cattle, and spoke Spanish well. He enjoyed roughing it as a *gaucho*. His nostalgic stories are written many years after the experiences as elegies for a way of life that has vanished. Many of his characters are types. Cunninghame Graham himself called his sketches 'rambling and incoherent reminiscences of a life that I have lived'. One or two stand out as expressions of his complex personality, especially 'La pulpería', where the narrator identifies with a drunk *gaucho* shouting 'Viva Rosas' and shouts the same thing, an outburst of passion that allows him to escape his European upbringing. Yet he certainly knew what he was writing about as few other Europeans did. There is a moment in 'Charlie the Gaucho' when he describes a corpse so vividly you actually see the flies. Writing of the wild pampa Indians he evokes how they were 'smeared over with a coat of ostrich grease, though never painted, and their fierce cries and smell were terrifying to the gauchos' horses, making them mad with fear.'

Cunninghame Graham also wrote numerous historical sketches – *The Horses of the Conquest*, 1930, dedicated to his Argentine horse 'Pampa'; *A Vanished Arcadia*, 1901, about the Jesuit empire; *The Conquest of the River Plate*, 1924; etc. He also wrote biographies like *A Brazilian Mystic: Being the Life and Miracles of Antonio Conselheiro*, 1920, based on the book by da Cunha (◊ Brazil); *Portrait of a Dictator: Francisco Solano López, Paraguay 1865–1870*; etc. He was a close friend to W.H. Hudson (◊ Argentina) and Joseph Conrad (◊ Venezuela). See Cedric Watts and Laurence Davies, *Cunninghame Graham: A Critical Biography*, Oxford University Press, Oxford 1979.

GREENE, Graham (1904–1991). See also under Mexico, Argentina and Panama. *Travels with my Aunt*, 1969 (Extract 1), is a light-hearted novel in which Henry Pulling, the narrator, ends up staying in Paraguay, after a trip up the **River Paraná** from Argentina. One of the themes is the joys of travel versus the boredom of home in suburban London. Travel abroad releases the imagination, as does story telling (one of Aunt Augusta's fortes). The narrator is a retired bachelor bank manager with a penchant for dahlias, who discovers real life through his aunt, and a new life in South America. Greene's Argentina and Paraguay are vital, unpredictable places where sudden death makes every moment of life count, as Visconti says, 'and every day you live will seem to you a kind of victory'. After years of boredom, Pulling can say 'I felt oddly elated to be alive.' Summing up his life Pulling says: 'It was as though I had escaped from an open prison . . . into my aunt's world of the unexpected character and the unforeseen event.' The novel is full of coincidences and dialogues; the plot concerns Pulling's discovery that his aunt is in fact his mother, and that she works more with the underworld than the respectable world he had known as a bank manager. In *Ways of Escape*, 1980, Greene wrote: '*Travels with my Aunt* is the only book I have written for the fun of it.'

LEWIS, Norman (see under Guatemala).

MEYER, Gordon (see under Argentina).

READ, Sir Herbert (1893–1968). Born in Yorkshire in England, after fighting in the first world war Read became a prominent art critic, and poet. His only novel, *The Green Child*, 1935 (Extract 8), is partly set in 'Roncador' (Paraguay). President Olivero returns to his childhood Yorkshire after his mock assassination in South America, still intrigued after

30 years by the Green Child. There is a confrontation, a challenge and a murder. Olivero sets off upstream with the Green Child and disappears under water. Part 2 reconstructs Olivero's South American years. After two years in a Cadiz prison, he is mistaken for a political leader in Buenos Aires, rides across the pampas to Roncador, a Guaraní-speaking republic – 'Roncador' means 'snoring' in Spanish. The name also obliquely refers to the explorer Colonel Fawcett's 'serra de Roncador', which Peter Fleming (◊ Brazil) claimed never existed. Olivero ends up a benign dictator, reviving the Jesuit ideal of organized work. He pens a new constitution. But, despite the success of this social experiment, he gets bored. Part 3 returns to Olivero and the Green Child in the subterrestrial kingdom, where the supreme science and wisdom is crystallography, and people yearn to be petrified. See James King, *The Last Modern: A Life of Herbert Read*, Weidenfeld and Nicolson, London, 1990.

ROA BASTOS, Augusto (1917–). Born in **Iturbe** on 13 June 1917, Roa Bastos left primary school to work. At 17 he joined the Paraguayan army and fought as a stretcher-bearer in the Chaco war. After the war he turned to journalism, travelled to Europe to report on the second world war, and in 1945 won a British Council scholarship to study journalism in the UK, publishing a book in 1946 on his English experience. In 1947 he exiled himself in Buenos Aires, with various jobs, from writing tangos to working as a waiter, and publishing short stories in 1953, and a novel *Hijo de hombre* in 1959 (*Son of Man*, 1965 – Extract 6) which explores the Paraguayan past through simple Paraguayan Guaraní-speaking people in a

mythic, almost lyrical way, with awful scenes about the pointless Chaco war. The main conflict in the *yerbales* (the land where the *yerba mate* shrubs grow) is between Miguel Vera, bourgeois intellectual, and Cristóbal Jara. Vera betrays the people, is unable to merge his theory with practice. The true son of man is the *pueblo*. In 1967 Roa Bastos published further short stories, and in 1974 his *Yo el supremo* (*I the Supreme*, 1986 – Extract 5), an ambitious novel recording anonymously the Paraguayan dictator Gaspar Francia's life (he ruled from 1814 to 1840), with documents, letters, fragments, and Francia's own punning mind-flow. Francia closed Paraguay off, decimated the Spaniards and created a self-sufficient economy, saving the country from being divided up by Brazil and Argentina. He was an astronomer, a bachelor, and admired by Thomas Carlyle. The novel recreates the totality of his life via monologue and contradiction that Roa Bastos called 'counter-history'. He incorporated Guaraní terms, and altered Spanish syntax to catch his country's bilingual status. The military coup in Argentina in 1976 forced Roa Bastos to move to Toulouse University. In 1989 he was able to return to Paraguay after General Stroessner had been ousted by Andrés Rodriguez.

VOLTAIRE, (1694–1778). Voltaire, whose real name was François-Marie Arouet, was born in Paris, where he also died. He was imprisoned in the Bastille, exiled in England, and fought over the issues of his age with wit and style. Late in his life he published Candide, 1759 (Extract 9), a picaresque account of Candide's coming to terms with reality after having been brainwashed by Dr Pangloss. The narrative is packed with sudden catastrophes, and unexpected journeys. Voltaire mocks the priests – and Pangloss – who have caught syphilis, which apparently originated in Latin America. Candide embarks from Cadiz for the New World and there hears about the Jesuits who had just been expelled by the Spanish Crown in 1767. Candide travels to Paraguay, on to Surinam (discovers slavery), and then to Cayenne in French Guiana where the myth of El Dorado is explained. Candide realizes that the new world is no better than the old, and returns. At the end, Pangloss's optimism is dead in Candide who has learnt to cultivate his own garden, avoid dullness, and engage in work to find happiness. Voltaire had approved of the Jesuit experiment as 'the highest degree of civilization' attained in all the New World.

WILDING, Michael (1943–). Born in Worcester, England, Wilding took up a teaching post at the University of Sydney in 1969, after graduating from Oxford. He is a short story writer, and champion of experimental fiction in Australia. He has written several novels, including his documentary novel The Paraguayan Experiment, 1985 (Extract 3), based entirely on archival material, down to the dialogues, about a group of Australian utopian socialists who emigrated to Paraguay in 1893 and set up their colony from scratch five leagues from **Villarica**. The novel charts their reason for leaving Australia, their arrival in Paraguay, to the break-up, due to alcohol, Guaraní women, and ideological clashes between the austere, teetotalism of the leader and his rivals.

CHILE

'The Chilean lives / amid trash and tempest, obscure / offspring of the harsh Homeland.'
Pablo Neruda, Canto General

Chile, or the República de Chile, could have derived its name from a chieftain, or a district. It means 'cold' in Quechua, or 'the Earth's best'. It has long borders along the high Andes with Argentina, and at the north with Peru and Bolivia. Nowhere is Chile wider than 180 km and it is 4260 km long. 756 945 sq km of territory held a population of 13.2 million in 1988. The capital is **Santiago**, founded in 1541 by Pedro de Valdivia, and today one of the smoggiest cities in the world. Other large industrialized cities include **Valparaíso** and **Concepción**. The majority of Chileans (66%) live in urban centres. Nicanor Parra ◊, black-humoured anti-poet, mocks these national barriers in 'The Borders of Chile' (Extract 1).

Benjamín Subercaseaux (1902–73) has written an essay defining Chile's relationship to its geography as *Chile: a Geographical Extravaganza*, 1971, though the Spanish title was *'loca'*, a mad geography. Despite this, it can be divided into three areas. The northern area, including the **Atacama desert**, is one of the driest in the world, where at **Iquique** over a period of 21 years only 1.52 mm of rain fell. This desert area has played a crucial part in Chile's rise from a forgotten, gold-less colony to one of the most stable countries of Latin America at the turn of the twentieth century. The first mineral discovery was nitrate, used as a fertilizer, for gunpowder and iodine. This desert mining was developed by English capital, with the help especially of a John Thomas North, the 'Nitrate King', who became fabulously wealthy, and who never learnt Spanish.

It was over who owned these deserts that an efficient Chilean navy declared war on Bolivia and Peru, the War of the Pacific in 1879–83, in which Chile won **Arica**, and Bolivia lost access to the sea. Nitrates from Chile enriched the upper class, but did little for the miners – as

Pablo Neruda ◊ noted in his poem to the saltpetre workers: 'And they showed me their rations / of miserable food, / the dirt floors in their homes, / the sun, the dust, the bedbugs, / and the immense solitude.' However, in the 1930s synthetic nitrates finished off this lucrative business. In Thornton Wilder's ◊ novel *The Eighth Day*, 1967, John Ashley, on the run from a murder he did not commit, works as an engineer on a mine in Chile, and notices how badly the Indians are treated. In 1911, in the same Atacama desert area, copper began to be mined with American capital creating the mine El Teniente. The three principal mines were US-owned, and over the century the threat of their nationalization by the left was continuous, so much capital did they syphon out.

The middle area of Chile is the **Mediterranean** area, where 90% of Chile's population live, and where its main cities are situated. This lowland region between the Andes chain and the coastal chain, is primarily agricultural, with cattle and famous vineyards. This is the land of the *fundos* or large estates inherited from the Spaniards and their system of *mayorazgo* (eldest son gets all) to ensure land remained in the same family. It is said that 600 Chileans owned 60% of the land. No land reform was carried out until 1962 under Alessandri, and then tepidly, until Dr Salvador Allende was elected in 1970. The handing over of the land to the *inquilinos* (tenants and farm workers) forms an important moment in Isabel Allende's ◊ first novel *La casa de los espíritus*, 1982 (*The House of the Spirits*, 1985 – Extract 2) when the landowning conservative patriarch Trueba returns to his *fundo* Las Tres Marías to find it no longer his.

The southern area of Chile begins at the **Bío-Bío River** in what is known as **La Frontera**, for until the 1880s this area belonged to the Araucanian, or, as they are known today, Mapuche Indians. This area of dense forests, with high rainfall, fiords, glaciers and conical volcanic peaks, contains small farms, German immigrant communities, especially in **Valdivia** and **Temuco** (near where poet Pablo Neruda was born). There are coal mines (in the **Lebu peninsula**) whose suffering miners have been recorded by Baldomero Lillo (1867–1923) in his untranslated novels *Sub terra*, 1904, and *Sub sole*, 1907. Fishing is very important (fish is a favourite of the Chilean diet), as are lumber and oil in **Tierra del Fuego**. But the climate is terrible.

A good description of the southern area, especially **Chiloé**, can be read in Darwin's (◊ Uruguay) *Voyage of the Beagle*. When Darwin visited **Concepción** there had just been a massive earthquake, another factor in Chile's 'mad' geography. Nancy Phelan also writes engagingly about this area in her *The Chilean Way*, 1974.

Pablo Neruda

Colonialism to Stable Independence

Chile is a *mestizo* country, with some 2% of Mapuche Indians. Through the nineteenth century there was a controlled immigration policy that favoured Germans, as I have noted. The Mapuche (Aracaunians) were fierce warriors who fended off the Spaniards. After Diego de Alvarado's abortive attempt to find gold in Chile in 1536–37, it was Pedro de Valdivia who conquered the country in 1540, but he was captured by the Mapuche, and lost his head – see Cunninghame Graham's (◊ Paraguay) 1926 biography. Alonso de Ercilla (1533–94), who fought for the Spaniards, wrote his epic poem in praise of these Indians, especially their leader Lautaro in *La Araucana* (1569–89, translated as *The Araucaniad*, 1945). Lautaro was one of Pablo Neruda's heroes in 1950 as he retells the story of the frustrated Spanish conquest of Chile. Lautaro, one of the first guerrilla leaders in the New World, apparently ate Valdivia's heart: 'Then we shared the bleeding heart. / I sank my teeth into that corolla, / fulfilling the rites of the earth'.

The **Bío Bío River** remained a frontier as the rest of Chile, then 'Nuevo Toledo', became a poor Spanish colony, with no gold. It was forced to develop agriculturally, and large tracts of land were handed out. After the French invasion of Spain (1808), following all the other Spanish colonies, there was a *cabildo abierto* (open town council) on 18

September 1810 that for the next three years set out a plan for independence, lifting trading restrictions, talking about abolishing slavery, opening newspapers, etc. Spain reconquered this colony in 1814, and it was Chilean exiles in Argentina, led by Bernardo O'Higgins who joined San Martín's army, crossed the Andes and liberated their country at **Chacabuco** in 1817 as San Martín proceeded north to meet Bolívar. O'Higgins remained as Director until 1823. Over the nineteenth century, without going into names and details, there was a battle between the two parties, the Catholic, land-owning conservatives (*pelucones*), and the reformist liberals (*pipiolos*). There were outbreaks of violence (in 1829) and a long period of conservative rule until 1861. But Chile was becoming rich through stability.

The country became a cultural haven. In 1829, a president called Diego Portales invited in the Venezuelan scholar and grammarian Andrés Bello (1781–1865), and he became the rector of the new **Universidad de Chile** in 1843. Bello wrote the Chilean Civil Code in 1855, a famous ode '*La agricultura de la zona tórrida*' in 1826, urging the young American nations to turn to work on the land, and a famous *Grámatica de la lengua castellana*, 1847. He also had a public feud with the Argentine writer and polemicist Domingo Sarmiento (◊ Argentina), then in exile in Chile from dictator Rosas in Argentina, who wrote his diatribe *Facundo* in **Santiago** in 1840. Claudio Gay, a French naturalist, was another invited in to Chile. From 1861 to 1891, the liberals ruled. It was during the radical, anti-British José Manuel Balmaceda's presidency that the young Nicaraguan poet Rubén Darío (◊ Nicaragua) chose to visit the cultural Mecca of Latin America and launch his revolutionary book *Azul* in **Santiago** in 1888. That same year Chile annexed Easter Island, some 3700 km away.

Over the nineteenth century, Chile had acquired territory in the north, islands in the Pacific and settled, with Edward VII's arbitration, a border dispute with Argentina (which in the 1980s nearly led to another war). A 'Christ of the Andes' was erected in 1902, made from a gun, to commemorate this agreement, and celebrated in a poem by the English poet Francis Berry (1915–) in *The Iron Christ*, 1938.

THE CHALLENGE FROM THE LEFT

However, despite this capitalistic rise, little was done for the workers, the poor, the *rotos*. In 1912, the socialist Labour Party was founded, and strikes and violent suppression of strikes began. Following the depression, there was a Popular Front candidate elected in 1938, but President Aguire Cerda died in 1941 before he could put his policies into practice. In 1948 the Chilean Communist Party voted for González Videla who was elected, and turned on it and banned the party. In his memoirs Pablo Neruda, a party member from 1945 until his death, described how he was forced underground, and crossed out of Chile over the Andes incognito. Videla was a 'traitor' and looms large in Neruda's *Canto General*, 1950. During the 1950s and 1960s, not enough was done to assuage the left, despite Frei's centrist government, and in 1970 Dr Salvador Allende was elected as the first Marxist ever to take power democratically. It was a euphoric moment for the left round the world, for Allende had many intellectual friends, from García Márquez (◊ Colombia), who swore that he would not write another novel till Pinochet fell, to Julio Cortázar (◊ Argentina). The period from 1970 to the final coup on 11 September 1973, after US-financed strikes and demonstrations, has been chronicled in many Chilean novels, from Isabel Allende's *The House of the Spirits*, to Ariel Dorfman's (1942–) *Hard Rain*, 1990, to those of Fernando Alegría ◊ and Antonio Skármeta ◊. General Pinochet remained in power after rounding up and exiling his opponents, leaving some 2500 'disappeareds' until he offered a plebiscite, thinking himself popular enough to survive, and lost, letting in the current president, Patricio Aylwin, in 1989. During the years of the dictatorship, Chile had become a model for the Chicago school economic theory, with low inflation and no debt.

Relating public events, or geographical considerations, to Chilean literature in no way includes all of Chile's writers, especially a strong and exciting poetic tradition that would include, among many others, Vicente Huidobro (1893–1948) and Gabriela Mistral (1889–1957), Nobel prize winner, whose **Elqui Valley** birthplace is a small museum, while at **Vicuña** there is the **Museo Gabriela Mistral**. See *Poets of Chile: A Bilingual Anthology, 1965–1985*, 1986, and *Chile: An Anthology of New Writing*, 1968. However, it is fair to claim that the inner history of Chilean life has been chronicled by José Donoso ◊ from his earliest novels in the 1950s, and by Jorge Edwards in his stories and novels. Tony Gould's *Death in Chile*, 1992, is a travelogue in quest of a dead writer friend, Cristián Huneeus, with interviews with Donoso, Parra and Edwards.

It was on the Chilean island of **Juan Fernández**, 1050 km off Valparaíso, that Alexander Selkirk, model for Defoe's Robinson Crusoe, was marooned from 1861 to 1864. **Easter Island**, 3790 km off Chile, also still belongs to it. Its mysteries were made famous by Norwegian explorer Thor Heyerdahl in 1955. Pablo Neruda wrote a wonderful posthumously published book, *La rosa separada*, 1973 (*The Separate Rose*, 1985) about the island.

BOOKLIST

The following selection includes all titles which are extracted in this chapter as well as those mentioned in the introduction which are available in English. In general, paperback editions are given when possible. The editions cited are not necessarily the only ones available. For most of the extracted works, the original publisher in English can be found in 'Acknowledgments and Citations' at the end of the volume, as can the exact location of the extracts and the editions from which they are taken. The date in square brackets is the original publication date of the work in its original language. Extract numbers are highlighted in bold for ease of reference.

Alegría, Fernando, *The Chilean Spring* [1975], Stephen Fredman, trans, Latin American Literary Review Press, Pittsburgh, PA, 1980. **Extract 6.**

Allende, Isabel, *The House of the Spirits* [1982], Magda Bogin, trans, Jonathan Cape, London, 1985/Knopf, New York, 1985. **Extract 2.**

Allende, Isabel, *Of Love and Shadows* [1984], Margaret Sayers Peden, trans, Black Swan, London, 1988/Knopf, New York, 1987. **Extract 4.**

Berry, Francis, *The Iron Christ*, Williams and Norgate, London, 1938.

Chile: An Anthology of New Writing, Miller Williams, ed, Kent State University Press, Kent, OH, 1968.

Darwin, Charles, *Voyage of the Beagle* [1839], Penguin, London, 1989.

Donoso, José, *Curfew* [1986], Alfred MacAdam, trans, Picador, London, 1990/Weidenfeld and Nicolson, New York, 1988. **Extract 7.**

Dorfman, Ariel, *Hard Rain*, Readers International, London, 1990.

Ercilla, Alonso de, *The Araucaniad* [1569–89], translated and published by Walter Owen, Buenos Aires, 1945.

Gould, Tony, *Death in Chile: A Memoir and a Journey*, Picador, London, 1992.

Huidobro, Vicente, *The Selected Poetry of Vicente Huidobro*, David Guss, ed, New Directions, New York, 1981.

Mistral, Gabriela, *Selected Poems of Gabriela Mistral*, Doris Dana, ed, Johns Hopkins University Press, Baltimore, MD, 1971.

Neruda, Pablo, *Canto General* [1950], Jack Schmitt, trans, University of California Press, Berkeley, CA, 1991. **Extract 9.**

Neruda, Pablo, 'A Pine-Cone, A Toy Sheep', Ben Belitt, trans, in *The Eye of the Heart*, Barbara Howes, ed, Allison and Busby, London, 1987. **Extract 8.**

Neruda, Pablo, *The Separate Rose* [1973], William O'Daley, trans, Copper Canyon Press, Port Townsend, WA, 1985.

Parra, Nicanor, 'The Borders of Chile', in *Emergency Poems*, Miller Williams, trans, Marion Boyars, London, 1977/New Directions, New York, 1972. **Extract 1.**

Phelan, Nancy, *The Chilean Way*, Travel Book Club, London, 1974.

Poets of Chile: A Bilingual Anthology 1965–1985, Steven F. White, trans, Unicorn Press, Greensboro, NC, 1986.

Saint-Exupéry, Antoine de, *Wind, Sand and Stars* [1939], Lewis Galentière, trans, Picador, London, 1987/Bantam, New York, 1945. **Extract 5.**

Skármeta, Antonio, *Burning Patience* [1985], Katherine Silver, trans,

Methuen, London, 1988/Panth-
eon, New York, 1987. **Extract 3.**
Subercaseaux, Benjamín, *Chile: A
Geographical Extravaganza* [1940],
Angel Flores, trans, Hafner, New

York, 1971.
Wilder, Thornton, *The Eighth Day*
[1967], Penguin, London, 1968/
Carroll and Graf, New York
1987.

Extracts

(1) CHILE: BARRIERS

Nicanor Parra, *The Borders of Chile*

*Poet Nicanor Parra's ironic prose-poem changes natural barriers
into political ones.*

It's not true that Chile is bordered by the Andes, by the Saltpeter
Desert, by the Pacific Ocean, by the meeting of two oceans: it's just the
opposite. It's the Andes that are bordered by Chile, it's the Pacific that
reaches the rim of Aconcagua.[1] It's the 2 oceans that break the
monotony of the south country into a thousand pieces. The Valdivia
River is the longest lake in Chile. Chile is bordered on the North by
the Fire Brigade, on the South by the Education Department, on the
East by the Nahuelbuta Range, and on the West by the emptiness that
makes the waves of the Ocean named above, on the South by González
Videla.[2] In the middle is a great cowpile surrounded by soldiers, priests
and education majors who souken[3] it up through copper water pipes.

[1]The largest volcano in Chile [translator's note]
[2]An ex-president of Chile. Elected by the left, he turned against them once he
was in office and forced a number of leaders of the left – including Neruda –
into exile. [translator's note]
[3]suck [translator's note]

(2) CHILE: COUNTRYSIDE AND DESERT

Isabel Allende, *The House of the Spirits*

Trueba, the patriarch, and sometimes narrator of Allende's first best-selling novel is a macho with a vile temper. He travels to his family's abandoned fundo on his way to restoring it and becoming head of one of Chile's richest families before the farm, Las Tres Marías, is expropriated by Salvador Allende's land reform.

Through the window of the train he watched the passing landscape of the central valley. Vast fields stretched from the foot of the mountain range, a fertile countryside filled with vineyards, wheatfields, alfalfa, and marigolds. He compared it with the sterile plateaus of the North, where he had spent two years stuck in a hole in the midst of a rough and lunar horizon whose terrifying beauty never ceased to interest him. He had been fascinated by the colors of the desert, the blues, the purples, the yellows of the minerals lying on the surface of the earth.

'My life is changing,' he said softly. He closed his eyes and fell asleep.

He got off the train at the station of San Lucas. It was a wretched place. At that hour of the morning there was not a soul on the wooden platform, its roof eaten away by inclement weather and ants. From where he stood he could see the whole valley through an impalpable mist that rose from the earth the night rain had soaked. The distant mountains disappeared behind clouds of a shrouded sky; only the snowy peak of the volcano could be seen in all its clarity, outlined against the landscape and lit by a timid winter sun. He looked around him . . . He combed the landscape for the town of San Lucas, but was only able to make out a far-off hamlet that was faded in the dampness of the morning.

(3) ISLA NEGRA

Antonio Skármeta, *Burning Patience*

Skármeta's young postman, who has seduced the innkeeper's daughter by quoting Neruda's love poetry, is witness to Neruda's illness at his coastal house at Isla Negra (not an island), and house arrest, as President Allende falls to General Pinochet.

In the area immediately surrounding Neruda's house, a group of soldiers had set up a barricade, and further away the roving lights of a military convoy flashed silently. It rained gently: a cold coastal drizzle more bothersome than wet. The postman took a short cut to the top of the hill. Keeping close to the ground, he surveyed the situation from there:

the poet's street was blocked from the north, and three recruits were watching the house from the area near the bakery. Everyone passing along this stretch of road was subject to search. In what seemed to be a relief from the tedium of patrolling an insignificant hamlet rather than an attempt to rout out subversive elements, the soldiers minutely examined every single document in people's wallets, and everyone carrying a bag was politely asked to reveal its contents one at a time: detergent, a package of needles, a box of tea, apples, a kilo of potatoes. They were then ushered on with a bored wave of the hand. In spite of the newness of the situation, the soldiers' behaviour seemed to Mario somehow strangely routine. The young enlisted men stood at attention and sped up their searches only when, from time to time, a lieutenant with a moustache and a threatening, booming voice would stop by.

Mario scrutinized these activities and manoeuvres until noon, when he climbed cautiously down the hill. Leaving his scooter behind, he made his way to the piers by taking an enormous detour behind the fishermen's huts. Barefoot, he slipped along under the shadows of the cliffs until he arrived at the beach in front of Neruda's house.

He stashed his bag in a cave behind a sharp-edged rock close to the dunes, and as prudently as possible, given the low, frequent flights of a helicopter scouting the shoreline, he rolled out the sheets of telegrams. For the next hour, he read them over carefully. When he had finished, he crumpled up the paper and hid it under a rock. The path leading up to the bell tower was short, but very steep. His advance was continually checked by the appearance of aeroplanes and helicopters that had already sent the seagulls and pelicans into exile. Their propellors allowed the helicopters to remain suspended in the air above the bard's house with such ease, they seemed like voracious beasts smelling something out.

(4) LONQUEN

Isabel Allende, *Of Love and Shadows*

An abandoned mine contains the bodies of murdered civilians (based on a real-life incident at Lonquen – see biographical entry). Allende describes the horror of her two protagonists as they begin to uncover the crime.

They piled up the stones they had removed, and closed the entrance, stunned, nervous, working with frenzy; it was as if in sealing the mine they could erase its contents from their minds and turn time back to the moment before they had known the truth; as if they could again live innocently in a radiant reality, removed from that awful discovery.

Francisco took Irene by the hand and led her to the ruined hut, the only visible refuge on the hill.

It was a mild night. In the virginal light, the landscape faded into nothingness, the outlines of the hills and the great shadowy eucalyptus trees disappeared. The shack was barely visible in the soft darkness, rising from the ground like an extension of nature. In comparison with the mine, the interior seemed as welcoming as a nest. They lay down in a corner on the wild grass and stared up at the infinity of the starry sky lighted by a milky moon. Irene put her head on Francisco's shoulder and released her distress in tears. He put his arm around her and they lay there a long time – hours, perhaps – seeking solace in the quiet and silence for what they had discovered, and strength for what they would have to bear. They rested together, listening to the faint murmur of leaves stirred by the breeze, the cries of nearby night birds, and the secret movement of rabbits in the meadow grass.

(5) Punta Arenas

Antoine de Saint-Exupéry, *Wind, Sand and Stars*

Saint-Exupéry describes southern Chile from his mail flying days, reaching Punta Arenas, Chile's most southerly city.

The pilot flying towards the Straits of Magellan sees below him, a little to the south of the Gallego River, an ancient lava flow, an erupted waste of a thickness of sixty feet that crushes down the plain on which it has congealed. Farther south he meets a second flow, then a third; and thereafter every hump on the globe, every mound a few hundred feet high, carries a crater in its flank. No Vesuvius rises up to reign in the clouds; merely, flat on the plain, a succession of gaping howitzer mouths.

This day, as I fly, the lava world is calm. There is something surprising in the tranquility of this deserted landscape where once a thousand volcanoes boomed to each other in their great subterranean organs and spat forth their fire. I fly over a world mute and abandoned, strewn with black glaciers.

South of these glaciers there are yet older volcanoes veiled with the passing of time in a golden sward. Here and there a tree rises out of a crevice like a plant out of a cracked pot. In the soft and yellow light the plain appears as luxuriant as a garden; the short grass seems to civilize it, and round its giant throats there is scarcely a swelling to be seen. A hare scampers off; a bird wheels in the air; life has taken possession of a new planet where the decent loam of our earth has at last spread over the surface of the star.

Finally, crossing the line into Chile, a little north of Punta Arenas, you come to the last of the craters, and here the mouths have been stopped with earth. A silky turf lies snug over the curves of the volcanoes, and all is suavity in the scene. Each fissure in the crust is sutured up by this tender flax. The earth is smooth, the slopes are gentle; one forgets the travail that gave them birth. The turf effaces from the flanks of the hillocks the sombre sign of their origin.

We have reached the most southerly habitation of the world, a town born of the chance presence of a little mud between the timeless lava and the austral ice. So near the black scoria, how thrilling it is to feel the miraculous nature of man!

(6) SANTIAGO

Fernando Alegría, *The Chilean Spring*

Alegría's narrating photographer describes the coup in Santiago that led to Allende's suicide in his palace, La Moneda, in 1973.

I returned to the Alameda and retraced my steps. The center of town was an armed camp. Some planes flew over. A helicopter went back and forth at great speed firing at the roofs of the Ministries. In the Alameda the traffic of armored vehicles, jeeps and military trucks kept up. Obviously the *Carabineros* were collaborating with the military, and together they were closing a pincer movement around La Moneda. I continued to walk casually and took pictures without anyone objecting. The soldiers and the police stared straight ahead and their faces disappeared into the metal circles of their helmets. They gave the impression of a military parade of combat uniforms. But near Santa Lucía that sensation changed. Now I felt that the enveloping movement came from very far away and was opening like a steel fan, embracing streets and avenues, from Americo Vespucio, Avenida Matta, Cerrillos Station and further away, closing the arc from the Panamerican highway, a green invasion, fast and efficient, against the gray sky, artillery, tanks, bayonets, a plodding movement over wet pavements, past shut-up buildings and houses, through the silent country, barely noticing the distant shining jets, keeping time with the boring rhythm of marches on the radio, searching out the bursts of machine gun and small weapons fire, but without ever seeing anyone, just uniforms advancing, because everyone had gone and Santiago was an open city, ready to disintegrate in a cloud of adobe and plaster dust.

(7) Santiago

José Donoso, *Curfew*

Donoso describes Santiago's Bellavista district where Matilde Urrutia, Neruda's widow, lived (La Chascona, now the Pablo Neruda Foundation), and where the folk-singing protagonist goes for her funeral.

Until quite recently, Bellavista looked like a quiet peasant village forgotten in the middle of Santiago, separated from the city by Forestal Park and the Mapocho river, cut off five blocks to the north by the hill with its ancient, rusty funicular railway. A curtained window facing the street, a door, two windows, another door, an alley, an occasional two-story house with a wooden balcony, a railing, or a widow's walk, tile roofs, painted columns, a palm tree standing erect behind a tenement, not particularly venerable trees lining the sidewalks, a domestic neighborhood of corner stores where cats nap on stacks of newspaper used to wrap candy or bread, a neighborhood that up until a short time ago offered no spectacle more exciting than the funeral processions that cross it from the east heading for the cemeteries behind San Cristóbal hill. Five years ago, Bellavista seemed immersed in the anachronistic anorexia of oblivion. The government, at that time, favored a different style, opulent and new, and Santiago was decorated with crystallized structures commanding panoramic views, to house a thousand blond families, a thousand hypothetical stores, a thousand dentists, a thousand unisex barbers, and when that megalomaniac dream suddenly dissolved, the buildings were abandoned on their never-completed avenues, dinosaurs from another paleontological period, discarded from a sinister papier-mâché operetta.

Reacting, in part, to that failure, a certain number of young people who had gone back to wearing long hair and beards began to take serious notice of the pleasant neighborhood of Bellavista: it was cheap, it was downtown, it was old without being oppressively ancient or museumlike. The houses, with their human dimensions, announced the survival of simple pleasures, of life without tension. In the afternoon, one neighborhood lady or another would drag her wicker chair out to the front door and sit waving to lifelong friends, and in the glow of the streetlights girls would play hopscotch in the street.

Some houses were discreetly restored. Stores appeared with modest pretensions about being 'different'. Young people walked the streets with musical scores and manuscripts under their arms, and long-skirted girls with hennaed hair attended happenings or trysts in tenements that aspired to be the Chilean Bateau-Lavoir, or dined at restaurants a bit more chic and a bit more expensive than their earlier avatars, or were measured for vests in weavers' shops.

Don Celedonio Villanueva, an erstwhile denizen of Montparnasse, used to visit the surrealist painter Camilo Mori and his wife, Maruja, in their studio when Mori was setting it up forty years ago, in the ornate little plaza that resembled a Disneyland interpretation of one of King Ludwig's castles. He declared he'd known for a long time this would be Bellavista's destiny. But Don Celedonio always 'knew' things beforehand. It was impossible to surprise him with predictions, or news of a political or social nature, or even with the title of a book he'd not read. The neighborhood's destiny seemed complete to him when Pablo Neruda moved into the most secluded house on a tortuously discreet cul-de-sac.

Neruda was a great inventor of geography: Isla Negra, which many suspected would never have existed without him; a Valparaíso that was completely his, which he superimposed onto the real city, erasing all other possible Valparaísos; a Temuco where it rained as it had never rained in Temuco; the violet sunsets of Maruri Street; the yellow mimosas of the Loncoche fields – and you ended up making the boring trip to Loncoche, where of course there were no more mimosas, so *ça ne valait pas vraiment le coup*, thundered Don Celedonio. Even this America to which Neruda's marvelous poetry has condemned us is more Nerudian than real – which, by the way, was what made it interesting.

People were destined sooner or later to follow Neruda to Bellavista – an ugly neighborhood, according to Don Celedonio.

(8) Temuco

Pablo Neruda, *A Pine-Cone, a Toy Sheep*

Neruda remembers Temuco, today capital of the Araucanía region, with some 220 000 inhabitants, where he went to school. Temuco is in southern Chile. This story is included in the anthology Eye of the Heart – see Booklist.

In the schoolhouse, the cold was glacial. Forty years ago, I sat quaking with cold, just as the boys in the new Liceo de Temuco do to this day. They have built a grand modern structure with large windows and no heating facilities: that's life for you, out on the frontier! We made men of ourselves in my day. There was plenty of reason to. Southern houses are all ramshackle, hastily clapped together out of freshly cut boards, with zinc roofing. Incessant great rainfalls made music on the roofs. Then, one fine morning a house facing the front would awake to find itself roofless: wind had carried it off two hundred meters. The streets were great quagmires; everywhere wagons fouled on the road. On the footpaths, picking our way from boulder to boulder, we slogged towards the school-house in the rain and the cold. Our umbrellas spun away on the wind. Raincoats were costly, shoes were soon waterlogged; gloves I despised. I shall never forget all the drenched stockings close to the braziers, the multitude of shoes sending up steam like small locomotives. Later, the floods came, sweeping away whole settlements – the most wretched of all, those who lived closest to the river. The earth rocked with tremblors. Sometimes on the highest ranges of all a plume of terrible light stood up: the Llaima volcano was active again.

And worst of all, fires. In 1906 or '07, I don't recall which, all Temuco went up in a holocaust. Houses blazed like match boxes; twenty-two street blocks were razed to the ground; nothing was left. But if there is one thing Southerners know how to build in a hurry, it is houses. They don't build for the ages; but they build. A man who has lived in the South all his life must expect to live through three or four holocausts. I remember myself first as a child planted on blankets in front of the house, watching it blaze for the second or third time.

But the saws sang. Timber was piled in the station again; there was a tang of fresh boards in the villages.

(9) VALPARAISO

Pablo Neruda, *Canto General*

Valparaíso, where Neruda had one of his three homes (La Sebastiana) in Chile, was one of the great ports of the world before the building of the Panama Canal. He describes it in this passage from his epic poem.

> It was the dawning of saltpeter on the pampas.
> The fertilizer's planet palpitated
> until Chile was filled like a ship
> of snowy holds.
> Today I behold whatever remained of all those
> who passed leaving no tracks
> in the Pacific's sands.
> Behold what I behold,
> the sullen detritus
> that the shower of gold left on my country's
> throat, like a necklace of pus.
> Wayfarer, may you be accompanied
> by this steadfast piercing stare,
> bound to Valparaíso's sky.

The Chilean lives
amid trash and tempest, obscure
offspring of the harsh Homeland.
Shattered glass, broken roofs,
obliterated walls, leprous quicklime,
buried door, dirt floor, barely clinging
to the vestige of the ground.
Valparaíso, filthy rose,
pestilential marine sarcophagus!
Don't wound me with your spiny streets,
with your crown of bitter alleyways,
don't let me see the child wounded
by your mortal swamp's misery!
You make me grieve for my people,
all my American homeland,
all that they've gnawed from your bones,
deserting you, girdled by the foam
like a miserable mangled goddess
on whose sweet broken breast
the famished dogs urinate.

Biographies and plot summaries

ALEGRIA, Fernando (1918–). Born in Chile on 26 September 1918, Alegría obtained his doctorate in Romance Linguistics. From the 1940s he lived in the USA – teaching at Berkeley 1947–67 and Stanford 1967–87. He was Cultural Attaché to Salvador Allende's government in 1970 in Washington, and resigned in 1973. Several of his novels have appeared in English, including *Lautaro, joven libertador del Arauco*, 1943 (*Lautaro*, 1944); a novel for younger readers, *Caballo de copas*, 1958 (*My Horse González*, 1964); and *The Funhouse*, 1984. His poems have been translated in *Changing Centuries: Selected Poems*, 1984, and *Instructions for Undressing the Human Race*, 1984. *El paso de los gansos*, 1975 (*The Chilean Spring*, 1980 – Extract 6) fictionalizes a photographer called Cristián and his experiences during the coup led by Pinochet which resulted in what appeared to be the murder of elected president Salvador Allende in September 1973. Alegría uses the observing photographer in the city (someone who actually existed), studies his family relationships and generational differences, and describes how he is slowly drawn from his American exile into an ethical/ political opposition. Alegría was in Chile at the time, interviewing Allende.

In 1992, Alegría published *Allende: A Novel*.

ALLENDE, Isabel (1942–). Allende was born in Lima on 2 August, but is Chilean. She was brought up by her mother, who early on gave her a notebook, in which Isabel Allende began writing. Her stepfather was a diplomat, so she grew up travelling round the world (Bolivia, the Middle East, including an English boarding school). She is a distant relation of Salvador Allende, Chile's socialist president. Marrying at 19, she worked as a journalist, and in television, before writing her first novel *La casa de los espíritus*, 1982 (*The House of the Spirits*, 1985 – Extract 2). This is a dynastic novel, centred on a land-owning Conservative tyrant Esteban Trueba and his strange, intuitive, and spiritualist wife Clara, with their daughter Blanca and grandchild Alba, and ending up with the murder of Salvador Allende and Pinochet's dirty dictatorship. The story is written from the woman's point of view (with fragments narrated by Trueba) in a style at times derivative of García Márquez, but compulsively readable, that brings in an abortion, love scenes between Blanca and folk-singing lefty Pedro Tercero García, severed heads, green hair, gay French counts, and much else. In 1984, Allende published *De amor y de sombra* (*Of Love and Shadows*, 1987 – Extract 4) dealing with the horrors of the Pinochet government and a crime of 1973 which occurred in **Lonquen** – 15 rural workers were shot and buried in an abandoned mine. Irene, a journalist, drops her boyfriend, an officer, for a photographer in opposition to the régime as they investigate the political murder of a young girl, fall in love, and escape the country. See under Venezuela for *Eva Luna*, and *Stories of Eva Luna*. Her fourth novel *El plan infinito*, 1991, was set in the USA. Allende currently lives in San Francisco with her second husband.

DONOSO, José (1924–). Born in **Santiago** on 5 October 1924 into a family of doctors and lawyers. He spent a year as a shepherd in **Magallanes**, and graduated from the **Universidad de Chile** and Princeton in 1951. He has lectured on English literature, edited the magazine *Ercilla* for four years, spent two years at the Iowa University Writer's workshop, and in 1968 he won the coveted Guggenheim. He went to live in Spain in 1967, and returned to Chile in 1981, with Pinochet still in power. His first novel was *Coronación*, 1957 (*Coronation*, 1965), followed by *Este domingo*, 1966 (*This Sunday*, 1967). Both are critical, realist novels of his bourgeois Chilean background. Then came *El lugar sin límites*, 1966 (*Hell has no Limits*, 1973), a taut novel about a transvestite and his daughter in a brothel, a study of machismo and emotion, set in the vineyards of central Chile. This was followed by *El obsceno pájaro de la noche*, 1970 (*The Obscene Bird of Night*, 1973), a bizarre exploration of madness and old age narrated by a schizophrenic writer. In *Casa de campo*, 1978 (*A House in the Country*, 1983), children are locked up in a house with sadistic servants. *La desesperanza*, 1986 (*Curfew*, 1988 – Extract 7) is set in **Santiago** under Pinochet, with Mañugo Vera, famous folk singer, returning for the funeral of Neruda's widow (Matilde Urrutia). He meets Judit Fox, a revolutionary from the obligarchy, an old flame, and begins a new affair. It is a novel about Vera's reintegration into Chilean local politics, with its curfews, and loss of privacy, rather than hiding comfortably in Europe. Donoso has also written short stories and novellas, including *Cuatro para Delfina*, 1982, four short novels exploring Pinochet's Chile with a common background of *nouveau-riche* businessmen, world recession, and cultural isolation. Donoso excels at satire, and

Isabel Allende

telling stories linking people to place and class through dialogue. He also wrote an amusing testimony of the Latin American literary revival or boom of the 1960s, *Historia personal del boom*, 1972 (*The Boom in Spanish American Literature: A Personal History*, 1977).

NERUDA, Pablo (1904–73). Neruda was born Ricardo Neftalí Reyes in **Parral**, central Chile, on 12 July 1904, son of a railway worker. His mother died a month after giving birth, and he grew up in **Temuco**. His solitary childhood in the local, damp woods has been evoked in his *Memoirs*, 1976. He adopted the pseudonym Neruda from a nineteenth century Czech writer. He published his first poems in 1919, collected in a book in 1921, the year he moved to **Santiago** to study to be a teacher of French. In **Santiago** he published *Veinte poemas de amor y una canción desesperada*, 1924 (*Twenty Love Poems and a Song of Despair*, 1969), nostalgi-

cally recalling two women in the wild nature of his provinces in mildly erotic imagery. By 1965 this book had gone into 67 editions, and sold over a million copies.

In 1925–26 Neruda lived in the south at **Ancud**. In June 1927 he was appointed honorary consul in Rangoon, Burma. In 1928 he moved to Colombo, Ceylon (Sri Lanka) and from 1930–32 was in Batavia, Java, where he married a Javanese woman, and had a daughter. During this isolated and lonely period of his life, Neruda wrote his most original poetry in *Residencia en la tierra*, 1935 (*Residence on Earth*, 1973). After a brief return to Chile in 1932, and meeting Federico García Lorca in Buenos Aires, Neruda was appointed Chilean consul in Barcelona in 1934, and then in Madrid in 1935. Here he edited a literary magazine, *Caballo verde para la poesía*, and befriended many of Spain's best poets. When the Spanish Civil War broke out he organized the Cultural Congresses in Valencia and Madrid in 1937, and in

Paris was Consul for Spanish emigration. He became involved with his second wife, Delia del Carril, in 1936. He was then appointed Consul General in Mexico in 1940–43, and became a close friend to Diego Rivera and other Mexican muralists. He changed his poetry to reflect the tragedy of Spain.

In 1943, on his way home, Neruda visited the Incan ruins of Machu-Picchu, and wrote *Alturas de Macchu Picchu* in 1945 (*The Heights of Macchu Picchu*, 1967). That same year, 1945, he was elected as a Communist Senator in Chile, and won the Premio Nacional de Literatura. For the rest of his life, Neruda was a party member. In 1951 he won the Lenin Peace Prize. In 1947 he and his party helped González Videla to presidency; Videla then turned against Neruda, who went into hiding, and escaped out of Chile incognito. This led to his uneven and ambitious rewriting of Latin American history and geography from his Marxist perspective in his *Canto*

general, 1950 (*Canto General*, 1991 – Extract 9). Interestingly, Che Guevera had a copy of this Latin American song in his rucksack when he was killed in Bolivia in 1967. In Capri in the early 1950s he met Matilde Urrutia who was to be his *compañera* for the rest of his life, and wrote his anonymous *Versos del Capitán*, 1953 (*The Captain's Verses*, 1972) for her. From the 1950s to his death Neruda wrote a succession of simple and sensual lyrics that include *Odas elementales*, 1954 (*Elemental Odes*, 1961 and *Selected Odes of Pablo Neruda*, 1990); *Estravagario*, 1958 (*Extravagaria*, 1972); *Plenos poderes*, 1962 (*Fully Empowered*, 1975); *Memorial de Isla Negra*, 1964 (*Isla Negra: A Notebook*, 1981); and many others collected singly, or in several available anthologies. He also wrote a play, and translated Shakespeare.

Neruda was hugely prolific. His complete works in Spanish ran to 3522 pages in 1975, not including eight posthumously published books.

Pablo Neruda's house 'La Chascona' in Bellavista, Santiago

Behind all Neruda wrote was a sensual cataloguing of place and people, a guiltless lovesong of things and food, that always resulted in some striking image, however uneven the poems. He was a great reader of his poems. In 1970, following the election of his friend Salvador Allende as president of Chile, Neruda, ill with cancer, was named ambassador in Paris. In 1971 he won the Nobel prize, and died in 1973, broken-hearted, twelve days after Allende. Only in 1990 were his wishes granted that the houses he bought, including **La Chascona** in **Bellavista, Santiago (F. Márquez de la Plata 0192), La Sebastiana** in **Valparaíso**, and the coast house at **Isla Negra**, be turned into a Pablo Neruda Foundation. See Manuel Durán and Margery Safir, *Earth Tones: The Poetry of Pablo Neruda*, Harvard University Press, Cambridge, MA, 1981.

PARRA, Nicanor (1914–). Born in **San Fabián de Alico** in southern Chile on 5 September 1914, Parra grew up in **Chillán** as the eldest son of a schoolteacher and seamstress mother. He came from a gifted musical family of eleven children. His sister, Violeta Parra, was one of the most exciting folk singers, and weavers, in Latin America until her suicide in 1967. He won a scholarship to a boarding school in **Santiago**, and studied maths at the **Instituto Pedagógico** of the **University of Chile**. In 1937 Parra published his first book of poems which won the Premio Municipal de Poesía in 1938, part-stimulated by Federico García Lorca. In 1938 he graduated in Mathematics and Physics, taught in a school, got married, and from 1943 to 1945 was at Brown University, Rhode Island, studying advanced mechanics. In 1948 he was appointed Director of the School of Engineering at the University of Chile, and won a British Council award to study cosmology at Oxford, where he lived until 1950. On his return to Chile in 1952, he became Professor of Theoretical Physics at the **University of Chile**. In 1954 he published his *Poemas y antipoemas*, translated into English in 1960. A more complete English version of *Poems and Antipoems* came out in 1967. Parra won the Premio Municipal in 1955. Since 1958 he has travelled extensively in Russia (in 1966 he published his translations of Russian poetry), China, Sweden and Cuba. In 1969 he collected all his poems except his first book as *Obra gruesa*, partly translated in *Emergency Poems*, 1972 (Extract 1), and also won the Premio Nacional de Literatura.

Many of Parra's prosaic, quirky, black-humoured antipoems develop out of classroom and teaching experiences, and the objectivity learnt from his work in science. He has described himself as anti-Neruda, stripping lyrical language of its excess metaphors. He writes colloquially and wants to communicate first of all. For Parra 'life has no sense'; his position is anarchistic. His later work used graffiti and is called *Artefactos* (1973) – a 'found' poetry that continues his attack on the lyrical poet's ego. During Pinochet's dictatorship he remained in Chile, writing *Sermones y prédicas del Cristo de Elqui*, 1979 (*Sermons and Homilies of the Christ of Elqui*, 1984), speaking through a religious fanatic called Domingo Zárate. Recently his *Antipoems: New and Selected*, 1985, appeared. Parra lives outside Santiago in **La Reina Alta**, and at **Isla Negra**, has been married at least three times, and has at least six children. See Edith Grossman, *The Antipoetry of Nicanor Parra*, University Press of New York, New York, 1975.

SAINT-EXUPERY, Antoine (1900–1944). Born in Lyons, France, Saint-Exupéry was killed in action as a pilot in the second world war. He was a pioneer mail courier, and inaugurated the flight from Comodoro Rivadavia to Bahía Blanca in Argentina, where he lived for 15 months. In *Terre des Hommes*, 1939 (*Wind, Sand and Stars*, 1939 – Extract 5) he flies to Chile, and lands accidentally in Concordia, Argentina, where he stays in a ruined palace that today bears a plaque in his honour. During a holiday in the Peninsula Valdés in Argentina he began his best-seller *Le Petit Prince*, 1945 (with his own illustrations). In 1930 he married a Central American, Consuelo Suncín.

SKARMETA, Antonio (1940–). Born in **Antofagasta** on 7 November 1940, Skármeta studied at the **University of Chile**, and Columbia, New York. He went into university teaching, and translating (Kerouac, William Golding, Mailer, etc) until the coup of 1973. In 1975 in Berlin, he taught film and drama. He recently returned to Chile. He has published five collections of short stories, selected in *Watch Where the Wolf is Going*, 1991, and three novels – *Soñé que la nieve ardía*, 1975 (*I Dreamt the Snow was Burning*, 1985); *La insurrección*, 1983 (*The Insurrection*, 1983); and *Ardiente paciencia*, 1985 (*Burning Patience*, 1987 – Extract 3). *Burning Patience* skilfully ties together a love affair between a village postman and an innkeeper's sexy daughter, Pablo Neruda's last years at his coastal home in Isla Negra, and the September coup of 1973. Neruda helps the postman seduce his girl by quoting his love poems by heart, until the girl's mother remembers that she was seduced the same way a generation before. It is a warm-hearted political fable, with neat touches of humour. Neruda's last weary years are poignantly described.

WILDER, Thornton (1897–1975). See also under Peru. Wilder was born in Madison, WI, and was educated in missionary schools before going to university at Oberlin College, Yale, and Princeton. He has written successful plays and novels. He travelled to Peru and Chile in 1941, sent by the US Department of State. He travelled by ship with the writer Sherwood Anderson (who died in Panama), and spent three months mainly in Bogotá, Quito, Lima and Arequipa. He knew a little Spanish and wrote a 21-page report on his official trip. After a publishing gap of 19 years, Wilder published his novel *The Eighth Day*, 1967 (not extracted due to copyright restrictions). The book is a dramatic exploration of who shot Breck Lansing. His best friend, John Ashley, was incriminated in a small mid-American mining town. The novel roams back and forward through the family histories as Ashley is helped to escape from prison and disappears in Chile, later presumed drowned off Costa Rica. We see the effect of this false sentence on the families as they try to make sense of life. A novel packed with life, and flashes of wisdom. Wilder places Ashley in a believable **Manantiales**, with its Indians and foreigners, and mines.

See Gilbert Harrison, *The Enthusiast: A Life of Thornton Wilder*, Ticknor and Fields, New York, 1983.

URUGUAY

Uruguay, or the República Oriental del Uruguay, is named after the river which forms its western border, hence Uruguay's other name, the Banda Oriental. This smallest independent state in South America is bordered in the North by Brazil, and along the Uruguay River by Argentina. It has a land area of 182 427 sq km, and 310 km of Atlantic shore. The population reached 3.1 million in 1990, with a high 79% living in the capital **Montevideo** (1 250 000 in 1985), and other urban areas. Mario Benedetti's early novel *La tregua*, 1960 (*The Truce*, 1969) catches the sad bureaucrat's world, while Juan Carlos Onetti ◊ has turned this grey urban world into 'Santa María', his fictional reflection of the city, with his immigrant protagonists with names like Larsen, and Brausen. Alan Judd's novel *Tango*, 1989, evokes this run-down but vital quality of Montevideo as his fat English bookseller farcically adapts to local chaos. The last Charrúa Indians – fierce nomads – were killed in 1832, and the country repopulated with European immigrants.

There is a 96% literacy rate. This is reflected in the excellent critical tradition of essayists, starting with José Enrique Rodó's *Ariel*, 1900 (*Ariel*, 1989) attacking the USA as Caliban, and defending the Mediterranean roots of Ariel's spiritual Latin America, to Emir Rodríguez Monegal, Angel Rama, and Eduardo Galeano (1940–), whose unofficial people's history of Latin America from his earlier *Open Veins of Latin America: 5 Centuries of the Pillage of a Continent*, 1974, to *Genesis*, 1985, *Faces and Masks*, 1987, and *Memory of Fire: Century of the Wind*, 1988, has been very influential. Galeano has also written fiction – *Días y noches de amor y de guerra*, 1978 (*Days and Nights of Love and War*, 1983).

Cattle farming has been the principal activity, for Uruguay lacks coal, petroleum and useful minerals. Cattle farming was based on huge wild herds controlled by *gauchos* until the fencing of the land in the 1870s. At first, exportation was of hide and jerked beef (anglicism for *charque*); then in the 1860s corned beef (Fray Bentos) with Bovril and Oxo plants for meat extraction, until the *frigoríficos* (deep freezing meat factories) took over.

The country consists of low rolling hills, with tall rich prairie grass, and more trees than Argentina. The woods – *montes* – produce *algarrobo* and *quebracho*. The ridges are called *cuchillas*. A fine description of late nineteenth century Uruguayan rural life, with its colourful *gauchos*, comes out in W. H. Hudson's ◊ novel *The Purple Land*, 1885 (Extract 4), and in Charles Darwin's ◊ observations (Extract 2). Tourism accounts for 10% of Uruguay's foreign exchange, especially from **Punta del Este**, where Argentines flock every summer (December to March), and where the writer Gordon Meyer ◊ lived, and placed many stories.

The land that became Uruguay in 1828 has been fought over by Portugal, then Brazil and Spain, then Argentina. The Portuguese had moved into Nova Colonia do Sacramento (today the well preserved fort village of **Colonia**) in the 1680s. **Montevideo** – 'I see a hill', a reference to the '*cerro*' – was founded in 1728 by the Spaniards to counter this incursion (the *cerro* is the hill dominating Montevideo, and a town district). The British under Sir Home Popham occupied Montevideo from 3 February to 9 September 1807. The same year the first newspaper was printed. In 1811 Montevideo was occupied by Spanish troops. This led to Uruguay's national hero, the *gaucho* José Gervasio Artigas's seige of Montevideo in 1811 that lasted nine years until he was exiled in Dr Francia's Paraguay. In 1820 Brazil occupied Montevideo. The defeat of Brazil at **Ituzainzó** in 1827 led finally to Independence on 27 August 1828. From the 1830s political and social life was chaotic, as the Uruguayans divided into two warring parties, the *colorados* (reds) and the *blancos* (whites) throughout the rest of the nineteenth century – a gory civil war, as W. H. Hudson shows in *The Purple Land*. In 1843 the Argentine dictator Rosas beseiged Montevideo for another nine years until 1851 (for that was where Argentine dissidents lived), when Garibaldi defended Uruguay against the Argentines.

The quality of Uruguayan life was changed by José Battle y Ordoñez, elected president in 1903, so that in later years Uruguay came to be called admiringly the 'Switzerland' of South America. He set about modernizing the country: he took over the banks; imposed an 8-hour working day, old-age pensions, unemployment funds and divorce. In fact he created a welfare state. He was also no friend of the Church: he ordered 'god' to be spelt in lower case, and banned buildings named after saints. In 1911, he was re-elected until 1915 and he died in 1929.

However, this modernization was at the expense of an expansion of bureaucracy and no raising of revenue from income taxes. An economic crisis based on over-heavy state enterprises, and government subsidies occurred in 1957, with fast-rising inflation and strikes. The urban guerilla group the Tupamaros – named after the Incan rebel Tupac Amaru – caught the public imagination with their Robin Hood beginnings. They kidnapped and killed an American officer Daniel Mitrione, revealed tax frauds by wealthy men, demanded blankets for the poor as ransom, and kidnapped a British ambassador (see Geoffrey Jackson, *People's Prison*, 1973). In 1973 the army stepped in, and violently repressed the guerrillas, an action which included the imprisonment of writer Juan Carlos Onetti. Most of Uruguay's intellectuals went into exile until elections were held again in 1985, and won by Dr Julio Sanguinetti. In the 1980s Uruguay had the highest proportion of political prisoners in the world (1 in 50 citizens), and over 350 000 political exiles. This politicization has entered the few Uruguayan novels translated, like Carlos Martínez Moreno's (1917–86) *El color que el infierno me escondiera*, 1981 (*El infierno*, 1988).

The essential drama of Uruguayan cultural life has been the contrast between the sprawling city and the empty, backward country, echoing the same conflict in Argentina, best embodied by Horacio Quiroga (◊ Argentina), Uruguayan, who rejected cosy urban life for living in wild nature in Misiones. Much writing stresses city alienation and immigrant malaise (see Florencio Sánchez's play *La gringa*, 1904, in *Representative Plays of Florencio Sánchez*, 1961), and with a rapidly declining currency, we are witnessing the last vestiges of a 'European' lifestyle.

BOOKLIST

The following selection includes all titles which are extracted in this chapter as well as those mentioned in the introduction which are available in English. In general, paperback editions are given when possible. The editions cited are not necessarily the only ones available. For most of the extracted works, the original publisher in English can be found in 'Acknowledgments and Citations' at the end of the volume, as can the exact location of the extracts and the editions from which they are taken. The date in square brackets is the original publication date of the work in its original language. Extract numbers are highlighted in bold for ease of reference.

Benedetti, Mario, *The Truce* [1960], Benjamin Graham, trans, Harper and Row, New York, 1969.

Borges, Jorge Luis, 'The Form of the Sword', in *Fictions*, Anthony Kerrigan, trans, Calder, London, 1965/Grove Press, New York, 1962 (as *Ficciones*). **Extract 7.**

Burton, Richard, *Letters from the Battle-Fields of Paraguay*, Tinsley Brothers, London, 1870. **Extract 6.**

Darwin, Charles, *Voyage of the Beagle* [1839], Penguin, London, 1989. **Extract 2.**

Galeano, Eduardo, *Days and Nights of Love and War* [1978], Judith Brisler, trans, Pluto, London, 1983/Monthly Review Press, New York, 1983.

Galeano, Eduardo, *Faces and Masks* [1984], Cedric Belfrage, trans, Quartet, London, 1987.

Galeano, Eduardo, *Genesis* [1982], Cedric Belfrage, trans, Methuen, London, 1987/Pantheon, New York, 1985.

Galeano, Eduardo, *Memory of Fire: Century of the Wind* [1986], Cedric Belfrage, trans, Quartet, London, 1989/Pantheon, New York, 1988.

Galeano, Eduardo, *Open Veins of Latin America: 5 Centuries of the Pillage of a Continent* [1971], Cedric Belfrage, trans, Monthly Review Press, New York and London, 1974.

Hudson, W.H., *The Purple Land* [1885], Duckworth, London, 1929. **Extract 4.**

Jackson, Geoffrey, *People's Prison*, Faber and Faber, London, 1973.

Judd, Alan, *Tango* [1989], Fontana, London, 1990.

Martínez Moreno, Carlos, *El infierno* [1981], Ann Wright, trans, Readers International, London, 1988.

Meyer, Gordon, *Summer at High Altitude*, Alan Ross, London, 1968. **Extract 5.**

Onetti, Juan Carlos, *A Brief Life* [1950], Hortense Carpentier, trans, Serpent's Tail, London, 1993/Grossman, New York, 1976. **Extracts 1 and 3.**

Rodó, José Enrique, *Ariel* [1900], Margaret Sayers Peden, trans, University of Texas Press, Austin, TX, 1989.

Sánchez, Florencio, 'La gringa' [1904], in *Representative Plays of Florencio Sanchez*, Willis Knapp Jones, trans, Pan American Union, Washington, DC, 1961.

Extracts

(1) COLONIA SUIZA

Juan Carlos Onetti, *A Brief Life*

Onetti's frustrated novelist narrator is seeking his reality, which will become Santa María, a city of lonely, lost failures. The 'Swiss colony' refers to Colonia Suiza, near Montevideo, and echoes the dated cliché about Uruguay being the Switzerland of South America.

There's an old man, a doctor, who sells morphine. Everything has to radiate from that, from him. Perhaps he isn't old, but he's tired, dried up. When you're better, I'll start to write. A week or two, no more. Don't cry. Don't be sad. I see a woman who suddenly appears in the doctor's office. The doctor lives in Santa María, near the river. I was there only once, hardly a day, in summer, but I remember the air, the trees in front of the hotel, the placid way boats came down the river. I know there's a Swiss colony near the city. The doctor lives there, and suddenly a woman enters his office. The way you went back and forth from behind a folding screen to take off your blouse and show the swaying gold cross suspended from its chain, the blue spot, the lump on your breast. Thirteen thousand pesos, at least, for the first outline. I'm going to leave the agency, we're going to live in the suburbs where you'd like to be, and maybe you'll have a child. Don't cry, don't be sad.'

I remembered talking, I saw my stupidity, my impotence, my false words filling the space occupied by my body, taking its shape. 'Don't cry, don't be sad,' I repeated as she quieted down on the pillow, barely sobbing, trembling.

Now my hand overturned the morphine ampule, overturned it again near Gertrudis' body, near her breathing, knowing that one thing had ended and another was beginning, inevitable; knowing it was necessary that I do not think about either and that both were only one thing, like the end of life and the beginning of putrefaction. The ampule was moving between my thumb and index finger, and I imagined the liquid had a perverse quality insinuated by its color, its capacity for movement, its ability to become still the moment my hand stopped moving, and then to shine serenely in the light, pretending it had never been agitated.

Slightly maddened, I played with the ampule, feeling my growing need to imagine and to draw close to me an indistinct doctor of forty years, the laconic and despairing inhabitant of a small city located between a river and a colony of Swiss farmers. Santa María because I had been happy there years ago, without reason and for twenty-four hours.

(2) MALDONADO

Charles Darwin, *Voyage of the Beagle*

Darwin was in Maldonado in 1832. The town had been sacked by the British in 1806. Today it has been swamped by Punta del Este.

Maldonado is situated on the northern bank of the Plata, and not very far from the mouth of the estuary. It is a most quiet, forlorn, little town; built, as is universally the case in these countries, with the streets running at right angles to each other, and having in the middle a large plaza or square, which, from its size, renders the scantiness of the population more evident and more unsociable. It possesses scarcely any trade; the exports being confined to a few hides and living cattle. The inhabitants are chiefly landowners, together with a few shopkeepers and the necessary tradesmen, such as blacksmiths and carpenters, who do nearly all the business for a circuit of 50 miles round. The town is separated from the river by a band of sand-hillocks, about a mile broad: it is surrounded on all sides, by an open slightly undulating country, covered by one uniform layer of fine green turf, on which countless herds of cattle, sheep, and horses graze. There is very little land cultivated even close to the town. A few hedges, made of cacti and agave, mark out where some wheat or Indian corn has been planted. The features of the country are very similar along the whole northern bank of the Plata. The only difference is, that here the granitic hills are rather more boldly pronounced. The scenery is very uninteresting; there is scarcely a house, an enclosed piece of ground, or even a tree, to give it an air of cheerfulness. Yet, after being imprisoned for some time in a ship, there is a charm in the unconfined feeling of walking over boundless plains of turf.

(3) MONTEVIDEO

Juan Carlos Onetti, *A Brief Life*

From Onetti's fictional town of Santa María (Montevideo) Díaz Grey watches the approach of the daily ferry from Buenos Aires.

Through the windowpanes and his eyeglasses, Díaz Grey would be looking at a noon of powerful sun melting into the winding streets of

Santa María. His forehead would be resting and sometimes slipping on the smoothness of the window glass next to the corner cabinets or the half-circle of the disorderly desk. He was looking at the river, neither wide nor narrow, rarely agitated; a river with lively currents that did not show on the surface, crossed by small rowboats, small sailboats, small motor launches and, according to an invariable schedule, a slow, broad ferryboat that cast off in the mornings from a coast of ombú trees and weeping willows, to plunge its prow into the unruffled water and, rocking, to approach Dr Díaz Grey and the city where he lived. A ferryboat loaded with passengers and a pair of automobiles fastened with cables, bringing the morning papers from Buenos Aires, perhaps carrying hampers of grapes, demijohns wrapped in straw, farm machines.

(4) Paysandu

W.H. Hudson, *The Purple Land*

Hudson's Richard Lamb, a typical English protagonist, slowly turns into a South American, later killing a cut-throat with pleasure. He settles into an estancia in northern Uruguay.

Continuing my journey through the Durazno district, I forded the pretty river Yí and entered the Tacuarembó department, which is immensely long, extending right away to the Brazilian frontier. I rode over its narrowest part, however, where it is only about twenty-five miles wide; then, crossing two very curiously named rivers, Rios Salsipuedes Chico and Salsipuedes Grande, which mean Get-out-if-you-can Rivers, Little and Big, I at length reached the termination of my journey in the province or department of Paysandú. The Estancia de la Virgen de los Desamparados, or, to put it very shortly, Vagabonds' Rest, was a good-sized, square brick house built on very high ground, which overlooked an immense stretch of grassy, undulating country. There was no plantation about the house, not even a shade tree or cultivated plant of any description, but only some large corrales, or enclosures, for the cattle, of which there were six or seven thousand head on the land. The absence of shade and greenery gave the place a desolate, uninviting aspect, but if I was ever to have any authority here this would soon be changed. The Mayordomo, or manager, Don Policarpo Santierra de Peñalosa, which, roughly done into English, means Polycarp of the Holy Land abounding in Slippery Rocks, proved to be a very pleasant, affable person. He welcomed me in that quiet Oriental politeness which is never cold and never effusive, and then perused the letter from Doña Isidora. Finally he said, 'I am willing, my friend, to supply you with all the conveniences procurable at this elevation; and, for the rest, you know, doubtless, what I can say to you. A ready understanding requires few words. Nevertheless, there is no lack of good beef, and, to be short, you will do me a great favour by making this house with everything it contains your own, while you honour us by remaining in it.'

After delivering himself of these kindly sentiments, which left me rather in a mist as to my prospects, he mounted his horse and rode off, probably on some very important affair, for I saw no more of him for several days.

I at once proceeded to establish myself in the kitchen. No person in the house appeared ever to pay even a casual visit to any other room. This kitchen was vast and barn-like, forty feet long at least, and proportionately wide; the roof was of reeds, and the hearth, placed in the centre of the floor, was a clay platform, fenced round with cows' shank-bones, half buried and standing upright. Some trivets and iron kettles were scattered about, and from the centre beam, supporting the roof, a chain and hook was suspended to which a vast iron pot was fastened. One more article, a spit about six feet long for roasting meat, completed the list of cooking utensils. There were no chairs, tables, knives, or forks; everyone carried his own knife, and at meal-time the boiled meat was emptied into a great tin dish, whilst the roast was eaten from the spit, each one laying hold with his fingers and cutting his slice. The seats were logs of wood and horse-skulls. The household was composed of one woman, an ancient, hideously ugly, grey-headed negress, about seventy years old, and eighteen or nineteen men of all ages and sizes, and of all colours from parchment-white to very old oak. There was a *capataz*, or overseer, and seven or eight paid *peones*, the other being all *agregados* – that is, supernumeraries without pay, or, to put it plainly, vagabonds who attach themselves like vagrant dogs to establishments of this kind, lured by the abundance of flesh, and who occasionally assist the regular *peones* at their work, and also do a little gambling and stealing to keep themselves in small change. At break of day everyone was up sitting by the hearth sipping bitter *maté* and smoking cigarettes; before sunrise all were mounted and away over the surrounding country to gather up the herds; at midday they were back again to breakfast. The consumption and waste of meat was something frightful. Frequently, after breakfast, as much as twenty or thirty pounds of boiled and roast meat would be thrown into a wheelbarrow and carried out to the dust heap, where it served to feed scores of hawks, gulls, and vultures, besides the dogs.

(5) Punta del Este

Gordon Meyer, *Summer at High Altitude*

Meyer lived for over two years in a house called 'Hendaya' in the pine woods off the resort town of Punta del Este.

In swift long-hand wind and sun are writing shadows on the white walls. Outside my window spring turns over its first pages. Thank god for that tasteless colourless Rioplatense spring, too feeble to wreck the heart with old fevers.

Today in the toylike harbour there was a little paint-chipping going on. Of course. Time to wake up. In a few months the Season will be here again. The international golf, polo, fishing, yachting, tennis, bridge. Above all: the social contest. Three months of it, ending in a hysteria of carnival. Then everyone pours away, because that also is the done thing. Then once more silence will descend on the peninsula, the hemisphere will swing into its idyllic autumn, and a few trees will bronze a little as they begin their yearly pretence of winter.

With also the climate of Cannes, or Biarritz, Punta del Este is nothing less than very nice. And nothing more. There is an elegant abandon of the formalities of society in the capital. Only some of the Argentines persist in dressing up. One of the done things for the new wealthy Argentine is to own a house in Punta del Este. The old Argentine landed aristocrat did this quite gracefully; it was merely one of his ways of living in his own metropolis. Now the new Argentine middle class has found another arena in which to compete with one another.

(6) Salto

Richard Burton, *Letters from the Battle-Fields of Paraguay*

Burton went up the Uruguay River in 1870 on his way to report on the War of the Triple Alliance between Paraguay and Brazil and Argentina, and stopped at Salto, where writer Horacio Quiroga (◊ Argentina) was born in 1878, and today a city of some 80 000.

Having time to spare, and my feet 'itching for a journey', I resolved to visit Salto, the terminus of Uruguay navigation. The river in this section becomes exceedingly picturesque. After passing a neat, clean Swiss colony which shows signs of roads, we find on the left bank those sandstone bluffs that have made travellers compare Father Uruguay with Father Rhine. A flat table, surrounded by rock precipices, falling into an earthslope, and brought up by thick dwarf forest below, is pointed to us as the 'Mesa de Artigas'. Tradition declares that the wild potentate, D. Pepe, who is described by all the travellers of the day, used here to cut his prisoners' throats and toss them from the plateau into the water. On both shores now begins a wealth of limestone; it is, however, hard as marble and expensive to burn. Frequent arroyos divide the fine grazing grounds, and the lomas or uplands are tasselled with the Coquito palm.

Presently we sight on both sides of the river the normal white sheet that argues a settlement. The right bank supports Concordia of Entre Rios; opposite it, in the Banda Oriental, lies Salto, 'the cascade', whose site is similar to that of Paysandú. Nor will the town require description. It has a pier, a Custom-House, three long parallel streets extending up the ridge, a main square, a Matriz, poor and yellow – the salteños appear more busy in temporal than in spiritual matters.

(7) Tacuarembo

Jorge Luis Borges, *The Form of the Sword*

Borges sets his story, written in 1942, in northern Uruguay, near the mountains that form the frontier with Brazil. The narrator is an Irishman who tells a tale of cowardice and betrayal in Ireland to reveal that he, Moon, was the coward. 'The Form of the Sword' is included in Fictions – see Booklist.

His face was crossed with a rancorous scar; a nearly perfect ashen arc which sank into his temple on one side and his cheek on the other. His real name is of no importance: in Tacuarembó everyone knew him as the Englishman of La Colorada. The great landowner of these parts, Cardoso, had not been interested in selling; I have heard that the Englishman had recourse to an unexpected argument: he told him the secret history of the scar. The Englishman had come from the frontier, from Rio Grande del Sur; there were those who said he had been a smuggler in Brazil. His fields were overgrown with underbrush; the wells were bitter; to remedy these faults, the Englishman worked alongside his peones. They say he was strict to the point of cruelty, but scrupulously fair. They also said he was a drinking man: a couple of times a year he would lock himself up in a room in the tower, and two or three days later he would emerge as if from a bout of insanity or from a battlefield, pale, tremulous, abashed – and as authoritarian as ever. I remember his glacial eyes, his energetic thinness, his grey moustache. He had scant dealings with anyone; true, his Spanish was rudimentary, contaminated with Brazilian. Apart from an occasional commercial letter or pamphlet, he received no correspondence.

The last time I made a trip through the Northern provinces a flash flood in the Caraguatá arroyo forced me to spend the night at La Colorada. I was only there a few minutes when I felt that my presence was inopportune. I tried getting into the good graces of the Englishman; I resorted to the least acute of all passions: patriotism. I said that a country with the spirit of England was invincible. My interlocutor agreed, but he added with a smile that he was not English. He was Irish, from Dungarvan. Having said this, he stopped himself, as if he had revealed a secret.

Biographies and plot summaries

BORGES, Jorge Luis (see under Argentina).

BURTON, Sir Richard (1821–1890). Burton was born in Torquay, UK. When he died in 1890 he was buried in Mortlake Cemetery under a tent-like tomb. Burton began to learn Arabic at Oxford before being rusticated. By the end of his life, he had learnt some 40 languages. In October 1842 he joined the Bombay Native Infantry, and soon could pass as a native. In 1853 he went on a pilgrimage to Mecca in disguise. In 1857 he was commissioned by the Foreign Office to search for the source of the Nile, and discovered Lake Tanganyika and Lake Victoria for Europeans. While in Goa (Portuguese India) Burton had learnt Portuguese, and was then sent as Consul to Santos, Brazil, where he lived from 1865 to 1868, finally leaving in 1872. He had previously translated the Portuguese epic poem the *Lusiads* by Camões, and left unpublished his translation of O *uruguai* by José Basilio de Gama, a

long anti-Jesuit poem dealing with the Spanish–Portuguese mission war from 1754 to 1759 in what is now Brazil. Burton wrote about his travels in the *sertão* in *The Highlands of Brazil*, 1869. *Letters from the Battle-Fields of Paraguay*, 1870 (Extract 6), dedicated to Domingo Fausto Sarmiento (◊ Argentina), is a detailed account of a boat trip up the Paraná River to observe the hopeless war waged by the Paraguayan dictator Solano López against the Brazilians and Argentinians. It includes a 77-page essay on Paraguay. Most of the travel book describes Argentina. Burton also translated (in 1886) a Brazilian novel, *Iracema* by José Martiniano de Alencar.

DARWIN, Charles (1809–1882). Born in Shrewsbury, UK, on 12 February, Darwin was the youngest son of a doctor and grandson of Erasmus Darwin. After local school he first went to Edinburgh, and then Cambridge, where in 1831 he obtained a degree in Theology without honours, but his mentor J. S. Henslow offered him a job as gentleman companion on Robert Fitzroy's surveying trip in the *Beagle*. Darwin was already a keen entomologist, and after first rejecting the offer, agreed to go, without pay. The *Beagle* finally set off on 27 December 1831, and the voyage was to last five years, until 2 October 1836. This long trip, mostly in South America, turned Darwin into the scientist who would later, after his marriage to his cousin Emma Wedgwood in 1839, be forced to make public his speculations concerning species (prompted by finches on the Galápagos Islands) with his *On the Origin of Species by Means of Natural Selection* in 1859.

From his return to England in 1836, Darwin hardly travelled except to spas, and remained with his family at Down House in Kent. In 1839, jointly with Fitzroy, Darwin published his vivid diary of his five-year trip (*Voyage of the Beagle* – Extract 2), which swings from delight at tropical nature to despair at his seasickness. It is a fresh account of a world not yet catalogued by modern science. Here we read about his first excursions into the Brazilian jungle near Rio, his horror at slavery, his mocking of peasants at **Maldonado** in Uruguay, his interview with dictator Rosas, his incredible horseback journey from Bahía Blanca to Buenos Aires across hostile Indian territory, his ascent of the Sierra de la Ventana, his shock at seeking naked Fuegians, and leaving Jemmy Button back in The Beagle Channel, his rides across waterlogged Chiloé Island, his stay in Valparaíso, his climb up into the Andes where he found sea shells, and many details on the animals, plants, and geology. In 1845 he published a second edition. Darwin is buried at Westminster Abbey in London. (Jemmy Button, referred to above, was the nickname of one of the three Fuegian Indians brought back to England by *Beagle* captain Fitzroy. Jemmy Button was then dumped back with his tribe and quickly reverted to his natural state. Chilean novelist Benjamín Subercaseaux wrote a novel about him called *Jemmy Button* [1950], Mary and Fred del Villar, trans, W.H. Allen, London, 1954/Macmillan, New York, 1955.

HUDSON, W. H. (see under Argentina). In 1885 Hudson published the novel *The Purple Land that England Lost* (Extract 4), suppressing 'that England lost' in its second edition of 1904. The novel is a pretext for descriptive set-pieces about horseback meanderings around Uruguay, gripped in a fever of civil wars. It is also about how Richard Lamb renounces his British upbringing and becomes a *criollo*, giving into his passions, falling for the easy-going women, and finally murdering a cut-throat. At the end Lamb is liberated from his Victorian straight-jacket. Uruguay has been saved from industrialization, and materialistic science, and Lamb thanks God that England did not colonize the country, despite its invasions of 1807. In early editions Hudson included a succint History of Uruguay as an appendix.

MEYER, Gordon (see under Argentina). From April 1964 to 1967, Meyer lived in 'Hendaya' in **Punta del Este** with his Uruguayan wife Mara Rincón.

ONETTI, Juan Carlos (1909–). Born on 1 July 1909, Onetti left school early, and worked in a succession of small jobs (a porter, selling football tickets, etc) in **Montevideo** and Buenos Aires. From 1941 to 1955, he worked for Reuters in Buenos Aires, and contributed to *Marcha* (founded in 1939). In 1957 he was appointed director of the **Municipal Library** in **Montevideo**. In 1974, after the military coup of 1973, Onetti was accused of 'pornography' concerning a story in *Marcha*, arrested and briefly imprisoned. He took three months to recuperate in a mental home. He went into exile in Spain in 1975, and still lives in Madrid, having taken Spanish nationality. He has been married four times, and has two children – one of them is Jorge Onetti, a novelist. Onetti published his first short story in 1932. In 1939 he published his short novel *El pozo* (*The Pit*, 1991) in which angry-young-man Eladio Linacero's scribbled memoirs open with a confession of how he humiliated a teenage girl who later died. The novel expresses Linacero's mysogyny, his hatred for the USA, and pessimism about life. In 1940 Onetti published the untrans-lated *Tierra de nadie*, and in 1943 *Anoche* (*Tonight*, 1991), set at the end of the Spanish Civil War during one long night, with Ossorio on the run, falling for a young girl and caught up in deadly local politics. In 1950, Onetti introduced his Faulkner-inspired country Santa María in *La vida breve* (*A Brief Life*, 1976 – Extracts 1 and 3), with recurring characters like the Doctor Díaz Grey, Larsen, Brausen and other low-life brothel-haunters and failures, uprooted immigrants and mediocre provincials. Faded youth, and broken promises instead of love and hope are the themes of this grey fictional world, prolonged in *El astillero* (*The Ship-yard*, 1968, and retranslated, 1991); *Juntacadáveres*, 1964 (*The Body Snatchers*, 1991); and three further untranslated novels. Juan Carlos Onetti's short stories are translated as *The Goodbyes and Other Stories*, 1990. See Djelal Kadir, *Juan Carlos Onetti*, Twayne, Boston, Massa-chusetts, 1977.

ARGENTINA

'Hard to believe Buenos Aires had any beginning. / I feel it to be as eternal as air and water.'
Jorge Luis Borges,
The Mythical Founding of
Buenos Aires

Argentina, or the República de Argentina, is named from the Latin for silver, like the Río de la Plata, following false rumours of a silver mountain in the late sixteenth century. Five times larger than France, Argentina borders with Chile, Uruguay, Paraguay, Brazil and Bolivia. From the tropical north to **Tierra del Fuego** in the south, Argentina stretches for 3693 km and its land area is 2 780 092 sq km. Domingo Sarmiento ◊ in his essay *Facundo*, 1845, called this vastness, and the distances between settlements, the 'curse' of Argentina (Extract 2). The population rose to 32.3 million in 1990. Of this population, 72% live in urban centres, with **Buenos Aires**, founded in 1536 but only the capital from 1853, reaching 10.7 million in the late 1980s, 36% of the total. The writer Ezequiel Martínez Estrada called Buenos Aires 'Goliath's head', in relation to the rest of the population. Rubén Darío (◊ Nicaragua), the Nicaraguan poet, arrived in Buenos Aires in its heyday in 1893 (Extract 12) and called it 'Cosmópolis' because it seemed so modern and rich. Most writers lived and live in this city as *porteños* (inhabitants of the 'port' of Buenos Aires). Ernesto Sabato's ◊ fiction is topographically exact, and Buenos Aires provides the background to his dramas (Extracts 20–22) with crucial scenes in the **Parque Lezama**; Julio Cortázar's ◊ city in his stories, and novels creates another image, but is also exact (Extract 11). For Jorge Luis Borges ◊ the city is its suburbs like Palermo where he grew up. Many of his poems and stories are rooted in local streets and areas (Extracts 8 and 9). Most of the writers extracted set fiction in Buenos Aires, from Gordon Meyer ◊ to Haroldo Conti ◊ to W.H. Hudson ◊.

Córdoba, with the oldest university after Lima in South America, founded in 1613, has a population of 982 000. In the 1950s Lawrence

Durrell ⟡ worked for the British Council there (and hated it, as revealed in his letters). Juan Larrea, the Spanish poet died in Córdoba, as did Manuel de Falla, García Lorca's composer friend. **Rosario** is the third city, with 954 600.

Unlike most of Latin America, 97% of the population is European, due to the elimination of the wild, nomadic Indians in the Desert Campaign 1879–83, under General Roca. Charles Darwin (⟡ Uruguay) has keen descriptions of these Indians, as does Cunninghame Graham (⟡ Paraguay). There was mass immigration from the 1850s, mainly Spanish ('*gallegos*') and Italians ('*tanos*'), followed by Poles, Turks, French, Russian Jews and Germans. Alberdi's slogan '*gobernar es poblar*' ('to govern is to populate'), backed up by Sarmiento, opened Argentina to '*gringos*' (originally referring to Italians in the protest poem *Martín Fierro*). Some 300 000 Indians lived in what is now Argentina before the Conquest. Interbreeding and negro slaves in the eighteenth century led to a *mestizo* population, replaced by the 3.5 million immigrants who arrived from Europe between 1860 and 1940. Literacy is very high, and 97% are Roman Catholics. Diet and customs are based on cattle farming, with the *gaucho* (the cowboy of the past), *asados* (barbecued beef), and *maté* drinking (from a straw in a gourd) typical. Argentines eat more beef per person than any other country in the world. These habits are reflected in Ricardo Güiraldes's ⟡ elegy to the *gauchos* in his novel *Don Segundo Sombra*, 1926 (Extract 35), in the earlier *Martín Fierro*, 1872 and 1879 (Extract 1), and in Francis Head's still fresh travel book *Rough Notes Taken During Some Rapid Journeys Across the Pampas*, 1826.

The **northwest** area, including Mendoza, La Rioja, San Luis, Tucumán, Salta and Jujuy, was the earliest colonized, as it lay nearer to Peru, but has not been incorporated into much literature (see Daniel Moyano, *El trino del diablo*, 1974; *The Devil's Trill*, 1988). **Tucumán** was founded in 1565, and is today the sugar-cane area of the republic. **Mendoza** is the wine-producing area. The Andes chain runs along the west as the border with Chile, reached from Mendoza through the Upsallata pass, under the tallest mountain in South America, **Aconcagua** (6959 m high). The **Chaco** (meaning 'hunting ground') region, an

---

Notes to map (facing page): [a]*Graham Greene's Honorary Consul's town;* [b]*See Mexican José Vasconcelos's description after his visit in the 1920s (Extract 31);* [c]*'Los 25 Ombúes', W. H. Hudson's birthplace, and now a museum;* [d]*See Charles Darwin and Gordon Meyer (Extracts 2 and 5 in Uruguay chapter);* [e]*Horacio Quiroga's house, now a museum, in the old Jesuit mission of San Ignacio;* [f]*See extract from W. H. Hudson's The Purple Land, 1885 (Extract 4 in Uruguay chapter).* Hollow circles = capital cities.

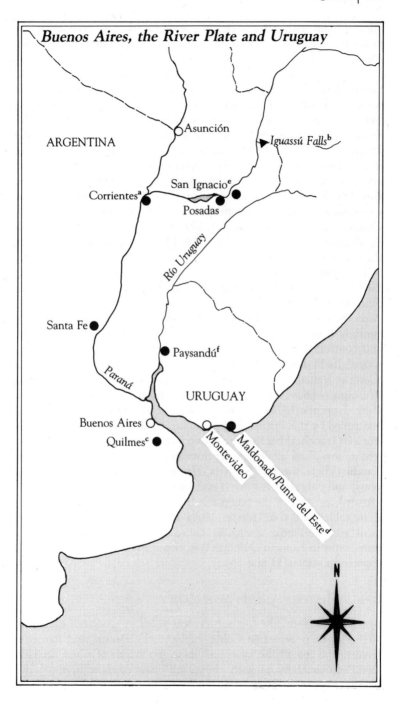

Buenos Aires, the River Plate and Uruguay

ARGENTINA

Asunción

Iguassú Falls[b]

San Ignacio[e]

Corrientes[a]

Posadas

Río Uruguay

Santa Fe

Paysandú[f]

Paraná

URUGUAY

Buenos Aires

Quilmes[c]

Montevideo

Maldonado/Punta del Este[d]

N

alluvial plain with *bañados* (water), savanna, thorny scrub and *quebracho* trees for lumber, is wild (see Julian Duguid ◊ Bolivia, and Gordon Meyer's *The River and the People*).

The third area is **Entre Ríos**, or **Mesopotamia**, which is mainly pasture land, lying between the Paraná and Uruguay Rivers. There were Jewish *gauchos* here, fictionalized by Alberto Gerchunoff in *Los gauchos judíos*, 1910 (*The Jewish Gauchos of the Pampas*, 1955). The fourth is **Patagonia**, ending in the glaciers and fiords of **Tierra del Fuego**, some 28% of the nation's territory but containing only 2.5% of its population. After the Indian campaign of 1879–83, pioneer colonizers came from Wales among other nations, with fruit farming in the **Río Negro** area, sheep stations, and oil discovered in 1907 near **Comodoro Rivadavia**. Natural gas is piped to Buenos Aires. Bruce Chatwin's (◊ Brazil) *In Patagonia*, 1977 (Extract 29), Charles Darwin's *Beagle* journal and W.H. Hudson's *Idle Days in Patagonia*, 1893, reflect the conditions of this area.

The *pampa húmeda* (or pampas in English), mainly the Provincia of Buenos Aires, includes **Buenos Aires** and **Bahía Blanca** (where Mallea ◊ has set his fictions dealing with isolation and loneliness – Extract 4). After the Indians were decimated, the land was handed over to the 300 families, known as the oligarchy, who became *estancieros* (ranchers), and controlled many aspects of national life. Their prestige is easily gauged in Manuel Puig's ◊ fiction set in the small pampas town of 'Coronel Vallejos'. A popular saga which is set in the pampas during Peronism is Diana Mills's *Reapers of the Wind: A Novel of Argentina*, 1989. From the 1870s with barbed wire, a railway network set up and controlled by the British, and *frigoríficos* (meat freezing plants), these *estancias* (ranches) became the country's main exporters of meat, wool, wheat, soya, and alfalfa. Apart from small mountain ranges at **Azul**, **Tandil** (where the Polish writer Witold Gombrowicz lived for many years, and published his diary) and **Sierra de la Ventana** (climbed by Darwin), no part of the pampas is higher than 30 m. The weather is changeable, with cold (*pampero*) and warm (*norte*) winds. The subtropical area bordering Paraguay, called **Misiones**, became almost a protagonist in Horacio Quiroga's ◊ stories of solitary pioneers and their disasters (Extracts 33 and 36).

EARLY HISTORY AND INDEPENDENCE

Juan Díaz de Solís, the first settler, was killed by Querandí Indians in 1516. In 1526 Sebastián Cabot explored the **Paraná** and **Paraguay Rivers**, and spread the falsehood about mountains of silver. In 1536 Don Pedro de Mendoza, with a large, self-financed expedition, founded Nuestra Señora de Buen Aire. But it was not until 1580 that Juan de

Garay secured **Buenos Aires**. For hundreds of years this region was the poorest, and least sought-after by the colonial Spaniards (*criollos*). It traded with the abundant animal skins, from cattle let loose that multiplied on the flat grass lands, and dried beef ('jerked beef', *charque*). In 1725 the population of Buenos Aires was 2200. Only in 1776 was a Viceroyalty created, to prevent Brazilian incursions, with the capital first at **Tucumán**, then **Córdoba**, and finally **Buenos Aires** with a population of 45 000 by 1800.

Independence followed the usual pattern in Latin America, but with less bloodshed. After the Napoleonic invasion of Spain in 1808 an open town meeting – the *cabildo* – voted to support the deposed Spanish monarch Ferdinand VII against Joseph Bonaparte. Only on 9 July 1816 was full Independence proclaimed. Earlier, the British invasion under Sir Home Popham, had helped create a national identity as they were evicted by the local population. The great liberator General José de San Martín decided to neutralize Spanish troops in Peru, crossed the Andes, liberated Chile, and with a fleet sailed for Peru, which he also liberated. He finally met up with Bolívar in Ecuador, and resigned because he favoured monarchic rule, dying in Boulogne, France (where there is a small museum).

The nineteenth century was virtually a civil war between 'civilization' and 'barbarism', to repeat Sarmiento's famous opposition in his *Facundo*, 1845. This meant a fight as to who would control the country: Buenos Aires, or a federal state. The *unitarios* turned to French and American Revolutions, and republicanism, and elected president Bernardino Rivadavia in 1826. But he was toppled by a rich *estanciero* called Juan Manuel Rosas, who became a 'federal' dictator from 1829 to 1852. He fought against the Europeanizing trends, forced people to wear ponchos and red ribbons, had the rough *gauchos* as his troops, a secret police called the Mazorca, exiled dissidents, and placed his portraits everywhere (even in W.H. Hudson's family *estancia* **Los 25 Ombúes**, now a museum).

The dictatorship of Rosas was opposed by all the intellectuals exiled in Montevideo and elsewhere: see José Mármol (1818–71), *Amalia*, 1851 (*Amalia: A Romance of the Argentine*, 1919); Esteban Echeverría's (1805–51) bitter allegory of the country as a slaughter-house killing off its poets in *El matadero*, 1838 (*The Slaughter House*, 1959); and especially Sarmiento, who wrote *Facundo* in exile in Chile in 1845. Rosas was defeated by General Urquiza – whose *estancia* **San José** in **Entre Ríos** is a museum – at the battle of **Caseros** in 1852. Rosas died and was buried in Southampton until he was recently brought back to Argentina by President Menem. Charles Darwin describes his interview with Rosas in his *Beagle* journal, and admired him. Following the defeat of Rosas, Argentina turned to immigration and Europe through

W.H. Hudson's birthplace, 'Los 25 Ombúes', in Quilmes near Buenos Aires, now a museum

successive presidents, starting with Bartolomé Mitre, classics scholar, translator of Dante and founder of the newspaper *La Nación* in 1870, president from 1862 to 1868 (there is a **Mitre Museum** in **Buenos Aires**). He was followed by the liberal educator and writer Domingo Sarmiento from 1868 to 1874 (there is a **Sarmiento Museum** in **Belgrano, Buenos Aires**). The classic work about nineteenth-century ranch life is Hudson's autobiography of his first 18 years, *Far Away and Long Ago*, 1918 (Extract 13).

PERON

The oligarchy was set up on the land with British help, from pedigree cattle, to the railway network (by 1912, 32 800 km of track). A new party was founded in 1916 called the Radicals (Unión Cívica Radical) to oppose the conservative oligarchy. The rebellious atmosphere in Buenos Aires at that time is captured in Roberto Arlt's only translated novel, *Los siete locos*, 1929 (*The Seven Madmen*, 1984). The Radicals finally came to power in 1916 under Hipólito Irigoyen, who ruled until toppled by a military coup in 1930, the beginning of the *década infame* of conservative–military corruption and rule.

In 1943 Juan Domingo Perón came to power. A follower of Mussolini's fascism, he based his power on labour and the army. After being imprisoned on **Martin García Island**, Evita Duarte, his charisma-tic mistress, organized a mass demonstration of the *descamisados* – 'shirtless ones' – and Perón, with the radio actress Evita at his side, was easily voted into power in 1946, and again in 1951 until his fall in a coup in 1955 (novelized by Gordon Meyer). Evita became a world figure, ran the Eva Perón Foundation, ranted against the oligarchy, but died young of leukaemia in 1952, aged 33. Thanks to Evita women got the vote in 1951. She even had plans for housewives to get paid. She became widely known in the UK through Andrew Lloyd Webber's musical *Evita*.

Perón was anti-British, resurrected the Falkland–Malvinas claims, bought out the British railroads, seized *La Prensa* (a prestigious conservative and anti-Peronist newspaper), controlled the universities, banned importation of foreign books and films, and threatened to expropriate land (see Tomás Eloy Martínez's ◊ novel, *The Perón Novel,* 1988 – Extract 32). Like Rosas before him, Perón alienated, exiled or imprisoned writers from Borges (demoted to poultry inspector) to Cortázar and Victoria Ocampo ◊. The church-burning mobs are vividly recreated in Ernesto Sabato's novel *Sobre héroes y tumbas*, 1961 (*On Heroes and Tombs*, 1981).

THE MILITARY

Since Perón's escape to Paraguay and then Franco's Spain, Argentina has been run by the powerful, nationalistic military. The threat of Cuba, and left-wing terrorism became a crucial factor after the civilian president Arturo Frondizi fell in a coup in 1962. Left-wing terrorist groups caught hold of the young people's imagination, as Graham Greene ◊ explored in *The Honorary Consul*, 1973. The Montoneros, and ERP (Ejército Revolucionario del Pueblo) started with Robin Hood tactics before turning to terrorism. In 1973 Perón was voted back in the person of Hector Cámpora, who then stood down to let the ageing Perón rule, with his wife Isabelita. This period has been recreated in Tomás Eloy Martínez's *The Perón Novel* and as farce in Luisa Valen-zuela's ◊ *Cola de lagartija*, 1983 (*The Lizard's Tail*, 1983), and Osvaldo Soriano's (1943–), *A Funny Dirty Little War*, 1983. Perón died in 1974 and Isabelita ruled under the shadow of right-wing thugs, until the military stepped in under General Videla in 1976 who instigated the 'dirty war', which ended with as many as 30 000 'disappeared', including many writers like Rodolfo Walsh, Haroldo Conti ◊, and Miguel Angel Bustos. The investigating 1984 Commission (CON-ADEP), headed by Ernesto Sabato, listed 8000 names (published by Faber in 1986).

This dark period is made vivid by many eye-witness novels translated into English, including Humberto Costantini's (1924–87), The Long Night of Francisco Sanctis, 1985; Enrique Medina's (1942–), The Duke: Memories and Anti-Memories of a Participant in the Repression, 1985; Alicia Partnoy's, The Little School: Tales of Disappearance and Survival in Argentina, 1986; Omar Rivabella's Requiem for a Woman's Soul, 1986; and novels by Vázquez Rial ◊ and Lawrence Thornton ◊. It is hard to separate fiction from facts, and Timmerman's Prisoner without a Name, Cell without a Number, 1981, Andrew Graham-Yooll's A State of Fear: Memories of Argentina's Nightmare, 1986, and the report Nunca Más, 1986, read as painfully as the novels cited above.

Recent history, including General Galtieri's invasion of the Falkland/Malvinas Islands (British from 1833) and the 1982 war, Raúl Alfonsín's 1983 radical presidency and taking the generals to court for human rights abuses (illustrated in Lawrence Thornton's Imagining Argentina), and Carlos Menem's right-wing Peronist 1989 electoral victory, awaits fictionalization, though Charles Gidley's recent romance The Crying of the Wind, 1992, develops along Argentine history from the 1960s to the 1980s.

THE VARIETY OF LITERARY TRADITIONS

Argentinian literature cannot be confined to realist writing mirroring and protesting political events. There are historical novels like Enrique Larreta's (1875–1961) The Glory of Don Ramiro: A Life in the Times of Phillip II, 1924 (his grand house is today the **Larreta Museum** – Spanish Art 'Enrique Larreta', Juramento 2291, Belgrano, Buenos Aires); Abel Posse's (1936–) hilarious mocking of Ferdinand and Isabel in The Dogs of Paradise, 1989; Juan José Saer's (1936–) recreation of the Discovery in The Witness, 1990; and Manuel Mújica Laínez's (1910–84) Bomarzo, a Novel, 1969, about an Italian garden of horrors, and The Wandering Unicorn, 1982 (his house in **Alta Gracia**, near **Córdoba**, is a museum/foundation). There is a long tradition of 'fantastic' writers from Borges to Cortázar to Bioy Casares ◊, to Silvina Ocampo's (1906–) Leopoldina's Dream, 1988, to Marco Denevi's (1922–) Secret Ceremony, 1961, to Enrique Anderson Imbert's (1910–) stories The Other Side of the Mirror, 1966, and Woven on the Loom of Time, 1990, to Manuel Peyrou's (1902–74) Thunder of the Roses, 1972, most conveying some kind of realism. There are many translated writers who just do not fit any categories, like Daniel Moyano (1930–1992), The Devil's Trill, 1988; Mario Satz (1944–), Sol, 1979; the poet Alejandra Pizarnik's extremist writings (translated in Alejandra Pizarnik, 1987); and Vlady Kociancich (1941–), The Last Days of William Shakespeare, 1990. The best introductions to this variety and sophistication are Norman di Giovanni's anthologies, Celeste Goes Dancing and Other

Ernesto Sabato

Stories, 1989, and *Hand in Hand Alongside the Tracks, and Other Tales*, 1992.

An Enigma

Argentina is an enigmatic country, as V.S. Naipaul (♢ Belize) in *The Return of Eva Perón*, 1982, noted. In 1947 it was as wealthy as Canada. It has abundant natural resources, and a vast territory. In the 1930s incredible wealth led to Argentines being considered as the most sophisticated people in the world. The vogue for the Tango, started by Carlos Gardel, caught the world's imagination until his death in a plane crash in 1935. Argentina has produced many writers like Borges, Sabato and Cortázar, revolutionaries like Che Guevara (the '*che*' is the verbal tic of Argentine Spanish), racing drivers, footballers, Nobel prize winning chemists, the Mothers of the Plaza de Mayo, and a way of life and educational system that is the envy of the rest of Latin America. But the nation has not progressed. Ezequiel Martínez Estrada's 1933 essay translated as *X-Ray of the Pampa*, 1972, remains the best exploration of Argentina.

BOOKLIST

The following selection includes all titles which are extracted in this chapter as well as those mentioned in the introduction which are available in English. In general, paperback editions are given when possible. The editions cited are not necessarily the only ones available. For most of the extracted works, the original publisher in English can be found in 'Acknowledgments and Citations' at the end of the volume, as can the exact location of the extracts and the editions from which they are taken. The date in square brackets is the original publication date of the work in its original language. Extract numbers are highlighted in bold for ease of reference.

Anderson Imbert, Enrique, *The Other Side of the Mirror* [1961], Isabel Reade, trans, Macdonald, London, 1968/Southern Illinois University Press, Carbondale, IL, 1966.

Anderson Imbert, Enrique, *Woven on the Loom of Time*, Carlton Vail and Pamela Edwards Mondragón, trans, University of Texas Press, Austin, TX, 1990.

Arlt, Roberto, *The Seven Madmen* [1929], Naomi Lindstrom, trans, David Godine, Boston, MA, 1984.

Bioy Casares, Adolfo, *The Dream of the Hero* [1954], Diana Thorold, trans, Quartet, London, 1987. **Extract 6.**

Bombal, María Luisa, *New Islands and Other Stories* [1935], Richard and Lucia Cunningham, trans, Farrar, Straus and Giroux, New York, 1982. **Extract 7**

Borges, Jorge Luis, 'The Mythical Founding of Buenos Aires', in Norman Thomas de Giovanni, ed, *Selected Poems 1923–1967*, Penguin Books, London, 1985/ Delacorte Press, New York, 1972. **Extract 8.**

Borges, Jorge Luis, 'The South', in *Fictions* [1944], Anthony Kerrigan, trans, Calder, London, 1965/Grove Press, New York, 1962 (as *Ficciones*). **Extract 9.**

Burton, Richard, *Letters from the Battle-Fields of Paraguay*, Tinsley Brothers, London, 1870. **Extract 30.**

Celeste Goes Dancing and Other Stories: An Argentine Collection, Norman Thomas di Giovanni, ed, Constable, London, 1989.

Chatwin, Bruce, *In Patagonia* [1977], Picador, London, 1979. **Extract 29.**

Conti, Haroldo, 'Lost', in *Translation: The Journal of Literary Translation*, Norman Thomas di Giovanni, trans, Spring 1987. **Extract 10.**

Cortázar, Julio, 'Text in a Notebook', in *We Love Glenda So Much and Other Tales*, Gregory Rabassa, trans, Harvill, London,

1984/Knopf, New York, 1983. **Extract 11.**

Costantini, Humberto, *The Long Night of Francisco Sanctis* [1984], Norman Thomas di Giovanni, trans, Fontana, London, 1987/ Harper and Row, New York, 1985.

Darío, Rubén, 'Song to the Argentina', in *Selected Poems*, Lysander Kemp, trans, University of Texas Press, Austin, TX, 1965. **Extract 12.**

Darwin, Charles, *Voyage of the Beagle* [1839], Penguin, London, 1989.

Denevi, Marco, *Secret Ceremony*, Harriet de Onís, trans, Time, Inc, New York, 1961.

Echeverría, Esteban, *The Slaughter House* [1871], Angel Flores, trans, Las Americas, New York, 1959.

Gerchunoff, Alberto, *The Jewish Gauchos of the Pampas* [1910], Prudencia de Pereda, trans, Abelard–Schuman, New York, 1955, and London, 1959.

Gidley, Charles, *The Crying of the Wind*, HarperCollins, London, 1992.

Graham-Yooll, Andrew, *A State of Fear: Memories of Argentina's Nightmare*, Eland, London, 1986.

Greene, Graham, *The Honorary Consul* [1973], Penguin, London, 1974/Viking Penguin, New York, 1983. **Extract 27.**

Greene, Graham, *Travels with My Aunt* [1969], Penguin, London, 1971/Viking Penguin, New York, 1977. **Extract 28.**

Güiraldes, Ricardo, *Don Segundo Sombra* [1926], Harriet de Onís, trans, Penguin, London, 1948/ New American Library, New York, 1966. **Extract 35.**

Hand in Hand Alongside the Tracks and Other Tales, Norman Thomas di Giovanni, ed, Constable, London, 1992.

Head, Francis, *Rough Notes Taken During Some Rapid Journeys Across the Pampas*, John Murray, London, 1826.

Hernandez, José, *Martín Fierro* [1872], Walter Owen, trans, Instituto Cultural Walter Owen, Buenos Aires, 1967. **Extract 1.**

Hudson, W.H., *Far Away and Long Ago*, [1918], Eland, London, 1982. **Extract 13.**

Hudson, W.H., *Idle Days in Patagonia*, Chapman and Hall, London, 1893.

Hudson, W.H., 'Ralph Herne', in *El Ombu* [1902], J.M. Dent, London, 1923. **Extract 14.**

Kociancich, Vlady, *The Last Days of William Shakespeare*, Heinemann, London, 1990.

Lowell, Robert, 'Buenos Aires', in *The Review*, No 8, August 1963. **Extract 15.**

Lowell, Robert, *Notebook*, Faber and Faber, London, 1970/Farrar, Straus and Giroux, New York, 1970.

Laretta, Enrique, *The Glory of Don Ramiro: A Life in the Times of Phillip II* [1908], L.B. Walton, trans, J.M. Dent, London, 1924/ Dutton, New York, 1924.

Mallea, Eduardo, *All Green Shall Perish* [1941], Harriet de Onís, trans, Calder and Boyars, London, 1969. **Extract 4.**

Manguel, Alberto, *News from a Foreign Country Came* [1991] Flamingo, London, 1992. **Extract 16.**

Mármol, José, *Amalia: A Romance of the Argentine* [1851–55], Mary J. Serrano, trans, Gordon Press, New York, 1977.

Martínez, Tomás Eloy, *The Perón Novel* [1985], Asa Zatz, trans, Pantheon, New York, 1988. **Extract 32.**

Martínez Estrada, Ezequiel, *X-Ray of the Pampa* [1933], Alain Swietlicki, trans, University of Texas Press, Austin, TX, 1972.

Medina, Enrique, *The Duke: Memories and Anti-Memories of a Participant in the Repression* [1976],

David William Foster, trans, Zed Books, London, 1985.

Meyer, Gordon, *Exiles*, Alan Ross, London, 1968. **Extract 17.**

Meyer, Gordon, *The River and the People*, Methuen, London, 1963.

Mills, Diana, *Reapers of the Wind: A Novel of Argentina*, Hodder and Stoughton, London, 1989.

Moyano, Daniel, *The Devil's Trill* [1974], Giovanni Pontiero, trans, Serpent's Tail, London, 1988.

Mújica Láinez, Manuel, *Bomarzo: A Novel* [1962], Gregory Rabassa, trans, Weidenfeld and Nicholson, London, 1970/Simon and Schuster, New York, 1969.

Mújica Láinez, *The Wandering Unicorn* [1965], Mary Fitton, trans, Chatto and Windus, London, 1983/Lester and Orpen Dennys, Toronto, 1982.

Naipaul, V.S., *The Return of Eva Perón*, Andre Deutsch, London, 1982.

Ocampo, Silvina, *Leopoldina's Dream*, Daniel Balderston, trans, Penguin, Toronto, 1988.

Ocampo, Victoria, 'The Lakes of the South', in *The Green Continent*, Harriet de Onís, trans, Poetry London Editions, 1947. **Extract 5.**

Partnoy, Alicia, *The Little School: Tales of Disappearance and Survival in Argentina*, Virago, London, 1988/Cleis Press, Pittsburgh, PA, 1986.

Peyrou, Manuel, *Thunder of the Roses* [1948], Donald Yates, trans, Herder and Herder, New York, 1972.

Pizarnik, Alejandra, *Alejandra Pizarnik: A Profile*, Frank Graziano and Maria Rosa Fort, trans, Logbridge–Rhodes, Durango, CO, 1987.

Posse, Abel, *The Dogs of Paradise* [1987], Margaret Sayers Peden, trans, Sceptre, London, 1992/Atheneum, New York, 1989.

Puig, Manuel, *Heartbreak Tango: A Serial* [1969], Suzanne Jill Levine, trans, Arena, London, 1987/Dutton, New York, 1973. **Extract 18.**

Puig, Manuel, *Pubis Angelical* [1979], Elena Brunet, trans, Faber and Faber, London, 1987/Random House, New York, 1986. **Extract 19.**

Quiroga, Horacio, 'The Incense Tree Roof', in *The Decapitated Chicken and Other Stories* [1917], Margaret Sayers Peden, trans, University of Texas Press, Austin, TX, 1976. **Extract 36.**

Quiroga, Horacio, *South American Jungle Tales* [1918], Arthur Livingstone, trans, Methuen, London, 1923/Duffield, New York, 1922. **Extract 33.**

Rivabella, Omar, *Requiem for a Woman's Soul*, Penguin, London, 1987/Random House, New York, 1986.

Sabato, Ernesto, *On Heroes and Tombs* [1961], Helen Lane, trans, Jonathan Cape, London, 1982/David Godine, Boston, MA, 1981. **Extracts 20 and 21.**

Sabato, Ernesto, *The Tunnel* [1948], Margaret Sayers Peden, trans, Jonathan Cape, London, 1988/Random House, New York, 1988. **Extract 22.**

Saer, Juan José, *The Witness*, Margaret J. Costa, trans, Serpent's Tail, London, 1990.

Sarmiento, Domingo F., *Life in the Argentine Republic in the Days of the Tyrants* [1845], Mrs Horace Mann, trans, Gordon Press, New York, 1976. **Extract 2.**

Satz, Mario, *Sol* [1976], Helen Lane, trans, Sidgwick and Jackson, London, 1979/Doubleday, New York, 1979.

Soriano, Osvaldo, *A Funny Dirty Little War* [1982], Nick Caistor, trans, Readers International, London, 1983.

Strachey, Isobel, *A Summer in*

Buenos Aires, Jonathan Cape, London, 1947. **Extracts 23 and 24.**

Thornton, Lawrence, *Imagining Argentina*, Bloomsbury, London, 1987/Bantam, New York, 1991. **Extract 25.**

J. Timmerman, *Prisoner without a Name, Cell without a Number*, Penguin, London, 1981.

Valenzuela, Luisa, 'Family for Clotilde', in *Open Door*, Hortense Carpentier and J. Jorge Castello, trans, Serpent's Tail, London, 1992/North Point Press, San Francisco, CA, 1988. **Extract 34.**

Valenzuela, Luisa, *The Lizard's Tail* [1983], Gregory Rabassa, trans, Serpent's Tail, London, 1987/ Farrar, Straus and Giroux, New York, 1983.

Vanasco, Alberto, 'Neither Saints Nor Sinners', in *Celeste Goes Dancing and Other Stories*, Norman Thomas di Giovanni, ed, Constable, London, 1989. **Extract 3.**

Vasconcelos, José, in *The Green Continent*, Harriet de Onís, trans, Poetry London Editions, 1947. **Extract 31.**

Vázquez Rial, Horacio, *Triste's History* [1987], Jo Labayni, trans, Readers International, London, 1990. **Extract 26.**

Extracts

(1) ARGENTINA: INDIAN HORSES

José Hernández, *Martín Fierro*

The outlaw Martín Fierro ('iron' in Spanish), gaucho, boasts about his horse skills, and the power of Indian horses after his and Cruz's stay with the wild Indians while on the run as deserters.

There isn't a danger in all the world,
But mounted well I'll meet;
The Indian's horse was a glossy black,
I was fit for anything on its back,
It could cover the ground like a leaping hound
with the 'bolas' round its feet.
    There was nothing it met on the open plain
That worried it in its stride;
The Indians teach them to run like light
Till they run down an ostrich flock in flight.

(2) ARGENTINA: THE PAMPAS

Domingo F. Sarmiento,
Life in the Argentine Republic

Sarmiento's pamphlet, published in 1845, was an attack on Facundo Quiroga, one of the gaucho henchmen of Rosas. The pamphlet opens with a vivid description of Argentina's pampas seen from exile in Chile.

The vast tract which occupies the Argentine Republic's extremities is altogether uninhabited, and possesses navigable rivers as yet unfurrowed even by a frail canoe. Its own extent is the evil from which the Argentine Republic suffers; the desert encompasses it on every side and penetrates its very heart; wastes containing no human dwelling are, generally speaking, the unmistakable boundaries between its several provinces. Immensity is the universal characteristic of the country; the plains, the woods, the rivers, are all immense; and the horizon is always undefined, always lost in haze and delicate vapours which forbid the eye to mark the point in the distant perspective where the land ends and the sky begins. On the south and on the north are savages ever on the watch, who take advantage of the moonlight nights to fall like a pack of hyenas upon the herds in their pastures and upon the defenceless settlements. When the solitary caravan of wagons, as it sluggishly traverses the pampas, halts for a short period of rest, the men in charge of it, grouped around their scanty fire, turn their eyes mechanically toward the south upon the faintest whisper of the wind among the dry grass and gaze into the deep darkness of the night, in search of the sinister visages of the savage horde which at any moment, approaching unperceived, may surprise them. If no sound reaches their ears, if their sight fails to pierce the gloomy veil which covers the silent wilderness, they direct their eyes, before entirely dismissing their apprehensions, to the ears of any horse standing within the firelight, to see if they are pricked up or turned carelessly backwards. Then they resume their interrupted conversation or put into their mouths the half-scorched pieces of dried beef on which they subsist. When not fearful of the approach of the savage, the plainsman has equal cause to dread the keen eyes of the tiger, or the viper beneath his feet. This constant insecurity of life outside the towns, in my opinion, stamps upon the Argentine character a certain stoical resignation to death by violence, which is regarded as one of the inevitable probabilities of existence. Perhaps this is the reason why they inflict death or submit to it with so much indifference and why such events make no deep or lasting impression upon the survivors.

(3) ARGENTINA: A SHANTYTOWN

Alberto Vanasco, *Neither Saints nor Sinners*

In Vanasco's short story, two skint friends find a wallet and after much soul-searching decide to give it back to the old couple who had vacated a seat on the packed bus out to Barracas. They locate them in a shanty town. This story is included in the anthology Celeste Goes Dancing and Other Stories – *see Booklist.*

Early the next day they caught a tram straight out to Lanús Este. Half an hour later the vehicle was creeping along unpaved streets lined with little houses flimsily built out of bits of wood and galvanized iron and open on all sides to the wind and the rain. Out in front were tiny yards of baked earth and straggly plants. From the tram window, Basilio and Jacinto saw ever more undeniable signs of extreme poverty and grim destitution filing past.

'Bye bye, little pile of money,' said Basilio as they arrived. 'Get out the wallet; we'll have to give it back.'

'Not so hasty. Maybe they own the whole neighbourhood,' replied Jacinto.

The tramline ended in a square, and they had to get out and make their way along a miry street for another three blocks, until they stood in front of the house they were looking for. It was not so much a house as a shanty made of mud bricks, a sort of rundown shack that had stubbornly held its ground while the suburb mushroomed all around it . . .

(4) BAHIA BLANCA

Eduardo Mallea, *All Green Shall Perish*

Novelist Mallea describes his home town Bahía Blanca in summer through Agata Cruz's journey there from her isolated farm, and disastrous marriage.

Behold Bahía Blanca, city of the south, lashed by Atlantic sands.

Like the cautious paw of the cat with the trusting kitten, summer plays with the city by the sea. Swiftly, a sunbeam moves down from the dome of City Hall and fiercely nullifies the square. All at once the still leaves of the sycamores are host to the joyous chirping of the siesta. Weary lawyers' assistants and their employers exchange glances of mutual, blunted envy. Tied to their old victorias, in four sparse rows around the municipal square, thirteen rachitic horses, heads drooping, stand for ever at ease. Throughout the square, young clerks from the offices of Notary Pontevín heatedly nourish their hatred of old clerks from the offices of Notary Balaguer. Idle shoeshine boys, café waiters, lottery brokers, ambitious schoolteachers, sedentary, dyspeptic accountants, on their own responsibility dare to defy the December sun and walk the streets. And in the Italian restaurant, among the odours of sawdust and pickled fish, provincial deputies – Asiatic and prophetic – enjoy a sumptuous lunch.

Here all is prosperity, all is commerce. Into the city – stony oasis on barren land – flow and are shipped out tons and tons of grain. International grain dealers, *criollo* concessionaires on commission, Hebrew experts, speculators, salesmen engage in their second-hand machinations for the home office. The controlling octopus is Buenos Aires. But in the midst of its rural moderation and monotony, this city swept by sandy winds is the promised land. What effort and energy, how many barren years of sacrifice and monotony have gone into the making of this shining prosperity! The intense summer heats, the winds, the dust swirling up Avenida Colón. The grey city, the oasis of the *quintas* of the well-to-do, the houses of the farmers who came to live in the city, the doctors who came to sacrifice themselves and make money, the cunning lawyers, the stores of agricultural implements, the consulates. The square, like a Sahara at siesta time, and proud O'Higgins Street full of foreigners and *elegantes* . . .

(5) BARILOCHE

Victoria Ocampo, *The Lakes of the South*

> *Victoria Ocampo, editor and owner of the literary magazine* Sur, *who learnt French before Spanish and worshipped Europe, here makes a rare journey into her own country down south to the lake district at Bariloche. 'The Lakes of the South' was published in the anthology* The Green Continent – *see Booklist.*

But finally last November I took the train at Constitución. There was the endless procession of hours and the everlasting ceremony of the damp towels against the windows, on a train that picked the most desolate places to stop, and maliciously halted there for hours on end, and where, instead of thirst-quenching fruit, I was offered chunks of petrified forest at ten cents apiece. And, into the bargain, I was ashamed to complain of my first-class accommodations after seeing the second-class; but at last one morning I found myself in Bariloche just as I had lost all hopes of ever arriving.

A few minutes before we entered the pleasant stone station I forgot my fatigue. The lake had come up to meet us. How blue it looked against the background of the snow-capped mountains, beside the bushes covered with flowers so red that they seemed land coral reefs! These bushes, the harbingers of spring in the Andes, whose name and existence I was unaware of (we call them *ciruelillos*; North Americans have given them the name of firebush), gave us a dazzling welcome all along the way, like Lake Nahuel Huapi itself. Not a breath of wind stirred it that day; vast and calm, it looked up at the sky without blinking, while the sky descended to its very depths.

By noon, on the road from Bariloche to Llao-Llao which skirts the lake and grows in wonders as it advances, I asked myself if I was on another planet . . . The giant *coihues* of the forests of Llao-Llao, those huge columns that terminate in a few small-leaved branches, seem trees that belong to another geological age, and it would not surprise us to see the long neck and tiny head of a dinosaur peering out from the bamboo-like *coihues* growing at their feet.

(6) Buenos Aires

Adolfo Bioy Casares, *The Dream of the Hero*

Bioy Casares places his quipping loungers in the Buenos Aires of the 1930s, at the height of its glamour and power.

They began feeling thirsty and, making jokes about their dryness, comparing their throats to an engine that has seized up, or to sandpaper, they reached El Aeroplano bar opposite plaza Díaz Vélez. Near their table there were two men drinking: one leaning against the bar and the other with his elbows on a table. The one at the bar was tall, cheerful and relaxed looking, with his hat tilted back. The other was not so thin and was blond, with very fair skin, thoughtful, sad, light blue eyes and a blond moustache.

'Listen, friend,' the fair-haired one was explaining in a loud voice, as though he wanted everyone to hear him, 'the fate of this country is pretty strange. Tell me, what is Argentina known for the world over?'

'Brilliantine,' replied the one at the bar. 'Tragacanth gum, that comes from India.'

'Come on now, don't be a fool. I'm being serious. Let's weigh it all up; I'm not talking about wealth, since before the economic recovery and the sanitation programme, we were already a complete wash-out compared with the Yankees; nor about physical size, since not even the most partisan can deny that Brazil is twice as big; nor about the quantity of cattle or agricultural produce, because if you think about it there's more in the smallest market in Chicago than in the great granary of our Republic; nor about maté, that drink that comes in sacks from Brazil and Paraguay; and I've no wish to bore the pants off you with tales of books, not even with the greatest glory of our scribblers, the criolladas – Martín Fierro brand – which were invented by none other than Hidalgo, a fellow from across the river.

The young man at the bar replied with a yawn:

'OK. You've told me what you're not going to talk about, now tell me what you are. I sometimes wonder, Amaro, whether you aren't becoming a real old Spanish windbag.'

'Don't ever say that to me, not even as a joke. It's precisely because I'm every bit as true a native of Buenos Aires as you, even though I don't wear my hat tilted back, that I'm confiding these truths to you, with a heart that is burning my fingers like the fried potatoes that are sold in Paseo de Julio. It's enough to make you despair, Arocena. What I'm talking about are not trivialities. I'm talking about things that are real, legitimate reasons for our pride, which spring from the heart of our people: I'm talking about the tango and about football.'

(7) Buenos Aires

María Luisa Bombal, *New Islands*

Bombal's novella describes the grand cemetery of Buenos Aires, the Recoleta, a city within the city in the middle of the most fashionable district in the barrio norte.

The same serene twilight suffusing the pampa washes over Buenos Aires, inundating in steel blue the stone and the air and the mist-covered trees in Recoleta Square.

Juan Manuel's mother walks confidently through a labyrinth of narrow streets. Never has she lost her way in this intricate city, for as a child her parents taught her how to find her bearings in any quarter. And here is their dwelling – the small cold crypt where parents, grandparents, and so many ancestors rest. So many in such a narrow chamber! If only it were true that each of them sleeps alone with his past and his present, isolated yet side by side! But no, that isn't possible. She lays her spray of orchids on the ground, rummaging through her purse for the key. Then, before the altar, she makes the sign of the cross and checks that the candelabra are well polished, that the white altar cloth is well starched. She sighs and descends into the crypt, holding nervously on to the bronze railing. An oil lamp hangs from the low ceiling, its flame mirrored in the black marble floor and shining on the bronze rings of the various compartments arranged sequentially by date. Here all is order and solemn indifference.

Outside, the drizzle starts up again. The raindrops rebound audibly on the concrete streets. But here everything seems remote: the rain, the city, the obligations that await her at home. And now she sighs, going over to the smallest and newest compartment – where Elsa's face reposes. Poor Juan Manuel, she thinks.

She tries unsuccessfully to feel sadness for her daughter-in-law's fate. But that rancor she admits only to the priest persists in her heart, despite the dozens of rosaries and the multiple short prayers her confessor orders her to recite as penance.

(8) Buenos Aires

Jorge Luis Borges,
The Mythical Founding of Buenos Aires

The poem from which these stanzas are taken plays with the river, the provincial past, the neighbourhoods. Borges placed poems in actual places like the Recoleta (the cemetery – see Extract 7), Plaza San Martín, and barrio sur, and called his 1923 collection 'Fervor de Buenos Aires'. 'The Mythical Founding of Buenos Aires' is included in Selected Poems – see Booklist.

On the coast they put up a few ramshackle huts
and slept uneasily. This, they claim, in the Riachuelo,
but that is a story dreamed up in the Boca.
It was really a city block in my district – Palermo.
A whole square block, but set down in open country,
attended by dawns and rains and hard southeasters,
identical to that block which still stands in my neighborhood:
Guatemala – Serrano – Paraguay – Gurruchaga.
A general store pink as the back of a playing card
shone bright; in the back there was poker talk.
The corner bar flowered into life as a local bully,
already cock of his walk, resentful, tough.
The first barrel organ teetered over the horizon
with its clumsy progress, its *habaneras*, its wop.
The cart-shed wall was unanimous for YRIGOYEN.
Some piano was banging out tangos by Saborido.
A cigar store perfumed the desert like a rose.
The afternoon had established its yesterdays,
and men took on together an illusory past.
Only one thing was missing – the street had no other side.
Hard to believe Buenos Aires had any beginning.
I feel it to be as eternal as air and water.

(9) Buenos Aires

Jorge Luis Borges, *The South*

The librarian in this autobiographical story has recovered from an injury that made him delirious (like Borges's own accident in 1938), and sets off from one of the main Buenos Aires stations 'south' to a childhood estancia, and an eventual duel with a drunken gaucho.

Reality favours symmetries and slight anachronisms: Dahlmann had arrived at the sanitorium in a hackney coach and now a hackney coach was to take him to the Constitución station. The first fresh tang of autumn, after the summer's oppressiveness, seemed like a symbol in nature of his rescue and release from fever and death. The city, at seven in the morning, had lost that air of an old house lent it by the night; the streets seemed like long vestibules, the plazas were like patios. Dahlmann recognized the city with joy on the edge of vertigo: a second before his eyes registered the phenomena themselves, he recalled the corners, the billboards, the modest variety of Buenos Aires. In the yellow light on the new day, all things returned to him.

Every Argentine knows that the South begins at the other side of Rivadavia. Dahlmann was in the habit of saying that this was no mere convention, that whoever crosses this street enters a more ancient and sterner world. From inside the carriage he sought out, among the new buildings, the iron grill windows, the brass knocker, the arched door, the entrance way, the intimate patio.

At the railway station he noted that he still had thirty minutes. He quickly recalled that in a café on the Calle Brazil (a few dozen feet from Yrigoyen's house) there was an enormous cat which allowed itself to be caressed as if it were a disdainful divinity. He entered the café. There was the cat, asleep. He ordered a cup of coffee, slowly stirred the sugar, sipped it (this pleasure had been denied him in the clinic), and thought, as he smoothed the cat's black coat, that this contact was an illusion and that the two beings, man and cat, were as good as separated by a glass, for man lives in time, in succession, while the magical animal lives in the present, in the eternity of the instant.

(10) Buenos Aires
Haroldo Conti, *Lost*

Conti, a writer who was 'disappeared' by the Argentine military in 1976, opens this story with his narrator describing the English clock tower in Buenos Aires near the main Retiro station (though it was renamed after the Falklands/Malvinas war: formerly Torre de los Ingleses, now Plaza de la Fuerza Aérea Argentina). This passage is extracted from the journal Translation – see Booklist.

To Oreste, Buenos Aires was the English Clock Tower, the Avenida de Mayo, Alem, and, somewhat unusually, the statue of Garibaldi in Plaza Italia, because the first time he ever set foot in the city – he was with his mother – they had got lost and that's where they ended up. They had their picture taken, and the man with the camera steered them to a tram that got them to Retiro Station. They managed to arrive in plenty of time, but all the same they were so flustered they almost boarded the wrong train.

Now, crossing Plaza Británica with its clock tower that somehow presided over his life and that he saw or glimpsed about Buenos Aires, here was his old melancholy welling up, and Oreste pictured his uncle in a corner of the waiting room of the Pacific (they still called it the Pacific) . . .

(11) Buenos Aires
Julio Cortázar, *Text in a Notebook*

Cortázar's narrator speculates about mysterious people who live all their lives on the underground in Buenos Aires, called the 'Subte'. 'Text in a Notebook' is included in the collection We Love Glenda So Much and Other Tales – see Booklist.

Curiously, what has bothered me most from the start has been finding out how they lived, without any reason for that life to be of the least importance to me. Almost immediately I rejected the idea of sidings or abandoned tunnels; the existence of all of them was manifest and coincided with the coming and going of the passengers between stations. It's true that between Loria and Plaza Once you can catch sight of a vague kind of Hades full of forges, sidings, piles of materials, and strange little huts with blackened windows. That kind of Nibelheim is glimpsed for a few seconds as the train shakes us almost brutally on the curves at the entrance to the station that's so bright in contrast. But it was enough for me to think of all the workers and foremen who share those dirty galleries to dismiss them as a usable redoubt; they wouldn't have exposed themselves there, not during the early days at least. I needed only a few observation trips to realize that nowhere, outside of the line itself – I mean the stations and their platforms and the trains in almost permanent motion – was there a place or conditions that could lend themselves to their life. I went along eliminating sidings, switch-offs, and storerooms until I arrived at the clear and horrible truth through what was of necessity left behind, residual, there in that twilight realm where the idea of being left behind kept returning time and time again. The existence that I am sketching out (some are probably saying that I'm proposing it) appeared to me to be conditioned by the most brutal and implacable necessity; out of the successive rejections of possibilities the only possible solution left was emerging. They, it had become only too clear now, aren't localized anywhere; they live on the subway, on the trains of the subway, moving continually. Their existence and their circulation like leukocytes – they're so pale! – favors the anonymity that has protected them so far.

Having reached this conclusion, I found the rest obvious. Except at dawn and very late at night, the Anglo trains are never empty because Buenos Aires people are night owls and there are always a few passengers coming and going before the station gates are closed. One might imagine now a last useless train that runs along following its schedule even though no one is getting on any longer, but I never got to see that. Or rather, yes, I did get to see it a few times but it was empty really only for me; the few passengers belonged to them, continuing their night through the fulfilment of inflexible instructions. I was never able to locate the nature of their necessary refuge during the three idle hours when the Anglo branch shuts down, from two to five in the morning. Either they stay on a train that's going onto a siding (and in that case the motorman has to be one of them) or they mingle episodically with the nocturnal cleaning people. This last is the least probable, for reasons of dress and personal relationships, and I prefer to suspect the use of the tunnel, unknown to regular passengers, that connects the Once station with the docks.

(12) Buenos Aires

Rubén Darío, *Song to the Argentine*

The Nicaraguan poet Darío lived in Buenos Aires from 1893 to 1898 ('Oh Cosmopolis!'), published his crucial Prosas profanas, 1896, and essays there, and worked for the great newspaper La Nación. There are references to the Tigre, to cafés (the Tortoni), estancias, Martín García Island (which has a monument to him) and local people. Later he wrote a celebratory 'song' on the centennial of Argentina's independence, from which these lines are taken. Extracted from Selected Poems of Rubén Darío – see Booklist.

The docks bristled with smokestacks;
new ideas and new muscles
landed at the seaports,
sent here by distant nations . . .
To offer thanks to God,
the liberal city preserves
the nave of its cathedral,
and the walls of all churches
will rise in every quarter,
all of them equally blest,
the synagogues, the mosques,
the chapels, and the pagodas . . .
Traffic, the city's bustle . . .
the passing of wheels and hooves,
the voice of domestic pianos,
profound human murmurs,
the sound of united voices,
cries and calls, all vibrant
(the pulsing of a taut string),
the feeling of a vital center
like the beat of a great heart
or the breathing of the capital's breast.
Let your proud hymn ring out,
free men of a free land!
Grandsons of the conquistadors,
renewed blood of Spain,
transfused blood of Italy,
of Germany, of the Basques . . .
of the new Europe that promises
a greater Argentine to come.

(13) BUENOS AIRES

W.H. Hudson, *Far Away and Long Ago*

In his old age in England, Hudson recalls an early visit in the
1850s to the slaughtering grounds of Buenos Aires, called the
'Saladero' ('salting meat').

The famous saladero, or killing-grounds, where the fat cattle, horses
and sheep brought in from all over the country were slaughtered every
day, some to supply the town with beef and mutton and to make
charque or sun dried beef, for exportation to Brazil, where it was used to
feed the slaves, but the greater number of the animals, including all the
horses, were killed solely for their hides and tallow. The grounds
covered a space of three or four square miles, where there were cattle
enclosures made of upright posts placed close together, and some low
buildings scattered about. To this spot were driven endless flocks of
sheep, cattle in herds of a hundred or so to a thousand, each moving in
its cloud of dust, with noises of bellowing and bleatings and furious
shouting of the drovers as they galloped up and down, urging the
doomed animals on. When the beasts arrived in too great numbers to
be dealt with in the buildings, you could see hundreds of cattle being
killed in the open all over the grounds in the old barbarous way the
gauchos use, every animal being first lassoed, then hamstrung, then its
throat cut – a hideous and horrible spectacle with a suitable accompani-
ment of sounds in the wild shouts of the slaughterers and the awful
bellowings of the tortured beasts. Just where the animal was knocked
down and killed, it was stripped of its hide and the carcass cut up, a
portion of the flesh and the fat being removed and all the rest left on
the ground to be devoured by the pariah dogs, the carrion-hawks, and a
multitude of screaming black-headed gulls always in attendance. The
blood so abundantly shed from day to day, mixing with the dust, had
formed a crust half a foot thick all over the open space: let the reader
try to imagine the smell of this crust and of tons of offal and flesh and
bones lying everywhere in heaps. But no, it cannot be imagined. The
most dreadful scenes, the worst in Dante's *Inferno* for example, can be
visualized by the inner eye; and sounds, too, are conveyed to us in a
description so that they can be heard mentally; but it is not so with
smells. The reader can only take my word for it that *this* smell was
probably the worst ever known on earth . . . It was the smell of carrion,
of putrefying flesh, and of that old and ever-newly moistened crust of
dust and coagulated blood. It was, or seemed, a curiously substantial
and stationary smell; travellers approaching or leaving the capital by
the great south road, which skirted the killing-grounds, would hold
their noses and ride a mile or so at a furious gallop until they got out of
the abominable stench.

(14) Buenos Aires

W.H. Hudson, *Ralph Herne*

Hudson's weakly plotted story has a British doctor going out to yellow-fever plagued Buenos Aires in the 1870s. 'Ralph Herne' is included in El Ombu – see Booklist.

After a voyage of thirty days, during which some intermediate ports were touched at, he arrived at Buenos Aires, which is far removed from the ocean, and can yet hardly be called an inland city, so vast and sea-like is the river on whose shores it stands. He had expected to find a sleepy sub-tropical Spanish town with people wearing the broadest of broad Panama hats, and smoking cigarettes, and lounging languidly about, as they invariably do in pictures of South American life. But he found instead a city of vast dimensions with all the streets adjoining the water filled with continuous streams of hurrying people, dressed very much as Londoners, and with the same rapt expression of devotion to business illuminating their countenances. The noise was simply deafening. The thunder of heavily-laden vans over the rough pavement of granite cubes, the perpetual jingling of innumerable tram-cars, ear-splitting cries from newsboys, and a thousand other sounds, made it a perfect pandemonium, compared with which the heart of London seems peaceful and quiet as a country village. He was past the age when noise is loved (according to the philosophers) for its own sake, but he had strong nerves, and all this unexpected stir and racket exhilarated him and filled him with very splendid ideas about the possibilities of the place. And at any moment, by stepping into a tram-car, he could have himself swiftly carried away, out of all this hurly-burly into quiet suburban lanes, with houses embosomed in vines and orange trees, standing in the middle of large gardens. There, too, were broad green parks and groves of towering eucalyptus, acacia and paradise trees, the last with graceful feathery foliage, and pale, lilac-coloured blossoms filling the warm air with delicate unfamiliar fragrance. Another thing he greatly wondered at in that Spanish-speaking land, so many thousands of miles from home, was the number of English people in it. There were churches, schools, newspapers, a club, a hospital and other things, all English; so that it seemed almost like one of the colonies to him, only with the difference in its favour that he was welcomed with as much warmth by everyone, and made as much of, as if visitors from the mother country were few and far between. The climate was delightful – the name says so – 'simply perfect' he was told by a resident he conversed with; and yet – strange contradiction! – there was a great deal of illness in the town, it was in fact a doctor's paradise, and Ralph at once determined to make it his home.

(15) BUENOS AIRES

Robert Lowell, *Buenos Aires*

US poet Robert Lowell later redrafted this poem and aptly retitled it 'Mania in Buenos Aires'. The following are the opening stanzas of the earlier version, taken from the magazine The Review *– see Booklist. The Hotel Continental still exists.*

In my room at the Hotel Continental
a thousand miles from nowhere,
I heard
the bulky, beefy breathing of the herds.

Cattle furnished my new clothes:
my coat of limp, chestnut-colored suede,
my sharp shoes
that hurt my toes.

A false fin de siècle decorum
snored over Buenos Aires
lost in the pampas
and run by the barracks.

(16) BUENOS AIRES

Alberto Manguel,
News from a Foreign Country Came

Manguel's narrator is the wife of a French military adviser on torture, hired by the Argentine generals; but before she discovers this she compares Buenos Aires to other cities in her life.

Buenos Aires turned out to be a patchwork of my other two cities, a mongrel Algiers in which the grimy arcades metamorphosed themselves into baroque French palaces, and the vast flat houses gathered around a cool courtyard hidden behind Napoleonic façades from the fifteenth district in Paris. Crowds like my African crowds sat in sidewalk cafés like Parisian cafés, and men with copper faces pushed past me in suits from the Avenue Matignon. The traffic and the apartment houses were Paris; the trees and the music in the suburbs were Algiers. I would sometimes stop at a corner, bewildered, transported to another country left behind long ago. Many times I felt homesick.

(17) BUENOS AIRES

Gordon Meyer, *Exiles*

In the story 'Exiles' (in the collection of the same name), Meyer describes a mad Italian who lives on Plaza Italia (with its statue of Garibaldi, who had fought against Rosas in Montevideo) in Buenos Aires, and who echoes his own exile.

In spring, you remember, from millions of points, those bell-shaped flowers, not unlike the throatwort, would bud, bloom, swing to and fro, chiming their noiseless chimes on the soft riverine heat; and long before summer's ferocious heat, had drowned the plaza in violet shadow. For the periphery of that plaza in which you then lived was a cordon of jacarandá trees, all leaning over slightly, like a corps-de-ballet, inclined from the waist, hands entwined over heads.

Other trees grew there – eucalypti, casuarinas, magnolias, and immensely tall palms exploding at their crowns into fronds overhanging like giant roosters' tails. All failed somehow to beautify the square. They were city-soiled. The jacarandá flowers, on the other hand, died before they could be sullied.

In the centre of the plaza, on an unlovely grey block, stood the monument. For some reason, in the cities of that country there always had to be a monument in plazas and every other vacant space. You came to think that there was a fear of natural spaces; they had to be dominated. And by a French sculptor, if possible – that was important.

(18) BUENOS AIRES

Manuel Puig, *Heartbreak Tango*

Puig's Nené writes home ('Coronel Vallejos', based on General Villegas where Puig was born) about her honeymoon in Buenos Aires.

When he started the car, my husband looked at my face and laughed, but he also felt emotional, because he had seen his mother crying too, poor lady, she seems to be real nice. I lowered my veil and fooled him. I didn't want him to see me with my makeup running. Luckily the dirt road had been flattened by the rain and we reached Lincoln at around midnight. There we spent the night, and after lunch the next day we continued on to Buenos Aires. By about seven o'clock we were already entering Buenos Aires, straight down Rivadavia Avenue, what lights! my husband pointed out the different districts we passed, Ciudadela, Flores, Caballito, what pretty names – no? – Independence Square, right to this lovely hotel, enormous, four stories high, and old but well preserved, it's on Callao Avenue and near to, of all places, Congress.

I had only been to Buenos Aires twice, once when I was little, and the other time when they admitted grandma to the hospital . . . Well, what I want to tell you is that I hardly knew the place, really. And the hotel is very steep but it's worth it, it's a good place for my husband because he has to receive businessmen here.

(19) BUENOS AIRES

Manuel Puig, *Pubis Angelical*

Puig's narrating woman, recovering in hospital from a cancer operation, recalls one of her lovers, a right-wing opera buff who worked at the Teatro Colón in Buenos Aires during the politicized 1970s.

By then I think that the trouble at the Theater was already starting. It was the season of '73, the Peronist government of Cámpora had already come to power. Pozzi was overjoyed with the atmosphere of freedom, especially the freedom of the press, and amnesty for prisoners. Before that twenty-fifth of May when Cámpora rose to power and let all the political prisoners go free, poor Pozzi had been incredibly busy with his prisoners. Now that he had some spare time I was already mixed up with this guy. But how can one make sense of something like this, that I should have offered myself to this person, despite the repugnance that he stirred up in me? . . .

And the intrigue at the Theater. During a performance of *Rigoletto*, at intermission, some thirty or forty hooligans came in through a passageway and began to sing several stanzas of the national anthem, at the top of their lungs. The audience, as always when the national anthem is sung at a public ceremony, stood up, from a combination of respect and fear which was nauseating. Respect toward the anthem and fear toward the intruders, do you understand? But how had they been able to get in? Someone in the management had to have been in complicity, no doubt about it. Without even finishing the song they started shouting in unison that the Teatro Colón was for Argentine performers, and out with the foreigners. It was a group of nationalists, of those who loathe anything foreign. And who wanted to demand that we engage only Argentine singers. But that was absurd.

(20) BUENOS AIRES

Ernesto Sabato, *On Heroes and Tombs*

In Sabato's novel chronicling porteño life in the 1950s, Fernando follows a blind man into the Banking District.

The man got off the train at the Plaza Mayo terminal before it made its final run to Palermo, and left the station via the exit leading to the Calle San Martín.

We began to walk down this street toward Cangallo.

At the intersection he turned off in the direction of the port district.

I was obliged to redouble my precautions, since on this lovely winter night there was almost no one out on the streets except the blind man and me. I therefore followed him at a prudent distance, taking into account the acute sense of hearing that such individuals have and the instinct that warns them that their secrets are in danger of being discovered.

The silence and the loneliness were as overwhelming as always at night in the Banking District. A far more silent and lonely district at night than any other – by contrast, doubtless, with the violent commotion typical of these same streets during the day: the noise, the indescribable confusion, the frantic hustle and bustle, the immense multitude rushing back and forth during Business Hours. But also, almost certainly, on account of the sacred solitude that reigns in these places when Money is taking its rest, once the last employees and office managers have gone home and an end has come to the exhausting and absurd daily round of activities whereby poor devils who earn five thousand pesos a month handle five million, and whereby veritable multitudes deposit, with infinite precautions, pieces of paper with magic properties which other multitudes withdraw from other little windows with inverse precautions. A completely unreal, phantasmagorical process, for even though they, the believers, regard themselves as realistic and practical persons, they accept these dirty pieces of paper on which, if one looks at them very carefully, one can make out a sort of absurd promise, whereby a gentleman who does not even sign with his own hand pledges, in the name of the State, to give something or other to the believer in exchange for the aforesaid dirty bit of paper. And the curious thing is that this individual believes this promise, since so far as I know, no one has ever demanded that this obligation be honored; and more surprising still, in exchange for these dirty bits of paper the person is generally handed another piece of paper that is cleaner but still more absurd, wherein another gentleman promises that in exchange for this paper the believer will be handed a certain quantity of the aforementioned dirty bits of paper: so that the whole thing is a sort of madness raised to the second power. And all this represents Something that no one has ever seen, something said to be deposited Somewhere, in the United States especially, in Steel caverns. And the fact that this entire process is of a religious nature is indicated first and foremost by words such as *credits* and *fiduciary*.

As I was saying, then, once such districts have been cleared of the frantic throngs of believers, they become more deserted than any other, since no one lives there at night and no one could live there, because of the absolute silence that reigns and the tremendous solitude of the gigantic lobbies of the temples of finance and the enormous underground caverns where the incredible treasures are kept, as meanwhile the powerful men who control this magic sleep uneasily, stuffed full of pills and drugs and haunted by nightmares of financial disasters. And also for the obvious reason that there is nothing to eat in these districts, nothing that would permit human beings, or even rats or cockroaches, to live there permanently; and finally, on account of the extreme cleanliness that exists in these redoubts of nothingness, where everything is symbolic or at most a mere piece of paper; and even these pieces of paper, which might conceivably provide nourishment for moths and other small insects, are kept in formidable steel safes, invulnerable to all living species.

(21) BUENOS AIRES

Ernesto Sabato, *On Heroes and Tombs*

Sabato's love story about Alejandra and Martín is placed in a topographically exact Buenos Aires, here the Plaza San Martín with its Kavanagh building.

Once outside, Alejandra headed for the square, walked up the grassy slope, and sat down on one of the benches facing the river.

They sat there for quite some time in a silence that she finally ended by saying:

'How restful it is to hate oneself!'

Martín contemplated the Torre de los Ingleses, with its clock marking off the time going by. The Cade wharf, with its great squat smokestacks, stood out behind it, and the Puerto Nuevo with its grain elevators and cranes: abstract antediluvian animals, with their steel beaks and their heads of giant birds bending down as though to peck at the ships.

Silent and depressed, he watched night descending over the city, the red lights at the top of the smokestacks and towers, the brightly lighted signs of the Parque Retiro, the streetlamps of the square beginning to gleam against the blue black sky. Meanwhile thousands of men and women streamed out of the maw of the subways and with the same daily despair entered the maw of the suburban trains. He contemplated the Kavanagh, where lights were beginning to go on in the windows. Perhaps up there too, on the thirtieth or thirty-fifth floor, a lonely man turned on a light to chase away the darkness of his little room. How many failures of two people to understand each other, as was happening to him and Alejandra, how many lonely lives there might be in that one skyscraper!

And then he heard what he had been fearing he would hear from one moment to the next:

'I have to go now.'

'Already?'

'Yes.'

They walked down the steep grassy slope together and once they had reached the bottom she said goodbye to him and began walking away. Martín followed her, keeping a few steps behind.

'Alejandra!' he shouted. (The voice was almost that of another person.)

(22) BUENOS AIRES

Ernesto Sabato, *The Tunnel*

Sabato's narrator, a misunderstood, obsessional artist who opens the novel from prison, confessing his murder of María, here gives us a glimpse into his behaviour in the Buenos Aires of the 1940s.

Even as she was leaving, assuring me, yet again, that she had no hard feelings toward me, I was sinking into paralyzing inertia. I stood in the middle of my studio, oblivious of everything around me, staring blankly ahead like a cretin, until suddenly I became conscious that I must *do* something.

I ran outside, but María was nowhere to be seen. I rushed to her house by taxi, theorizing that she would not go directly home and that I could wait for her there. For more than an hour I waited in vain. I called her house from a bar. I was informed that she was not in and she had not been home since four o'clock (the hour she had left to come to my studio). I waited several hours more. I called again. I was told that María would not be home until late that evening.

Frantic, I looked for her everywhere, that is, in the places where we used to meet or walk: La Recoleta, Avenida Centenario, Plaza Francia, the port. I could not find her anywhere, and finally it dawned on me that logically she would be anywhere other than the places that reminded her of our happiest moments.

Again I rushed to her house, but by then it was so late I was sure that María must be home. I phoned once again. She had, in fact, returned, but she was in bed and could not come to the telephone. I left my name anyway.

Something between us had been shattered.

(23) BUENOS AIRES

Isobel Strachey, *A Summer in Buenos Aires*

Strachey evokes a confitería, or tea house, called the 'Paris'.

They drove along a broad avenue leading to the centre of the town passing by a vast monument to liberty reaching up, dazzling white, into the vivid sky, and a spacious park of pillared rose gardens, fountains and arbours. They passed palatial houses built in French style round courts and gardens, all their façades blankly shuttered; with an occasional white-coated man-servant lounging at the front door with a dog. Young men dressed in black stood idly on the pavements regarding the passers-by, few of whom were women. The traffic moved violently along comprising large open taxis with ceaselessly bleating horns, trams with cow-catchers and jangling bells, and rattling horse-cabs swerving in and out of the rest.

The Confiteria Paris had a magnificent interior of mirrored walls and marble floor and a heavy sweet fragrance of little buns and cakes piled on a baroque counter which wound along the glittering walls. These led into another larger hall containing little marble-topped tables with gilt chairs, long windows shaded with embroidered linen curtains and statues in the style of Ingres or Chardin in rounded alcoves in the painted walls. The tables hummed with fashionably dressed Argentines drinking coffee and chocolate, while a string quartet played mazurkas in a recess.

(24) BUENOS AIRES

Isobel Strachey, *A Summer in Buenos Aires*

Hurlingham, modelled on the London riverside club, is the hub of Anglo–Argentine social life.

The night train for Rosario and the north hurried past suburban level crossings, streets of rococo villas, large houses half hidden by the thick vegetation of their gardens, pieces of waste ground and clusters of huts built with empty kerosene tins and corrugated iron and hung with lines of washing. A narrow asphalt road followed the railway line between rows of trees. Violet and Miguel sat facing each other in their narrow compartment, rocked like shuddering dolls in a toy perambulator and smiling in happy complicity . . .

'Look,' he said, taking her arm, 'we have passed Hurlingham and the polo ground. You have never seen it, have you?'

'I went there once with Colonel Hamilton and the children,' she replied. 'We watched the polo while he played golf.'

There had been a lot of English people sitting in front of the club-house in deck-chairs, wearing striped blazers and calling loud and cheerful greetings to each other with an air of the close intimacy of a family party and a jolly almost aggressive appreciation of leisure spent in green and spacious surroundings.

(25) BUENOS AIRES

Lawrence Thornton, *Imagining Argentina*

Thornton's Carlos Rueda, theatre director with a gift for dreaming the truth about the 'disappearances' of the late 1970s in Buenos Aires under the military, discovers the Mothers of the Plaza de Mayo.

The Plaza de Mayo was less than a mile from the theater on the most direct route from Carlos' house. Though it cost him an extra twenty minutes coming and going, he had avoided the area since Cecilia's disappearance because the Casa Rosada, the seat of the government, lay just across the street from the Plaza. Carlos tried not to think about it as he and Esme walked along the Avenida Victor Ruiz. All of his attention was on the obelisk rising from the Plaza, which was topped with the statue of a woman in flowing robes who carried a spear. They were still too far to see the circular promenade, and for a moment his eyes drifted from the obelisk to the spires and cupolas of the buildings beyond, the thrust of palms and jacarandas and palo borracho trees, the bell tower of the odd church. But when they crossed the traffic of the roundabout his gaze fell level with the Plaza where upward of fifty women were walking in a slow, ritualistic procession. Each wore a white scarf which bound them together in some as yet unknown sorority. Were it not for the scarves they could have been a cross-section of the city's women: some clearly middle class, who could have been his neighbors; some poor Indians whose skin shone like polished wood. They all carried signs so that at a distance they appeared like a gathering of religious zealots brandishing cryptic phrases from the Book of Revelations, advertising the apocalypse.

As soon as he and Esme reached the edge of the Plaza he understood that the signs were epitaphs and that the women were bound by motherhood. Photographs of the disappeared were centered in each sign, and beneath them were inscriptions written in large black letters . . .

(26) BUENOS AIRES

Horacio Vázquez Rial, *Triste's History*

This novel about a death-squad thug opens with a bitter elegy to Buenos Aires.

On its northern, eastern and every flank except for the one that trails off into the *pampa* like a grubby, ragged strip of lace spattered with settlements and hamlets, the city looks out on to the mighty, open river with its one discernible shore and its ominous yellow waters beyond which may lie the world or nothing; solitary, sprawling, vast amid the vastness, Buenos Aires is the south, the meeting point of certain unmemorable destinies, of certain irrevocable encounters, where murderous and other devious assignments are hatched and sometimes dispatched under the shady auspices of smalltime political bosses, born of the murky grey of the concrete buildings and the pigeons

– which scavenge in the smog dotted with the twisted hands of little old ladies reduced by loneliness to scattering crumbs that are not exactly leftovers, vainly sowing the tarmac and paving stones with a few dozen seeds disputed by hundreds of flapping wings hovering without ever settling on the ground –

Buenos Aires is the south: in the south beyond the south, beyond the fictitious limits of what properly constitutes the capital's urban sprawl, in a zone thick with silence and with shabby, ramshackle houses once upon a time set in their own grounds and now, in 1942, swallowed up by a rash of flimsy modern blocks and the modest beginnings of what in ten or twenty years' time would become a swarming shanty town: there, in the depths of a rambling one-storey slum dwelling turned by a time-honoured chain of letting and sub-letting agreements into a tenement: there, in the last of the dozen rooms occupied by a dozen families and assorted groupings, with shared use of the one bathroom without hot water and a stove with three coal-fired burners: there, in that unsavoury hole, early one ice-cold morning, Cristóbal Artola was born . . .

(27) CORRIENTES

Graham Greene, *The Honorary Consul*

*Greene's protagonist, Dr Plarr, who will seduce the Honorary
Consul's ex-prostitute wife, describes Corrientes, where he lives,
and where Greene once spent 12 days.*

Doctor Plarr's practice prospered. He never regretted leaving the harsh
competition of the capital, where there were too many doctors with
German, French and English degrees, and he had grown fond of the
small city by the great Paraná river. There was a local legend that those
who once visited the city always returned, and it had certainly proved
true in his case. One glimpse of the little port with its background of
colonial houses, seen for an hour one dark night, had drawn him back.
Even the climate did not displease him – the heat was less humid than
he remembered it in the land of his childhood, and when the summer
broke up at last with an enormous eruption of thunder, he liked
watching from the window of his apartment the forked flashes dig into
the Chaco shore. Nearly every month he gave a dinner to Doctor
Humphries, and sometimes now he would take a meal with Charley
Fortnum who was always either sober, laconic and melancholy, or
drunk, talkative, and what he liked to term 'elevated'. Once he went to
Charley Fortnum's camp, but he was no judge of a maté crop and he
found the heaving motion of Fortnum's Pride as he was driven around
hectare by hectare – Charley called it 'farming' – so disagreeable that he
refused the next invitation. He preferred a night at the Nacional when
Charley would talk unconvincingly of a girl he had found.

Every three months Doctor Plarr flew down to Buenos Aires and
spent a weekend with his mother who was growing more and more stout
on her daily diet of cream-cakes and *alfajores* stuffed with *dulce de leche*.

(28) FORMOSA

Graham Greene, *Travels with my Aunt*

*Greene's narrator, a retired suburban banker, discovers the
thrills of life through travel in wild, unpredictable Argentina and
Paraguay. Here he describes the town of Formosa, on the Chaco
in northern Argentina and capital of Formosa province, with a
population of 95 000. The narrator is on his way by boat to
Asunción.*

It was two days later that we came to Formosa on a day which was as
humid as all the others had been. The heat broke on the cheek like
little bubbles of water. We had turned off the great Paraná river the

night before near Corrientes, and now we were on the Paraguay. Fifty yards across the water from the Argentinian Formosa the other country lay, sodden and empty . . . It certainly seemed an ideal town for smugglers with only a river to cross. In Paraguay I could see only a crumbling hut, a pig and a small girl.

I was tired of walking the deck, so I went ashore too. It was a Sunday and quite a crowd had collected to see the boat come in. There was a pervading smell of orange petals, but it was the only sweet thing about Formosa. One long avenue was lined with oranges and trees bearing rose-coloured flowers, which I learned later to be *lapachos*. The side-streets petered out a few yards away into a niggardly wild nature of mud and scrub. Everything to do with government business, justice or amusement lay in one avenue: a tourist hotel of grey cement on the water's edge had been half-built, for what tourists? little shops selling Coca-Cola: a cinema which advertised an Italian Western: two hairdressers: a garage with one wrecked car; a *cantina*. The only house of more than one storey was the hotel, and the only old and beautiful building in the long avenue proved, as I came closer to it, to be the prison. There were fountains all down the avenue but they didn't play.

The avenue must lead me somewhere, I thought, but I was wrong. I passed the bust of a bearded man called Urquiza who, judging from the carved inscription, must have had something to do with Liberation from what? – and ahead of me I saw rise up above the orange trees and the *lapachos* a marble man upon a marble horse who was certainly General San Martín – Buenos Aires had made me familiar with his features and I had seen him upon the sea-front at Boulogne too. The statue closed the avenue as the Arc de Triomphe closes the Champs Elysées; I expected some further avenue beyond, but when I reached the statue I found the hero sat on his horse in a waste of mud at the furthest limit of the town. No strollers came so far, and the road went no further. Only a starving dog, like a skeleton from the Natural History Museum, picked his way timorously across the dirt and the rain pools towards me and San Martín. I began to walk back.

(29) GAIMAN, PATAGONIA
Bruce Chatwin, *In Patagonia*

Chatwin leaves Buenos Aires for Patagonia and the Welsh colony village of Gaimán. The Welsh arrived in 1865, landing at Puerto Madryn.

I took the night bus on the Chubut Valley. By next morning I was in the village of Gaimán, the centre of Welsh Patagonia today. The valley was about five miles wide, a net of irrigated fields and poplar windbreaks, set between the white cliffs of the barranca – a Nile Valley in miniature.

The older houses in Gaimán were of red brick, with sash windows and neat vegetable gardens and ivy trained to grow over the porches. The name of one house was *Nith-y-dryw*, the Wren's Nest. Inside, the rooms were whitewashed and had brown painted doors, polished brass handles and grandfather clocks. The colonists came with few possessions but they clung to their family clocks.

Mrs Jones's teashop lay at the far end of the village where the bridge crossed over to the Bethel. Her plums were ripe and her garden full of roses.

(30) GOYA

Richard Burton,
Letters from the Battle-Fields of Paraguay

Burton takes a boat up the Paraná River and describes Goya (with a population today of some 47 000), a port on the way to Paraguay. It was the refuge of a priest who ran off with Camila and who was finally caught by dictator Rosas and executed (see María Luisa Bemberg's 1984 film Camila, and an untranslated novel by Enrique Molina, Una sombra donde sueña Camila O'Gorman, 1973).

Early on the next morning we passed the Costa Tala, where the river widens to an enormous girth; and at 7 am we reached Goya. Here both banks are very flat, the bright green vegetation is very tall, and the stream is three and a half leagues wide – a long riverine island, one of a mighty many, splitting it into an eastern and a western channel. Large ships ascend the latter; the former is comparatively shallow. Many craft go up the Bocas de Abajo or lower mouth to the port, and descend again, losing six to seven leagues, rather than encounter the Boca de Arriba. The name Goya is a corruption of Gregoria, the wife of a Portuguese settler, and must not be made with Mr Mansfield 'Goyaz', a province of the Brazil. Dating from 1820, it is one of the most thriving places in the Upper Paraná, and the Correntinos look upon it as a small Buenos Aires. I afterward visited the Puerto, on a sandy spit, close to the Arroyo de Goya. Here are the large white capitania and flagstaff, and six or seven brick houses; the rest are sheds, including a large graseria (where fat is boiled down), and a kind of chalet, which receives steamer-passengers. Carts and horses transport them to the Pueblo, a mile or so up stream, where an obelisk and white towers rise above green orchards. It is an industrious commercial little hive of 3000 souls, who export their hides and wool, oranges and cheeses; the latter are famed through the land, and so are the 'china' girls, who are said to press them by the simple process of supersession. The climate is feverish, and the place is too near the lowlands of the Sta Luzia River.

(31) THE IGUASSU FALLS

José Vasconcelos, *La raza cósmica*

Vasconcelos, ex-Minister for Education of the Mexican revolutionary government in the 1920s, travelled to the stunning Iguassú Falls on the borders of Argentina and Brazil. This passage (originally from La raza cósmica) is extracted from the anthology The Green Continent – see Booklist.

From the moment one steps on to the terrace of the Hotel Foz de Iguassú, one sees in front and a little below the magic fringe of the green woods and the white jets and curtains of water. The first thing that catches the eye is the little Argentine hotel with its red roof, set in its emerald lawn. Then as the eye sweeps the horizon, a succession of miracles appears. The sensation is so powerful that there is nothing to say, the sight imposes silence.

These falls come from a great lateral bifurcation of the Iguassú, which divides into a number of streams seeking a channel. They drop over the precipice and all come together again at a lower level. Beyond this the gorge fills up with trees, and above its rocky crenellation rises the plumy forest, crowned with the tall tufts of the palm trees . . . Almost at once the serene central semicircle of waters appears, drops first to a platform which boils with foam, then hurls itself into space again in a mass whose impact makes the earth shake. From where we stand it is impossible to see this gigantic down-pouring in all its extension – only the swollen masses of water which roll incessantly. As they fall, the streams intermingle, intertwine, or come together in a single mass; they boil and quiver, crash, and send up clouds of foam and mist which envelop everything as on the first day of creation. Something of primeval chaos exists in this spot, which from time immemorial has been known as the Devil's Throat.

(32) LA FORESTAL, THE CHACO

Tomás Eloy Martínez, *The Perón Novel*

Martínez's account of Perón's life is also a history of Argentina's liberation movements of the 1970s. Here he describes a minor incident in Perón's early life in the Chaco village of La Forestal.

According to the census of 1914 our population was eight million inhabitants, with one third born outside Argentina. Much of the country's basic industry was in foreign hands. In Patagonia, the newly arrived adventurers from Europe quickly fleeced the gullible *criollos*. The British in northern Sante Fe had an empire almost as large as their native land. It was called La Forestal. Their business consisted of cutting down the vast red *quebracho* forests from which they extracted tannin. The concession, which stretched from San Crisóbal to the borders of the Chaco, covered over five million acres and contained seven or eight towns where, I believe, some 10 000 men worked.

Everything under those skies belonged to the English: the stores, the water, the jungles, the security forces, and the women. Fortunately, they paid little attention to the women; they lived in big houses surrounded by golf courses and formal gardens and gave parties with entertainment provided by famous musicians who were brought in direct to that wilderness from the Teatro Colón. I heard that they hired Toscanini's entire orchestra in 1903 and that in 1915 – shortly before the tragedies that brought me to those parts – they arranged a recital by Caruso. Our little *criolla* women gave them indigestion. They preferred the love of other insipid blondes.

In July 1919, the towns rose up demanding higher wages and hygienic housing. La Forestal organized its own repressive army. They released the most hardened criminals from prison, put them in uniform, and gave them guns. Torture and murder began. The company shut off the strikers' water and electricity. The army stepped in once again.

One Saturday that same July, when my shift at the arsenal seemed more interminable than usual, I was handed a wire from Captain Descalzo. They were sending him to La Forestal to restore order, and he wanted me to go with him. He had already arranged my transfer and the appointment of a replacement. Lieutenant Perón could not refuse.

Descalzo put me in command of a detachment of twenty soldiers and assigned me to the village of Tartagal, where some 400 families lived. I have never forgotten those jungles. One rode through their denseness and saw swarms of birds like cobwebs in flight. Swamps stretched on both sides of the road and there were gleaming little towers that looked like bonfires. They were anthills. The *quebrachos* were in the distance, trees 50 to 100 feet tall, with twisted, knotty branches. Brick-colored dust hung in the atmosphere, drying everything it touched because of the tannin. No man survived in that environment more than twenty-five years. The English did tours of duty of eight to ten months. The *criollo* peons had no choice but to endure that hell until they died.

(33) Misiones

Horacio Quiroga, *South American Jungle Tales*

Quiroga lived as a pioneer in San Ignacio (his house and garden are now a museum) near Misiones, so called because the Jesuits had their empire in the region. He wrote local jungle stories in the Kipling manner about parrots, giant tortoises, rays, raccoons, and flamingoes.

In South America there is a river called the Yabebirí; and it flows through the city of Misiones. In this river there are many rays. A kind of mud fish like the salt-water skate; and the river, indeed, gets its name from them: 'Yabebirí' means the 'river of ray fish'. The ray is a wide, flat fish with a long, slender tail. The tail is very bony; and when it strikes you it cuts, and leaves poison in the wound. There are so many rays in the river that it is dangerous even to put your foot into the water. I once knew a man who had his heel pricked by a ray. He had to walk more than two miles home, groaning with pain all the way and fainting several times from the poison. The pain from a ray bite is one of the sharpest pains one can feel.

(34) Pinamar

Luisa Valenzuela, *Family for Clotilde*

This story, published in the collection entitled Open Door (see Booklist), is about a father–son rivalry and is set in the seaside resort of Pinamar – the 'in' place according to the 1991 South American Handbook.

He dug his penknife into the trunk of a pine tree. He wanted to go away, anyplace. If only Pinamar were a port, then he could at least imagine trips . . .

It was Sunday morning. With his jacket over his shoulder, Rolo walked through the trees surrounding the house, along the border of thickly clustered acacias, to the garden of the rear cottage. He had forgotten about the new tenant, but there she was to remind him, reclining on a deck chair in the shade, showing a great deal of white flesh and gleaming red hair. Rolo stopped short.

'Hi, darling, Where're you off to?' She had a warm, soft voice.
'To Mass,' he answered grudgingly.
'To Mass?' Coming from her, the word sounded new and mysterious.
The sun was burning bright. Rolo wanted to stretch out in the cool
air under the pines and simply listen to her. Instead he said, 'Yes, to
Mass. You may think our chapel small and ugly and unfinished, but
that's not what counts if you want to go to Mass.'
'Hmm. And if you were to stay here at my side and sip a gin and tonic,
wouldn't that be nicer than going to church?
'No.'
'Well, your good father would prefer to sit here with me. He isn't like
you. He doesn't go to Mass. Yesterday afternoon he passed by here on
horseback five times. Just a little while ago I saw him in a bathing suit;
he must be off for a swim . . . Stay a bit.'
She had deep-set dark-gray eyes. Rolo ran off without answering her.

(35) SAN ANTONIO ARECO
Ricardo Güiraldes, *Don Segundo Sombra*

*Güiraldes opens his novel, about intitiation into manhood
through the hard outdoor life of the gaucho, with a description of
San Antonio Areco, 140 km north north west of Buenos Aires,
where the Güiraldes family still has its estancia La Porteña, and
where there is the Güiraldes Museum.*

At the outskirts of the town, some ten blocks from the village square,
the old bridge throws its arch across the river, linking the houses and
gardens to the placid fields.
　　That day, as usual, I had come away to hide in the shade of a rock
and hook a few catfish that I could trade at La Blanqueada for sweets,
cigarettes or cash. But I was not in good spirits; I felt strangely sullen
and unsociable, and had not rounded up the gang that usually loafed
and fished with me . . . I was thinking. Thinking of my fourteen years
of life as a *guacho* – the name everyone around there probably gave me –
an abandoned orphan. With eyes half-shut, to keep out the things I did
not want to see, I pictured the town's forty blocks, the low flat houses,
the monotonous streets forever parallel or at right angles to each other.
In one of those blocks, no better and no worse than all the others, was
the house of my so-called aunts – my prison.

(36) San Ignacio, Misiones

Horacio Quiroga, *The Incense Tree Roof*

San Ignacio, site of one of the grandest Jesuit missions, was
where Quiroga lived. 'The Incense Tree Roof' is to be found in
The Decapitated Chicken and Other Stories – see Booklist.

In the state of Misiones, around and amidst the ruins of San Ignacio,
the second capital of the Jesuitical empire, rises the present town of the
same name – San Ignacio. It is composed of a number of small
properties hidden from each other by trees. At the edge of the ruins, on
a bare hill, rise a few rude houses bleached blinding white by the sun
and lime but graced at sunset with a magnificent view of the valley of
the Yadebirí river. There are stores in the district, more than the heart
could desire, to the point that it is impossible for a new road to open up
without a German, a Spaniard, or a Syrian setting up shop on the spot.
All the public offices are located within the space of two blocks: the
police station, the justice of the peace, the city offices, and a
coeducational school. As a note of local color, there is a bar
constructed on these same ruins – overrun, as you know, by vegetation
– a bar created in the days of the fever for yerba maté, the tea that
became the national drink of the area, when the plantation foremen
coming down the Upper Paraná toward Posadas eagerly debarked in
San Ignacio to sit, blinking tenderly, before a bottle of whiskey. I have
related the characteristics of that bar in another story so we won't go
into that again today.

But in the time we're talking about, not all the public offices were
actually located in the town. Between the ruins and the new port, a
half-league from each, on a magnificent mesa chosen for the private
delight of its inhabitant, lived Orgaz, the chief of the Bureau of
Records, and this public office was located in his house.

Orgaz's house was made of wood, with a roof of incense tree shingles
layered like slate. This is an excellent arrangement if you use dry
shingles that have been drilled for nail holes ahead of time. But when
Orgaz raised his roof, the wood was newly split, and he drove the nails
right through the shakes, with the result that the wooden shingles split
and curled up at the ends till the bungalow roof resembled a sea urchin.
Every time it rained, Orgaz had to change the position of his bed eight
or ten times, and all his furniture was marred with whitish water spots.

Biographies and plot summaries

BIOY CASARES, Adolfo (1914–).
Bioy Casares was born in **Buenos
Aires** on 15 September 1914, and
lives there now. He was the son of a
landowner, and was part educated at
home. In 1940 he married the poet
and short story writer Silvina Ocampo
(1906–), and became a member of
the editorial board of Victoria Ocampo's ◊ influential literary magazine
Sur. In 1932 he met and befriended
Jorge Luis Borges ◊ and co-authored
nine books with him between 1942
and 1970, sometimes under the
pseudonym of Honorario Bustos
Domecq (*Extraordinary Tales*, 1971;
Chronicles of Bustos Domecq, 1976,
and *Six Problems for Don Isidro Parodi*,
1981) which unfairly left him in
Borges's shadow. In 1990 he won
Spain's Premio Cervantes.

Bioy Casares is fascinated by
women, by detective stories whose
format he often borrowed, and by the
'fantastic', and is a playful narrator
with an ironic sense of humour.
Although he began publishing fiction
in the late 1920s his first important
novel, of a science fiction kind, was
La invención de Morel, 1940 (*The In-
vention of Morel and Other Stories*,
1961), set on an island where there is
an experiment to create humans by
projecting them as if on a screen. This
was followed by *Plan de evasión* in
1945 (*A Plan for Escape*, 1975), *El
sueño de los héroes*, 1954 (*The Dream
of the Hero*, 1987 – Extract 6), set in a
realistic **Buenos Aires** where the
working-class hero Gauna is saved in
a knife fight by El Brujo once, but not
the second time, when he dies. A
parable about fate and god. He then
published *Diario de la guerra del cerdo*,

1969 (*Diary of the War of the Pig*,
1972); *Dormir al sol*, 1973 (*Asleep in
the Sun*, 1978); and *Aventuras de un
fotógrafo en la Plata*, 1989 (*The Adventures of a Photographer in La Plata*,
1991), a laconic novel dealing with
erotic adventures in **La Plata**. With
his wife Silvina Ocampo and Jorge
Luis Borges, Bioy Casares edited the
Antología de la literatura fantástica,
1940 (*The Book of Fantasy*, 1988).

BOMBAL, María Luisa (1910–1980).
Born in Viña del Mar, Chile, on 8
June 1910, Bombal was educated in
France from 1922 to 1931, and stu-
died literature and philosophy at the
Sorbonne. From about 1933 to 1941
she lived in **Buenos Aires**, where in
1934 she wrote *La última niebla* (*The
House of Mist*, 1947), at one time
sharing a flat with Pablo Neruda (◊
Chile). Between 1937 and 1940 she
wrote screen plays for Sonofilm. In
1938 her second novel *La amortajada*
(*The Shrouded Woman*, 1948) was
published, and she wrote her short
stories, translated by Richard and
Lucía Cunningham as *New Islands and
Other Stories*, 1982 (Extract 7). Her
fictional world deals with erotic
spoiled women trapped in a man's
world, and escaping through fantasies. The tone is melodramatic, and
the language taut and poetic. On a
visit back to Santiago, she tried to
shoot her lover Eulogio Sánchez dead,
was jailed, and banished from Chile.
In 1940, representing Chile at a PEN
Club meeting, she met and later married Count Raphael de Saint-Phalle,
living in the USA for 30 years. She
died in Chile on 6 May 1980.

BORGES, Jorge Luis (1899–1986). Borges was born in **Buenos Aires** on 24 August 1899, son of a teacher and failed writer (whose mother had been born in England) and a mother who ruled her son's life, translated Herbert Read and Virginia Woolf, and died in 1975 at the age of 99. He had a sister Norah, a painter. Borges was brought up bilingually, and at the precocious age of six began writing. He grew up among his father's extensive library, an emotional symbol of the universe that accompanied him all his life. In 1914 the family moved from **Palermo** (the park in Buenos Aires that was once dictator Rosas's private estate) where they were living to Europe to find a cure for his father's failing eyesight (inherited by Borges himself), and stayed in Geneva until 1919, then a year in Lugano, then Mallorca. When Borges returned to **Buenos Aires** in 1921 it was as an *ultraísta* poet, writing avant-garde poems based on daring metaphors. He later repudiated these 'timid extravaganzas'. From this time on he lived near the **Plaza San Martín** in a flat on **Maipú 994**. He spent time in the summers in **Adrogué** (background to his story 'Death and the Compass') and on the Uruguay River at Enrique Amorim's house 'Las Nubes' in Salto, Uruguay. He first published poems – *Fervor de Buenos Aires*, 1923; *Cuaderno San Martín*, 1929 – and right through his life saw himself as a poet (*Selected Poems 1923–1967*, 1972 – Extract 8), dealing sincerely with limited themes, like reading, his Buenos Aires *barrios*, or his ancestors.

Borges wrote his first stories in the early 1930s, and concentrated on what became his famous stories following a near fatal accident in 1938, the same year his father died. These stories were first published in *Sur*, and became *Ficciones*, 1944 (*Fictions*, 1965 – Extract 9); *El Aleph*, 1949 (*The Aleph and Other Stories, 1933–1969*, 1970); and, less startlingly new, *El informe de Brodie*, 1970 (*Doctor Brodie's Report*, 1972) and *El libro de arena*, 1975 (*The Book of Sand*, 1977). It took Borges a while to be appreciated in all his subversive subtlety, and then only after sharing the Formentor Prize with Samuel Beckett in 1961. His best fictions are cunning mystifications and artifices, in a terse prose that plays with metaphysics and logic, conveying an underlying tone of melancholia, even humiliation. His modernity is akin to Kafka's and asserts the almost self-indulgent pleasures and the grim necessity and flimsiness of fantasy in a brutalizingly empirical world. His prose style, and conceits, have created a clear post-Borges school of writing.

In the 1940s Borges worked as a librarian, and professor. In 1946 he was demoted by Perón to inspector of poultry, and after Perón's fall in 1955 appointed as Director of the National Library on **Calle México**. By 1955 Borges had become almost totally blind, and was aided by loyal secretaries and friends. He married disastrously in 1967, and then again just before his death in Geneva in 1986 to María Kodama. His later life was uneventful, composing his poems and stories orally. Borges received many honours, but not the Nobel Prize. He enjoyed talking, and there are numerous books of interviews. His love of English literature, especially of Stevenson, Kipling, Chesterton, and Hudson, can be seen in subtle essays like *Other Inquisitions*, 1964. He wrote many books with friends, like Adolfo Bioy Casares ◊, from spoof detective stories to a history of Buddhism. The **Jorge Luis Borges Foundation**, with his library, can be visited at Rodríguez Peña 1236, 7a, Buenos Aires. Family litigations question his will, and even his body, buried in Geneva. See E. R.

Jorge Luis Borges

Monegal, *Jorge Luis Borges: A Literary Biography*, E.P. Dutton, New York, 1978.

BURTON, Sir Richard (see under Uruguay).

CHATWIN, Bruce (see under Brazil).

CONTI, Haroldo (1925–1976). Conti was born in **Chacabuco** outside Buenos Aires on 25 May 1925. He grew up there. He went to a Salesian seminary until 1944, when he left and took various jobs. In 1955 he married, and had two children. In 1960 he won the *Life* magazine story prize. He built his own boat and began sailing in the Tigre Delta and up to Brazil, reflected in his fiction. In 1971 he

visited Cuba, began to participate in left-wing politics, worked as a journalist, and made short documentary films. During the military crackdown he was kidnapped on 4 May 1976 and never seen again. All his letters, diaries and manuscripts also disappeared. He wrote three books of short stories and four novels, including *Sudeste*, 1962, and *Alrededor de la jaula*, 1967, all untranslated.

CORTAZAR, Julio (1914–1984). Born in Brussels on 26 August 1914, Cortázar was the son of an Argentine diplomat. In 1918 his separated mother moved back to **Buenos Aires** and Cortázar grew up in suburban **Bánfield**, but he never lost his French 'r'. After university he taught at a school, then at the **University of Mendoza** (Cuyo) in 1944, where he lectured on French literature, and, under the pseudonym Julio Denis, published a book of sonnets in 1938, his first short story in 1941, as well as critical essays on Keats, Rimbaud and Artaud in reviews such as Victoria Ocampo's ◊ *Sur*. He clashed with the Peronist authorities and lost his lecturing post in 1945. From 1945 to 1949 he ran the **Cámara del Libro** in **Buenos Aires**. He then trained as a translator (and later translated Defoe, Poe, Gide, Giono, etc) and interpreter, and moved to Paris in 1951 with a scholarship, where he lived, working for UNESCO the rest of his life, taking out French citizenship in 1981. He married the translator (and now his executor) Aurora Bernárdez in 1953. In later years, Cortázar supported Cuba (first visited in 1962), then Allende's Chile, and especially Sandinista Nicaragua. He worked for the Bertrand Russel Peace tribunal, and ceded royalties to different left-wing groups.

In 1951, Cortázar published his

Julio Cortazar

first book of stories, *Bestiario*, under his own name. Seven subsequent volumes followed (he published 82 stories) all finely crafted and realistically set, dealing with a sudden shift out of banal everyday life into a baffling and disturbing 'otherness' that is often more psychological than supernatural. He learnt from the French surrealists how to shake the lazy reader into an awareness that 'something' threatens his complacency. His use of the short story does not change over time, and he rearranged them in terms of themes, not chronology. He is expert at the devious narrator whose version of events is not quite trustworthy. The following stories ex-

ist in English: *End of the Game and Other Stories*, also under *Blow Up and Other Stories*, 1967, from *Final del juego*, 1956, and *Las armas secretas*, 1959; *All Fires the Fire, and Other Stories*, 1971, from *Todos los fuegos el fuego*, 1966; *A Change of Light and Other Stories*, 1980, from *Alguien que anda por ahí*, 1977; and *We Love Glenda so Much and Other Tales*, 1983 (Extract 11), from *Queremos tanto a Glenda*, 1981. In 1966 Antonioni filmed 'Las babas del diablo' as *Blow-Up*.

Cortázar published his first novel *Los premios* in 1960 (*The Winners*, 1965), a very readable account of a heterogeneous group from all sectors of Argentine society who have won lottery tickets for a cruise to Europe, which never sets sail. Instead there is an investigation into what is happening on board, and why the poop is out of bounds. Different relationships develop, until the most appealing character, Medrano, a dentist, goes too far and is killed. The novel is realistic, but has an avant-garde character, Persio, who comments on events from a philosophical viewpoint. Cortázar's second novel *Rayuela*, 1963 (*Hopscotch*, 1966), is a cult work, concerning a francophile Argentine, a failed poet called Horacio Oliveira in Paris, and his quest for La Maga's love and meaning and creativity with fellow bohemians. It can be read several ways, and it has a huge appendix of snippets, newspaper cuttings, poems, and extra chapters. Certain sections stand out as brilliant short stories, such as the scene with the avant-garde pianist Berthe Trépat, or the death of La Maga's baby Rocamadour. Half the novel takes place in Paris, until Oliveiro is deported back to **Buenos Aires**, where he clowns his way with friends to a possible suicide. A third novel came out in 1968, *62 – modelo para armar* (*62: A Model Kit*, 1972) with a gallery of exiles in London and Paris searching again for love and meaning. It is experimental, with bizarre scenes involving stuffed dolls, and the Courtauld Institute in London. In 1973 he published *Libro de Manuel* (*A Manual for Manuel*, 1978), about a group of revolutionaries who kidnap a penguin in Paris, with inserted newspaper clippings. A last strange novel emerged in 1979, *Un tal Lucas* (*A Certain Lucas*, 1984).

Cortázar was an unrepentant modernist, with a theory about two kinds of readers – one who preferred conventional plots and characters, the other who searched for a fuller sense of life through experimentation. All his novels are grounded in realistic detail. Cortázar has published two books of poems, idiosyncratic collage works, one translated as *Around the Day in Eighty Worlds*, 1986, and, just before he died, political essays – translated in *Nicaraguan Sketches*, 1989. Behind his multifaceted work lies a restless youthfulness, even dissatisfaction that evokes both intense seriousness, and black humour and laughter. He refers to zen, boxing, the Tango, Borges, and French surrealists in a prose that is never boring to read. He died in Paris in 1984, and is buried in Montparnasse cemetery.

DARIO, Rubén (see under Nicaragua).

GREENE, Graham (1904–1991). See also under Mexico, Panama and Paraguay. Greene dedicated his Argentinian novel *The Honorary Consul*, 1973 (Extract 27), to Victoria Ocampo ◊ in memory of his stays in her houses in **San Isidro** and **Mar del Plata**. It is located in a nameless provincial Argentine town (**Corrientes**), a port looking on to the **Chaco**. Dr Eduardo Plarr, a misfit trying to obliterate his past, is an Anglo–Argentine, with a Paraguayan mother living in **Buenos Aires**. He flies down to have tea with her in Buenos Aires in the **Richmond** on **Florida Street**. His friend the Honorary British Consul, Charlie Fortnum, marries a young whore Clara, whom Plarr lusts after and gets as his mistress. Paraguayan guerrilla friends of Plarr kidnap the Consul instead of the American ambassador out visiting the Jesuit ruins. The Consul is shot in the heel trying to escape from their hideout in a poor *barrio*, and Plarr is called in. He is shot as he tries to negotiate with the police. The action is vividly portrayed through dialogue. Argentina is a 'crazy country', a place 'too vast for human beings'. As a novel about a man trying to escape from his 'sense of wasted time' through lust, as a dialogue about priests, religion and guerrilla war, this is typical Greene fiction. At the end, Plarr is jealous that the ageing alcoholic Consul actually 'loves' Clara, the reformed whore carrying Plarr's baby. Greene knew about the Tupamaros, and that Jackson the British ambassador had been kidnapped in Montevideo. He stayed for a fortnight in **Corrientes**.

GUIRALDES, Ricardo (1886–1927). Güiraldes was born in **Buenos Aires** on 13 February 1886, but spent the first four years of his life in Paris, so that French became his first language. He was educated privately, and gave up trying to become an architect. He returned to Paris in 1910–12, 1919–20, and 1922, and died there in 1927. In 1913 he married. He published short stories in 1915 dealing with *pampas* life around his family *estancia* **La Porteña**, near **San Antonio Areco** with its **Güiraldes Museum**. He published his poems the same year. An untranslated autobiographical novel, *Raucho*, 1917, describes a young man's trip to Paris, and his longing to return to the *pampas* despite the good life. His second novel *Rosaura*, 1917, is about a village girl who kills herself after being spurned by a rich lover. In 1923 he wrote *Xamaica*, also untranslated, a travel book about his boat trip from Buenos Aires to Jamaica. In 1924 Güiraldes part-funded the avant-garde magazines that gathered together modern writers in Argentina. He also discovered that he had Hodgkins disease. In 1920 he began what was to become his masterpiece, *Don Segundo Sombra*, 1926 (*Don Segundo Sombra: Shadows on the Pampas*, 1935 – Extract 35), based on a real *gaucho* he had known as a boy. The novel is narrated by a Fabio Cáceres, who is initiated into the complexities of the *gaucho* life by his guru Don Segundo, hardening himself into becoming a man, to discover that he is no orphan, but the son of the local landowner. The novel is a carefully crafted elegy to the free life of the *gaucho* (now over), and a detailed recall of its customs. Güiraldes was fascinated by Oriental philosophies after visiting the Far East, and was a Sunday painter.

The Güiraldes Museum near San Antonio Areco

HERNANDEZ, José (1834–1886). Hernández was born on 10 November 1834 in **San Isidro** in the province of Buenos Aires. He fought for the *gauchos* against the domination of Buenos Aires, founding a paper in 1869 called *Río de la Plata*. He wrote an angry protest poem in three weeks, hiding in a hotel in **Buenos Aires**, about the fate of *gauchos*, that he called *El gaucho Martín Fierro*, 1872 (Extract 1) and that has become Argentina's national poem (usually known as *Martín Fierro*). Fierro is a guitar-playing, singing *payador* who is conscripted, and has to abandon wife and hut. After killing a negro, he is on the run from the law, and joins up with fellow convict Cruz. Hernández wrote a follow-up called *La vuelta de Martín Fierro*, 1879, that has the two *gauchos malos* in Indian territory witnessing the barbarism of the wild Indians, until they save a *cautiva*, a white woman made wife of a *cacique*. The second part is less dramatic, less angry and breaks up into sections dealing with aphorisms about country life, and songs from Fierro's sons. Hernández died in 1886 on his *quinta* (small estate) 'San José' in **Belgrano**. The long poem in *gaucho* slang has been translated four times into English in 1923, 1935, 1967 and 1974.

HUDSON, W. H. (1841–1922). Hudson was born on 4 August 1841 on his American immigrants' *estancia* **Los 25 Ombúes** in **Quilmes** near Buenos Aires, which is today the **G. E. Hudson Museum** (William becomes 'Guillermo', Henry, 'Enrique'). He was educated at home on the family *estancias*, first where he had been born, then for financial reasons in the rented 'Las Acacias' at **Chascomús**. The first 18 years of his life form the subject of his wonderful autobiography of growing up wild on the *pampas* – *Far Away and Long Ago*, 1922 (Extract 13). It is the best book to read on nineteenth-century Argentine life, with vivid details about the flora and fauna, the yellow fever epidemic, Buenos Aires, the dictator Rosas's dwarf, etc, written when Hudson was ill and old in England, after a series of hallucinatory flashbacks. He is moving on his relationship with his American-born mother, an illness that forced him to read books, and his anguished discovery of Darwin (◊ Uruguay). When his parents died, Hudson had to work as a farm hand on the *pampas*, and began collecting bird-skins which he sent to the Smithsonian in Washington, as well as writing notes which were regularly published in London in the *Proceedings* of the Zoological Society, including a clash with Darwin over *pampas* woodpeckers which humiliated Hudson. During these years, Hudson travelled down to **Patagonia** (still hostile Indian territory), but accidentally shot himself in the knee, as vividly recollected in *Idle Days in Patagonia*, 1893. He also roamed Uruguay (background to *The Purple Land*, 1885), did his military service, took notes on birds (collected in his *Birds of La Plata*, first in conjunction with Sclater in 1888–89, then recast as his own in 1920). He saved money to visit England, and left Argentina for good in 1874, aged 33.

In London, without contacts, and very poor, Hudson found that science had progressed beyond the kind of field naturalist he had become, into Darwinian laboratory work. So he turned to writing fiction, and natural history sketches, to earn money. In 1885 he published *The Purple Land* (see under Uruguay). *A Little Boy Lost*, 1905, is about an orphan seeking his mother in the *pampas*. *El Ombú*, 1902, reprinted as *South American Sketches*, 1909, is a gripping story narrated by an old *gaucho* about a cursed house under the ombú tree on the *pampas*. The flow of vivid anecdotes – barefeet monks with spurs, English soldiers after their defeat in Buenos Aires, a general driven mad by bathing in the blood of a live bull – heightens Hudson's pessimism about happiness on earth, for time robs all his characters of hope. 'Ralph Herne' (Extract 14) describes an English doctor going out to **Buenos Aires** for the first time during the yellow fever epidemic, and adapting to life there.

See under Venezuela for *Green Mansions*, 1904. Hudson wrote a utopian novel (*A Crystal Age*, 1887) and collected his nature notes on Argentina in *The Naturalist in La Plata*, and on England, with many comparisons with Argentina, in *Birds in a Village*, 1893; *Nature in Downland*, 1900; *Birds and Man*, 1901; *Hampshire Days*, 1903; *The Land's End*, 1908; *Afoot in England*, 1909; etc. Hudson married his older landlady in 1876. He worked hard for the Royal Society for the Protection of Birds. He died in 1922 and is buried in Worthing, Sussex, in the UK. See Ruth Tomalin, *W. H. Hudson: A Biography*, Faber and Faber, London, 1982.

LOWELL, Robert (1917–1977). Born in Boston, Lowell was educated at Harvard and Kenyon College, was imprisoned during the war as a conscientious objector, and in 1970 moved to the UK. His first book of poems came out in 1944. In *Notebook*, 1970, 'the story of my life' between June 1967 and June 1970, his poem 'Mania in Buenos Aires, 1962' (a fuller version was published in *The Review*, 8 August 1963 – Extract 15) opens with Lowell in the **Hotel Continental**, 'a thousand miles from nowhere' in a snoring city 'run by the barracks'. He comments disparagingly on the official statues and coups, he mocks the **Recoleta Cemetery** and walks the streets of Buenos Aires so much his feet bleed. In June 1962, the Congress for Cultural Freedom sent Lowell with wife Elizabeth Hardwick and daughter Harriet to visit Brazil (and Elizabeth Bishop). In September Lowell went alone with Keith Botsford on to **Buenos Aires**, lunched at the **Casa Rosada**, and 'insulted' a general. He insisted on visiting every statue in the city. At a party given by Rafael Alberti, Lowell wrestled on the floor, but was soon 'straightjacketed' and put in the **Clinic Bethlehem**. Lowell criticized Caracas in Venezuela, and sneered at El Presidente Leoni with his bodyguards. In 1967 Lowell and Elizabeth Hardwick visited Caracas for the Congress for Cultural Freedom. In January 1968, he visited Ivan Illich in Cuernavaca in Mexico, and wrote poems about Toltec temples, Aztec women and the Emmaus monastery. He also wrote a poem about Che Guevara 'gangstered down'. See Ian Hamilton, *Robert Lowell: A Biography*, Faber and Faber, London, 1983.

MALLEA, Eduardo (1903–1980). Born on 14 August 1903, Mallea was the second of three children to a surgeon and his musical wife, in **Bahía Blanca**. In 1916 the family moved to **Buenos Aires**. Mallea started to study law in the **University of Buenos Aires**, but dropped out. In 1926 he published his first volume of short stories. In 1928 he joined the newspaper *La Nación*, and by 1931 he was editing its cultural supplement. In 1936 he published his second book of stories. He married the poet Helena Muñiz Larreta in 1944. Mallea formed part of the editorial group of the magazine *Sur*. After the fall of Perón,

W.H. Hudson

he was named ambassador to UN-
ESCO in Paris for 1955–58. Over his
life he made numerous journeys to
Europe. His childhood and intellectual formation have been well described in his autobiography *Historia
de una pasión argentina*, 1937 (*History
of an Argentine Passion*, 1983). His
main theme has been a quest through
character and psychology of what it
means to be an Argentine. He diffe-
rentiated between two Argentinas –
the visible, frivolous mask, and the
invisible, more spiritual one. *Fiesta en
noviembre*, 1938 (*Fiesta in November*,
1969) echoes the murder of García
Lorca in Spain with that of a poet in
Argentina set against an empty cocktail party. In *La bahía de silencio*, 1940
(*The Bay of Silence*, 1944), the main
character, Martín Tregua, agonizes
over where Argentina is going after
failing as a newspaper editor, disliking
Europe, and going through an affair

before falling for a married woman. *Todo verdor perecerá*, 1941 (*All Green Shall Perish*, 1969 – Extract 4) anatomizes a sterile marriage and the inner resentful loneliness of Agata, who breaks away from her husband Cruz until she kills him by opening the windows wide when he is ill. *Chaves*, 1953 (*Chaves*, 1970) follows another taciturn man, a saw-mill worker, and explores his anguished mind.

MANGUEL, Alberto (1948–). Manguel was born in **Buenos Aires** on 13 March 1948. He has lived in France, England, Spain, Tahiti and, from 1982, in Canada. His anthologies include *Other Fires: Stories from the Women of Latin America*, 1986, and *Black Water: The Anthology of Fantastic Literature*, 1983. His first novel, written in English, *News from a Foreign Country Came*, 1991 (Extract 16), is the story of a family ignorant that the father, the Captain, has been a torturer. A Frenchman schooled in the Algerian war between white *colons* and the Arabs, this man is invited to **Buenos Aires** to help fight against subversion. The novel opens in Canada, with a girl Ana and a servant Rebecca from Argentina. Then the mother, Mariane, is killed by a bomb and the novel returns in time to her girlhood in Algeria, her religious longings, her sexual awakenings, photography, Arabs, and her love for the older man, the Captain, with a mysterious military job. They have a late daughter. In Buenos Aires Mariane is ignorant of the disappeared until she tries to find her husband at work to help a friend and walks into a room where he is lecturing the military on torture and pain. The backdrop is Perón, Evita, Perón's death, the disappeared, a meeting of the Mothers de la Plaza de Mayo.

MARTINEZ, Tomás Eloy (1934–). Born in **Tucumán**, Martínez has worked as a journalist, as well as publishing fiction and lecturing in the USA. His second novel *La novela de Perón*, 1985, (*The Perón Novel*, 1988 – Extract 32), written in exile in Venezuela where he lived until 1985 after the military coup of 1975, explores the complex biography of Juan Domingo Perón, dictator and then elected president of Argentina from 1946 until his overthrow in 1955, and subsequently re-elected with the support of the guerrilla left in 1973 until his death in 1974. The novel is part-documentary, based on hours of taped interviews with General Perón in his Madrid home in exile. However, Martínez, though using actual historical people, invents their relationships and dialogues with Perón, from his third wife Isabelita to the sinister spiritualist López Rega, his private secretary and founder of the right-wing death squads. There are sections dealing with life-loving guerrillas. The book closes with the massacre of left-wing *montoneros* on the road to **Ezeiza** international airport. The novel is a good introduction to Perón and the Argentina he controlled for so many traumatic years. Martínez has written an account of the massacre of guerrillas at **Trelew**.

MEYER, Gordon (1919–1968). Born in London on 3 October 1919, Meyer was educated at Cranleigh, and Oxford, without finishing his degree. He fought the war in the navy, serving on motor torpedo boats. He worked in the wool business, divorced, first went out to Argentina in 1954, and re-married. An illness got him writing his first stories (in *Blackwoods*) in 1958. In 1961 he spent a year on Rhodes. His first novel *Sweet Water and Bitter*, 1962, is narrated by an

Englishwoman, and deals with her marriage to an Argentine against the backdrop of Peronism, and machismo, with an idyllic affair on **Victoria Island** on **Lake Nahuel Huapí**. In 1963 he published *Death in the Campo*, three novellas which won the *London Magazine* short story prize. The title story is a detailed account of the dying of an Englishman's lover's old mother in the dusty *pampas* town **Cañada de Gómez**. 'The House of Dolls' deals with a university professor staying in a German-run boarding house in **San Martín de los Andes**, in the lake district in southern Argentina. It is a chilling discovery of incest. 'Quits', the best story, diagnoses a failing relationship between a snobby Argentine dilettante, and his promiscuous, painter mistress. It is psychologically acute in its presentation of feeling and its relation to weather, and consciousness. Meyer pays particular respect to mood and half-thoughts.

In 1964 Meyer moved to Punta del Este, Uruguay, and married a third time. In 1966 he published his travel book *The River and the People*, about a journey up the River Paraná to Paraguay and a visit to an *estancia* on the Chaco, interspersed with delightful erudition about the Jesuits, Eliza Lynch, the Paraguayan dictator Solano López's Irish mistress, and their dramatic downfall. In 1966 Meyer also published *Exiles* (Extract 17), a selection of short stories, mainly set in Argentina and Uruguay, anatomizing the collision of European and Latin American sensibilities through affairs, relationships, and living in exile. In 1967 he travelled round Italy, and England, and published a second travelogue, *Summer at High Altitude*, about a hair-raising train and bus trip to Bolivia, and his research into the sudden expulsion of the Jesuits from their paternalistic

empire. Meyer died of cancer in London in 1968. See Jason Wilson, 'The Weather and the Women: The South American Writings of Gordon Meyer', *London Magazine*, June/July 1991.

OCAMPO, Victoria (1890–1979). Ocampo was born in **Buenos Aires** in 1890, eldest of six girls (a sister was Silvina Ocampo, the writer) to a rich *estanciero*. She was educated by governesses, and lived a lot in France, so that her first language was French. After her early marriage failed, she went into journalism and wrote on women's issues for the newspaper *La Nación*, modelling herself on Virginia Woolf, whom she met. In 1931 she founded *Sur* and it ran until 1970, the most prestigious literary magazine in Latin America at the time. She was clever with her secretaries (José Bianco, Enrique Pezzoni), launched Borges and many others, and she brought over to Argentina, and translated (*Sur* was also a publisher), writers such as Graham Greene, Albert Camus, Tagore, Waldo Frank, André Malraux and some, like Pierre Drieu la Rochelle, who became her lovers. She was actively anti-Peronist, and briefly imprisoned for her views. In 1942 she published an essay on her hero T. E. Lawrence, translated into English as *338171 T. E. (Lawrence of Arabia)*, 1963. Her untranslated *Testimonios, 1935–1977* are a personal record of her literary life. In 1977 she was the first woman elected to the Argentine Academy. **Villa Ocampo**, her large house in **San Isidro** outside Buenos Aires was donated to UNESCO. Her house in **Mar del Plata**, designed by Le Corbusier, is a cultural centre. See Doris Meyer, *Victoria Ocampo: Against the Wind and the Tide*, George Braziller, New York, 1979.

PUIG, Manuel (1932–1990). Puig was born on 28 December 1932 in **General Villegas**, in the province of Buenos Aires, and brought up by his mother in cinemas, escaping the humdrum life of his *pampas* town, an experience at the core of his first novel *La traición de Rita Hayworth*, 1968 (*Betrayed by Rita Hayworth*, 1971). He dropped out of university, and went to Rome in 1956 with a scholarship to study film in Cinecittá – he worked with De Sica, and wrote scripts in English. He worked for Air France at Kennedy Airport for three years (his English was good enough to write *Eternal Curse on the Reader of These Pages*, 1982, in English).

In 1967 Puig returned to **Buenos Aires** and published *Boquitas pintadas*, 1969 (*Heartbreak Tango: A Serial*, 1973 – Extract 18), lifting the lid off his home town fictionalized as 'Coronel Vallejos', dealing with a village Don Juan dying of TB, and sexual secrets. The novel follows four women at school together, but later separated by class differences, a mur-

der, and Hollywood ideals of love. The time is 1947, and the action moves between **Cosquín** in the Cordoban hills, the *pampas* town and **Buenos Aires**. This was followed by *The Buenos Aires Affair*, 1973 (*The Buenos Aires Affair: A Detective Novel*, 1976), and *El beso de la mujer araña*, 1976 (*Kiss of the Spider Woman*, 1979), dealing with a homosexual and a guerrilla in prison in Argentina, and their bizarre relationship based on telling films, and a need for affection, with footnotes by Puig exploring homosexuality. *Kiss of the Spider Woman* was filmed in 1985 by the Brazilian director Hector Babenco. In 1979 Puig published his account of 1970s Argentina through a woman dying in a hospital in Mexico recalling her lovers, from a guerrilla to a fascist thug in *Pubis angelical* (*Pubis Angelical*, 1986 – Extract 19), interspersed with Hollywood fantasies about women looking for a more glamorous life. Puig's fiction deals with the provincial lower-middle classes of Argentina, whose fantasies are conditioned by the radio, colour magazines, and the cinema, and who express themselves in ready-made images, always expecting more from reality than they ever get. As a novelist Puig gives us the raw material of these lives through documents, letters, phone calls, monologues, dialogues, as if the narrator refuses to judge. Yet all his fiction is a parody of small-town life.

In 1973 Puig left Argentina to live in New York, then Rio and finally in Cuernavaca, Mexico, where he died in hospital after a routine operation in 1990. His last novel is *Cale la noche tropical*, 1988 (*Tropical Night Falls*, 1992).

QUIROGA, Horacio (1878–1937). Quiroga was born on 31 December

Horacio Quiroga's house, near San Ignacio in Misiones, now a museum

1878 in Salto, Uruguay, the youngest of an Argentine consul's four children. His father was killed in a hunting accident, and Quiroga grew up with his Uruguayan mother in Salto and Montevideo. In 1896 his stepfather committed suicide. By then, Quiroga had turned into a literary dandy, publishing his first stories. In 1900 he travelled to Paris, where he met the Nicaraguan poet Rubén Darío (◊ Nicaragua), but ran out of money and returned home jaded with Parisian glamour. In 1901 he published his first book of poems and stories. In 1902, he accidentally shot a good friend dead. He was then appointed a teacher at a school in **Buenos Aires**. In 1903 he travelled as a photographer to study the Jesuit ruins near **San Ignacio** in subtropical **Misiones** with an official expedition

led by the poet Leopoldo Lugones. This journey changed his life: he left the artificial city and bought land in the **Chaco**, to grow cotton. The venture failed, and Quiroga returned to teaching. In 1906 he bought 185 hectares near **San Ignacio**, Misiones, and built his own house overlooking the jungle and the Paraná River – today it is a **museum**.

In 1908 Quiroga's first novel was published. In 1909 he married one of his pupils, and settled in San Ignacio, where he was appointed judge and recorder of deaths and births. The couple had two children. From 1910 to 1916, Quiroga tried out several ventures – making coal from wood, alcohol from oranges, etc – but all failed. In 1915 his young wife killed herself. Quiroga moved to **Buenos Aires** with his children to become

Uruguayan Consul. His first great collection of stories *Cuentos de amor, de locura y de muerte*, 1917 (*The Decapitated Chicken and Other Stories*, 1976 – Extract 36) included many stories set in **Misiones**. Quiroga intended to jolt his reader either through horror – blood-sucking spiders, murderous Mongolic children – or by testing his characters against the violent nature of subtropical Misiones, with its snakes and powerful rivers. *Cuentos de la selva*, 1918 (*South American Jungle Tales*, 1922 – Extract 33) showed Quiroga's sympathy for animals, and animal intuitions in humans. In 1920 he published *El salvaje*; in 1924 *El desierto*; and in 1926 *Los desterrados* (*The Exiles and Other Stories*, 1987), describing local characters in Misiones. In 1927 he married one of his daughter's friends, 29 years younger than himself, and in 1929 published his second novel. In 1931 he moved back to his house in San Ignacio with his three children. He published his last book, *Más allá*, in 1935. In 1937, ill with cancer, he poisoned himself with cyanide.

Quiroga was one of the first Latin American writers to turn to his country's hinterlands and look for a more meaningful way of understanding himself and his culture. He was a pioneer both in his active life, and as a writer in the Poe tradition. As a keen amateur naturalist, he sought to write a literature based on direct experience where intense moments of crisis, or danger, reveal the flaws or destinies of his characters. A rebel against comfortable urban life, he enjoyed manual work, built his own houses and canoes and grew his own food.

SABATO, Ernesto (1911–). Born on 24 June, in **Rojas** in the province of Buenos Aires, Sabato graduated in physics and mathematics from **La Plata University** in 1937 with a doctorate in physics. In 1935 he visited Europe as a delegate to the Communist Party Youth Congress in Brussels, and in 1938 he won a scholarship to research in the Curie Laboratory in Paris, and in 1939 at the Massachusetts Institute of Technology in Boston. Back home in 1940 he taught at the University of La Plata and, after a crisis in 1941, gave up his scientific career and became a writer. In Paris he had befriended the surrealist Oscar Domínguez. He began by publishing wide-ranging essays in 1945, written for *Sur*. He has continued to popularize ideas, with attacks on rationalism, Sartre, the French 'new' novel, and Borges, in favour of a deeper exploration of personality, with his untranslated study of a novelist's creativity, *El escritor y sus fantasmas*, 1963. Sabato's first novel *El túnel*, 1948 (*The Tunnel*, 1988 – Extract 22) has Pablo Castel, an obsessive painter in Peronist **Buenos Aires** confessing why he murdered his mistress. We get a powerful picture of a psychotic, set in actual Buenos Aires and an *estancia* on the coast. *Sobre héroes y tumbas*, 1961 (*On Heroes and Tombs*, 1981 – Extracts 20 and 21), describes a failed love affair between Martín and neurotic Alejandra from the upper class, and her maniacal father. The novel is realistically situated in **Buenos Aires** (especially **Parque Lezama, La Boca**, and several cafés) and goes back in history to the civil wars with Lavalle, and on to Peronist church burning, with an enigmatic initiation into the secret society of the blind. It is an exciting introduction to Argentine life and history. His last novel, *Abaddón el exterminador*, 1974, has recently appeared as *The Angel of Darkness*, 1992.

After the restoration of democracy

in Argentina in 1983, Sabato was appointed head of the commission to investigate the *desaparecidos* (CONADEP), which published *Nunca Más* in 1984 (*Nunca más*, 1986). With failing eyesight, Sabato has turned to painting. He lives in **Santos Lugares**.

SARMIENTO, Domingo (1811–1888). Sarmiento was born in **San Juan** on 15 February 1811, one of 15 children. He died in Asunción, Paraguay, but is buried in **Buenos Aires**. Exiled in Chile in 1831–36, and again in 1840 by Rosas, he argued about grammar with the conservative Andrés Bello and produced a quickly written biography of a *gaucho caudillo* Facundo Quiroga, relating him to Argentina's geography, its empty *pampas*. This came out as *Civilización y barbarie: Vida de Juan Facundo Quiroga*, 1845 (*Life in the Argentine Republic in the Days of the Tyrants*, 1868 – Extract 2) as a serial in a Chilean newspaper. The title of this fertile essay, 'Civilization and Barbarism', made Sarmiento the defender of European values over the 'barbary' of the local nomadic Indians, and wild *gauchos* supporting the dictator he detested, Rosas (in power 1829–51). He saw an Argentina peopled with hard-working European immigrants, with canals, and universities, becoming as rich as the USA. *Facundo* is the classic account of the dilemmas of progress in Latin America, with a complex description of lawlessness, and education as the panacea to the ills, as much as a defence of the city against the countryside. Part essay, part polemical pamphlet, part poem and part novel, *Facundo* explains *gaucho* customs, and violence. Sarmiento was the first in a line of wide-ranging essayists that led in 1933 to Ezequiel Martínez Estrada – *X-Ray of the Pampa*, 1972.

In 1846 Sarmiento travelled to France, Spain and Africa, and in 1847 was in Switzerland, Germany, the UK and the USA. His experiences are written up in *Viajes*, 1854 (see *A Sarmiento Anthology*, 1948 and *Travels: A Selection*, 1963, and *Sarmiento's Travels in the United States in 1847*, 1970). In 1848 he married (although already a father). In 1851 he fought with Rosas's conqueror, General Urquiza, and again exiled himself to Chile in 1852–55. In 1855 Sarmiento returned to Argentina, edited a newspaper, and in 1860 entered politics as a senator, then minister. In 1862 he became governor of **San Juan**, was ambassador to the USA (1865–68), and in 1868–74 was the first civilian president of his country. He wrote compelling memoirs of his youth in San Juan, especially moving on his mother – *Recuerdos de provincia*, 1850. His complete works run to 52 volumes. There is a **Sarmiento Museum** in **Belgrano** (Calle Cuba), Buenos Aires. See A. W. Bunkley, *The Life of Sarmiento*, Princeton University Press, Princeton, NJ, 1952.

STRACHEY, Isobel (1907–1987). Isobel Strachey was born on 21 May 1907 at Castle Donington, Derbyshire, but was brought up in Argentina where her father worked on the British-owned railways. She married the painter John Strachey, wrote several novels, and many short stories. Her second novel *A Summer in Buenos Aires*, 1947 (Extracts 23 and 24), shows how Violet Bell, English governess to a widowed colonel in **Buenos Aires**, refuses marriage to her boss and runs off with an aristocratic, polo-playing Argentine who seduces her in the train on the way to his *estancia*. The well observed novel deals with the transformation of

Violet into Violeta, freeing herself – temporarily – from her Englishness. It opens with Violet admiring her naked breasts in a mirror as she recalls her English background and puritan mother. She is forced to chose between a 'feverish life' in Buenos Aires or a dreary job in the UK. An awkward plot obliges her to return with her mother. While at the *estancia* with her lover she dares to go to a carnival alone and receives men without chaperones. Galloping across the *pampas* arouses a 'precarious elation'. She becomes sunburnt, with a 'carelessly slouching body', while before she had been 'prim, plump and pink'. She asks herself 'Surely life should not be so easy?' and objects to how men are so free, 'Why is it that in the Argentine the men have unlimited freedom of behaviour and the women none?'. The background details are sure: the action takes place around 1925 with the new Radical government in place and deals with the rich Argentines, with scenes at **Tigre**, the **Confitería Paris**, the races and the **Jockey Club**. Her novel *For Change of Scene*, 1959, is also set in Buenos Aires. Strachey died in London.

THORNTON, Lawrence. Born in California, Thornton has a PhD and teaches at UCLA. His first novel, *Imagining Argentina*, 1987 (Extract 25), tells about a children's theatre director and playwright who painfully discovers a gift for imagining truths about some of the 'disappeared' in Argentina during the 'dirty war' (1976–81) after first his wife Cecilia, and then his daughter Teresa, are abducted by thugs in green Falcon cars. The novel, narrated by a retired journalist, passionately defends 'imagination' during a *junta*'s 'orgasmic rush of violence'. Carlos Rueda, his

protagonist, gets involved with the Mothers of the Plaza de Mayo, and the stories they tell him, in harrowing detail. Rueda searches in his imagination to find out what has happened to his wife: at times his vision fails; he is beaten up; his theatre is closed; and finally his daughter is kidnapped and murdered. The reality his imagining evokes is a 'world where anything seemed possible'. He cleverly unmasks the murderer of real-life Dagma Hagelin. The novel ends up in the historic trials in which Strassera accuses the *junta* generals of their crimes, and shouts '*Nunca más*' ('Never again').

VALENZUELA, Luisa (1938–). Born in **Buenos Aires** on 26 November 1938, Valenzuela is daughter of writer Luisa Mercedes Levinson. She married early, had a daughter and divorced, working as a journalist for *La Nación*. She has lived in Europe, and, from 1969, in New York. Since 1990 she has lived in **Buenos Aires**. Her first novel in 1966 and a 1967 book of stories are translated as *Clara: Thirteen Short Stories and Novel*, 1976. In 1975 she published short, black-humoured and satirical stories set in the foul 1970s in Argentina, *Aquí pasan cosas raras* (*Strange Things Happen Here*, 1979). Her 1983 novel *Cola de lagartija* (*The Lizard's Tail*, 1983) was a fictional biography of López Rega, sinister occultist controlling Perón, Isabelita, and the Triple A death squads in the 1970s. The novel borders on farce, with Luisa Valenzuela entering her own fiction's ominous atmosphere of fear. *Open Door*, 1988 (Extract 34) is an anthology of her strange, experimental work.

VANASCO, Alberto (1925–). Born in **Buenos Aires**, Vanasco was brought up on a farm in **San Juan** until 1934. His various jobs have included teaching mathematics. He has translated the US novelist J. D. Salinger, is a poet, a playwright, a novelist, a science fiction writer, and a short-story writer.

VASCONCELOS, José (1882–1952). Vasconcelos was born in Oaxaca, Mexico, on 27 February 1882 and died in Mexico City. During the Mexican revolution he supported Madero against the dictator Porfirio Díaz in 1910, became rector of the university in 1921, and in 1924 Minister for Education – see his autobiography of these years, *Ulises criollo,* 1935 (*A Mexican Ulysses,* 1963). When Obregón came to power Vasconcelos was again appointed Minister for Education, and commissioned mural painters (Diego Rivera, Siqueiros, Orozco, Dr Atl, etc) to bring art to the people on public walls. He began the Revolution's impressive literacy campaign by installing schools all over rural Mexico. He resigned in 1929, and travelled round Europe, and Argentina (see Extract 31) until 1940. *La raza cósmica,* 1925, studies the melting-pot of races which Latin America will create in the context of Vasconcelos's travels to Argentina, Brazil, and other countries.

VAZQUEZ RIAL, Horacio (1947–). Born in **Buenos Aires**, son of republican Spanish exiles, Vázquez Rial exiled himself in Barcelona after the 1975 coup where he went to university, and completed a doctorate on population surveys in the River Plate region. He lives in Barcelona, has written an essay, a book of poems, and six novels, including *Historia del Triste,* 1987 (*Triste's History,* 1990 – Extract 26), a modernist biography of a clear-witted thug who joins a death squad run by priests and fascists, and who is finally caught and imprisoned. The history of the Argentine disappeared washes over him, but we readers see what happened to Haroldo Conti ◊. The novel is packed with real names, and a vivid sense of a disgusting force unleashed by the right in the 1970s. Vázquez Rial has also written a guide in Spanish – *Buenos Aires,* 1988.

ACKNOWLEDGMENTS AND CITATIONS

The author and publisher are very grateful to the many literary agents, publishers, translators, authors, and other individuals who have given their permission for the use of extracts and photographs, supplied photographs, or helped in the location of copyright holders. Every effort has been made to identify and contact the appropriate copyright owners or their representatives. The publisher would welcome any further information.

EXTRACTS

MEXICO: (1) B. Traven, *The Rebellion of the Hanged*, Penguin, London, 1970, pp 5–6. (2) Carlos Fuentes, *A Change of Skin*, André Deutsch, London, 1987, pp 3–4. By permission of André Deutsch. (3) Graham Greene, *The Lawless Roads*, Penguin, London, 1971, p 173. By permission of Laurence Pollinger Ltd on behalf of the Estate of Graham Greene. (4) Rosario Castellanos, *Another Way to Be: Selected Works of Rosario Castellanos*, University of Georgia Press, Athens, GA, 1990, pp 61–62. Copyright © 1990 by the University of Georgia Press. By permission of the University of Georgia Press. (5) Malcolm Lowry, *Under the Volcano*, Penguin, London, 1962, pp 9 and 11. By permission of Jonathan Cape, Random House UK Ltd. (6) B. Traven, *The Treasure of the Sierra Madre*, Picador, London, 1983, pp 213–214. (7) Juan Rulfo, *Pedro Paramo*, Grove Press/John Calder, New York/London, 1959, pp 1–2. Copyright © 1958 by Grove Press, Inc, renewed © 1987 by Grove Press, Inc. By permission of Grove Weidenfeld, New York. (8) Mariano Azuela, *The Underdogs*, Signet, New York, 1962, pp 144–145. (9) D.H. Lawrence, *The Plumed Serpent*, Penguin, London, 1950, pp 120–121. (10) James M. Cain, *Serenade*, Picador, London, 1985, p 108. (11) Katherine Anne Porter, 'Hacienda', *Flowering Judas*, The Modern Library, New York, 1935, pp 227–229 and 231. Copyright 1935 and renewed 1963 by Katherine Anne Porter, reprinted by permission of Harcourt Brace Jovanovich, Inc. (12) Alexandre von Humboldt, *Political Essay on the King-dom of New Spain*, Oklahoma University Press, Norman, OK, 1972, pp 114–115. Copyright © 1972 by Alfred A. Knopf, Inc. By permission of the University of Oklahoma Press. (13) William Burroughs, *Queer*, Picador, London, 1986, p 52. By permission of Pan Macmillan. (14) Raymond Carver, *In a Marine Light: Selected Poems*, Picador, London, 1988, p 119. By permission of Collins Harvill, an imprint of HarperCollins Publishers Limited. (15) Len Deighton, *Mexico Set*, Panther, London, 1985, pp 355–356. By permission of Random House UK Ltd. (16) Bernal Díaz, *The Conquest of New Spain*, Penguin, London, 1963, pp 214–215. Copyright © J.M. Cohen 1963. By Permission of Penguin Books Ltd. (17) Carlos Fuentes, *Constancia and Other Stories for Virgins*, André Deutsch, London, 1990, pp 117–119. By permission of André Deutsch Ltd. (18) Carlos Fuentes, *Where the Air is Clear*, Farrar, Straus and Giroux, New York, 1977, pp 40–41. By permission of A.M. Heath on behalf of Carlos Fuentes. (19) Margo Glantz, *The Family Tree*, Serpent's Tail, London, 1991, p 152. By permission of Serpent's Tail Ltd. (20) Jack Kerouac, *On the Road*, André Deutsch, London, 1958, pp 300–301. Copyright © Jack Kerouac, 1955, 1957. By permission of Penguin Books Ltd. (21) D.H. Lawrence, *The Plumed Serpent*, Penguin, London, 1950, pp 55–56. (22) José Emilio Pacheco, *Battles in the Desert and Other Stories*, New Directions, New York, 1987, p 105. DR © 1963 Ediciones Era, SA. Copyright © 1987 by Katherine Silver. By permission of New Directions Publishing Corporation. (23) Octavio Paz, *Selected Poems*, New Directions, New York, 1984, pp 17–18. Copyright © 1979 by Octavio Paz and Eliot Weinberger. By permission of New Directions Publishing Corporation. (24) Charles Tomlinson, *Notes from New York and Other Poems*, Oxford University Press, Oxford, 1984, p 59. © Charles Tomlinson 1984. By permission of Oxford University Press. (25) Richard Ford, *The Ultimate Good Luck*, Flamingo, London, 1990, pp 9–10. By permission of HarperCollins Publishers Ltd. (26) Malcolm Lowry, *Dark as the Grave Wherein my Friend is Laid*, Jonathan Cape, London, 1969, pp 207–208. By permission of the Peters Fraser & Dunlop Group Ltd. (27) José Rubén Romero, *Notes of a Villager: A Mexican Poet's Youth and Revolution*, Plover Press, Kanehoe, HI, 1988, pp 73–75. By permission of Plover Press. (28) Paul Bowles, 'Señor Ong and Señor Ha', *Collected Stories*, Black Sparrow Press, Santa Barbara, CA, 1980, pp 173–174. Copyright © 1947, 1946 by Paul Bowles. By permission of Black Sparrow Press. (29) Aldous Huxley, *Eyeless in Gaza*, Chatto and Windus, London, 1936, pp 495–496. Acknowledgments are due to Mrs Laura Huxley and The Hogarth Press. By permission of Random House UK Ltd. (30) Saul Bellow, *The Adventures of Augie March*, Penguin, London, 1966, pp 401–402. By permission of A.M. Heath Ltd on behalf of Saul Bellow. (31) Octavio Paz, *Selected Poems*, Penguin, London, 1979, p 21. Copyright © 1973 by Octavio Paz and Florence H. Williams. Translation by William Carlos Williams. By permission of Penguin Books Ltd. (32) Graham Greene, *The Power and the Glory*, Penguin, London, 1962, pp 7–8. By permission of Laurence Pollinger Ltd on behalf of the Estate of Graham Greene. (33) Agustín Yañéz, *The Edge of the Storm*, University of Texas Press, Austin, TX, 1963, pp 4–5. Copyright © 1963 The University of Texas Press. By permission of The University of Texas Press. (34) Charles Olson, *Mayan Letters*, Jonathan Cape, London, 1968, p 71. By permission of Random House UK Ltd. **GUATEMALA:** (1) Rodrigo Rey Rosa, *Dust on Her Tongue*, Peter Owen, London, 1989, p 32. By permission of Peter Owen Ltd. (2) Norman Lewis, *The Volcanoes Above Us*, Arena, London, 1989, pp 48–49. © 1957 by Norman Lewis. By permission of Rogers, Coleridge & White Ltd on behalf of Norman Lewis. (3) Mario Payeras, 'Story of a Maestro', in *And We Sold the Rain: Contemporary Fiction from Central America*, Ryan, Peterborough, 1989, pp 35–36. By permission of Ryan Publishing Co Ltd, London. (4) Norman Lewis, *The Volcanoes Above Us*, Arena, London, 1989, p 74. © 1957 by Norman Lewis. By permission of Rogers, Coleridge & White Ltd

on behalf of Norman Lewis. (5) Norman Lewis, *The Volcanoes Above Us*, Arena, London, 1989, pp 28–29. © 1957 by Norman Lewis. By permission of Rogers, Coleridge & White Ltd on behalf of Norman Lewis. (6) Aldous Huxley, *Beyond the Mexique Bay*, Penguin, London, 1955, p 55. Acknowledgments are due to Mrs Laura Huxley and The Hogarth Press. By permission of Random House UK Ltd. (7) Sergio Ramírez, *To Bury Our Fathers: A Novel of Nicaragua*, Readers International, London, 1984, p 60. By permission of Readers International. (8) Rose Macaulay, *Staying With Relations*, Collins, London, 1930, pp 16–17. By permission of the Peters Fraser & Dunlop Group Ltd. (9) Paul Bowles, *Up Above the World*, Arena, London, 1984, pp 19–21. By permission of first publisher, Peter Owen Ltd. (10) Rubén Darío, *Autobiografía*, translated from the Spanish by Jason Wilson. (11) Miguel Angel Asturias, *Men of Maize*, Verso, London, 1989, pp 163–165. By permission of Verso. **EL SALVADOR:** (1) Francisco Gavidia, 'The She-Wolf', in *Clamor of Innocence: Stories from Central America*, City Lights Books, San Francisco, CA, 1988, pp 97–98. (2) Roque Dalton, *Miguel Mármol*, Curbstone, Willimantic, CT, 1987, pp 258–259. By permission of Curbstone Press. (3) Joan Didion, *A Book of Common Prayer*, Penguin, London, 1977, pp 10–11. By permission of George Weidenfeld & Nicolson Ltd. (4) Jacinta Escudos, 'Look at Lislique, See How Pretty It Is', in *And We Sold the Rain: Contemporary Fiction from Central America*, Ryan, Peterborough, 1989, pp 1–2. By permission of Ryan Publishing Co Ltd, London. (5) Manlio Argueta, *Cuzcatlán*, Chatto and Windus, London, 1987, pp 47–48. (6) Manlio Argueta, *One Day of Life*, Chatto and Windus, London, 1984, pp 146–148. Translation copyright © 1983 by Bill Brow. By permission of Random House, Inc. (7) Roque Dalton, 'San Salvador', in Joan Didion, *Salvador*, Chatto and Windus, London, 1983, p 33. *Salvador* © Joan Didion 1983. By permission of Sheil Land Associates Ltd. (8) Joan Didion, *Salvador*, Chatto and Windus, London, 1983, pp 35–36. © Joan Didion 1983. By permission of Sheil Land Associates Ltd on behalf of Joan Didion. (9) Claribel Alegría, *Ashes of Izalco*, Curbstone, Willimantic, CT, 1989, pp 10–11. By permission of Curbstone Press. (10) Paul Theroux, *The Old Patagonian Express*, Penguin, London, 1980, pp 141–142. By permission of Aitken & Stone Ltd on behalf of Paul Theroux. **BELIZE:** (1) Aldous Huxley, *Beyond the Mexique Bay*, Penguin, London, 1955, p 30. Acknowledgments are due to Mrs Laura Huxley and The Hogarth Press. By permission of Random House UK Ltd. (2) Graham Greene, *Getting to*

Know the General, Penguin, London, 1985, p 123. By permission of Laurence Pollinger Ltd on behalf of the Estate of Graham Greene. (3) V.S. Naipaul, *The Overcrowded Barracoon*, Penguin, London, 1976, pp 227–228. By permission of Aitken & Stone Ltd on behalf of V.S. Naipaul. (4) Robert Stone, *A Flag for Sunrise*, Picador, London, 1982, p 65. Acknowledgment is due to Martin Secker & Warburg Ltd as publisher. By permission of Octopus Publishing Group. **HONDURAS**: (1) Salarrué, 'We bad', in *Clamor of Innocence: Stories from Central America*, City Lights Books, San Francisco, CA, 1988, pp 68–69. (2) Roberto Sosa, *The Difficult Days*, Princeton University Press, Princeton, NJ, 1983, pp 41 and 47. Copyright © 1983 by Princeton University Press. By permission of Princeton University Press. (3) O'Henry, *Strictly Business and Other Stories*, Hodder and Stoughton, London, 1973, pp 310–312. (4) Paul Theroux, *The Mosquito Coast*, Penguin, London, 1981, p 109. By permission of Aitken & Stone Ltd on behalf of Paul Theroux. (5) Constantino Suasnavar, in Dudley Fitts, ed, *Anthology of Contemporary Latin-American Poetry*, New Directions, Norfolk, CT, 1942, p 221. Copyright © 1942, 1947 by New Directions Publishing Corporation. By permission of New Directions Publishing Corporation. (6) Julio Escoto, 'April in the Forenoon', in *And We Sold the Rain: Contemporary Fiction from Central America*, Ryan, Peterborough, 1989, pp 84–85. By permission of Ryan Publishing Co Ltd, London. (7) Norman Lewis, *The Volcanoes Above Us*, Arena, London, 1989, pp 16–17. © 1957 by Norman Lewis. By permission of Rogers, Coleridge & White Ltd on behalf of Norman Lewis. **NICARAGUA**: (1) Rubén Darío, *Selected Poems of Rubén Darío*, University of Texas Press, Austin, TX, 1965, p 116. Copyright © 1965 The University of Texas Press. By permission of The University of Texas Press. (2) Ernesto Cardenal, *Marilyn Monroe and Other Poems*, Search Press, London, 1975, p 67. By permission of Search Press Ltd. (3) Julio Cortázar, *Nicaraguan Sketches*, W.W. Norton, New York and London, 1989, pp 111–112. (4) Salman Rushdie, *The Jaguar Smile*, Picador, London, 1987, pp 15–17. By permission of Pan Books Ltd. (5) Robert Stone, *A Flag for Sunrise*, Picador, London, 1982, p 145. Acknowledgment is due to Martin Secker & Warburg Ltd as publisher. By permission of Octopus Publishing Group. (6) Thomas Belt, *The Naturalist in Nicaragua*, John Murray, London, 1874, pp 234–235. (7) Ernesto Cardenal, *From Nicaragua With Love: Poems (1979–1986)*, City Lights Books, San Francisco, CA, 1986, pp 17–19. (8) Ernesto Cardenal, *Marilyn Monroe and Other*

Poems, Search Press, London, 1975, p 53. By permission of Search Press Ltd. (9) Sergio Ramírez, 'A bed of Bauxite in Weipa', in *Stories*, Readers International, London, 1986, p 49. By permission of Readers International. (10) Sergio Ramírez, *To Bury Our Fathers: A Novel of Nicaragua*, Readers International, London, 1984, pp 8–9. By permission of Readers International. **COSTA RICA**: (1) Ernesto Cardenal, *Marilyn Monroe and Other Poems*, Search Press, London, 1975, p 45. By permission of Search Press Ltd. (2) Carlos Gagini, *Redemptions: A Costa Rican Novel*, San Diego State University Press, San Diego, CA, 1985, pp 21–23. By permission of San Diego State University Press. (3) Paul Theroux, *The Old Patagonian Express*, Penguin, London, 1980, pp 203–204. By permission of Aitken & Stone Ltd on behalf of Paul Theroux. (4) Carmen Naranjo, 'And We Sold the Rain', in *And We Sold the Rain: Contemporary Fiction from Central America*, Ryan, Peterborough, 1989, pp 150–151. By permission of Ryan Publishing Co Ltd, London. **PANAMA**: (1) Henryk Sienkiewicz, 'Lighthouse-Keeper of Aspinwall', in *The Masterpiece Library of Short Stories*, Vol XIII, The Educational Book Company, London, undated, pp 311–312. (2) Jane Bowles, *Two Serious Ladies*, Virago, London, 1979, pp 38–39. By permission of publisher Peter Owen Ltd. (3) Aldous Huxley, *Eyeless in Gaza*, Chatto and Windus, London, 1936, p 491. Acknowledgments are due to Mrs Laura Huxley and The Hogarth Press. By permission of Random House UK Ltd. (4) John Keats, 'On First Looking into Chapman's Homer', *The Poetical Works of John Keats*, Oxford University Press, Oxford, 1967, p 39. (5) Malcolm Lowry, 'Through the Panama', in *Hear Us O Lord from Heaven Thy Dwelling Place*, Lippincott, New York, 1961, pp 56–58. By permission of the Peters Fraser & Dunlop Group Ltd. (6) Iain Banks, *Canal Dreams*, Abacus, London, 1989, pp 35–36. © Iain Banks 1989. By permission of Macmillan London and Sheil Land Associates Ltd on behalf of Iain Banks. (7) William Burroughs, *Queer*, Picador, London, 1986, pp 113–114. By permission of Pan Macmillan. (8) Graham Greene, *The Captain and the Enemy*, Penguin, London, 1989, pp 116–117. By permission of Laurence Pollinger Ltd on behalf of the Estate of Graham Greene. (9) Graham Greene, *Getting to Know the General: The Story of an Involvement*, Penguin, London, 1985, pp 87–88. By permission of Laurance Pollinger Ltd on behalf of the Estate of Graham Greene. (10) Graham Greene, *Getting to Know the General: The Story of an Involvement*, Penguin Books, London, 1985, p 66. By permission of Laurence Pollinger Ltd on behalf of the Estate of Graham Greene.

COLOMBIA: (1) Gabriel García Márquez, 'Tuesday's Siesta', *No One Writes to the Colonel and Other Stories*, Picador, London, 1983, pp 66–67. By permission of Jonathan Cape, Random House UK Ltd. (2) Joan Didion, *The White Album*, Penguin, London, 1981, pp 195–196. By permission of Weidenfeld and Nicolson Ltd. (3) Christopher Isherwood, *The Condor and the Cows*, Methuen, London, 1949, p 36. (4) Gabriel García Márquez, *One Hundred Years of Solitude*, Jonathan Cape, London, 1970, pp 24–25. By permission of Jonathan Cape, Random House UK Ltd. (5)Gabriel García Márquez, *Love in the Time of Cholera*, Jonathan Cape, London, 1988, pp 15–17. By permission of Jonathan Cape, Random House UK Ltd. (6) Armando Solano, in *The Green Continent*, Poetry London Editions, London, 1947, pp 386–387. (7) Jorge Isaacs, *María: A South American Romance*, Harper and Brothers, New York and London, 1990, pp 286–287. (8) José Eustacio Rivera, *The Vortex*, Putnam, New York, 1935, pp 39–40. (9) Gabriel García Márquez, *The General in His Labyrinth*, Jonathan Cape, London, 1991, pp 244–245. By permission of Jonathan Cape, Random House UK Ltd. (10) Paul Bowles, 'Call at Corazón', *Collected Stories*, Black Sparrow Press, Santa Barbara, CA, 1980, p 66. Copyright © 1947, 1946 by Paul Bowles. By permission of Black Sparrow Press. VENEZUELA: (1) Robert Lowell, *Notebook*, Faber and Faber, London, 1970, pp 53–54. By permission of Faber and Faber Ltd. (2) Alexandre von Humboldt, *Travels*, Penguin, London, 1993. © 1993 Jason Wilson. (3) Henri Charrière, *Papillon*, Grafton, London, 1980, pp 537–538. By permission of HarperCollins Publishers Ltd. (4) Lisa St Aubin de Terán, *Keepers of the House*, Penguin, London, 1983, pp 182–183. By permission of A.M. Heath Ltd on behalf of Lisa St Aubin de Terán. (5) Joseph Conrad, *Nostromo*, Penguin, London, 1963, p 83. (6) Alejo Carpentier, *The Lost Steps*, Penguin, London, 1968, pp 59–60. By permission of A.M. Heath Ltd on behalf of Alejo Carpentier. (7) Pablo Neruda, *Canto General*, in *Selected Poems*, Jonathan Cape, London, 1970, p 173. By permission of Random House UK Ltd. (8) Sir Walter Raleigh, 'The Discovery of the Large, Rich and Beautiful Empire of Guiana', in *Selected Writings*, Penguin, London, 1986, pp 94–95. (9) Rómulo Gallegos, *Canaima*, North American Association of Venezuela, Caracas, 1984, p 11. By permission of Mrs Sonia Gallegos. (10) Ramón Díaz Sánchez *Cumboto*, University of Texas Press, Austin, TX, 1969, pp 8–9. By permission of The University of Texas Press. (11) Joseph Conrad, *Nostromo*, Penguin, London, 1963, pp 17–18. (12) W.H. Hudson, *Green Mansions*,

Duckworth, London, 1922, pp 32–33. (13) Isabel Allende, *Eva Luna*, Hamish Hamilton, London, 1989, pp 129–131. By permission of Hamish Hamilton Ltd. ECUADOR: (1) Jorge Icaza, *Huasipungo*, Dennis Dobson, London, 1962, pp 14–15. (2) Charles Darwin, *Voyage of the Beagle*, Penguin, London, 1989, pp 269–270. (3) Herman Melville, 'The Encantadas', in *Billy Budd and Other Stories*, Penguin, London, 1967, pp 131–133. (4) Demetrio Aguilar Malta, *Don Goyo*, Humana Press, Totowa, NJ, 1980, pp 59–60. By permission of Humana Press. (5) William Burroughs, *Queer*, Picador, London, 1986, pp 91–92. By permission of Pan Macmillan. (6) Jorge Carrera Andrade, *Selected Poems*, State University of New York Press, New York, 1972, p 35. Translation copyright © 1972 by the State University of New York. By permission of the State University of New York Press. (7) Kurt Vonnegut, *Galápagos* Grafton, London, 1987, pp 17–19. Copyright © 1985 by Kurt Vonnegut. By permission of Delacorte Press/Seymour Lawrence, a division of Bantam Doubleday Dell Publishing Group, Inc, and Random House UK Ltd. (8) Henri Michaux, 'Ecuador', in *Selected Writings: The Space Within*, New Directions, New York, 1952, pp 13–17. Copyright © 1968 by New Directions Publishing Corporation. By permission of New Directions Publishing Corporation. (9) Moritz Thomsen, *The Saddest Pleasure*, The Sumach Press, London, 1991, p 7. By permission of Random House UK Ltd. (10) Adalberto Ortiz, *Juyungo*, Three Continents Press, Washington, DC, 1982, pp 43–44. By permission of Three Continents Press. PERU: (1) Mario Vargas Llosa, *Who Killed Palomino Molero?*, Faber and Faber, London, 1987, pp 64–65. By permission of Faber and Faber Ltd. (2) Nicholas Shakespeare, *The Vision of Elena Silves*, Collins Harvill, London, 1989, pp 3–4. By permission of HarperCollins Publishers Ltd. (3) José María Arguedas, *Deep Rivers*, University of Texas Press, Austin, TX, 1978, p 9. By permission of The University of Texas Press. (4) Mario Vargas Llosa, *The Time of the Hero*, Grove Press, New York, 1966, pp 109–110. By permission of Faber and Faber Ltd. (5) Mario Vargas Llosa, *The Real Life of Alejandro Mayta*, Faber and Faber, London, 1986, pp 52–53. By permission of Faber and Faber Ltd. (6) Pablo Neruda, *The Heights of Macchu-Picchu*, Jonathan Cape, London, 1966, pp 25–27. By permission of Random House UK Ltd. (7) Antonio Cisneros, *Peru: The New Poetry*, London Magazine Editions, London, 1970, p 61. By permission of Alan Ross, *London Magazine*. (8) Peter Matthiessen, *At Play in the Fields of the Lord*, Collins Harvill, London, 1988, pp 129–130. By permission of HarperCollins Publishers Ltd. (9) Peter Matthiessen, *The Cloud Forest: A Chronicle of the South American Wilderness*, Collins Harvill, London, 1988, p 150. By permission of HarperCollins Publishers Ltd. (10) César Vallejo, 'On the Other Side of Life and Death', in *The Eye of the Heart*, Allison and Busby, London, 1987, pp 144–146. (11) Cirio Alegría, *Broad and Alien is the World*, Nicholson and Watson, London, 1942, pp 5–6. By permission of The Merlin Press Ltd. **BOLIVIA:** (1) R.C. Hutchinson, *Rising*, Penguin, London, 1982, pp 2–3. Copyright © R.C. Hutchinson 1976. By permission of Curtis Brown Ltd, London. (2) Gordon Meyer, *Summer at High Altitude*, Alan Ross, London, 1968, pp 152–153. By permission of Alan Ross. (3) Jon Cleary, *Mask of the Andes*, Collins, London, 1982, p 318. By permission of HarperCollins Publishers Ltd. (4) Julian Duguid, *Green Hell*, Jonathan Cape, London, 1931, pp 142–143. (5) Gordon Meyer, *Summer at High Altitude*, Alan Ross, London, 1968, pp 57–58. By permission of Alan Ross. (6) Gordon Meyer, *Summer at High Altitude*, Alan Ross, London, 1968, pp 108–109. By permission of Alan Ross. (7) Peter Matthiessen, *The Cloud Forest: A Chronicle of the South American Wilderness*, Collins Harvill, London, 1988, pp 72–73. By permission of Harper-Collins Publishers Ltd. **GUYANA:** (1) Edgar Mittelholzer, *My Bones and My Flute*, Longman, London, 1991, p 1. (2) Wilson Harris, *The Eye of the Scarecrow*, Faber and Faber, London, 1970, pp 16–17. By permission of Faber and Faber Ltd. (3) Roy Heath, *Orealla*, Flamingo, London, 1986, p 60. By permission of A.M. Heath Ltd. (4) Roy Heath, *Orealla*, Flamingo, London, 1986, pp 246–247. By permission of A.M. Heath Ltd. (5) V.S. Naipaul, 'A Handful of Dust: Return to Guiana', *New York Review of Books*, 11 April 1991, p 15. By permission of the *New York Review of Books* and Aitken and Stone Ltd. (6) Charles Waterton, *Wanderings in South America*, Nelson, London, 1903, pp 145–146. (7) Evelyn Waugh, *A Handful of Dust*, Penguin, London, 1951, p 168. By permission of the Peters Fraser & Dunlop Group Ltd. (8) Charles Waterton, *Wanderings in South America*, Nelson, London, 1903, pp 221–225. (9) Shiva Naipaul, *A Hot Country*, Hamish Hamilton, London, 1983, pp 1–3. By permission of Aitken and Stone Ltd. (10) Evelyn Waugh, *A Handful of Dust*, Penguin, London, 1951, pp 169–170. By permission of the Peters Fraser & Dunlop Group Ltd. (11) Wilson Harris, *Tumatumari*, Faber and Faber, London, 1968, pp 20–22. By permission of Faber and Faber Ltd. **SURINAM:** (1) Alejo Carpentier, *Explosion in a Cathedral*, Penguin, London, 1971, pp 249–250. By permission of A.M. Heath Ltd. (2) Paul Marlee, *Guinea-Pig*,

Karnak House, London, 1990, pp 75–76. By permission of Karnak House. (3) Shiva Naipaul, *Beyond the Dragon's Mouth: Stories and Pieces*, Hamish Hamilton, London, 1984, p 356. By permission of Aitken and Stone Ltd. (4) Paul Marlee, *Guinea-Pig*, Karnak House, London, 1990, pp 13 and 104. By permission of Karnak House. (5) Voltaire, *Candide*, Penguin, London, 1947, pp 85–86. Copyright © John Butt 1947. By permission of Penguin Books Ltd. (6) Paul Marlee, *Guinea-Pig*, Karnak House, London, 1990, p 106. By permission of Karnak House. **FRENCH GUIANA:** (1) Charles Waterton, *Wanderings in South America*, Nelson, London, 1903, pp 139–143. (2) Henri Charrière, *Papillon*, Grafton, London, 1980, p 427. By permission of HarperCollins Publishers Ltd. (3) Henri Charrière, *Papillon*, Grafton, London, 1980, pp 66–67. By permission of HarperCollins Publishers Ltd. **BRAZIL:** (1) V.S. Pritchett, *Dead Man Leading*, Chatto and Windus, London, 1937, pp 4–5. By permission of the Peters Fraser & Dunlop Group Ltd. (2) James Hamilton-Paterson, *Gerontius*, Vintage, London, 1990, p 163. By permission of Macmillan London Ltd. (3) Cyro dos Anjos, *Diary of a Civil Servant*, Fairleigh Dickinson University Press, Cranbury, NJ, 1988, p 94. By permission of Associated University Presses. (4) Frank Tuohy, *The Warm Nights of January*, Macmillan, London, 1960, pp 47–49. By permission of the Peters Fraser & Dunlop Group Ltd. (5) Graciliano Ramos, *Childhood*, Peter Owen, London, 1979, pp 120–121. By permission of Peter Owen Ltd. (6) Darcy Ribeiro, *Maíra*, Picador, London, 1985, p 41. By permission of Pan Macmillan Ltd. (7) Márcio Souza, *Mad Maria*, Avon Books, New York, 1985, pp 9–10. (8) H.M. Tomlinson, *The Sea and the Jungle*, Duckworth, London, 1912, pp 143–144. (9) Sir Arthur Conan Doyle, *The Lost World*, John Murray, London, 1960, p 98. (10) Euclides da Cunha, *Rebellion in the Backlands*, University of Chicago Press, Chicago, IL, 1944, pp 422–423. Copyright © 1944 by the University of Chicago. By permission of The University of Chicago Press. (11) Dalton Trevisan, 'Death on the Square', in *The Vampire of Curitiba and Other Stories*, Knopf, New York, 1972, pp 61–62. (12) Antônio Torres, *The Land*, Readers International, London, 1987, pp 4–5. By permission of Readers International. (13) James Hamilton-Paterson, *Gerontius*, Vintage, London, 1990, pp 196–197. By permission of Macmillan London Ltd. (14) Antônio Callado, *Don Juan's Bar*, Knopf, New York, 1972, pp 121–122. (15) Elizabeth Bishop, 'The Burglar of Babylon', *The Complete Poems, 1927–1979*, Chatto and Windus, London, 1983, pp 95–96. Copyright © 1979, 1983 by

Elizabeth Bishop. By permission of Farrar, Straus and Giroux, Inc. (16) Antônio Callado, *Don Juan's Bar*, Knopf, New York, 1972, p 84. (17) Peter Fleming, *Brazilian Adventure*, Penguin, London, 1987, p 53. (18) Rudyard Kipling, 'Brazilian Sketches', in Blair Niles, ed, *Journeys in Time*, Coward-McCann, New York, 1946, pp 366–367. (19) Joaquim Maria Machado de Assis, *Epitaph of a Small Winner*, Penguin, London, 1968, pp 164–165. First published in UK by Chatto and Windus. By permission of Random House UK Ltd. (20) Moritz Thomsen, *The Saddest Pleasure*, The Sumach Press, London, 1991, p 32. By permission of Random House UK Ltd. (21) Erico Veríssimo, in *The Green Continent*, Poetry London Editions, London, 1947, pp 342–343. (22) Caio Abreu, *Dragons*, Boulevard, London, 1990, pp 70–71. Boulevard Books are distributed by Harrap Publishing Group. By permission of Boulevard Books. (23) Jorge Amado, *Shepherds of the Night*, Collins Harvill, London, 1989, pp 212–213. By permission of HarperCollins Publishers Ltd. (24) Jorge Amado, *Tent of Miracles*, Collins Harvill, London, 1989, pp 3 and 9. By permission of Harper-Collins Publishers Ltd. (25) Moritz Thomsen, *The Saddest Pleasure*, The Sumach Press, London, 1991, p 101. By permission of Random House UK Ltd. (26) Henry Bates, *The Naturalist on the Amazons*, J.M. Dent, London, 1863, p 184. (27) Mário de Andrade, *Macunaíma*, Quartet, London, 1984, pp 74–75. By permission of Quartet Books Ltd. (28) Frank Tuohy, *The Animal Game*, Macmillan, London, 1957, pp 97–98. By permission of the Peters Fraser & Dunlop Group Ltd. (29) Bruce Chatwin, *The Viceroy of Ouida*, Jonathan Cape, London, 1980, p 51. By permission of Random House UK Ltd. (30) R. Magalhães Júnior, 'The Immunizer', in William Grossman, *Modern Brazilian Short Stories*, University of California Press, Berkeley, CA, and London, 1967, p 6. Copyright © 1967 The Regents of the University of California. By permission of the University of California. (31) João Ubaldo Ribeiro, *Sergeant Getulio*, André Deutsch, London, 1980, pp 1–2. By permission of André Deutsch Ltd. (32) Clarice Lispector, *The Apple in the Dark*, Virago, London, 1985, pp 116–117. **PARAGUAY**: (1) Graham Greene, *Travels with My Aunt*, Penguin, London, 1971, pp 213–215. By permission of Laurence Pollinger Ltd on behalf of the Estate of Graham Greene. (2) Gordon Meyer, *The River and the People*, Methuen, London, 1963, pp 95–96. By permission of Aubrey Meyer. (3) Michael Wilding, *The Paraguayan Experiment: A Documentary Novel*, Penguin, Sydney, 1985, pp 71–72. By permission of Penguin Books Australia Ltd. (4)

Norman Lewis, *The Missionaries*, Secker and Warburg, London, 1988, pp 148–150. Published by Vintage in 1992. Copyright © 1988 by Norman Lewis. By permission of Rogers, Coleridge & White Ltd on behalf of Norman Lewis. (5) Augusto Roa Bastos, *I the Supreme*, Knopf, New York, 1986, pp 98–99. By permission of Faber and Faber Ltd. (6) Augusto Roa Bastos, *Son of Man*, Gollancz, London, 1965, pp 7–9. (7) R.B Cunninghame Graham, *South American Sketches*, University of Oklahoma Press, Norman, OK, 1978, pp 210–211. (8) Herbert Read, *The Green Child*, Robin Clark, London, 1989, pp 82–83. By permission of Quartet Books Ltd. (9) Voltaire, *Candide*, Penguin, London, 1947, p 62. Copyright © John Butt 1947. By permission of Penguin Books Ltd. **CHILE**: (1) Nicanor Parra, 'The Borders of Chile', in *Emergency Poems*, New Directions, New York, 1972, p 107. Copyright © 1972 by Nicanor Parra. By permission of New Directions Publishing Corporation. (2) Isabel Allende, *The House of the Spirits*, Jonathan Cape, London, 1985, pp 141–142. By permission of Random House UK Ltd. (3) Antonio Skármeta, *Burning Patience*, Methuen, London, 1988, pp 111–113. By permission of Methuen and Co. (4) Isabel Allende, *Of Love and Shadows*, Black Swan, London, 1988, pp 197–198. First published in UK by Jonathan Cape. English translation copyright © 1987 by Alfred A. Knopf, Inc. By permission of Random House UK Ltd. (5) Antoine de Saint-Exupéry, *Wind, Sand and Stars*, Bantam, New York, 1945, pp 71–72. First published in the UK by William Heinemann Ltd. By permission of Octopus Publishing Group. (6) Fernando Alegría *The Chilean Spring*, Latin American Literary Review Press, Pittsburgh, PA, 1980, pp 113–114. By permission of Latin American Literary Press. (7) José Donoso, *Curfew*, Picador, London, 1990, pp 17–19. (8) Pablo Neruda, 'A Pine-Cone, A Toy Sheep', in Barbara Howes, ed, *The Eye of the Heart*, Allison and Busby, London, 1987, pp 226–227. (9) Pablo Neruda, *Canto General*, edited and translated by Jack Schmitt, University of California Press, Berkeley, CA, 1991, pp 280–281. Copyright © 1991 Fundación Pablo Neruda, Regents of the University of California. By permission of the University of California Press. **URUGUAY**: (1) Juan Carlos Onetti, *A Brief Life*, Grossman, New York, 1976, pp 10–11. (2) Charles Darwin, *Voyage of the Beagle*, Penguin, London, 1989, p 71. (3) Juan Carlos Onetti, *A Brief Life*, Grossman, New York, 1976, pp 14–15. (4) W.H. Hudson, *The Purple Land*, Duckworth, London, 1929, pp 46–49. (5) Gordon Meyer, *Summer at High Altitude*, Alan Ross, London, 1968, pp 11–12. By permission of Alan Ross.

(6) Richard Burton, *Letters from the Battle-Fields of Paraguay*, Tinsley Brothers, London, 1870, p 218. (7) Jorge Luis Borges, 'The Form of the Sword', in *Fictions*, Calder and Boyars, London, 1975, pp 106–107. By permission of George Weidenfeld and Nicolson Ltd. **ARGENTINA:** (1) José Hernandez, *Martín Fierro*, Instituto Cultural Walter Owen, Buenos Aires, 1967, p 141. (2) Domingo F. Sarmiento, *Life in the Argentine Republic*, Gordon Press, New York, 1976, p 1. (3) Alberto Vanasco, 'Neither Saints Nor Sinners', in *Celeste Goes Dancing and Other Stories*, Constable, London, 1989, p 70. By permission of Constable and Company Ltd. (4) Eduardo Mallea, *All Green Shall Perish*, Calder and Boyars, London, 1967, pp 83–84. By permission of Marion Boyars Publishers Ltd. (5) Victoria Ocampo, in *The Green Continent*, Poetry London Editions, London, 1947, pp 122–123. (6) Adolfo Bioy Casares, *The Dream of the Hero*, Quartet Books, London, 1987, pp 179–180. By permission of Quartet Books Ltd. (7) María Luisa Bombal, *New Islands*, Farrar, Straus and Giroux, New York, 1982, pp 99–100. Translation copyright © 1982 by Farrar, Straus and Giroux, Inc. By permission of Farrar, Straus and Giroux, Inc. (8) Jorge Luis Borges, 'The Mythical Founding of Buenos Aires', *Selected Poems*, Penguin, London, 1972, pp 61–63. Copyright © 1968, 1969, 1970, 1971, 1972, and 1985 by Emece Editores, SA, and Norman Thomas di Giovanni. Translation by Alastair Reid. By permission of Penguin Books Ltd. (9) Jorge Luis Borges, 'The South', in *Fictions*, Calder and Boyars, London, 1975, p 154. By permission of George Weidenfeld and Nicholson Ltd. (10) Haroldo Conti, 'Lost', in *Translation: the Journal of Literary Translation*, Spring 1987, p 66. Translation copyright by Norman Thomas di Giovanni. By permission of Norman Thomas di Giovanni. (11) Julio Cortázar, 'Text in a Notebook', in *We Love Glenda So Much and Other Tales*, Harvill Press, London, 1984, pp 102–103. By permission of HarperCollins Publishers Ltd. (12) Rubén Darío, *Selected Poems of Rubén Darío*, University of Texas Press, Austin, TX, 1965, pp 123–125. By permission of The University of Texas Press. (13) W.H. Hudson, *Far Away and Long Ago*, J.M. Dent, London, 1918, pp 286–287. (14) W.H. Hudson, 'Ralph Herne', in *El Ombu*, J.M. Dent, London, 1923, pp 191–192. (15) Robert Lowell, 'Buenos Aires', *The Review*, No 8, August 1963, p 34. (16) Alberto Manguel, *News from a Foreign Country Came*, HarperCollins, London, 1991, pp 173–174. By permission of HarperCollins Publishers Ltd. (17) Gordon Meyer, *Exiles*, Alan Ross, London, 1968, pp 221–222. By

permission of Alan Ross. (18) Manuel Puig, *Heartbreak Tango: A Serial*, Arena, London, 1987, pp 124–125. By permission of Random House UK Ltd. (19) Manuel Puig, *Pubis Angelical*, Faber and Faber, London, 1987, pp 81–82. By permission of Faber and Faber Ltd. (20) Ernesto Sabato, *On Heroes and Tombs*, David Godine, New York, 1981, pp 241–242. Copyright © 1981 by Ernesto Sabato. By permission of David R. Godine, Publisher. (21) Ernesto Sabato, *On Heroes and Tombs*, David Godine, New York, 1981, p 217. Copyright © 1981 by Ernesto Sabato. By permission of David R. Godine, Publisher. (22) Ernesto Sabato, *The Tunnel*, Jonathan Cape, London, 1988, pp 77–78. By permission of Random House UK Ltd. (23) Isobel Strachey, *A Summer in Buenos Aires*, Jonathan Cape, London, 1947, p 47. By permission of Random House UK Ltd. (24) Isobel Strachey, *A Summer in Buenos Aires*, Jonathan Cape, London, 1947, pp 168–169. By permission of Random House UK Ltd. (25) Lawrence Thornton, *Imagining Argentina*, Bloomsbury, London, 1987, p 37. By permission of Bloomsbury Publishing Ltd. (26) Horacio Vázquez Rial, *Triste's History*, Readers International, London, 1990, pp 13–14. By permission of Readers International. (27) Graham Greene, *The Honorary Consul*, The Bodley Head, London, 1973, pp 73–74. By permission of Laurence Pollinger Ltd on behalf of the Estate of Graham Greene. (28) Graham Greene, *Travels with My Aunt*, Penguin, London, 1971, pp 201–202. By permission of Laurence Pollinger Ltd on behalf of the Estate of Graham Greene. (29) Bruce Chatwin, *In Patagonia*, Picador, London, 1979, pp 24–25. By permission of Random House UK Ltd. (30) Richard Burton, *Letters from the Battle-Fields of Paraguay*, Tinsley Brothers, London, 1870, pp 260–261. (31) José Vasconcelos, in *The Green Continent*, Poetry London Editions, London, 1947, pp 152–153. (32) Tomás Eloy Martínez, *The Perón Novel*, Pantheon, New York, 1988, pp 112–113. (33) Horacio Quiroga, *South American Jungle Tales*, Methuen, London, 1923, p 5. By permission of Methuen and Co. (34) Luisa Valenzuela, 'Family for Clotilde', *Open Door*, North Point Press, San Francisco, CA, 1988, pp 162–163. By permission of Curtis Brown Ltd, and Serpent's Tail Ltd. (35) Ricardo Güiraldes, *Don Segundo Sombra*, Penguin, London, 1971, p 3. (36) Horacio Quiroga, 'The Incense Tree Roof', in *The Decapitated Chicken and Other Stories*, University of Texas Press, Austin, TX, 1976, pp 145–146. Translated by M. Sayers Peden. © 1976 The University of Texas Press. By permission of The University of Texas Press, Austin.

PICTURES

Front cover and spine – Indian burial ground in the Bolivian Andes by Andrew Wood; Back cover – Pablo Neruda's house 'La Chascona' by Tomasina Wilson; p 5 – Octavio Paz by Rafael Doniz; p 9 – Graham Greene by William Karel; p 52 – Carlos Fuentes by Grove Studios, London; p 81 – Norman Lewis by Don McCullen; p 79 – Paul Bowles by Roy Round. Courtesy of Peter Owen Publishers Ltd; p 82 – Rodrigo Rey Rosa by Cherie Nutting. Courtesy of Peter Owen Publishers Ltd; p 129 – Ernesto Cardenal, © Sigrid Rothe. Courtesy of Search Press Ltd; p 157 – Gabriel García Márquez by the Douglas Brothers; p 173 – García Márquez's birthplace by Alastair Dingwall; p 194 – Joseph Conrad courtesy of Raffles Hotel, Singapore; p 245 – Gordon Meyer by an unknown journalist from *La Nación*, Buenos Aires; p 269 – Wilson Harris, © 1989 Dr Peter Stummer. Courtesy of Wilson Harris; p 330 – Rudyard Kipling courtesy of Raffles Hotel, Singapore; p 332 – Graciliano Ramos courtesy of Peter Owen Publishers Ltd; p 335 – Frank Tuohy by Mark Gerson; p 355 – Pablo Neruda courtesy of University of California Press; p 369 – Isabel Allende © Lieberman Photography, San Francisco; p 370 – Pablo Neruda's house by Tomasina Wilson; p 432 – Julio Cortázar by René Burri/Magnum; p 434 – Güiraldes Museum by Tomasina Wilson; p 441 – Quiroga's house by Tomasina Wilson.

INDEX

This is an index to authors and other prominent people. (E) = extract. Bold type = biographical entry.